The European Past

SECOND EDITION

VOLUME II

Reappraisals in History
Since Waterloo

EDITED BY

Shepard B. Clough
Professor of History, Columbia University

Peter Gay
Professor of History, Yale University

Charles K. Warner
Professor of History, University of Kansas

John M. Cammett
Professor of History, City University of New York

The Macmillan Company

ACKNOWLEDGMENTS

Henry A. Kissinger, "The Congress of Vienna: A Reappraisal," from *World Politics*, Vol. VIII, No. 2 (January 1956), pp. 268-280. Reprinted by permission.

Robert A. Kann, "Metternich: A Reappraisal of His Impact on International Relations." Reprinted from *The Journal of Modern History* Vol. XXXII, No. 4 (December 1960), pp. 333-339 by permission of the University of Chicago Press. Copyright 1960 by the University of Chicago Press.

William Langer, "The Pattern of Urban Revolution in 1848," from *French Society and Culture Since the Old Regime*, edited by Evelyn Acomb and Marvin L. Brown, Jr. Copyright © 1966 by Holt, Rinehart, and Winston, Inc. Reprinted by permission of Holt, Rinehart, and Winston, Inc. Pp. 90-112.

Friedrich Meinecke, "The Year 1848 in German History: Reflections on a Centenary," from *The Review of Politics* Vol. X, No. 1 (January 1948), pp. 475-492. Copyright 1948, by the University of Notre Dame. Reprinted by permission.

Jacques Barzun, "Who Are the Romanticists?" from *Classic, Romantic, and Modern*, by Jacques Barzun, pp. 7-17, by permission of Little, Brown and Co.—Atlantic Monthly Press. Copyright © 1943, 1961 by Jacques Barzun.

Peter Viereck, "Romanticism and Nazism," from Peter Viereck, *Metapolitics—The Roots of the Nazi Mind* (New York: Capricorn Books, 1961), pp. 17-20, 29-34, 37-40, 50-53, 68-70, 192-194. Copyright 1941, by Alfred A. Knopf, Inc. Copyright 1961, by Peter Viereck. Reprinted by permission of the author.

Robert W. Lougee, "German Romanticism and Political Thought," from *The Review of Politics*, Vol. XXI, No. 4 (October 1959), pp. 631-645. Copyright, 1959, by the University of Notre Dame. Reprinted by permission.

Basil Willey, "What Was Darwin's Theory?" from Basil Willey, "Darwin's Place in the History of Thought," *Darwinism and the Study of Society—A Centenary Symposium*, Michael Banton (ed.) (London: Tavistock Publications, 1961; Chicago: Quadrangle Books, 1961), pp. 2-5. © Michael Banton, 1961. Reprinted by permission of Quadrangle Books.

Cyril Bibby, "Huxley and the Reception of the 'Origin,'" from *Victorian Studies* (Darwin Anniversary Issue), Vol. III, No. I (September 1959), pp. 76-86. Reprinted by permission of *Victorian Studies* and the author.

George E. Simpson, "Darwin and 'Social Darwinism,'" from *Antioch Review*, Vol. XIX (Spring 1959), pp. 33-45. Reprinted by permission.

Samuel Bernstein "From Utopianism to Marxism," from *Science and Society*, Vol. XIV, No. I (Winter 1949-1950), pp. 58-67. Reprinted by permission. Copyright 1950 by Science and Society, Incorporated.

George Lichtheim, "The Doctrine of Revolution," from George Lichtheim, *Marxism: An Historical and Critical Study* (New York: Fredrick A. Praeger, Inc. 1961), pp. 51-62. Reprinted by permission. Copyright George Lichtheim, 1961.

John Lewis, "Capital and the Nature of Capitalist Crisis." Reprinted by permission of International Publishers Co. Inc. Copyright © 1965. From *The Life and Teachings of Karl Marx* (New World Paperbacks, 1965), pp. 186-205.

Albert Guérard, "The Judgement of Posterity." Reprinted by permission of the publishers from Albert Guérard, *Napoleon III*. (Cambridge, Mass.: Harvard University Press), Copyright, 1943, by The President and Fellows of Harvard College, pp. 281-293.

Sir Lewis Namier, "The First Mountebank Dictator," from Sir Lewis Namier, *Vanished Supremacies: Essays on European History 1812-1918*. (London: Hamish Hamilton Ltd., 1958). Reprinted by permission. Copyright Sir Lewis Namier, 1958.

Alan Spitzer, "The Good Napoleon III," from *French Historical Studies*, Vol. II, No. 3 (Spring 1962), pp. 308-329. Reprinted by permission of *French Historical Studies* and the author. Copyright 1962 by the Society for French Historical Studies. Quotations appearing in French in the original essay have been translated by the editors.

Antonio Gramsci, "Neglected Agrarian Revolution." from Antonio Gramsci, *Il Risorgimento*, translated by Charles Delzell, from *The Unification of Italy, 1859-1861*, edited by Charles F. Delzell. Copyright © 1965 by Holt, Rinehart and Winston, Inc. Reprinted by permission of Holt, Rinehart and Winston, Inc.

Rosario Romeo, "Liberal-Capitalist Rebuttal to Gramsci's Thesis," from Rosario Romeo, "La tesi del Gramsci e il problema dello suiluppo del capitalismo," in *Risorgimento e capitalismo*, translated by Charles Delzell, from *The Unification of Italy, 1859-1861*, edited by Charles F. Delzell. Copyright © 1965 by Holt, Rinehart and Winston, Inc. Reprinted by permission of Holt, Rinehart and Winston, Inc.

John M. Cammett, "The Gramsci-Romeo Debate," from *Science and Society*, Vol. XXVII, No. 4 (Fall 1963), pp. 441-457. Reprinted by permission.

Hans Rothfels, "Problems of a Bismark Biography," from *The Review of Politics*, Vol. IX, No. 3 (July 1947), pp. 362-380. Copyright, 1947, by the University of Notre Dame. Reprinted by permission.

Franz Schnabel, "The Bismark Problem," from Hans Kohn (ed.), *German History: Some New German Views* (Boston: The Beacon Press, 1954) pp. 65-83. All rights reserved. Reprinted by permission.

Alfred von Martin, "Bismark and Ourselves," from Hans Kohn (ed.), *German History: Some New German Views* (Boston: The Beacon Press, 1954), pp. 94-101. All rights reserved. Reprinted by permission.

Philip Magnus, "Talking Turkey," from Philip Magnus, *Gladstone, A Biography* (London: John Murray, 1954) pp. 238-255. Reprinted by permission.

Paul Smith, "Disraeli: First Modern Conservative?" from *Disraelian Conservatism and Social Reform* (Toronto: University of Toronto Press, 1967), pp. 2-5, 11-18, 22-36, 319-325. The footnotes have been omitted. Reprinted by permission.

J. A. Hobson, "The Economic Aspects of Imperialism," from J. A. Hobson, *Imperialism, A Study* (London: George Allen & Unwin, Ltd., 1902), 3rd edition revised 1938, pp. 51-61, 80-93. Reprinted by permission of the publisher and The Macmillan Company, New York.

D. K. Fieldhouse, "Imperialism: An Historiographical Revision," from *The Economic History Review*, Vol. XIV, No. 2 (1961), pp. 187-195. Reprinted by permission.

Fritz Fischer, "Economic Expansion and World Power." Reprinted from *Germany's Aims in the First World War* by Fritz Fischer. By permission of W. W. Norton & Company, Inc. Copyright 1961 by Droste Verlag und Druckerei GmbH, Dusseldorf. Translation copyright © 1967 by W. W. Norton & Company, Inc., and Chatto & Windus, Ltd. Pp. 11-24.

Joachim Remak, "Europe on the Eve: How Deep the Trouble?" From *The Origins of World War I* by Joachim Remak. Copyright © 1967 by Holt, Rinehart and Winston, Inc. Reprinted by permission of Holt, Rinehart and Winston, Inc. Pp. 60-97.

Imanuel Geiss, "The Outbreak of the First World War and German War Aims," from *The Journal of Contemporary History*, Vol. I, No. 3 (London: George Weidenfeld & Nicolson Ltd., 1966), pp. 71-87. Reprinted by permission.

John Maynard Keynes, "The Case Against the Versailles Treaty," from *The Economic Consequences of the Peace* by John Maynard Keynes, copyright 1920 by Harcourt, Brace & World, Inc.; renewed, 1948, by Lydia Lopokova Keynes and reprinted by permission of Harcourt, Brace & World, New York, Macmillan & Co. Ltd., London, and the Estate of Lord Keynes.

Etienne Mantoux, "The Question of Reparations," from *The Carthaginian Peace or The Economic Consequences of Mr. Keynes* (London: Oxford University Press, 1964; New York: Charles Scribner's Sons, 1952). Reprinted by permission of Mme. Paul Mantoux.

Wolfgang Sauer, "National Socialism: Totalitarianism or Fascism?" from *The American Historical Review* Vol. LXXIII, No. 2 (December 1967), pp. 404-424. Reprinted by permission of Wolfgang Sauer.

David Schoenbaum, "The Third Reich, Social Opportunity and Society," from *Hitler's Social Revolution* by David Schoenbaum. Copyright © 1966 by David Schoenbaum. Reprinted by permission of Doubleday & Company, Inc. Pp. 284-301.

J. P. Nettl, "Industrialization in the Soviet Union 1929-1940," from The Soviet Achievement by J. P. Nettl, © 1967 by J. P. Nettl. Reprinted by permission of Harcourt, Brace and World and Thames and Hudson Ltd.

Leonard Schapiro, "The Basis and Development of the Soviet Polity," from *Fifty Years of Communism in Russia*, Milorad M. Drachkovich (ed.) (University Park: The Pennsylvania State University Press, 1968), pp. 48-63. Reprinted by permission.

A. J. P. Taylor, "War for Danzig," from *The Origins of the Second World War* by A. J. P. Taylor, Copyright © 1962 by A. J. P. Taylor. Reprinted by permission of Atheneum Publishers, New York, and Hamish Hamilton Ltd., London.

Zygmundt Kulak, "A. J. P. Taylor and the Origins of World War II," from *Polish Western Affairs*, Vol. IV, No. 2 (1963), pp. 370-378. Reprinted by permission.

Lawrence Stone, "Theories of Revolution," from *World Politics* (January 1966), pp. 5-22. Reprinted by permission.

Martin Nicolaus, "The Unknown Marx," *New Left Review*, No. 48 (March-April 1968). Reprinted by permission of the author.

Barrington Moore, Jr., "Why We Fear Peasants in Revolt," from *The Nation* Vol. 203, No. 9. (September 26, 1966), pp. 271-274. Reprinted by permission.

Preface to the Second Edition

This edition of *The European Past* is informed by the same purpose as the first edition; that is, to present recent evaluations and conflicts in the interpretation of important historical topics. Increasing numbers of both scholars and students, with good reason, have been drawn to the study of modern history. Consequently, changes in this edition are more extensive than is usual in a revision. Some twenty-six selections in the first edition have been deleted, and twenty-eight new essays have been added. The majority of the new ones are recent contributions which have appeared since the publication of the first edition of *The European Past*. Several topics are altogether new; among them are "The Crisis of the Seventeenth Century," "Towards the Origins of Modern Revolution" (Volume I), and "Fascism," "Stanlinism," and "Twentieth-Century Revolutions" (Volume II).

S.B.C.
P.G.
C.K.W.
J.M.C.

Preface to the First Edition

It has been the object of the editors of this book to introduce new materials and a new approach to the study of European history. Included in these two volumes are historical essays which present revaluations or conflicts of interpretation centered around thirty-two important historical topics.

Sometimes controversies evolve from differences in method; sometimes from fundamental differences in the philosophy of history; sometimes from the selection of different data. In every case, however, the reader is introduced to the frontiers of research in history. He is given a sense of the "sifting and winnowing" involved in historical judgment and provided with an opportunity to make informed judgments of his own.

Controversies or reinterpretations produced by different historical questions have, of course, been used to some degree in other books of readings. But the typical "case study" frequently offers a hodgepodge of primary and secondary materials in such fragmentary form as to vitiate their meaning. The selections presented in this book aim at conveying a sense of depth of the subject being treated.

It will be noticed that the largest part of the selections included here have been published during the last twenty years. All come from the current generation of scholars or their teachers. This choice has been deliberate. The great classic controversies of the last century or the earlier years of this one which fill the pages of some books of readings are not, of course, without interest. But if history is a cumulative study which permits us to know more and more about the past, is not the latest history the best gauge of whatever consensus has been reached on a given issue?

The selections presented here are either articles from scholarly journals, most often reproduced in their original length, or they are meaningful portions of monographs or broader studies. An innovation has been to offer, where possible, an historiographical essay as one of the selections under a particular topic. Where this has not been possible, background information is included in the topic introduction. Several of the essays have been translated expressly for this book.

The editors wish to acknowledge the research assistance of James Friguglietti, the secretarial help of Patricia Cutler Warner, and the translation assistance of Cambridge Editorial Research, Inc.

S. B. C.
P. G.
C. K. W.

Contents

THE NEW STATESMEN

IMPERIALISM

EUROPE AND THE AFTERMATH OF NAPOLEON

1 / The Congress of Vienna and the Metternich Era

The two selections that follow cover an event, the Congress of Vienna, which set up a system, often called the "Metternichian system," that ordered the relations between the states of Europe and a period 1815-1848, during which the "system" functioned.

The first selection is by Henry Kissinger. Though widely known as an analyst of contemporary international affairs, Kissinger is also the author of a highly praised study, *A World Restored: Metternich, Castlereagh, and the Problems of Peace 1812-1822* (1957). In his essay below, Kissinger concentrates on the workings of the congress. At the same time he offers an interesting combination of theory and history. He begins by defining the elements of a practicable optimum in international settlements and concludes that the success of the Congress of Vienna was due to circumstances which made the achievement of such an optimum possible. Kissinger does not discount entirely the part played by the diplomats. Although he rejects "the myth about Talleyrand's role at the congress," he praises the abilities of Metternich and Castlereagh and "the skill of the diplomats in *making use of their opportunities*" (italics added). For Kissinger, "the effectiveness of diplomacy depends on elements transcending it," and his warning against ascribing the achievements of the Congress of Vienna "to the very process of negotiation, to diplomatic skill, and to 'willingness to come to an agreement'" is, in effect, a rejection of standard interpretations of the congress.

The second selection, by Robert Kann, an authority on the history of the Hapsburg Empire,[1] examines Metternich in a broader context than the Congress of Vienna by evaluating his impact on international relations during his chancellorship and commenting on the relationship of his policies to the problems of our time. In this last respect, Kann's essay represents a qualified reappraisal of the recent rehabilitation of Metternich and his era.

The reader should remember that late nineteenth- and early twentieth-century historiography—which was in the liberal or nationalistic tradition or a combination of the two—saw the Congress of Vienna as an attempt "to turn the clock back," the

[1] R. Kann, *The Multinational Empire: Nationalism and National Reform in the Hapsburg Monarchy, 1848-1918* (New York: Columbia, 1950); *The Hapsburg Empire: A Study in Integration and Disintegration* (New York: Praeger, 1957); *A Study in Austrian Intellectual History: From Late Baroque to Romanticism* (New York: Praeger, 1960).

3

Concert of Europe as an instrument to maintain the *status quo,* and the suppression of the revolutions of 1848 as thwarting the progressive forces of liberalism and nationalism. Metternich was the villain in the center of this stage, and after he fled it in 1848, his place was taken by the Emperor Francis Joseph with assistance from Tsar Nicholas I.

This is an oversimplified picture of what people believed, but in its broad outlines it was the accepted one, and it is perpetuated to some degree today in popular histories. The shift away from this point of view began after World War I with the opening of the Hapsburg and Austrian State Archives and the publication in 1925 of *Metternich,* a massive and scholarly biography by Heinrich Von Srbik, which shed new light on Metternich and his policies. But in the sense that each age rewrites history in terms of its own experience, the real rehabilitation of Metternich began after World War II.

To the generations which have seen two world wars separated by only two decades of uneasy peace, the "fifty-year peace" in Europe which followed the Congress of Vienna is impressive enough. The Crimean War, of course, ended this period and was a blow to the spirit of Metternich's system, but the Concert of Europe survived it.[2] And although the existence of the concert became increasingly precarious, the continuation of Metternich's "European conscience" has been credited with preventing the outbreak of a general European war during the hundred years between Waterloo and 1914.

The same generations which have seen two world wars have, also understandably, looked at nationalism with something less than the approbation of pre-1914 historians. From this point of view, Metternich's eighteenth-century cosmopolitanism carried into the nineteenth century has seemed more relevant than before. There have been new insights into his steadfast opposition to the unification of Germany and Italy and his determination that the Hapsburg Empire should play a leading role in Europe. In our own time, the dismemberment of that empire, so hopefully undertaken in 1919 in the name of "self-determination" (a solution to the ethnic problems of the empire that Metternich would have considered anarchic) has ended after many vicissitudes in Russian penetration of Central Europe and the Balkans. By contrast, as Kann points out, Metternich's "skillful containment of Russia" was one of his more successful policies.

Again this an oversimplified picture, but it should help the reader understand the rehabilitation of Metternich to the point where his policies seem to relate to the problems of our time.[3] As we pointed out earlier, Professor Kann's essay qualifies this assumed relationship. Although not uncritical, Kann is an admirer of Metternich

---

[2] All major powers were represented at the Congress of Paris (1856), which ended the Crimean War, and questions of general European concern unrelated to the war were acted on. All major powers were also represented at the Congress of Berlin (1878, which ended the Russo-Turkish War. But before then, peace settlements made between the belligerents after the Austro-Prussian War (1866) and the Franco-Prussian War (1870) had all but destroyed the concert idea. The London Conference of 1913, where the major powers dictated the peace terms of the First Balkan War to the belligerents, appears as a revival of the concert system, but it was ineffective in keeping peace either in the Balkans or Europe.

[3] For a notable example of this line of thinking, see Peter Viereck, *Conservatism Revisited* (New York: Scribners, 1949; rev. ed. New York: Collier Books, 1962). In this book and in "New Views on Metternich," *The Review of Politics* (1951), pp. 211-28, Viereck also offers evidence that Metternich was more aware of the new social and political forces than most historians give him credit for, and sees him as more of a political philosopher than, for example, Kann does. Viereck's book or article can be read with profit in connection with this topic.

and maintains that "as to the significance of his life's work for the present world . . . he surpasses most of the outstanding statesmen that came before or after him." Kann believes, however, that this significance rests on an "almost unique contribution . . . the creation of a system of international politics according to supra-national and supra-party principles and based on supposedly self-evident reason." As to the relation of Metternich's policies to our times along the lines suggested above, he has important reservations which raise interesting questions of historical causation and analogy.

THE CONGRESS OF VIENNA: A REAPPRAISAL

Henry A. Kissinger

It is only natural that a period anxiously seeking to wrest peace from the threat of nuclear extinction should look nostalgically to the last great successful effort to settle international disputes by means of a diplomatic conference, the Congress of Vienna. Nothing is more tempting than to ascribe its achievements to the very process of negotiation, to diplomatic skill, and to "willingness to come to an agreement"—and nothing is more dangerous. For the effectiveness of diplomacy depends on elements transcending it; in part on the domestic structure of the states comprising the international order, in part on their power relationship.

Any international settlement represents a stage in a process by which a nation reconciles its vision of itself with the vision of it by other powers. No state can doubt its own good faith; it is the vehicle of its social cohesion. But, equally, no power can stake its survival entirely on the good faith of another; this would be an abdication of the responsibility of statesmanship. The whole domestic effort of a people exhibits an effort to transform force into obligation by means of a consensus on the nature of justice. But the international experience of a state is a challenge to the universality of its notion of justice, for the stability of the international order depends on the reconciliation of different versions of legitimacy. Could a nation achieve all its wishes, it would strive for absolute security, a world order free from the consciousness of foreign danger, and one where all problems have the manageability of domestic issues. But since absolute security for one power means absolute insecurity for all others, it is obtainable only through conquest, never as part of a legitimate settlement.

An international settlement which is accepted and not imposed will therefore always appear *somewhat* unjust to any one of its components. Paradoxically, the generality of this dissatisfaction is a condition of stability, because were any one power *totally* satisfied, all others would have to be *totally* dissatisfied and a revolutionary situation would ensue. The foundation of a stable order is the *relative* security—and therefore the *relative* insecurity—of its members. Its stability reflects, not the absence of unsatisfied claims, but the absence of a grievance of such magnitude that redress will be sought in overturning the settlement rather than through an adjustment within its framework. An order whose structure is accepted by all major powers is "legitimate." An order containing a power which considers its structure oppressive is "revolutionary." The security of a domestic order resides in the preponderant power of authority, that of an international order in the balance of forces and in its expression, the equilibrium.

But if an international order expresses the need for security and an equilibrium, it is constructed in the name of a legitimizing principle. Because a settlement transforms force into acceptance, it must attempt to translate individual demands into general advantage. It is the legitimizing principle which establishes the relative "justice" of competing claims and the mode of their adjustment. This is not to say that there need be an exact correspondence between the maxims of legitimacy and the conditions of the settlement. No major power will give up its minimum claim to security—the possibility of conducting an independent foreign policy—merely for the sake of legitimacy. But the legitimizing principle defines the marginal case. In 1919, the Austro-Hungarian Empire disintegrated not so much from the impact of the war as from the nature of the peace, because its continued existence was incompatible with national self-determination, the legitimizing principle of the new international order. It would have occurred to no one in the eighteenth century that the legitimacy of a state depended on linguistic unity. It was inconceivable to the makers of the Versailles settlement that there might by any other basis for legitimate rule. Legitimizing principles triumph by being taken for granted.

Although there never occurs an exact correspondence between the maxims of the legitimizing principle and the conditions of the settlement, stability depends on a certain commensurability. If there exists a substantial discrepancy *and* a major power which feels disadvantaged, the international order will be volatile. For the appeal by a "revolutionary" power to the legitimizing principle of the settlement creates a psychological distortion. The "natural" expression of the policy of a status-quo power is law—the definition of a continuing relationship. But against a permanently dissatisfied power appealing to the legitimizing principle of the international order, force is the only recourse. Those who have most gain from stability thus become the advocates of a revolutionary policy. Hitler's appeal to national self-determination in the Sudeten crisis in 1938 was an invocation of "justice," and thereby contributed to the indecisiveness of the resistance: it induced the Western powers to attempt to construct a "truly" legitimate order by satisfying Germany's "just" claims. Only after Hitler annexed Bohemia and Moravia was it clear that he was aiming for dominion, not legitimacy; only then did the contest become one of pure power.

The major problem of an international settlement, then, is so to relate the claims of legitimacy to the requirements of security that no power will express its dissatisfaction in a revolutionary policy, and so to arrange the balance of forces as to deter aggression produced by causes other than the conditions of the settlement. This is not a mechanical problem. If the international order could be constructed like a mathematical axiom, powers would consider themselves as factors in a balance and arrange their adjustments to achieve a perfect equilibrium between the forces of aggression and the forces of resistance. But an exact balance is impossible, and not only because of the difficulty of predicting the aggressor. It is chimerical, above all, because while powers may appear to outsiders as factors in a security arrangement, they appear domestically as expressions of a historical existence. No power will submit to a settlement, however well-balanced and however "secure," which seems totally to deny its vision of itself. There exist two kinds of equilibrium then: a general equilibrium which makes it risky for one power or group of powers to attempt to impose its will on the remainder; and a special equilibrium which defines the historical relation of certain powers among each other. The former is the deterrent against a general war; the latter the condition of smooth cooperation. An international order is therefore rarely born out of the consciousness of harmony. For even when there is an agreement about legitimacy, the conceptions of the requirements of security will differ with the geographical position and the history of the contending powers. Out of just such a conflict over the nature of the equilibrium the Congress of Vienna fashioned a settlement which lasted almost exactly a century.

For the problem at Vienna was not simply how to protect Europe against a renewed French onslaught. There was general agreement about the extent of France compatible with the peace of Europe, but this only sharpened the disagreements *within* the victorious coalition about the relative spheres of influence of Austria, Prussia, Russia, and Great Britain. And this contest was made all the more intractable because each of the protagonists meant something different by the term "equilibrium" so frequently invoked. When the British Foreign Minister, Castlereagh, spoke of the equilibrium, he meant a Europe in which hegemony was impossible; but when Metternich appealed to the equilibrium, he included a Germany in which Prussian predominance was impossible. Russia's demand for Poland threatened the equilibrium of Europe and Castlereagh could, therefore, hardly believe that any other problem was worth discussing before the Tsar's pretensions were thwarted. Prussia's insistence on Saxony merely imperiled the balance within Germany, but this was enough to absorb the full energy of Metternich. Castlereagh was interested in creating a Central Europe which would be strong enough to resist attack from both the West and the East; Metternich desired the same thing, but he was also concerned about Austria's relative position *within* Central Europe. To Castlereagh, the Continental nations were aspects of a defensive effort; but to the Continental nations the general equilibrium meant nothing if it destroyed the historical position which to them was the reason for their existence. To Castlereagh, the equilibrium was a mechanical expression of the balance of forces; to the Continental nations, a reconciliation of historical aspirations.

This led to a diplomatic stalemate, made all the more intractable because Britain and Austria had secured most of their special objectives during the war so that few bargaining weapons were left to Russia and Prussia, a stalemate which could be broken only by adding an additional weight to one side of the scales. Since the sole uncommited major power was France, the former enemy emerged as the key to the European settlement. Thus grew up a myth about Talleyrand's role at the Congress of Vienna, of the diabolical wit who appeared on the scene and broke up a coalition of hostile powers, who then regrouped them into a pattern to his liking by invoking the magic word "legitimacy" and from an outcast emerged as the arbiter of Europe.[1] To be sure, since the Treaty of Paris had settled France's boundaries, Talleyrand could afford perhaps the most disinterested approach. His wit and caustic comments became famous, so that Gentz could say of him that he had both the laughers and the thinkers on his side. But these efforts would have availed little,

---

[1] It is a legend spread by those who confuse results and causes and by professional diplomats wont to ascribe to mere negotiating skill what is possible only through the exploitation of more deep-seated factors. It has gained currency because Talleyrand, whose monarch had not come to Vienna, was obliged to write voluminous reports, and in order to cement his shaky domestic position, the former Foreign Minister of Napoleon tended to emphasize his indispensability. See, for example, Harold G. Nicolson, *The Congress of Vienna,* New York, 1946; Duff Cooper, *Talleyrand,* New York, 1932; Crane Brinton, *The Lives of Talleyrand,* New York, 1936; Guglielmo Ferrero, *The Reconstruction of Europe,* New York, 1941.

had not the threat of France been eclipsed by the danger from the East, had not the differences among the Allies become greater than their common fear of France. So long as the Coalition still believed that the memory of the common wartime effort would provide the motive force of a settlement, Talleyrand was powerless. Once this illusion was shattered, the issue became one of the limits of self-restraint, whether a power would fail to add a factor to its side merely for the sake of the appearance of harmony. The logic of the situation provided the answer: France came to participate in European affairs, because they could not be settled without her.

As the plenipotentiaries were assembling in Vienna, however, the course of events seemed by no means this clear. It was still thought that the settlement would be rapid, that France would appear as but a spectator, that the rest of Europe would only be called upon to ratify an instrument drafted in relative harmony. This was reflected in the procedural scheme agreed to at preliminary conferences between Austria, Prussia, Russia, and Great Britain which placed the effective control of the Congress in the hands of the "Big Four." Talleyrand protested strenuously against the exclusion of France and the minor powers from the deliberations of the Congress, but despite his brilliance and sarcasm, he achieved only a few minor concessions. It was decided to adjourn the formal opening of the Congress until November 1, 1814, and to have the pending questions examined in the meantime by the eight signatories of the Treaty of Paris, the "Big Four" plus France, Spain, Portugal, and Sweden. The "Big Four" left no doubt, however, that they intended to continue their private discussions and to treat the "Eight" merely as a ratifying instrument or as one for settling peripheral issues.

Talleyrand's first sally failed, because a logical inconsistency is not sufficient to dissolve coalitions. Only after the claim of special righteousness, which is characteristic of coalitions, had disappeared in a conflict which indicated that the relations of the Allies among each other were simply those of contending powers, could Talleyrand emerge as an equal partner. But first one more effort to determine whether the Tsar could be induced to limit his claims without the threat of force had to be made. So well had Castlereagh established himself as the prime contender for the European equilibrium that it was he who entered the arena to try the Tsar's resolution.

There ensued a strange and unreal series of interviews between Castlereagh and Alexander; strange, because their bitterness was accompanied by protestations of unending friendship, and unreal, because Alexander and Castlereagh could never agree on basic premises. In order to obtain a framework for negotiation, the protagonists constantly shifted positions, pretending to agree with the other's principles, but interpreting them in a manner which reduced them to absurdity. Thus Castlereagh at one stage became an avid defender of a completely independent Poland, while Alexander on another occasion defended his Polish plan as a contribution to European security. That Alexander did not propose to let protestations of Allied unity deprive him of his Polish spoils became apparent on the occasion of his first interview with Castlereagh on the day after his arrival.[2] For the first time, he avowed his Polish plans in detail. He proposed to keep all of the Duchy of Warsaw with the exception of a small portion to be ceded to Prussia.

---

[2] Castlereagh's report. See Charles Webster, *British Diplomacy, 1813-1815*, London, 1921, pp. 197ff., October 2, 1814.

These claims, Alexander agrued, were not the result of ambition, but the outgrowth of a moral duty and motivated by the sole desire of achieving the happiness of the Polish people. In short, since they were not advanced in the name of security, they could not threaten anyone. Castlereagh, in reply, urged that a Russian appendage extending deep into Central Europe would constitute a constant source of disquiet for the rest of Europe. But the Tsar left no doubt that he was unwilling to withdraw from his Polish possession. The interview between Castlereagh and Alexander had thus made evident that persuasiveness would not suffice and that the next stage of the negotiations would have to be based on force or the threat of force.[3]

While Castlereagh was negotiating with the Tsar, he made every effort to assemble such a force. As an abstract problem in diplomacy his task seemed simple. But although the equilibrium might be indivisible, it did not appear so to its components. The Tsar could not be resisted without a united front of the rest of Europe, but the powers of Europe were not at all in accord regarding the real danger. They did not wish to see the general equilibrium overturned, but they were not prepared to resist at the sacrifice of that part of it on which their historical position depended. A strong Russia might dominate Europe, but a too powerful Prussia would outstrip Austria and a united Germany might menace France. Hardenberg, the Prussian minister, was more interested in Saxony than in Poland; Talleyrand was almost as afraid that the problem of Poland would be settled *without* him as that it would be settled *against* him; and Metternich, while not indifferent to the extension of Russia into Central Europe and of Prussia into Central Germany, did not wish to resist openly since this would cause the brunt of the effort to fall on Austria, the most exposed power, while surrendering the policy of close cooperation with Prussia which Metternich considered the key to Austrian security. "I barricade myself behind time," Metternich told the Saxon envoy, "and make patience my weapon."[4]

Thus Castlereagh's effort to create a united front against Russia led to an ambiguous series of constellations, of half-hearted coalitions and tentative betrayals, of promises of unyielding support coupled with hedges against bad faith. Matters were finally brought to a head by Prussia, the power which could least afford delay. For although the treaties of Kalish, Teplitz, and Chaumont had guaranteed Prussia its territorial extent of 1805, they had never specified where Prussia might find the requisite territories, particularly if it lost its Polish possessions to Russia. The available compensations, composed of former provinces or former satellites of France, primarily in the Rhineland, were inadequate. And they were undesirable because of their geographic separation from the main part of the Prussian monarchy and the Catholic religion of their inhabitants. Thus Prussia came to look toward Saxony, coveted since the time of Frederick the Great, contiguous with its own territories and with a predominantly Protestant population. But Prussia's negotiating position was the weakest of those of the major powers. Unlike Russia, it was not in possession of its prize. Unlike Austria, it had not made its participation in the war dependent on obtaining its special conditions. If now the Polish question was settled

---

[3] The exchange continued through October in a series of memoranda: Castlereagh to the Tsar, October 12, 1814, see Duke of Wellington, *Supplementary Despatches, Correspondence and Memoranda,* 15 vols., ed. by his son, London, 1855-1872, IX, p. 332; the Tsar's reply, October 30, p. 386; Castlereagh's reply, November 8, p. 410.
[4] Wilhelm Schwarz, *Die Heilige Allianz,* Stuttgart, 1935, p. 13.

before that of Saxony, Prussia would have paid the penalty for its total commitment; of having fought the war with so much fervor that its participation had never been negotiable, of neglecting the peace because the war, in effect, had become an end in itself. And Prussia required Austrian acquiescence in the annexation of Saxony, because the organization of Germany, the indispensable condition of Prussia's security, would become illusory if Austria emerged on the Saxon issue as the protector of the secondary German powers.

It is not surprising, therefore, that On October 9, 1814, Hardenberg submitted a memorandum agreeing to an "intermediary system based on Austria, Prussia and Britain," and directed against Russia.[5] But he made Prussia's cooperation on the Polish question dependent on Austrian agreement to the annexation of Saxony and to the provisional occupation of Saxony by Prussia as a token of good faith. In its tentative quest for allies, in its pedantic effort to achieve the advantage of every course of action, the Hardenberg memorandum merely served to illustrate Prussia's dilemma: Russian support might gain it Saxony, but not legitimacy; while Austrian support might yield it Poland, but not Saxony. The Hardenberg memorandum was a plea not to leave Prussia dependent on the good will of the Tsar; to create a European order based on Austro-Prussian friendship, but also on Prussian possession of Saxony.

But this effort to combine incompatible policies provided Metternich with the means to separate the Polish and Saxon question by one of his intricate maneuvers. On October 22, he transmitted two notes to Hardenberg and Castlereagh whose tone of grudging agreement to Hardenberg's proposal obscured the fact that the moral framework which was being created to resist in Poland would prove equally effective to resist in Saxony and that Hardenberg, in his effort to hedge his risks, had made his defeat inevitable. For Castlereagh in his overriding concern with the balance of power and Hardenberg in his obsession with Saxony overlooked two subtle and mutually inconsistent reservations in Metternich's despatches: that Prussia's annexation of Saxony should not lead to a "disproportionate aggrandizement," a condition clearly impossible of fulfillment if Prussia regained her Polish provinces,[6] and that Austria's agreement on the Saxon point was conditional on the *success* of the effort to thwart the Tsar's design on Poland[7]—which, in turn, would leave Prussia isolated in the inevitable contest over the interpretation of the first reservation.

But while Metternich was preparing the moral framework for an effort to separate Prussia and Russia, Castlereagh was looking only to Poland, as if the European equilibrium could be created with the necessity of a mathematical equation. On October 23, he finally succeeded in getting Prussia to agree to a common plan of action against Russia on the basis of Metternich's memoranda.[8] The three powers undertook to force the issue by confronting the Tsar with the threat of bringing the Polish question before the full Congress if a reasonable settlement could not be obtained by direct negotiations. They proposed three acceptable solutions: an independent Poland as it existed prior to the first partition, a rump Poland on the

[5] Comte d'Angeberg, *Le Congrès de Vienne et les Traites de 1815,* Paris, 1863-1864, II, p. 1934.
[6] Text of note to Castlereagh, *ibid.,* II, pp. 1939ff.
[7] Text of note to Hardenberg, *ibid.,* I, pp. 316ff.
[8] Castlereagh's report, Webster, *op. cit.,* p. 212, October 29, 1814.

scale of 1791, or the return of the three partitioning powers to their former possessions.[9]

The threat of an appeal to Europe in Congress was the last effort to settle the European equilibrium by a combination *within* the anti-French coalition. When Metternich called on the Tsar to present the ultimatum on the Polish question, he was dismissed haughtily and even challenged to a duel. And when, on October 30, the three sovereigns left to visit Hungary, Alexander appealed to his brother monarchs against their ministers. He failed with the Austrian Emperor, but it did not prove too difficult to convince the stodgy and unimaginative Prussian King that the secret negotiations of the three ministers were an act of bad faith. When the monarchs returned to Vienna, Hardenberg was ordered, in the presence of the Tsar, to refrain from any further separate negotiations with his Austrian and British colleagues. In this manner, on November 5, the contest over Poland ended for the time being. The effort to achieve an international order based on agreement and not on force seemed to have returned to its starting point.

But this was a mistaken impression. For if Castlereagh's failure had proved that the equilibrium could not be achieved through a demonstration of its necessity, Metternich's almost imperceptible complementary effort had created the moral framework for reopening the issue by an appeal to legitimacy. The procrastination which had proved so maddening to Castlereagh had in fact been Metternich's most effective means to overcome his dilemmas, for delay strengthened Austria's chief bargaining weapon, that legitimacy can be conferred but not exacted, that it implies agreement and not imposition. So the weeks had passed while Europe complained about the frivolity of the Austrian minister and the old school of Austrian diplomats raged that their "Rhenish" minister, whom they nicknamed Prince Scamperlin, was betraying the Empire to Prussia. But in the admiration for the famous phrase of the Prince de Ligne: "Le Congres danse, mais il ne marche pas," it was overlooked that the Congress was dancing itself into a trap.

When Hardenberg offered Metternich his cooperation, he believed that he was clinching his gains and that he was obtaining a guarantee of Saxony, however the Polish negotiations ended. But because Metternich's reply had made Austrian agreement to the annexation of Saxony conditional on the *success* of their common measures, the effort to connect the two issues became a means to separate them. For if the Polish negotiations succeeded, Prussia would lose her moral claim to Saxony in the eyes of Europe. If Prussia regained her Polish possessions, the annexation of Saxony would represent the "disproportionate aggrandizement" against which Metternich had warned Castlereagh. But if the Polish negotiations failed, Prussia would lose her moral claim to Saxony in the eyes of Austria. Prussia's isolation was assured none the less surely, because the fact of resistance was almost as certain to alienate the Tsar as its success. Having demonstrated Austria's European concern by yielding in Saxony, intransigence could now be defended by the requirements of the European and not the German equilibrium. And Castlereagh, having obtained Austrian support in the Polish negotiations, would no longer be able to treat the Saxon issue as an internal German affair. There could be no doubt of the attitude of France or of the smaller German states. Prussia, in its effort to obtain reinsurance, had only succeeded in achieving its isolation.

When, on November 7, Hardenberg informed Metternich of the King's orders and

[9] Memorandum re procedure, *ibid.*, pp. 213ff.

of the difficulty of carrying out the agreed plan with respect to Poland, Metternich finally had the moral basis for action.[10] Austria was interested in the closest relationship with Prussia, he replied, but no longer at the price of the destruction of Saxony.[11] After being forced to tolerate Russian aggrandizement in Poland, Austria could not acquiesce in Prussian aggrandizement within Germany without upsetting the equilibrium completely. Metternich suggested an alternative plan which maintained a nucleus of Saxony, while giving a large part of it to Prussia, together with other compensations in the Rhineland. But all protestations of friendship could not hide the fact that Prussia was outmaneuvered, that Metternich had lost out in Poland only to win in Saxony and then partially to restore the situation in Poland by means of Saxony.

It did not matter that, on November 8, the Russian military governor of Saxony turned over the provisional administration to Prussia, or that the Prussian military were threatening war. Russia, at the periphery of Europe, might rest its claim on Poland on the fact of possession, but a power situated in the center of the Continent could survive only as the component of a "legitimate" order both within Germany and in Europe. Thus, although by the middle of December the Congress of Vienna seemed to have reached a complete stalemate, behind the scene a fundamental transformation was preparing itself. A stalemate is not total until all the factors are engaged and France was still uncommitted. The contests during October and November had exploded the myth of Allied unity and the threat of France no longer loomed larger than that of the erstwhile ally. While Castlereagh was despairing about the Polish failure and accusing Metternich of never having really intended to resist,[12] a combination was forming on the Saxon question which was to give a new direction to the contest. For the coalition which could resist in Saxony was, by definition, also the coalition which could resist in Poland. And the claims of power defeated in one quarter would, almost necessarily, limit the assertions of arbitrariness in the other. So it was proved, after all, that the equilibrium was indivisible, although the solution did not come about through a consciousness of this. It was not in the name of Europe that Europe was saved, but in the name of Saxony.

But before this new combination could be formed, domestic pressures on Castlereagh nearly wrecked Metternich's finely spun plan. An insular power may fight its wars in the name of the European equilibrium, but it will tend to identify the threats to the equilibrium with threats to its immediate security. Because its policy is defensive and not precautionary, it will make the cause of war depend on an overt act which "demonstrates" the danger. But the danger to the equilibrium is never demonstrated until it is already overturned, because an aggressor can always justify every step, except the crucial last one, as the manifestation of limited claims and exact acquiescence as the price of continued moderation. To be sure, Britain had entered the fray against Napoleon at an early stage and continued the contest with great persistence. But the threat to the equilibrium had become manifest

---

[10] D'Angebert, *op. cit.,* I, p. 406 (Hardenberg's note to Metternich). There is yet another indication, although no proof, that Metternich never intended the Polish negotiations as anything but a means to isolate Prussia on the Saxon question: his dismal defeat during his interview with Alexander. At no other time in his career did Metternich choose a frontal attack, negotiate so ineffectively, or surrender so easily.

[11] Text, *ibid.,* I, p. 505.

[12] Webster, *op. cit.,* pp. 248ff.

through an attack on the Low Countries and a challenge to Britain's command of the seas. Now the issue was Poland, however, a "distant" country both geographically and psychologically. It was not clear until it was "proven" that the Rhine was best defended along the Vistula or that there existed any threat to peace except France. In this frame of mind the Cabinet considered the Polish dispute an irritating outgrowth of Continental rivalry, threatening a peace dearly won, and dealt with it primarily under the aspect of its impact on British domestic politics.

On October 14, Liverpool, the British Prime Minister, wrote Castlereagh that the "less Britain had to do with [Poland] ... the better" and he transmitted a memorandum by the Chancellor of the Exchequer, Vansittart, who simply denied the reality of the Russian danger. With the petulance of mediocrity convincing itself that the easy way out is also the course of wisdom, Vansittart argued that the absorption of Poland would add an element of weakness to the Russian state while proving conducive to British commerce.[13] Finally, on November 22, the Cabinet sent its first instructions to Castlereagh since his arrival in Vienna: "It is unnecessary," wrote Bathurst, "for me to point out to you the impossibility of ... consenting to involve this country into hostilities ... for any of the objects which have hitherto been under discussion at Vienna."[14]

Thus, at the crucial point in the negotiations, Castlereagh was deprived of his only means of exerting pressure and at a moment when the issue was becoming one of pure power. For Prussia was being drawn by Metternich's temporizing into precipitate action. As it observed its moral and material basis slipping away, its tone became increasingly bellicose. Its military were openly speaking of war and even the more moderate Hardenberg hinted at extreme measures. But if possession without legitimacy was illusory, legitimacy through force proved chimerical. Castlereagh was merely defining Prussia's dilemma when he told Hardenberg that "he [Hardenberg] could not regard an unacknowledged claim as constituting a good title and that he never could in *conscience* or *honor* ... make the mere refusal of a recognition a cause of war...."[15] In this situation Castlereagh did not propose to follow his Cabinet's instructions. To announce British disinterest would remove the major deterrent to war and, in its effort to guarantee peace, the Cabinet would have brought about what it feared most. Or else, a British withdrawal from the contest would have led to an Austrian surrender and to a complete overturn of the equilibrium.

So it happened that Castlereagh and Metternich found themselves on the same side in a battle whose moral framework had been defined by the wily Austrian Minister. The more intransigent Prussia's attitude, the stronger became Metternich's position. Without the necessity for abstract discussion, Austria emerged as the protector of the secondary powers. When Metternich proposed an alliance to Bavaria and Hanover and the construction of a German League without Prussia, he was simply giving expression to a general consensus. It was at this point, when the last vestiges of the Alliance were disappearing, that Talleyrand reappeared on the scene. He emerged because Metternich put him on the stage and his eloquence was but a reflection of Metternich's desire for anonymity, for Metternich was not interested in appearing as the agent of Prussia's humiliation. It was Metternich's desire that events

[13] *Ibid.*, pp. 220ff.
[14] *Ibid.*, pp. 247ff.
[15] *Ibid.*, p. 255. December 7, 1814.

should come about "naturally," because that would minimize the danger of personal schisms; it was Talleyrand's effort that they should appear "caused," for that would cement his shaky domestic position.

Talleyrand was given his opportunity by Metternich, who communicated to him the Austrian note to Hardenberg and thus made clear that the Big Four had not been able to settle the issue.[16] Talleyrand replied in a trenchant memorandum, which asserted the superiority of the claims of legitimacy over the requirements of the equilibrium and denied the possibility of deposing kings, because sovereigns could not be tried, least of all by those who coveted their territories. It was not for Prussia to state what she would take, Talleyrand argued boldly, but for the "legitimate" King of Saxony to define how much he would yield.[17] It was a masterly summary of all the inconsistencies of two months of acrimony, but this was not its significance. Talleyrand had served France better by remaining "available" than by writing memoranda. The real importance of the exchange lay in the fact that France was once again part of the concert of Europe.

Only a short step separated Talleyrand from full participation in the deliberations. Castlereagh, who had hoped to avoid so drastic a step, finally agreed on December 27. When, On December 31, Castlereagh and Metternich proposed that henceforth Talleyrand participate in the meetings of the Big Four, it was clear that the special claims of the Alliance had ceased before Prussia had gained the fruit of its war effort. Even the Tsar, in Castlereagh's words, "would not advise Prussia to resist now that he has secured his own arrangement in Poland." Thus driven back on its last resources, Prussia threatened war.

But the reaction merely served to indicate Prussia's impotence. Castlereagh replied sharply that "such an insinuation might operate upon a power trembling for its own existence but must have the contrary effect upon all alive to their own dignity; and I added that if such a temper really prevailed, we were not deliberating in a state of independence and it was better to break up the Congress."[18] That same day, Castlereagh proposed a defensive alliance between France, Austria, and Britain. To be sure, Talleyrand was required to guarantee the Low Countries and to reaffirm the provisions of the Treaty of Paris. But Talleyrand's greatest achievement at Vienna was precisely this exhibition of self-restraint, this refusal to attempt to sell French participation in the alliance for a territorial advantage, an effort which would have united all the other powers against him. As a result he gained something more important, the end of the isolation of France and the real recognition of its equality.

If the defensive alliance provided the crisis of the Congress of Vienna, it also paved the way for its resolution. In any negotiation it is understood that force is the ultimate recourse. But it is the art of diplomacy to keep this threat potential, to keep its extent indeterminate, and to commit it only as a last resort. For once power has been made actual, negotiations in the proper sense cease. A threat to use force which proves unavailing does not return the negotiation to the point before the threat was made. It destroys the bargaining position altogether, for it is a confession not of finite power but of impotence. By bringing matters to a head, Prussia found itself confronted by three powers whose determination could not be

---

[16] Clemens Metternich, *Aus Metternichs Nachgelassenen Papieren,* 8 vols., ed. by Alfons von Klinkowstroem, Vienna, 1880, II, pp. 503ff.
[17] *Ibid.*, pp. 510ff., December 19, 1814; D'Angeberg, *op. cit.*, pp. 546ff.
[18] Webster, *op. cit.*, p. 278, January 1, 1815.

doubted, although the treaty itself remained secret. And the Tsar proved a lukewarm ally. A series of partial settlements had isolated Prussia because "satisfied" powers will not fight for the claims of another, if an honorable alternative presents itself.

Castlereagh, therefore, took up the proposal of Metternich's memorandum of December 10 by which Prussia was to obtain part of Saxony and extensive territories in the Rhineland. It soon became apparent that Prussia would not carry out her threat of war. By January 3, 1815, after Metternich and Castlereagh had refused to negotiate without Talleyrand, Hardenberg, to save face, himself recommended Talleyrand's participation.[19] On January 5, Castlereagh could report that "the alarm of war is over."[20] The Saxon question was henceforth officially discussed by the now Big Five and was resolved largely through unofficial negotiations in which Castlereagh played the role of the intermediary between Metternich and Talleyrand on the one side and the Tsar and Hardenberg on the other.

In his endeavor to achieve a final settlement, Castlereagh had to resist an attempt by Prussia to move the King of Saxony to the left bank of the Rhine and an effort by Austria to save the Elbe fortress of Torgau for Saxony. But with the aid of the Tsar, he convinced Prussia that in the interest of the European equilibrium she would have to assume the defense of the Rhineland, and he made clear to Austria that the defensive alliance extended only to an actual attempt to overthrow the European equilibrium, not to internal German arrangements.[21] The danger of war had also made the Tsar more pliable. When Castlereagh suggested some concessions in Poland in order to make the Saxon arrangement more palatable to Prussia, Alexander agreed to return the city of Thorn to Prussia. On February 11, a final agreement was reached. In Poland, Austria retained Galicia and the district of Tarnopol, while Cracow was constituted a free city. Prussia retained the district of Posen and the city of Thorn which controlled the upper Vistula. The remainder of the Duchy of Warsaw with a population of 3.2 million became the Kingdom of Poland under the Tsar of Russia. In Germany, Prussia obtained two-fifths of Saxony, Swedish Pomerania, much of the left bank of the Rhine, and the Duchy of Westphalia. Austria had already been assured compensation in Northern Italy and predominance in all of Italy though the establishment of dependent dynasties in Parma and Tuscany.

On June 9, 1815, the final acts of Vienna were ratified by Europe assembled in congress. It was the only meeting of the Congress of Vienna.

There are two ways of constructing an international order: by will or renunciation, by force or legitimacy. For twenty-five years Europe had been convulsed by an effort to achieve order through force and to contemporaries its lesson was not its failure but its near success. Under Napoleon Europe had been unified from the Niemen to the Bay of Biscay but its cohesion was supplied by the power of the Grande Armée. It is not surprising, then, that in their effort to create an alternative the statesmen of Vienna looked back to a period which had known stability and that they identified this stability with its domestic arrangements. Nor was this assessment as ludicrous as a self-righteous historiography made it appear later on. For one of the reasons which had impelled Napoleon ever further was his

[19] *Ibid.*, p. 280.
[20] *Ibid.*, p. 282.
[21] *Ibid.*, p. 295, January 29, 1815.

often repeated conviction that the survival of his dynasty in a world of "legitimate" monarchs depended on the success of his arms. In short, Napoleon confronted Europe with a revolutionary situation because he considered the unimpaired maintenance of the other sovereign states as incompatible with his own existence.

By contrast, one of the reasons for the success of the Vienna settlement was precisely the absence of such an ideological gulf. When a power considers the domestic notion of justice of another sovereign state a mortal threat to its own survival, no basis for negotiation exists. Safety can then only be found in physical extent; diplomacy is reduced to maneuvering for position and such adjustments as do occur have but a tactical significance: to prepare the ground for the inevitable showdown. This is not to say that domestic structures must be identical before meaningful negotiations can take place. It is enough that there exists no power which claims both exclusiveness and universality for its notion of justice. For diplomacy the art of relating powers to each other by agreement can function only when each major power accepts the legitimacy of the *existence* of the others.

In Vienna, of course, the consensus went further than this. There existed a general agreement about the nature of "just" domestic arrangements, which by limiting risks made for flexibility of relationship. The problem of relating a state's vision of itself to the vision of it by the powers, defined in the beginning as one of the key problems of an international settlement, was rarely simpler than at Vienna. This was the reason for the success—for the possibility—of "secret diplomacy," that intangibles were understood in the same manner. To be sure, the results of the Vienna Congress reflected to no small degree the skill of the diplomats in making use of their opportunity. Both Metternich and Castlereagh were extraordinary negotiators capable of shaping a conference to their ends: Castlereagh through his ability to reconcile different points of view and a singlemindedness which enabled him to keep discussions focused on essentials; Metternich through the art of defining a framework which made concessions appear, not as surrenders, but as sacrifices to the common cause. But whatever the skill of the diplomats, the second reason for the success of the Congress is no less fundamental: that in the face of all protestations of friendship and of a real measure of ideological agreement the importance of power-relationships was never lost sight of. The conviviality of the statesmen must not obscure the fact that the European order emerged from the threat of war and the formation, however temporary, of two hostile alliances. The issue was decided not only by the persuasiveness of the statesmen but by the relative strength of the opposing camps.

The settlement proved all the more lasting because the negotiators at Vienna did not confuse the atmosphere of the conference table with the elements of stability of the international system. A statesman cannot make the survival of his charge entirely dependent on the continued good will of another sovereign state; not only because he has no control over the continuation of this good will, but more importantly because the best guarantee for its remaining good is not to tempt it by too great a disproportion of power. The Vienna settlement took into account this relationship of security and legitimacy. It did not rest on unsupported good faith, which would have put too great a strain on self-limitation; nor on the efficacy of a pure evaluation of power, which would have made calculation too indeterminate. Rather, there was created a structure in which the forces were sufficiently balanced, so that self-restraint could appear as something more than self-abnegation, but which took account of the historical claims of its components, so that it met general acceptance. No power felt so dissatisfied that it did not prefer to seek its remedy *within* the framework of the Vienna settlement rather than in overturning it. Since the international order did not contain a "revolutionary" power, either ideologically or in power terms, its relations became increasingly spontaneous, based on the growing certainty that a catastrophic upheaval was unlikely. The result was a century without a major war.

METTERNICH: A REAPPRAISAL OF HIS IMPACT ON INTERNATIONAL RELATIONS

Robert A. Kann

One of the supposed truisms of history is that the test of greatness in political action is its applicability to present-day conditions. When calling the roll of the eminent Western statesmen in the field of international relations in the last centuries—from Richelieu and Kaunitz to Cavour and Bismarck, to take only a few outstanding examples—one begins to wonder if this concept is not an oversimplification. Of the many who acknowledge the great contributions of these men to the policies of their countries, only a few would claim that their methods are in any way germane to the problems of our day. It appears that historical changes during the last generations make it necessary to differentiate between great action and action applicable in the modern world.

In the case of Prince Clemens Metternich, the "coachman of Europe," from the Congress of Vienna in 1814 to his enforced abdication from power at the beginning of the revolution of 1848, the situation seems to be rather the reverse. His character appears to many to have been as controversial as that of Richelieu, Talleyrand, or Bismarck; in his domestic policies he has found fewer defenders than any one of them. His greatness is still questioned today, though probably less so than half a century ago. Yet, as to the significance of his life's work for the present world, entirely irrespective of the issue of his personal greatness, he surpasses most of the outstanding statesmen that came before or after him.

Why is this true? So sweeping an assertion must of necessity be limited in its application. It is not to be applied to Metternich's role as the leading Austrian statesman for almost four decades, nor even to his suppression of nationalism and constitutionalism in Central Europe. Metternich's active influence on the idea of the police state, censorship, and cultural isolationism, so frequently associated with Austrian internal administration in the Restoration era, has been generally overrated. The same certainly cannot be said of the national and constitutional issues in the Germanies, the Hapsburg Empire, and Italy. Here, however, Metternich did not act very differently from many of his ministerial colleagues throughout the Restoration period, both within and outside Austria. Like him, they conceived the chief task in domestic administration to be the preservation of ancient empire structures in a fast-changing world. Whatever Metternich did in these spheres has of course become part of the flow of cause and effect in the stream of history. Yet, whether he showed greater skill or perhaps less long-range insight than others, in these respects he appears more as the tool than the free agent of history.

The significance of Metternich for our times rests on a very different and almost unique contribution, a contribution which is perhaps comparable to that of only one Western statesman after him—Woodrow Wilson. The comparison seems strange. What does Metternich, the slightly frivolous, enlightened cavalier, never fully at home in the emotional, romantic era, have in common with the austere, puritan thinker Wilson? The answer is simple: the creation of a system of international politics according to supra-national and supra-party principles and based on supposedly self-evident reason. No attempt will be made here to stress this similarity further in personal terms. Wilson in many ways the liberal, Metternich the conservative; Wilson the deep thinker and luckless manager of international relations, Metternich the conventional though not shallow writer, the brilliant operator of foreign affairs and diplomatic agencies—there is no need to dwell on these great differences in character and the even greater ones in the political environment. What stands out, however, is the fact that both men forged a program not primarily tied to the national community, a program not conceived solely as a second step to an interrelationship between the great powers, as was the case with Bismarck or Cavour. Wilson, while by no means neglecting the interests of his country, perceived them first and last within the international community, just as Metternich in more modest terms simultaneously kept in view the Concert of Europe and, as a mere part of the whole, the Hapsburg Empire.

Among the formal international agreements in the three centuries from the Westphalian peace treaty to the present, these two systems share another—in this case negative—aspect that sets them apart from most other actively promoted systems of international relations of this period: the lack of a crusading or anti-crusading idea. True enough, the Wilsonian philosophy was permeated with the ideals of a supra-national democratic humanitarianism, but this had little to do with party ideology of any kind. In the same sense one might say that, appearances notwithstanding, Metternich's anti-revolutionary, anti-national, and anti-constitutional doctrine was in fact deeply rooted in an enlightened absolutism that placed equilibrium between the powers first and recognized ideological factors only insofar as they might disturb this equilibrium. One may well rate Wilson's political ideals far higher than Metternich's, and yet one cannot help being impressed by the latter's operation of a system of clear thought, reasonably free from the stresses of day-to-day political battles and the conflicts of specific personal interests. In this respect it is significant that the man whose name has been, and in all likelihood always will be, associated with this system of political thought clearly rejected the notion that international political doctrine and strategy should be linked to a specific individual and thus be weakened in their general validity.[1]

An admission that this "system"—the term used by Metternich's friends and foes alike—was clear, dispassionate, and rational within the limits of obvious human frailties implies but faint praise. Surely the chancellor did not produce an

---

[1] See "Aus Metternichs nachgelassenen Papieren," edited by his son Prince Richard Metternich-Winneburg (8 vols.; Vienna, 1880-84) (hereafter cited as *NP*), VIII, 186 and 196-97, where Metternich deplores the tendency to link an idea to a specific individual and thereby weaken its impact. This applies in particular to the political phenomenon of Louis Napoleon in December 1848. See also (*ibid.*, pp. 462 ff.) Metternich's letter of Jan. 17, 1849 to Prince Felix Schwarzenberg on the desirability of a depersonalized concept of government as he saw it practised in England. See further the biography by H. v. Srbik, *Metternich* (3 vols.; Munich, 1925-54), I, 321-26, and the following passages from *NP* referred to in it: VII, 517, 612, 639; VIII, 200, 286, 239.

intellectual masterpiece of political strategy comparable to Machiavelli's *Prince*. Metternich was a voluminous and facile writer, but his lengthy ruminations on the nature of politics are not distinguished by any particular originality of thought. His correspondence on current events is far superior to his theoretical memoranda. In any event, the truly brilliant writings to which the system owed its frame derive primarily from Metternich's closest collaborator in the state chancellery, Friedrich von Gentz. This should in no way detract from the significance of Metternich's life work, which is based on a rare combination of thought and action, a sublime interplay between rigidity of doctrine and flexibility of application. This point was to some extent overlooked by Metternich's eminent biographer, Heinrich von Srbik, who represented Metternich's doctrines as a powerful work of political philosophy and his diplomacy as a kind of minor skill, not quite worthy of his hero. The observer of later days may well rate the rigidity and consistency of Metternich's political thought lower while he may appraise the flexibility of its execution considerably higher.

Basically, Metternich's theories consist in the combination and interpretation of a few simple and well-established concepts.[2] He believed in a principle of legitimacy in international relations which may not be quite as broad as has been claimed in a brilliant analysis by Henry Kissinger, who considers it an international order of limited conflicts always adjustable by negotiation between litigating powers.[3] It was something more than a restoration of divine right absolutism; it was a stable order determined by the consensus of the recognized great powers of the day. Here it is well to remember that after the French Revolution of 1789 and the Napoleonic wars this order was not an established one but was merely restored or manufactured. As such it required this consensus, that is, the compromise between the great powers; and thus it could never be an exact replica of the old one. It was the good fortune of Metternich that the limited ideological differences between the great powers of this period made such a compromise possible. Compromise is indeed the salient feature in the second of Metternich's great principles: equilibrium among the great powers of the European pentarchy—at that time the world pentarchy—of Austria, France, Great Britain, Prussia, and Russia. Here again the notion of equilibrium, in the sense of a balance of power as attempted by the Westphalian peace treaty and actually achieved by the treaties of Utrecht, Rastadt, and Baden after the war of the Spanish Succession, was no more a new concept than legitimacy would have been in terms of divine right theory. What was new was the application of this concept: its extension from the sphere of power politics into that of ideological differences as represented by British constitutionalism and utilitarianism; a Tsarist mixture of metaphysically inspired enlightened absolutism and imperialism; a French drive for imperial restoration in very uncertain domestic political terms; a Prussian push for supremacy in the German orbit; and an Austrian effort to maintain a mediator's position within the framework of "the unified decentralized state."[4] A mediatorship of this sort in the service of the equilibrium could function only if it were assured of two further factors, related to but not

---

[2] See in particular Srbik, I, 317-42.
[3] Henry A. Kissinger, *A world restored: Metternich, Castlereagh and the problems of peace, 1812-1822* (New York, 1957), pp. 1-3, 137, 204. See also R. A. Kann, *A study in Austrian intellectual history: from late Baroque to Romanticism* (New York, 1960), pp. 259-302.
[4] Srbik, I, 434-36; see also Metternich's memorandum of Oct. 1817, *NP*, III, 66-75.

similar to those previously mentioned. There were security and stability. To Metternich, security required not only military preparedness but also a compromise between the powers. He fully realized that the absolute security of one power is in purely military terms a threat to that of others. While it is true that in an age of codified great-power dominance his concept cannot be described as collective security in the broad modern sense, it is entirely proper to refer to Metternich's security concept as based primarily on the consensus of the joint powers.

More controversial is the concept of stability, the interpretation and application of which has greatly contributed to Metternich's ill repute in the liberal camp. It is that part of his philosophy which is commonly associated more than any other with the notion of a blind restoration of the old regime and all that it involves in terms of direct and indirect restrictions of human liberties, of social emancipation and freedom of opportunity. Actually, Metternich never identified stability with the status quo, nor was he opposed to the idea of slow evolutionary reform in itself. Yet, such reforms were applied primarily to the realm of international politics, where he felt at home and was thus able and willing to make concessions, and not to the social-economic sphere, where change at home as well as abroad meant to him approaching the danger zone of revolution.[5]

What has particularly exasperated his critics is the kind of verbiage which seemingly intends to obscure the fact that he thought of consensus as deriving from government power not subject to control by public opinion, and freedom of thought as pertaining to an external forum and not merely to individual conscience.[6] It is perhaps noteworthy that these later, primarily nationalist critics took rationalizations of this kind for mere hypocrisy, whereas an extremely bitter contemporary liberal opponent like Heinrich Heine in his preface to *Französische Zustände* gives Metternich credit for the fact that he never "played the demagogue . . . that one always knew where one stood with him. . . .One knew that he did not act either out of love or petty hatred but grandly in the spirit of his system. . . ."[7] Apparently Heine knew the difference between hypocrisy and flexibility. For all Metternich's outstanding diplomatic skill and perspicacity, without this flexibility his entire political theory would have been fragile indeed.

It must be remembered, of course, that Metternich was spared the difficulty of the democratic and, to a degree, even of the totalitarian governments of today—namely, the necessity of obtaining at least a measure of public support for his policy. It was perhaps not so much the reactionary character but the seeming stability of the regime in Austria as well as his personal prestige that made him more impervious to the impact of public opinion than any contemporary leading statesman, Tsar Alexander I not excluded.[8]

---

[5] See the highly illuminating memorandum of June 1853 to his successor Count Buol in *NP*, VIII, 347-50 where he readily agrees to "manipulation" in the political sphere but categorically refuses what he terms "capitulation" in the social one.

[6] See for instance the strange concoction of the terms freedom, order and tyranny, all wrapped into one, in his so-called Political Testament of 1849-55, *NP*, VII, 633-42, and especially 636-39, or his remarks addressed to Count Auersperg (Anastasius Grün) in 1838 on the identification of freedom of expression with freedom of thought. See Srbik, I, 397-98.

[7] Heinrich Heine, *Sammtliche Werke* (12 vols.; Hamburg, 1851-65), VIII, *Französische Zustände*, Preface of 1832, pp. 19, 20.

[8] Though personally not oblivious to the effect of public opinion, Metternich conceived of it primarily as a gauge to measure the destructive forces of revolution. See, for instance, *NP*, VIII, 238-39, written in 1850.

Lack of concern for the impact of public opinion, however, determines only one facet of diplomacy, and even that presumably only for a short period of time. Yet, by today's standards, Metternich's success was a long-range one and may well be measured in decades. This in spite of the fact that his disregard for mass support did not work entirely to his advantage. After all, there was a reverse side to this problem as well; namely, the lack of such strength as could have been drawn from such backing. It was precisely with the beginning of Metternich's tenure of office after the peace of Schönbrunn in 1809 that Austrian policy dismissed what Metternich considered the mere props of diplomacy. In its stead he introduced a foreign policy that was to be put into action after he was sure not only that Austria would not be isolated, but also that agreement existed as to the aims of the powers with which he wanted to cooperate. Hence, Austria's late but not belated joining of the anti-Napoleonic coalition in 1813 which, for all practical purposes, substituted a guarantee of success for the weight of popular support in the war of 1809.[9] This cautious policy was prompted largely by the strategic central position of Austria and the complexities of her ethnic-historic structure, threatened in the event of defeat by complete dismemberment, a danger to which the other key members of the great alliance, Great Britain and Russia, were not exposed.

But such a policy, slow and perhaps hesitant in execution, did not lack daring and imagination in planning. It should always be remembered that Metternich was the first to perceive the opportunity for the containment of France and was the last to agree to the destruction of Napoleon. He did so because he felt that a Napoleon, curbed in his foreign policy, would still be strong enough to check revolution, while his lesser successors would have to move into a power vacuum. Whether this belief, shattered by Napoleon himself during The Hundred Days in 1815, was correct is less important than his willingness to adjust the concept of legitimacy to stability rather than restoration.

Flexibility was demonstrated above all by the entire foreign policy of Metternich during that strange period of great-power conferences from 1815 to 1822. Somber features in this picture are not lacking. Yet, though criticism of the oppressive measures of the Concert of Europe against Naples and Spain may be justified in itself, the main point should not be overlooked that in a sense this policy was a price paid—perhaps all too willingly then—for the containment of Russia in close collaboration with Great Britain. Here again the chief evidence of flexible skill is the fact that Metternich cooperated sincerely and successfully with British statesmen whose philosophy of government was much more divergent from his own than that of Alexander I and his brother. Indeed, in 1821 it was no idle boast on Metternich's part when he wrote, "If I were not master of making [the Russian troops] retreat just as I made them advance, do you think I should ever have set them in motion?"[10]

It is quite true that after 1822 Metternich's grip on the European situation relaxed, slowly at first, then at an increasing speed. The ever more obvious deficiencies of the settlement of Vienna in regard to the rising issues of constitutionalism, liberalism, and nationalism (which are outside the province of this discussion) are not solely responsible for this fact. Even in the purely diplomatic sphere it became impossible to keep two alliance systems with different *raisons*

---

[9] See Metternich's reflections in regard to Austria's policy at the beginning of the Crimean War, *ibid.*, 364-71.
[10] *Ibid.*, 467; letter by Metternich to Count Stadion, quoted from Kissinger, p. 280.

d'être permanently in line. And surely the quadruple—later quintuple—alliance, primarily concerned with the preservation of the territorial status quo, and the holy alliance, emphasizing the necessity of domestic governmental patriarchies, proved to be wholly incompatible. Metternich's policy from the Congress of Verona in 1822 to his downfall at the very beginning of the March rising in 1848 is a continuous chain of rearguard actions to delay, to cover, and to argue away the breakdown of the Concert of Europe and all it stood for.

It cannot be denied that he achieved a limited success in his relations with the Orleans monarchy in France after the great July revolution of 1830, and a more modest but perhaps more difficult one, the Münchengraetz agreement with Russia of 1833, which for a time checked further Russian advances in the disintegrating Ottoman East. Undoubtedly, these policies helped also to give a limited renewal to Austria's lease on life in the German and Italian spheres. Metternich had, after all, succeeded in maintaining the great-power position of Austria, but the glorious period from 1812 to 1822 when the Hapsburg Empire, anticipating the late Victorian position of Great Britain, acted as European mediator and arbitrator in the service of peace had passed. Austria—very much against Metternich's original intension—had been forced to shift from an overall key position in the center of Europe to a kind of Austro-Russo-Prussian entente system. Her status, deprived of the flexibility desired by the state chancellor, was thus fatally weakened, even during Metternich's lifetime, by the deterioration of her relations with Russia resulting from the Crimean war crisis. This in turn presaged and to a point predetermined the loss of her position in Italy and Germany within less than a decade.

In a sense this steady undermining of Austria's position as a great power testifies to the eminence of Metternich the statesman, since what looked for a time like the operation of an infallible system turned out to be merely the temporary success of an eminent man. As the genuine Austrian that the Rhenish aristocrat had become, he was certainly pleased by his success, but never intoxicated by victory, always cognizant that he fought a delaying battle which he could not win in the end.[11]

What does it all add up to? An evaluation of Metternich's policies and of their relationship to the problems of our times might perhaps most conveniently move from the less controversial to the more controversial. Unfortunately for Metternich's reputation, this entails stronger and wider support for the negative criticism of his policies. There have been few who have maintained seriously that even within the standards of his own time the prince understood the impact of the social changes brought about by the Industrial Revolution and the gradual emancipation of the peasants, the Declarations of Independence and of Rights, the continental pattern of constitutional government, the rise of liberal nationalism. While he himself naturally enough believed in the correctness of "the system," he realized better than many of his more uncritical admirers that it had not stood the test of the times. Had he gone one step farther and realized that it was not merely the upheavals of the period but something less impersonal as well that had made things go wrong, he would not have been the man he was.

In the political field the verdict is somewhat less clear than in the social one. Unquestionably, the territorial settlement of 1814-15 was in a state of dissolution in the east by the end of Metternich's tenure of office. In western and central Europe

[11] See, for instance, *NP*, III, 347-48 (1820), and 472 (1821); V, 193-96 (1831).

the then established boundaries could still be held in a precarious kind of balance, but here the constitutional principles of the system were in rapid flux. Above all, the balance of power between east, west, and central Europe became increasingly disturbed. Here, however, it may well be argued that times like ours, subject to ever more rapid political change, might take a more tolerant view of the relative brevity of the preservation of established treaty provisions and principles.

Such comparisons of the relative similarity of historical situations should, of course, be based on complete confidence concerning the chain of historical causation itself. True enough, the bulk of evidence concerning the course of European political history from Metternich's time to ours is in. Yet before we can pass judgment on the character of the impact of his policies on our times, we would have to be very sure that he really exercised such an influence. To answer this question of causation in a fully satisfactory way is actually a far more difficult task than that of forming value judgments. Here we have to face the fact that we can assume but we cannot prove the degree to which Metternich influenced later events.

An assumption of this kind is usually based on three interrelated facts: the containment of Russia, the preservation of the Hapsburg Empire, and above all the establishment and maintenance of peace. Hardly anybody will argue that Metternich's skillful containment of Russia was successful in the long run. Still, it is sometimes asserted that his policy at this particular time might well serve as a model for policies in our day. I do not believe this to be true. If historical analogies are meaningful, we must, of course, make a generous allowance for differences in historical situations. When we come to deal with personalities as different as Alexander I and his brother, and Messrs. Stalin and Khrushchev, the allowance must be very generous indeed. If we add to these differences the more important ones in ideology, we have reached a point where historical comparisons become unprofitable. Metternich's Eastern policy may have been wise or unwise; it teaches us no specific lessons.

Anyone who, like this writer, feels that the disintegration of the Hapsburg Empire at the end of World War I was a major tragedy in international relations cannot fail to be impressed by the argument that Metternich secured the preservation of Austria and therewith the European equilibrium, so tragically destroyed in 1918. While the effect of Austria's disintegration was demonstrably one major factor, though surely not the only one, responsible for the European crises that have continued since that time, the premise that Metternich's achievements helped to secure the great-power position of Austria up to that point is far more problematical. There can be no doubt that he made an outstanding contribution to the restoration of the Hapsburg Empire from the depths of defeat in the Napoleonic wars to the key position she held for a decade after 1812 and to her continuation as a great power for some time subsequent to this. Yet restoration and preservation are by no means the same. Whether Metternich's part in establishing Austria's domestic policies and ideological alignments actually contributed to the preservation of the empire up to 1918 or, from a long-range viewpoint, possibly shortened her lease on life, is a question of extraordinary complexity. It merges with the more comprehensive question whether social and cultural change can be stopped at a certain point by governmental authority and, if so, for how long. Historians thus far have not found satisfactory answers.

The Russian and the Austrian problems are both linked to the supreme quest for the preservation of peace, the decisive test in any evaluation of Metternich. On the assumption (which, however, has not been proved) that Metternich's policies are largely responsible for the course of international relations from the Congress of Vienna to the outbreak of the war in 1914, the arguments present themselves as follows: Metternich's system secured for a full century the preservation, if not of peace, at least of an era without major war. Other schools of thought refuse to give Metternich credit at this point on the basis of the familiar and unanswerable argument that the extent of historical causation cannot be proved. More fruitful, however, is the examination of another line of thought which denies that peace was actually preserved during the century from 1815 to 1914. Here we may come close indeed to the core of the Metternich problem.

By and large, historiography prior to the first world war took an unfriendly, even hostile attitude toward Metternich's foreign policy. This, of course, was due to several factors. Established western liberalism, central European neo-liberalism of the third quarter of the nineteenth century, and the German nationalism of the second empire, represented best perhaps by Treitschke's philosophy of history, rejected Metternich's doctrines and devices for obvious and specific reasons. Beyond this, however, one may well say that the people who reached manhood around 1848 and died before 1914 did not feel that they lived in an era of peace. To them the Crimean War, the Austro-Prussian War, and the Franco-Prussian War were big wars, and in view of the relative number of troops engaged and casualties suffered they had good reason to think so. Only the tragedy of two world wars has changed that picture. This, indeed, is the period when the reversal in the evaluation of Metternich, initiated by such eminent historians as Guglielmo Ferrero and Heinrich von Srbik, commences.[12]

It is psychologically quite understandable that the impact of the dark forces of our time should challenge the historian to portray Metternich in a favorable light. Undoubtedly such a shift in the frame of reference explains the motivation of those who contend that Metternich made a lasting contribution to peace. It neither proves nor disproves the contention itself. One thing only is certain. Metternich himself wanted peace, and peace not merely in terms of a Bismarckian saturation of power but on the basis of the status quo, adjusted by negotiations as he conceived them. Thus the living lesson of his work pertaining to international relations is not embedded in any particulars of political strategy but in principles which may be summarized as follows: moderation in success and perseverance in defeat, steadfastness of purpose as the intrinsic premise of compromise irrespective of conflicting ideologies, consensus based on reason and not on emotion. Surely not these principles in themselves but failure to apply them successfully is responsible for Metternich's equivocal position in history. Yet how could he have applied them successfully without linking them gradually to some kind of system of popular sovereignty? And how could he have done so without repudiating the tradition he stood for?

[12] Guglielmo Ferrero (Eng. trans), *The principles of power* (New York, 1942) and *The reconstruction of Europe* (New York, 1941). The third volume of Srbik's biography deals with the historiographical evaluation of Metternich. See also A. Wandruszka, "Der Kutscher Europas. Fürst Metternich im Urteil der Historiker von Heute," *Wort und Wahrheit*, XIV (1959), 459 ff.

2 / 1848: An Opportunity Lost?

In a much quoted phrase, G. M. Trevelyan has called the year 1848 "the turning point at which modern history failed to turn." In 1848, liberals in France, Germany, Italy, and the Austrian Empire carried out revolts against their authoritarian rulers and demanded constitutions, and—in several cases or to some degree—universal suffrage and republican governments. In Italy and Germany, the revolutionaries aimed at national unification—as well. In the Austrian Empire, Kossuth and the Hungarians fought for an independent state. At Prague, the Slavonic Congress asked that the empire be converted into a federation of nations enjoying equal rights. In France, where there was no problem of national identity, social and political considerations predominated. There the revolutionaries established the Second French Republic, and in its provisional government, Socialists, such as Louis Blanc, held office. By the end of 1849, however, all these revolutions had been effectively crushed.

In France, the Second Republic did not formally become the authoritarian Second Empire until 1852. But in December 1848, the election of Prince Louis Napoleon as president of the Republic gave comfort to the partisans of order, for all that Louis Napoleon had been elected directly by universal suffrage and had shown concern with social problems. In Italy and Germany, the work of unification was undertaken by the "new statesmen," Cavour and Bismarck. Although they made concessions to moderate, liberal opinion, *Realpolitik* rather than idealism guided their policies, and the unification of their states was achieved largely through force of arms. In the Austrian Empire reaction was the most complete. With the institution of the repressive Bach system, it seemed as though the hands of the clock had been turned back—thus Whig or liberal history's interpretation of 1848 as "an opportunity lost." Perhaps the most eloquent expression of this point of view comes from Trevelyan.

That year as we can now see, was an ill year for the future of mankind. The failure of the Continental Liberals to establish some measure of free government and national self-expression at a time when Europe was ripe for such a change was a disaster on the grand scale. It lies at the root of many of the evils of the present day, and the year 1848 is, negatively, one of the governing dates of modern history. An opportunity was lost which did not recur. It was a moment when Parliamentary institutions and free political life might have been established on the Continent in time to become acclimatized before the social questions and class divisions of modern industrialism became unfavourably acute. If Germany had then been liberalized, it can scarcely be doubted that Russia would have reformed in time. And the new nations as Mazzini prophetically saw them, might have begun their racial life on a basis not of militarism and mutual hatred, but of complete opposition to the militant attitude of mind. The very feebleness of the military preparations of the patriots . . . illustrates the point. Conscription and government by bayonets, being at that time associated with the denial of nationalism, were unpopular with the men of '48. But owing to the failure of their efforts, national aspirations took another mold and were re-expressed in terms of military power.[1]

In 1944, Sir Lewis Namier, never one to shun historical controversy, subjected the older view of 1848 to a blistering attack in the Raleigh Lecture on History at the British Academy. In his interpretation of 1848, Namier stressed the "early manifestations of aggressive nationalisms, especially of German nationalism which derives from the much belauded Frankfort Parliament rather than from Bismarck and 'Prussianism' ". The belief that "there was something especially noble and precious and liberal minded about the collectivity of Germans at that time" is, according to Sir Lewis, "one of the legends of history. . . . With 1848 starts the Great European War of every nation against its neighbors."[2]

The next two selections, which postdate Namier's interpretation, reflect the increasing concern of historians with the nature and causes of revolution. In the first, William L. Langer, an outstanding historian of European diplomacy, argues that the revolutions of 1848 "led to grave political and social conflicts, to say nothing of national antagonisms and wars that might otherwise have been avoided." In each case, says Langer, reforms would probably have been forthcoming without revolutionary action. In striking contrast to England, the civil police in the continental capitals was everywhere "inadequate for the task." The European powers were therefore almost entirely dependent on regular military forces. Professor Langer asserts that social and political conditions in the mid-nineteenth century made the use of troops for police work "extremely hazardous."

The second selection, by the distinguised German historian, Friedrich Meinecke, concentrates on the revolution of 1848 in Germany. Though his is a moderate interpretation, Meinecke views the German revolution much more favorably than does Langer. He admits that the nationalism of the liberals of Frankfort might have led "into the storm center of a great European war." But he points out earlier that in the revolution the German people kept to "a comparatively high moral level" and warns against being misled by "the criminal excesses reached in our day" into condemning the elemental national craving of the men of '48. For theirs was a genuine hunger for something indispensable."

In general, Meinecke thinks that the failure of the German revolution of 1848 was a tragedy, inevitable because of political and social factors operative at the time and because of historical factors reaching back into the German past. Meinecke's interpretation both tempers the newer, harsher view of German nationalism in 1848 and challenges, with its theme of "inevitable tragedy," the older interpretation of an "opportunity lost."

[1] G. M. Trevelyan, *Manin and the Venetian Revolution of 1848* (London: Longmans, Green & Co., 1923), pp. vii-viii.

[2] L. B. Namier, *1848: The Revolution of the Intellectuals,* The Raleigh Lecture on History–1944. From the *Proceedings of the British Academy,* XXX (London: Geoffrey Cumberledge), p. 33.

THE PATTERN OF URBAN REVOLUTION IN 1848

William Langer

Although the centennial celebrations of 1948 spawned many publications and brought into new relief many aspects of the European upheavals of the mid-nineteenth century, relatively little attention has been devoted to the comparative study of these revolutions. The objective of this essay is to examine the outbreaks of February and March 1848 so as to determine what, if anything, they had in common, and to raise the question whether these famous revolutions were inevitable or even beneficial.

Although there were disturbances in the countryside as well as in many cities, the events in the four great capitals, Paris, Vienna, Berlin, and London, were crucial. It is true that these government centers had been but little touched by the new industrialism and that therefore the proletariat of the factories played but a very subordinate role, especially in the early days of the revolutions. Yet the capitals were the seats of traditional industry, with a huge population of craftsmen, tradesmen, and specialized workers of all kinds. London and Paris, in particular, harbored thousands of different industries without having much of a modern industrial proletariat. The workers were mostly what might be termed *menu peuple* (lesser bourgeoisie).

This does not mean that the capital cities were less restless than the new factory towns. In all of them life had become unsettled and precarious, for everywhere the traditional artisan was exposed to the competition of machine industry, located chiefly in the provincial towns. Wages, if they did not actually decline, remained low, while employment became steadily more uncertain. The plight of the urban workers following the economic crisis of 1846-1847 is well known and its bearing on the revolutions of 1848 has been duly stressed by Professor Labrousse and others. Basically it was inevitable that the early stages of industrialization should have brought instability and hardship, but the situation in mid-century was greatly aggravated by the fantastic growth of the European population; this growth entailed an unprecedented movement of rural workers to the cities, which for centuries had held the promise of opportunity.

In the years from 1800 to 1850 the growth of the European capitals was stupendous, with the result that at the end of the period a large proportion of the population was not native born. It consisted largely of immigrants, permanent or temporary, coming either from nearby areas, or from abroad. In the 1840s alone about 250,000 persons came into London, 46,000 of whom were Irishmen, who were particularly disliked and feared by the English workers because of their incredibly low standard of living. In addition, there were substantial numbers of Belgian and German workers.

As for Paris, the researches of Louis Chevalier and others have thrown a flood of light on the nature of the population and the conditions of life. The number of inhabitants just about doubled between 1800 and 1850, due very largely to

Footnotes omitted.

immigration. Thus, between 1831 and 1836 about 115,000 arrived, and from 1841 to 1846 another 98,000. Most of the newcomers were from the neighboring *départements*, but there were many foreigners as well. Accurate statistics are lacking, but there appear to have been upward of 50,000 Germans (mostly tailors, shoemakers, cabinetmakers) in Paris, to say nothing of large numbers of Belgian and Italian workers and sizable contingents of political refugees from many lands.

The situation in Vienna and Berlin was much the same. The population of the Austrian capital numbered about 400,000, 125,000 of whom had been added between 1827 and 1847. In 1845 there were some 130,000 Czech, Polish, and Italian immigrants. In Berlin the populations rose from 180,000 to 400,000 between 1815 and 1847, due largely to the heavy immigration from the eastern provinces.

In all cities the steady influx of people created an acute housing shortage. This was less true of London than of the continental capitals, for there the government offices had long since moved from the Old City to Westminster and the well-to-do had built new homes in the West End and along the main highways to the west and northwest. The 125,000 people who still lived in the Old City were for the most part clerks, runners, cleaners, and other employees of the great banks and business houses. In the continental capitals, however, the exodus of the upper classes from the old central districts had only just begun. The new and fashionable sections of northwestern Paris were still far from complete, while the oldest part of the city was incredibly congested, "an almost inpenetrable hive of tenements and shops." The efforts of Rambuteau, the *préfet* of the Seine, to open up the dingiest areas by constructing larger arteries, involved the destruction of much cheap housing little of which was replaced elsewhere. Under the circumstances rents rose rapidly. Most immigrant workers were lucky to find even miserable quarters in the center of the town or in the workers' sections of eastern Paris. "The difficulty of finding lodgings," wrote a contemporary, "is for the worker a constant ordeal and a perpetual cause of misery."

In Vienna and Berlin, as in Paris, a great many immigrant workers found refuge in the lodging houses, which enjoyed a golden age at this time. In the low-grade places men and women were housed together, and it was by no means uncommon for eight or nine persons to be crowded into one room. The old Innere Stadt of Vienna, still surrounded by its seventeenth-century walls, was so hopelessly congested that some members of the aristocracy were obliged, most reluctantly, to build new "villas" beyond the Kärntner Tor, while practically all industry, with the exception of the old-established silk trade, was compelled, by government decree, to locate in the suburbs. In Berlin, too, the rapidly developing textile and metallurgical industries were concentrated in the northern areas, while the upper classes lived mostly in the western and southwestern sections. Berlin was notorious for its wretched lodging houses and workers' barracks.

Considering the great instability of the changing social order, it is not surprising that many of the newcomers in the cities failed to find the hoped-for employment. Thousands were chronically out of work, reduced to living in dank cellars or unheated garrets, and often driven by desperation into robbery or other crimes. In Paris, as in most other cities, about a quarter of the population was indigent, dependent on government or private relief. The situation thus engendered was particularly dangerous because as yet in many cities the rich and poor lived cheek-by-jowl. The Paris apartment house, whose lower floors were occupied by the well-to-do while the *petite bourgeoisie* took over the upper stories and the paupers were left the crannies under the eaves, are familiar to us from Balzac's novels, but it must be remembered that in almost every part of Paris prosperous residential areas and pockets of slums were intermingled. There was no strictly aristocratic quarter and no strictly workingmen's quarter. Even in metropolitan London fashionable streets were often backed by abandoned "rookeries." Such existed even in the West End, in the vicinity of Buckingham Palace.

Overall conditions in the crowded cities of the early or midnineteenth century were such as to create chronic social tension. Riots by the hungry or unemployed were all too common, as were also clashes between native and foreign workers. It is obvious that these outbreaks could and at times did assume such proportions as to threaten governments, if not the entire social order.

To combat disturbances European governments had traditionally relied upon their military forces. Napoleon's "whiff of grapeshot" was an example of the use even of artillery in breaking up a hostile demonstration. More common, however, was the employment of sabre-charging cavalry. Nicholas I of Russia, though confronted with the most formidable and urgent social problem in Europe, escaped revolution in 1848 by ruthless application of these tactics. His internal defense force, quartered throughout the country, numbered some 200,000 men and beat down any threat of insurrection. The secret police and the Cossack brigades showed the world how to maintain order and vindicated Nicholas's claim to be the gendarme of Europe.

But in western Europe these methods of brutal repression had by the nineteenth century become as difficult to apply as they were objectionable. To ride or shoot down unarmed citizens was hardly the answer to political or social problems, to say nothing of the fact that conscripted soldiers showed ever greater unwillingness to fire upon the people. In Britain, where the problems created by the industrial revolution were most acute, the government had, before 1848, worked out a different procedure or policy. In connection with the very formidable and menacing Chartist demonstrations of 1839 and 1842 freedom of speech and assembly were generally respected, but the authorities made it perfectly clear that any effort to subvert the government or the social order would be ruthlessly suppressed. Furthermore, General Charles Napier, in charge of the forces in the industrial areas of the north, by adroitly placing his troops and by bringing additional soldiery from Ireland to ensure against defection, succeeded in creating a genuine deterrent.

As for London, much greater advances had been made in the direction of public security. In 1829 the first modern civil police force had been established, consisting of selected, uniformed, trained and well-paid constables numbering by 1848 about 5500 men. Despite much popular hostility, the London police soon made itself respected and indeed worked out the tactics of what today are called "riot control formations," that is, the organization and employment of squad or platoon wedges to penetrate mobs, arrest leaders, and break up demonstrations, and of echelons to pry rioters away from buildings and force them to move in specified directions.

Chartist Demonstration in London

Some insight into the problems confronting continental governments in February and March 1848 can be gained by reviewing the great Chartist demonstration and petition scheduled for April 10 in London as the culmination of a series of disturbances in Glasgow, Manchester, and even in the capital that echoed the revolutionary events on the continent in the preceding weeks.

In the councils of the Chartist movement there were some who, as in 1839, favored revolutionary action and the use of violence in the event that the great petition were again rejected by parliament. But the majority of the leaders, long since convinced of the government's determination to suppress any attempt at insurrection, still hoped to attain their ends by peaceful demonstration. The plan then was to stage a monster meeting followed by the procession of thousands of workers to the House of Commons. The great day was to be April 10, when contingents of Chartists marched from various assembly points in the metropolis to Kennington Common, in southwestern London. When they gathered, at about 11:00 A.M., the police were already at hand. Feargus O'Connor, the leader, was warned that while the meeting itself was permissible, the law forbade large demonstrations designed to intimidate Parliament and that therefore the crowd would be permitted to recross the river only in small groups. O'Connor, a demagogue braver in words than in deeds, at once urged his followers to accept the police ruling. There was some speechmaking, but presently the whole meeting was washed out by rain. The demonstrators straggled back over Blackfriars Bridge, while the petition, with its millions of signatures, was taken to Parliament by a small delegation riding in three cabs. The day ended without even a window having been broken.

There is every reason to think that the London police could by itself have dealt with the Chartist demonstration. But the government had been unwilling to take the chance and had, with the full support of the propertied classes, made preparations far beyond anything the situation called for. The aged Duke of Wellington had been put in command of the troops, which were brought in from the surrounding areas. At the same time, a call was sent out for special constables, to which all respectable elements, from peers to business and professional men, down to clerks, railroad officials, shopkeepers, and others responded in great numbers. It is said, and was so reported in the *Times*, that no less than 150,000 of these constables were enrolled. They sand-bagged and garrisoned the Bank of England, the Post-Office, India House, and other valuable properties, while the troops, which were kept out of sight as much as possible, occupied the Tower and other strong points. On the river three ships were held in readiness, with steam up, to transport troops or supplies to any threatened spot. The Chartists, as they marched to their rendezvous, could hardly fail to notice the reception that awaited them in case of serious unrest.

So much certainly was to be learned from the London experience: (1) an efficient police force was capable of dealing with even large-scale demonstrations; (2) a government acceptable to the citizenry could count on the support of huge numbers of volunteers; (3) the troops could be kept in reserve, to be used only in an emergency; (4) a clean-cut policy and adequate preparations would serve as an effective deterrent. Harriet Martineau, in her account of the Kennington Common meeting, was not far off the mark when she declared exultantly: "From that day it was a settled matter that England was safe from revolution."

It is true, of course, that the British government had the advantage in facing the Chartist threat not only of previous experience but of the experience of the continental governments that had succumbed to revolution. Nonetheless, it will be useful to review the outbreak of insurrection in Paris, Vienna, and Berlin in the light of what could and was done in another country in what were roughly comparable circumstances. For it is probably a mistake to argue that Britain, because it had no revolution in 1848, was in some mysterious way different and therefore exempt from major social ructions. If there was a great deal of talk of revolution on the continent in the years preceding 1848, there was hardly less of such talk in England. Friedrich Engels, it will be recalled, in 1845 held that social revolution was unavoidable.

The 1848 Revolution in Paris

The events of February 1848 in Paris, which ended with the downfall of the Orleans Monarchy, were conscientiously analyzed by M. Crémieux more than fifty years ago. They were far too complicated to be satisfactorily summarized in a brief essay. Certain features, however, should be highlighted. It is well known, for instance, that Louis Philippe and his chief minister, M. Guizot, were surprised by the insurrection by which they were overtaken. This surprise is at least understandable, for even though opposition to the regime had been mounting it certainly did not suggest the possibility of a major upheaval. The opposition, insofar as it was organized and directed, was in the main a parliamentary opposition calling for very modest changes: liberalization of the electorate, limitation of political patronage, extension of civil liberties. It is hardly an exaggeration to describe this opposition as a family affair, the struggle of one faction against another within the same social framework. Its leaders did not plan revolution, nor even desire it. For months they had been carrying on a campaign of propaganda and agitation centering about a program of political banquets. But these methods, if they were not directly imitated from the British, were at any rate the counterpart of the great pressure campaigns conducted across the Channel by Daniel O'Connell and Richard Cobden, namely the campaigns that led to the emancipation of the Catholics, to the great Reform Act of 1832, and to the repeal of the Corn Laws in 1846. These victories over a well-entrenched ruling class were watched with the utmost interest by liberals all over the Continent. When Cobden in 1847 made a tour of the continental countries he was everywhere fêted by the enlightened, educated circles, all of which took heart from the British experience. Considering that in the French Chamber most of the prominent members had, by 1848, aligned themselves with the opposition, there is no reason to suppose that in the not too distant future the resistance of even Guizot and Louis Philippe would have crumbled.

Only a few words need be said in this context of the more popular opposition, that of the disfranchised writers, artists, tradesmen, and workers who, ever since their disillusionment with the July Revolution of 1830, had been organized in secret societies and some of whom, certainly, were quite prepared to rise in revolt in the name of democracy or socialism. The unemployment, want, and unrest in Paris were such that a great social uprising seemed to some, like Tocqueville, a real and immediate threat. It will be remembered that the monster opposition banquet that had been planned for the first *arrondissement* was moved to a hall in the aristocratic quarter and that, when it was prohibited by the authorities, the opposition leaders were positively relieved. Far from wanting a popular disturbance, the opposition was intent on remaining within the bounds of legality. But in actuality the popular opposition, while noisy and threatening, was so limited in numbers, so divided and weak, so unprepared as to be quite innocuous. It may be recalled that popular leaders like Louis Blanc positively dreaded an insurrection, knowing that the lower classes were bound to be defeated.

The question now arises: How well equipped and prepared was the government to deal with major disorders? It had faced a series of formidable disturbances in the years 1830-1834 and a concerted attempt at insurrection in 1839. Its security forces were briefly as follows. The regular uniformed police force (*sergents de ville*) numbered only a few hundred men, but was reinforced by an essentially military *Garde municipale*. This body, recruited largely among army veterans, consisted of sixteen companies of infantry and five squadrons of cavalry (a total of 3200 men), splendidly accoutered, thoroughly drilled, and so notorious for its brutality as to be passionately hated by the population.

The *Garde municipale* was roughly the equivalent of the London metropolitan police, except that it was more pronouncedly military in character. It, in turn, was expected to rely for support on the *Garde nationale* which, again, was intended to play the same role as the London special constables. The *Garde nationale* was, however, a permanent force, more or less regularly trained and excercised, for the most part uniformed and armed. It consisted of one legion for each of the twelve *arrondissements,* plus one elite cavalry legion and four suburban legions—all told a force of no less than 84,000 men. All able-bodied men were liable for service in the *Garde nationale* but actually only those who paid a certain annual tax were enrolled. It was understood that the *Garde* was an essentially bourgeois formation designed for defense of the regime. Only after it had gone into action against insurgents was the regular garrison expected to take part. This garrison consisted of some 30,000 troops, quartered in barracks scattered throughout the city.

In the July Revolution of 1830 the commander of the forces, Marshal Marmont, had been faced by the refusal of his troops to fire on the populace. The danger of defection in the event of civil strife was a continuing one and for that very reason the government relied chiefly on the *Garde nationale* to quell the disturbances of the 1830s. It proved to be a matter of prime importance, then, that the devotion of the *Garde* to the king had weakened greatly by 1848. Ever since 1835 the upper classes had evaded service, while the legions of the poorer *arrondissements* had become seriously disgruntled. The king was certainly not ignorant of these developments. Indeed, after 1840 he did not even review the *Garde*, though to show his displeasure in this way was probably unwise. The estrangement between the ruler and the formations that were supposedly the mainstay of his regime was to be the crucial factor in the events of February 22-24, 1848.

The crowd that assembled on the Place de la Madeleine on the rainy morning of February 22 was altogether nondescript and evidently moved more by curiosity than by any set purpose. It surged aimlessly to and fro until in the later morning a group of students from the Left Bank led the way to the Chamber of Deputies, where the first minor clashes took place before the crowd was pressed back over the river to the Place de la Concorde. The king and the government clearly did not take the demonstration seriously, for preparatory measures that had been decided on were countermanded, probably from fear that action by the troops would only roil the populace and possibly from uncertainty as to the reliability of the forces. In this connection it is interesting to note that on this very first day of unrest the troops tended to stand aloof. They watched idly while the crowd broke street lanterns and overturned omnibuses, and in some cases stood inactive while barricades were being thrown across the streets.

From the outset the *Garde municipale* acted with its usual energy and ruthlessness and, as might be expected, enraged the populace. It might conceivably have broken up the demonstrations by its own efforts, had it been given appropriate orders. But these were not forthcoming, so the *Garde* found itself reduced to purely defensive operations. Since the disorders continued to spread, the king on the morning of February 23 reluctantly called out the *Garde nationale*, only to find, to his horror, that even the legions from the well-to-do sections had joined the opposition to the Guizot regime and insisted on immediate reforms. The effect of this revelation was to precipitate the rather unceremonious dismissal of Guizot. Had the king then called at once on the opposition leaders, Thiers and Barrot, to form a ministry and had he, at the same time, accepted the modest reforms demanded by the opposition, the situation might well have been saved. But Louis Philippe disliked Thiers and was loath to accept changes. In the sequel he was to agree to a reform ministry but without consenting to reforms and, belatedly, to show a determination to resist that, at an earlier hour, might have stood him in good stead.

For the time being, both the *Garde* and the troops were left without adequate directives. In the growing disorder the officers lost confidence while the men became demoralized. Meanwhile the center of disturbance shifted to the crowded *arrondissements*, where the barricades went up by the hundreds. On the evening of February 23 there took place the "massacre" of the Boulevard des Capucines, when a surging crowd of National Guards and people collided with a detachment of troops which, hard pressed, opened fire, leaving some fifty persons dead on the pavement. Only after this tragic episode, which raised the resentment of the populace to fever heat, did Louis Philippe entrust command of both the troops and the *Garde nationale* to Marshal Bugeaud, victor of the Algerian campaigns and a soldier renowned for his toughness, who had been itching for a chance to put the "rabble" in its place. Bugeaud started out bright and early on the morning of February 24 in an attempt to reopen communications between the key points of the city. Yet before noon he proclaimed a cease-fire. The reasons for this *volte-face* on the part of a fire-eating commander have been the subject of much debate, but need not detain us here. The fact is that the weariness and demoralization of the troops, the almost complete defection of the *Garde nationale*, and above all the hundreds of barricades must have shown him the futility of his effort. The king made a last desperate but vain attempt to rally the support of at least part of the *Garde nationale*, after which he was driven to the inevitable decision to abdicate.

In review it must be reiterated that the revolution that developed in Paris was neither planned nor desired. The outbreaks were disjointed, isolated, leaderless, and utterly without plan or coordination. The king, through poor judgment, distrust, and indecision, allowed the disturbances to develop to the point at which suppression became impossible. When he failed to conciliate the *Garde nationale*, he sealed the fate not only of the regime but of the dynasty.

Revolution in Vienna

The situation in Vienna was strikingly similar to that in Paris, despite the vast disparity between France and the Hapsburg Monarchy in terms of political and social development. Opposition to the Metternich system had been growing apace during the 1840s and by 1848 had reached the point at which even the old feudal estates were calling for change and, more importantly, influential officials, army officers, and intellectuals were agitating for reforms along the lines of Western liberalism. The government suffered much from the fact that the Emperor was incompetent to rule, while the imperial family was divided on questions of policy. Certainly Prince Metternich had many enemies, a situation that obliged him to acquiesce in the establishment of the *Gewerbeverein* and the *Leseverein*, organizations that soon became strongholds of the liberal, reforming factions. It is rather hard to believe that, in the natural course of events, Metternich would not soon have been forced out of office and a more liberal, progressive policy adopted.

Naturally the news from Paris, the reports of the ease with which Guizot and Louis Philippe had been driven out by popular demonstration, greatly reinforced the pressure on the Vienna court. A veritable whirlwind of petitions called for an end to repression and the introduction of a liberal system. Most prominent among these was the petition submitted by the 4000 Viennese students, many of whom came from the lower classes, and all of whom suffered under the restrictions of the Metternich system. This, like other petitions, was rejected, largely because of the unwillingness of the Archduke Louis, chief of the council of state, to consider making concessions under pressure.

The Viennese government in no sense faced a threat of revolution. The loyalty of the entire population of the dynasty—even to the half-witted Emperor—was such as to astound contempories. The opposition was, as in France, directed against the ministry, hoping that its policy of immobility or stagnation could be gotten rid of by peaceful pressure. The only real danger of upheaval lay in the workingmen of the suburbs, who like workers elsewhere in Europe were suffering, and who, by the spring of 1848, were in such ferment that the government was obliged to set up public works and open soup kitchens to alleviate the unemployment and want. But not even the workers were revolutionary in the sense of having an organization or program. The workers were desperate but knew no course of action besides wrecking the hated machines and occasionally plundering the foodshops.

Besieged by deputations and all but buried under petitions, the government, fearing disturbances, ordered the garrison troops in readiness. These forces numbered about 14,000, mostly quartered in barracks just outside the walls. On these the government would have to rely in case of serious disorder, for the police forces were altogether inadequate. The civil police was almost exclusively a secret police, assigned to the surveillance of dangerous and subversive persons and organizations. Under its supervision was a *Militar-Polizeiwache* consisting of 1100 to 1200 men. On paper, at least, there stood between these police forces and the regular troops something akin to the French *Garde nationale*, namely, a *Bürgerwehr* (Citizens' Guard) that, during the French occupation in 1809 had served a useful purpose but that had since 1815 sunk to the status of a ceremonial guard, noted chiefly for the excellence of its band-music. Officially, the *Bürgerwehr* comprised 14,000 men of the upper and middle bourgeoisie, electing its own officers and serving at its own expense. Only about a third of the force was equipped with firearms.

The events of March 13 in Vienna were as confused as the February days in Paris. It was a bright spring morning and many people, including elegantly-dressed ladies, assembled before the palace of the Estates of Lower Austria, because it was known that this influential body was about to proceed to the palace with yet another petition. Presently a large body of students arrived, hoping to enlist the support of the Estates for their own petition. No one knew just what to do. While waiting, some of the students began to make speeches. There was much milling about in the narrow Herrengasse and in the courtyard of the palace. Eventually, toward noon, the president of the Estates appealed to the Archduke Albert, commanding the troops, for relief from popular pressure. The soldiers had a hard time making their way to the center of disturbances. Presently, tiles and other missiles were thrown at them from roofs and windows; guns went off, no one knew how or why; there were five dead. Like the much more horrible "massacre" of the Boulevard des Capucines, this episode was enough to set off a whole series of desultory clashes between the military and the people. At the same time crowds of workers from the suburbs began to invade the Inner City until the gates were closed against them. Some remained outside the walls, howling like hungry wolves. Most of them, however, returned to the suburbs to engage in an orgy of incendiarism and plunder.

Franz Grillparzer, the great Austrian dramatist, was an eyewitness of the events of March 13 and pictured the initial demonstrations at the Standehaus as a pleasant, good-natured fracas. The whole thing, he wrote in his recollections, could have been snuffed out by two battalions of soldiers, but no troops, in fact not even the police, were to be seen. The military, when at last it appeared, did too much. After the first bloodshed and after the arrival of the workers from the suburbs, the situation became much more ominous. During the afternoon the demand for Metternich's dismissal became deafening. At the same time there were violent clashes between the troops and the populace, led by the students. Efforts to storm the arsenal led to considerable bloodshed, while at the Schottentor the workers actually managed to secure control of the entrance. In the elegant suburb of Wieden the mob sacked Metternich's villa and other aristocratic homes.

In the hope that order might still be restored, a group of prominent citizens in the late afternoon persuaded the Lord Mayor, Count Czapka, to call out the *Bürgerwehr*, of which he was the commanding officer, and if possible induce the military to withdraw from the city while the *Bürgerwehr* took over. The chronology is hopelessly confused and it is hardly worthwhile trying to fix it. Archduke Albert, the commander of the forces, who himself had been badly injured by a block of wood thrown at him from a window, did in fact evacuate the inner city. For the next several, critical days, the garrison troops stood idle and useless on the parade ground just outside the walls.

The *Bürgerwehr*, meanwhile, was to play the same role as that of the Paris *Garde nationale*. A deputation of *Bürgerwehr* officers at once proceeded to the palace to demand the dismissal of Metternich (allowing the court until 9:00 P.M. to make up its mind) and the arming of the students. These were hard decisions for the court to make, for the emperor was feeble-minded and his relatives were badly divided. Several of the archdukes, led by Archduke John, had long since convinced themselves that Metternich must go and that real reforms must be undertaken. On the other hand, Archduke Louis abominated reforms and was urged by Metternich and Field Marshal Prince Windischgrätz to stand firm. The whole disturbance, argued the aged chancellor, was nothing more than a riot that could be easily mastered by the police and the troops. What led to the downfall of Louis Philippe was his eagerness to dismiss Guizot. Where a policy of concessions would lead no one knew. As for Windischgrätz, he had had years of experience dealing with serious workers' outbreaks in Prague and other Bohemian cities. He was sure that energetic action by the military could quickly suppress the disturbances. To dismiss Metternich, he held, would be nothing short of shameless cowardice.

In the end, "the impotent scarecrows" (Kudlich) were unable to withstand the pressure of *Bürgerwehr*, students, and members of the Estates. In the evening Metternich was obliged to resign and permission was given for the immediate arming of the students, who alone were thought to have any influence with the rampaging workers. In the course of the night thousands of muskets were dealt out to students and citizens. These, in turn, formed patrols and managed to restore some semblance of order.

No good purpose would be served by pursuing the story further. At the end of the first day the court had surrendered to the liberal elements, if only in order to master the radicalism of the workers—that is, to put an end to an unwanted revolution for which the indecision of the court was largely to blame. A few words should, however, be said of the immediate aftermath. Like Louis Philippe in his belated appointment of Marshal Bugeaud, the Viennese court made a hopeless attempt to save the situation by naming Prince Windischgrätz civil and military governor of Vienna (noon, March 14). He was to proclaim martial law, while the government was to revoke all the concessions made under popular pressure on the preceding day. The field marshal apparently thought the situation too far gone, and his efforts to assert his authority did, in fact, prove altogether futile. The court was no longer in a position to refuse the demand for the organization of a national guard, which was to include a separate student corps (*Akademische Legion*). This new national guard was intended to comprise about 10,000 reliable citizens, but popular pressure led to the enrollment of some 30,000, in addition to the 7000 students in the special legion. Windischgrätz was, for the time being, quite helpless. On the following day (March 15) the court had to agree to a constitution, with which the first phase of this rather incredible revolution was brought to a close.

Revolution in Berlin

The story of the Berlin revolution—our last case study—provides a classic example of how *not* to deal with revolutionary situations. Berlin, like other capitals, was in a process of rapid economic transformation and was, in addition, a veritable hotbed of radical philosophical thought. Yet, politically, the population was strikingly inexperienced and apathetic. The rapidly developing liberal movement in Prussia had its stronghold not in Berlin, but in the Rhineland and in provincial cities such as Königsberg and Breslau. The famous United Diet of 1847 had revealed the wide divergence between the aspirations of the rising middle class and the outmoded, traditionalist notions of the ruler. But even then the liberals, for all their discontent, were far from advocating revolution. Like their counterparts elsewhere in Europe, they relied on agitation and pressure to bring about a constitutional regime. A sober evaluation of the evidence suggests that they were probably justified in their expectations. By the beginning of 1848 even so recalcitrant a prince as Frederick William IV was beginning to yield to the constitutionally-directed importunities of his ministers.

Berlin is supposed to have had, in 1848, some 40,000 to 50,000 industrial workers in the textile and metallurgical trades, and certainly far more in the traditional artisan occupations. As elsewhere, the workers suffered acutely from the rapid economic changes; five-eighths of the laboring population is supposed to have been in extreme want. In the years just preceding 1848 some workers' associations had sprung up and some revolutionary groups, such as the *Zeitungshalle*, had emerged. But these were exceptional. The workers were, for the most part, illiterate and apathetic so far as politics were concerned. Class consciousness and subversive activity were practically nonexistent.

It was no doubt inevitable that news of the Paris insurrection should have led to much excitement and that, somewhat later, reports of Metternich's fall should have evoked widespread enthusiasm. From March 6 on, there were many meetings, speeches, resolutions, and petitions, all advancing the familiar liberal demands. The general tone of both meetings and petitions was one of hope and good will. And rightly so, for the Prussian government, like those of the South German states, was on the verge of giving way to popular pressure. There was, to be sure, strong conservative opposition, led by Prince William of Prussia, the king's brother. But there were even stronger forces convinced that fundamental changes were inescapable and that Prussia's future position in Germany depended on leadership of the liberal movement. As early as March 12 the king, albeit reluctantly and with mental reservations, made the basic decision to accept a constitution and a responsible ministry.

Had the Prussian government provided Berlin with an adequate civil police, there is no reason to suppose that the popular meetings and processions would have gotten out of hand. But, incredible though it may seem, in this city of 400,000 there was no police to speak of, nor even anything akin to a civic or national guard. Officially there was a gendarmerie consisting of 40 sergeants and 110 men, but these gendarmes were employed almost exclusively in the law courts, markets, places of amusement, and so forth. For the preservation of public order the government relied on the garrison troops (about 12,000 in number). In short, the government could deal with serious disturbances only by the methods employed in Russia, methods altogether unsuited to the conditions of a large western city. This had become clear during the so-called *Potato Revolution* of April, 1847—large-scale food riots during which some barricades had been erected and severe clashes between troops and people had taken place. At that time the city authorities had petitioned for a modest constabulary, to act in the first instance. But the government had been unwilling to delegate such authority. It therefore remained dependent on the armed forces, which, because of their ruthless and brutal action, were intensely hated by the populace, and which, in turn, despised the "rabble."

As popular excitement grew, the authorities brought more and more troops into the city. Clashes were almost inevitable. They began to take place on March 13 and the ensuing days, with some loss of life and much burning resentment, accompanied by insults and provocations on both sides. Already on March 9 the city authorities renewed the request for formation of a civil constabulary, which was belatedly granted on March 16. Civic guard units (*Bürgerschutzkommissionen*) were hastily enrolled. There was to be a force of 1200 men, patrolling in groups of ten to twenty, armed only with truncheons. It was, however, understood that henceforth the military should act only if called upon by officers of the civic guard. In a word, they were expected to play the same role as the special constables in London.

Actually this improvised constabulary played but a sorry role in the Berlin uprising. The men had little more than good will. Neither the military nor the populace paid much attention to them. On the contrary, their efforts met with derision. The crowds grew increasingly restless and the troops more and more eager to beat them into submission. Hence the growing demand on the part of the people for the withdrawal of the military from the city and the formation of a real national guard, which would have been tantamount to the king's putting himself at the mercy of his subjects. This he was naturally unwilling to do, but on March 18, just as a monster demonstration at the royal palace was being organized, the king issued the famous "patent" by which he promised the early convocation of the United Diet, expressed his acceptance of constitutional government, and announced his leadership of the liberal, national movement in Germany. Since this document met most of the popular demands, it called forth general enthusiasm. Huge crowds gathered in the palace square, while the recently established civic guards stood in array before the portals of the palace. Then the sight of troops massed in the courtyard of the palace led to renewed cries for withdrawal of the soldiers. The commotion became so great that the king ordered General von Prittwitz, the commander of the troops, to clear the square. The general's cavalry squadron was so hard pressed by the crowds that infantry was sent out to relieve him In the din and confusion two rifle shots rang out. No one was hurt, but the crowds suddenly panicked. Like the Paris populace after the massacre of the Boulevard des Capucines, the Berliners were convinced that they had been betrayed: that they had been lured to the palace by promises of reforms, only to be fallen upon by the hated military. Scattering before the advancing troops, they spread all sorts of alarming stories through the city. Everywhere barricades began to go up, and before evening fighting had broken out in many sections of the metropolis.

The king and his military advisers were always convinced that the insurrection of March 18-19 was instigated and planned by foreign agents—French, Swiss, Poles, 10,000 of whom were reputed to have arrived in the city. But this comfortable theory was not supported by solid evidence. No one doubts that there were a great many foreigners, mostly workers, in Berlin, nor that many German workers had spent some years in Switzerland or Paris. Furthermore, there were certainly some confirmed revolutionaries who provided what inspiration and leadership they could. But the insurrection showed little, if any, evidence of planning or organization. All strata of the Berlin population were involved in one way or another. The students played a far less significant role here than in Vienna, but they do seem to have been instrumental in bringing workers from the suburbs to help man the barricades. But judging from the losses, the actual fighting was carried on largely by young artisans, the traditional craftsmen of the city.

Prittwitz had at his disposal a total force of about 15,000, consisting of cavalry, artillery, and infantry, with which he proceeded to act with great energy. The insurgents, on the other hand, had but few muskets or munitions and had to make do with improvised weapons. Under these circumstances they could not hope adequately to defend the barricades, many of which were but lightly constructed. Instead, they hurled paving stones and tiles from the roofs or poured boiling water from the windows. The troops invaded the houses, pursued the rebels to the garrets, and there either cut them down or dragged them away captive. The advantage throughout lay with the military, and indeed by midnight of March 18 Prittwitz had established effective control over the center of the city. This is not to say that the completion of the operation would not have been an arduous business. Prittwitz seems to have hoped that he could persuade the king to go to Potsdam, after which he would have concentrated his troops outside the city for establishment of a blockade. Eventually, if necessary, he planned to snuff out the insurrection by bombardment of the disaffected quarters. The king, however, wanted to put an end to the fighting at almost any cost. Hence his pathetic appeal "To my dear Berliners," drafted in the night, offering to discuss the situation with representatives of the people and to withdraw the troops once the barricades had been taken down.

The picture at court on the morning of March 19 was one of utter confusion: The king, in a state of near collapse, was evidently unable to appreciate all the implications of his decisions or in general to provide consistent leadership. Beset on all sides by officials and deputations of citizens and, furthermore, misled by unconfirmed reports that barricades were already being dismantled, he ordered the withdrawal of the troops to their barracks except for guards at the palace and the arsenal. Through misunderstanding even these critical places were presently abandoned. It seems likely that the king intended to leave Berlin as part of Prittwitz's plan. But all arrangements for his departure were hopelessly upset when, early in the afternoon, a great procession arrived at the palace bearing the bodies of some 200 victims of the street-fighting, their wounds exposed. Eventually the crowd made its way into the courtyard of the palace. On vociferous demand of the throng the king was obliged to appear and even to doff his cap in reverence to the people's dead. Nothing, certainly, could have demonstrated more clearly the complete capitulation of the monarchy. The people, on the verge of defeat in battle, had secured not only the removal of the troops to their barracks but also the establishment of a civic guard. (The King agreed to this immediately after his humiliating appearance on the balcony.)

The *Bürgerwehr*, as the new civic guard was called, was to be organized by districts, each to have roughly 100 men. Only those who had full citizen rights (*Bürgerbrief*) were eligible for enrollment and the old traditional marksmans-guild (*Schützengilde*) was to provide the kernel of the hastily constructed force of 6000 men. Several thousand muskets were immediately supplied from the arsenal. By 6:00 P.M. on March 19 the élite *Schützengilde* and the newly recruited *Bürgerwehr* were able to take over guard duty at the palace. Frederick William had placed himself entirely under the protection of his subjects. He was as defenseless, wrote the American minister in Berlin on March 21, "as the poorest malefactor of the prisons." Early in the morning of March 21 the entire Berlin garrison was withdrawn from the city. For the moment the revolution was triumphant.

Conclusion

By the mid-nineteenth century the economic and social transformation of western and much of central Europe had reached the point at which basic political changes had become imperative.

There was much pressure on the part of the propertied middle classes for such changes, as is shown most vividly by the fact that in both Paris and Vienna the national guard, designed to protect the existing regime, lent their support to the cause of reform.

Yet there was remarkably little organization or planning for revolution. The colorful heroism of a few revolutionary leaders and the occasional spectacular outbreaks of radical elements are apt to be misleading.

The proponents of liberalism and reform expected to attain their ends by peaceful organization and action. They were fascinated by the achievements of O'Connell and greatly heartened by the triumph of Cobden and the free-trade movement.

After 1846 the forces of liberalism were so formidable and insistent as to be almost irresistible.

It was the unpardonable fault of the Continental princes to have failed to gauge the strength of the opposition and to have refused to accept the inevitable. This was particularly true of Louis Philippe, because the reforms called for in France were of a modest nature and the failing loyalty of the national guard must certainly have been known to him.

Ways to avoid serious upheaval were demonstrated not only by the preventive measures taken later in London, but also by the timely concessions made by King Leopold of Belgium, through which his government secured the support of the opposition which enabled it to present a united front to efforts at radical insurrection.

The alternative to concession was systematic repression, as practiced in quite different forms in Britain and Russia. But prevention of insurrection called above all for vigorous action The situation in the European capitals, with their dislocated artisan economy, widespread unemployment, fluid population, and appalling living conditions, was necessarily explosive. It was imperative, therefore, to prevent ordinary assemblages of people from degenerating into mob action and eventual revolution.

Everywhere on the Continent the civil police was inadequate for the task. As of old, governments still relied on their military forces to prevent major disorders. But the use of troops for police duty, always undesirable because too drastic, had by 1848 become extremely hazardous. For even though the aristocratic officer corps might spoil for a chance to put "the rabble" in its place, the common soldier in conscript armies was understably reluctant to shoot at unarmed citizens. In the July Revolution Marshal Marmont saw most of his forces melt away. Even in England it was sometimes thought advisable to bring troops from Ireland, lest the English troops assigned to quell disturbances in the industrial areas prove unreliable.

In these circumstances it behooved governments to move promptly and energetically. In all the capitals the initial demonstrations were amorphous, aimless, unaggressive. Yet nowhere did the authorities show the required determination. Troops were left to act as best they could; higher direction was almost completely lacking.

As a result, faily innocuous aggregations of people quickly turned into bellicose mobs. Open conflict between people and troops ensued, and presently military operations in the narrow, congested quarters of the city became all but impossible. Insurrection fed on itself. Radical elements were able to take advantage of a situation that they by themselves could never have created.

Thus, by ineptitude and indecision the governments provoked revolutions that were as unexpected as they were unwanted, even by the opposition. In discussing this period stress should be laid on the failure of monarchy rather than on the forces of revolution.

To explain this failure presents something of a challenge. We must attribute it chiefly, I think, to the feeling of insecurity common to almost all princes in the period after the French Revolution. Their fear of the actually ineffectual secret societies and their dread of a world conspiracy against the throne and the altar are well-known. Moreover, they were apprehensive of the newly aroused people, the more so in view of the frightful barricade fighting in Paris in July 1830 and, in the 1840s, the growing threat of a desperate proletariat.

The liberal middle classes, too bear a heavy responsibility for the disastrous revolutions that ensued. In retrospect, it seems almost incredible that the Paris national guard should have carried its dislike of the regime and its desire for reforms to the point of standing aside, allowing the insurrection to develop and opening the door to political and social upheaval that, in turn, provided the opportunity for a repressive dictatorship. In Vienna the *Bürgerwehr* played an equally dubious role, setting the stage for the radicalism of the summer of 1848 and the ensuing counterrevolution.

Finally, one may fairly ask whether the revolutions of 1848 were necessary or even desirable. The work of reform was carried through more rapidly and more smoothly in countries such as Britain, the low countries, Scandinavia and even Russia, in which there were no revolutions. In the last analysis the Continental revolutions, while they achieved some measure of reform, led to grave political and social conflicts, to say nothing of national antagonisms and wars that might otherwise have been avoided. In view of the period of reaction that almost everywhere followed the revolutions it would seem that these upheavals actually delayed many urgently needed changes. Without the revolutions many later tensions might have been forestalled or at least attenuated, and Europe might have escaped a veritable harvest of both internal and external strains and animosities.

THE YEAR 1848 IN GERMAN HISTORY:
REFLECTIONS ON A CENTENARY

Friedrich Meinecke

The popular uprising of the March Days of 1848 in Berlin, superficially viewed, remained an episode, and the men who were fighting for progress along various lines failed, and were bound to fail, in their aims. The German revolution, said Friedrich Engels in his instructive articles of 1851-52 (which he published in America above the signature of Karl Marx), was a necessity, but its temporary suppression was similarly unavoidable. We shall still have to substantiate this, but must turn our gaze first upon the Berlin revolution, and upon the positive comment which it may offer for our contemporary historical situation. Yet for this too it is necessary to search somewhat deeper.

We must set before ourselves today more sharply than before, the problem of critical alternatives in the history of Germany, in order to gain a deeper insight into the infinitely complex web of her dark destiny. The natural task of Germany in the nineteenth century was not only to achieve unification, but also to transmute the existing authoritarian state *(Obrigkeitsstaat)* into commonwealth *(Gemein-schaftsstaat)*. To that end, the monarchial-authoritarian structure had to be made elastic—if possible, through peaceful reform—so that the result would be an active and effective participation of all strata of society in the life of the state. This was imperatively demanded by the new configuration which was in process within the German society, and which was undermining the former aristocratic foundations of the authoritarian monarchy. An upper middle class arose, the lower middle class increased in large strides, and the beginning of the industrial proletariat in the middle of the century gave notice of its mighty growth to come. Now, the task of reorganizing and harmonizing within a new commonwealth a people in social transition, bursting with vitality, remained largely unfulfilled, although many liberal and democratic concessions were granted by the old authorities. Which then were the decisive points in this development? When were possibilities first seen, attempts made or frustrated, which could have brought Germany forward upon the path to the commonwealth?

I see, above all, three such moments. The first occurs toward the end of the Prussian era of reform, in the year 1819—the year of the Carlsbad Decrees— when with the dismissal of Wilhelm von Humboldt and Boyen, their most fruitful constitutional projects were also buried, and the authoritarian and militaristic principle triumphed in Prussia. The second crisis, when this principle once more won out in the end, was the year 1848. And the third point of decision was the Prussian era of conflict and the year 1866, which, while seeing some progress made toward satisfying the desire for national unity and strength, allowed the liberal and democratic ideas only a partial or apparent success. For it separated the way of the upsurging popular movements from the authoritarian-militaristic citadel of the entire national life.

Of these three fundamental decisions of the nineteenth century, the first was fought out in the more restricted circle of the ruling class itself, between highminded and farsighted statesmen on the one hand and a monarch of limited understanding on the other. The third crisis developed as a duel between the liberal upper middle class and Bismarck, in which that tremendously skilful campaigner understood how to win over at last a large part of the opposition. At no time in the years before 1866, was the weapon of a revolution seriously considered by Bismarck's progressive antagonists; they were fearful of it, in accordance with the instincts of an upper bourgeoisie. The second crisis—that of 1848—offers therefore a unique, and for us today, a moving spectacle: here the whole people, not Prussians alone, but Germans of every class, stepped into the arena, and an actual revolution came about.

Revolutions, fearful as the invasion of irrational forces may be, or turn out to be, have in certain cases their deep historical justification. Such was the case in Germany, and especially in Prussia, in the year 1848. Admitttedly the old order, now attacked by the revolution, was not in all aspects characterized by decay or ossification. the *Biedermeierzeit* with its lovely spiritual flowering had gone before. The Zollverein, since 1833 a work of the Prussian bureaucracy, had made secure the indispensable preconditions for the rise of modern economic forces, and thereby also for the social transformation from which the revolution itself had sprung. The psychopathic romanticist who now sat on the throne of the Hohenzollerns was himself inspired with a deep love for German civilzation *(Deutschtum),* and was at some pains to bring about a German unity in its own way. But this way contradicted most sharply the urgent needs of the time. It was upon illusions that he based his attempts to reform the wretched organization of the German Bund and to fulfill the promise of a constitution (made in 1815) by the assembling of the united provincial diets in 1847. For the strongly aristocratic composition of these provincial estates, and the narrow powers which were all that the king would concede to them, were completely inadequate to satisfy the claims of popular representation which grew out of the process of social change. And in everyday life one felt everywhere the old absolutist-militarist police state, unbroken in spite of the isolated concessions to liberalism which the king, giving with one hand and rescinding with the other, might make. But behind the reaction against his personal and self-contradictory rule, and behind all individual grievances, there stood as a deepest source of discontent the feeling that the Prussian military and Junker state must be reorganized from the ground up—that the old authoritarian state must give way to a new commonwealth.

In fact this emotion, spurring on toward revolution, was not actually evoked but only powerfully stimulated, by the February revolution in France and the scattered revolts that were flaring up throughout Germany and even in Metternich's own Vienna. The remarkable circumstance that everywhere they succeeded at once, without encountering resistance, would demonstrate that the moral position of the rulers themselvès was already noticeably shaken, that they no longer possessed an unquestioning and naive faith in the viability of the old order. Such a faith was necessary, if the governments were to use against the revolution the physical instrumentalities of power, still amply available to them. When later they realized that these resources were still at their disposal, the authorities did not hesitate to act accordingly, and to suppress the revolution with reaction. But as things were in March, 1848, they all, as Frederick William IV later expressed it, "lay flat on their bellies."

He, the king himself, most of all. And this in spite of the fact that he had actually launched, on the 18th of March, the physical auxiliaries of his power—his faithful army—successfully against the people's barricades in Berlin. Yet on the very next day, he permitted, through his own order, these troops—though undefeated—to abandon the inner city which they had conquered, and thereby exposed the person of the king to the severest of humiliations at the hands of the rebels. Let us leave aside entirely the tangled complexity of these events, which have been investigated time and again, and emphasize only this. So feeble and contradictory a policy could not have been conducted by any prince, who, with a pure and undiminished faith in his old world, was simply defending it against a new. This new world had already to some degree insinuated itself, secretly and unsuspected, into his own thinking, distracting and weakening his power for effective action. Sooner or later the new was bound to win out, in spite of many setbacks to come, and to replace the authoritarian state by some form of democracy.

Such an interpretation may be justified, as we look back over the whole century that separates us from the year 1848, and as we think of the task now before us—the task of casting aside all relics of the authoritarian state (of which the Third Reich was, in fact, but a malignant outgrowth), and building up a sound and vigorous democracy. The easy victory—to be sure, not a military but a political and psychological victory—by which the street-fighting in Berlin prevailed over the old military monarchy, suggested symbolically that the latter's downfall was written in the stars; that one day the sovereignty of the people would become a reality. But, at the same time, it was no more than a symbol. For the new world was as yet quite untested and immature, and the old world still possessed many unexploited resources—even the chance of remaining victorious for some time to come. Bismarck and his work, after all, had sprung from it, at once magnificent and ephemeral. But let us now mark clearly the indications of that immaturity in which the new world of democracy then continued to find itself.

First a glance at Berlin. The men on the barricades of the 18th of March certainly fought bravely and fiercely, more fiercely than the Parisians before them had fought on the 24th of February. Such was the opinion of the Frenchman Circourt, who had come to Berlin as the representative of the new republican government, and had witnessed both engagements. But was it really the whole of the Berlin populace that stood behind the fighting or accompanied it with good wishes? Pastor Bodelschwingh, son of the minister whose task it was to pass on the royal command for retreat on the

19th of March, wrote in 1902: [1] "We youngsters were running about on the streets that Sunday morning (March 19). With the uprising repelled, there reigned a joyful mood among the greater part of our population; everywhere from the houses the troops were plied with food." Of course, most of the individual bits of evidence which we possess concerning the 18th and 19th of March, are colored to some extent by the sympathies of the witness, and so this testimony of Bodelschwingh should not be taken too literally either. But even less does it deserve to be entirely discarded. And a glance at the general attitude of the German upper middle class in the years 1848-49 reveals all the more clearly that large sections of this class were still greatly desirous of tranquility, and continued to be loyal to the old authorities.

It is necessary to go more deeply into these questions, in order to explain the paradoxical fact that the German revolution of 1848 could everywhere succeed so easily at first, and then in the sequence of events be overthrown with comparatively little effort. To understand this, the character, attitudes, and moral habits of the German people as it was at that time, and those of the various social strata within it, must be taken into consideration. And our contemporary need to attain to an inner relationship with this first attempt at German democracy gives this problem all the more importance.

The German people had only just emerged from the years of thinking, writing, and striving. But the thinking and dreaming continued likewise within the framework of new achievements and new desires. This ideological groundswell is common to all parties and classes within the German people, from Frederick William IV and his devout Christian-German friends—the extremists of reaction—all the way to the extremists of revolution: the men whose forceful minds conceived the Communist Manifesto of 1848, Karl Marx and Engels. For did not Hegel live on with them—a Hegel in reverse and yet preserved *(aufgehoben)*? Was it not true of both these thinkers, who claimed to regard all ideologies as merely secondary efforts of fundamental economic forces, that in them there came to life something distinctly ideological—an unqualified belief in the determining power of the laws of development—set up at a time when they themselves found only a tiny handful of followers? In any case, we ought no more gainsay the strong impulse of idealism which worked in these men, than that operating in Dahlmann and Gagern—the champions of the liberal nation-state—or in the brothers Gerlach, defenders of a divinely ordained corporative state. The German revolution of 1848, admittedly, shows not only an all-pervading spirit of idealism, which often outstripped reality and became ideological. It also brought to bear what in actual effect was more powerful—the reality itself, the massive and elemental interests of individuals and social groups. And, because it *was* a revolution, it likewise saw the release of base passions, and outrages of all kinds, perpetrated by the Right as well as by the Left. But if 1848 is compared with other revolutions—and particularly with the most ignominious of all revolutions, that of 1933—it can be stated that the factor of human depravity played a comparatively insignificant role. This must not be obscured by the fact that the extremist parties took pleasure in accusing one another of disgraceful conduct. Theirs were for the most part "atrocity stories." Neither was there anything which could be termed a "brutalized soldiery," nor were the barricades and the free corps of Hecker and Struve manned by a mere "mob." The German people, considered as a whole, kept in those days to a comparatively high moral level.

---

[1] Pastor Bodelschwingh is known as the founder of Bethel. The author wrote to him in 1902, requesting information about the revolution of 1848; the above quotation is from his reply.

It must be admitted that their level of life no longer possessed the spiritual grandeur of the age of Goethe. This decline was unavoidable in any case, since the urgent task of establishing a new political and social way of life compressed men into mass or group patterns, and made it more difficult for the individual to gather within himself the creative force from which proceeds all great culture. But what mattered now was, whether this people would prove to possess the maturity, the strength, the insight and steadfastness, that its new task demanded. Certainly, as we have noted, it was written in the stars that one day the new world would triumph over the old, popular sovereignty over the authoritarian state. But could the victory be achieved at this juncture? The fact that the revolution failed does not necessarily prove that the people were not ready; this may have been due to the coincidence of accidental factors. How bitter were the complaints, in the very midst of events, that just such a personality as Frederick William IV should have been for the revolution its "man of destiny"—a man who had actually, out of weakness, bowed before it at the outset, but who had then stubbornly resisted it; and by his refusal of the imperial office on April 3, 1849, had allowed the nation's call for the creation of the liberal nation-state to die away. Certainly another man in his place could have attempted another and possibly more propitious solution of the German problem. Then, however, the success of the attempt would once more have depended, in the last analysis, upon the world situation. This aspect of the problem we shall take up later. Suffice it now to ask again: was the German people really prepared for the task ahead?

Basic attributes and historical experiences, working together, had made the German people parochial, not only outwardly but inwardly as well, to a degree hardly equalled in any other nation of Europe. The princely territorial state, multiplied a hundredfold to the point where it exhibited absurd extremes of dwarfishness, depended everywhere upon a landed gentry which served the state and, in return, held sway over those beneath them. All this had mingled with the German bloodstream and had rendered the German people obedient and lacking in poltical self-reliance. In this very multiplication of authority, we see the chief means by which the mentality of the authoritarian state penetrated so deeply into the pores of German life.

One need only compare this with the development of England and France, where the royal absolutism—in England short-lived anyhow—had indeed helped to create a unified nation, but had never been able to instil so lasting and thoroughgoing a habit of obedience, as had the multiplicity of small German principalities. How far an original or native trait had helped to bring this about, can only be conjectured. Was it perhaps the spirit of fealty described by Tacitus? But the example of the Germans in Switzerland and their historical development since the Middle Ages indicates that there were other potentialities of a political nature inherent in the German character. Free of princely and therefore of rigid rule, subject only to patrician and—by the same token—more pliable authority, Switzerland was enabled to develop the native democratic tenet of her original cantons into the governing principle of her commonwealth, and thus to build upon historical foundations a modern democracy. No, the German need not submit to any fatalistic dread that because he is a German, he may for ever and ever be condemned to the habits of servility implanted by the authoritarian state. But it takes time, much time, again to tear free of it. Then too, this state has borne the German people, along with evil fruits, many and varied benefits, and thus fashioned much of ethical value that might well be carried over into the new world of the democratic commonwealth.

Good and evil alike, then, grew out of this disposition toward obedience, whose origin may well be placed primarily in the political fragmentation referred to above.

Even where a larger political entity was growing up, as in Prussia, the extreme insistence upon this subservient attitude brought out in a manner especially striking the contrast between its good and evil effects Prussia was, indeed, a state with two souls: the one austere and narrow, withdrawing into itself; the other culturally alive, striving, in Boyen's phrase, toward a threefold alliance of *"Recht, Licht und Schwert."* This Prussia, at once forbidding and attractive, now exerted her influence upon the rest of Germany. But how much was this influence again bound to confuse and distract all the aims of revolutionary Germany! The singleness of revolutionary purpose which would have been necessary for a victory over the old order, was thus rendered at the outset far more difficult to achieve. Now the German people, breaking loose from its previous subservience, did indeed reach out tumultuously for unity, power and freedom—only to find itself divided anew when it sought to determine the methods by which these were to be accomplished. How deep was the disintegrating and paralyzing effect of the Austro-German *(grossdeutsche)* problem, which implied what to some seemed an avoidable, to others an inevitable sacrifice of a portion of their fellow-countrymen *(Brudersstamm),* and the break-up of a German national community; how strongly has this problem contributed to the negative result of the revolution! It is hardly necessary, in addition, to recall the particularism of the intermediate German states. In fact, it was not merely the egotistic instincts of the princes, of their court councillors and court provisioners, but particularistic tendencies as well, conscious or unconscious, in the people themselves, which came into conflict with the new yearning for unity.

These were the factors of secular growth, going back as far as the Middle Ages, which weakened and divided in advance any unified revolutionary purpose in the German people. To these, however, were now added problems of the most modern type, arising out of the new configuration of society. It is true that the one part of the people which now broke away from the old attitudes of obedience, and rose up against the authoritarian state and against the splintering apart of the nation, was agreed upon the demand for greater unity, power and freedom; but it fell out once again over the emphasis and interpretation to be placed upon one or another of these three words. For behind the national revolution there was unfolding a social revolution, a class struggle between the old, the newer, and the newest social strata. This fact was recognized most clearly at the time by Marx and Engels, the champions of the newest class—the industrial proletariat—which had only just arisen and was still by no means very numerous. Between this youngest and (as Marx and Engels dogmatically proclaimed) potentially most important class, and that which had ruled so far—the nobility and the higher bureacracy—there lay the two clearly distinct divisions of the bourgeoisie: the upper and lower middle class. The first was of more recent origin; the other dated far back, though it was not nearly as old as the peasantry—who, together with agricultural laborers, still made up by far the preponderant majority of the people as a whole. (The committee on economic affairs of the Frankfurt Parliament estimated that they consituted virtually four-fifths of the total population at that time.) The share of the rural population in the revolution was certainly not unimportant, but created no particularly complicated issue for the fate of the revolution as a whole Since a general land reform through the dismemberment of the large estates was not yet seriously envisioned, the agrarian problem of 1848 entailed only the casting-off of all remaining feudal encumbrances upon the peasant class and the peasant holdings. That was a comparatively simple task. Even conservative statesmen realized the necessity of solving this question at once, and when the peasants saw that steps in this direction were being taken or being planned, they calmed down again. They still shared sufficiently in the old habits of subservience, in any case. The young Bismarck could well consider using them as tools in the counter-revolution.

Side by side with the working class, the lower middle class provided most of the revolutionary energy. Craftsmen and workers formed the bulk of the fighters on the barricades. Had they not risen up, the revolution could not have achieved dynamic force at all, and all the idealists and theorists of the general movement (reaching into the upper middle class) would have remained officers without an army. There would have been no parliament in the Paulskirche, no draft for a German constitution with an hereditary Prussian emperor at its head. The craftsmen in Germany at that time were badly off. It was related in the Paulskirche that there was one small town with seventy tailors, of whom only seven were able to find employment. Some hardship was caused by guild restrictions which continued here and there. But a genuine guild spirit revived again, as is evidenced in the desperate struggle waged against the new machine by workers who were losing their livelihood, in the excesses committed by the waggoners against the railroads and by the boatsmen against the Rhine river steamers. These were all, in fact, merely symptoms of the basic feature of an age in which the machine, and the modern technology, had revolutionized the entire life of the western peoples, by creating new human masses and new, unsuspected and distressing situations among these masses.

In such a crisis, the old authoritarian state proved unable for a long time to provide effective aid. Its officialdom was vacillating between benevolence and a narrow, pedantic attitude; its police a nuisance; its army—though possessed in the militia *(Landwehr)* of a more popular aspect—aroused bitter opposition by the arrogance and drill-ground manner of the regulars and their officers. Democracy as a cure for all these sufferings was the magic word that echoed through the ranks of the lower bourgeoisie—a class so quietist by nature and so restless now. The working classes took up the same slogan, and added to it their own socialistic demands. The younger generation within the upper middle class in many places espoused the democratic cause with enthusiasm, and imbued it with the impulse of idealism. It was, to be sure, an exceedingly immature and primitive democracy of which these Germans dreamed, more a rejection of the old authoritarian state than a positive affirmation of the people's state resting upon a fully developed common spirit among all classes. The distrust and arrogance with which the various classes regarded one another, once more divided the very groups which had just made common cause against the old authorities. Let us illustrate this and other facts aforementioned, with certain experiences which the young Rudolf Virchow had in the March Days of Berlin.

Eight days before the 18th of March, he had returned from Upper Silesia, where he had been sent as a doctor to study the "hunger-typhus." He was indignant at the inability of the Magistrates to take effective measures, and had long been convinced that the absolutist system of government was untenable. He assisted in the building of barricades on the 18th of March, and, armed with a pistol, placed himself at the one which blocked the Friedrichstrasse from the Taubenstrasse. Only six days later, he had to admit in a letter to his father: "Already there begins a reaction among the citizenry (Bourgeoisie) against the workers (the people). Already they are speaking of a rabble, already plans are being made for withholding equal distribution of political rights among the various groups in the nation." But, he added, the popular party would be alert and powerful, and would see to it "that no bourgeoisie should enjoy the fruits of a battle it had not waged."

One realizes here the closeness of the relationship between events in Berlin and the revolutions of 1830 and 1848 in France. But the problems of the German revolution were nevertheless much more complicated than those of the French uprisings. For the social revolution in Germany and its underlying class struggle was intertwined with the national revolution in a way which finally led to the failure of both. France no longer had need of a national revolution. She had long since achieved her unity, and her centralized power apparatus remained through one regime after another. In Germany both social equality and national consolidation were still to be achieved, with endless pains. And the need of the nation for unity and power was just as elemental and as deeply rooted in history as was the cry for domestic freedom and equality arising from those classes which the authoritarian state had so far kept down. Dahlmann in Frankfort even voiced the opinion that within the German desire for both power and freedom, the stronger impulse was now directed toward power, which had thus far been denied. The criminal excesses reached in our day by the need for power in Germany should by no means mislead us into condemning the elemental national craving of the men of '48. For theirs was a genuine hunger for something indispensable. Even Goethe had once acknowledged this fact, after the battle of Leipzig. "Art and science," he said to Luden, "are universal, and in view of these the bonds of nationality disappear. But the consolation they afford is but hollow comfort, and cannot replace the proud consciousness of belonging to a great, strong, feared and respected nation." Basically all the cravings of the year 1848 were permeated by kindred feelings and experiences. There was a general desire to leave behind the constricting and now intolerable bonds of the past, as one leaves behind a dark and airless dungeon. Just as the little man felt himself generally neglected and mistreated by the authoritarian state, so did the more cultivated German, who saw himself as a member of a great national community, and yet hemmed in by the irritating boundaries and the often ridiculous parochialism of thirty-eight greater or smaller authoritarian states. And equally neglected and thrust aside did he feel himself and his whole people to be within the entire body of European states.

All three of these desires [the liberal, the national, the European] were now, it was fondly hoped, to find their fulfillment through the Frankfurt National Assembly which, elected by universal and equal suffrage, convened on the 18th of May. Let us consider its social composition; it was noticeably different from what one might have expected as the result of the democratic suffrage imported from France. It contained no workers, only one genuine peasant, few members of the lower middle class, but many lawyers and judges—and, as is well known, many professors; nor were representatives of business and industry lacking. This indicates the still remaining respect of the lower for the upper strata of society, especially for the academically educated and in general for what is termed the upper bourgeoisie. But the same masses who now cast their votes for these people, were simultaneously in a state of unruly and turbulent commotion, which must necessarily have boded evil for the upper middle class interests and ideals. One had to rely on such an energetic thrust from below, in order to succeed at all to Frankfurt and the Paulskirche. But now it was a question, indeed, whether one could continue to employ these energies as indispensable weapons against the rulers, and yet keep them within limits, so as to guard against anarchy and the overturn of the social order.

In the last analysis, it was the danger of communism which appeared to threaten the whole bourgeoisie—not only the upper but the lower middle class as well. How real even the latter felt this threat to be, is exemplified by the bloody clash between the civil guard and the workers in Berlin on October 16, 1848. Communistic slogans and demands rang out from the enraged masses. A clearly conceived program, such as that of Marx and Engels, was in truth limited at first to the narrowest circles. But in a broader perspective, it appears that the very existence of a communist movement was perhaps decisive, or at least instrumental, in determining the course of events in 1848—and, in the first instance, the attitude and policy of the Paulskirche. For it was in view of this communist threat that the middle class and its representation in the majority parties of the Paulskirche again and again were forced over toward the Right, toward some kind of compromise with the old authorities and their military resources. The same threat was instrumental in preventing the maintenance of a unified revolutionary purpose within the whole people, to which perhaps the government might at last have been forced to submit. We use the little word "perhaps," because historical questions of this sort cannot be treated like a mere problem in mathematics; because in every case where we have to consider the historical possibility of another kind of development than that which actually took place, an unknown "X" disturbs the calculation.

In any event, the parties of the majority—right and left center—which desired to establish a liberal, constitutional nation-state with an hereditary Prussian emperor as its head, found themselves in an extremely contradictory and precarious position. They needed the resources of a revolution just as much as those of a counter-revolution. But their position did not enable them to make full and unqualified use of either, without endangering the very basis of their undertaking. In their effort, however, to pursue a middle course and to bring both revolutionary and counter-revolutionary resources simultaneously or alternately into play, they incurred the danger, in turn, of becoming powerless themselves, and of seeing their cause wrecked against the forces of the stronger contender of the two—the counter-revolution. This, viewed as a whole, was to be their fate. Let us briefly point out here only the critical stages.

From France the signal had been given in February for the revolution; from France again the signal was given for the counter-revolution in June. In a terrible, three-day street battle, Cavaignac smashed the Paris workers. To be sure, the German middle class heaved a sigh of relief; but for them the ebbing of the revolutionary wave which now followed in Germany as well, was gain and loss alike—while for the reactionary forces of the authoritarian state, this turn constituted a clear gain. With the decline of communist fortunes, those of national liberalism sank as well.

This same dynamic course of events then unfolded during September. When the Prussian government concluded with Denmark the truce of Malmö, which seriously threatened the German claim to Schleswig, the aroused majority in the Paulskirche at first rejected it outright; but shortly thereafter, in view of the impracticable consequences of a refusal, the assembly, once more grown meek, ratified the agreement. And when an uprising from the Left now led to street fighting in Frankfurt itself and endangered the assembly, it was forced to turn for help to Prussian and Austrian troops (from the federal fortress at Mainz), in order to prevent a general landslide to the Left. Once more the fortunes of the authoritarian state rose, once more those of national liberalism sank. And they dropped still lower when the governments of Austria and Prussia, in October and November respectively, put down with their own military forces the rebellious democracy in Vienna and Berlin.

Under such circumstances was born the constitutional project of the Frankfurt National Assembly, culminating in the choice of the King of Prussia as hereditary emperor on March 28, 1849. Doubtless it was a proud achievement of the noblest aspiration toward national unity and freedom. But it lacked the basis of power which would have been necessary to put it through against the particularistic and reactionary forces of the authoritarian state. It was defeated at once when Frederick William IV, on April 3, 1849, refused to accept the new crown offered to him—a crown which in his view could appear only as a product of the revolution, a Danaean gift. And when the genuine revolution now reared its head again, and the disappointment which broad masses of the people experienced over the failure of Frankfurt exploded in the May uprisings in Pfalz and Baden, the equally disillusioned middle class—in order not to be engulfed altogether by revolution and the social upheaval that might follow—was forced once more, as in September, 1848, to lean on the authoritarian state. It had now exhausted its own role as an independent power factor, and had to be satisfied with the scant dole of liberal and national concessions which the insight of those who ruled Prussia might still be willing to grant. The May uprisings, on the other hand, were easily put down by Prussian troops. The fighters of the revolution, be they idealists of the urban educated class, little people of the lower bourgeoisie, or workers, proved completely inadequate to wage a military campaign against the disciplined and dependable fighting force of the authoritarian state.

Upon these rocks was wrecked the German revolution. Only a unified revolutionary purpose, reconciling workers with bourgeoisie and upper with lower middle class, might have been able (as we have noted) to force another result and so to weaken the army's tradition of loyalty as to overthrow the old authorities. But the social transformation of the people, which brought on disruption within the entire middle class, had in fact made impossible from the first the growth of such a spirit of revolutionary unity. Without this social transformation, however—without a rising upper middle class, a lower middle class threatened with disintegration, and an aspiring working class—the revolution itself would have been impossible. Thus strangely and tragically intertwined were the inner necessity of this revolution and its inevitable failure.

We have deliberately emphasized the question whether the year 1848 could already have brought a commonwealth to the German people. For it is this very question which above all burns in our hearts in the dark situation of today. Only as a genuine and healthy commonwealth could Germany win in Europe and in the world a position strong enough to be maintained through all the crises of Europe. The Bismarckian Reich, magnificent as was its undertaking to combine the vital elements, old and new, within state and society, was yet unable to achieve that intense common spirt which is indispensable as an essential bond within the whole, and as the basis of any vigorous democracy.

There has been much talk since Ranke of a primacy of foreign policy, which is supposed to exercise a formative and dominating influence upon domestic affairs. I believe that this doctrine, while containing an indisputable kernel of truth, today requires revision and certain qualifications. The motives as well as the effects of foreign policy—and particularly whether its success is to be lasting or only temporary—depend to a considerable extent upon the inner coherence and sturdiness of the individual state; upon the type and degree of common spirit which animates it. The Bismarckian Reich, it is true, was built up under a primary impulse of foreign policy—that is, out of the necessity to erect a strong and independent power in the center of Europe. In addition, it certainly lacked no appreciation of the fact that this power must also possess inner coherence, and rest on a sense of national community. But the synthesis which Bismark attempted to forge between authoritarian state and commonwealth failed the test in the years of decision, when the world wars came. Too much of the authoritarian state remained in Bismarck's work.

But in what way, we must now inquire, is the year 1848 related to the primacy of foreign policy and to the world of European power politics in general? We have already seen that among the aims of the year 1848, there was also present the hope of raising Germany to the status of a great power. And this need was felt not only in the ranks of the middle class—of the party of liberal reform, the advocates of an hereditary imperial crown. More or less consciously, it inflamed also the will of many of those who wished to make of Germany "the republic one and indivisible." The Left too had its power politics—still a totally irresponsible variety—but one already spurred on in no small measure by desires and aspirations, though they were of course, assumed to advance democracy. Hence war was appraised as an instrument for winning a lasting peace among the democratically united peoples of Europe. This idea of forming an aggressive front is to be encountered often enough—for example, in the proposal of an alliance with democratic France against autocratic Russia. And was it not the Left itself in the Paulskirche—in the September crisis after the truce of Malmö—which demanded the continuation of a national war against Denmark, a war threatening to widen into a European war? It was the opinion of Karl Marx that a world war must assist his cause. Thus democrats were willing enough in such cases—though at first with merely verbal audacity—to take up the sword, the assumption being that in the future it should not be carried by the "brutalized soldiery" of an authoritarian state, but by a people's army. We realize now, that an intensification, a victory of the domestic revolution in Germany, could have led—and perhaps necessarily—into the storm center of a great European war. A realization, once more, that is deep with tragedy.

This danger of a European war, in fact, was like a lowering black storm-cloud overshadowing the whole of the revolution of 1848, and even subsequent events. All the problems of this year which were specifically national, were inflammatory in the highest degree. To gain Schleswig, a war had to be started as early as April, 1948; but it stirred immediate opposition in Russia, England, and Sweden, which eventually did bar the way to this prize. The Polish-German problem of Posen led, even in its first stage, to bloody fighting within the province itself; but it could as easily have eventuated in a Russian intervention. The great Austro-German question, the exclusion of Austria from the federative state envision in the Paulskirche, was most clearly burdened with the heavy mortgage of an imminent war against Russia and Austria. And France? There from the outset a common conviction prevailed that a united and powerful Germany could not be tolerated. French "security," they felt, would be endangered by such a development. Thus a new struggle over the Rhine frontier was threatening. In the French mind, offensive and defensive motives were in this case—as, perhaps, ever since then!—inextricably intertwined. But were they not also similarly present in many ways in the German mind? There was no lack here either of expansionist fantasies, though at first they were confined to individual imaginations.

Thus did the German revolution of 1848, and especially the work of the Paulskirche—the imperial constitution of 1849—contain certain warlike possibilities, which through the succeeding century became realities, and finally ended in the collapse of Germany. At that time they remained mere possibilities, because the German revolution (with the exception of the Danish war) spent itself internally; because internally it could still be held in check through the exercise of the resources of authoritarian power. But by this means were restrained not only the war-breeding impulses toward unity and power, but also the urge to freedom of the German people;

the insistence upon becoming a popular, national commonwealth. Once more an inter-relationship altogether tragic—one whose significance seizes us especially today.

The fact must however be acknowledged that a large part of this fatal interaction lay in the existence of the Prussian military and authoritarian power. Only Prussia—as the party of the hereditary imperial crown at Frankfurt perceived—was able and destined to fulfill the hopes of the whole nation for unity and power; but at the cost of the nation's hope for freedom, if Prussia remained what she was. She was indeed a state with two souls; yet the Junker-militarist principle inherited from Frederick William I and Frederick the Great was stronger in her than the principle of the Prussian reform era, which had pointed toward the commonwealth. If Prussia should remain what she was, even within a Germany united under her leadership, then it was to be feared that the Junker-militarist principle would permeate the whole, in one way or another. Instead of Prussia merging into Germany, Germany would merge with Prussia—if not formally, at least in essence. This danger the sponsors of the hereditary imperial crown at Frankfurt clearly recognized—as I had occasion to point out more specifically forty years ago—and therefore they demanded that Prussia sacrifice her political unity and allow herself to be divided into provinces directly under the Empire. But this the strong and proud spirit of the Prussians rejected categorically, and thus the partisans of the hereditary imperial crown—as they cast their votes for Frederick William IV—had to comfort themselves with the uncertain hope that the force of events would some day take effect and integrate Prussia within Germany.

The force of events decided otherwise. The militaristic principle continued to dominate almost the whole of a century, until it overreached itself in hybrid form; and Prussia was not dissolved from within, but destroyed from without. The tormenting problem today is this: will *Finis Borussiae,* also mean *Finis Germaniae?* To desire once more to become a great power in the traditional sense, would be to begin all over again the tragedy of the century gone by. This time let us learn at last from history! In order to avoid new catastrophes—not only for Germany, but for Europe, yes, even for the whole world—new forms of international solidarity must be discovered. And they are in fact already being sought today, with the purpose of safeguarding the morally justified and eternally valid need of a nation for strength. Goethe's phrase (from which we quoted) has indeed expressed this demand: to exist as a nation, fully respected by other nations, to whom a like respect is due. The contribution which Germans themselves have to make to the accomplishment of this infinitely difficult task, is at the same time the permanent legacy of the revolution of 1848. The weaknesses resulting from time and destiny, from which this revolution suffered and through which it failed, we have brought honestly into the open. May we succeed, as men who have been tempered by misfortune, in reaching the goal of that pure and noble yearning: national unification within a democratic commonwealth.

INTELLECTUAL CURRENTS

3 / The Two Problems of Romanticism

Romanticism has been used as one of those convenient signposts by which historians of ideas mark off different cultural epochs such as the Renaissance, the Scientific Revolution, or the Enlightenment, Employed in this way, romanticism is generally presented as a revolt against the Enlightenment, taking place roughly in the first half of the nineteenth century and distinguished by "a reaction against scientific method," "a preference for emotion," "an exaggeration of individualism," "a return to the Middle Ages," "a movement back to nature" —to mention only some of the popularly ascribed characteristics which Jacques Barzun, in the first selection below, says are *not* romanticism.

Thus the first problem romanticism presents is one of definition. Here there are difficulties; the chief ones seem to be that if romanticism is considered a movement, how can a unity be made out of its obvious diversity and contradictions, and, if it is to be fixed within chronological limits, how do we account for the "Romantics" or "Romanticists" who fall outside the agreed-on boundaries.[1] The conflicting definitions of romanticism by contemporaries and by the generations of scholars and literary critics who have succeeded them compound these difficulties.

Such considerations led the late Arthur O. Lovejoy, before his death dean of American historians of ideas, to try to clear up ". . . or to diminish this confusion of terminology and of thought which has for a century been the scandal of literary history and criticism."[2] In a famous paper written in 1923, he asked scholars to abandon the idea of romanticism as a "real entity" and instead "learn to use the word 'Romanticism' in the plural" by discriminating between the various romanticisms that appeared in different countries at different times and, indeed, within the same country at different times.[3]

---

[1] The obvious solution is to label them "precursors." Thus J. J. Rousseau (1712-1778) "the precursor of romanticism" falls squarely within the chronological limits of the Enlightenment.

Difficulties inherent in the "precursor" label, however, are well demonstrated by the "movement back to nature." The English nature poets wrote in the seventeenth century, and English or "natural" landscape gardening began then. The first use of the term "noble savage" has been attributed to Thomas Dryden (1631-1700). These difficulties underscore the usefulness of Jacques Barzun's distinction between "intrinsic romanticism" and "historic romanticism."

[2] Arthur O. Lovejoy, "On the Discrimination of Romanticisms" in *Essays in the History of Ideas* (Baltimore: The Johns Hopkins Press, 1948), p. 234.

[3] *Ibid.*, pp. 234-35. The original paper was delivered at the fortieth annual meeting of The Modern Language Association of America, December 27, 1923 and first published in *PMLA*, XXXIX (1924), 229-53.

In another influential and controversial paper, "The Meaning of Romanticism for the Historian of Ideas," Lovejoy repeated that "there is no such thing as Romanticism . . . one may perhaps speak of—not a, but several, Romantic movements"[4] and warned that "Nothing, then, but confusion and error can result from the quest of some suppositious intrinsic nature of a hypostatized essence called 'Romanticism.' "[5] But Lovejoy did outline and sketch "a quite different sort of inquiry" which might answer the questions implicit in the title of his paper, "make for the elimination of confusion . . . , the understanding of the history of the past century and a half, and . . . the understanding of the contemporary intellectual, moral, and political situation."[6]

Its starting point is a massive historical fact which no one is likely to deny—namely, that in the last quarter of the eighteenth century, especially in the 1780's and 1790's there were discovered, invented or revived, chiefly in Germany, a large number of ideas which had been relatively, though not always absolutely, unfamiliar or uninfluential through most of the seventeenth and eighteenth centuries; and that the total impact of what we may call, for short, the new ideas of the 1780's and 1790's (including revivals of old ideas under "new"), as they developed, ramified, and were diffused during the following decades, profoundly altered the habitual preconceptions, valuations, and ruling catchwords of an increasingly large part of the educated classes in Europe, so that there came into vogue in the course of the nineteenth century and in our own a whole series of intellectual fashions—from styles in poetry and styles in metaphysics to styles in government—which had no parallels in the preceding period.[7]

Another landmark in the continuing discussion of romanticism was the publication in 1943 of *Romanticism and the Modern Ego* by Jacques Barzun, one of America's leading intellectual historians and social critics. As its title suggests, Barzun's study of romanticism is a wide-ranging one which relates its subject to current political, cultural, and social problems. Barzun concedes the variety and contradictions of romanticism, but he addresses himself to the problem of definition. His distinction between "historic romanticism" and "intrinsic romanticism" and his linking of all Romanticists "in the double problem of making a new world and making it in the knowledge that man is creative and limited" come as close as is likely possible to a general definition of Romanticism.[8] The first

[4] Arthur O. Lovejoy, "The Meaning of Romanticism for the Historian of Ideas," *Journal of the History of Ideas,* II (1941), 261.
[5] *Ibid.,* p. 260.
[6] *Ibid.,* p. 260.
[7] *Ibid.,* p. 260.
[8] One is tempted to say he solves the problem of definition, but the problem of definition continues to be discussed. A noteworthy contribution is René Wellek, "The Concept of Romanticism in Literary History. I. The Term 'Romantic and Its Derivatives'; II. The Unity of European Romanticism," *Comparative Literature,* I, No. 1 (Winter 1944), 1-23; No. 2 (Spring 1949), 147-72.
Wellek argues against Lovejoy for the usefulness of the terms "pre-romanticism" and "romanticism" and seeks to demonstrate that "the major romantic movements (i.e. English, French, and German) form a unity of theories, philosophies and style, and that these, in turn, form a coherent group of ideas, each of which implicates the other."
A recent study, W. T. Jones, *The Romantic Syndrome* (The Hague: Martinus Nijhoff, 1961) is an interesting attempt to establish an empirical methodology for the study of works of art and of scientific and philosophical theory which is illustrated by a definition of the concept of "romanticism." The approach combines cultural anthropology with the history of ideas, and other "syndromes"—the Medieval, the Renaissance, and the Enlightenment, as well as the Romantic—are described.

selection below, covering these points, comes from a recently revised edition of Barzun's book.

The second problem with romanticism is a more specialized one than the problem of definition and possibly a more controversial one. It is the problem of the relation of German Romantic thought to the militant German nationalism which began in the second half of the nineteenth century and culminated in the nazism of Adolf Hitler. Interestingly, the controversy over this relationship was also initiated by Arthur Lovejoy. The reader will notice in the quotations above from "The Meaning of Romanticism for the Historian of Ideas" that Lovejoy ascribed to the ideas of the 1780's and 1790's a continuing influence into the nineteenth and twentieth centuries and believed that his inquiry would bear on the contemporary situation. Thus in the second part of his paper, Lovejoy established a relationship, though expressed in reserved and highly abstract terms, between the development of three ideas of the 1780's and 1790's (diversitarianism, holism or organicism, and voluntarism or dynamism) and "the monstrous scene presented by Germany and Europe today."[9]

With the publication in 1941 of *Metapolitics: From The Romantics to Hitler* by Peter Viereck, the discussion took a more forthright turn. In the selection below, reprinted from a recent, revised edition of *Metapolitics*, Viereck, today a well-known historian, Pulitizer Prize-winning poet, and spokesman for a vital, conservative philosophy, seeks to establish "the long but unbroken chain linking Fichte's nineteenth-century theories with Hitler's twentieth-century practice." Viereck integrates an abstraction like organicism with the all-embracing quality of German Romanticism to show how even an "ivory tower" poet like Novalis—to use one of Viereck's most original examples—could become so affected by romanticism as to take a position which logically leads to some part of Nazi ideology or practice. Other examples cited by Viereck, if more obvious, are no less striking.

It was not to be expected that either Lovejoy's or Viereck's arguments would go unchallenged. No small part of Jacques Barzun's *Romanticism and the Modern Ego*, which followed closely on the publication of their views, is devoted to a refutation of the connection between romanticism and modern collectivism[10]—and there were other critics.[11] The third selection below, however, has been chosen as a more recent contribution to what has turned out to be a continuing discussion. On one hand it might be called a compromise view, for while Robert Lougee, professor of history at the University of Connecticut, its author, concedes connections between German Romantic thought and several aspects of nazism or fascism, he feels that the Fascist organization of state and a number of features associated with it "demonstrate divergencies from the very foundation of Romantic thought." On the other hand, the author concludes with the original proposition that, "In the history of political thought, romanticism as a precursor of conservatism plays a role equivalent to that of the natural rights philosophy as a precursor of liberalism. To give romanticism another part to play, is to obscure its historical significance."

[9] Lovejoy, "The Meaning of Romanticism . . . " pp. 270-78.
[10] Generally in chaps. I, II, and VIII; more specifically with respect to the German connection, *Romanticism and the Modern Ego*, pp. 44-51; *Classic Romantic and Modern*, pp. 30-35.
[11] With respect to Lovejoy's argument, see Leo Spitzer, "Geistesgeschichte vs. History of Ideas as Applied to Hitlerism," *Journal of the History of Ideas*, V, No. 2 (April 1944), 191-203. Arthur O. Lovejoy, "Reply to Professor Spitzer," is in the same issue, pp. 204-19.

WHO ARE THE ROMANTICISTS?

JACQUES BARZUN

Who are the romanticists and what is the common bond that makes them bear a common name?

In English, the noun "Romanticism" gives two adjectives—romantic and romanticist. They are not commonly differentiated, but it is to be desired that they should be. We should then be able to tell apart the two distinct fields of application I have begun to distinguish: romanticism as an historical movement and romanticism as a characteristic of human beings. We should then say: "My friend X is a romantic" and "the poet Byron is a romantic*ist.*" When we say *the romanticists* at large we should mean a number of men who lived at a particular time and place, and who did certain things that fixed them in the mind of posterity. However, much they differ ideally or fought among themselves, Byron, Wordsworth, Shelley, Victor Hugo, Leopardi, Mickiewicz, and Schiller were romanticists. They received the name whether they liked it or not. Indeed, many romanticists vigorously disclaimed the title, like Delacroix, or accepted it for only half their work, like Goethe. In this sense, romanticism is a mere tag and not an adequate description. You cannot infer a man's personal characteristics, much less his opinions, from his correct labeling as a romanticist. What you can infer, we shall shortly see. Meantime, think of romanticist as a term comparable to "Man of the Renaissance." If someone had addressed the living Leonardo da Vinci and asked him: "Are you a typical *Renaissance-mensch?* he would have said, "What nonsense are you talking about?" Nevertheless, in any survey of the period, there is Leonardo, "typical of his age," and there is also the very different Michelangelo, his antagonist, but no less typical. They have been caught in the chronological net and historiography has stamped them with a convenient label.

With romanticism, the problem is complicated by the fact that during the romantic period small groups of writers or thinkers appropriated the general name to themselves. In Germany, for instance, scholars distinguish between Early and Late Romantic. But in neither of these groups will you find Schiller and Goethe. They stand apart, and yet Goethe's *Faust* is a bible of Romanticism. If you wish to find another German romanticist, Heine, you must look for him among the "Young Germany" group. This is the petty politics of cultural history. In French romanticism likewise, you will at one time find Victor Hugo and Stendhal on opposite sides, each representing a different shade of literary policy. In England, no one was called a Romanticist while living. All this is of great interest to the biographer or the historian of the several arts. But to use these temporary distinctions, as some have done, in order to blur the outlines of an era is to be guilty of obscurantism through pedantry. When the educated man has a true general conception of romanticism, it will be time to refine upon its details. For our present purpose, historic romanticism can be defined as comprising those Europeans whose birth falls between 1770 and 1815, and who achieved distinction in philosophy, statecraft, and the arts during the first half of the nineteenth century.

Some of course were born outside these arbitrary limits of time, like Goethe. There are others whose fame came after the terminal date, like Blake. A few more resist classification with the main body. So long as they are few these irregularities will not disturb anyone who remembers that we are dealing with an historical grouping. History does not arrange its products in bunches; it is man who seeks to put order into the disarray of history. Hence the ragged edges, but they are the edges of something central and solid.

We have then a group of men known as romanticists and living as contemporaries between 1770 and 1850. What, besides time, binds them together? It is at this point that we pass from *historic* romanticism to what may be called, *intrinsic* romanticism. I have suggested that if an attitude becomes noticeable or dominant in a given period, its elements must be latent in human beings, or in certain human beings, all the time. In individual instances we call it this or that kind of temperament. For example, it is probable that there are Puritans at all times and places; but when a great many occur at the same time and place, then we have a Puritan period. In the same manner there are heroic ages and ages of luxury, ages of classicism, of rationalism, of renaissance, of decadence—and of romanticism. Not that each of these represents a fixed type; rather it is a combination of human traits which for one reason or another happens to be stressed, valued, cultivated at a given historical moment. Why one attitude is preferred to another is something for the cultural historian to explain after the event, but *that* it is preferred is the reason for our being able to speak of a romantic period.

This distinction between *permanent* elements in human nature and their periodic emphasis in history is the first of the devices by which we can make more exact and serviceable our use of the name "romantic." If, for instance, we hear William James called a romantic, we are entitled to say: "James was not contemporary with Byron; what precisely have you in mind when you classify them under the same head?" If, as is likely, the answer given is: "I call him romantic because of his irrationalism," the field is then open to argument over the correctness of the description and over the propriety of making one belief or opinion taken at random symptomatic of a whole temperament or philosophy. The libraries are full of books, usually written in wartime, and which show that from Luther to Hitler, or from Fichte to Mussolini, or from Rousseau to Stalin "one increasing purpose runs." The demonstration is made by stringing together on one line of development all thinkers who "believe in the will" or "believe in hero worship" or "believe in the divine right of the people." In these works the intention of human ideas is disregarded for the sake of finding a collection of scapegoats.

The history of ideas cannot be written so, like an invoice of standardized goods. It is a subject requiring infinite tact On the one hand, diversity must be reduced to clear patterns for he sake of intelligibility; on the other, the meaning of each idea must be preserved from falsification by constant reference to its place and purport in history. It is strictly meaningless to speak of someone as "a believer in a strong state"—strong for what, for whom, by what means, against whom?

The same is true of irrationalism, which is only one of the alleged symptoms of the romantic temper. Granting that the connection between romanticism and irrationalism exists, in what direction does it point? And, to begin with, what is the meaning of irrational? To hear critics wax indignant over irrationalism in such highly organized persons as James, Nietzsche, Bergson, and Freud, one would suppose that they repudiated reason and behaved like maenads. One almost expects that their writings will be ungrammatical and demented. Instead of which one finds an extraordinary concentration of thought, a great skill in raising and meeting objections, and a solicitous care for order and form.

What is true of these four moderns who are supposed to be the fountainheads of neo-romanticism is true of their predecessors of over a century ago. They were not men of one book or one idea. Hence any reduction of their thougts or accomplishments to a single notion is inevitably belied by the facts. It is an explanation doomed to swift and complete refutation at the hands of anyone possessing even a fragment of firsthand knowledge about the subject.

At this point I may state dogmatically what I shall show in the sequel, that romanticism is not equivalent to irrationalism, nor sentimentality, nor individualism, nor collectivism, nor utopian aspirations, nor love, nor hate, nor indolence, nor feeble-mindedness. Consequently if any of these human traits particularly excite one's disapproval one must call them by their proper names, and not shirk responsibility for the judgment by terming their manifestations "romantic."

If anyone should doubt that these attributes have been made the distinguishing marks of romanticism, let him simply turn to the sampling of usage given in Chapter X, or else consult any of a dozen popular biographies of the so-called "romantic figures." For pleasure and instruction one could do far worse than to go to the conscientious work by L. and R. Stebbins on the romantic composer Carl Maria von Weber. It is the best, most scholarly, and most intelligent book on the subject; but dealing as it does with a figure from the romantic period, it accurately betrays the prevailing idea of that movement. On the jacket of the book we find the unthinking echo of what is said within: "Weber was no romantic composer, but a serious hard-working musician." In other words, a romantic composer is one who does no work, and it is a wonder how the romantic school of music managed to produce what it did.

Dip into the book itself and you come across equally bewildering generalizations, such as this concerning a German duke of obviously unbalanced mind: "He ... was either insane or the embodiment of the nth degree of early German romanticism—which, indeed, amounts to much the same thing." Here romanticism is insanity, but in the next sentence this sweeping condemnation is mitigated: "Certainly, he exemplified the school both in aversion to effort and in a behavior which followed the impulses of his subconscious without curb." In other words, the noble duke was a rake and an idler, like thousands of other men before and since the romantic period. What was specifically romantic about him? We are never told, and an earlier definition seems to describe the movement very differently. "There was a time," we are informed, when "a man could say, godlike, 'life is thus; but thus I will not have it. Standing on the intolerable reality I recreate.' This is the essence of romanticism."

Not satisfied with this essence, however, the biographers look for another in the possible "causes" of their romantic subject, in this case, Weber: "Was he a romanticist because of his convictions, or because he was dragged about by an unpredictable father, had no proper education and was nurtured on his mother's stories of the Catholic church?" There being no reasonable answer to such questions, another, equally plausible, is put: "Schelling's romanticized teachings exerted a strong influence upon him. Would a different philosophy have shaped a classicist instead of a romantic composer?" This is followed by a still deeper muddle: Schelling and Weber have each been philosophizing, but "it was impossible to write or speak openly of liberty . . . the contemplation of eternal problems was postponed for a freer age, and romanticism provided the usual escape." Schelling, I may mention in passing, was the famed author of a work on Human Freedom.

Now for a few comments on romanticism and the affections: "Their friendship was of a romantic nature and lasted until death . . ." "He fell in love many times." [but] , not with the easy sentimentality of his fellow romantics. . . ." And to conclude, some judgments of value about a man who is admitted on all hands to be an ornament of the romantic school: "The German romanticist proscribed labor, but there never was a man who worked harder than Weber; the German romanticist was an introvert with a subjective mind, but Weber liked society and saw his creations with an objective eye." And lastly: "One cannot lightly disregard the judgments of the great romantics, Meyerbeer and von Weber."

The juxtaposition of these sentences gives them, of course, a ludicrous air, though this is not intended, nor do I mean to discredit the biography. If the book were mere journeyman work, the authors' treatment of romanticism might matter less. But their opinions are educated opinions, and the point of singling out sentences is that they faithfully represent the usual view. Not one reader in a thousand would dwell skeptically upon them as they occur in the midst of interesting and well-documented paragraphs. These pronouncements seem to state the accepted fact; which only means that their mutual inconsistency and inherent falsity have been so often repeated that we no longer notice anything wrong.

According to this so-called educated opinion, romanticism is insanity, escape, introversion, sentimentality, and laziness; but a given romantic is objective, hard-working, steadfast in friendship, a creator of lasting works and one whose judgment is not lightly to be disregarded. I pass over the superficial psychology that makes of a shiftless father, a Roman Catholic mother, or the German philosopher Schelling the decisive factor in the production of a romanticist musician. The belief here seems to be that a man's outlook is picked up by chance or put on casually like hat and gloves. This is part and parcel of that other belief that somehow a romantic is a creature wholly different from other men, the men we know and see at work. Which makes it a matter for surprise to the biographer when his romantic subject behaves rationally, works hard, shows lasting affection, and acts with judgment and integrity in his art.

Seeking a demonstration of widespread error in a particular book is not irrelevant to the promised definition of intrinsic romanticism. Just as in dealing with historic Romanticism it was important to show the difficulties that come from equating the upsurge against liberalism with Romanticism, so in dealing with intrinsic romanticism it is important to show the impossibility of matching up the term with the current commonplaces about irrationalism, sentimentality, and the like. I will go even further and say that none of the usual scholarly definitions, whether sympathetic or not, seems satisfactory. Romanticism is not a return to the Middle Ages, a love of the exotic, a revolt from Reason, an exaggeration of individualism, a liberation of the unconscious, a reaction against scientific method, a revival of pantheism, idealism and catholicism, a rejection of artistic conventions, a preference for emotion, a movement back to nature, or a glorification of force. Nor is it any of a dozen more generalities which have been advanced as affording the proper test. It is not any of these things for the simple reason that none of them can be found uniformly distributed among the great romanticists. Mention any such characteristic and a contrary-minded critic will name you a Romanticist who did not possess it; he may even produce one who clearly strove for the opposite. It is this truth that has led a number of critics to abandon the search—and to abuse romanticism all the more for not yielding up its secret on first inspection.

This is not to say that many of the tendencies enumerated in the textbooks were not present in the romantic age. They obviously were, and it is in romantic work that scholars have found them. But a collection of features defines nothing unless it is common to nearly all the individuals examined. The error has consisted in supposing that what unites an age are common opinions and common traits. If this were true what would become of the war of opinions which characterizes every age? If it were true, how could John Dewey and T. S. Eliot belong to one and the same culture? If it were true, how could there be any traditions handed down through time? There would be, on the contrary, blocks of unanimous people holding the stage for a century or so, followed by other solid blocks of an opposite complexion.

In other words, what we want as a definition of intrinsic romanticism is the thing that gave rise to—and that incidentally explains—all the other attitudes I have enumerated. Why did some romanticists attack Reason, why did some turn catholic, why were some liberal, others reactionary? Why did some praise the Middle Ages and others adore the Greeks? Clearly, the one thing that unifies men in a given age is not their individual philosophies but the dominant problem that these philosophies are designed to solve. In the romantic period, as will appear, this problem was to create a new world on the ruins of the old. The French Revolution and Napoleon had made a clean sweep. Even before the Revolution, which may be taken as the outward sign of an inward decay, it was no longer possible to think, act, write, or paint as if the old forms still had life. The critical philosophers of the eighteenth century had destroyed their own dwelling place. The next generation must build or perish. Whence we conclude that romanticism is first of all constructive and creative; it is what may be called a solving epoch, as against the *dis*solving eighteenth century.

Because the problem of reconstruction was visible to many men does not mean that they all proposed the same solution, or saw all its aspects in the same way. The divergences were due to differences of temperament, geographical situation, and special interest. A poet such as Wordsworth or Victor Hugo saw the emptiness of eighteenth-century diction and the need of creating a new vocabulary for poetry; a philosopher such as Schopenhauer saw the illusoriness of eighteenth-century hopes of progress and the need of recharting moral reality, with suggestions for better enduring it; a political theorist like Burke, who apprehended the wholesale destruction of the social order, had to propose an alternative means of change; a thinker like Hegel, who was at once philosopher, political theorist, and esthetician, saw creation as the result of conflict in history and in the mind, and proposed nothing less than a new logic to explain the nature of change. He then showed how to use it for rebuilding on more lasting premises.

These men clearly cannot be made into a romantic *school*, but they equally clearly partake of a romanticist *temper*. More than that, they share certain broad predilections in common, such as the admiration for energy, moral enthusiasm, and original genius. It is because an era faces one dominant problem in varying ways that certain human traits come to be held in greater esteem than they were before. The task of reconstruction manifestly does demand energy, morality, and genius, so that the new passion for them was thus not a whimsical or useless trait in the romantics, but a necessity of their position.

By the same logic, one is led to see that romanticism was far from being an escape from reality on the part of feeble spirits who could not stand it. The truth is that these spirits wanted to change the portions of reality that they did not like, and at least record their ideals when the particular piece of reality would not yield—both these being indispensable steps toward reconstruction. Our modern use of the term "escape" is unfortunately vitiated by smugness and double meanings, and one should refuse to argue its application with anyone who will not first answer this question: "Suppose a primitive man, caught in a rainstorm, who has for the first time the idea of taking shelter in a cave: is he facing reality or escaping it?" The whole history of civilization is wrapped up in this example, and a universal test for distinguishing creation from escape can be deduced from it. The mere fact that a man is seen making for a cave or heard declaring his intention to build a hut is not enough; what is he going to do *then?* What is the relation of that single act to his whole scheme of life? Applying this test to romanticism, we shall see that on the whole it was infinitely more constructive than escapist.

But, it may be said, other periods faced with the task of creation have not produced cultures resembling romanticism. The very system which preceded romanticism and came to an end with the eighteenth century was created around 1650 and it took the form that we call classical. True enough; so to understand romanticism we must add to the fact of its creative mission the further fact that it conceived its mission in a certain way. It conceived it in the light of a great contradiction concerning man. I mean the contrast between man's greatness and man's wretchedness; man's power and man's misery.

It would be tedious to give citations from one romanticist after another in which this contrast is noted and commented on. But one cannot help being struck by the repetition of this independent "discovery" in the works of the romantic epoch. It obtrudes itself in many forms and contexts, whether or not one is seeking common elements in the many-sided activities of this generation of men. Moreover, there are other supporting facts outside the period that are worth remembering. Where do we find the most famous expression of this contrast in the nature of man? Surely in the *Thoughts* of Pascal, historically not a romantic, but a seventeenth-century author whose whole temper, social and religious, made him a dissenter in his own time. Whom does the classicist Voltaire most persistently attack in his own eighteenth century? It is Pascal. Voltaire wrote an *Anti-Pascal* and looked upon him as the most dangerous enemy of the Enlightenment. In much the same spirit Condorcet brought out an altered edition of the *Thoughts.* When does Pascal emerge in his full stature? and with his full meaning?—not until 1843, in the first half of the romantic nineteenth century.

The core of the conflict is Pascal's view of man's fate—the antithesis of greatness and misery—which leads him to an analysis of art and society as merely conventional and relative; justice on one side of a river, Pascal points out, becomes injustice on the other. In short, man is first of all a creature lost in the universe and he *makes* his shelter, physical, social, and intellectual. This was bound to be also the view of the later romanticists, who found themselves at odds with the remnants of the old regime, without protection from the universe, and forced to build a new order.

But in a thinking reed, as Pascal terms man, the contradictory state of having powers and of feeling one's weakness is not one to be dumbly endured. Some resolution must be found even while the protective social order is being built.

Indeed, many men feel that the imperfect social order is inadequate to resolve the inner conflict. Hence the search for a philosophy, a religion, a faith, which will transcend and unify the felt disharmony. Pascal himself, as we know, found this faith in ascetic Christianity. The romanticists, a hundred and fifty years after Pascal, found it in many different objects of belief—pantheism, Catholicism, socialism, vitalism, art, science, the national state. To fill out the list would be to give a catalogue of the contributions of romanticism. What matters here is the interconnection of all these faiths through their roots in the double problem of making a new world and making it in the knowledge that man is both creative and limited, a doer and a sufferer, infinite in spirit and finite in action.

* * *

ROMANTICISM AND NAZISM

Peter Viereck

* * *

Why has the word "romanticism" always been so hard to pin down? Surely not because it lacks connotations. On the contrary, romanticism has too many. On hearing it, the mind is certainly conditioned to an immediate reaction. Yet what one pictures is as vague, blurred, misty in outline as those moonlit landscapes which romantic poets cherished. Such intuitive "feeling for" the meaning of romanticism is completely adequate for the romantic himself. For his critics, a concept must be found which is more precise, consistent, clear.

A precise response to the word "romantic" is impossible if only because there have been too many authoritative definitions. Romanticism has been defined at great length—and differently in each case—by Goethe, the Schlegel brothers, Novalis, Heinrich Heine, Eichendorff, Victor Hugo, Stendhal, Coleridge, Carlyle, Georg Brandes, Irving Babbitt, and many others equally authoritative. They all conflict.[1]

---

[1] Among early nineteenth-century Germans, the two most fruitful examples of conflicting viewpoints toward romanticism are, on the one hand, the articles by A. W. Schlegel, Friedrich Schlegel, Novalis, and Schleiermacher in the periodical *Athenäum* (3 vols., Berlin, 1798-1800)—and, on the other hand, Heinrich Heine: *Die romantische Schule* (Hamburg, 1836).

Among more recent discussions of romanticism, the following books and magazine articles are suggested to the reader as the minimum of a preliminary introduction to a study of the subject. Georg Brandes: *Main Currents in Nineteenth-Century Literature* (6 vols., London, 1901-24), Vol. II, on Germany. G. A. Borgese: *Storia della Critica Romantica* (2nd ed., Milan, 1920). Hans Böhm, ed.: *Gedankendichtung der Frühromantik*, Vol. XXVII of *Kunstwart-Bücherei* (Munich, 1935); an anthology of the romantic school's new ideas. Paul Kluckhohn: *Die deutsche Romantik* (Leipzig, 1924). Richard Benz: *Die deutsche Romantik* (Leipzig, 1937). Friedrich Gundolf: *Romantiker* (2 vols., Berlin, 1930-1). L. A. Willoughby: *The Romantic Movement in Germany* (London, 1930). Ricarda Huch: *Die Romantik* (2nd ed., Leipzig, 1924). H. N. Fairchild: *The Romantic Quest* (New York, 1931). Hans Kohn. *Force or Reason* (Cambridge, Mass., 1937). Mario Praz: *The Romantic Agony* (London, 1933). Fritz Strich: *Deutsche Klassik und Romantik* (Munich, 1922). Irving Babbit: *The New Laokoön* (Boston and New York, 1910), and *Rousseau and Romanticism* (Boston and New York, 1919). Arthur O. Lovejoy: "On the Discrimination of Romanticisms," in *Publications of the Modern Language Association*, New York and Menasha, Wisconsin, Vol. XXXIX (1924). "Romanticism: A Symposium," by J. C. Blankenagel, G. R. Havens, H. N. Fairchild, K. McKenzie, F. C. Tarr, and Elizabeth Nitchie, in *P.M.L.A.*, Vol, LV (March 1940). Jacques Barzun: "To the Rescue of Romanticism," in *American Scholar*, New York, Spring 1940 (which I recommend as a brilliant defence of romanticism and for a viewpoint directly opposite to my own).

Consequently I cannot hope to avoid conflicting with much of them. But one may seek some common denominator by inquiring whether the authorities do not so much disagree as contemplate romanticism on different planes of reference.

The American philosopher Arthur Lovejoy, perhaps the most penetrating modern authority on romanticism, stresses that the word "romanticism" has become almost meaningless and speaks, instead, of many quite different "romanticisms."[2] It seems to me that these differences have two chief causes: First, the opposite creeds within the fold of German romanticism itself. (One example of such opposites is the bohemian individualism of the romantic school's earliest phase versus the totalitarian collectivism of a Fichte, Hegel, and Hitler.) Second, the differeneces between German romanticism and the romanticisms of France, England, and America.

Often two different romanticisms are really the same great romantic movement applied to different planes. In the case of bohemian individualism versus totalitarianism, one is on the plane of the ego and the other on that of the state. But both—and this is the point to be stressed—apply to their respective planes the identical romantic philosophy of ceaseless lawless expansion and of self-justified self-worship.

The second cause for confusion we can take in our stride, for we are concerned chiefly with German romanticism. So-called romantic movements did also exist in France and England. Sometimes these did indeed stand for the same things as the original romanticism, that of Germany, but never as a wide-spread national movement. To a large extent I accept the following statement:

Romanticism is Germanic and reached its purest expression in those territories which are freest from Roman colonization. Everything that is regarded as an essential aspect of the romantic spirit, irrationalism, the mystic welding together of subject and object, the tendency to intermingle the arts, the longing for the far-away and the strange, the feeling for the infinite and the continuity of historic development—all these are characteristic of German romanticism and so much so that their union remains unintelligible to the Latins. What is known as romanticism in France has *only its name in common* with German romanticism[3]

Romanticism is typically "Germanic" in its broadest versions, but never exclusively so and with many exceptions. Even further, one may treat romanticism not only as the "purest expression in those territories freest from Roman colonization" but also, and more important, as a cultural and political reaction against the Roman-French-Mediterranean spirit of clarity, rationalism, form, and universal standards. Thereby romanticism is really the nineteenth century's version of the perennial German revolt against the western heritage.

In other words, romanticism, no matter how far afield it may seem from current Nazi politics, is the most influential modern phase of Germany's old "two souls in one breast," the German cultural schizophrenia which made nazism possible.

* * *

[2] Lovejoy, *loc. cit.* (pp. 229-53). For further aspects of romanticism, see also the following works of Lovejoy: *Bergson and Romantic Evolutionism* (Berkeley: University of California; 1913): *The Great Chain of Being* (Cambridge, Mass., Harvard University Press; 1936), lectures 10 and 11; *Optimism and Romanticism* (Baltimore: Mod. Lang. Assoc.; 1927); reprinted from *P.M.L.A.*, Vol. XLII, no. 4, December 1927, pp. 921-45.

[3] Gustav Pauli, quoted in Vol. IV of Georg Dehio *Geschichte der deutschen Kunst* (4 vols., Berlin, 1919-34).

In mankind's ordinary, Euclidean mathematics, the whole must always equal the sum of its parts. In romantic mathematics, the whole is greater than the sum of its parts. This first romantic postulate may be restated as the ideal of organic synthesis on all planes, what some philosophers call the hypothesis of "emergence" or "creative synthesis."

Let us keep in mind, throughout, the historical background of the original romantic school. The romantics were partly right in attributing the vicious side of the great French Revolution—namely, its chaos and its consequent ghastly bloodshed—to the disruptive effects of destructive rationalist analysis.

The original romantic school and modern nazism triumphed in part for the same reason. Both were welcomed by many as a synthesizing counter-poison to the alleged disintegrating effects of an aggressive rationalism. The French and Russian world-revolutions were the respective *bêtes noires*. The French and the Jews were the respective bogy men.

Romanticism was the most influential literary movement in German history, penetrating and transforming every single aspect of human society. It had the courage to call its aim "a universal synthesis." This synthesis was applied philosophically and religiously, scientifically, poetically, politically.

Philosophically and Religiously.—The philosophy or religion most typical of the romantic school is vitalistic pantheism. This is illustrated by the very title of the book by the influential romantic philosopher Schelling: *World-Soul* (1798). The universe is greater than the sum of all its parts and contains a vital omnipresent spirit which analysis can never find. Schelling defines the entire universe as a single indivisible "organism."[4] Romantic philosophy, especially Schelling's was moulded by Goethe, himself only temporarily a romantic. Goethe loved to hyphenate "God-Nature" ("*Gott-Nature*") as one unified organism. A. W. Schlegel's university lectures on vitalism helped to romanticize the youth of Germany and Austria. Today Henri Bergson's philosophy of the *élan vital* is the famous French application of Germany's old romantic tradition of vitalism.

Scientifically.—Science was told to treat nature organically rather than mechanically. Analysis has been invariably coupled with the adjective "destructive" by romantics. By dissolving the whole into its component parts, scientific analysis is accused of losing that invisible force which makes the whole greater than the total parts. Synthesis was set up for science as the counter-ideal to mechanistic analysis. This was the message of Fichte's theory of science. Its importance is shown by the fact that the German romantic school's official magazine in 1800 hailed Fichte's organic theory of science as one of the three "greatest tendencies of the age." The other two were the French Revolution (the counter-credo to romanticism) and the romantic Part One of *Wilhelm Meister* (Goethe's prose counterpart to the Part One of *Faust*)[5]

Poetically.—The repercussions of the organic view upon literary content are obvious. A simple example is the amount of space which all romantic literature devotes to deeply felt scenic beauty. Vitalistic pantheism is what makes romantic poets of all nations feel so "at one" with so-called nature. Less obvious but no less significant are the repercussions of the organic view upon technical form.

[4] Friedrich W. Schelling: *Von der Weltseele* (2nd revised ed., Hamburg, 1806; 1st ed., 1798).

[5] *Athenaüm*, Vol. II, last issue.

The difference between neo-classic and romantic techniques is the difference between the static and the flowing. The typical neo-classic poem is atomistic; it consists of distinctly divided lines or couplets. The romantic's typical poem is quite as organic a unit as his universe or his political society.

In our own English literature the two most familiar examples of this contrast are Dryden and Pope versus Shelly and Keats. Pope's famous *Essay on Man* consists of self-sufficient rhymed couplets ("heroic couplets") making perfectly good sense each by itself. The opening ten couplets can be read in reverse or mixed-up order and still remain satisfactory. In contrast, the couplets of Keats and Shelley flow into one another so that their order cannot possibly be changed: they are organically welded.

Politically.—When this organic approach was applied to state or nation or race instead of to universe or science or poem, the result was poltical romanticism. Without it Hitler's Third Reich is inconceivable. But the political application only followed after the aesthetic application, under the stress of the wars against France; and so our earlier attention to aesthetic and philosophic romanticism, far from being irrelevant to nazism, is its historical introduction.

Rousseau, the Swiss semi-romantic, coined the two contrasting phrases: "general will" and "will of all." These his German admirers used all too successfully to bolster up their organic view of the nation. The will of all is the mere sum of citizens' individual (atomistic) wills, what modern democracy deems synonymous with the will of the people. The general will is the indivisible state-organism's vaster will, what nazism deems synonymous with the will of the people.[6]

Living at the height of French rationalism, against which he only partly revolted, Rousseau never intended the general will as the sheer mysticism it became in Germany. The catch is that no objective criterion exists for deciding correctly what man or party is the true interpreter of the state's voice. Counting noses in election is ruled out as mere will of all. Consequently, the general will, though never so intended by the more liberal Rousseau, became in Robespierre's French Revolution the mask for the republican Reign of Terror and became in Hitler's German Revolution the mask for limitless anti-republican despotism.

Innumerable writers of all lands have used terms treating the nation as an indivisible organism, but these were generally only useful and picturesque metaphors for the need of national unity. To German political romantics, however, the organic state was not metaphor but concrete reality. The recognized political oracle of the German romantic school was Adam Müller, just as the Schlegel brothers were the joint literary oracle. Adam Müller called the state "a vast individual enveloping all the little individuals" and called human society "solely a single noble and complete person." He wanted the state to cease being an "instrument in the hands of a person" and to become, instead, "a person itself, a freely evolving whole," to which all citizens must piously sacrifice their mere individual freedoms.[7]

Novalis is usually remembered as the greatest of romantic ivory-tower poets; but he, too, illustrates the all-embracing quality of Germany's romanticism, which applied the principles of its "universal-poesy" to all planes, including politics.

---

[6] Jean Jacques Rousseau: *Le Contrat Social.*
[7] Friedrich Meinecke: *Weltbürgertum und Nationalstaat* (7th ed., Munich and Berlin, 1928), pp. 148-9. Reinhold Aris: *Die Staatslehre Adam Müllers in ihrem Verhaltnis zur deutschen Romantik* (Tübingen, 1929) shows Müller's crucial and neglected importance in political romanticism.

Impatient foreign critics have again and again dubbed nazism "political insanity." That is praise rather than insult to many a German romantic. Novalis rhapsodized that "collective insanity," in contrast with individual insanity, "ceases to be insanity and becomes magic." Its magic is holy; he elsewhere compares it with that of God: "From each true state-citizen glows forth the soul of the state, just as in a religious community a single personal God manifests Himself as if in thousands of shapes." Novalis defines each citizen as a mere "limb" of the state organism, which is "alive and personal."[8]

More familiar examples are Hegel's evolving state organism, incarnating God's idea, and Fichte's totalitarian national-socialism. Hitler's speeches and *Mein Kampf* are a lowbrow version of political romanticism. Here the race instead of the state is the mystic whole greater than the total of its parts, welded by purity of blood. The democratic parliamentary system would atomistically divide this welded unit into separate parties. The Volk unit's general will speaks only through its oracle of the Führer.

This romantic metaphysics of race organically unites possessors of the same blood even when they live in separate states. Thus were sown in nineteenth-century thought the seeds of ceaseless future wars. In order to justify war against sovereign states with German minorities, the Nazi periodical *Rheinfront* said in 1937:

Primarily we are not citizens of states but racial comrades. The certificate of state citizenship is an easily exchanged possession, but membership within one's Volk is something immutable, granted by God. . . . The law of blood-brotherhood . . . produces a great community of German kind which has its members in all states of the world and which finds its proud refuge and kernel in the Reich of Adolf Hitler.[9]

* * *

The State.—The organic view was valuable in unifying so loose a federation as the Germany of the eighteenth century and of the pre-Bismarck nineteenth century. Such an all too "atomistic" Germany was, we must remember, the historical context of the romatic revolt against atomism. By itself, the organic assumption, as propagated by the proto-romantics like Herder, was not agressively nationalist nor morally and physically destructive. None of this (no revolt against external law) was in the typical quotations previously cited from Novalis and Adam Müller.

The quotations from them made the bare statement that the state is a single superhuman individual. If we read on in these two, we watch this needed unifying force become a force of chaos at the subtle point where the mathematical fallacy passes into the repetition. Novalis goes on to say: *"All* culture springs from a man's relations with the state."[10] Adam Muller goes on to say that nothing inorganic should fetter these superhuman individuals, the states—no human law, no league of nations.

Novalis wanted a special uniform for the citizens of the state, especially for those who most fully incarnated the "state soul." The wearers of this uniform have

---

[8] Novalis quoted in the Böhm anthology: *Gedankendichtung,* p. 71, and in Meinecke, *op. cit.,* pp. 65, 67-8.

[9] Josef Huenerfauth in *N.S.Z. Rheinfront,* quoted in *New York Times,* Sunday Magazine Section, November 21, 1937, p. 16.

[10] Novalis (pseudonym of Friedrich von Hardenberg): *Works,* ed Miner, II, 272.

turned out to be Hitler's Storm Troopers, a not illogical development which would have horrified Novalis and every single one of the other early romantics.

The self-justified state, like the Faustian man, must not let ethical discrimination hamper its experience of life's totality. So we are not surprised to find Adam Müller end with bloody hymns to war. The result of Hegel's state-worship, too, was that the state became the ethical end in itself in much influential German political thought. All individuals, all the external restrictions of international morality, and all the concretely existing internal parts of the state must be sacrificed to its mathematically non-existent whole, which is mystically greater than its total parts.

Volk.—Gradually this exalted organic unity of political romanticism was applied to the plane of race instead of the state. Modern nordic racism is to a surprising extent a product of nineteenth-century German romanticism. It took the Germans to revive the old Jewish concept of a Chosen People who have been defeated, dispersed, and cruelly partitioned but are messianically destined.

No romantic unity must have its organic oneness divided by external lines. The poem's unity must not be divided by classical lines nor the Volk's by class lines. No part of the Volk's totality must be despised. In the Nazi labour camps all youths, rich and poor without exception, are forced to dwell together six months in the same Spartan circumstances. The aim is to give them, in Hitler's words, "a true national community feeling ... and above all a proper respect for manual labour." (No mention, of course, of respect for mental labour.)

Though most early romantics, unlike Fichte, still retained functional class lines, they strove successfully to wear down cultural class lines. They it is who discovered and enthroned the previously despised folk-literature. They convinced Germany that the basic and best German Kultur lay in the folksongs, epics, and symbolic myths which they collected amid the aristocratic sneers of the classicists. These writings were claimed to be not the works of individual authors but of the impersonal force of Volk, a sort of collective author. This was Herder's folksong theory. The Grimm brothers, collecting the famous *Grimm Fairy Tales,* did most to convert Germany to this theory.

All individuals, but especially educated individuals, were ruled out as the authors of folk art. Education allegedly made individuals too artificial, too unprimitive. Only the indivisible primeval "Volk-soul" had the required creative powers.

The mysterious dormant powers of the "common people," the mute inglorious Miltons that bloom to blush unseen, have perhaps been exaggerated. In any case, the romantic Grimm theory has been completely discredited by the most thorough later examinations. These have exposed folksongs and the quaint, apparently "native" folk-costumes as slow seepages downward from court and educated circles, as simplified borrowings from above and almost never as creations.[11]

The first romantic generation, the Jena school of the Schlegels, Tieck, Novalis, was less important in propagating Herder's ideas of folk art than was the second generation, the Heidelberg romantic school of the Grimm brothers and Arnim and Brentano. The latter two writers published the most famous German folksong collection (*The Boy's Magic Horn*) during Napoleon's rule over Germany. Later the great Prussian Minister Stein commended this single book of poems for its

[11] John Meier: *Kunstlieder im Volksmunde* (Halle an der Saale, 1906); and *Kunstlied und Volkslied in Deutschland* (Halle a. d. S., 1906). Hans Naumann: *Grundzüge der deutschen Volkskunde* (Leipzig, 1922).

important part in arousing Volk patriotism to overthrow the French! So we see how close is the connection between poetry and politics in romantic Germany.[12]

Arnim and Brentano declared they had taken these folksongs down orally from the lips of the common people. Germans believed this, basing their worship of Volk to an incredible extent on this single epoch-making book and its surrounding folk-wisdom cults. Since then the book's so-called folksongs have been traced. Almost all were found copied from books of individual poets of the upper and middle classes. Some of the best and most "natural" and "primitive" of these songs, supposedly collected from the ancient lore of the race, were secretly written by the talented Brentano himself.[13]

In England the same gullible age went into ecstasies over those primitive products of the Celtic soul, Macpherson's forged *Poems of Ossian*. The worshipful attitude toward Volk gave tremendous impetus to both democracy and nationalism, the two greatest political forces of the nineteenth century, but also—via nationalism—to nazism.

* * *

Herder was the first to make German romanticists enthusiastic for the "organic, plantlike unfolding of Volk-souls."[14] This was toward the close of the eighteenth century, and his words referred not merely to Germany but to all Volk-souls. Here romantic politics was still in the eighteenth-century tradition of cosmopolitan humanitarianism. This was sloughed off during the transition from books to bullets. The right to "unfold organically" became restricted to the German "Volk-soul" alone. Father Jahn, the youth leader of the Napoleonic era, best personified this transition.

The early romantics, from Herder up to the wars with the French Revolutionaries and Napoleon, saw the Volk-soul chiefly as a medium for beautiful literature, as the Rousseauist lispings of the "noble savage." But Jahn and Fichte were more interested in beating France and French thought than in art for art's sake. They, and German leaders ever after, used this folk-literature as a political medium to inculcate nationalism in the young.

Herder was the highminded founder of the Volk cults of both Germans and Slavs. He anthologized and encouraged the national literatures of every Volk impartially. His goal was the peaceful co-operation of all nationalisms. Ironically, his national anthologies later became the fountainheads of both aggressive Pan-Germanism and aggressive Pan-Slavism.

The crowning irony is Herder's theory that an age of really passionate nationalism would make war impossible forever. Past wars he explained as the products of unnational atomistic states. But an organic national state would so enjoy the fruits of its unfolding Volk-soul that it would want all other Volk-souls to have the same enjoyments and would encourage them, too, to unfold without restriction. Herder envisaged a utopia of perpetual peace in which passionate nationalisms unfolded sweetly side by side like different-coloured roses in one common garden.

[12] L. A. von Arnim and Clemens Brentano, eds.: *Des Knaben Wunderhorn* (3 vols., Heidelberg, 1808, 1819). Stein's comment cited in Johannes Janssen: *Johann Friedrich Böhmers Leben* (3 vols., Freiburg in Breisgau, 1868), I, 439.
[13] Karl Bode: *Die Bearbeitungen der Vorlagen in "Des Knaben Wunderhorn"* (Berlin, 1909; Vol. LXXVI of Palaestra series).
[14] H. O. Ziegler: *Die moderne Nation* (Tübingen, 1931).

This goal has all our sympathies, but we question Herder's faith in nationalism as the means. From Rousseau's untenable faith in the natural goodness of man, Herder derived his untenable faith in the goodness of nations who act "naturally." His are the romantic postulates: acting "naturally" meant unfolding organically the instincts of the national ego and being "freed" from the artifical restraints of external law. But to classicists and conservatives the essence of freedom is these traffic lights of universal external law. Without these the natural and instinctive unfolding—whether on the plane of individual or nation—means unchecked egoism and the war of all against all.

The goal of Herder's nationalism was negated when Jahn angrily denounced the "love of the German for his foreign brethren" and glorified aggressive war.[15] Yet Jahn and all later Volk nationalists through Hitler are inconceivable without Herder. That is why Nazi schoolbooks make Herder a chief hero. The Nazi and Wagnerian cult of the organic instinctive Volk could not have existed without him. Yet he would be jailed as a pacifist and internationalist if he lived in Germany today.

The trouble is the old and very human one that we cannot reach our goals without using means tough enough to be effective. And then—the means have the disconcerting habits of getting the bit in their teeth.

From a Herder to a Hitler! Was this corruption of nationalism inevitable or merely a tragic accident? Probably inevitable, but we can never really know. What we do know is that this corruption is a basic motif of the last hundred years. Not only in Germany but in all lands nationalism passed from the humane, the peaceful, and the tolerant to the war of all against all. From Herder to Hitler in Germany, from Mazzini to Mussolini in Italy, from Wordsworth to Kipling in England.

The gradual stages of this downward transition should not be slurred over as negligible nuances. The descent inside Germany appears in three distinct stages: from the literary romantics down to the active leader Jahn; from Jahn down to the racial determinism and Aryan cult of Wagner and Houston Chamberlain; from the talkers Wagner and Chamberlain down to the rock bottom of the active leader Hitler.

Each stage is accompanied by an ever broader class and mass appeal, requiring an ever lower and less educated and more demagogic common denominator. The first Volk-worshippers of the romantic school are like Marie Antoinette playing in the artificial "naturalness" of her Arcadian little shepherdess costume. Their nationalism was the sophisticated affectation of literary snobs and life-starved professors. Through them, nationalism saturated German literature and universities and history books. Through the universities, the books, the student leagues, Jahn's storm-trooper gymnasts, and the battlefields of Leipzig and Waterloo, German nationalism saturated the middle classes. Then Wagner, anticipating a more industrialized age, transferred nationalism from middle class to proletariat, from capitalism to economic socialism. With Hitler and Goebbels nationalism has reached the broadest and lowest possible common denominator.

The greatest demagogues of our age have won their proletariat—at least for the time being—to a national socialism. Until Hitler, nationalism seemed almost a class monopoly of the bourgeoisie. Hitler called "this bourgeois world . . . a class doomed by fate to decline." He shrewdly observed that the earlier "Pan-German movement

---

[15] Quoted in H. von Treitschke: *History of Germany in the 19th Century* (New York, 1919), V, 249, 244.

was nationalistic but unfortunately *not social enough* to win the masses."[16] Therefore . . .

* * *

The gymnast Jahn and the poet Arndt were called "the popularizers of the teachings of the Volk-Soul."[17] A parliamentary committee of the German Diet classified Jahn's *German Folkdom* of 1810 with Ficht's *Speeches to the German Nation* of 1808 as "the spiritual godfathers of the newer Germany."[18] Both works were written while French troops still occupied Germany; this background accounts for the fanatic bitterness of Jahn's and Fichte's nationalism.

Fichte's work was limited in its appeal by its abstruse metalphysics. Jahn's book offered a more practical program, in colorful demagogic style. General Blücher, the German co-victor at Waterloo, called Jahn's book "the Germanest verbal gun *[sic]* "[19] *German Folkdom* is halfway between scientific scholarship and demagogics—that half-way point which sounds so thrilling and convincing to the half-educated.

Jahn's credo was that the unconscious force of Volk shapes all history. To describe this force Jahn coined the word "folkdom" (*Volkstrum*), today one of the most important Nazi words. Folkdom he called "that which the Volk has in common, its inner existence, its movement, its ability to propagate. Because of it, there courses through all the veins of a Volk a folkic thinking and feeling, loving and hating, intuition and faith."[20]

Cosmopolitanism Jahn spurned because "humanity appears nowhere by itself pure and simple but only as incarnated by folkdoms."[21] The Greeks and Germans are "humanity's holy people."[22] Later Hegel devoted many volumes to describing how Greeks and Germans, in turn, incarnated God's idea. "How odd of God to choose the Jews," German nationalists seem to wail, when the Germans would make a Chosen People so much superior.

Jahn attempted no new philosophic foundation. Almost all his ideas derive from the German romantics, in whom he was steeped. The romantic school's organic assumption, when applied to the plane of nation and in the context of the war with France, produced Jahn's book *Folkdom*.

Folkdom is devoted to methods for nationalizing Germany's way of life or, rather, "awakening" its allegedly innate nationalism. Without Hitler's cynicism, the book foreshadows *Mein Kampf* by its shrewd outline of propaganda techniques and educational indoctrination. So does Jahn's appeal for biological Volk purity.[23] "Animal hybrids have no genuine power of propagation, and hybrid peoples have just as little posterity." "The purer a people, the better; the more mixed, the

---

[16] Hitler: *Mein Kampf*, (ed. cit.), pp. 984, 158.
[17] F. Schnabel: *Deutsche Geschichte im Neunzehnten Jahrhundert* (4 vols., Freiburg, 1929-37), I, 306.
[18] J. Friedrich: *Jahn als Erzieher* (Munich, 1895), p. 48.
[19] Jahn, *op. cit.* Euler's introduction), I, xlvi-xlvii.
[20] Euler, *op. cit.,* p 111. Jahn, *op. cit.,* I, 154, 156.
[21] Jahn, *op. cit.,* I, 158.
[22] *Ibid.,* I, 162.
[23] Theune, *op, cit.,* p. 124.

worse." Every Volk should lead an isolated existence. The founding of a world government "is the last moment of humanity."[24]

Volk is the only true basis of a state. "A state without Volk is nothing, a soulless artifice." wrote Jahn. "A Volk without a state is nothing, a lifeless frivolous phantom like the vagabond gypsies and Jews. Only state and Volk in one make a Reich. Its power of survival is its folkdom."[25] Today that sounds more trite than startling, although attempts to change the map of Europe on that basis will always mean chaos and war. Metternich, the Hapsburg Chancellor and urbane "good European," first viewed more with amusement than horror "that newfangled notion of nationality."[26] But even in his own day it became the most frightening reality of modern progress.

* * *

In the pre-Hitler past, *Realpoltik* was perhaps equally practised (tacitly) by all nations. But with frank perversity and perverse frankness, nineteenth-century Germany, like the Italy of Machiavelli, went furthest in rationalizing this deplorable practice into a glorious ideal of theory. Fichte's *Speeches to the German Nation,* during the War of Liberation, are the philosophic foundation of modern German *Realpolitik.* He preached a double moral standard: what is wicked for the individual to do becomes holy if done by the state. Unlike the individual, the state should use for victory, if needed, all possible frauds, violations of law, and violent crimes. The collective Volk-ego should be bound by no external laws or limits.

The historical background for Fichte's *Speeches* explains why so extreme a *Realpolitik* caught the German imagination at that particular time. This historical context was the coming War of Liberation against Napoleon. So great were the hates of German romantics for what they called the French tyranny, and so great seemed the odds against its overthrow, that even the most bloody and scoundrel-like means seemed justified.

The historical situation led the romantics to the extremest statements of the Germanic racial myth that had yet appeared. German nationalism and Francophobia were widespread only among the middle class, to which most romantics belonged, and even there only among a noisy minority. Both the aristocrats and the peasant masses were apathetic to the crusade Jahn and Fichte preached. The German masses realized they were in many ways better off under Napoleon's semi-liberal Jacobin rule than under their German feudal masters. Therefore the romantic-school publicists of the War of Liberation turned to a tactic which Hitler has directly borrowed from them. They preached nordic self-worship and race hatred of everything French in order to stir to white heat the apathetic public feeling against Napoleon. Moreover, unlike modern propagandists of the Goebbels school, the romantics sincerely believed the Germanic myth they preached.

Often their race hate included not only France but also the German Jews. That fact, too, appears less mysterious when viewed not in vacuo but in its historical context. Napoleon, as son of the French Revolution, made a point of freeing German Jews for the first time from their mediaeval ghetto restrictions.

[24] Jahn, *op. cit.,* I, 164-8.
[25] *Ibid.,* I, 160.
[26] W. Monypenny and G. Buckle: *Life of Benjamin Disraeli* (new ed., 2 vols., New York, 1929), I, 997-1003.

Consequently many Jews were more loyal to Napoleon than to their native Germany and have made poor nationalists ever since. From those days on, following the tradition of Fichte and Jahn, German psychology closely links racial myth and *Realpolitik*, the former justifying the use of the latter.

Fichte in his *Speeches* says: "Between states, there is neither law nor right save the law of the strongest"; Germany, living more metaphysically than all other races, is "the Volk, metaphysically destined, which has the moral right to fulfil its destiny by *every* means of cunning and force." Starting the myth of racial purity, Fichte calls the Germans the most unmixed of all peoples and the closest to the mystic powers of nature. Their unique purity and their romantic idealism make the Germans not merely "a Volk" but "*the* Volk."

This superiority justifies "*the* Volk" in seizing whatever *Lebensraum* it needs and expelling or enslaving other Volk. In doing this, Germans must not be deterred by legality or by their own written promises, for *the* Volk is above all such scraps of paper and above such sentimental rubbish as international morality. *The* Volk must impose a German peace on Europe. This peace must be based not on treaties and written pledges but on brute force alone, a self-justified force.

These axioms of Fichte's *Realpolitik* were developed into a philosophic glorification of war by his fellow-romanticist Hegel. Thence they were carried even further by Treitschke and Houston Chamberlain and all the other philosophers and historians who form the long but unbroken chain linking Fichte's nineteenth-century theories with Hitler's twentieth-century practice[27]

GERMAN ROMANTICISM AND POLITICAL THOUGHT

Robert W. Lougee

The retreat from liberalism and the rise of fascist totalitarianisms in the interwar period occasioned widespread inquiry into the intellectual sources of the phenomenon. Writers have frequently discovered the "roots," to use the fashionable metaphor, in romanticism, particularly, German romanticism. Sharp controversies have arisen over the propriety and validity of attributing modern political lunacy ultimately to the romantic mind. A prior question may well be asked, what exactly are the elements of romantic thought which have political significance. This paper seeks to identify and analyze these elements.

Four aspects of romantic thought merit analysis for this purpose. They are the romantic epistemology, the romantic philosophy of history, the romantic notion concerning the one and the many, and the romantic spirit of protest. The term romantic is not limited here strictly to the Jena, Heidelberg, or any other literary school. It applies to those writers who, in the late eighteenth and early nineteenth centuries, represented that latter phase of the movement which brought German intellectual life to flower, who possessed a new feeling for life of extraordinary

[27] J. G. Fichte: *Speeches (Reden an die deutsche Nation)*. This and the preceding paragraph follow H. W. Steed's convenient summary of Fichte in Kolnai, *op. cit.*, pp. 8-9.

depth and richness of promise, and who stood in opposition to the Enlightenment and the concept of man as a subject only of outer sense experience.[1]

The romantic epistemology was a reaction against the rationalism of the eighteenth century. By the middle of this century reason was conceived as agent rather than as being, or as Lessing put it, the power of reason is to be found not in the possession, but in the acquisition of truth. The method of the Enlightenment was to take the positive or the given, analyze it into its elements, and then perceive how the elements were combined in the given phenomenon. The aim was to establish generally valid principles. Such a method had been used in scientific studies in the seventeenth century and now in the eighteenth century was applied to political and economic problems.

Unlike the thinkers of the Enlightenment, the romantic writers did not consider analysis an indispensable tool in discovering knowledge. This is not to say that they were unbridled irrationalists given to incessant flights of fancy, but simply that they preferred to experience deeply and directly, to feel, to emphasize, to grasp as a whole the meaning and significance of the given situation. The positive or the given as it appeared to them was their point of departure. Hence their suspicion of concepts as artificial, as nonexistential. Hence their disdain for a mechanical world view in which simple, understandable laws are used to describe and explain all nature. Hence their indifference to the logical contradiction between different elements of their thought, or, indeed, their evident pleasure in discovering and accepting as reality what to the logical conceptual mind must appear as polar opposites.

Herder had contributed to this theory of knowledge. He had taught that

... every kind of human knowledge has its own characters, that is, its nature, time, place and period of life; Greek culture, for example, grew according to the times, the place, and the circumstances and sank as these passed.[2]

Whence it follows that the uniqueness of human situations forbids the application of principles derived by the analysis of some other situation. The essence of a given situation is to be grasped by specific study and finally by *Einfuhlung* —a feeling into it. His philosophy of history was that not will and reflection but given forces and circumstances engender historical change and make things happen as they do.

Why did Alexander push to India? Because he was Philip's son and, given the preparations of his father, the deeds of his nation, his age and character, and his reading of Homer, he had no other course.[3]

No one expressed the romantic sense of the inadequacy of the new knowledge of the Age of Reason better than Novalis who wrote bitingly of the

men who were restlessly engaged in eliminating poetry from nature, from the soil, from human souls and from the sciences; destroying every trace of the sacred, heaping sarcasm on all great men and events, and depriving the world of its variegated color. Light, because of its mathematical obedience and its movement,

---

[1] Paul Kluckhohn in *Deutsche Literatur,* Reihe Romantik (Leipzig, 1931), I, Introduction.
[2] Herder, *Ideen zur Philosophie der Geschichte der Menschheit* in *Werke,* IV, Meyers Klassiker-Ausgaben (Leipzig und Wien, n.d.), 169.
[3] *Ibid.,* 166.

became their favorite subject. They enjoyed light more because it could be analyzed than because it could produce colors, and so they named after it their great preoccupation, the Enlightenment.[4]

Much of the spirit of German romantic irrationalism was in Burke who taught the Germans more than almost any other Englishman. He wrote of "the happy effect of following nature, which is wisdom without reflection." He abhorred "the nakedness and solitude of metaphysical abstraction" in anything concerning human affairs and discovered the evil genius of the *Tiers État* in 1789 in the predominate group of village lawyers, who perhaps knew their laws and regulations but not the nature of living, human reality.[5] Joseph Görres carried this spirit into later romanticism and in a clever figure ridiculed the rationalist way of thought as considering the world with a *"geschliffenen Insektenauge,"* that is, as seeing things not as wholes but as parts like the eye of an insect.[6]

The romantic theory of knowledge is explicit or implicit on nearly every page of the chief romantic political thinker, Adam Müller. The key to his *Elemente der Staatskunst* is his distinction of concept (*Begriff*) and idea (*Idee*). A concept is a word or definition which describes the state or some other institution as it appears from one viewpoint or from a given point in time. As the picture of a sunset cannot catch the subtle play and change of shape and color so does the concept fail to contain what is living and vibrant in the object. If the thought (*Gedanke*) however expands,

. . . if it moves and grows as the object moves and grows, then we name the thought not the concept but the idea of the thing, of the state, of life. Our usual theories of the state are heaps of concepts and therefore dead, useless, impractical; they are not in step with life, because they turn on the error that the state may perfectly and once and for all be conceived; these theories do not allow for movement whereas the state moves on without end.[7]

Those statesmen who have really taught us something have not taught from textbooks or from statistics, "the tiresome speculation of the study," but have based their teaching on life and movement.[8] The quintessence of the romantic view of knowledge is expressed in Müller's advice to the student of politics whom he urges to study things as they are, to get first hand experience with laws and institutions. A real feeling for these things, he says, is worth vastly more than the "watchmaker-type" of understanding, for as all higher branches of knowledge, political science is to be experienced (*erlebt*) not merely cold learned (*erlernt*).[9]

The romanticists, thus, clearly rejected analysis and speculation as the best means of acquiring ultimate knowledge. They were realists who wished to catch the flow of being first hand, so to speak, and not after it was filtered through a conceptual network. Political theorizing of any kind must be anathema to this view. Romantic thought was contemptuous of liberalism and of enlightened absolutism as well, for both represent the intervention of the rational mind into the destinies of nations.

[4] Novalis, *Die Christenheit oder Europa, Sämliche Werke* (München,1924), III, 17.
[5] Burke, *Reflections on the Revolution in France, Works* (London, 1815-27), V, 78, 36, 90.
[6] R. Saitschick, *Joseph Görres* (Freiburg in Breisgau, 1953), 152.
[7] Adam Müller, *Die Elemente der Staatskunst* (Wien, Leipzig, 1922), I, 20.
[8] *Ibid.*, 6.
[9] *Ibid.*, 16.

Ludwig von Gerlach and his circle, the "romantic conservatives," were anti-liberal and anti-absolutist. "Right, eternal and historical, in church and state and in opposition to arbitrary action of any kind . . . in opposition to absolutism from above and from below—this was the tendency of our struggle.[10] This line of thought stood in opposition to many nineteenth century political developments—centralization and the waxing activities of a rationalistic bureaucracy, constitutions and bills of rights based on general principles of natural laws, the growth of democracy with its mechanical principle of reaching decisions by electoral divisions, and more broadly to the whole tendency of modern culture to rationalize, systematize, mechanize.

The romantic philosophy of history was complementary to the romantic epistemology. The insistence that reality must be grasped directly and not through abstractions led naturally to an interest in history which is the full play of reality in time. The romanticist did not, as the men of the Enlightenment, use history as a laboratory to test different theories, but as the means of perceiving and knowing the whole through an acquaintance with the different stages of its development and of gaining an appreciation of the various forces at work in fashioning that whole. They sought, that is, to know in the romantic sense of the word.

Their conception of history contained at least four mutually consistent but distinct ideas. In the first place, it assumed that historical change is the product of historically given circumstances and not the consequence of arbitrary intervention. To borrow the terminology of a more recent period, they held that history was the product of *Entwicklung* rather than *Entscheidung*, of gradual development rather than arbitrary decision.[11] Adam Müller made the point by rejecting the application of Archmides' principle to political change. Archimedes had said, "Give me a fixed point outside of the earth, and I shall move the earth out of its hinges." Müller argued,

. . . do not all unfortunate errors of the French Revolution coincide in the illusion that the individual could really step out of the social contract, that he could overthrow and destroy from the outside anything that does not please him, that the individual could protest against the work of thousands of years, that he need recognize none of the institutions he encounters, in brief, it is the illusion that there really exists a fixed point outside the state which anyone can reach and from which anyone can mark new paths for the body politic, from which he can transform an old body into a completely new one and can outline for the state in place of the old, imperfect, but well tried constitution, a new one which will be perfect at least for the next fortnight.[12]

By rejecting arbitrary intervention in history he did not mean to preclude historical guidance through a higher *Entscheidung*, through the immanence of the divine. Indeed, for the later theological stage of romanticism, God has had a historical role much as in the Christian philosophy of history.

Secondly, their interpretation of history was non-theological. There is no distant utopia or gradual approach to perfection. Perfection is possible at every stage and is often attained. Amid the most suitable conditions Homer produced the perfect epic, Herder believed. Later poets turned to drama and other forms and brought them to

[10] Ernst Ludwig von Gerlach, *Denkwurdigkeiten* (Schwerin, 1903), I, 234.
[11] E. Lemberg, *Geschichte des Nationalismus in Europa* (Stuttgart, 1950), 270.
[12] Müller, *Die Elemente*, 26.

perfection. "Phidias created his mighty Jupiter and no higher Jupiter was possible.[13] Likewise, social and political forms as well as artistic come to maturity and perfection in their season and then give way to others which are not higher or better but simply different. This is what Burke meant when he wrote of "the great mysterious incorporation of the human race" which "is never old or middle-aged or young, but in a condition of unchangeable constancy, moves on through the varied tenor of perpetual decay, fall, renovation, and progression.."[14] History is cyclical rather than linear, a view of enormous significance for modern conservative theory.[15]

Thirdly, romanticists emphasized the culturally and historically creative role of the simple people of the folk. The folk were idealized, spiritualized. The folk-spirit, *Volkgeist*, is the medium out of which great events and great works are precipitated. Whence came Greek culture, Herder asked.

By no master was it forced upon them; through the sound of the lyre at holy ceremonies, games, and dances, through self-discovered knowledge and skills, mostly through repeated intercourse with one another and with other peoples; by these means the people assumed now this, now that direction, custom, and law.[16]

In a magnificent passage on the Arabians in the *Ideen* Herder suggested how the origin, character and spirit of a folk is bound up with its historical destiny.

The way of life of this folk, to whom cities appeared as dungeons, its pride in its origins, in its God, in its rich and poetic speech, in its noble steeds, in sword and bow, in everything else which it possesses and believes holy—all this prepared the Arabs for a role which, when their time came, . . . they played well.[17]

Eichendorff expressed the idea succinctly.

In history nothing is arbitrary. That which is enduring is not the despotic work of the few, but rather is generated from within the folk itself.[18]

Adam Müller held that ultimately the constitution of the state must be founded not on the will of a majority but on the "temper of a people."[19]

Fourthly, the romantic philosophy of history perceived a world order—or perhaps disorder—in which striving, creation, and recreation is constantly going on without reference to any immutable norms or principles, that is, a world order beyond the operation of natural laws valid without regard to time and place. Troeltsch found this view a principal point of distinction between Western thought and German romanticism. On the one hand he saw "an eternal, rational and divinely ordained system of Order, embracing both morality and law" and on the other "individual, living, and perpetually new incarnations of an historically creative mind," a conception of history as "an ever moving system, which throws up unique

---

[13] Herder, *Ideen*, 169, 170.
[14] Burke, *Reflections*, 79.
[15] A. Mohler, *Die Konservative Revolution in Deutschland* (Stuttgart, 1950), 104 ff.
[16] Herder, *Ideen*, 107.
[17] *Ibid.*, 459.
[18] Eichendorff, *Über die Folgen von der Aufhebung der Landeshoheit der Bischöfe und der Klöster in Deutschland* in *Deutsche Literatur*, Reihe Romantik, X, 37.
[19] Adam Müller, *Friederich der Grosse und Preussen*, in R. Kohler, ed., *Adam Müller Schriften zur Staatsphilosphie* (Munchen, n.d.), 107.

individualites as it moves and is always shaping individual structures on the basis of a law which is always new . . . ."[20]

Likewise Adam Müller wrote of the "Chimera of natural law" and utters the pungent exclamation, "A natural law which differs from the positive law!"[21]

In short, the romantic mind was a historical mind. It regarded history not as a chronicle of times past to be used for statistical or illustrative purposes, but rather as a living revelation of Spirit, the principal source of inspiration and knowledge. It was a dedication to history as a living reality, expressing itself unconditionally in each of its forms and periods. It was historicism. The coronation of history as the queen of the sciences was performed by Friedrich Schlegel in his lecture, *Über die neuere Geschichte.* Even the higher philosophy, he wrote,

may not, without peril, neglect looking constantly to the history of the development of man and of his spiritual powers, for otherwise it unfailingly loses itself in incomprehensible things . . . . History . . . if it knows how to conceive and represent the spirit of great times and great men and events, is itself a true philosophy . . . . A sense for the excellent and highest in what is brought to us by poetry and art, comes clearly only when we know how to place ourselves in the spirit of the time out of which the art or poetry arises or which it represents.

We must turn to the past to understand the present. Only knowledge of the past will give us "a quiet and firm perspective on the present, a measure of its greatness or smallness, and a basis of judgment of it."[22]

This romantic philosophy of history has been a vital source of conservative thought. It has been an argument against sudden and basic changes in the given social and cultural pattern. It has been directed against revolution and all movements which aim at reform or planning without regard to the historically given. It has favored those theocratic social conceptions which regard man as under divine dispensation and accordingly as well off as he ought to be in any given moment of time. It has worked against those doctrines of progress which teach that man is headed upwards from the swamp and brambles to the higher Elysian fields. Yet, the romantic philosophy of history has been equally opposed to the dogmatists of utter reaction, for history is movement and change, not stagnation. The emphasis on the creative role of the people of the nation must be considered an important source of modern nationalism.

The romantic conception of the individual and the social group—the one and the many—is distinctive and, for the Western mind, remarkable. The romanticist placed the highest value on the individual, his freedom, and his self-development and self-realization. Yet, he placed an equally high value on the group, which he considered as a living organism whose laws of organization placed the constituent individuals in a relation of mutual dependence. Unlike the Western mind which tends to set the individual and the group in opposition and assume that either the one or the other must have primacy, the romantic mind found the two completely and necessarily complementary.

---

[20] From Troeltsch's essay on Natural Law and Humanity which occurs as an appendix in E. Barker, *Natural Law and the Theory of Society* (Cambridge, 1934), 204.

[21] Müller, *Die Elemente,* 40.

[22] F. Schlegel, *Über die neuere Geschichte* in *Deutsche Literatur,* Reihe Romantik, X, 30.

Romantic individualism must be sharply distinguished from atomistic individualism. The social contract theories prevalent in the eighteenth century generally assumed that the individual in nature enjoys a position of independence from his fellows, and that he has natural rights which do not derive from any association. But to be independent is not to be unique, and these theories assumed that all individuals behave more or less in the same way and, therefore, like atoms, respond alike to general laws or forces. Romantic individualism, on the contrary, stressed the uniqueness of individuals, a uniqueness which placed them beyond conformity to any general law or principle. Schnabel has pointed out that before the romantic period all thought had assumed some point of reference outside of the individual, in God, in humanity, in classical culture, in the majority. The romanticists, in contrast, labored to individualize the world. Man became a law and measure unto himself.[23] The term *Persönlichkeit* came to be used "as a designation for a person with uniqueness and peculiarity of nature and with the implication that developing one's own individual nature is a primary objective."[24]

A *Persönlichkeit* is one who is distinct, not subordinate, cannot be counted or numbered with others. Goethe was an inspiration for this kind of individualism. Wilhelm Meister, in his long travels and involved experiences, sought to discover and to express his real self. Wilhem writes to Werner,

What good were it for me to manufacture perfect iron while my own breast is full of dross? What would it stead me to put properties of land in order, while I am at variance with myself? To speak it in a word the cultivation of my individual self, here as I am, has from my youth upwards been constantly though dimly my wish and my purpose.[25]

Kant had contributed to the freeing of the individual personality from what seemed to many of his generation as mechanistic determinism. His doctrine of the practical reason and the presence of the moral law within assured the individual of his freedom. Fichte taught in the *Wissenschaftslehre* the ultimate reality of the self-active ego which creates nature in order to realize itself. This ego may be grasped only by him who proclaims his freedom from the phenomenal world of cause and effect and perceives the universal ego through inner vision, that is, by looking within, he may more truly see all that seems to be without.

Pietism preached the "inward godly life of the individual" and thereby "brought into immediate consciousness the infinite worth of the individual human race.[26] It is scarcely surprising that one of the foremost preachers of the new individualism should have come from the pietistic Herrnhuters—Friederich Schleiermacher. The greatest Protestant theologian since Calvin elaborated a religious system which revolved around the notion of the fundamental worth of the individual's piety and religious experience. His *Monologen* repeatedly stresses the absolute quality of the inner freedom of the individual. "So freedom, art thou of all things the innermost, the first, and most fundamental. When I return into myself, in order to regard you, my gaze wanders out of the realm of time and is made free from any necessity; any heavy feeling of slavery is dissipated...."[27]

[23] F. Schnabel, *Deutsche Geschichte im Neuhnzehten Jahrhundert* (Freiburg in Breigau, 1929-37), I, 243,244.

[24] P. Kluckhohn, *Persönlichkeit und Gemeinschaft* (Halle, 1925), 2.

[25] *Wilhelm Meister's Apprenticeship* (Carlyle translation, Boston, 1883), 261.

[26] Kluckhohn, *Persönlichkeit*, 5.

[27] Schleiermacher, *Monologen* in *Deutsche Literatur* Reihe Romantik, IV, 33.

The same age which displayed such striking individualism, reacted against the isolation of the individual. From the mid-1790's romantic writers more and more stress the role of the individual as a vital part of a larger organic whole. This stress did not aim at subordinating the individual to the group but rather at coordinating him with it. Still less did it aim at eliciting likeness of contribution or equality of treatment. Rather the group was thought strong according to the uniqueness and diversity of its elements. The assumption was that the individual by being completely true to himself would best represent and contribute to the character of the whole. As Schleiermacher wrote, ". . . it has become clear to me that every man ought in his own way to represent manhind."[28]

The romantic relation of the one and the many must be considered in light of the prevailing conception of reality as a product of the tension of polar opposites. Goethe had written of the "inner totality" as consisting of the unity of "inner and outer thought and deed, necessity and freedom." Adam Müller's early work, *Die Lehre vom Gegensatz,* had expounded this thesis and his later writings applied it. In the *Elemente* the ideal society combines youth and age, the juristic (that is, the orderly) and the economic (That is, the aggressive), war interests and peace interests, progress and stability, and the like.[29] Novalis held that individuality itself arose from the assimilation and blending of diverse individualities.

In order to build himself into an individuality, one must know how to assume and assimilate other individualities unto himself, and in this way will become a substantial individuality himself.[30]

In leading the romanticists to their peculiar conception of individual and group no influence was more direct or greater than the lectures on *Die Bestimmung des Gelehrten* which Fichte held at Jena during the summer semester of 1794. There the "social impulse" is given a central place.

This impulse arises from reciprocal action, the reaction of opposites upon one another, the give and take between them, . . . not for a mere causality, which is but the activity of the one against the other; the question here is not subordination, as in the material world, but of coordination.[31]

Accordingly,

. . . the social impluse belongs among the basic impulses of man. Man is constructed to live in society; he is not perfect if he lives in isolation, indeed it is a self-contradiction.[32]

The flowering of the organic conception owed much to Schelling who published his *Ideen Zu einer Philosophie der Natur* in 1797. In this work the organic conception stands in the sharpest distinction to the mechanical, causal thought of the eighteenth century. The whole world is considered as an organism and every part related. In the *Ideen Zu einer Philosophie der Natur,* he wrote, "organization is the very essence of things, not phenomena, but object itself.[33]

---

[28] *Ibid.,* 40.
[29] Müller, *Die Elemente,* 98,99.
[30] Kohler, v.vi.
[31] Fichte, *Werke* (Medicus edition, Leipzig, n.d.), I, 20.
[32] *Ibid.,* 18.
[33] J. Baxa, *Einfuhrung in die romantische Staatswissenschaft* (Jena, 1923), 17,28.

The organic conception was applied to the state and society, terms not sharply distinguished in this period, by virtually every romantic writer who considered this subject. Fichte expressed it in his *Foundations of Natural Law.*

Just as in the product of nature every part, whatever it is, can exist only in this one union and outside of this one union would not exist—indeed outside any organic union it would not exist, for without the interaction of organic forces keeping each other in equilibrium no lasting form would exist, but an eternal struggle of being and not being would exist which we can not even imagine—similarly man obtains only in the union of the state a definite place in the chains of things, a point of rest in nature; and everyone obtains this definite place in face of others and of nature by being a part of this definite association.[34]

Müller considered the state, and by this he seems more nearly to mean society,

... not a mere factory, a farm, an insurance institution or mercantile society; it is the intimate association of all spiritual wealth, physical needs, of the whole of physical and spiritual wealth, of the total external and internal life of a nation in a great energetic infinitely active and living whole.[35]

In Novalis' thinking the mediaeval state or the *Ständestaat* had the character of a well-articulated, self-harmonious whole. The guilds were the limbs and strength of the state, the nobles the moral element, priests the religious, scholars the intelligence, kings the will. Görres called for a *Ständestaat* based on "the teaching, military, and food-producing classes." Similarly, Franz Baader called for an organic *Ständestaat* rather than a mechanically organized state. "Association means inequality between those bound together, because between equals only a heaping together or an aggregation takes place."[36]

The notion of the unique individual in organic harmony with the whole has been a fertile source of political and social ideas. It has been an argument against statism and leveling. It has suggested a society of self-developed individuals, but also of classes and estates with unique privileges and responsibilities, integrated into a functioning whole. This is virtually an image of the Old Regime, yet a model for modern corporate organization and even some forms of collectivism, although a modern collective consists more nearly of disciplined units than naturally associated individuals. Certainly, the organic view has been an inspiration for some lines of thought which oppose laissez-faire economic individualism. Adam Müller's guild socialism was not without influence on the *Katheder Socialisten* and has enjoyed a revival in the twentieth century.

A striking characteristic of romanticism is its penchant for *Zeitkritik.* Baxa wrote of the romanticist as "an extremely critical spirit, . . . troubled with standing doubts about the sense and purpose of his existence."[37] A critical spirit naturally accompanied the romantic temper which rejected many accepted norms. The romanticist, accordingly, had a wide latitude for criticism of existing society and culture. His conception of organic historical development was often a basis for critical judgment. The question was asked whether an institution, or idea, or even a whole period was a "genuine" product of historical evolution, or whether it

---

[34] Fichte, *Werke,* II, 212.
[35] Müller, *Die Elemente,* 37.
[36] Baxa, *Einführung,* 159, 160.
[37] *Ibid.,* 7.

reflected the spirit of its time, and whether it were true to itself and its innermost tendencies, rather than being an artificial excrescence on the face of time. Such a basis of judgment was, of course, not without its contradiction—perhaps the deepest contradiction in romantic political thought. For, on the romanticist's own conception of history, how can an event or development take place outside of history, that is, not be genuine? Liberalism and democracy and the modern political theory based on the concept of natural rights undoubtedly are as much rooted in the earth of historical environment and as much the product of historical forces as the rise of a feudal aristocracy in the Middle Ages and its perpetuation into modern times.

Romanticists varied widely in their specific criticisms, but there was a widespread feeling that the times were degenerate, a conviction that a pristine golden age had passed and ought to be regained. For many, the Middle Ages seemed to be such an age and hence the virtual cult of mediaevalism. As events turned more and more people away from the Revolution, romantic writers, many of whom had at first been enthusiastic admirers of what seemed to be a great movement of liberation, came to regard the Revolution and the whole background of rationalistic thought and commercial activity which had helped to produce it, as a blow at the human soul and a source of modern degeneration. Novalis, referring to the contention of the modern spirit with the old, expressed the form, if not the political substance of the romantic *Zeitkritik.* "This great inner schism . . . was a remarkable indication of the harmfulness of culture at a certain stage."[38] The romantic *Sehnsucht,* the longing for all that which is wished and that which is lost, represented a dissatisfaction and rejection of what is and as Schnabel has remarked became "the basic mood" of modern man and led to his characteristic *"Geist der Opposition."*[39]

The romantic protest was often radical and activist, manifesting not only a contempt for, but a rebellion against the status quo. Novalis wrote:

The fate which oppresses us is the sluggishness of our spirit. By enlargement and cultivation of our activity, we change ourselves into fate. Everything appears to stream in upon us, because we do not stream out. We are negative, because we choose to be so; the more positive we become, the more negative will the world around us be, until at last, there is no more negative and we are all in all. God wills gods.[40]

The admonition to stream out is at the heart of all modern radical romantic thinking, the basis of modern activism.

Müller's radicalism is somewhat more specific and almost eschatological in flavor. "I speak not of things present, but of things to come," he writes.

We must completely destroy this lascivious and sensuous private life, together with the cold, dried-out formality of our public life; let them die together, in common death will their atoms again be reconciled; our grandchildren will live in a new and better creation; at the least it is for us to maintian a learned interest, a philosophical lust for the general upheaval.[41]

[38] Novalis, *Die Christenheit,* 10.
[39] Schnabel, *Deutsche Geschichte,* I, 240, 24ɔ.
[40] Novalis, *Fragmente* in *The German Classics,* ed., Kuno Francke (New York, 1913), IV, 188.
[41] Adam Müller, *Friederich der Grosse,* 100.

The romanticist's interpretation of modern times as degenerate and the eschatological nature of his protest must be regarded as a powerful source of the seemingly self-contradictory movement of radical conservatism. The romantic protest was against change which seemed the product of artificial and not natural historical evolution. The revolt was not against the historically given, but against that which obscured, or blocked, or diverted the historical stream. This is the kind of revolution which has been made by modern conservatives.

What is the "responsibility" of romanticism in light of the foregoing? To be sure the idea of "revolution from the right," activism, contempt for liberal thought, the enthusiasm for the *Volk* and local color, the tendency toward corporate action, the note of irrationalism, these are certainly features which romanticism has in common with Nazism and Fascism. On the other hand, the Fascist organization of society around a dictatorial leader, and party, the ruthless demands for conformity, the nihilistic disregard for "historically" established patterns, morals, and institutions, the creation of new and strained theories and concepts—such as the doctrine of race—by which to interpret history and order society, these demonstrate the divergencies from the very foundation of romantic thought.

Romantic literature, because of its rich and multifarious nature, may, like Scripture, be a source of inspiration—and of ammunition—to the most diverse political views and arguments. Nevertheless, like Scripture, romantic thought has prevailing tendencies. Insofar as these prevailing tendencies have political significance, they clearly tend mostly to the support of a conservative view of the world—to the conservatism of principle, that is, not to a conservatism of interest. In the history of political thought, romanticism as a precursor of conservatism plays a role equivalent to that of the natural rights philosophy as a precursor of liberalism. To give romanticism another part to play, is to obscure its historical significance.

4 / Social Darwinism and Darwin: Are They Related?

The period from 1850 to 1870 has been called the Age of Science, not because science reached levels of discovery or application since unsurpassed, but because, for the first time, science or "natural philosophy" displaced philosophy as the prime concern of intellectuals. In the preceding half-century, scientists had been content to experiment. Now, as the century reached the halfway mark, they began to generalize and produce bold thought-provoking theories and—this is important, theories which could be understood by the educated layman. Their ideas were eagerly seized on in popular lectures by such great scientists as Clerk-Maxwell and Faraday, or in scientific best-sellers like Humboldt's *Cosmos* (1849-58).[1]

In this stimulating atmosphere, Charles Darwin published *The Origin of Species* in 1859. His theory of evolution exceeded them all in its provocativeness, impact, and diffusion. As a result, a book meant for scientists and those interested in scientific ideas alarmed the churches and brought the forces of organized religion to bear against Darwin. This battle settled, evolution was taken over by the "social philosophers" and converted into "Social Darwinism," a congeries of theories and other writings which applied conclusions drawn from *The Origin of Species* to human society and made them the popular, social philosophy for a period extending into our own century.

The three selections that follow, all taken from papers prepared for the centenary of *The Origin of Species*, admirably illustrate the process just described. The first, by Basil Willey, a distinguished historian of ideas, explains what was original in Darwin's theory, what Darwin meant to prove, and how he has been misunderstood on both points.

The second selection, by Dr. Cyril Bibby, author of a definitive study of Huxley,[2] is concerned with the impact of the *Origin*. Dr. Bibby shows the popular interest in the debates Darwin's theory stirred up and how the indomitable Huxley, Darwin's advocate, crushed the opposition of the churches and the scientist Owen. But in several interesting passages, Dr. Bibby records some unique misgivings Huxley had

---

[1] For the ideas in this paragraph the editors are indebted to the excellent first chapter of Robert Binkley, *Realism and Nationalism, 1852-1871* (New York and London: Harper and Brothers, 1935).

[2] *T. H. Huxley—Scientist, Humanist, Educator* (London: Watts, 1959).

about his victory and how, great humanist that he was, he fought racist distortions of Darwin's doctrines and broke with his friend Herbert Spencer over them. Spencer, who coined the phrase "survival of the fittest," saw in evolution justification for an extreme laissez-faire government.

While the second selection indicates the beginnings of Social Darwinism, the third selection, by anthropologist George Simpson, is devoted to a critical discussion of Social Darwinism, past and present, pro and con. Professor Simpson also addresses himself to the prickly question of whether or not Darwin was a Social Darwinist himself, a connection Basil Willey or Dr. Bibby would seem to disavow.

WHAT WAS DARWIN'S THEORY?

Basil Willey

Samuel Butler used to complain that so many Darwinians spoke of Evolution as if it were Darwin's own invention, whereas Darwin's theory was merely that evolution had come about mainly by natural selection. By now it is generally realised, I suppose, that Darwin's importance lay not in promulgating evolution itself, but in showing how it worked and making people believe in it. According to Butler, "Buffon planted, Erasmus Darwin and Lamarck watered, but it was Mr. Darwin who said 'That fruit is ripe,' and shook it into his lap." This is misleading if it is taken, as Butler meant it to be taken, as an aspersion on Darwin's originality. Darwin did not arrive at his results by reading the works of his precursors, but by studying Nature herself with that infinite patience in observation, coupled with a certain visionary power, which together constitute what we call "genius." In fact, although Darwin had read his grandfather's *Zoonomia* in youth, he knew much less than many of his critics about the previous history of evolutionary thought, and was rather surprised when various "anticipations" were pointed out to him. Butler, the *advocatus diaboli* in this case, was nearer the truth when he wrote (in *Life and Habit,* 1878):

Less than twenty years ago we never met with, or heard of, anyone who accepted evolution, ... unless it was that someone now and again said that there was a very dreadful book going about like a rampant lion, called "Vestiges of Creation" ... Yet now, who seriously disputes the main principles of evolution? ... It is not he who first conceives an idea ... but he who makes the people accept the main conclusion ... who has done the greatest work as regards the promulgation of an opinion. And this is what Mr. Darwin has done for evolution.[1]

Although I am sure that the present audience will not need to be reminded, I should like, before sketching the earlier history of "the development idea," to remind myself of how Darwin, in the famous book whose centenary we are celebrating, summarised his own conclusions. Here are his words, which were inserted in the last chapter of the sixth edition of the *Origin of Species:*

I have now recapitulated the facts and considerations which have thoroughly convinced me that species have been modified, during a long course of descent. This

---

[1] Samuel Butler, *Life and Habit,* 1924 ed., p. 276.

has been effected chiefly through the natural selection of numerous successive, slight, favourable variations; aided in an important manner by the inherited effects of the use and disuse of parts; and in an unimportant manner ... by the direct action of external conditions, and by variations which seem to us in our ignorance to arise spontaneously.[2]

A simple-seeming statement: yet behind it stretch years of dogged and devoted labour, and beneath its every phrase lie the volcanic fires of controversy. "That species have been modified"—but the immutability of species, and their origin in special acts of divine creation, was so generally held by theologians and naturalists alike before 1859, that Darwin, writing to J. D. Hooker in 1844 could say: "At last gleams of light have come, and I am almost convinced (quite contrary to the opinion I started with) that species are not (it is like confessing a murder) immutable. ... I think I have found out," he goes on, "the simple way by which species become exquisitely adapted to various ends."[3] All we need add, in order to complete this preliminary précis of Darwin's position, are the following points: the tendency of all offspring to vary, however slightly, from the parent stock; the enormous fecundity of living creatures, leading to the Malthusian struggle for existence, and the survival of the fittest. Nature, like man when breeding domesticated animals and plants, takes advantage of the favourable variations as and when they are thrown up, and suppresses the unfavourable. Creatures that happen to put forth variations advantageous to them in the struggle, survive and perpetuate themselves; the rest dwindle or perish. Since this Conference is concerned with Darwinism and the Study of Society, I ought also perhaps to mention at this point (what is familiar to you all) that it was the reading of Malthus on Population in 1839 which gave the final shake to the slowly-forming crystal of Darwin's theory. On his return from the voyage of "The Beagle" (1831-6) he had begun systematically to arrange his observations and to collect every possible fact bearing upon the variation of creatures under domestication. He soon saw that "selection was the keynote of man's success in making useful races of animals and plants," but how selection could operate in nature remained as yet a mystery to him. Then (as he says in the *Autobiography*):

In October 1838 ... I happened to read for amusement [an odd form of diversion, one might think] Malthus on *Population*, and being well prepared to appreciate the struggle for existence which everywhere goes on from long-continued observation of the habits of animals and plants, it at once struck me that under these circumstances favourable variations would tend to be preserved, and unfavourable ones to be destroyed. The result of this would be the formation of new species. Here then, I had at last got a theory by which to work. ...[4]

In the Cambridge Centenary and Jubilee volume of 1909 (*Darwin and Modern Science*), J. Arthur Thomson pointed out that Malthus also furnished a clue to A. Russel Wallace, and that Herbert Spencer, before 1859, had published an article in the *Westminster Review* on the theory of population, in which he had "come within an ace of recognising that the struggle for existence was a factor in organic evolution." Thomson's comment is that Darwin, Wallace and Spencer had all been

[2] Darwin, *Origin of Species*, World's Classic edition, 1951, pp. 549-50.
[3] Francis Darwin, *Life and Letters of Charles Darwin*, 1887, vol. II, p. 23.
[4] Lady Nora Barlow (editor), *The Autobiography of C. Darwin*, London, 1958, p. 120.

"led from a social problem to a biological theory," and that to grasp this correlation with contemporary social problems is more important than to ferret out hints and "anticipations" from older books which Darwin had mostly not read. He further quotes an interesting passage from the article "Biology" in *Chambers' Encyclopaedia*, in which the writer (P. Geddes) argues that the replacement of Paley by Darwin, as chief interpreter of the order of nature, is not just the replacement of anthropomorphism by science, but of an eighteenth century kind of anthropomorphism by a nineteenth century kind. For

"the place vacated by Paley's theological and metaphysical explanation," says Geddes, "has simply been occupied by that suggested to Darwin and Wallace by Malthus in terms of the prevalent severity of industrial competition, and those phenomena of the struggle for existence which the light of contemporary economic theory has enabled us to discern, have thus come to be temporarily exalted into a complete explanation of organic progress."[5]

This shows what happens when Darwin gets into the clutches of a smart intellectual. We are apt to surrender outright to such swift generalisations, yet how misleading is the suggestion that Darwin saw Nature in terms of the Industrial Revolution! Though a benevolent man, he never bothered about "the condition of England question"; his thoughts hovered over the Galapagos Islands and the coast of Peru much more than over Manchester or Birmingham. On one point only his mind was fixed: how new species are formed; and Malthus meant nothing to him save for his fruitful hint on this process. As Thomson rightly adds, moreover, Darwin at once proceeded to *verify* the formula, and its validity does not depend on what suggested it. It can be safely said, on the other hand, that any debt of Darwin's to social theory was repaid with usury, for many sociologists and others afterwards tried to interpret human history on Darwinian lines, either approving or disapproving of competition and *laissez-faire* according to their political and economic views. Opinion was divided between those who thought that, to secure the best results, the struggle between individuals, classes and nations should go on; and those who held that man, whatever his ancestry, was now an ethical being, and must transcend and control the struggle in the interest of ideal ends.

[5] J. Arthur Thomson, "Darwin's Predecessors"; Ch. II in *Darwin and Modern Science,* Cambridge 1909, p. 15.

* * *

HUXLEY AND THE RECEPTION OF THE "ORIGIN"

Cyril Bibby

The most important book of its century, Darwin's *Origin of Species,* catalysed a complete rearrangement of ideological patterns over a wide range of human thought. It is an interesting question why the book's impact was so immense. It was partly, no doubt, that its thesis bore so closely on vital matters of belief and speculation; partly the masterly manner in which vast numbers of facts were marshalled into overwhelming array; partly the deceptive blandness of style and simplicity of statement which allowed readers to imagine that they really understood the book. And yet theories of evolution were not new: they had cropped up repeatedly among the Greeks and Romans, and in more recent times had been proposed by both Lamarck and Darwin's own grandfather. Not even the theory of natural selection was entirely new: although Darwin was unaware of it, he had been in some measure anticipated by W. C. Wells in 1813 and in more detail by Patrick Matthew in 1831.[1] Why, then since these earlier evolutionists had made comparatively little impression and been but little reviled, was Darwin at once so successful and so abused?

It is a fairly sound general rule that excessive indignation and unreasoning abuse arise from fear and insecurity, and, though the England of 1859 was calm on the surface, on the level of ideology she was deeply apprehensive. The European revolutions from 1789 on were not forgotten; it was not many years since England had suffered widespread riots and arson; there had recently been the Eureka Stockade revolt in Australia and the Mutiny in India; Napoleon III was at war in Italy. In 1845 Newman had seceded to Rome and given the national church a severe fright; in 1846 the English translation of Strauss's *Leben Jesu* had brought a shock from another direction; soon the Christian Socialists were actively spreading novel views; in 1850 came the "Papal Aggression"; in 1853 F. D. Maurice's *Theological Essays*, which led to his ejection from his Chair at London's King's College, gave yet another jolt, in 1858 H. L. Mansel produced his defence of orthodoxy, *The Limits of Religious Thought*, one effect of which was to remind Huxley of the man in Hogarth's election scene, sawing away his opponent's inn sign without noticing that he himself was sitting on it. There was much to indicate the need for closing the ranks of conventional thought against subversive ideas.

This may explain the virulence of some of the opposition to Darwin, but it does not explain all the opposition. To many scientists, including some very eminent ones, the evidence in favour of the transmutation of species appeared inadequate to overturn the traditional (and still scientific) view of independent creation. And today, when one usually thinks of evolution in biological terms, it is well to remember that the very word "biology" was coined only in 1813 and that in this context "scientists" must very largely mean naturalists." For geologists, in particular, the succession of strata in the rocks, each with its characteristic fossil content, was not implausibly explained as the result of a succession of cataclysms and subsequent creations, a view held even by the master-geologist, Cuvier himself. The Pentateuchal myth, arising among a people influenced by the culture of the recurrently flooded valleys of Tigris and Euphrates, could be presented quite credibly as a record (or folk-memory) of the most recent cataclysm. And, when someone as intelligent as Newman could assert the value of Revelation was shown by the fact that without it we should never have been able to discover that Noah had preserved the animals in his ark, it is not surprising that the common view of creation was still that versed by Milton a couple of centuries earlier:

> The earth obey'd, and straight,
> Op'ning her fertile womb, teem'd at a birth
> Innumerous living creatures, perfect forms,
> Limb'd and full grown.

[1] W. C. Wells, *Two Essays: One upon Single Vision with Two Eyes; the Other on Dew...* (1818): Patrick Matthew, appendix to *Naval Timber and Arboriculture* (1831).

To the average believer, Darwin appeared to be not simply promulgating a new scientific theory, but destroying the foundations of belief; and, when a great comparative anatomist like Richard Owen asserted the theory to be untrue, it is not surprising that he and his like were greeted with open arms as scientific advisers to the Establishment.

It was fortunate for the Darwinians that Owen was a man too vain to think that he might be mistaken. Instead of admitting that Huxley was right and he was wrong in the debate about the degree of similarity between man and ape, Owen lost the opportunity to give way gracefully, and so made his position increasingly untenable by a stubborn refusal to face facts. When the fall came, it was in consequence the more resounding, and the *Punch*-reading public was treated to a series of cartoons and squibs reflecting the controversy. One, headed "The Gorrilla's Dilemma," had this touching first stanza:

> *Say am I a man and a brother,*
> *Or only an anthropoid ape?*
> *Your judgment, be't one way or t'other,*
> Do *put into positive shape.*
> *Must I humbly take rank as quadruman*
> *As OWEN maintains that I ought:*
> *Or rise into brotherhood human,*
> *As HUXLEY has flatt'ringly taught?*
> *(XLIII [18 Oct. 1862], 164)*

Owen's defeat was reflected in another set of verses, headed "Monkeyana" and addressed from the Zoological Gardens over the signature of "Gorilla":

> *Then HUXLEY and OWEN,*
> *With rivalry glowing,*
> *With pen and ink rush to the scratch;*
> *'Tis Brain versus Brain,*
> *Till one of them's slain;*
> *By Jove! it will be a good match!* ...
>
> *Next HUXLEY replies*
> *That OWEN he lies*
> *And garbles his Latin quotation;*
> *That his facts are not new,*
> *His mistakes not a few,*
> *Detrimental to his reputation.*
>
> *To twice slay the slain*
> *By dint of the Brain*
> *(Thus HUXLEY concludes his review),*
> *Is but labour in vain*
> *Unproductive of gain,*
> *And so I shall bid you "Adieu!"*
> *(XL [18 May 1861], 206)*

For the lower orders, less likely to smile over *Punch* than to chortle over the vigorous burlesque pamphlets of the time, there was "A report of a SAD CASE Recently tried before the Lord Mayor, OWEN *versus* HUXLEY, In which will be found fully given the Merits of the great Recent BONE CASE" (1863), with page after page of this sort of thing:

Policeman X—"Well, your Worship, Huxley called Owen a lying Orthognathous Brachycephalic Bimanous Pithecus; and Owen told him he was nothing but a thorough Archencephalic Primate."
Lord Mayor—"Are you sure you heard this awful language?"

It is difficult today to understand the enormous interest taken by the public of the 1860's in science, when scholars and streetsweepers alike knew that Huxley had proved right and Owen wrong. As Huxley won battle after battle, he rapidly became science personified and the most influential scientist there has ever been in public affairs; his own immense personal prestige seemed like a guarantee that Darwin's theory was correct.

Yet, when powerful and varied ideological interests are defeated so quickly and so completely as in this case, there are likely to be contributory causes deep down below the surface appearance of things. It is true that Darwin's patient accumulation of evidence provided a much more powerful brief than any predecessor had prepared. (Huxley noted, "Mr. Darwin abhors mere speculation as nature abhors a vacuum. He is as greedy of cases and precedents as any constitutional lawyer."[2]), but not even the scientific world would have been so quickly convinced had it not been already in a sense awaiting conviction.

Below the public surface of geological orthodoxy, firmly based on catastrophism, there had never ceased to flow many private rivulets of doubt. On the Continent, from Fracastoro and Leonardo in the sixteenth century and Steno in the seventeenth to Desmarest in the eighteenth, there had been those who suspected that the past of the earth could be explained in terms of forces presently observable. In 1785 England saw the publication of James Hutton's *Theory of the Earth,* a splendidly argued exposition of uniformitarian geology. Hutton failed to make much impression, but meanwhile more canals were being cut and before long a great burst of railway construction made it easy for Englishmen to make geological observations at home, in addition to those made during increasingly popular European travel and on long sea cruises. When the first volume of Charles Lyell's *Principle of Geology* appeared in 1830, to be discounted by most of the geological mandarins, many of the younger men were immensely impressed by its argument that the earth had slowly evolved into its present form, and the second volume dealt with plant and animal life in a manner which somehow only just failed to assert its evolution. No doubt there were many who still believed, and more who affected to believe, that old John Lightfoot of Cambridge had been correct in asserting the "Man was created by the Trinity on 23rd October, 4004 B.C., at nine o'clock in the morning," but some were beginning to think in terms of millions and hundreds of millions of years rather than in thousands. Long before the *Origin* appeared, the impregnable rock of Scripture was suffering slow erosion, ultimately as effective as the erosion which the uniformitarian geologists postulated for the earthly rocks. Geological theory, despite its firm surface, was in a flux within, and the impact of Darwin's book was sufficient to crack it wide open.

Biology, too, new as it was, was already on the verge of a fundamental reassessment. Erasmus Darwin's *Zoönomia* (1794) made as little impression on most

[2] "The Darwinian Hypothesis," *Collected Essays* (1893), II, 20.

people as it did on the young Charles Darwin, "the proportion of speculation being so large to the facts given,"[3] and even Lamarck's much better based *Philosophie zoologique* (1809) was little known in England. Darwin, indeed, denied that men's minds were already prepared for his theory, asserting that he "never happened to come across a single one who seemed to doubt about the permanence of species," but he immediately followed this with the more signficant remark that "innumerable well-observed facts were stored in the minds of naturalists, ready to take their proper places as soon as any theory which would receive them was sufficiently explained" (*Autobiography*, p. 124). Increasingly, with accumulating biological knowledge, the idea of independent creation had become less credible, and many, even outside the professional ranks of biology, were beginning to entertain the possibility of evolution.

This may help in part to explain the ready response which Darwin's book received among those who were not too deeply committed to orthodoxy. Even Sir Charles Lyell, "up to that time a pillar of the anti-transmutationists (who regarded him, ever afterwards, as Pallas Athene may have looked at Dian, after the Endymion affair),[4]" declared himself a Darwinian and was a tower of strength. As for the younger men, T. H. Huxley and Alfred Newton [5] were probably not the only ones to declare their vexation at not having thought out so simple an explanation of things for themselves. Far away in New Zealand Samuel Butler received the book as a flash of illumination; at home the first edition was sold out on the day of publication and the second soon after; in Europe translations rapidly appeared in many languages and the vast literature of "Darwinismus" soon called up regular German bibliographies. People were ready for an evolutionary explanation of things and natural selection provided a credible mechanism simple enough to be understood by scientist and layman alike.

The major battle between evolution and orthodoxy, highlighted by the 1860 Oxford clash between Professor Huxley and Bishop Wilberforce, has been often enough described. What is sometimes comparatively neglected is that there were many clergy quite ready to come to terms with the new scientific outlook. Even Newman, despite his conversion to Rome, saw no especial intellectual difficulty in accepting organic evolution (with, or course, certain theological reservations about the human soul), and in the Church of England there were men who accepted the idea from the start. This was a time when, as G. M. Young has remarked, "English society was poised on a double paradox . . . Its practical ideals were at odds with its religious professions, and its religious belief was at issue with its intelligence."[6] Charles Kingsley was one of those who were anxious to bring their religion into line with their intelligence and their practice into line with their religion—once, indeed, he commented to Grant Duff, in his curious stammer, "We shall never do any good, till we have got rid of those o—dious words Re—ligion and Christi—anity."[7]

Kingsley's views come out very clearly in his fascinating correspondence[8] with Huxley. The two had first met in 1855, and four years later Kingsley wrote to

---

[3] *The Autobiography of Charles Darwin,* ed. Nora Barlow (London, 1958), p. 49.

[4] *Life and Letters of Charles Darwin,* ed. Francis Darwin, 3 vols. (1887), II, 231.

[5] Alfred Newton (1829-1907) was appointed first professor of zoology and comparative anatomy at Cambridge in 1866.

[6] "Portrait of an Age" in *Early Victorian England* (London, 1934), II, 426.

[7] Mountstuart E. Grant Duff, *Notes from a Diary, 1886-1888* (1900), I, 170.

[8] In the muniments of the Imperial College of Science and Technology.

express appreciation of Huxley's review of Darwin's book in *Macmillan's*. In the following year, when Huxley suffered the death of his first child Noel, the clergyman sent him a letter of consolation which evoked from Huxley a baring of the soul quite exceptional for so self-controlled a man, and thereafter they were close friends. Kingsley had no qualms whatever about accepting Darwin's theory, and Huxley wrote "it is clear to me that if that great and powerful instrument for good or evil, the Church of England, is to be saved from being shivered into fragments by the advancing tide of science—an event I should be very sorry to witness, but which will infallibly occur if men like Samuel of Oxford are to have the guidance of her destinies—it must be by the efforts of men, who, like yourself, see your way to the combination of the practice of the Church with the spirit of science. . . . I don't profess to understand the logic of yourself, Maurice, and the rest of your school, but I have always said I would swear by your truthfulness, and sincerity, and that good must come of your efforts" (23 Sept. 1860).

Soon, indeed, it was Huxley who was the restraining influence, and by the spring of 1863 he was warning Kingsley that there was as yet no evidence that selection could produce specific sterility: "From the first time that I wrote about Darwin's book in the *Times* and in the *Westminster* until now, it has been obvious to me that this is the weak point of Darwin's doctrine. He *has* shown that selective breeding is a *vera causa* for morphological species; he has not yet shown it a *vera causa* for physiological species" (30 Apr. 1863). It was in this year that Kingsley's satire *The Water Babies* appeared, with its suggestion that, if any water baby were ever found, it would be divided between Professors Huxley and Owen for examination (p. 44).[9] How well Kingsley kept in touch with scientific developments is indicated by his incidental reference to *Archaeopteryx* (p. 47), discovered only shortly before his fairy tale went to press. Many a nursemaid must have read to her charges the account of how Professor Ptthmllnsprts (presumable "Put-them-all-in-spirits") "got up once at the British Association, and declared that apes had hippopotamus majors in their brains as men have" (p. 94)—but perhaps few of them recognized the reference to Huxley's 1860 assertion that the brain of the ape contained a *hippocampus minor*. And, as Kingsley continued, this was a shocking thing to say, "for, if it were so, what would become of the faith, hope, and charity of immortal millions?" Even more illuminating is the account of "the great and famous nation of the Doasyoulikes," living "at the foot of the Happy-go-lucky Mountains, where flapdoodle grows wild," who by a slow process of retrogressive evolution eventually became apes. "Yes," said the fairy solemnly, "there are two sides to every question, and a downhill as well as an uphill road; and if I can turn beasts into men, I can, by the same laws of circumstance, and selection, and competition, turn men into beasts" (p. 140).

Huxley told Kingsley, "I am quite as ready to admit your doctrine that souls secrete bodies as I am the opposite one that bodies secrete souls—simply because I deny the possibility of obtaining any evidence as to the truth or falsehood of either hypothesis . . . If you tell me that an Ape differs from a Man because the latter has a soul and the ape has not, I can only say that it may be so . . . until you satisfy me as to the soundness of your method of investigation, I must adhere to what seems to my mind a simpler form of notation—*i.e.*, to suppose that all phenomena have the same substratum (if they have any), and that soul and body, or mental and

[9] Page references are to the Watergate Classic ed. (1948).

physical phenomena, are merely diverse manifestations of that hypothetical substratum" (22 May 1863). As for retrogressive evolution, Huxley was in agreement that "So far from a gradual progress toward perfection forming any necessary part of the Darwiniam creed, it appears to us that it is perfectly consistent with indefinite persistence in one state, or with a gradual retrogression."[10]

Nevertheless, this fallacious notion of inevitable progress towards perfection as a necessary corollary of natural selection greatly helped the acceptance of Darwinism. The validity of a scientific theory is nowise determined by its consonance or conflict with popular opinion, or by the readiness of experts to move in its direction, or by the personal characters of its proponents or opponents, or by its convenience as ideological camouflage for vested interests. All these, however, may markedly influence the speed with which a new theory gains ground, and this was conspicuously the case with Darwin's theory. Had there not been widespread readiness to accept some sort of evolutionary ideas; had not the geological work of Lyell and others prepared the minds of scientists for the idea that massive changes can be brought about by small causes granted only sufficient time; had not Darwin already established a reputation for meticulous work and earned the admiration of fellow-scientists for his conscientiousness and their affection for his modesty, and had not Huxley been so brilliant an advocate and so dauntless an agent-general; and had not the idea of "the survival of the fittest" so admirable provided a sort of pseudo-scientific sanction for the apologists of laissez-faire capitalism, there is no knowing how long the opposition to Darwin might not have maintained its strength. As things were, the worst of the abuse was spent within a decade, and after another decade what opposition remained was thoroughly respectful. Several genuine gaps in Darwin's evidence happened to be quite quickly filled—the discovery of *Archaeopteryx* provided one of the hypothecated "missing links," study of *Amphioxus* cast light upon the borderland between vertebrate and invertebrate, embryological research went apace, and the massively accumulating fossil evidence (especially in America) tended to crush opposition by its mere weight. And, with geologising become the favourite hobby of half the country clergymen, criticism was disarmed where it might most have flourished.

As early as 1863 Kingsley was writing to Maurice, "Darwin is conquering everywhere and rushing in like a flood, by the mere force of truth and fact.[11] What was really happening was that the general idea of evolution was running in like a flood, Darwin having opened the floodgates, but the flood was not pure Darwin and the force was not merely that of truth and fact. In 1861 came Maine's *Ancient Law,* in 1863 Huxley's *Man's Place in Nature* and Lyell's *Antiquity of Man,* in 1865 McLennan's *Primitive Marriage* and Tylor's *Early History of Mankind,* in 1866 Marx's *Kapital* and Bagehot's *English Constitution.* Evolutionary assumptions and ways of thinking rapidly spread through anthropology, history, and theology, and in the process Darwin's own great personal contribution became obscured. "I cannot understand why you scientific people make such a fuss about Darwin," remarked Matthew Arnold to John Judd in 1871, "Why, it's all in Lucretius."[12] In the same year St. George Mivart published his *Genesis of Species* and claimed that evolution

---

[10] "Criticisms on 'The Origin of Species,' " *Collected Essays,* II, 90-91.
[11] *Charles Kingsley: His Letters and Memories of His Life,* ed. Mrs. Kingsley, abr. version (1883), p. 253.
[12] J. W. Judd, *The Coming of Evolution* (1910), p. 3.

was not merely compatible with Roman Catholicism but actually approved by the Jesuit Father Suarez—a claim which at once sent Huxley to the Latin text and led him, as he said, to "come out in the new character of a defender of Catholic orthodoxy, and upset Mivart out of the mouth of his own prophet."[13] In his "Mr. Darwin's Critics" Huxley declared roundly, "If Suarez has rightly stated Catholic doctrine, then is evolution utter heresy. And such I believe it to be" (*Collected Essays*, II, 147). Huxley was quite right, but it is an interesting commentary on the trend of opinion that within twelve years of the appearance of Darwin's book he had to be *proclaiming* its heresy. Nine years later he reminded the Royal Institution that "it is the customary fate of new truths to begin as heresies and to end up as superstitions; and, as matters now stand, it is hardly rash to anticipate that, in another twenty years, the new generation ... will be in danger of accepting the main doctrines of the 'Origin of Species,' with as little reflection, and it may be with as little justification, as so many of our contemporaries, twenty years ago, rejected them."[14]

Darwin's doctrines, unfortunately, were not simply accepted, but badly distorted. The idea that natural selection led inevitably to the "survival of the fittest" appealed greatly to the "Whites," who were so evidently surviving better than the "Blacks" in the world of the nineteenth century. So, just as in earlier days the apologists of slavery were able to quote selected Bible texts, now the spokesmen of "White" supremacy were able to pick passages from Darwin. To Darwin himself the slavery system was an abomination, and Huxley urged by lecture and in print that the results of miscegenation depended upon the social setting and that there was no reason to assume that primitive peoples were incapable of advancement,[15] but pseudo-Darwinian justification of racial discrimination continued to make headway. Similarly, despite Huxley's repeated insistence that intellectual ability was not the prerogative of any one social class, that "he did not believe that if 100 men were picked out of the highest aristocracy in the land and 100 out of the lowest class there would be any difference of capacity among them,"[16] that "the 'points' of a good or of a bad citizen are really far harder to discern than those of a puppy or a short-horn calf,"[17] the movement for eugenic reform developed a markedly anti-artisan bias, somewhat corrected only in the last couple of decades.

Even more crude was the distortion of Darwin to justify ruthless competitive capitalism. Men might starve, and women and children slave away for a mere pittance in the mines and mills, but all would be for the best in the end—the fittest would survive and the race thereby improve. Perhaps it is not the whole truth to call this the distortion of Darwin, for Herbert Spencer had arrived at evolutionary ideas quite independently and the phrase "survival of the fittest" was his own. As early as 1852 he had delivered to the British Association a paper "A Theory of Population, deduced from the General Law of Animal Fertility," and in the same year he developed in the *Leader* a view of evolution much on Lamarckian lines. Unfortunately, once the opposition to Darwin had been thoroughly defeated and discredited, all sorts of bastard speculation seemed legitimised; and, as a friend of Darwin and Huxley, Spencer was able to appear to the undiscriminating as a

---

[13] *Life and Letters of Thomas Henry Huxley,* ed. Leonard Huxley (1900), I, 392.
[14] "The Coming of Age of 'The Origin of Species,' " *Collected Essays*, II, 229.
[15] *Birmingham Daily Post* (7-12 Oct. 1867).
[16] *Daily Chronicle* (8 June 1887).
[17] "Evolution and Ethics, Prolegomena," *Collected Essays*, IX, 23.

spokesman of the new knowledge. When Huxley told the Birmingham and Midland Institute, as his "Administrative Nihilism" (1871) put it, that the extreme laissez-faire view favoured "neither a monarchy, an aristocracy, nor a democracy, but an *astynomocracy,* or police government" (*Collected Essays,* I, 259), Spencer developed an attack on his friend. Seventeen years later the two were still at loggerheads on this issue, and Huxley's "Struggle for Existence in Human Society" (*Collected Essays,* IX, 195-236) led, as he had realised that it would, to a quarrel with Spencer. From the point of view of the moralist, Huxley maintained, the animal world is at about the level of a gladiators' show, and the ethical man must not fight out the struggle for existence like any other animal but devote his best energies to setting limits to the struggle. As late as 1893, in his Romanes Lecture on "Evolution and Ethics," he was still trying to combat this sort of misapplication of evolutionary theory, but the Spencers and the Nassau Seniors won. As Huxley remarked, in language worthy of Engels, "men have become absorbed in the mere accumulation of wealth; and as this is a matter in which the plainest and strongest form of self-interest is intensely concerned, science (in the shape of Political Economy) has readily demonstrated that self-interest may be safely left to find the best way of attaining its ends."[18]

The impact of the *Origin of Species* was immense, but it was not only scientific and theological orthodoxy which it shattered. Everything was put into flux, and some of the directions of flow were in an ethical and political sense reactionary. Now, a century later, we have the task of disentangling the true from the false, the applications from the misapplications, the good effects from the bad effects, and a mighty task it still is.

[18] "Administrative Nihilism," *Collected Essays,* I, 268.

DARWIN AND "SOCIAL DARWINISM"

George E. Simpson

Like Holy Writ, Darwinism is susceptible to many interpretations. Aristocrats and democrats, Marxists and racists, militarists and pacificists, social scientists and biological scientists have read and re-read, interpreted and re-interpreted Darwin.

In *The Origin of Species* Darwin attributed the diverse forms of life and the evolution of complex animals from simpler ones to "a Ratio of Increase so high as to lead to a Struggle for Life, and as a consequence to Natural Selection, entailing Divergence of Characters and the Extinction of less-improved forms." In *The Descent of Man* he thought that the "ape-like" progenitors of man, like other animals, must have tended to increase beyond their means of subsistence and thus to have been involved in a struggle for existence and to the "rigid law of natural selection." Groups composed of the largest number of individuals possessing physical variations best adapted for gaining subsistence or for defending themselves would survive in greater numbers and produce more offspring than groups less well-endowed.

In dealing with the struggle for existence in early human tribes, Darwin acknowledged the influence of the physical nature of the country, and he attributed some importance in this struggle to the size and stature of the men. Greater importance, however, was given to intellectual powers (which, he said, tend to be inherited), to superiority in the arts, and to social and moral qualities. Such faculties as sympathy, fidelity, and courage were held to have been acquired through natural selection, "aided by inherited habit."

Kropotkin contended that Darwin's followers, including Herbert Spencer and T. H. Huxley, "reduced the notion of struggle to its narrowest limits." Huxley's paper on the "Struggle for Existence and Its Bearing Upon Man" stated that among primitive men, as among animals, "the weakest and stupidest went to the wall, while the toughest and shrewdest, those who were best fitted to cope with their circumstances but not best in another way, survived. Life was a continuous free fight, and beyond the limited and temporary relations of the family the Hobbesian war of each against all was the normal state of existence."[1]

Early Social Darwinism

The application of Darwin's principle of natural selection to human society, with special emphasis on competition and struggle, became known as "Social Darwinism." This doctrine, congenial to the intellectual climate of the end of the nineteenth century, was endorsed by the advocates of unrestricted competition in private enterprise, the colonial expansionists, and the opponents of voluntary social change. Among others, Ernst Haeckel provided scientific sanction for this point of view.

The theory of selection teaches that in human life, as in animal and plant life, everywhere and at all times, only a small and chosen minority can exist and flourish, while the enormous majority starve and perish miserably and more or less prematurely .... The cruel and merciles struggle for existence which rages through living nature, and in the course of nature *must* rage, this unceasing and inexorable competition of all living creatures is an incontestable fact; only the picked minority of the qualified fittest is in a position to resist it successfully, while the great majority of the competitors must necessarily perish miserably. We may profoundly lament this tragical state of things, but we can neither controvert nor alter it. "Many are called, but few are chosen." This principle of selection is as far as possible from democratic; on the contrary it is aristocratic in the strictest sense of the word.[2]

Herbert Spencer and William Graham Sumner were prominent in advancing the doctrine of the social Darwinists. Despite differences in their philosophies, both saw the poor as the "unfit." Because they are the result of the operations ot the laws of evolution, they cannot be assisted and efforts to help them through legislation,

---

[1] Quoted in P. Kropotkin, *Mutual Aid,* New York, McClure Phillips & Co., 1902, p. 4. (Huxley's paper was published in 1888.) George Nasmyth *(Social Progress and the Darwinian Theory,* New York, G. P. Putnam's Sons, 1916, p. 33) points out that Huxley wrote of ethical factors and limits to the struggle in later periods of history.

[2] Ernst Haeckel, "Freedom in Science and Teaching," p. 93. Quoted in George Nasmyth, *op. cit.,* p. 6.

public charity, and social reconstruction are evil.[3] According to Spencer, "The whole effort of nature is to get rid of them, and make room for better . . . . If they are sufficiently complete to live, they do live, and it is well they should live. If they are not sufficiently complete to live, they die, and it is best they should die.[4]

Although Darwin pointed out that militarism and war occasion reverse selection by exposing the biologically soundest young men to early death or preventing them from marrying during the prime of life and, at the same time, by providing those with poorer constitutions with greater opportunity to marry and propogate their kind, many of the social Darwinists praised war as a means of furthering social progress. Among these, one of the most influential was Ludwig Gumplowicz, Austrian jurist and sociologist. In his doctrine, social and cultural evolution was due solely to the struggle of social groups, with inter-group war functioning socially as the struggle for existence and the survival of the fittest function in the case of individuals.[5] An English scientist, Karl Pearson, wrote: "History shows me one way and one way only, in which a high state of civilization has been produced, namely the struggle of race with race, and the survival of the physically and mentally fitter race. If men want to know whether the lower races of man can evolve a higher type, I fear the only course is to leave them to fight it out among themselves."

Ninteenth century imperialists, calling upon Darwinism in defense of the subjugation of "backward" races "could point to *The Origin of Species* which had referred in its sub-title to *The Preservation of Favored Races in the Struggle for Life*. Darwin had been talking about pigeons but they saw no reason why his theories should not apply to men, and the whole spirt of the naturalistic world-view seemed to call for a vigorous and unrelenting thoroughness in the application of biological concepts."[6] Darwinian theory was utilized to justify the conflicts of rival empires, the ententes and the alliances of the "balance of power." Bismarck in Germany, Chamberlain in England, and Theodore Roosevelt in the United States found in social Darwinism a sanction for their theories of force and expansion.

Another aspect of social Darwinism at the turn of the century was the eugenics movement. Like other early social Darwinists, the eugenicists equated the "fit" with the upper classes and the "unfit" with the poor. Believing that disease, poverty, and crime are due largely to heredity, they warned against the high reproductive rates of the lower classes. As Hofstadter shows, they differed from earlier social Darwinists in that they failed "to draw laissez-faire conclusions, and depended for a part of their own program upon state action."

Was Darwin a Social Darwinist?

Students of Darwin's work are divided on the question of whether he was a social Darwinist. Hofstadter remarks that "there was nothing in Darwinism that inevitably made it an apology for competition or force. Kropotkin's interpretation of Darwinism was as logical as Sumner's." George Nasmyth, a pacifist who popularized

---

[3] John W. Bennett, review of Richard Hofstadter, *Social Darwinism in American Thought*, University of Pennsylvania Press, 1944, in *American Anthropologist* 47 (1954), p. 448.
[4] Herbert Spencer, *Social Statics*, New York, D. Appleton & Co., 1864, pp. 414-415.
[5] Howard Becker and Harry E. Barnes, *Social Thought from Lore to Science*, I, 2nd ed., Harren Press, Washington, D.C., 1952, p. 713.
[6] R. Hofstadter, *op. cit.*, pp. 146-147.

the work of Kropotkin and of Jacques Novicow, went further and claimed that social Darwinism was founded upon "a gross distortion of Darwin's own theory of social progress." Nasmyth contrasted Darwin's theory of society, "held together from within by the cementing power of the moral sense and social instincts," with "the philosophy of force, as represented in the sociology of Spencer, Ward, and Ratzenhofer, in which society is held together only by the external force exerted by some other society, this society having been constituted and held together in some miraculous way." Nasmyth goes so far as to say that "the inclusion of the entire human race within the bounds of the moral law—the federation of the world—becomes, therefore, in the true Darwinian theory, the ultimate goal of human evolution." He felt that Darwin had exposed the harsh reasoning of those who attributed social advance to competition, war, and opposition to reform. Asserting that Darwin had emphasized the importance of charitable actions, he added that such actions "tend to take the form in modern legislation of old age pensions, mothers' pensions, sickness and accident insurance and other social measures. . . . "

Other scholars have reached an opposite conclusion. Sweezy thinks the evidence that Darwin gave "the sanction of his great reputation to the reactionary doctrines now associated with his name under the term social Darwinsim" is unmistakable.[7] As proof he cites this passage in *The Descent of Man*:

With savages, the weak in body or mind are soon eliminated; and those that survive commonly exhibit a vigorous state of health. We civilized men, on the other hand, do our utmost to check the process of elimination; we build asylums for the imbecile, the maimed, and the sick; we institute poor-laws; and our medical men exert their utmost skill to save the life of everyone to the last moment. There is reason to believe that vaccination has preserved thousands, who from a weak constitution would formerly have succumbed to small-pox. Thus the weak members of civilized societies propagate their kind. No one who has attended to the breeding of domestic animals will doubt that this must be highly injurious to the race of man.

Bernhard Stern quoted the following passage from the same work in his claim that Darwin subscribed to the eugenic creed:

The advancement of the welfare of mankind is a most intricate problem; all ought to refrain from marriage who cannot avoid abject poverty for their children; for poverty is not only a great evil but tends to its own increase by leading to recklessness in marriage. On the other hand, as Mr. Galton has remarked, if the prudent avoid marriage while the reckless marry, the inferior members tend to supplant the better members of society.

According to Stern, such a view applies natural selection mechanically to man, disparages the contribution of preventive medicine, and attacks the poor laws "as coddling the poverty stricken who are identified as inferior stock."[8]

While Geoffrey West thinks that Darwin himself was more elastic in his view of natural selection than most of his interpreters, "the effect of his treatment of the Struggle is infinitely more one of competition that co-operation. . . . Popular

[7] P. Sweezy, "Social Darwinism," *Science and Society,* 6 (1942), p. 76.
[8] Bernhard Stern, "Social Darwinism," *ibid.,* p. 76.

Darwinism may be a crude but it is scarcely an unfair or inaccurate presentation of the broad effect of Darwin's basic writings."[9]

Although he calls attention to passages in *The Descent of Man* which emphasize the role of the co-operative spirit, Sir Arthur Keith expresses surprise that Darwin took "the action of his law of Natural Selection in bringing about the extermination of the less civilized by the more civilized peoples in such a spirit of indifference.[10] Montagu's appraisal of Darwin's position seems judicious.

To the present writer, Montagu's appraisal of Darwin's position seems judicious.

If it is true that the appeal to Darwinian theory for support of a social system based on ruthless competition and exploitation of colonial peoples represents a misinterpretation of evolutionary theory, the conclusion seems inescapable that Darwin himself was the first to make this misinterpretation. The few passages in which Darwin mentions altrusim and cooperation come exclusively from *The Descent of Man*, where in a book of a thousand pages they are virtually crowded out by numerous statements that appear to stand in direct and unequivocal contradiction to them.[11]

Social Darwinism In Recent Years

Adolf Hitler's racism and Nazism have been called perversions of Darwinism. Hitler's virulent doctrines were the culmination of a half-century of social Darwinistic thinking in Germany. One of his most influential immediate predecessors was General Friedrich von Bernhardi, who said of the Germans that "no nation on the face of the globe is so able to grasp and appropriate all the elements of culture, to add to them from the stores of its own spiritual endownment, and to give back to mankind richer gifts than it received."[12] Inspired by Heraclitus, Goethe, Treitschke, Frederick the Great, Clauss Wagner, von Schlegel, Schiller, and Clausewitz, Bernhardi glorified war as a biological necessity, as the greatest factor in the furtherance of culture and power, and claimed that the Germans could fulfill their great and urgent duty toward civilization only by the sword.

Hitler's doctrines are so well-known that extended reference to them here is unnecessary. According to *Mein Kampf,* the "Aryan" alone "furnishes the great building-stones and plans for all human progress," The Aryan had subjugated "lower races" and made them do his will, the Jew's "intellect is never constructive." "the mingling of blood .... is the sole reason for the dying-out of old cultures," and hyperindividualism had cheated Germany of world domination and a peace "founded on the victorious sword of a lordly people. . . ." Hitlerism represents the most extreme variety of social Darwinism and the one which has had the most powerful effects on the destinies of modern peoples.

[9] Geoffrey West, *Charles Darwin,* Yale University Press, 1938, pp. 327-328.

[10] Sir Arthur Keith, *Darwin Revalued,* London, Watts & Co., 1955, p. 264.

[11] Ashley Montagu, *Darwin, Competition, and Cooperation,* Henry Schuman, 1952, p. 96. On page 132 of this work, Montagu says that Nasmyth "errs in claiming Darwin not to be a social Darwinist."

[12] F. von Bernhardi, *Germany and the Next War,* New York, Longmans, Green & Co., 1914. Originally published in 1912.

Echoes of social Darwinism are found in some of E. A. Hooton's writings. During World War II he wrote:

Now if there is anything which can complete the ruin of the human animal which has been victimized by the machine, it is public charity and institutionalized care.... The reason why medicine has worked such biological havoc in civilized society is that it is coerced and intimidated by an imbecilic manifestation of humanitarian policy, which demands that human life be regarded as sacred.... The great European democracies, France and England handled this postwar anthropological situation with the same humanitarian stupidity which is a consistent policy of the United States.... They listened to the voices of the proletariat and allowed themselves to be weakened further by governments of socialistic and communistic imcompetents who preached economic and personal equality and worshipped worthlessness.... We must rid ourselves of the false prophets of cultural salvation and witless preachers of human equality.... The future of man is dependent on biology. We must have fewer and better men, not more morons and machines.[13]

More recently, W. H. Sheldon's studies of constitutional types have included social Darwinistic views of race and war.[14]

* * *

Sheldon claims that where conditions are "both soft and unregulated, our best stock tends to be outbred by stock that is inferior to it in every respect." He urges that we adopt

the view that war is the cheapest way out of the mess we have got into. Grim, decimative war carried to the point of settling on a power basis the question of political organization of the planetary population.... Birth control movements, except when universally enforced by political power, constitute only another monkey trap. Since as yet a central political power has not been established for our time, any talk of birth control now is like pacifism. This is to build the second story of the house before the first.

An interesting type of social Darwinism in modern dress combines a knowledge of genetics with racism, mutualism, and a formula on race mixture. Citing the United States as "an experiment in the study of the values of races," C. D. Darlington attributes the strength of this country partly to genetic recombination between diverse races but "also, perhaps even more, to the unrecombined diversity." He contends that

from the point of view of supporting a population of human beings there can be no doubt that the white-plus-Negro society is more efficient than the Indian was or ever could be. And the disparity is still increasing. Why? A white society alone would probably be little more numerous than the whites in the mixed society. A Negro society alone, even if not cut off from all intercourse with whites (to judge

---

[13] E. A. Hooton, *Why Men Behave Like Apes and Vice Versa,* Princeton University Press, 1940, pp. xvi-xix, xxv.
[14] W. H. Sheldon, E. M. Hartl, and E. McDermott, *Varieties of Delinquent Youth,* New York, Harper and Brothers, 1949, pp. 813, 836, 881.

from the experiment in Liberia) would cetainly support far fewer Negroes than there are in the mixed society. The advantage of the white-plus-Negro society is that its two racially dissimilar elements are able and willing (although only just willing) to help one another. The American Indian has been found not to be able and willing to help the other two. Their capacity and his capacity are both, of course, racial and genetic. They are determined and limited by heredity.

People, like water and vinegar, Darlington says, are different. He believes that "the future of mankind rests with those genetically diverse groups, whether races or classes, which can practice mutual help and show mutual respect. Neither of these habits can be assisted in the long run by a make-believe of equality in the physical, intellectual and cultural capacities of such groups." In his view, all races and classes have something to contribute and a plea is made for (a) "a balance . . . between the genetically differentiated elements of every nation and of all the nations of the world," and (b) "a balance . . . between inbreeding and outbreeding."[15]

Criticisms of Social Darwinism

The Russian sociologist, Jacques Novicow (1849-1912), was one of the first writers to devote himself to the refutation of the doctrine that unmitigated struggle for existence is the chief factor in human progress. In Novicow's view, the struggle for existence becomes in human society primarily an intellectual rather than a physical type of conflict. He predicted that intellectual conflict within societies would increase, be accompanied by an increase of justice and sympathy and a decrease of hatred, and bring about the survival of the best individuals.

In 1902, Petr Kropotkin wrote of the two aspects of animal life in Eastern Siberia and Northern Manchuria which had impressed him most—the severity of the struggle for existence against a formidable Nature, and the absence of the bitter struggle for existence among animals of the same species in spots where animal life was abundant. Under the former conditions, the distinctive feature was under-population rather than over-population. Wherever he observed scores of species and millions of individuals (colonies of rodents, flights of birds, a migration of fallow-deer), he saw mutual aid and mutual support which led him to conclude that this feature was highly important for the maintenance of life and the preservation and further evolution of each species. He saw further that when animals have to struggle mightily against scarcity of food (e.g., semi-wild cattle and horses, wild ruminants, squirrels), the portion of the species affected by the calamity "comes out of the ordeal so much impoverished in vigor and health that no progressive evolution of the species can be based on such periods of keen competition." Consequently, Kropotkin was unable to accept the view that the struggle for the means of subsistence, of every animal against all other animals of its own species, and of every man against all other men, was a natural law. Instead he was convinced that the practice of mutal aid has created the conditions of social life "in which man was enabled to develop his arts, knowledge, and intelligence."

Dobzhansky and Allen point out that natural selection in man comes about through the survival of the genetically fit, not of the genetically fittest. Calling

---

[15] C. D. Darlington, *The Facts of Life*, Macmillian, 1953, pp. 292-294.

Spencer's "survival of the fittest" an effective slogan in the campaign to get the theory of evolution accepted, they say it greatly overstated the fierceness of the struggle for existence.[16]

Ashley Montagu has called attention to the criticisms of one-sided Darwinism made by a number of outstanding modern biologists, including S. J. Holmes, Patrick Geddes, J. Arthur Thomson, George Gaylord Simpson, Theodosius Dobzhansky, Marston Bates, Warder C. Allee, William Patten, John Muirhead Macfarlane, Ralph Lillie, and Herman J. Muller. According to these scientists, co-operative forces are biologically more important and vital than struggle.[17] Attempting to resolve the competition-co-operation issue, Montagu writes:

Competition of every kind exists in the state of nature and has, of course, played an important role in the evolution of the varieties of life, but so has co-operation. In the struggle for existence one group may be competitively more successful than another because it is more co-operative. Certainly, so far as the persistence or continuation of every group is concerned, natural selection favors the *co-operative* as opposed to the *disoperative* struggling for survival.[18]

The Present Status of the Concept of Natural Selection

The view that "life is a struggle for existence in which only the fit survive, the fittest being those who have whatever it takes to survive" has been called "the Darwinian fallacy."[19] The concept of natural selection has not been discarded, but it has undergone revision. While the process of combative competition and struggle may occasionally result in one type producing a larger number of surviving progeny than another, this is not always the case. If the selection is severe, the reserves of genetic variability are soon depleted.[20]

In the evolutionary sense, fitness means that one genotype leaves more surviving progeny than another in the same environment. According to Dobzhansky: "The superiority may result from the fact that individuals of one genetic type are stronger and more resistant to environmental hazards, and live longer than individuals of other genetic types. Or one type may be more sexually active or more fecund than another. Individual vigor and fecundity are not necessarily correlated, and a superior fecundity may compensate or even overcompensate for deficient vigor.[21]

To J. B. S. Haldane the application of Darwinism to contemporary capitalist society would be that the poor are fitter than the rich because they leave more offspring behind them in each generation.[22] Replying to Mr. Haldane, Bernhard Stern called attention to the importance of social tradition (e.g., knowledge of birth

[16] Theodosius Dobzhansky and Gordon Allen, "Does Natural Selection Continue to Operate in Modern Mankind?", *American Anthropologist*, 58 (August, 1956), p. 593.

[17] Ashley Montagu, *Darwin, Competition and Cooperation*, pp 48-69

[18] Ashley Montagu, *The Direction of Human Development*, New York, Harper and Brothers, 1955, p.27.

[19] Ashley Montagu, *Darwin, Competition and Cooperation*, pp. 17-18.

[20] T. Dobzhansky and Gordon Allen, *op. cit.*, p. 593.

[21] T. Dobzhansky, "Heredity, Environment, and Evolution," *Science*, vol. III (Feb. 17, 1950), pp. 164-165.

[22] J. B. S. Haldane, "Concerning Social Darwinism." *Science and Society*, 5 (1941), pp. 373-374.

control, influence of religious tradition, changing attitudes concerning family life) in determining family size.[23]

Darwin's opposition to birth control, on the ground that "overmultiplication was useful, since it caused a struggle for existence in which only the strongest and the ablest survived," seems outmoded. Geoffrey West remarks that now "intelligent birth control is as much a factor for survival as co-operation."

In shaping the genetic equipment of homo sapiens in the past, natural selection contributed to the development of culture. Culture has been such a successful nonbiological adaptive instrument that man has become specialized to live in man-made environments.[24] Despite the claims of the social Darwinists, social improvement seems to be due mainly to advances in technology and social organization rather than to breeding or selective elimination. Self-preservation is no longer a sufficient motive for living. Modern man determines what "the conditions and standards of a tolerable existence" are.[25]

In no human society has it been possible to breed genetic types selectively which would be adapted to different statuses. Societies change at different rates, but even during relatively stable periods social life is a complex matter. Those who show the greatest adaptability have an enormous advantage in meeting the demands of life in any type of society.[26]

While the present view of natural selection emphasizes the role of co-operation in the life of modern societies, competition is not held to be unimportant. Unmitigated competition and democracy are inconsistent, and democratic societies seek to make competition socially useful.[27]

Montagu remarks that regardless of whether competition "in its aggressive combative sense, ever had any adaptive value among men, which is greatly to be doubted, it is quite clear that it has no adaptive value whatever in the modern world." Homo sapiens may not survive, but if he doesn't, extinction will be due not to Nature but to his own devices, to his inability to adjust to a cultural world of his own creation.

Conclusion

One hundred years after the publication of *The Origin of Species*, and eighty-eight years after the appearance of *The Descent of Man*, natural selection remains an important concept in biology, anthropology, sociology, even in international relations. Modern man is subject to selection, natural and artificial. If this were not so, all human geneotypes would produce surviving children in the same ratio as the occurrence of these genotypes in existing populations. Today the adaptive value of co-operation is more widely acknowledged and the role of ruthless aggression as a factor in the evolution of man, society, and culture is given smaller significance.

[23] Bernhard Stern, "Reply on Social Darwinism,"*Science and Society*, 5 (1941), pp. 275.

[24] T. Dobzhansky, "Evolution at Work," *Science*, 127 (May 9, 1958), p. 1097.

[25] David Bidney, "The Concept of Cultural Crisis," *American Anthropologist*, 40 (October, 1940), p. 546.

[26] A. Montagu, *Man's Most Dangerous Myth*, 3rd ed., Harper, 1953, p. 74.

[27] On Célestin Bouglé's criticisms of the social Darwinistic arguments against democracy, see H. Becker and H. E. Barnes, *op. cit.*, II, pp. 846-847.

Social Darwinistic thinking has not disappeared, but increasingly the "nature, red in tooth and claw" version of natural selection is regarded as an outdated brand of Darwinism.

5 / Marx and Marxism: Three Recent Evaluations

In a short introduction it is difficult to survey the vast literature on Marx and Marxism. The theoretical and publicistic writings of Karl Marx and Friedrich Engels are in themselves voluminous. But during the stormy period when Marxian socialism fought its way to ascendancy in the Socialist movement, their writings, in turn, engendered a whole literature of criticism and interpretation by Socialists of all shades of opinion, some of whom claimed Marxism for their own, while others rejected it violently. It was probably this doctrinaire struggle that led Marx, sometime before his death in 1883, to declare that by certain interpretations of his writings he was no Marxist.

How much more might he have emphasized this declaration during the period that begins with the triumph of Marxism-Leninism in Russia. Here again Marxism has spawned a vast literature which, in this instance, has transformed it into a system as all encompassing as those of an Aristotle or an Aquinas and elevated Marx to the role of an infallible prophet. On the other hand, the antipathy of the free world to totalitarianism and the identification of Marxism with state communism have combined to produce volumes of writings that only obscure the essential Marx. Therefore we must turn to trained scholars, such as those represented in the selections that follow, for an unemotional evaluation of Marx and Marxism. As the philosopher Sidney Hook puts it, "Whether one accepts or rejects Marx's ideas they constitute a critical part of the critical tradition of the West."[1]

The first two selections deal with the *Communist Manifesto,* that powerful epitome of Marx's philosophy and program. The first of these is a paper which Samuel Bernstein originally read before the American Historical Association in 1948, the centennial year of the publication of the *Manifesto.* Bernstein sympathetically maintains that "after the lapse of a century, we can conclude that little of it is dated" and that it still has "a forecast and message." While acknowledging Marx's and Engel's debt to their precursors, as indeed they did themselves, Berstein argues for the uniqueness of the *Manifesto.*

The second selection, which is a chapter from George Lichtheim's *Marxism: An Historical and Critical Study,* covers a much narrower area than Bernstein's broader synthesis. Lichtheim concentrates on the years immediately preceding the publication of the *Manifesto,* examining Marx's and Engel's writings during this period and the conditions influencing them. He deals in particular with Marx's

---

[1] Sidney Hook, "The Communist Manifesto One Hundred Years After," *New York Times Magazine,* February 1, 1948, p. 38.

thoughts about what form the coming revolution in Germany should take. Still, this study offers interesting contrasts with some of Bernstein's points, particularly Lichtheim's conclusion that "The *Manifesto* spells out the implications of a world-view which owed more to 1789-94 than its authors would have been willing to admit."

John Lewis, in the third selection, turns to a discussion of *Das Kapital,* the work of the mature Marx and the main source of his fame. Although uncritical in the extreme, Lewis provides a handy summary of the main thesis of this gigantic work. For Marx, capitalism was both a great liberating force and a source of constant insecurity and instability. It was a historical process of constant tension between the "law of motion" of the system and many countervailing forces. Among the more controversial points made by Lewis are his assertions that Marx did not attempt to provide "a final theory of capitalist economic crisis" and that Marxism "has acquired a relevance to the modern world and its problems denied to other theories of the nature and problems of contemporary capitalism."

FROM UTOPIANISM TO MARXISM

Samuel Bernstein

The Communist Manifesto had antecedents. An example of the eighteenth century that has often been cited is Maréchal's *Manifesto of the Equals.* It was an expression of communist thinking that had its roots in eighteenth century theory and French revolutionary practice. In the first half of the 19th century there were Georg Büchner's *Der hessische Landbote* of 1834, which, in the spirit of sans-culottism, appealed to the oppressed to rise up against their oppressors, and the communist catechism of Moses Hess in 1844, which called for a society that would free man from the reign of money.[1] The previous year the leading Fourierist, Victor Considérant, published his paper *The Manifesto of Peaceful Democracy,*[2] containing a statement of principles of the Fourierist School. These manifestoes, however, have long been relegated to obscurity. Only the *Manifesto* of Marx and Engels, published in London in February 1848, to-day commands the attention of the world.

The earlier manifestoes vigorously indicted existing conditions. But their programs were at best expressions of a hope which depended for its realization either on an individual will or on the force of reason. The social systems, projected in them, did not grow out of the historical process, for man was placed outside of historical change. *The Communist Manifesto,* on the other hand, proclaimed a new conception of history in which the modern working class, arising out of new productive relations, held the promise of the future. Consequently, it heralded a new epoch in the socialist movement.

The *Manifesto* was written as the program of the Communist League, an international organization with its headquarters in London and nuclei in France,

---

[1] For the German text of the catechism see Auguste Cornu, *Moses Hess et la gauche hégeliénne* (Paris, 1943), p. 109-18.
[2] *La démocratie pacifique,* August 1, 1843.

Belgium, Switzerland and Germany. Under the influence of Marx and Engels the League renounced Weitling's chiliastic anarchism and French egalitarianism and accepted instead the doctrines on which both men had been in agreement since 1844. In 1847 it commissioned Marx and Engels to draft a manifesto. The manuscript was sent to the printer a few weeks before the outbreak of the February Revolution in Paris.

The Manifesto of the Communist Party, to use its full title, did not at once win partisans. In fact, from 1848 to 1871, it had only a limited popularity. But it already existed during this period in English, French, Danish, Polish and Russian translations. The first English translation appeared in 1850 in the paper of George Julian Harney, the Chartist.[3] The *Manifestò* won increasing notice after the Paris Commune, which in no small way helped to publicize the names of Marx and Engels. *Woodhull & Claflin's Weekly* in New York republished the first English translation in 1871.[4]

As Marxism was made into a program by socialist parties, it became the subject of bitter controversy. Governments tried to stifle it by legislation and police measures. Intellectuals not only assailed its basic principles; they also charged that it was a paraphrase of earlier works. Thus Charles Andler contended without a shred of evidence that Engels' *Condition of the English Working Class* was a compilation out of Buret's *De la misère des classes laborieuses en Angleterre et en France.*[5] The most consistent attack has been made against *The Communist Manifesto.* At least a half dozen men, notably Georg Brandes, Georges Sorel, Morris R. Cohen and Harold J. Laski, have either charged or implied that Marx and Engels had plagiarized Victor Considérant's *Manifesto of Peaceful Democracy.*[6] It can be said at the outset that no solid evidence has ever been submitted to substantiate the charge. But since it has been repeated on several occasions, a brief inquiry into it is in order.

Considérant's indictment of bourgeois society was both eloquent and arresting. In place of the old feudalism, he said, a monied aristocracy had arisen, which imposed a new type of servitude and stood as a threat both to the working and middle classes. Capital became concentrated in the hands of a few who invaded everything, and society tended to be divided into two large classes: a small number owning everything and the large number having nothing. The new feudalism henceforth formed the real government. Considérant predicted that unless a solution was found for this "social hell," as he called it, revolutions would follow.

---

[3] *The Red Republican,* November 9-30, 1850.

[4] December 30, 1871.

[5] *Le Manifeste communiste: introduction historique,* p. 35 and 79.

[6] For example, Georg Brandes wrote in his *Ferdinand Lassalle* (English translation, New York, 1925), p. 115, that the Communist Manifesto was "almost a mere translation from Victor Considérant." Different versions of the charge have appeared from time to time. See e.g. Georges Sorel *La décomposition du marxisme* (Paris, n.d.), p. 32; Morris R. Cohen,*The Faith of a Liberal* (New York 1946), p. III. The charge is also implied in Harold J. Laski, *Karl Marx; an Essay,* reprinted with *The Communist Manifesto* (New York, 1943), p. 17 by the League for Industrial Democracy. Anarchists added their strident voices to the chorus. Thus W. Tcherkesoff insisted at one time (see *Precurseurs de l'Internationale* (Bruxelles, 1899), p. 97) that Marx and Engels had stolen their theories from Louis Blanc, and at another (See Pierre Ramus, ed., *Die Urheberschaft des Kommunistchen Manifests* (Berlin, 1906), p. 9-20) that they had filched the essential parts of their *Manifesto* from Considérant. Enrico Labriola endorsed Tcherkesoff's second conclusion. See *ibid.* pp. 21-24.

Considérant, however, failed to reveal both the laws of change of the society he arraigned and the causes of its breakdown. The disturbing picture he drew, in his *Manifesto* as in his earlier works, strikingly resembled the portrayals of socialist contemporaries. The kind of capitalism they were all confronted with was the financial, speculative variety of the July Monarchy. Since credit was political enonomy's standard for valuing men, their solution of the pressing social problems, their hope of achieving their different versions of justice, depended on the organization of credit under capitalism, and not on the socialization of the means of production and distribution, as Marx and Engels contended. All the leading utopians, in common with Considérant, were alarmed at the growing power of concentrated capital, and at its perversion of the egalitarian and libertarian principles of the French Revolution. Turning their backs on the new situation born out of the technological revolution, all of them looked with confidence either to their social panaceas or to the new utopias they planned to erect.

For they did not count on the rising proletariat to lead the way to socialism. Considérant, like other socialists, to be sure, accented the existence of a class struggle in history. In this he was not original, as we shall show later. His survey of the class conflict in fact bears a strong likeness to that of the Saint-Simonians, Bazard and Enfantin.[7] In common with them, he held that as humanity marched forward the spirit of fraternity intervened to cushion the conflict. Classes would ultimately approach one another and travel arm in arm toward the goal ahead. This conception of class relations, terminating in collaboration and harmony, rested on the belief that human history developed rationally and uninterruptedly, and it implied a confidence in the readiness of the upper class to accept the dictates of history. Thus Considérant did not show, as Marx and Engels did, how the future emerged out of practical human activity which shaped the course of history. Having faith in the irresistible triumph of reason. Considérant set up ideal conditions for the future, whose convincing power, he believed, would inspire men to establish them.

It is important to observe, in the light of the charge of plagiarism, that, in contrast to Marx and Engels, Considérant regarded the political question as secondary to the social question. He saw no connection between economic factors and state forms, for the existing political régime did not seem to him incompatible with social progress. Democratic principles like equality before the law and the elective system of representation had already been won, he contended. It was only a matter of developing them. And who would develop them? Not the proletariat, according to Considérant, for the class struggle was not the propulsive force in his system. The principles will develop in accordance with social evolution, marked out by the progress of "the dogma of fraternity," to use Considérant's phrase. The authors of the *Manifesto* had in mind a socialist like Considérant when they said of the utopians that they "endeavor, by small experiments, necessarily doomed to failure, and by the force of example, to pave the way for the new social gospel."[8]

All indications point to the conclusion that Considérant's historical outlook was not much further advanced than that of eighteenth century perfectibilists, that he relied on an abstract principle of justice, manifesting itself in history to give rise to a cooperative order. His own blueprint of it was in line with the dreams of utopians

[7] *Doctrine de Saint-Simon, Exposition Première année,* 1829 (Paris, 1924), p. 238-39, publiée par C. Bouglé et Elie Halévy,
[8] Karl Marx, *Selected Works* (Moscow, 1935), I, p. 238.

in general. His *Manifesto of Peaceful Democracy* discloses that his view of society was a static instead of a dynamic one; that like Proudhon, his contemporary, he was at bottom a conservative in the sense that he aspired to solve existing incompatibilities by balancing interests. "Thus," wrote Engels in 1843 in an estimate of the Fourierist phalanx, "after all the beautiful theories of association and free labor; after a good deal of indignant declaration against commerce, selfishness, and competition, we have in practice, the old competitive system upon an improved plan, a poor law bastille on more liberal principles."[9] It is, therefore, incomprehensible, in the light of the evidence, how students of socialist theory, who aspire to remain on the level of science, can accuse Marx and Engels of having copied Considérant.

This does not rule out their indebtedness to their precursors. In fact they were the first to acknowledge it. No one ever wrote more warmly of the great utopians than Frederick Engels;[10] and, while rejecting the remedies of econonmists like Simonde de Sismondi and Thomas Hodgskin, for example, Marx esteemed their penetrating judgments on capitalist production.[11] In contrast to their forerunners, Marx and Engels held this histoical development could not be brought to a halt by an *a priori* social device. For the anatomy of capitalism revealed to them its laws of growth and decline. Within it were being ripened the conditions of the future and the class that would achieve it.

Now Marx and Engels did not discover the existence of a class struggle. "Long before me," wrote Marx to Weydemeyer in 1852, "bourgeois historians had described the historical development of this class struggle and bourgeois economists the economic anatomy of the classes."[12] We have seen that the class struggle was a running theme in the writings of the utopians. But the theme had already been present in eighteenth century literature. Adam Smith, in the chapter on "The Wages of Labor," described the latent and open antagonism between masters and workmen.[13] His French contemporaries, the Physiocrats, had a class theory of their own, which helped them explain the circulation of the net product.[14] Significant was their contention that the productive class alone provided the life blood of society and that a parasitic class alienated a portion of the net product. Opponents of the Physiocrats, for instance Necker and Linguet, clearly recognized an existing antagonism between capitalists and wage earners. But their class theory did not point to a solution of the antagonism.[15]

The French Revolution cast the spotlight on class distinctions. Henceforth political and economic thinkers linked the class conflict with the evoluton of the forms of property. Thus, as early as 1792, Antoine Barnave approached the historical materialistic outlook and held that property relations were behind class divisions and the distribution of power.[16] Saint-Simon, who had also been

---

[9] Marx-Engels, *Gesamtausgabe*, Part I, Vol. II, p. 438.

[10] See e.g. *Herr Eugen Dühring's Revolution in Science* (New York [1935]), Pt. iii, ch. 1.

[11] *Histoire des doctrines économiques* (Paris, 1925), VI, p. 86-87; VII, 137-40, 149-52, 179-83, 205-207.

[12] *Selected Correspondence*, p. 57

[13] *An Inquiry into the Nature and Causes of the Wealth of Nations*, Book 1, ch. 8.

[14] See e.g. [Quesnay], *Tableau économique avec ses explications* (1760).

[15] Necker, "Sur la législation et le commerce des grains," *Oeuvres complètes* (Paris, 1820), I, p. 126 ff. Linguet, *Thérorie des loix civiles* (London, 1767), II, p. 461 ff.

[16] *Oeuvres* (Paris, 1843) I, p. 13.

influenced by the French Revolution, went beyond Barvave. Instead of considering property in general the basis of the class conflict, Saint-Simon saw it conditioned by property in the means of production. And he concluded that politics was the science of production.

The class struggle was also a central theme in the writings of English socialists and economists in the first half of the nineteenth century. Notable examples were Charles Hall's *The Effects of Civilization on the People in European States* (London, 1805), Thomas Hodgskin's *Labor Defended against the Claims of Capital* (London, 1825), and the numerous articles of the Chartist, James Bronterre O'Brien.[17]

The class struggle, therefore, had been regarded as a factor in social relations long before Marx and Engels. What the two did that was new was to exhibit it as a law of social change, leading to the historic moment when the proletariat won political supremacy in the nation and piloted it toward socialism.

How had the two men arrived at this conclusion? Marx reached it via a criticsm of Hegel's theory of the State and of the science of economics with its static categories, as the classical economists had conceived them; Engels, through the study of industrial and labor conditions in England. The first concluded that legal relations and state forms were not explainable by the progress of the human mind; their roots had to be sought in the material conditions of life. From his studies and observations in England the second acquired the conviction that increasing concentration of wealth and the sharpening of the class conflict would finally bring about the establishment of a system of production, founded on the collective activity of men.

The paths travelled by Marx and Engels converged and there began one of the most remarkable partnerships in history. Marx supplied his learning and his creative genius; Engels, his knowledge of labor conditions, his business experience and his skill in marking out foundations. The two closely studied classical German philosophy, English and French political economy and French and English socialism; and both devoted themselves to practical activity.

The principles they arrived at by 1848 were formulated in *The Communist Manifesto.* Though it is the statement of the Communist Party's credo, it also has the polemic quality of several of their earlier works. In the third chapter Marx and Engels took exception to the socialist and communist schools that did not represent a realistic position in relation to the general body of the proletarians. Their own view of communism, to be sure, only assimilated aspects of earlier social movements; but it also overcame their limitations; and in this respect it was qualitatively distinct from all earlier social systems. The earlier socialist and communist writings, said Marx and Engels in the *Manifesto,* "attack every principle of existing society. Hence they are full of the most valuable materials for the enlightenment of the working class." The practical measures of these writings, the two men continued, "point solely to the disappearance of class antagonisms which were, at that time, only just cropping up, and which, in these publications, are recognized in their earliest, indistinct and undefined forms only. These proposals therefore, are of a purely utopian character."[18]

Looking at the *Manifesto* after the lapse of a century, we can conclude that little of it is dated. The program toward the end of the second chapter was written in the

[17] See e.g. *Bronterre's National Reformer,* 1837, nos. I-II.
[18] Marx, *Selected Works* (Moscow, 1935), I, p. 239

anticipation that the revolution, which had already begun in Milan and Palermo, would make the proletariat the political arbiter in the most advanced countries of Europe. Then there is chapter four which sketches briefly the attitude of communists towards the various opposing parties. These parts of the *Manifesto* have a bearing on the general political climate in which it was written, and can be useful for forming an estimate of the period.

The third chapter of the *Manifesto,* already referred to, reflects the theoretical controversies before 1848, and establishes the differences between the teachings of Marx and Engels and those championed by other socialists and communists at that time. Since the tenets of pre-Marxist socialists have reappeared in different versions since 1848, the third chapter can continue to serve as a basis for modern Marxist criticism. The authors of the *Manifesto* took their stand against those they characterized as reactionary socialists who today have their counterpart among elements that dream of reimposing a fixed hierarchical order of the past; they dissociated themselves from the partisans of conspiracy, "the alchemists of revolution," as Marx called them, who were detached from the working class and who counted on a small, secret group to seize power; and they could not find common ground either with a socialist reformer like Proudhon who desired to redress social grievances, "in order to secure the continued existence of bourgeois society,"[19] or with socialist and communist doctrinaires, of whom Considérant and Cabet were notable examples, who appealed to philanthropists to help them set up models of the terrestrial paradise.

By contrast with these socialists and communists, Marx and Engels did not permit themselves to be distracted from reality by an apocalyptic contemplation of the future. For the social systems they rejected they substituted "the critical examination of conditions, of the advance and general results of the real social movement."[20] From their investigation of the historical process they concluded that the rise and decline of classes and institutions were subject to contradictions. The *Manifesto* lauds the great achievements of the bourgeoisie, and we are inclined to agree with a recent student that in all literature there "are probably no passages which paint the achievements of capitalism in more glowing terms than those devoted to the subject in the *Manifesto.'*[21] But it already speaks of this class as in a funeral oration. The proletariat, arising out of the new productive relations, stood ready to become its heir and successor, for the proletariat, in the opinion of Marx and Engels, held the promise of a vast human potential. The experience of the French and English proletariat in the thirties and forties had already taught them that. If on the eve of the revolutionary storm of 1848 they underestimated the reserve, expanding power of capitalism, if they did not foresee the growth of the world market after the decline of the economic crisis, during which the *Manifesto* was composed, if, as Engels said later, they failed to include in their calculations both Russia and the United States, they were nevertheless prophetic. In accordance with the laws of social development, as they saw them operating in history, they regarded the proletariat as the dynamic class.

The conviction was the outcome of a new conception of history, that has come to be known as historical materialism. As a guide to historical study, it is best

[19] *Ibid.,* p. 235.
[20] Karl Marx, *Herr Vogt* (Paris, 1927), I, p. 126.
[21] Paul M. Sweezy, "Origins of Present Day Socialism," *A Centenary of Marxism* (New York, 1948), p. 80, edited by Samuel Bernstein and the Editiors of *Science and Society.*

shown in the writings of Marx and Engels on the Revolution of 1848.[22] This historical philosophy starts from the thought that men make their own history, "but in the first place," as Engels wrote, "under very definite presuppositions and conditions. Among these the economic ones are finally decisive. But the political, etc., ones, and indeed even the traditions which haunt human minds, also play a part, although not the decisive one."[23] In the letter, from which we have just cited, Engels admitted that he and Marx were "partly to blame for the fact that younger writers sometimes lay more stress on the economic side than is due to it. We had to emphasize this main principle in opposition to our adversaries, who denied it, and we had not always the time, the place or the opportunity to allow the other elements involved in the interaction to come into their rights."[24]

The historical materialistic conception pointed the way to socialism. The socialist society, instead of being a hope or conjecture, was the outcome of the tortuous turns and twists of history in which the class struggle was the moving force. Socialism as the solution of the class conflict was rational, not as the achievement of reason, but rational in the sense that it was the denouement of the historical process. Historical movement did not consist in the march from one idea to another, but in the transition from one system of production to another.

Marx and Engels explained why the transition to socialism could be made only by the proletariat. "In the conditions of the proletariat," they wrote, "those of old society at large are already virtually swamped. The proletarian is without property,"[25] by which Marx and Engels meant the ownership of the means of production. Modern industry revolutionized the worker's psychology and life pattern, revealed to him the cold, cash nexus between himself and his master, and removed for him the halo surrounding existing conditions. In contrast to the classes that had previously risen to power and set up defenses for their newly acquired position, the proletariat had nothing of its own to protect. Its task was to put an end to all the safeguards of private property as the only way of getting control of the productive forces of society. Moreover, unlike all previous movements which were "movements of minorities," the movement of the proletariat, said the authors of the Manifesto, "is the self-conscious, independent movement of the immense majority, in the interest of the immense majority. The proletariat, the lowest stratum of our present society, cannot stir, cannot raise itself up, without the whole superincumbent strata of official society being sprung into the air."[26]

The historical perspectives in the Manifesto, its confidence in the workers' achievement of socialism represented a leap from the realm of fantasy, where system makers dwelt, to the realm of objective historic conditions which transformed circumstances and men. The final paragraph of chapter one in the Manifesto later elaborated in the first volume of Capital, boldly outlines the process by which capitalist contradictions will finally lead to the triumph of the proletariat over the bourgeoisie. "In place of the old bourgeois society, with its classes and class antagonisms," said Marx and Engels in closing chapter two, "we shall have an association, in which the free development of each is the condition for the free

[22] Marx, The Class Struggles in France (1848-1850) and The Eighteenth Brumaire; Engels, Germany; Revolution and Counter-Revolution.
[23] Marx-Engels, Selected Correspondence (New York, 1935), p. 475-76.
[24] Ibid., p. 477.
[25] Selected Works I, p. 216.
[26] Ibid., I, p. 217.

development of all."[27] This is the forecast and message of *The Communist Manifesto.*

[27] *Ibid.*, p. 228.

THE DOCTRINE OF REVOLUTION

George Lichtheim

After what has been said it is scarcely surprising that one should have to revert from sociology to Hegelian philosophy—and from France to Germany—in tracing the doctrine of revolution, unfolded in Marx's writings on the eve of 1848: the date of the *Communist Manifesto* and of the abortive European democratic rising. It has become customary to treat the *Manifesto* as the theoretical expression of that "proletarian revolution" which is supposed to have triumphed in Russia in 1917 after some hopeful preparatory experiments on French soil between 1848 and 1871. More will have to be said about the link between the French and the Russian experience. For the moment the question is what "the revolution" signified for Marx (and for Engels) on the eve of 1848. And here the first point to be noted is that they were primarily concerned with Germany. This may seem obvious, seeing that they were in the forefront of the German radical movement which briefly occupied the stage in 1848-9. But it is frequently overlooked; all the more reason for emphasising it.

The only revolution possible in Germany at that stage was a "bourgeois-democratic" one, a fact quite obvious to Marx and Engels (though not to all their associates) by 1847 at the latest.[1] With the wisdom of hindsight it is easy today to perceive that in actual fact the revolution never emerged from the theoretical sphere, but in the 1840's this outcome was not easily predictable. In retrospect one can also discern a difference of emphasis on this point between Marx and Engels, the former being less inclined to hope for a successful democratic rebellion against the absolutist regime, preparatory to a normal development on Western lines. Indeed Marx never seems to have believed that such an outcome was likely on German soil, while Engels frequently insisted that it was inevitable, and moreover that it was the duty of the Communists to promote it and not let themselves be deflected by the anti-capitalist and anti-liberal tirades of those "true socialists" whose sentimental longing for a partnership between the monarchy and the working class merely served to prolong the death agony of the old regime.[2]

[1]Cf. Engels, *On the History of the Communist League,* MESW II, pp. 306-23. The urgency of such a revolution from the viewpoint of the German middle class is emphasised in Engels's "Der Status Quo in Deutschland" (MEGA I/6, pp. 231-49), written in March 1847, but not published before 1932. In view of the stress laid in this important essay on the need to promote a bourgeois revolution in Germany, for the sake of the country's national development, it is not surprising that modern Communist literature tends to be silent about it.
[2]Engels, "Der Status Quo in Deutschland," MEGA I/6, p. 231; cf. also the relevant passage in the *Communist Manifesto,* MEGA I/6, pp. 525 ff (Eng. trans. in MESW I, pp.33 ff). A textual comparison shows that those passages which stress the progressive character of a capitalist development in Germany, and the reactionary nature of all counter-tendencies, including socialist ones, are taken over from Engels's unpublished manuscripts of 1847, including his *Grundsaetze des Kommunismus,* of which more later. For Engels's substained animosity toward Hess, Gruen, and the "true socialists" generally, cf. MEGA I/6, pp. 33-116.

Where both men agreed was in holding that *if* there was to be a successful revolution in Germany, it would need to mobilise the masses; but this left open the question who was to direct it. That the German middle class was quite incapable of promoting a radical break with the past did not become apparent for some years, and when it had, the theoretical and tactical differences between Marx and Engels automatically ceased to be relevant.

But this is to anticipate. In 1844-7, and *a fortiori* before he had formed his lifelong partnership with Engels in the autumn of 1844, Marx was occupied with the problem of fitting the imminent German revolution into the conceptual framework he had just elaborated, and here his reading of recent French history suggested a possible solution. Paradoxically, the very backwardness of Germany made it seem plausible to suppose that the Germans would not content themselves with the kind of revolution that Western Europe had undergone. True, in many respects Germany had only just reached a stage already attained in France or Britain, notably in economics.[3] But precisely because his native country was so far behind, Marx thought that the coming revolution might be all the more radical. It would then transcend the sociopolitical level reached in Western Europe and for the first time place the proletariat upon the stage of history:

It is not the *radical* revolution, *universal human* emancipation, which is a utopian dream for Germany, but rather the partial, merely political, revolution, which leaves the pillars of the building intact. What is the basis of a partial, merely political revolution? Simply this: *a part of civic society* emancipates itself and attains *general* domination, a particular class, from its *particular situation,* undertakes the general emancipation of society.... But in Germany every class lacks not only the consistency, the incisiveness, the courage, the ruthlessness required to turn it into the negative representative of society, but also that generosity needed to identify itself, if only for a moment, with the popular mind.... The middle class hardly dares to conceive the idea of emancipation from its own standpoint, and already the development of social conditions, and the progress of political theory, declares this standpoint to be antiquated or at least problematical.

In France, partial emancipation is the basis of complete emancipation. In Germany, universal emancipation is the *conditio sine qua non* of any partial emancipation. In France it is the reality, in Germany the impossibility, of a step-by-step emancipation which must give birth to complete liberty.... Where then is there the *positive* possibility of German emancipation? In the formation of a class with *radical chains...* a class which is the dissolution of all classes, a sphere of society which has a universal character because its sufferings are universal, and which claims no *particular right* because the wrong committed against it is not a *particular wrong* but wrong *as such* .... When the proletariat declares the *dissolution of the existing social order* it does no more than proclaim the *secret of its own existence,* for it constitutes the *effective* dissolution of this order.... As philosophy finds its *material* weapons in the proletariat, so the proletariat discovers its *intellectual* weapons in philosophy, and once the lightning-flash of the idea has penetrated this naive popular soil, the emancipation of the *Germans* to *manhood* will become reality.... The emancipation of the *German* is the emancipation of *man. Philosophy* is the *head* of this emancipation, and the *proletariat* its *heart.* Philosophy cannot realise itself without abolishing the proletariat, and the proletariat cannot emancipate itself without realising philosophy.[4]

    [3] "Zur Kritik der Hegelschen Rechtsphilosophie" (1844), MEGA I/I, p. 611.
    [4] *Ibid.,* pp. 617-21.

This famous passage is commonly cited as proof that in 1844 Marx was not yet a Marxist: in other words, that he had not yet developed the "materialist" outlook which after 1850—and in particular from the 1870's onward—was to become the hallmark of orthodoxy. This seems a curious way of approaching the subject. Whatever may be said about the evolution of doctrine, there is no "Marxism" apart from Marx's own writings, and the above passage is certainly one of his most characteristic early statements. Moreover, so far from being a passing aberration, it represents the very essence of his pre-1848 theorising about the coming revolution. It is true that in later years he took a less exalted view of the part which thought had to play in transforming the world, just as the concept of a social revolution which would transcend philosophy by "realising" its aims, disappeared from his writings; but it was never repudiated, nor could it have been, for it is precisely what he meant by the "union of theory and practice." Without this central idea, Marxism is just another species of materialist determinism, and this is indeed what the later socialist movement largely succeeded in making out of it. But the transformation was never complete; at the core of the system, however much it might be watered down by its own author and others to suit the positivist fashion of the later nineteenth century, their remained something resembling the original vision of a world made new by a unique event fusing thought and action, theory and practice, philosophy and the revolution, into a creative drama of human liberation. It is literally true that apart from this quasi-metaphysical *tour de force* the whole subsequent history of the Marxist movement must remain incomprehensible.

It is worth noting that while in his essay of 1844 Marx stood Hegel's conservative philosophy of the state on its head, he did so by carrying to its furthest extreme Hegel's own rationalist mode of thinking. Although the language of the lengthy passage just quoted is reminiscent of Feuerbach—notably the emphasis on the "emancipation of man"—the logic behind it is Hegelian: the present order of things stands condemned because it is irrational. Elsewhere in the same essay the existing state of affairs is declared to be "beneath the level of history" and "beneath criticism," from which it follows that its dissolution is both imminent and urgent. No more than Hegel did Marx doubt that what was irrational was also unreal. The most irrational, and consequently the least real, of all possible phenomena was a state of affairs such as that in pre-1848 Germany which, unlike the *ancien régime* of 1789, could not even claim to represent the traditional social order, but was a pure anachronism due to the backwardness of Germany and its lack of social development. To criticise this state of affairs—to lay bare its contradictions—was to demonstrate why such a condition of things could not be maintained much longer.

But in order to become effective, criticism had to abandon its purely theoretical status and turn into an instrument of revolution. If the youthful Hegel had in a general manner developed the notion that Reason must go out into the world and, as it were, work for its living in order to come to itself, Marx goes so far as to postulate a theoretical critique which makes an end of philosophy—in the traditional sense of the term—by "realising" its aims. Such a critique is indeed no longer philosophy, if by that term is meant contemplation, and on these grounds it has sometimes been said that Marx at this point ceased to be a philosopher. This suggestion fails on two counts: in the first place, Marx had never written anything but critiques, though it was only in 1844 that he extended his criticism of institutions to the point of fusing theory and practice; secondly, this fusion was no less philosophical—indeed metaphysical—for being directed against the ruling ideas of the age. To say that the coming revolution would make an end of philosophy by fulfilling its ultimate aims—liberty and equality—was to make as grandiose a claim as any that had been put forward since German Idealism was launched by Hegel and Schelling in the 1790's. Where Marx breaks away from the idealist scheme is in placing thought within a material context: philosophy by itself cannot transform the social order simply by holding up a scheme of perfection or a conceptual image of "true" reality; it needs an ally, and can find it only in a class whose existence proclaims "the effective dissolution of this order." This is a radical inversion of the idealist conception, but hardly a repudiation of philosophy as such. The "critical theory" of 1844 is still philosophical in essence; its criterion of judgment is the irrationality of religion—lengthily developed in the same essay—and the deeper irrationality reflected in the need for religious consolation. At no point is it suggested that the coming revolution is to be welcomed simply because it is inevitable. Rather its inevitability is deduced from the intolerable conflict between the demands of reason and the unreasonableness of the *status quo*.

These general considerations find their counterpart in a doctrine of revolution behind which it is not difficult to perceive the general model of Jacobinism, as modified and brought up to date to suit the theoretical requirements of the 1840's. The "critical theory" is intended as the theory of a political revolution patterned on that of 1789-94, but with this difference: instead of "the people" we now—almost for the first time—encounter "the proletariat."

The essential precondition of the hoped-for German revolution is defined as "the formation of a class with *radical chains* . . . . a class which is the dissolution of all classes." Marx as good as admits that as yet no such stratum exists east of the Rhine, though it is beginning to form, thus raising backward Germany to the West European level. Its inevitable growth is expected to furnish "philosophy," i.e., the radical intellectuals, with the instrument required to overturn the existing order. That of course was substantially what had occurred in France in 1789, with the important difference that in the meantime the industrial proletariat had taken over from the traditional urban plebs. By the same token, the question why the French Revolution had in the end failed to achieve the ultimate aims of its most advanced spokesmen could now at last be answered in the light of recent socialist-communist literature: the Jacobins had been unable to transcend the framework of bourgeois society. Yet "partial emancipation" (the downfall of the *ancien régime*) had been secured, and "complete emancipation" (socialism) was sure to follow. In backward Germany, still lagging far behind, this order had to be reversed: only the revolutionary proletariat, led by the intellectual vanguard, could accomplish even the "partial emancipation" implicit in the "merely political" revolution already victorious in France; only a class whose inhuman condition proclaimed "the dissolution of the existing social order" could enable "philosophy" to realise its aims. Because that class was bound to reject the social order root and branch, "philosophy finds its material weapons in the proletariat." The coming revolution would be total because its aim was nothing less than the radical transformation of man's being in the world.

For all its utopian overtones—not to mention the strained conjunction of Hegelian and Feuerbachian concepts—Marx's essay of 1844 discloses a clear enough realisation that the German bourgeoisie would not in fact make the revolution which in his view was required to bring Germany up to the West European level. And if it failed, the task necessarily devolved upon the class which was already forming in the womb of bourgeois society, but had not yet found political expression. Hence the revolution, though "bourgeois" in origin, would have to be led by the proletariat! Three-quarters of a century later a similar mode of reasoning served to fortify Lenin in his faith that the hour had struck for Russia to proclaim the world revolution: not *although* but *because* she was the most backward of the great European nations! In so doing he was compelled to repudiate not only Social-Democratic orthodoxy, but post-1850 Marxism as well; he was not, however, being untrue to the spirit of the early Marx, though reflection might have prompted doubt whether philosophical manifestoes are meant to be taken literally and used as political guide-posts. In 1844 Marx had not yet emancipated himself from either Feuerbach or Hegel, and even the *Communist Manifesto* of 1847-8 (though written with far greater comprehension of history and economics) presents far too sweeping a synthesis of philosophy and revolutionary strategy to be of use as a political textbook. All this, however, belongs to a different chapter. In the 1840's there was no real chance of anyone in Europe—least of all in Germany—taking such formulations literally. Indeed the German proletariat so confidently invoked by Marx scarcely existed. The actual historical *locus* of revolutionary politics was Paris, and in Paris the era of proletarian insurrections in the service of bourgeois democracy was drawing to a close.[5]

If the utopian extrapolation from Feuerbach's philosophy was to be abandoned—and by 1847, when the *Manifesto* was in preparation, Marx had already cast some of his youthful ideological baggage overboard—there arose a further difficulty: to say that the coming German revolution could only be a bourgeois one[6] was equivalent to saying that it would bring the liberals to power. This awkward conclusion could be qualified by asserting that the proletarian revolution would follow in the wake of this first upheaval;[7] but there remained the task of making these paradoxes plausible to those outside the narrow circle of the Communist leadership. Already there loomed the problem of inducing the "masses" to follow the lead of a "vanguard" which could afford to take the long view because it incorporated the science of revolution. In 1848-9 these preoccupations were to be drowned in a torrent of happenings that fell far short of accomplishing even the modest opening phase of the two-stage upheaval envisaged in the *Manifesto*. Subsequently the rise of Social-Democracy, and the virtual abandonment of the old strategy by Marx himself, served to obscure the solution with which the founders of Marxism had briefly toyed in those turbulent years. Here again it remained for the Russian Revolution to revive a dormant issue that Western socialists had long believed to be dead.

While the *Manifesto* skipped entire stages of the sacrosanct historical process in order to telescope two different revolutions into one, its authors could at least point to the example set by the French socialist and communist sects of the period. In common with them, Marx and Engels thought in terms of the revolutionary experience of 1789-94, when moderate factions were displaced by more radical ones, until the whole democratic movement had advanced far beyond its original

[5] Cf. Marx, *The Class Struggles in France 1848-50* (preface by Engels), MESW I, pp. 118 ff. After the failure of the 1848-9 movement, Marx gradually relinquished his faith in historical short-cuts, but the repudiation was never quite complete and overt. Engels went further, as we shall see.

[6] *Manifesto of the Communist Party*, MESW I, p. 65.

[7] *Ibid.*

starting-point. It was more difficult to justify the implicit assumption that European capitalism in 1847 was already outmoded and ripe for socialisation. This was to mistake the birth-pangs of the new order for its death-throes—a misunderstanding only possible in an age in which the memory of the French Revolution had accustomed people to expect the imminent collapse of the existing social order. That the latter was still largely pre-capitalist, hence in urgent need of radical *bourgeois* measures, was a circumstance not wholly lost upon Engels, who had seen enough of England to be able to correct any misconceptions Marx might have entertained on this point. Yet paradoxically it was Engels who in 1844-5 persuaded Marx to regard Britain as the laboratory of the first genuinely proletarian-socialist revolution.[8] By 1847, with the *Manifesto* in preparation, it became urgent to formulate the theoretical grounds of this forecast, and here again it was Engels who took the lead.

He did so in a document which has not received its due share of attention, despite the fact that Marx utilised it in drafting the final text of the *Manifesto*.[9] Taken together with his earlier writings it may be said to outline a conception of history and a doctrine of revolution significantly different from that of Marx. That this is not an academic matter becomes evident when one compares these early writings with the works of the mature Engels, which from the 1870's onward became the theoretical foundation of German Social-Democracy. The internal consistency is striking; so is the persistence of certain guiding ideas which do not occur in Marx and in some respects even run counter to the general tendency of his thinking. Thus Engels makes considerable play with the "industrial revolution"—a concept which Marx had not yet begun to employ.[10] In other respects too the tenor of his argument is a good deal more technocratic than that of the *Manifesto*. At the risk of some schematisation the difference can be described as that between a socio-political concept oriented on French political experience, and a doctrine derived from the contemplation of industrial strains in early Victorian England. Thus it is plain in reading Engels that he is mainly concerned with the role of the proletariat in the "industrial revolution," and behind this theme there already looms the notion that the "proletarian revolution" is destined to set free the "productive forces" at present held back by the institutions of bourgeois society. Echoes of this technological enthusiasm recur in the *Manifesto*, as does the emphasis on the revolutionary role of capitalism in doing away with pre-industrial forms of society; but where Marx stresses the catastrophic character of the process, Engels is inclined to emphasise its liberating and progressive side: the emancipation of the productive forces already set in train by the "industrial revolution" remains incomplete under capitalism because private property stands in the way. Communism represents its

---

[8] Cf. Engels, "Umrisse zu einer Kritik der Nationaloekonomie," in *Deutsch-Franzoesische Jahrbuecher*, 1844, MEGA I/2, pp. 379 ff. It was the essay which first drew the two men together. In the following year, Engels's *Condition of the Working Class in England* presented the socialist solution as the necessary outcome of the British situation—on the grounds that a revolution was preparing which would bring the Chartists to power and thus precipitate a social transformation.

[9] Engels, "Grundsaetze des Kommunismus," MEGA I/6, pp. 503-22. The text was first published by Eduard Bernstein in 1913. Cf. also Gustav Mayer, *Friedrich Engels*, The Hague, 1934, vol. I, pp. 283-5, where it is briefly dismissed as a "casual sketch." For a thorough analysis of the document and its implications cf. H. Bollnow, "Engels' Auffassung von Revolution und Entwicklung," in *Marxismusstudien*, Tuebingen, 1954, vol. I, pp. 77-144.

[10] Engels, *loc, cit.*, p. 503; cf. also Bollnow, *loc. cit.*, p. 79.

consummation, and the proletarian revolution is primarily envisaged as the act whereby *the industrial revolution escapes from bourgeois control.*[11]

If this idea was destined to become a key concept of Leninism, another aspect of Engels's thought turns up a generation earlier in the ideology of German Social-Democracy, namely his stress upon the inevitability of the coming sociopolitical transformation. The latter being the necessary consequence of the industrial revolution in its relentless unfolding within the womb of bourgeois society, its tempo depended primarily upon the degree of economic development already reached under capitalism. The more industrialised a country, the more numerous its working class, and the nearer the date of socialisation, whether peaceable or violent. In 1847 Engels still thought that Britain would lead the way, with Germany far in the rear, and the backward agrarian countries waiting to be transformed by the example of the more advanced.[12] A generation later this perspective was extended to Germany, and then to Europe in general. Engels is thus in a very real sense the father both of Social-Democratic orthodoxy and of the Leninist faith in industrialisation. He could even be viewed as a distant precursor of Fabian socialism, were it not for his scepticism about the likelihood of a peaceful transition, and his dislike of the pre-1848 "socialists" who (unlike the "communists") urged measures falling short of the abolition of private property in the means of production.[13] It may be that gradualism is not a necessary consequence of determinism. The prevalence of the latter in Engels's thinking is unquestionable, and helps to explain not merely some of his more obvious divergencies from Marx, but also the fact that in the subsequent development of the socialist movement it was Engels rather than Marx who supplied guidance at the tactical level.

As against the complex dialectic of existence and essence, reality and "alienation," which Marx develops in his writings between 1843 and 1848, Engels sketches a simpler and more harmonious picture. Neither the *Condition of the Working Class* (1845) nor the fragmentary *Grundsaetze* (1847) is weighed down by philosophical ballast. In conformity with their author's lifelong adherence to the optimistic world-view of the Enlightenment,[14] the emancipation of society through "communism" (i.e., through the abolition of private property in the means of production) is envisaged as a unilinear process in which modern man—man as formed by the industrial revolution and the attendant triumph of science over religious superstition—achieves complete self-realisation. In contrast to Marx, the accent falls upon the satisfaction of human needs rather than upon the transformation of (human and social) nature. The coming revolution is destined to remove the barriers to freedom and equality; its inevitability arises from the conflict between the productive forces unleashed by the new technology, and the inadequacy of the existing institutions. The Marxian *complexio oppositorum* of

---

[11] Engels, *ibid.,* pp. 510-11. The terms "Produktionskraefte" and "Produktivkraefte" are employed interchangeably by Marx and Engels in their early writings to denote the powers latent in the economy; in this they followed the example of the French economists of the period who spoke of "forces productives." Cf. Marx's use of these terms in the original French text of his *Misery of Philosophy* (1847). (*Misère de la Philosophie, Réponse à la Philosophie de la Misère de M. Proudhon;* in MEGA I/6, pp. 117-228 passim.)

[12] Engels, *loc. cit.,* p. 516.

[13] *Ibid.,* pp. 519-21. In the 1840's socialism was commonly regarded as a philanthropic middle-class movement; hence the preference shown by Marx and Engels for the term "communism."

[14] Cf. Gustav Mayer, *Friedrich Engels,* passim; Bollnow, *loc. cit.,* pp. 101 ff.

bourgeoisie and proletariat has no real place in this picture; although duly mentioned in passing, it is external to the real purport of Engels's argument which operates with the concepts of the Enlightenment in its most recent, positivistic, phase. In close parallel with these methodical assumptions, the role of the "subjective factor" is reduced almost to vanishing point: determination rules throughout, the active agents of progress being disembodied entities such as technology, science, or the industrial revolution as such. Other abstractions prominently displayed include society, machinery, the productive forces, capital, industry, the class struggle, and finally the new society, in which all these factors will be united in a new and superior harmony.[15]

On the eve of the 1848 upheaval, this optimistic and positivist doctrine was no more than an ingredient in the explosive theoretical mixture which Marx was preparing in the *Manifesto*. The time had not yet come for the socialist movement to step into the liberal inheritance. In 1848 most radicals commonly employed Jacobin terminology. For the tiny Communist League, then about to seize partial control of the radical stirrings in Germany, Marx's philosophy of total revolution, with its chiliastic overtones familiar to readers brought up in the Judeo-Christian tradition, was more appropriate than the hopeful anticipations entertained by Engels. Not that the two men were conscious of important differences in outlook. When it came to drafting the *Manifesto,* Engels characteristically yielded to the unquestioned authority of his senior associate. The first published document of German Communism thus bore the imprint of revolutionary French thinking, down to points of style and phrasing whose Jacobin, or Babouvist, ancestry could not possibly be mistaken. The *Manifesto* indeed is as much a French as a German document, and its incomparable rhetorical power owes more to the synthesis of these two European traditions than conventional critics have been willing to concede. For the same reason it does not translate well into English. In this seemingly external and insignificant fact it is possible to discern the latent element of a problem which was to become important when Marxism ceased to be a Continental European doctrine and tried to accommodate itself to the traditions of the English-speaking peoples. In the age of the democratic revolution, which in Western Europe climaxed in 1848, it was natural for the first generation of socialists to think of the coming transformation in terms derived from their own political experiences. On the Continent of Europe, these experiences were determined by the struggle against absolutism which ran parallel to the new conflict of classes. The birth-pangs of the industrial revolution thus aggravated a tension which had no real counterpart in Britain, let alone North America. Notwithstanding the Chartist movement, the "social revolution" meant different things to Continental democrats still struggling to throw off the inherited deadweight of autocracy, and to English radicals not burdened with this particular problem. "Red republicanism" was confined to Europe, and within Europe it centered on France, where democracy's first battle had been fought and won on the barricades. The Communist League of 1848 was the inheritor of this tradition, and the *Manifesto* spells out the implications of a world-view which owed more to reminiscences of 1789–94 than its authors would have been willing to admit.

[15] For the peculiarities of Engels's style, cf. Bollnow, *loc. cit.,* pp. 105-14. That his sentence constructions disclose a distinctive manner of harmonising an optimistic world-view with a deterministic philosophy of revolution, must be apparent to anyone familiar with the original texts. It is scarcely accidental that this style (down to peculiarities of grammatical and syntactical construction) later recurs in Bernstein and Kautsky.

THE LIFE AND TEACHING OF KARL MARX

John Lewis

Capital

It has been said that Marx was one of those thinkers who spend their lives writing a single important book under a number of different titles. What is quite certain is that this single book was never intended to be a treatise on economics, or "political economy" as it was then called. It was, on the contrary, a critique of all economic systems, and his aim was neither to lay down the principles that every kind of economy must conform to, nor was he attempting to explain the working of the capitalist system as if there was a certain finality or absoluteness about its laws, which was the aim of the orthodox economist. On the contrary, Marx wrote *Capital* to show not how capitalism works but how forces immanent in it bring about its destruction and its supersession by socialism.

For Marx the history of economic thought does not show us a succession of attempts—some mistaken, others nearer the mark—to answer the same question, which concludes with what the writer believes to be the right answer. It is rather an enquiry into the particular questions which successive schools of political economy sought to answer. And these were quite different from period to period, depending in each case on the social and historical situation at the time. This is a matter of history and can only be settled by historical methods, since the problems stated and answered related to given conditions and to a particular stage in social development.

This was how Marx looked at things; and he also saw that the questions which arose at any particular time were always asked by particular groups appearing on the scene with some new contribution to make, brought into existence as a class and given their task and its problems by the development of the economy in which they came to be. In this way the mercantilists appear with the rise of foreign trade and pose the questions and make the demands required by it, and the physiocrats appear with the development of capitalist farming and frame their questions and answers in terms of the agricultural situation and its needs.

Marx discovered at the very outset of his career that men tend to project certain ideas derived from their actual condition beyond themselves and then to consider these as eternal principles ruling their lives, to which they are compelled to give allegiance. This indeed is how all transcendental and absolute ideas arise, particularly those of religion. Marx regards capitalist economics as a religious phenomenon—to use a philosophical phrase, as the hypostatisation of economic abstractions. He says that the political economists who treat capitalist institutions as the only natural ones "resemble the theologians, who also establish two kinds of religion. Every religion but their own is an invention of men, while their own religion is an emanation from God."

Therefore *Capital* has to be seen not as a treatise on economics, written to demonstrate the labour theory of value, the theory of increasing misery and the falling rate of profit, nor as a book of predictions, all of which must necessarily come about independently of human understanding, will and resolve. It is a dramatic history that is designed to involve its readers in the events it describes, so that they find themselves stepping on to the stage of history and participating in and bringing to an issue the working out of human destiny.

Marx laboured at his task for forty years. From the moment that he began to study economic questions in 1843 until his death in 1883 he was continuously engaged in this work. From an immense mass of material the finished volumes began to take shape, but only the first received its final form and was published in his lifetime.

Among this pile of preliminary work we find the manuscript of the third volume of *Capital* written in 1865 even before the first volume was published.[1] This is important because it has frequently been alleged that when the theory of value, expounded in the first volume, was seen to ignore the question of price fluctuation, he desperately tried to remedy matters by writing another volume.[2] But Marx knew perfectly well what he was doing—in the first volume he works out the basic principles without complications, and then proceeds to show how they explain the actual working of the capitalist system as we know it. Until the essential law of the unmodified system has been established we shall never be able to understand or predict the consequences of particular modifications. Thus in Carnot's "heat engine" which demonstrates the basic theory of energy-exchanges in the steam engine—and nowhere in the history of science is the close relation of technological progress and enlargement of theory more closely demonstrated—the theoretical balance is nowhere realised in practice; but it is nevertheless the key to practice. So with Marx, who in Volume I works out the money expression of value, and in Volume III the different conception of *price of production,* which is derived from values according to certain rules. Not only does this theory not contradict the theory of value, it is based directly upon it.[3]

It is understandable that economists concerned with the actual working of the present commercial system should dislike the emphasis which Marx lays on value. His system and theirs differ in fundamental scope and aim. Capitalist economics is a theory of exchange and of how profit is made and utilised for further investment; Marx is concerned with a theory of production. If the labour theory of value can be used to understand the movement of history and to make a revolution, the price theory can be used to understand the movement of stocks and shares and to make money. There is confusion, therefore, between a system characterised by the production of use-values as a means merely to the creation and accumulation of exchange-values (in the form of profit), and a system based on the direct and purposive creation of use-values for their own sake.

Once Marx has made plain by his theory of value how and for what purpose surplus value is obtained he is on the way to discover the "law of motion" of the whole capitalist system. Capitalism can and must work for the purpose of accumulating profit; hence the necessity for maintaining (or restoring) the conditions in which profit can be made. This is the prerequisite for the very existence of the system and to it everything else must be sacrificed.

Marx knew perfectly well that in a capitalist system commodities are not

[1] In the long letter to Engels written on August 2nd, 1862, Marx makes it perfectly clear that he had worked out the whole of his theory long before Vol. I of *Capital* was published. We have all the manuscripts of this year, which also contain the long section on rent which subsequently appeared in Vol. III.

[2] This is the well-known criticism of Bohm-Bawerk in *Karl Marx and the Close of His System* from which most subsequent economic criticism of *Capital* derives.

[3] In the manuscript of 1857-58, the *Grundrisse* written ten years before the appearance of *Capital,* we find a full discussion on another question, the tendency of the rate of profit to fall which Marx is often said not to have adequately treated.

exchanged on the basis of their real value as measured in terms of labour-time. He expressly points out that the prices of commodities diverge more and more from their values. So much the worse for capitalism! For this divergence of prices from values is evidence of the ever-growing irrationality of the system. Marx is also able to show on the basis of his theory how the flagrant injustice and waste of the capitalist system have arisen, how as industrialisation became complete capitalism would necessarily move into a period of growing and insuperable difficulties. The labour theory of value enabled him to understand both how it was that the holding down of the workers' standard of life to a bare subsistence was *up to a certain point* the necessary condition of rapid industrialisation, and how it was that, after full industrialisation, this same pressure to minimise costs (wages) and maximise profit for further capitalisation turned into a barrier to the further expansion of production. This leads straight to the discovery of the central contradiction of capitalism which Marx reaches in Volume II and discusses at considerable length in Volume III.

The first volume was published in the beginning of September, 1867, in an edition of one thousand copies, by Meissner of Hamburg. It received several favourable reviews in the English press. The *Saturday Review* declared that Marx had the gift of lending even the driest economic question a certain fascination. Another reviewer said that Marx "in no way resembled the majority of German scholars who wrote their books in a language so dry and obscure that the heads of ordinary mortals are cracked by it."

Engels now undertook a whole campaign to publicise the first volume of *Capital* and wrote several anonymous reviews for the German papers. The historian Beesly was a friend of Marx; as a sub-editor of the *Fortnightly Review* he had promised to accept a review by Engels. But the editor, John Morley, sent it back with the remark that the subject was too abstruse for a journal of that character. All these notices of Engels were written to give the public some idea of the main purpose of *Capital*, which was at last to furnish socialist aspirations with a scientific basis, "which neither Fourier nor Proudhon nor even Lassalle have been able to give them."

The French edition was completed in 1875 and published with alterations and additions by Marx. The first Russian edition came out in 1872. The English translation by Samuel Moore and Edward Aveling appeared in 1886, three years after the death of Marx.

Marx had prepared the material for the second and third volumes, and there was also a mass of material on *Theories of Surplus Value,* but his failing health prevented him from putting them into shape. After his death this was done by Engels, and Volume II, *The Process of Circulation of Capital,* appeared in 1886 and Volume III, *The Process of Capitalist Production as a Whole,* in 1894. *Theorien über den Mehrwert* (Theories of Surplus Value) was published in Stuttgart 1905-10. This was to have formed the fourth volume of *Capital.*

Volume I (*A Critique of Political Economy*) begins by stating that the wealth of a capitalist society presents itself as an enormous accumulation of commodities for sale. The commodity is now examined in all its aspects and especially in its relations to other commodities in commercial exchange: the commodity under capitalism, including essentially labour power itself as a typical commodity; and the commodity in the form of surplus value realising its value in money (another commodity), creating a mass of profit for further investment and further profit.

This is the whole rationale and mechanism of capitalism.

Capital is not therefore concerned with the labour process as such but with labour as creating surplus value—the never-ending process of profit-making itself, which has no limit. In Marx's vivid words: "By transforming money into commodities which form the material elements of a new product or serve as factors in the labour process, and by incorporating living labour power with their dead substance the capitalist transforms value (past labour, dead labour) into capital, into self-expanding value, into a monster quick with life, which begins to 'work' as if love were breeding in its body." He goes on to show how this form of society rouses to life mighty productive forces of social labour and thus creates the material base for a new and higher form of society.

What then is the driving force and the essential mechanism of this new level of economic organisation? It is by no means merely the securing of profits by an exploiting class for its own pleasure. The surplus value which the capitalist obtains through the wage system is dedicated to the further expansion of capital investment.[4] Capitalism is a machine for converting surplus value into the means whereby more surplus value is obtained for the purpose of investing it in order to obtain still more and so on, *ad infinitum.*

"Accumulate! Accumulate! That is Moses and all the prophets! Industry furnishes the material which saving accumulates. Therefore you must save; you must reconvert the largest possible proportion of surpus value or surplus product into capital. Accumulation for accumulation's sake. This was the formula by which the classical political economist gave expression to the historical mission of the bourgeois period."[5]

Marx was anxious to show that this method of obtaining surplus value and realising it was not mere cheating, was not, as many socialists were inclined to believe, the simple process of selling a commodity for more than you gave for it, or more than its real value as measured by the cost of production.

"The transformation of money into capital is to be explained on the basis of the laws immanent in the exchange of commodities, is to be explained in such a way that the starting-point is an exchange of equivalents (i.e. even if the price obtained is no more than the value of the commodity). Mr. Money-bags who is as yet only an embryo capitalist, must buy his commodities at their value, and must sell them at their value; and nevertheless at the end of the process he must draw more value out of circulation than he puts into it at starting."[6]

Marx achieves the highest artistic force and eloquence in the passages where he discloses the essence of capitalist exploitation. One cannot easily forget the picture illustrating the conversion of money into capital. The whole process of exploitation takes on a perfectly equitable appearance, and its very essence is the spirit of freedom of which the liberal is so proud. "There alone rule Freedom, Equality, Property, and Bentham are supreme. Freedom because both buyer and seller of a commodity, say of labour power, are constrained only by their own free will. They contract as free agents, and the agreement they come to is but the form in which they give legal expression to their common will. Equality, because each enters into relation with the other, as with a simple owner of commodities, and they exchange equivalent for equivalent. Property, because each disposes only of what is his own.

---

[4] Marx was prepared to assume that 80 per cent of surplus value was reinvested as new capital in the nineteenth century. *Capital*, I. 611.

[5] *Capital*, I.606.

[6] *Capital*, I.144

And Bentham, because each looks only to himself. The only force that brings them together and puts them in relation with each other is the selfishness, the gain and the private interests of each. Each looks to himself only, and no one troubles himself about the rest, and just because they do so, do they all, in accordance with the pre-established harmony of things, or under the auspices of an all-shrewd providence, work together to their mutual advantage, for the common weal and in the interest of all."[7]

Capital thereafter is largely taken up with an extended exposition of how the capitalist maximises surplus value by intensifying the exploitation of labour. There is first an inherent tendency to appropriate the whole twenty-four hours of theoretically possible labour-time, less the ever shorter period necessary to produce a bare subsistence. The thirst for surplus value is insatiable. Capital, vampire-like, only lives by sucking living labour, "it oversteps not only the moral, but even the merely physical maximum bounds of the working day. It usurps the time for growth, development and healthy maintenance of the body. It steals the time required for the consumption of fresh air and sunlight."[8]

Marx enforces and illustrates this characterisation of exploitation with a documented picture compiled from factory reports with their prosaic description of misery and filth, their remorseless enumeration of the abnormal conditions of nineteenth-century labour. After reading this volume the orthodox textbooks of economics never seem the same to us again: we can always see through their argument the realities of the economic processes they describe and explain in the abstract terms of their science.

Theory is always linked with actual fact, based on a documented picture of modern industrialism as it actually was. Those moving and remorseless chapters dealing with the expropriation of the peasants, the struggle between the worker and the machine, the length of the working day, are magnificently written. As we read them we feel that we have been taken through the real structure of our civilisation and been shown not only the degradation of the workers but also of the masters. Yet it maintains a strong feeling of objectivity and restraint which is the source of much of its authority and persuasiveness.

The increasing mechanisation of industry also has the effect of dehumanising the worker, mutilating him into a fragment of a human being, degrading him to become a mere appurtenance of the machine, divorcing him from the *intellectual* potentialities of the labour process. Thus the whole development of capitalism results in a condition in which "the worker does not use the instrument of labour, but the instrument of labour uses the worker."

This is the "despotism of capital." Within the factory the massed machines feed upon and slowly destroy their living appendages, who exist only to promote the expansion of capital and only so long as they can find employment for this purpose. The unseen, dictatorial powers of the economic mechanism, "work out with an iron necessity towards an inevitable goal." Clearly this is Marx's portrait of hell!

Nor is this merely a picture of a single capitalist country; it is Marx's picture of the capitalist world as dominated by a process of production motivated by

[7] *Capital*, I.155
[8] *Capital*, I.250. Marx was well aware of the counteracting forces to this tendency in trade union activity and legislation which, he stated, could considerably alleviate the condition of the workers.

capitalism's boundless drive for self-expansion. The great incubus of accumulated capital does not function as a means for fulfilling human needs as, rationally, it obviously should; but dominates and oppresses the men who continuously increase it (and not their own welfare) by their labour. Marx again recalls Feuerbach. "Just as in the sphere of religion man is dominated by the creature of his own brain, so in the sphere of capitalist production, he is dominated by the creature of his own hand.[9] The productive powers of labour thus "appear as self-dependent powers of capital lording it over labour and standing in direct opposition to the labourer's own development."[10]

The first volume of *Capital*, far from being an elaborate exposition of economic abstractions, has the dimension and spirit of an epic account of the rise and development of a new, immensely impressive and yet appalling system out of feudalism with its more primitive but more human technique, putting "an end to all feudal, patriarchal, idyllic relations. It has pitilessly torn asunder the motley feudal ties that bound man to his 'natural superiors,' and has left remaining no other nexus between man and man than naked self-interest, than callous 'cash payment.' It has drowned the most heavenly ectasies of religious fervour, of chivalrous enthusiasm, of philistine sentimentalism, in the icy water of egotistical calculation.[11] Capitalism has swept all this away, "wrecking it and overspreading it; accelerating, reorganising, reassembling, in ever more ingenious complexity, ever more formidable proportions; breaking out of the old boundaries of nations; sending its commerce across oceans and continents to bring the people of distant cultures into its system, and as it lays hold on the destinies of races, reshaping their very personalities and their aspirations. And all this without their really grasping what has happened to them, and independently of their will."[12]

It is important to realise that Marx is not awarding praise or blame in his account of the development of capitalism. The evils of capitalism do not spring from the malevolence of capitalists. If this were so, a little more personal kindness might remove its harshness and injustice. In the Preface to the first volume Marx explains that individuals are dealt with only in so far as they are personifications of economic categories, embodiment of particular class relations and class interests. He points out that it is classical political economy itself that has shown us the irresistible mechanism of supply and demand, production costs and profitability, profit margins and foreign markets. "If to classical economy the proletarian is but a machine for the production of surplus value; on the other hand, the capitalist in his eyes is only a machine for the conversion of this surplus into additional capital."[13]

Yet this does not lessen his indignation at the resulting crucifixion of mankind upon the cross of gold. He describes the passion for gain as "at once the most violent, the basest and the most abominable of which the human breast is capable." He utterly exposes the selfishness and hypocrisy of those who try to convince mankind that the existing order is really man's highest achievement, that it is impossible to devise anything better. He had a peculiar psychological insight which sensed, as few have been able to, the capacity of men to remain oblivious or indifferent to the pains they inflict on others in the pursuit of economic

[9] *Capital*, I.634.
[10] *Capital*, III.1027.
[11] Communist Manifesto.
[12] Edmund Wilson, *To the Finland Station*.
[13] *Capital*, 1.606.

self-interest. He reveals with tremendous force the self-satisfaction and obtuseness of those men of property who consider themselves the salt of the earth. He succeeds at one and the same time in showing the inevitability of capitalism and more, how indispensable it was for the progress of the race, that although it is an evil compared with socialism it was a huge advance over primitive backwardness, savagery, feudalism and patriarchalism; that the socialisation of production and centralisation of industry required for socialism could have been achieved in no other way than by capitalism. And all this is demonstrated in a work which is justly considered one of the most remarkable models of implacable objectivity in the investigation of social phenomena.

What passion breathes in the pages of *Capital*, dealing with the history of primitive accumulation, the expropriation of the peasants from the land, the merciless reckoning with the expropriated! Here the dry facts of the exploitation of the masses whose whole life was converted into a simple means for expanding the value of capital were transformed into lines that breathe indignation and wrath, sarcasm towards the oppressors and warm partisanship on behalf of the oppressed. How far is passion compatible with objectivity? It is impossible to bring any accusation of inaccuracy or falsification against Marx. He is polemical not because he is tendentious in the sense of deliberately distorting the facts to make out his case, but because he accurately portrays all the contradictions that exist in life. His doctrine is passionate because it is true. He comes forward as representative of the class most vitally interested in the replacement of capitalism by socialism, the class that holds the future in its hands. But socialism up to the time of Marx had been no more than a utopian dream. In *Capital* he puts it on a firm scientific foundation and shows that it is the necessary and logical result of the whole course of development of civilisation. This meant a new conception of world history; chaos and arbitrariness give way to scientific theory. History is not the effect of fate, or accident, or heroes imposing their will on events. Its laws of development are now discerned. Until they were revealed, until man had learned to see, he was helpless in the clutch of circumstance. Laws of development, yes, but unlike the laws of nature they do not operate apart from the will and actions of people, but through the understanding and resolve, through the action of large groups of human beings, of classes. The peoples themselves make their own history, but with intelligent understanding of the conditions in which they find themselves, of the perils and demands of the situation which confronts them.

Thus Marx was able to see the capitalist economy in the perspective of historical development, as having a beginning and also as having an end. He designates the succession of systems "as so many epochs in the progress of the economic formation of society. The bourgeois relations of production are the last antagonistic form of the social process of production—antagonistic not in the sense of individual antagonism, but of one arising from conditions surrounding the life of individuals in society; at the same time the productive forces developing in the womb of bourgeois society create the material conditions for the solution of the antagonism. This social formation constitutes therefore the closing chapter of the prehistoric stage of human society.[14]

[14] Marx, Preface to *Critique of Political Economy*.

The Nature of Capitalist Crisis

The second volume of *Capital* never had the careful revision and tightening of the argument, the sharpening and pruning of the sentences and paragraphs that give such drive and power to the first volume. It was prepared by Engels from the draft manuscript which Marx himself had not worked up with his accustomed care into its final form. It does not sparkle with quite the same intellectual brilliance. Yet it is indispensable to Marx's argument.

While nearer to the contemporary facts of capitalist economy and less deliberately abstract than the first volume, it is also more theoretical in its treatment. Volume I moves on a high level of abstraction in spite of its historical section and factual material on factory conditions. But Marx knew quite well that the theories formulated here required modifications when applied to the actual operation of capitalism; and it is in Volumes II and III that this application, with the necessary modifications, is found. It is here that the *tendencies* arising from the nature of capitalism, as revealed in the first volume, are shown deflected by the counteractive forces of complex conditions. Yet as with Carnot's heat engine, and Galileo and Newton's laws of acceleration and motion, the operations of nature and the mechanical constructions of man are only rendered intelligible and made possible by abstract laws which neglect friction. In the same way, it is the basic principles enunciated in the first volume that explain the complex working of capitalism in real life.

In Volume I, Marx had shown how surplus value is obtained and how capital accumulates. What now has to be worked out in some detail is how in the world of trade and commerce commodities are realised in the form of hard cash. This would be impossible but for the credit system and the banks, which enable individual capitalists and business concerns continually to advance each other the credit they need and take up the available money, so that the uninterrupted progress of production and the sale of commodities are ensured both for the capitalist and for society as a whole.

What has further to be shown is how the commodities are thrown on to the market to compete with other commodities in the system of free competition, how in the confusion and anarchy of the market the manufacturer maintains his profit. What adjustments of wages and prices are required? How does the capitalist know what to produce and how much? What controls the amounts of labour and capital devoted over the whole system to each commodity in terms of the vagaries of individual demand?

Out of this seeming chaos a whole must result which will permit the capitalist to continue his business and at the same time satisfy the needs of society. In other words, the operations of capitalist economic law must keep in motion the circular movement of production, sale, profit and reallocation of resources for the next (and probably modified) circuit. The permanent circulation of production and consumption of society as a whole must be kept in movement within the confusion of innumerable deviating movements of individual capital.

All this is far more concrete than the matters dealt with in the first volume; nevertheless, it requires less concrete illustration, it is more theoretical. Marx's immensely important and lucid exposition anticipates much of later economic writing, to an extent insufficiently recognised by many economists.

Marx therefore proceeds to the investigation of precisely how the circular movement of investment, production, profit-making, accumulation of capital and reinvestment, whereby capital constantly changes from the money form into the commodity form and back again, proceeds. And this is being carried out by thousands of individual capitalists each concerned solely with his own interests and making his decisions as dictated by the laws of the market. How out of this anarchy do we arrive at the circulation of production and consumption in society as a whole?

Now, for the circular movement to continue without interruption, as is necessary if production, employment and the consuming power of the workers is to be maintained, it is absolutely necessary for each and every capitalist to sell the product of his enterprise. It is precisely here that contradictions arise because of the extremely complex conditions required for the circulation of the entire mass of commodities produced under capitalism.

Marx proceeds to show how the very process of capitalist *development* (i.e. profit-making for reinvestment and therefore for the general *expansion* of production) infringes upon these conditions and calls forth an interruption in the entire process of *re-production*,[15] and this must lead to periodic economic crisis.

In the second volume, therefore, Marx raises the question of economic crises. Capitalism is not, as was generally supposed, a stable system. On the contrary it is constantly throwing itself out of equilibrium "because the forces of production can never be utilised beyond the point at which surplus value can not only be produced but also realised in a society in which the great majority are poor".[16]

Marx does not, however, either in Volume II or in Volume III, in which the same problem is further discussed and the analysis of its complex nature carried farther, attempt to provide a final theory of capitalist economic crisis. He does not, because there can be no such complete theory. There are many kinds of crisis; many different and interacting causes, and many modifying influences. But whatever form crisis takes, it is the manifestation of the basic contradiction of capitalist society and it is this contradiction that Marx lays bare. Of the various ways in which it works itself out, Marx discusses several, but others have since appeared and have been analysed in their turn. Even with regard to any particular crisis the interacting forces present a complicated picture in which every cause was once itself an effect and every effect becomes a cause, so that the reciprocal and interacting forces can be described from more than one point of view—as overproduction or underconsumption or disproportion, and so on. These explanations may be equally valid and their varied viewpoints illuminating. No one explanation need be selected as the true one. What *is* important is that they all reveal from their different angles, the same incompatible ends to which capitalism inevitably drives.

But Marx is able to make quite clear what is *not* the real cause of crisis: It is not simple underconsumption, the inability of the consumers to buy back the total product of consumers goods, as if the taking of excessive profit left the consumer without enough purchasing power to buy the commodities thrown on the market,

---

[15] The meaning of "reproduction" is important for the understanding of the problem as Marx presents it. In *simple* reproduction the profit is reinvested and the cycle of further utilisation of resources and sale of the products continues with the same quantity being produced each year. But under developing capitalism we get *extended* reproduction—that is to say, more and more commodities are produced and there is also growth in the number and scale of plants and factories. According to Marx the contradictions of capitalism become more severe in the process of extended reproduction.

[16] *Capital*, II.363.

and if employers were not so short-sighted as to keep wages down everything would be well.[17]

Marx points out that so far from this being the case, economic crisis follows a period of trade expansion which has led to the absorption of the unemployed, so that their competition for jobs no longer keeps wages down. Wages rise, profitability falls and crisis supervenes. If, therefore it were to be said "that the working class receive too small a portion of their own product, and the evil would be remedied by giving them a larger share of it, or raising their wages, we should reply that crises are precisely always preceded by a period in which wages rise generally and the working class actually gets a larger share of the annual product."[18]

Marx concludes that although underconsumption is not in itself the real cause of crisis, that is not to say that it does not play a necessary role among other causes in bringing it about.

In the third volume of *Capital* Marx examines further aspects of the problem of economic crisis, which he relates not only to underconsumption, but also to the falling rate of profit, and the basic disequilibrium of an economy that always attempts to expand production without any reference to the consumption which alone can give it meaning.

But first of all he has to deal with an important source of difficulty in the capitalist economy—the falling rate of profit, and the tendency for the rate to fall. Firstly, how are the profits, after they have been turned into money, to be distributed? The employer, the merchant, the loan capitalist and the landowner, have all played their parts in the production and sale of commodities, and now each demands his share in the profit. Marx shows how each in fact receives a share in accordance with the size of his capital.

But the rate of profit does not necessarily rise with the development of capitalism; and Marx next sets out to show that there is in fact a tendency for it to fall, and this can prove an important factor in the increasing disequilibrium of the capitalist system. An important section of Volume III is devoted to this question. Marx argues that this tendency appears when increased mechanisation leads to a smaller proportion of labour to machinery being employed.[19] When such a fall in the rate of profit occurs the process of further investment is arrested and crisis is precipitated; while, operating as a long-term tendency, it will constitute a progressively increasing drag on the process of expansion of capital.

Marx does not fail to point out that there are many counteracting tendencies to this factor in slowing down investment, such as the rise in labour productivity, cheapening of machinery and raw materials, and advantageous terms of foreign trade.

It has already been pointed out that in the first volume he is constructing a simplified model to make clear his basic theory of surplus value and how it

[17] In the nineteen-twenties there was vigorous propaganda by the Independent Labour Party, based on the assumption that a high-wages policy could cure unemployment. Similar theories were again advanced in the economic crisis of 1929.

[18] *Capital*, II.476. The crisis of 1931 verified this. The *Economist* for June 2nd, 1934, published a chart showing a rise in wages in France, Germany, Britain, Japan and the United States between 1929 and 1931, while prices were falling fast. This "was bound to diminish the amount of labour and other factors of production which could be employed at a profit, and to lead to an enormous increase in unemployment of men and machinery".

[19] In Marx's terms the ratio of constant to variable capital is raised, resulting in what he calls a higher composition of capital.

originates, throwing into relief the basic influences which were shaping the configuration of the whole system, and incidentally showing that economic exploitation is not based on violence, robbery and cheating, but that everything that happens in capitalist society is the result of definite and regularly-operating laws and not of arbitrary forces or the decisions of evil-minded men.[20] In the second and third volumes Marx has moved from the basic level to the surface, to the world of bankers and shops, of the stock exchange and the market. Therefore having explained the nature of value and the relation to price or exchange value in the first volume, he is now perfectly willing to handle the problem of particular prices and to show the effect of a variety of conditions on his simplified model by the method of successive approximations.[21]

But it remains true that "the law of value dominates the movements of prices, since a reduction or increase of the labour time required for production causes the prices of production to fall or rise."

It is necessary to be clear that *Capital* is not intended to be a descriptive and analytical study of the fixed structure of the capitalist economic system, but to show that structure as changing, as in flux, as a system having a determinate cycle of growth and decay. Marxism reveals the law of motion of capitalist society, the processes of its own self-movement. Social reality is not a fixed structure but a changing one, and change is effected by strains set up in the system by its own working at any stage. Marxism overcomes the fatal incapacity to see the present as a phase in historical development and subject to inevitable change and transformation.

It is in the light of this fact that everything in the three volumes of *Capital* must be understood. We are not considering an alternative system of explanation for the permanent economic facts and functions of an industrial society. We are treating all the items—profit, prices, money, exchange, the commodity, investments—as *factors of change*. Hence the crucial chapters will be those which show that the normal working of the system inevitably leads to disequilibrium and crisis.

Marx had already reached his first disclosure of this in Volume II, and now in Volume III it assumes a more and more important place in his analysis of capitalist development.[22] The classical economist had tended to identify the rule of economic law with the postulation of an underlying stability and harmony in the economic system. To this view Marx opposed the notion that capitalism was not a stable but an unstable system. It had been described by the economists as a self-regulating system—the variations in the price of capital, labour and commodities, under the pressure of supply and demand, keeping the whole system working efficiently. Marx now points out that the very forces which operate to maintain equilibrium generate counter-forces which periodically disrupt that equilibrium; that the measures which capitalism is forced to take when the first symptoms of disequilibrium appear are themselves "the forcible solutions of existing contradictions, violent eruptions which

[20] *Capital*, III.286.
[21] As had already been pointed out it was supposed by Böhm-Bawerk (*Karl Marx and the Close of His System*) that when he came to Volume III Marx realised that his basic theory was incorrect and produced a new one which was totally incompatible with it. Unfortunately for this view, Marx had written most of Volume III before he wrote Volume I, and saw no such incompatibility. The theory as it is worked out in the later volume essentially depends upon that in Volume I. Böhm-Bawerk's contention that the theory of prices contradicts the theory of value is the very opposite of the truth.
[22] *Capital*, III.292 f.

restore the disturbed equilibrium for a while." The crisis is thus not merely the expression of a breakdown of equilibrium, but itself the process by which the broken equilibrium asserts itself. The sequence of events and decisions, slowing down of investment and production, dismissals, reduction of wages, and falling prices, all operate to keep the system functioning. If they were not put into operation, the system would crash. The forces making for the stability of the system are the forces which disrupt it.

But Marx does not single out *one*, decisive cause of economic crisis—underconsumption, finance and credit, over-investment and so forth. Each crisis in turn may have its origin in something different, and all of them may well involve financial disruption *and* over-investment, *and* underconsumption. To ask for any such single solution would be to require a too mechanical and over-simplified answer. What is clear is that crises are an inevitable product of capitalist society, a product of the many-sided relation between the productive forces and the productive relation of capitalism.

"The real barrier of capitalist production is capital itself. It is the fact that capital and its self-expansion appear as the starting and closing point, as the motive and aim of production; that production is merely production for capital, and not vice versa, the means of production mere means for an ever-expanding system of the life process for the benfit of the society of producers. The barriers within which the preservation and self-expansion of the value of capital resting on the expropriation and pauperisation of the great mass of producers can alone move, these barriers come continually in collision with the methods of production, which capital must employ for its purposes, and which steer straight towards the unrestricted extension of production, towards production for its own self, towards an unconditional development of the productive forces of society. The means, this unconditional development of the productive forces of society, comes continually into conflict with the limited end, the self-expansion of the existing capital. Thus, while the capitalist mode of production is one of the historical means by which the material forces of production are developed and the world market required for them created, it is at the same time in continual conflict with this historical task and the conditions of social production corresponding to it.[23]

There is thus a contradiction between production considered as producing values (consumption goods) and as producing profit; ultimately capital goods are never produced and investment in capital goods does not take place except with a view to their ultimate utilisation in turning out consumption goods.

Capitalism attempts to expand production, since accumulated profits must be invested, without any reference to the consumption which alone can give it meaning. The two sides of the economy, which are mutually dependent, since production lacks any objective unless it issues in consumption, are, in the capitalist world, separated logically as well as in time and space; on the one hand we have production and exploitation, on the other the ultimate realisation of surplus value in sales. But the latter is limited by the consuming power of society, whereas the former is only limited by available resources. Consuming power is not of course determined by need, but by available spending power, and since for every competitive business concern costs are an evil and must be as far as possible reduced, the consumption of the great mass of the population is kept at a minimum. The consuming power is further restricted, as Marx pointed out, by the

[23] *Capital,* III.293.

tendency to accumlate, the urgent pressure to accumulate surplus value which is the driving force of the whole capitalist system.[24]

Therefore the forces of production can never be utilised beyond the point at which surplus value can not only be produced, but also realised in a society in which the great majority are poor. There is an inherent tendency for growth in consumption to fall behind the growth in the output of consumption goods. "The last cause of all real crisis always remains the poverty and restricted consumption of the masses as compared to the tendency of capitalist production to develop the productive forces in such a way that only the absolute power of consumption of the entire society would be their limit."[25]

It is clear that it is not within the competence of capitalism to plan its production in relation to its consumption, both maximising the former and at the same time distributing the requisite purchasing power for its appropriation by the consumers. For "capital and its self-expansion appear as the starting and closing point, as the motive and aim of production," which is not, and cannot be under capitalism, the satisfaction of consumption. "Production is merely production for *capital*, and not vice versa, the means of production are means for an ever-expanding system of the life-process for the benefit of the *society* of producers."[26]

Marx immediately points out, however, the immensely important role of capitalism as "the historical means by which the material forces of production are developed and the world market for them created." Yet at the same time it is in continual conflict with this historical task.

Two closely connected questions of some importance remain for discussion. Did Marx attempt to show the inevitability of the total breakdown of capitalism in some final crisis? This is not so, for Marx never forgot the importance of the counteracting tendencies which interfere both with the tendency to a falling rate of profit and the decline of consumption power. Marx did not prophesy breakdown:[27] he was concerned to analyse actual trends, not to speculate on their hypothetical outcome.

Marx always took due note of such countervailing tendencies as the increasing productivity of labour (in relation to the falling rate of profit), the growth in organised labour's economic and political strength. Nor did the view that the whole working class would inevitably sink into pauperisation play any part in the Marxian argument. Marx seems to indicate that something like this would happen among the reserve army of the more or less permanently unemployed, but there is no evidence that he expected real wages to fall until the entire working class was at, or below subsistence level. The pressure on wages is, of course, real enough; but it represents an abstract tendency which asserts itself only in the absence of counteracting forces. Marx sees among such forces not only resistance to worsening conditions, but a growth in working-class solidarity, trade union and organisational strength, and political militancy, which by revolutionary action prevents final collapse by effecting the transformation to socialism.

The investigation of the causes of disequilibrium within capitalism as a dynamic system which generates its own complusive drive to expansion and at the same time

[24] *Capital*, III.286.
[25] *Capital*, III.560.
[26] *ibid*.
[27] The question of inevitable breakdown has been exhaustively discussed by Kautsky, Bowden, Rosa Luxemburg, and in recent times by Sweezy *(Theory of Capitalist Development)*.

its own fetters on expanding production, has acquired a relevance to the modern world and its problems denied to other theories of the nature and problems of contemporary capitalism. Many economists see with apprehension the dependence of the American economy on a gigantic arms programme, and anticipate catastrophe extending far beyond America to Europe and the rest of the world, should the armaments race cease and the cold war be allayed. Obvious to most economists today is what has been called "creeping stagnation," a falling of the rate of increase of productivity to a level incompatible with a rising standard of living and the overcoming of the continuing evils of capitalist civilisation.

The immense importance of *Capital* is now recognised by many economists and social theorists who by no means accept Marx's general position. Schumpeter calls it "one of the greatest individual achievements of sociology to this day."[28] Professor W. Leontief of Harvard speaks of Marx's brilliant analysis of the long run tendencies of the capitalist system. "The record is indeed impressive: increasing concentration of wealth, rapid elimination of small and medium sized enterprises, progressive limitation of competition, incessant technological progress accompanied by an evergrowing importance of fixed capital, and last but not least the undiminishing amplitude of recurrent business cycles—an unsurpassed series of prognostications."[29]

[28] Schumpeter, *Socialism, Capitalism and Democracy.*
[29] Proceedings of the 50th Annual Meeting of the American Economic Association.

THE NEW STATESMEN

6 / Napoleon III: Some Conflicting Verdicts

Professor Alan Spitzer, in the third selection in this section, has so well traced Napoleon III's varying fortunes in the hands of historians that there is no need to discuss here the details of an historical controversy that has produced so many divergent judgments on his personality and policies. Also, the three selections taken together treat nearly all of the factors that make for the differing evaluations of Louis Napoleon's reign. The enigmatic personality of the emperor, the *coup d'état* which liberals of the 1848 tradition found impossible or hard to forgive—even after Caesarism gave way to a briefly realized liberal empire—the gap between idea or ideals and performance, the economic and social programs of the empire and its foreign policy are all commented on.

The first selection comes from the concluding chapter of Albert Guérard's sensitive and sympathetic study of Napoleon III. It reflects what Spitzer calls the "generally favorable" interpretation of the Second Empire that has prevailed in this country and England during the last two decades. That, in the words of Spitzer, "a hostile tradition does certainly survive," is proved by the second selection. Sir Lewis Namier takes issue with some of the points made in Guérard's book and hits hard at what he considers the dictatorship of Napoleon III.

In the third selection, a model of what a critical, historiographical essay should be, Spitzer, besides reviewing the literature on Napoleon III, makes some original and trenchant judgments of his own which are a valuable contribution to the understanding of a controversial period in French history.

THE JUDGEMENT OF POSTERITY

Albert Guérard

Je me souviendrai éternellement des bontés de l'Empereur et de l'Impératrice et je resterai jusqu'à mon dernier jour fidèle à leur mémoire. . . . Malgré les vaines et stupides clameurs de la rue et toutes les lâches défaillances de ces derniers temps, l'Empereur peut attendre avec confiance le jugement de la postérité. Son règne restera l'un des plus glorieux de notre histoire. LOUIS PASTEUR[1]

[1] Letter to Marshal Vaillant, September 5, 1870; in Paul Guériot, *Napoléon III* (Paris 1933-34), II, 322.

"The Emperor may await with confidence the judgment of posterity. His reign will remain among the most glorious in our history." These words written by Louis Pasteur in a glow of indignation and despair will be read by most with a pitying, melancholy smile. At the close of this study, upon which I have been engaged for thirty years, I have no hope of altering the verdict of the unthinking. Legends, it seems, are indestructible. To the end of time, people will believe that William Tell did shoot the apple; that Frederick the Great was the incarnation of the German national spirit and the hero of the Protestant faith; that Napoleon I was the crowned soldier of the Revolution, a good European, and invincible on the battlefield; that Bismarck was a flawless realist; and that Karl Marx, single-handed, transformed Socialism from vague Utopia into rigorous science. In this world of unchallenged convention, Napoleon III stands irremediably condemned.

If we pass from loose tradition to careful research, the scene changes altogether. Within the last fifty years, Napoleon III has won the respect and sympathy of practically every critical historian. The old Carlylean tone of contempt is found only in popular works or textbooks at third or fourth hand. Even the frankly biased account by the *petit bourgeois* Radical Charles Seignobos, a period piece of the Gambetta age, and that by Albert Thomas in an orthodox "Socialist" series are completely different in tone from the apocalyptic vituperations of Victor Hugo.

On the other hand, I hate the word *glorious* which Pasteur applied to the reign of Napoleon III. It is not consonant with the character of the scientist, one of the most unassuming of men; it does not stand for the best in the Second Empire. In the Napoleonic sense of martial fame, we had better forget *glory* altogether. The Crimean War was a costly blunder; Napoleon III himself was horror-stricken on the battlefields of Italy, and whatever sickly laurels he may have won fell to dust at Sedan. If glory evokes gorgeous display, the glittering court, the gay uniforms, the gilded Grand Opera, behold, this also is vanity. All this tarnished splendor has acquired with the years a kind of baroque charm, futile and pathetic; but it is appealing only because it is dead.

What Pasteur had in mind, the true *glory* of Napoleon III, is that he was profoundly devoted to the cause of the masses, the inarticulate, the humble, the forgotten. This was his "democracy," his "socialism," a deeper reality than any constitutional form or any pseudo-scientific doctrine. In this he stands almost unique in the long line of French sovereigns. In comparison, the truly *glorious* rulers, Francis I, Richelieu, Louis XIV, Napoleon I, are cold and harsh; they prized France merely as their pedestal. Only three kings are remembered because there was in them a touch of tenderness for the common folk: Louis XII was called "the Father of the People," but he has become very shadowy; Louis XVI said to Turgot, "You and I alone love the people"—but his good will was a feeble reed; Henry IV is still a cherished memory, and most of all perhaps for his homely slogan, "A chicken in the pot every Sunday." In his early career, Henry of Navarre was even more of an adventurer than Louis Napoleon; when he came to power, he did not grant France any "liberties" of the Parliamentary kind; and he was no paragon of puritanical virtue. Yet to many readers, the comparison will seem absurd: Henry remains a universal favorite, the frank admirers of Napoleon III are few and apologetic. Why this difference? First of all, Henry was murdered—a great boon. Then, in those days, there were bitter factions but no organized parties; so his successors, while reversing his policies, did not find it essential to blacken his memory. And, above all, Henry had the advantage of *style*. He might be frivolous, but he was bluff and hearty. He was, in the words of the old song, "the triple-threat man, who could drink, fight, and make love," all with a delightful touch of bravado. He was "French of the French," if your ideal of France is to be found in Alexandre Dumas rather than in Alfred de Vigny. Napoleon III had no dash and very little humor; he was gentleness and silence. Yet he too was recognized by the people as their friend and their leader.

II

His faith in the people, his desire to serve the people, assumed a threefold form. In European affairs, it became *the principle of nationalities,* the right of self-determination ascertained by plebiscites. In the economic and social field, it manifested itself as *Saint-Simonian socialism:* order and prosperity, for the purpose of improving the welfare of the most numerous and poorest class. In politics, it sought realization as *direct democracy,* brushing aside those intermediate powers which invariably bolster privilege.

Upon the first two articles of his faith, we shall insist no more. He was a better European than Bismarck or Gambetta, and a better socialist than Karl Marx, because he was less narrow than they, and not poisoned with hatred and pride. The things he labored for, confusedly, haltingly, shall come to pass if this war is not to be eternal: all nationalities free and equal within a United Europe, industrial wealth for the service of the many, not for the profit of the few. These were Utopias yesterday; they are at this hour the only alternative to strife and chaos. The third part of his creed, direct democracy, is more controversial. Rightly understood, it might be his most substantial contribution to the making of modern Europe.

The ideal of Napoleon III was a national, non-partisan government. This conception is sharply opposed to the multi-party system, which is the foundation of all Parliamentary regimes; and it is even more directly antagonistic to the single-party system, which is Totalitarianism. Strictly speaking, until the fall of the Empire, Bonapartism was not a party.

The State, according to this view, represents only those interests which cannot be divided without destruction, and in which every one, whatever his private opinions may be, necessarily has a share. These can be summed up in one word, *security:* international security, which, ideally, means a just and durable peace, and, immediately, national defense; security at home, that is to say law and order. Its necessary instrument is a disciplined force, the army and the police. The head of the State, not for glory, but for service, is a man in uniform. This collective security should be above controversy: *Salus populi suprema lex esto.* The secondary task of the government is to promote *general* prosperity, through those improvements which do not exclusively serve private interests—public works, the development of natural resources. Whatever is factional or sectional is not the proper domain of the State; the government should be not the agent of a victorious party, but the *greatest common denominator* of all private interests.

Security, order, prosperity, are strictly material ends. The government which limits itself to their service is frankly a materialistic government. These things, by definition, are Caesar's. All that we can reasonably demand of Caesar is that he should perform his restricted task honestly and well. We should not expect the police or the postal authorities to be idealistic; their sole duty is to be non-partisan and to be efficient.

Saint-Simonian socialism, generously Utopian as it appears, is yet in perfect harmony with this materialistic conception of the State. If the aim of the State is the *common* good, if the State be indeed a *commonwealth*, leaving private interests to private initiative, then automatically it will be devoted to "the welfare of the most numerous class," which is also the poorest. Those who are above that common level do not need the State; they can take care of themselves. In concrete terms, it is the business of the State to prevent famine, but not to provide luxuries. It should "extinguish pauperism": it should not seek to create millionaires. So long as millionaires can grow richer without causing destitution, the State does not interfere with them. But if there be a connection between luxury at one end and famine at the other, then the State has the right and the duty to move. The common good, the good of the common man, must first be served.

This conception of the State as above parties is recognized to a large extent in the most orthodox of Parliamentary regimes. We deprecate partisanship even in elected office holders: a Mayor should be the Mayor of the city, not of the victorious faction. The spoils system is the natural consequence of the party spirit, for if all men must take sides, solidly, for the Blacks or the Greens, and if the other side is necessarily wrong in all things, then it is our duty to "turn the rascals out"—generals, engineers, and judges as well as governors, sheriffs, and dog-catchers. Yet we are now ashamed of the spoils system, and we are striving to eliminate it from public administration. In a crisis such as war, we have no doubt that common interests must take unquestioned precedence. Now the State should consider itself as constantly at war; not against other States—such a criminal thought never guided Napoleon III—but against disorder, disease, and want. Within that sphere, and for the duration of that eternal fight, there should be no parties.

Napoleon III was not averse to parties because he had an autocratic temperament: on the contrary, no one could be more considerate in his relations with other men, and even with dogs. He condemned parties because, in his opinion, they had irremediable faults. Even when they were perfectly honest, their squabbles paralyzed necessary action; this had been evident under Louis Philippe and the Second Republic. But could they ever be perfectly honest? Parties are inconceivable without partisanship, which is the deliberate warping of one's thought. If a man seeks to remain impartial and free, he cannot commit himself to any party organization. Worst of all, party rule, if logically carried out, is of necessity tyrannical. The party in power attempts to impose its full program upon the defeated. To be sure, the minority hopes to conquer power in its turn; party government is thus a series of wrongs offset by other wrongs, which is an extremely wasteful method of never attaining the right. These are not the excesses of the party spirit, but its very essence. The only legitimate field of government action should be the nonpartisan.

If we could afford to be as paradoxical as Einstein, we should say that this field is restricted, yet indefinitely extensible. The *greatest common denominator* may grow. We have attempted to show that Napoleon III did not believe in the "minimal State" of the philosophical anarchists. It was with him an article of faith that the government should not be defensive merely, but positive, dynamic, an instrument for the common good. In him, the policeman and the humanitarian were not at odds. The "guardian of the peace"[2] was also an agent of progress.

But, if the sphere of the government is constantly expanding, there ever remains a domain beyond: the free, boundless, teeming domain of opinions—religious, social, political, artistic. So long as a thought is merely an *opinion,* even if it be passionately held by a majority, it has no right to turn itself into a *law,* binding upon the minority. Most Americans are Christians; a majority of them are Protestants. They have steadily refused to establish a State religion, or to make their creed part of the Constitution, for, by so doing, they would be outlawing dissenters, depriving Jews, Buddhists, or agnostics of their full citizenship. *There are things that are not Caesar's.* This Napoleon III fully understood, and therein lies the radical difference between his democracy and modern dictatorships. For *they* believe in the single-party system, imposing its will upon all dwellers in the land and in every domain, the ideal as well as the material. Not only must men, under their rule, obey the same traffic regulations, but they must think and feel alike, or else they are crushed into silence.

Beyond the expanding *greatest common denominator* of security, order, prosperity, the regime of Napoleon III was definitely pluralistic. It did not matter that the Empress should be at heart a Legitimist, Morny an Orleanist, Prince Napoleon a Republican, and the Emperor himself a Socialist: if they obeyed the law and sought to promote the general welfare, they could be faithful servants of the community. Persigny, because he was a *mere* Bonapartist, was properly voted crazy. Pluralism is not identical with liberty—one might conceive of pluralistic tyrannies existing side by side—but it is the indispensable condition of liberty. The country which seeks to impose spiritual unity, by forcible or insidious means, is not free. Authority, on the other hand, is not antagonistic to liberty. The police is the protector of our innermost freedom; it makes it possible for us to differ in peace.

The Empire prohibited political meetings almost up to the end, because it was frankly committed to the suppression of factional strife. It did not abolish the liberty of the press; the blunders of a few policemen and censors should not blind us to that essential fact. Journalists were made responsible for misstatements and personal insults, but throughout the Empire there were papers which were openly Legitimist, Orleanist, Republican, anticlerical, or Ultramontane in their sympathies. Prévost-Paradol, who opposed the Empire until 1870, recognized as early as 1853 that the result of "the Tyranny" was actually to raise the intellectual and literary level of discussion. Vociferations were discouraged; incontrovertible facts stated with moderation had a chance to be heard; criticism could be sharp and even bitter, if it remained courteous. Those keen-edged weapons, allusion and irony, recovered a favor and an effectiveness they had lost since the days of Voltaire. The fearless expression of delicate thought has two enemies: the dead silence imposed by a despot, the universal tumult of full license; the second is the worst. Not merely expression, but thought itself is drowned by competitive bellowing; in the stillness of a jail, a man can at least hear himself think. The Second Empire was neither a jail nor a pandemonium; men could reflect, and talk.

More deadly to liberty than any censor are respectable conventions, unchallenged conformities. In Victorian England, wrote Hilaire Belloc, "a sort of cohesive public spirit glued and immobilized all individual expression. One could float imprisoned as

---

[2] In French, *gardien de la paix, agent de police, sergent de ville,* and in some cases *gendarme* all mean "police officer."

in a stream of thick substance, one could not swim against it." The public spirit of the Second Empire was not cohesive, and that is why its activity was so intense and so many-sided. Never, not even in the great moments of the Renaissance and the Enlightenment, were *all* schools of thought so vigorously represented. Within the solid framework of the materialistic state, the richest spiritual anarchy prevailed; and in that domain, anarchy should be the only law. Many years ago, in *French Prophets of Yesterday*, I attempted to catalogue that unexampled surge of intellectual energy. But no critical guide can do full justice to a period in which Catholics and Protestants of all shades, Humanitarians, Freethinkers, Voltairian Rationalists, Saint-Simonians, Positivists, mystics, devil-worshippers, scientists, anarchists, socialists, believers in Art for Art's Sake, went fearlessly to the end of their thought.

"Frivolous" France under the Second Empire could be amused by fancy–dress balls, by grand reviews in dashing uniforms, by Offenbach operettas, by the sauciness of Theresa or the antics of Princess Metternich, by the light wit of Alphonse Karr, Aurélien Scholl, Albert Wolff, Arsène Houssaye, Paul de Kock, Henri Rochefort, Meilhac and Halévy. But, with the hubbub of politics almost completely hushed, she could also be stirred, as we are not, by philosophical and religious controversy. A lecture by Renan at the Collège de France was an event of national importance. His *Life of Jesus,* quiet and scholarly, gave rise at once to hundreds of passionate attacks and defenses. There were police regulations, but no taboos. No cranny of human experience was left unexplored. And under that apparent chaos, there ruled a deep and definite hierarchy of values.

Napoleon III was, to borrow Gamaliel Bradford's phrase, a "damaged soul"; and, after 1860, a damaged soul imprisoned in a damaged body. Grave, thoughtful, kind, devoted to noble causes, determined withal, fearless, and surprisingly practical, he had in him also the tortuousness of the eternal plotter, the vagueness of the Utopian, the weakened fiber of the sensualist, the fatalism of the gambler. Some characters in history are obvious in their greatness, mediocrity, or turpitude: even though our sympathies may widely differ, we feel that we can focus Washington, Victoria, Gladstone, and even Napoleon I. Napoleon III is not one of these. His elusive physiognomy changes altogether with the light that is turned upon it. At one moment, he appears impressive: the only political leader in the nineteenth century whose thought could still be a guide for us today. At other times, the caricature drawn by Kinglake and Victor Hugo seems almost convincing: the middle-aged rake in imperial trappings, sinister even in his futility. The most searching, the most persistent light of all, the one in which he was seen by every one who approached him, reveals him as gentle, not merely in speech and smile, but to the very depths of his being.

And the unique regime he fashioned was no less enigmatic: strangely attractive, not in its glitter, not even in its daring, but in its "humanity," yet damaged also, and from the very first. The Roman Expedition in 1849, the fusillade on the fourth of December 1851, were causes of confusion not wholly dispelled to this day. They inflicted upon Caesarian Democracy as Louis Napoleon conceived it wounds which at the end of twenty years still refused to heal. In addition to these tragic accidents, there were antinomies in the very structure of the Empire which made its survival precarious. The most obvious, however, was only apparent: the conflict between authority and liberty. Neither of these principles can cover the whole of life, and the Empire, more clearly than other regimes, defined their respective spheres. More dangerous was the Napoleonic heritage; a government which was modern, peace-minded, democratic, industrial, socialistic, grew out of the "Legend," which was the crude exaltation of military adventure. Napoleon III was entirely different from Napoleon I, whom he had used purely as a Promethean myth; but so long as the Bonapartes ruled, it would have been hopeless to eliminate the Napoleonic Virus—as hopeless as it was for Prussia to cast off the ruthless cynicism of Frederick the Great. There are forms of ingratitude that history will not tolerate: you cannot build upon the glory of the Founder and then denounce that glory as a thing of evil.

This leads us to the fatal flaw in the Empire, the restoration of heredity. Louis Napoleon was not fully conscious of the contradiction it implied. His thought was a unique historical complex, and he sincerely believed that his blood, his tradition, his doctrine, and the will of the people were in miraculous harmony: *vox populi* and *vox Dei*, in unison, would inevitably utter the same word, *Napoleon*. This mystic delusion was at one time shared by many; but a delusion it was, and could not endure. Yet for the first twenty years of his political career, Louis Napoleon resisted the temptation. His first "Dream of a Constitution" (*Rêveries politiques*) in 1832, and the definite project he submitted to the people in 1851, provided for an elected Chief of State.

Had he given up power at the end of ten years, according to his own proposal, his term of office, although far from flawless, would have justified the highest praise. Heredity is a harmless fiction if the sovereign is but a figurehead; it becomes an absurdity if he attempts to be the active and responsible leader of the nation. Because the dynastic Empire had been restored, France had to submit, after 1861, to the rule of a man intelligent no doubt, well-meaning, experienced, but ailing, and unable to exercise for good the power he still claimed to wield. She might have been autocratically governed, in the name of a child, by a high-spirited but narrow-minded woman. She might have been exposed to the uncongenial and capricious dictatorship of Prince Napoleon. If, on the other hand, Napoleon III had yielded in time, if he had accepted in 1863-64 the offer of Adolphe Thiers and restored a Parliamentary monarchy, he would have become a mere Louis Philippe in gaudier trappings; he would have sacrificed the principle which was his *raison d'être*, Caesarian democracy.

History is not chemistry; there is no method that will enable us to analyze with irrefutable definiteness the elements of a complex situation. We have tried honestly to do so, and we are aware that the result cannot be called scientific knowledge. There entered into the making of Louis Napoleon's career accidents, a personality, and a principle; heterogeneous as they were, they remain indissolubly fused.

It is with the principle that we are chiefly concerned. That principle is *direct democracy*. The experiment failed, not because the principle could be proved wrong, but because it was not applied in its full and honest simplicity. Caesarism reverted to heredity; the opposition, of the Right and of the Left, was bent on restoring factional strife, as if that alone deserved the name of Liberty. Three forces united in raising Louis Napoleon to supreme power: the Imperial Legend, the dread of disorder, and humanitarian democracy. All three were very real, but the third was the deepest in French opinion, and in Louis Napoleon's own soul. The regime which he conceived resembles the American far more than it does British Parliamentarism on the one hand, Totalitarian Dictatorship on the other. It might be well for France, when she resumes the normal course of her destiny, to borrow her inspiration from the United States rather than from England. If she did so, the Constitution of 1852 would be for her a better starting point than the Constitution of 1875. And she would be fortunate indeed if she found again, under such a regime, a leader with the unfailing gentleness, the quiet intellectual courage, the profound generosity, of Napoleon III.

THE FIRST MOUNTEBANK DICTATOR

Sir Lewis Namier

Recurrent situations in history reproduce analogous forms; there is a morphology of politics. But to the basic repetition and the individual variations of organic growth an element is added peculiar to man: imitation engendered by historical memory. The modern dictatorship arises amid the ruins of an inherited social and political structure, in the desolation of shattered loyalties—it is the desperate shift of communities broken from their moorings. Disappointed, disillusioned men, uprooted and unbalanced, driven by half-conscious fears and gusts of passions, frantically seek a new rallying point and new attachments. Their dreams and cravings projected into the void gather round some figure. It is the monolatry of the political desert. The more pathological the situation the less important is the intrinsic worth of the idol. His feet may be of clay and his face may be a blank: it is the frenzy of the worshippers which imparts to him meaning and power.

Such morbid cults have by now acquired a tradition and ideology, and have evolved their own routine and political vocabulary. With Napoleon I things were serious and real—the problems of his time and his mastery of them; he raised no bogies and whipped up no passions; he aimed at restoring sanity and at consolidating the positive results of the Revolution; and if, in superposing the Empire on the Republic and in recreating a Realm of the West, he evoked the memories of Caesar and Charlemagne, the appeal was decorative rather than imitative. There would have been no occasion for his dictatorship had not the living heritage of French history been obliterated by revolution; but his system has left its own unhealthy legend, a jackal-ghost which prowls in the wake of the "Red spectre." Napoleon III and Boulanger were to be the plagiarists, shadowy and counterfeit, of Napoleon I; and Mussolini and Hitler were to be unconscious reproducers of the methods of Napoleon III. For these are inherent in plebiscitarian Caesarism, or so-called "Caesarian democracy," with its direct appeal to the masses: demagogical slogans; disregard of legality in spite of a professed guardianship of law and order; contempt of political parties and the parliamentary system, of the educated classes and their values; blandishments and vague, contradictory promises for all and sundry; militarism; gigantic, blatant displays and shady corruption. *Panem et circenses* once more—and at the end of the road, disaster.

The first coups of Louis-Napoleon, at Strasbourg in 1836 and at Boulogne in 1840, were miserable failures, like Hitler's Munich *Putsch* of 1923. Both men were treated with humane and neglectful forbearance, and in the enforced leisure of their comfortable prisons they composed their programmatic works—Des Idées *Napoleoniennes* and *Mein Kampf.* Not even at a later stage did the political leaders realize the full gravity of the situation—thinking in terms of their own and not in those of the masses, they could not descry either in Louis-Napoleon or in Hitler a possible ruler or dictator. Louis-Napoleon escaped from his prison at Ham in 1846, and settled in London. On the outbreak of the February Revolution he hastened to Paris, a professed supporter of the Republic; but when requested by the Provisional Government to leave the country, he complied, and the Chartist crisis of April found him acting the special constable in London. In the by-elections of 4 June he was returned to the Constituent Assembly by four *départments,* but rather than face an imbroglio, he withdrew. "When one is weak, one has to submit and await better days," he wrote to his cousin Napoleon ("Plonplon") in 1844; and on 5 June 1848: "In these moments of exaltation, I prefer to remain in the background." Re-elected in September by five constituencies, he took his seat, and read out a brief address affirming his devotion "to the defence of order and the strengthening of the Republic." "These correct words, spoken in a toneless voice, were received with perfunctory applause," writes his latest biographer, Mr. Albert Guérard.[1] He looked

disarmingly unobtrusive. His torso was long and his legs short; he moved awkwardly, with a shuffling gait; his head sat heavily on his broad and round shoulders; his countenance was pale and immobile; his eyes were small, heavy-lidded, of an undefinable grey. . . . He was not downright ludicrous; he was not exactly commonplace; he certainly was not impressive.

When the Assembly, enmeshed in constitutional doctrine and democratic dogma, decided to have the President of the Republic elected by popular vote, and not by the Legislature, the door was opened for a Bonapartist restoration. To preclude it, an amendment was moved debarring members of former ruling families.

Every eye turned towards Louis-Napoleon, for the amendment was aimed at him alone. He went up to the tribune and, in a few halting sentences, uttered with a strangely un-French accent, he protested against "the calumnies constantly hurled at his head," stammered, ended abruptly and shuffled back to his seat.

The amendment was withdrawn, its mover himself describing it, "after what we have just seen and heard," as superfluous. On 10 December 1848, in the Presidential election, Louis-Napoleon received 5,400,000 votes against the 1,800,000 of his four opponents; Lamartine—poet, orator, and leader in the provisional Government—found himself at the bottom of the poll, with a mere 17,000. "The world is a strange theatre," remarks Alexis de Tocqueville; "had Louis-Napoleon been a wise man or a genius, he would never have become President of the Republic."

"The remote lack-lustre gaze of his grey eyes, now that it was fraught with destiny, could be declared sphinx-like or prophetic," writes Guérard. And Pierre de La Gorce, historian of the Second Empire, says that the change which success produced in the public estimate of the same traits of Louis-Napoleon's character was like a picture advertising a hair-restorative: "before" and "after." Between these two appraisements, the taciturn, shadowy, impassive figure of Napoleon III has puzzled the century which has gone by, as the shrieking, convulsed, hysterical figure of Hitler will puzzle the one to come. "A sphinx without a riddle," was Bismarck's

---

[1] Albert Guérard: *Napoleon III.* Harvard University Press, London: Cumberlege, 1945.

summing up of Napoleon III; "from afar something, near at hand nothing"; "a great unfathomed incapacity." And N. W. Senior reports Tocqueville having said to him in January 1852:

Louis-Napoleon is essentially a copyist. He can originate nothing; his opinions, his theories, his maxims, even his plots, all are borrowed, and from the most dangerous of models—from a man who, though he possessed genius and industry such as are not seen . . . once in a thousand years, yet ruined himself by the extravagance of his attempts.

But Napoleon III, said Grimblot to Senior in 1855, "lacked industry and capacity"—and on this point most contemporaries are agreed.

When we were together in England [continued Grimblot] I saw much of him. We have walked for hours in the Green Park. His range of ideas is narrow, and there is always one which preoccupies him . . . and shuts out the others . . . He learns little from his own meditations, for he does not balance opposite arguments; he learns nothing from conversation, for he never listens.

And an unnamed friend of Senior's, in 1858: ". . . as he is ignorant, uninventive, and idle, you will see him flounder from one failure to another." Guizot, Thiers, Montalembert, Falloux, Duvergier de Hauranne, Victor Hugo, Ampère, Beaumont, they all despised *celui-ci;* but the opposition of the intellectuals was tolerated because as Tocqueville put it, their writings were not read "by the soldier or by the *prolétaire";* and "the principle of his régime was to rest on the army and the people, and to ignore the existence of the educated classes."

"Within the last fifty years," writes Guérard, "Napoleon III has won the respect and sympathy of practically every critical historian." Sympathy, perhaps; but respect is based on a man's actions, and not on his dreams and intentions. La Gorce summing up a life's work, wrote about Napoleon III in 1933: "Baleful (*funeste*) he was: still, hardly have I written the word than I would like to soften it, for he was good and even enlightened; but no sooner did the light break through than it was clouded." Nor does Guérard's book, the product of years of study, yield a very different result, though the story is often lyricized, especially in an attempt to represent Napoleon III as a far-sighted reformer, a "Saint-Simon on horseback" whose régime is of the most "vital importance." Moreover praise is offered of his plebiscitarian dictatorship, of "direct democracy" as contrasted with "parliamentary practices." None the less, the picture which emerges of Napoleon III is hardly fit to inspire respect in the reader.

Guérard seeks to understand Napoleon III, but finds no solution to the enigma. "His elusive physiognomy changes altogether with the light that is turned upon it." His mind was "complex, perhaps tortuous"; "perhaps unfathomable, perhaps simply nebulous"; there was "no flash of intuition, no capacity for sudden decision." Princess Mathilde, Louis-Napoleon's cousin and at one time his betrothed, exasperated by his taciturnity, wished she could "break his head, to find out what there is in it"; and both she and her brother, Prince Napoleon, "ascribed his caution to mental hesitancy or flabbiness of will." He had grown up "in an atmosphere of elegiac resignation," writes Guérard; and in his youth he was "retarded in development, 'gently stubborn,' as his mother called him." He was a "damaged soul." But, like La Gorce, Guérard stresses Napoleon III's "profound and unaffected kindliness," his gravity, courtesy, and gentleness—"a man of '48," "a democratic humanitarian." In his own eyes Napoleon III was "a providential man," "an instrument of the Divine Purpose"; but even that faith "was gently obstinate,' not blatant." "I am sure that the shade of the Emperor protects and blesses me," he wrote from Ham in 1842. Even in his obsessionist ideas he lacked energy and ruthlessness. How then did such a man succeed?

By the time the Napoleonic disaster had assumed "dramatic value and epic grandeur," in the late twenties, Romanticism adopted "the Napoleonic theme," writes Guérard; and in the thirties the Emperor turned "into a hero of folklore." The July Monarchy, prosaic and dull, could not afford to dramatize conservatism without playing into the hands of the Legitimists, nor move to the Left, for fear of the Republicans; but they tried to surfeit France with Napoleon's glory, "retrospective, and therefore safe." As was proved by Louis-Napoleon's failure at Boulogne, this was then "but a legend . . . something to be enjoyed rather than to be believed in or acted upon . . . a sufficient motive for a pageant, but not for a revolution." How did it ever come to life? Even in the early months of the Revolution "Bonapartism was advancing . . . with a strict minimum of ideology, organization, and expenditure"—"it held itself in reserve." But had it ever more than a minimum of ideas and resources? To Guérard, Louis-Napoleon is not "merely the passive heir of the Legend"—he reshaped it "in his own image" and by his pamphlets

created in the public mind that paradoxical association between Bonapartism and humanitarian democracy which was Louis-Napoleon's special contribution to politics. It was not exclusively the Emperor's nephew, it was also the man who had written *On the Extinction of Pauperism,* who was chosen by the people in December 1848.

"The chief quality in Louis-Napoleon's style is its directness. . . . His words are historical documents." Not many who have read those pamphlets are likely to endorse such praise. La Gorce says that they are neither good nor bad, but significant; turgid, contradictory, and baffling, both naive and cunning; they develop commonplaces "with a sustained solemnity"; but occasionally, he claims, there occurs an original idea. Some of us have failed to discover any. In fact, had the electorate been sufficiently advanced to read Louis-Napoleon's writings, fewer might have voted for him—but what percentage is likely even to have heard of them?

According to Guérard, Louis-Napoleon was elected on his own program of "authoritarian democracy," known, understood, and "freely endorsed by 5,400,000 votes." All political parties stood for "the privileges of some élite": with the Legitimists the criterion was social superiority, with the Orleanists property, with the Republicans profession of their creed. Bonapartism, it is claimed, brushed aside the "intermediate powers and special interests"—Parliament and plutocracy—in order to realize the "unformulated doctrine" of the people: "direct contact between sovereign and masses." This kind of argument formed indeed the stock-in-trade of Louis-Napoleon. In his *Idées Napoléoniennes* "the tutelary and democratic power of the plebeian hero . . . who was the true representative of our revolution" is contrasted with the aristocratic or oligarchic character of the British Parliamentary system; "aristocracy requires no chief, while it is in the nature of democracy to personify itself in one man." And the Second Empire in its depreciation of *les anciens partis,* its strictures on "sectional interests," and its bombast about the integration of all truly national interests and "the organization of modern society," is a forerunner of the single-party totalitarianisms.

But such animadversions on Parliament call for no rebuttal. Oligarchy is of the essence of Parliament which requires an articulated society for basis. Elections presuppose superiorities; these may be based on birth, wealth, education, service, personal standing; or the rise may be achieved through local bodies, party organizations, trade unions, etc. But acknowledged superiorities there must be: and these were much impaired in the France of 1848. Three years later their absence was adduced in justification of the *coup d'État;* Louis-Napoleon, in a pamphlet "La Révision de la Constitution," which he sent to the British Ambassador, Lord Normanby, naming himself as its author, denounced Parliamentary Government as "totally unfit for a country like France, without aristocracy, without bodies politic, in short without any local sources or influence or power except the creatures and instruments of the Central Executive."

With such "official candidates" he himself managed in time to pack his Assemblies. But in May 1849 the electorate, which had given him an overwhelming majority half a year earlier, returned an assembly consisting of some 300 Orleanists, 160 Legitimists, 160 Republicans, and a mere handful of Bonapartists; "partisan elections, worse confounded by local influences and local issues," writes Guérard, "were but a shattered mirror, and could not reflect the country as a whole." Obviously millions of men, politically unschooled, will in a free election put their mark against the name they happen to know. Of the five names in the Presidential election "Napoleon" alone had nation-wide currency; in Parliamentary elections a similar advantage accrued to the local notables. Louis-Napoleon's person mattered little, his pamphlets even less, and of his program only as much as could be read into his name, a greater engine of propaganda than even the modern Press and the wireless. Through the freak of a plebiscite the ghost of Napoleon entered the body politic of a sick, deeply divided community: the peasants were hostile to the big landowners and their exiled kings, and had no use for the urban bourgeois and *intelligentsia;* the Legitimists loathed the Orleanists; and everybody abhorred and feared the "Reds," so much so that even of those who knew Louis-Napoleon in the flesh and despised him—the politicians—many supported him. They thought that because he was intellectually their inferior, they would be able to run him or get rid of him; the German Conservatives—Junkers, industrialists, generals, Nationalists— thought the same about Hitler. "The elect of six millions executes, and does not betray, the will of the people," declared Louis-Napoleon, nicely rounding off the figure. But too much should not be read by historians into that verdict.

"The workmen of the great cities," writes Guérard,". . . refused to recognize the Empire as a genuine form of democracy." Their strength and spirit were broken in the June Days of 1848, long before Louis-Napoleon appeared as the "saviour of society" (Cavaignac was his Noske). But exploiting the feeble riots of June 1849, engaged in *par acquit de conscience,* Louis-Napoleon proclaimed: "It is time that the good be reassured, and that the wicked should tremble." And after the *coup d'État* his shady associates staged their own Reichstag Fire. There had been hardly any opposition, the workers refusing to fight; but as some kind of insurrection was required to justify the coup and extensive repressions, resistance was encouraged and beaten down. Next, an accidental shot on the boulevards provoked a fusillade; the ground was strewn with dead. "These were not insurgents," writes Guérard; "it was a quiet, well-dressed crowd, which was watching the military parade as a show." And the sequel? "Mixed commissions," often of an atrocious character, condemned thousands of innocent men to death, transportation, or exile. Where was then, one may ask, Louis-Napoleon's renowned kindliness? He had written in his *Idées Napoléoniennes:* "The Imperial eagle . . . . was never stained with French blood shed by French troops. Few governments can say as much about their flag!" Not he about his own any longer.

The plebiscitarian Caesar "had not grown up with the French aristocracy, the French court, the French army, the French people," writes Guérard. "He remained on the throne an enigma, an adventurer, an exile." And like Napoleon I, he "was saddled with the Bonapartes." One of them, Pierre, son of Lucien, was "a fit subject for a picaresque romance." But Louis-Napoleon himself and his favorite cousin, Napoleon, "in their exalted sphere had in them something of the Pierre Bonaparte element: they too are disquieting, they elude normal classification; they are both Caesars and *déclassés*"; while Morny, an illegitimate son of Napoleon III's mother, and Walewski, a bastard of Napoleon I, both leading Ministers of the Second Empire, were "the perfect models of aristocratic adventurers." Morny was a man of affairs—promoter, speculator, and profiteer *par excellence*—"his secret information and his great influence as a statesman were freely used to foster his private schemes." And he was not the only one of that type in the doubtful *équipe* of the Second Empire, which, says Guérard, "was free from bourgeois pettiness, but also lacked some of the bourgeois virtues. " The view that it was not a régime but a racket is not altogether unfounded.

The gaudy Empire "on its glittering surface . . . was a military régime"; "the great reviews . . . were an essential part of its political strategy"; "the days of bourgeois drabness were over"; gold braid and epaulets, much martial display, conspicuous waste and maladministration. "War was made into a blend of the circus, the tournament, and the quest. There was a dash of gaiety about it all . . . the spirit of Cyrano and d'Artagnan." Louis-Napoleon "believed in the army, but not in war . . . He believed implicitly that he was born a soldier . . . it was faith without works." His technical knowledge did not prevent him from fumbling even in peace-time manoeuvres. "At Magenta . . . he was sluggish, almost paralysed. When Frossard came with the news: 'Sire, a glorious victory!' the queer 'victor' could hardly credit his luck: 'And I was going to order a retreat!' " "The Empire . . . in its warlike aspect was an imitation, and feeble at the core." Napoleon III "was unmilitary in his ineradicable gentleness. . . . A philanthropist at the head of any army is a pathetic absurdity."

A "philanthropist" and a "policeman": for the army at home was "a vast police force in reserve," "held in readiness against any possible uprising of the democratic great cities." "Napoleon III the Policeman was not in contradiction with Napoleon III the Socialist"; "racketeer, policeman, reformer . . . were mingled in that equivocal figure." In the social reformer, "the romanticist whose dreams were of the future . . . and translated themselves into terms of engineering," who realized that "modern industry is collectivistic" and through the Imperial power wanted to give it a collective sense, Guérard tries to find atonement for Napoleon III's failure in all other spheres. Still, the *éloge* is hardly convincing; Napoleon III talked the humanitarian jargon of his generation and shared its mechanic interests and hobbies, but no convincing evidence is adduced of original ideas or personal achievements. And, intermixed with vast unproven claims, appears the admission that his economic and social policies "are no less perplexing than his management of foreign affairs"—which is saying a great deal.

For Napoleon III's foreign policy was shallow and utterly confused. He believed in peace and was out to tear up the Treaty of Vienna; he believed in nationality and claimed for France her "natural frontiers"; he wanted Italy free but not united; in eighteen years he waged three major European wars and sent three expeditions overseas, without ever seeming to know what he was after. At first luck covered up, to some extent, his muddles and blunders. But after 1860 "the series of setbacks, wrong guesses, false moves on the part of the Government was unbroken"—Poland, Denmark, Sadowa, Queretaro, Mentana; the Emperor and his people were losing faith in his star. There was perplexity, aimless drift, and obscure dismay. By 1867 French hegemony was at an end; France felt intolerably humiliated, the Emperor was infinitely weary. "L'Empire a été une infatuation," writes La Gorce, "il a été l'incohérence, il a été aussi . . . l'imprévoyance."

But here is a last attempt at justification: "Everywhere," writes Guerard, "in Paris, in provincial France, in Algeria, the true monuments of the Second Empire are its public works." (Faust, who sold his soul for power, concludes his life over public works.) "The transformation of Paris, his personal conception . . . was so nobly conceived that after half a century it was still adequate." The pulling down and rebuilding of capitals is again a recurrent feature in the history of despots and dictators, from Nero to Mussolini and Hitler. Self-expression, self-glorification, and self-commemoration are one motive. But there is also a deeper, unconscious urge, born of fear: of things lurking in the dark, narrow streets of old cities, the product of organic, uncontrolled growth. Let in light and air and suffer nothing which is not of the despot's will and making! With Napoleon III such fears found a conscious rationalization: open spaces were needed for a "whiff of grapeshot." When his empire fell not one shot was fired.

The careers of Napoleon III and Hitler have shown how far even a bare minimum of ideas and resources, when backed by a nation's reminiscences or passions, can carry a man in the political desert of "direct democracy"; and the books written about Napoleon III show how loath posterity is to accept the stark truth about such a man. And yet a careful examination of the evidence merely confirms the opinion of leading contemporaries about him: the enigma was not so much in him as in the disparity between his own spiritual stature and the weight of the ideas centred on him. Dream pictures are best projected on to a blank screen—which, however, neither fixes nor brings them to life.

How much can be safely said of Napoleon III? Biographers agree that there was something in him which defies definition and description: obviously the unstable, the shapeless, the void cannot be delineated. He was reticent, secretive, conspiratorial; at times his power of silence created the appearances of strength. Narrow and rigid in his ideas, out of touch with reality, he was a dreamer entertaining vast, nebulous schemes, but vacillating, confused, and therefore complex and ineffective in action. There was in him a streak of vulgarity. He was sensual, dissolute, undiscriminating in his love-affairs: his escapades were a form of escapism, a release. He was benign, sensitive, impressionable, suggestible, yet "gently obstinate." He talked high and vague idealism, uncorrelated to his actions. He had a fixed, superstitious, childish belief in his name and star. Risen to power, this immature weak man became a public danger. His silence was self-defence: to cover up his inadequacy and to preserve him from the impact of stronger personalities, of demands which he would have found difficult to resist, of arguments to which he had no reply; it also helped him to avoid commitments. Ampère describes him as "what is called a good-natured man" in that "he likes to please everyone he sees." Tocqueville, for a few months his Foreign Minister, and Beaumont, an ambassador, were aghast at his vast chimerical, unscrupulous, confused schemes and ideas; when argued with he would keep silent without giving in—"he abandoned nothing." He would bide his time—which with him meant inactive waiting without any approach to reality. He tumbled into situations, neither designed nor deliberately created by him. When forced to act, the day-dreamer would try to draw back: so it was before the *coup d'État,* and again in 1859—in fact in almost every crisis. But if the initiative had passed out of his hands he would drift anxiety-ridden, fumbling, wishing to call a halt, and mostly unable to do so. Under stress his personality seemed to disintegrate.

* * *

THE GOOD NAPOLEON III

Alan B. Spitzer

H.M. THE EMPEROR NAPOLEON III.—In respectful memory of a beneficent and far-sighted man, died January 9th, 1873. He has found peace; one day he will find true justice.—The Hon. Secretary of the Souvenir Napoleonien in England, Ernest Weal.—In Memoriam notice, *The Times* (London), January 9, 1962.

In the past two decades the standard interpretation of the Second Empire, in England and America at least, has become generally favorable.[1] This approach, often presented as a revision of earlier partisan judgments is based both on fresh research and on changing conceptions of what is politically right and desirable. The classic Bonapartist, republican, and socialist interpretations have been qualified or discarded, but political norms, not always articulated, continue to shape evaluations of the regime.[2]

Much of the recent literature on Napoleon III reflects the conviction that he needs to be rescued from a tendentious historiography. The very persistence of this idea is of some interest when one considers for how long and by how many historians it has been expressed. To mention a distinguished example: Pierre de La Gorce began his classic history of the Second Empire with the observation,

The reign of Napoleon III has been judged up to the present only preferentially or in hatred. It has twice undergone the trial of falsehood: the falsehood of

[1] The most notable recent examples of this tendency are: Albert Guérard, *Napoleon III* (Cambridge, 1943) and *Napoleon III, A Great Life in Brief* (New York, 1955); Lynn M. Case, *French Opinion on War and Diplomacy during the Second Empire* (Phila., 1954); Roger L. Williams, *Gaslight and Shadow* (New York, 1957); Theodore Zeldin, *The Political System of Napoleon III* (London, 1958); and, to some extent, J. M. Thompson, *Louis Napoleon and the Second Empire* (New York, 1955). This essay was completed before the author could obtain a copy of T. A. B. Corley *Democratic Despot. A Life of Napoleon III* (London, 1961). This work also presents a qualified favorable reinterpretation of the Second Empire, concluding, "For Napoleon the 'end' was not, as in Solon's phrase, death, but that posthumous reputation he so desired. Who shall say that this end is not well in sight?"

[2] My own approach to the Second Empire starts from the Left.

adulation in the days of power, the falsehood of calumny in the days of misfortune. [EDITORS' TRANSLATION] [3]

De La Gorce's attempt at an objective and critical analysis won general acclaim but it too has been challenged by his successors. F. A. Simpson in his *Napoleon and the Recovery of France* deplored a Catholic bias in de La Gorce and then developed an interpretation which has been influential in establishing the favorable image of Louis Napoleon.[4] Indeed, Albert Guérard could assert in 1943 that "within the last fifty years Napoleon III has won the respect and sympathy of practically every critical historian."[5] Nevertheless, Guérard's successors continue to break lances for the man who, in the words of Roger Williams, has been "the victim of an indifference which has been translated by most writers about him into terms of contempt."[6] In a subsequent issue of *History Today*, the journal in which Williams' remarks appeared, Theodore Zeldin wrote, "It is time, therefore, that the abuse of his enemies should be appreciated in its true light and not accepted as impartial history merely because they happened to be distinguished men."[7]

A hostile tradition does certainly survive. In a sense the unfortunate Emperor is forever represented as Victor Hugo's Napoleon the Little and his partisans as Daumier's "Ratapoil," the rakish, seedy, and sinister adventurer. These images persist in the republican historiography introduced by Taxil Delord's implacable *Histoire du Second Empire*[8] and in the socialist interpretations of Albert Thomas and his successors. [9]

[3] Pierre de La Gorce, *Histoire du Second Empire* (7 vols.; 12th ed., Paris, 1912), I, i; *cf.*, Blanchard Jerrold, *The Life of Napoleon III* (4 vols., London, 1874-1882), III, 8; H. Thirria, *Napoléon III avant l'Empire* (2 vols., Paris, 1895), I, i-iii; Henry Berton, *L'Evolution constitutionelle du Second Empire* (Paris, 1900), I, 739; Paul Guériot, *Napoleon III* (2 vols., Paris, 1933-34), II, 319-321; Hendrik N. Boon, *Rêve et réalité dans l'oeuvre économique et sociale de Napoléon III* (La Haye, 1936), pp. 164-165; Octave Aubry, *The Second Empire*, trans, A. Livingston (Phila., 1940), 604; J. B. Barbier, *Outrances sur le Second Empire* (Paris, 1946), pp. 7-9. For a somewhat dated survey of the literature on the Second Empire see Robert Schnerb, "Napoleon III and the Second French Empire," *Journal of Modern History*, VIII (September, 1936), pp. 338-355.

[4] F. A. Simpson, *Louis Napoleon and the Recovery of France, 1848-1856* (London, 1923), viii. De La Gorce has recently been damned as an apologist of the Second Empire: E. Jeloubovskaia, *La Chute du Second Empire et la Naisance de la Troisième République en France*, trans. J. Champenois (Moscow, 1959), pp. 5, 9.

[5] Guérard, *Napoleon III*, p. 282.

[6] Roger I. Williams, "Louis Napoleon. A Tragedy of Good Intentions," *History Today*, IV (April, 1954), 219.

[7] Theodore Zeldin, "The Myth of Napoleon III," *History Today*, VIII (February, 1958), 105.

[8] Taxil Delord, *Histoire du Second Empire* (6 vols.; 5th ed., Paris, 1869–1875). *Cf.* Gabriel Hanotaux, *Histoire politique*, Vol. V of *Histoire de la nation française*, ed. G. Hanotaux (Paris, 1929). For another example of a broadly unfavorable treatment see René Arnaud, *The Second Republic and Napoleon III*, trans. E. F. Buckley (London, 1939). The author claims to stand between Seignobos and de La Gorce. The attitude toward the Second Empire of the academic left (under the Third Republic) is succinctly expressed in the following comment on Bergson's eulogy of Emile Ollivier at the Académie in 1918, " . . . a philosopher for fops or dandies has dared to deliver not the eulogy, but a shameless panegyric, of M. Emile Ollivier. . . . This very Academy . . . listened without wincing to the insolent challenge to the public conscience made by M. Bergson." *Annales Révolutionnaires*, X (1918), 287-288. See also Henry Jaudon. "Emile Ollivier," *Revue bleue*, LVI (Feb. 1918), 80-84. For Bergson's speech see Henri Bergson, *Discours de Reception de M. Henri Bergson Séance de l'Académie française du 24 Janvier 1918* (Paris, 1918).

[9] E.g., Albert Thomas, *Le Second Empire (1852-1870)*, Vol. X of *Histoire Socialiste*,

Possibly the most influential republican evaluation of the reign of Louis Napoleon was engraved by Charles Seignobos on that monument to Sorbonnard historiography, the Lavisse series. He concluded his history of the Empire:

The Empire imposed on France by a military coup d'état had no other active force at its service than the army; the nation had not become imperial and only assisted the Empire through inertia; the electors voted for it because it was there. The government was nothing but a group of civil servants superimposed on the nation without becoming integrated with it; it remained an official machine without any moral authority; the great mass of the indifferent obeyed it; but where there was political life it was always opposed. With the army gone the Empire collapsed without a struggle, without opposition to the pressure of the mob. Its chiefs fled abroad, nobody tried to defend it. [EDITORS' TRANSLATION][10]

Perhaps the gap between orthodox republican historiography and the modern revisionists can be measured by two evaluations of Seignobos. While Robert Schnerb refers to his "sufficiently objective analysis" of the Second Empire,[11] Albert Guérard describes his work as "the frankly biased account by the petit bourgeois Radical Charles Seignobos, a period-piece of the Gambetta age."[12]

The attitudes distressing to Guérard persist, but the extent of partisan animus among contemporary French historians of the Empire can be exaggerated. The monographs of Maurain, Schnerb, Duveau, Guiral, and others probably do add up to a negative presentation of the regime, but they are scrupulously documented, fair, and balanced efforts.[13]

Unfavorable judgments never did go unchallenged in France. Aside from Bonapartist apologia, of which the most distinguished was Émile Ollivier's massive and influential justification of the Liberal Empire,[14] scholarly works favorable to the Empire have appeared frequently in the twentieth century—from Lebey's treatment of the early period to Paul Guériot's well-received volumes, which

ed. J. Jaurès (Paris, 1906); and Vol. XI of the same series, Jean Jaurès, *La Guerre Franco-Allemande;* Paul Louis, *Histoire du mouvement syndical en France* (2 vols., Paris, 1947), I, 41-42, 98-99; Alexandre Zévaès, "Les Candidatures ouvrières et révolutionnaires sous le Second Empire," *La Révolution de 1848,* XXIX (mars 1932-février 1933), 132-154. Jeloubovskaia, *La Chute du Second Empire.* This work is written partly as a corrective to what the author considers to be a tradition of unscientific apologetics. She presents both imperial domestic and foreign policy simply as the political manifestations of capitalist class interests.

[10] Charles Seignobos, *Le Déclin de l'Empire et l'établissement de la 3e République,* Vol. VII of *Histoire de France Contemporaine,* ed. E. Lavisse (Paris, 1921), p. 248.

[11] Schnerb "Napoleon III and the Second French Empire," pp. 338-339.

[12] Guérard, *Napoleon III,* p. 282.

[13] Jean Maurain, *La Politique ecclésiastique du Second Empire de 1852 à 1869* (Paris, 1930), and *Un Bourgeois français au XIXe siècle. Baroche, Ministre de Napoléon III* (Paris, 1936); Georges Duveau *La Vie ouvrière en France sous le second Empire* (Paris, 1949); Pierre Guiral, *Prévost-Paradol* (Paris, 1955); Jacques Droz, Lucien Genet, and Jean Vidalenc, *L'Époque Contemporaine. I. Restaurations et Révolutions* (1815-1871) ("Clio," Paris, 1953). In the *Peuples et Civilization* series the volume by Charles Pouthas, *Démocraties et Capitalisme* (1848-1860) (Paris, 1948) shows no discernible bias; the succeeding volume, by Henry Hauser, Jean Maurain, and Pierre Benaerts, *Du libéralisme à l'Impérialisme* (Paris, 1939) presents an unfavorable picture of the later Empire.

[14] Emile Ollivier, *L'Empire libéral, études, récits, souvenirs* (17 vols., and I table; Paris, 1895-1915).

characteristically concluded on the note of Louis Pasteur's eulogy of the Emperor.[15]

Louis Napoleon has enjoyed an even better press abroad. Notwithstanding occasions of great unpopularity in England and America, he has never, from the time of Bagehot's defense of his coup d'état,[16] lacked defenders—in fact, the major monographs in English have been predominantly sympathetic. A line of hostile interpretation does exist—running from Kinglake's conspiracy theory of the origins of the Crimean War[17] through H. A. L. Fisher's and G. P. Gooch's whiggish distaste for Bonapartist authoritarianism,[18] to various critiques of Louis Napoleon's diplomacy[19] and to J. Salwyn Schapiro's description of the imperial system as a harbinger of Fascism.[20]

The critical literature has been outweighed by works justifying the Empire to the foreign reader. Blanchard Jerrold's semi-official biography based upon materials in the possession of the imperial family was an early example of books exhibiting sympathy for Louis Napoleon and for his tragic Empress, who for many years continued to make documents accessible to sympathetic investigators.[21] The most influential academic reinterpretation was expressed in F. A. Simpson's two distinguished volumes, *The Rise of Louis Napoleon* and *Louis Napoleon and the Recovery of France,* first published in 1909 and 1923, respectively.[22] After Simpson, the current outside of France has continued to flow strongly in Louis Napoleon's favor, swelling into the lush prose of Robert Sencourt:

... even in his weakness and his mistakes, he, as a Bonaparte, proved that there was in him, as in his more famous predecessor, an elasticity, a resilience, which make him a power when he seemed to have left the world branded as a failure. He completed the career of Napoleon I. Who has completed his own?[23]

---

[15] André Lebey, *Louis-Napoléon Bonaparte et la Révolution de* 1848 (2 vols.; Paris, 1907-08); Guériot, *Napoleon III,* II, 322.

[16] Walter Bagehot, "Letters on the French Coup d'Etat of 1851," *Literary Studies* (2 vols.; London 1911), Vol. I.

[17] Arthur William Kinglake, *The Invasion of the Crimea: Its Origin and an account of Its Progress down to the Death of Lord Raglan* (6 vols., London, 1863-1880). For the most recent of the scholarly refutations of Kinglake, see Brison D. Gooch, "A Century of Historiography on the Origins of the Crimean War," *American Historical Review* LXII (October, 1956), 33-58.

[18] H. A. L. Fisher, *Bonapartism* (Oxford, 1914), pp. 142-163, 198-200; Philip Guedalla's popular success was, if not critical, patronizing. Philip Guedalla, *The Second Empire* (London, 1960). This recent work is close in tone to a nineteenth-century liberal response to the Empire.

[19] E.g., Franklin Charles Palm, *England and the Rise of Napoleon III* (Durham, 1948); A. J. P. Taylor, *The Struggle for the Mastery of Europe, 1848-1918* (Oxford, 1954), pp. 25, 133, 204 ff.; René Albrecht-Carrié, *A Diplomatic History of Europe Since the Congress of Vienna* (New York, 1958), pp. 82-83, 132-138.

[20] J. Salwyn Schapiro, *Liberalism and the Challenge of Fascism* (New York, 1949), pp. 316 ff.; See also J. P. Mayer, *Political Thought in France* (London, 1943), pp. 45-69 Karl-Heinz Bremer, "Der Sozialistische Kaiser," *Die Tat,* XXIX (Juni, 1938), 160-171; and for a brief assessment of the similarities and differences with Fascism, see Frederick B. Artz, "Bonapartism and Dictatorship," *South Atlantic Quarterly,* XXXIX (Jan. 1940), 48-49.

[21] The flow of works on the tragic Empress, the Gilded Beauties of the Court, and the Prince Imperial still provides a certain moisture.

[22] F. A. Simpson, *The Rise of Louis Napoleon* (London, 1909); Simpson, *Louis Napoleon and the Recovery of France* (London, 1923).

[23] Robert Sencourt, *Napoleon III: The Modern Emperor* (London, 1933), p. 369.

The recent works of Guérard, Williams, Zeldin, Case, and (to a lesser extent) J. M. Thompson have continued the revision of an excessively critical image of the Second Empire. These works are not uncritical, but they tend to emphasize the desirable consequences of the regime and to present partial justifications for its alleged failures. The arguments most often advanced in the line of this positive revisionism might be represented in the following rather unfair pastiche:

The Second Empire has been too narrowly viewed in the light of republican or socialist predilections. A more just evaluation would recognize that the faction-ridden systems which the Second Empire replaced were only destroyed after they had failed to satisfy the national aspirations for order and unity. The new 18th of Brumaire entailed a certain amount of temporary unpleasantness, but it provided that political stability which was the indispensable context for economic and social advances scarcely possible under any alternative regime. Despite inherited disabilities the Liberal Empire was evolving towards a viable parliamentary system with the support of the vast majority of the nation. Doctrinaire critics overlook the real progress that was made in the face of complex difficulties and with that refractory human material whose last chance to be welded into a truly unified people disappeared with the Empire. Even the condemnation of Louis Napoleon's apparently disastrous foreign policy must be qualified with reference to the pressures of irresponsible political factions and of public opinion which demanded victories abroad without sacrifice at home. And one must take into account Louis Napoleon's vision of a European policy—a noble conception frustrated by the short-sighted Machiavellianism of other princes.

A full discussion of this interpretation would touch on political, economic, social, literary, religious, educational, and diplomatic history. This article will consider only certain questions of economic, political, and foreign policy evoked by the recent literature.

In judging the economic development of the Empire, although it poses the most complex problems of research and interpretation, historians are in agreement unusual in the historiography of the period. Not all would accept Sainte-Beuve's identification of Napoleon III as a "Saint-Simon on horseback,"[24] but most admit to some real connection between imperial policies and the striking advance of the French economy. Georges Pradelié's monograph in the *Que sais-je?* series is representative of French historiography in its conclusion that, while France suffered in the long run from Louis Napoleon's foreign and domestic political policies, it owes to him a considerable legacy of national wealth and of effective economic institutions.[25]

The difficulty for a just assessment of the economic contributions of the Empire lies in the obligation to distinguish the economic consequences of government policy from the effects of other factors and to work out the relationship of short-run economic change to long. When, for example, Guerard and Pradalié commended the Second Empire for the accumulation of wealth which made possible the rapid payment of the indemnity after the Franco-Prussian war, they gave to Louis Napoleon's reign all of the credit for that viability which enabled France to make comparable efforts after 1815 and again after the World Wars of

---

[24] Guérard, *Napoleon III*, pp. 193 ff.
[25] Georges Pradalié, *Le Second Empire (Que sais-je?)* (Paris, 1957), p. 124; and for the same assessment see Marcel Blanchard, *Le Second Empire* (Paris, 1950), pp. 7-8.

the twentieth century. Notwithstanding Guérard's disclaimers he seemed to attribute to Napoleon III the fruits of a century of French secular economic growth.[26]

One might argue that the years of the Empire happen fortuitously to coincide with a period of French, or indeed, world-wide, industrial expansion that would have occurred under any political circumstances. Similar considerations might be applied in favor of the Empire. To evaluate the break with protectionism merely by its consequences in the period 1860-1870 is to ignore the possibly beneficial long-run effects of competition on a traditionally overprotected economy.[27] Other complications arise from varying views of the economic curve of the years 1852-1870. Partisans of the Empire emphasize the burgeoning years between 1852-1857. Opponents look to the depression of 1867-1870.

Most historians have agreed, despite their different points of view, that the signs of economic growth are impressive in relation both to other periods and to other states. The years 1852-1857 particularly were an exception to a long history of relative stagnation, and the French rate of growth was unmatched by that of any other state.[28] The combined value of French exports and imports almost tripled between the beginning and the end of the Empire, surpassing the rate of expansion for any other European state in those years.[29] Perhaps even more impressive is the evidence of the structural changes which helped to propel France into the industrial era. The Second Empire saw the establishment of what Perroux calls the "generating industries ... industries whose establishment was decisive for the forming of a French market," [EDITORS' TRANSLATION] and the striking growth of the railroads and the "great credit institutions."[30]

To establish the existence of these changes is not to demonstrate Louis Napoleon's responsibility for them, but significant relationships between imperial policies and constructive change are persuasively presented in such works as David Pinkney's *Napoleon III and The Rebuilding of Paris,* Louis Girard's *La Politique des Travaux Publics du Second Empire,* and Marcel Blanchard's articles on the railroad policies of the Empire.[31] At any rate, a majority of historians grant Louis Napoleon some of the credit for the unprecedented stimulus to capital formation, credit expansion, and a spirit of enterprise foreign to the crabbed, unimaginative Orleanist economic tradition, and essentially believe with Girard that France still enjoys a

---

[26] Guérard, *Napoleon III,* p. 196.

[27] For assessments of the economic consequences of the Second Empire, See Émile Levasseur, *Histoire du commerce de la France* (2 vols.; Paris, 1911-1912); Germain Martin, *Histoire économique et financière,* Vol. X of *Histoire de la nation française,* ed. Gabriel Hanotaux (Paris, 1927), Marcel Marion, *Histoire financière de la France depuis 1715* (5 vols., Paris, 1914-1928), V. Arthur L. Dunham, *Anglo-French Treaty of Commerce of 1860 and the Progress of the Industrial Revolution in France* (Ann Arbor, 1930); Shepard B. Clough, *France: A History of National Economics, 1789-1939* (New York, 1939); Henri Sée, *Histoire économique de la France* (2d. ed., 2 vols.; Paris, 1951), II.

[28] Rondo Cameron, "Economic Growth and Stagnation in France, 1815-1914," *The Journal of Modern History,* XXX (March, 1958), I.

[29] Sée, *Histoire économique,* II, 288. According to Levasseur Belgium was the only state to surpass France. Levasseur, *Histoire du commerce,* II, 331.

[30] Francois Perroux, "Prise de Vues sur la croissance de l'économie française, 1870-1950," *Income and Wealth,* Series V, ed. Simon Kuznets (London, 1955), p. 55.

[31] David H. Pinkney, *Napoleon III and the Rebuilding of Paris* (Princeton, 1958); cf. J. M. and Brian Chapman, *The Life and Times of Baron Haussmann* (London, 1957); Louis Girard, *La Politique des travaux publics du Second Empire* (Paris, 1952). Marcel Blanchard, "La politique ferrovaire du Second Empire," *Annales d'histoire économique et sociale VI* (Novembre. 1934), 529-545.

legacy of "the works set up by the French of the Second Empire." [EDITORS' TRANSLATION] [32]

The relevance of these conclusions to a justification of the Empire depends not so much on economic fact as on political value. Did the economic benefits outweigh the accompanying graft, favoritism, and speculation? Did the Morny who floated impressive enterprises compensate for the Morny who enjoyed a slice of Jecker's Mexican investments? Did the improved salubrious and magnificant product of Haussmann's municipal renovation cancel out the inequities, the inconveniences, and the aberrations in taste that attended the rebuilding of Paris? The answers can be founded only on individual postulates of Right and Progress.

Whatever uniformity obtains for such judgments does not extend to evaluations of Louis Napoleon's social welfare policies, perhaps because the evidence is even more difficult to assess, perhaps because the implicated values are so strongly held and so sharply conflicting.

Louis Napoleon's sympathy for the masses has been one of his strongest claims to the affections of historians. J. M. Thompson dwelt on his sincere intention to provide the workers with "their just share of the national wealth," [33] and concluded that Louis Napoleon "... never ceased to clutch the inviolable shade of social equality and justice which still eludes a less corrupt and prejudiced age." [34] This interpretation, of Louis' intentions at least, is widely shared—even Karl Marx, who was scarcely charitable to "the hero Crapulinsky," granted that, "Bonaparte looks on himself as the representative of the peasants and of the people in general, against the bourgeoisie, who wants to make the lower classes of the people happy within the framework of bourgeois society." [35]

More recently, Guérard and H. N. Boon, among others, have identified Louis Napoleon as a Socialist, and in 1938 the German historian, Karl-Heinz Bremer, praised the pioneering authoritarian socialism of the Second Empire, which is not precisely what its recent admirers have in mind. [36] Admiration for Louis Napoleon's brand of socialism has, however, generally been confined to non-socialists. The hostile socialist histories of the Second Empire are analogous to the "ungrateful" electoral behavior of the contemporary French worker, which produced the paradox of "a leader ... rejected by those whom he was most anxious to benefit." [37]

The apparent working-class preference for republican institutions in spite of the imperial benevolence is often praised, or damned, as a triumph of abstract ideological considerations over strictly material demands. Some historians have argued, however, that the intentions of the government were essentially manipulative, that occasional social reforms were only the means to authoritarian political ends, that the state remained the agency of the possessing classes, that real

---

[32] Girard, *La Politique des travaux publics*. See also Sée, *Histoire économique*, II, 251, "If Napoleon was only a fleeting apparition from the political point of view, by contrast from the economic point of view his reign marked an epoch; it is he who opened the road for capitalism in France and from there to the whole of the continent." There are similar views in Pierre DuPont-Ferrier, *Le Marché financier de Paris sous le Second Empire* (Paris, 1925).

[33] Thompson, *Louis Napoleon and the Second Empire*, p. 103.
[34] *Ibid*, p. 239.
[35] Karl Marx, *The Eighteenth Brumaire of Louis Bonaparte*, Vol 35, *Marxist Library*, ed. C. P. Dutt (New York, 1936) p. 117.
[36] Guérard, *Napoleon III*, p. 198; Boon, *Rêve et réalité*, p. 154; Bremer, "Der Sozialistische Kaiser," pp. 161-164.
[37] Guérard, *Napoleon III*, p. 218.

wages fell, and that the workers showed an increasingly mature awareness of their own material interests when they repudiated the system at the polls.[38]

How the workers actually conceived their interests and how these conceptions influenced their political behavior remain complex and difficult questions. Georges Duveau's remarkable study of working class life under the Empire delineated the "caractère équivoque" of proletarian political response in which sympathy for the Emperor might accompany hostility to the *patronat*, or resistance to the Empire be expressed not so much from the viewpoint of a worker as from that of a democrat in the tradition of the old radical artisanate.[39] Duveau concluded that, in the obscurity of the contemporary industrial climate, the worker searched for his solutions "in his moral heritage and in utilizing, rather than fighting, the propaganda of the traditional parties which tried to capture his attention." [EDITORS' TRANSLATION][40] Other historians have seen an increasing consciousness of class interests developing independently of traditional political alignments. Workers supported Louis Napoleon in 1848 precisely because he was not identified in their eyes with bourgeois interests but they eventually repudiated his paternalism, not so much for some republican ideal but because of their inchoate urge to defend their interests according to their own lights.[41]

On the basis of his findings that real wages remained stagnant during the Empire, Duveau concluded that the general progress of the French economy widened the social gap between the workers and an enriched bourgeoisie.[42] But this in itself cannot explain working-class political behavior because workers reacted not alone to this secular development but also to short-term business fluctuations, to political change, and to the government's successes and failures in international relations. Even in the years of economic depression and social conflict from 1867 to 1870 working-class behavior was variously motivated. The textile workers, for example, combined with their patrons in a campaign against imperial tariff policy,[43] yet in 1870 the alliance was shattered by strikes of unprecedented size and violence.[44]

The government's ambiguous response to the textile strikes indicates some of the complexities of an analysis of the relation between imperial policies and working-class politics. There is evidence of a certain amount of imperial sympathy for the strikers, but the strikes were ultimately met with the intervention of troops.[45] On many other occasions contradictions between Louis Napoleon's benevolence and the actual response of the government to working-class aspirations had been apparent. J. M. Thompson observes that the Emperor's sincere pursuit of

---

[38] This is essentially the position of Édouard Dolléans, *Histoire du mouvement ouvrier* (4th ed., 2 vols., Paris, 1948), I, pp. 251-360; *cf.* I. Tchernoff, *Le Parti Républicain au coup d'état et sous le Second Empire* (Paris, 1906), pp. viii-ix, 404, 410, 493-494; Jeloubovskaia, *La Chute du Second Empire, passim.*

[39] Duveau, *La Vie ouvrière*, pp. 100-103.

[40] Duveau, *La Vie ouvrière*, p. 550.

[41] Fernand L'Huillier, *La Lutte ouvrière à la fin du Second Empire* (Paris, 1957), pp. 74 ff.; Sreten Maritch, *Histoire du mouvement social sous le Second Empire à Lyon* (Paris, 1930), pp. 266-267.

[42] Duveau, *La Vie ouvrière*, pp. 385-416.

[43] Claude Fohlen, *L'Industrie textile au temps du Second Empire* (Paris, 1956), pp. 410-429.

[44] *Ibid.*, pp. 439-440; L'Huillier, *La Lutte ouvrière*, pp. 64-72.

[45] *Ibid.*, p. 70.

social justice assumed an economic expansion essentially dependent upon bourgeois enterprise, and was "mortgaged to capitalism." The idealistic ends were sacrificed to the indispensable means. "Workers' associations and meetings might be prohibited in the name of public order, strikes broken to protect the labour market, wages kept down to stimulate production and public works. The Empire might become the victim of its own *élan vital*, the Emperor the prisoner of his prosperity and progress."[46] It is probable that working-class attitudes were affected more by the actual operation of the imperial system than by Louis Napoleon's conceptions of how it ought to operate.

To understand how Louis Napoleon's government qualified and perverted his most generous conceptions one must be aware of the differences between the Emperor's ideals and interests of the groups that shared power with him. The Emperor is often praised for standing above the factions and governing for the good of all, but his policies were shaped and executed by men whose values were those of the conservative, propertied minority.[47] Guérard regretted that the conservatives were able to "muscle in and to endorse a winner whose principles were the very reverse of theirs,"[48] but Zeldin has shown that the imperial system continuously co-operated with local notabilities and that it recruited its parliamentary candidates "from the highest ranks of society, from the great landowners, wealthy mayors and so on."[49] This élite was scarcely enthusiastic for socialism, even of the Bonapartist brand. If the Empire, as Guérard, Williams, and Zeldin claimed, was not the instrument of the political Right, it certainly did business with and through the traditional supporters of the "party of order."

At the very peak of the imperial structure there was the court, a group which must figure in any examination of the obstacles between Louis Napoleon's good will and positive reform. The imperial entourage is often blamed for major blunders including the fatal decision for war with Prussia. J. M. Thompson is one of the few reasonably sympathetic historians of the Second Empire to point out that the political power of the imperial court was a necessary product of the imperial system. "In a government which left so little initiative to its constitutional bodies, it becomes of special importance to inquire into the relations between the Emperor and those who were his immediate associates: the Empress, his Bonaparte relations, the friends of his youth, his ministers and ambassadors."[50] The extra-constitutional influences exerted by these close associations were contradictory and inconsistent,

---

[46] Thompson, *Louis Napoleon and the Second Empire*, p. 239. Duveau, *La Vie ouvrière*, p. 549, "The Emperor wished to govern for the masses and with the aid of the masses ... but, not without reason, he was worried over the loyalty of the working-class and finally, on the whole, he checked the workers instead of collaborating with them." [EDITORS' TRANSLATION]

[47] Duveau concedes the caesarist socialism of Louis himself, but emphasizes the fact that he surrounded himself with "civil servants still imbued with the old Orleanist spirit and, guessing the contradictions which beset the Emperor, they didn't hesitate to dictate to him frequently. Hence in the turnings of the cogwheels of the Imperial machine (there were) misses and jolts which had their repercussions in the worker's world." [EDITORS' TRANSLATION] Duveau, *La Vie ouvrière*, p. 16.

[48] Guérard, *Napoleon III*, p. 138.

[49] Persigny, quoted by Zeldin, *ibid.*, p. 11. For the view that one of the grave weaknesses of the regime was its failure to rally the established élite, see Simpson, *Louis Napoleon and the Recovery of France* pp. 372-373, and Hanotaux, *Histoire politique*, pp. 477, 551.

[50] Thompson, *Louis Napoleon and the Second Empire*, p. 246.

reflecting personal and ideological cross-purposes, and from them stemmed some of the vagaries of imperial policy.

Perhaps of even greater significance was the cumulative influence of the minor officials who actually executed policy. Indeed, the Empire can well be described, not as a dynastic direct democracy, but as the quintessential administrative state. According to Brian Chapman's useful survey, *The Prefects in Provincial France*, the apogee of prefectoral authority was attained under the Second Empire.[51] In a sense the prefects made the regime, for, according to Chapman, they contrived the Red Scare of 1851, which was a crucial element in Louis Napoleon's coup d'état. This interpretation is reinforced by Howard Payne's detailed analysis of the role of the bureaucracy in preparing for the coup d'état and in inviting Louis Napoleon to seize supreme power and crown the edifice of the administrative state.[52]

In another article Payne described the consolidation and reinforcement of the centralized police system and concluded that "despite the contemporary elaboration of theories of unlimited police powers they were in practice limited to an extent far removed from the totalitarian models of the twentieth century."[53] This observation does not really vitiate the cumulative force of Payne's descriptions of the increase in authority and scope of the imperial police. Louis Napoleon can be defended against rather forced comparisons with the Nazis, but the fact that nineteenth-century dictators fell short of twentieth-century totalitarians can scarcely be a conclusive answer to their liberal critics.

Napoleon III is perhaps most effectively defended against charges of authoritarianism by reference to the evolution of the Liberal Empire after 1860. The Emperor himself is the great protagonist of this transformation, not only creating new institutions but summoning up new men to operate them. Among these men Emile Ollivier was pre-eminent—the hero of those who would trade the doctrinaire insistence on republican forms for the substance of imperial liberties.[54]

The ambiguities of a constitution which stipulated ministerial responsibility but did not specify its locus, which envisioned a cabinet based on a parliamentary majority but acceptable to, and presided over by, the Emperor, have been defended as necessary aspects of a difficult transition. Both Williams and Zeldin compare the constitutional progress of the Liberal Empire to the complex adjustment of executive to legislature worked out over a much longer period in

---

[51] Brian Chapman, *The Prefects and Provincial France* (London, 1955), p. 38; see also, Pierre-Henry, *Histoire des préfets* (Paris, 1950), pp. 171-194. Zeldin emphasizes the crucial electoral role of the prefects, "It was not Napoleon, nor Persigny but the prefects, who had the greatest single influence in choosing the official candidates," Zeldin, *The Political System of Napoleon III*, p. 19.

[52] Chapman, *The Prefects and Provincial France*, p. 37; Howard C. Payne, "Preparation of a Coup d'état: Administrative Centralization and Police Powers in France, 1849-1851," *Studies in Modern European History in Honor of Franklin Charles Palm*, eds., F. J. Cox, R. M. Brace, B. C. Weber and J. F. Ramsey (New York, 1956), p. 197.

[53] Howard C. Payne, "Theory and Practice of Political Police during the Second Empire in France," *Journal of Modern History*, XXX (March, 1958), 14-23.

[54] At the conclusion of a chapter devoted to Ollivier, Williams writes, " . . . recalling the despair of the Republicans after the plebiscite in 1870, is it not possible that the reforms were sufficiently promising for the reconciliation of liberty and order that the Republicans after 1870 never dared admit it?" Williams, *Gaslight and Shadow* p. 298; cf., Berton, *L'Évolution constitutionelle du Second Empire*, pp. 381; Pierre de La Gorce, *Napoléon III et sa politique* (Paris, 1933), pp. 156 ff.; Pierre Saint Marc, *Émile Ollivier* (Paris, 1950), pp. 227 ff.; Bergson, *Discours . . . de l'Académie française.*

seventeenth-century England.[55] It would be consistent with this analogy to argue that Louis himself had led France back into the seventeenth century. Perhaps his enemies exaggerated the "crime" of the Second of December, but it is fair to recall that the builders of the Liberal Empire had razed the parliamentary edifice of the Second Republic. The prospects of the parliamentary Empire might have been matched by those of the Republic, had it been allowed the twenty years which the Empire used to return to its point of departure. It is certainly plausible to suppose that a Republic dominated by Thiers and the"Burgraves" would have lacked the democratic ambiance of Bonapartist caesarism.[56] Still, arguments from English analogy might lead one to assume as good a chance for a fruitful evolution under a conservative parliamentary Republic before 1870 as for resolution of the contradictions of a parliamentary empire after 1870.

There is little point in pursuing this rather arid conjecture, but there is some point in examining the actual recruitment for the Liberal Empire, which did not, after all, staff itself with something very different from a reconstituted party of order. Ollivier's ministry of the Right and Left center did not include the great Orleanist paladins but did take in a range of qualified Orleanists and diluted Bonapartists who would have been perfectly at home in earlier oligarchies.[57] Some of the enemies of liberal institutions were dropped, but in the person of Rouher went a powerful partisan of free trade and with Haussmann the personification of public works, to be replaced by protectionists and scrupulous economizers. The last section of Girard's book on public works under the Empire, entitled "L'Abdication de la finance Saint-Simonienne," presents as a concomitant of liberalization the repudiation of the buccaneering and creative finance of the great period of imperial public works.[58]

According to Maurain the evolution of the Liberal Empire represented not only the triumph of the reconstituted party of order but also of the clergy: "The clerical party which, under the authoritarian Empire, had exercised only an indirect influence on the government, often powerful, but always limited, thus (now) took possession directly." [EDITORS' TRANSLATION][59] Maurain's analysis of the ecclesiastical policies of the Second Empire challenged the representation of the regime as the last hope for a true political community, for he concluded that its shifts and expedients only sharpened the classic conflict between clericals and anti-clericals until, "after 1869, the dispute for power was, as in 1849, between the

---

[55] Williams, *Gaslight and Shadow*, p. 279. Zeldin, *The Political System of Napoleon III*, p. 152. "... since so many people believed that France was not ripe for the institutions of nineteenth-century England, it was perhaps not as silly as it might appear to start with those of seventeenth-century England."

[56] See the characterization of Orleanist liberalism in E. Beau de Loménie, *Les Responsabilités des dynasties bourgeoises* (3 vols., Paris, 1943), I, 171, 185, 200; and in Maurain, *Baroche*, p. 357. "The chiefs of the old party of order ... liberal in politics because hostile to the personal government of the Emperor . . .were very conservative in social matters and refractory to the humanitarianism of Napoleon III."

[57] Zeldin, *The Political System of Napoleon III*, pp. 144-151. De La Gorce quotes one of the deputies of the Right as remarking "In the present cabinet ... only the Duke d'Aumale in the War Ministry and the Prince de Joinville in the Navy Ministry are missing." [EDITORS' TRANSLATION] De La Gorce, *Histoire du Second Empire*, VI, 5.

[58] Girard, *La Politique des travaux publics*, pp. 359 ff.

[59] Maurain, *La Politique ecclésiastique du Second Empire*, p. 939.

clerical party of order and the anti-clerical republicans." [EDITORS' TRANSLA-TION][60]

An examination of these conflicts and of the social tensions attendant upon the growth and concentration of French industry reinforces the supposition that the bitter class and political struggle of 1871 must have owed something to the Empire.

Evaluations of domestic developments during the last years of the Second Empire are often affected by the knowledge that imperial foreign policy was to end in disaster. For many critics of the regime, the catastrophe of 1870 damns all of its works. The friends of the Empire, on the other hand, reject this judgment as the narrow standard of the cult of success, and some even defend those policies which led directly to the destruction of the Empire.

Historians generally agree that, notwithstanding autonomous foreign and domestic pressures which shaped imperial foreign policy, the major plans and the ultimate decisions were the Emperor's.[61] This grave responsibility has weighed heavily in the scales of his critics, but it has also served as a kind of palliation for some of his apparent blunders. His partisans emphasize his personal good will—expressed, for example, in his sincere attempt to mitigate the effects of a suicidal international *Realpolitik* by the formation of a new Congress of Europe. Binkley's volume in the Langer series coined the term *Federative Polity* to represent those tendencies which rampant nationalism was to destroy and which Louis Napoleon's foreign policy strove unsuccessfully to preserve and to extend.[62] Binkley's conviction that the Emperor was "the last good European in a position of authority" is widely shared.[63]

The image of Louis Napoleon's visionary internationalism owes a great deal to hindsight. Demolished by a rival which had scarcely begun to realize its satanic strengths, imperial France may not seem terribly threatening in retrospect, but the policies she pursued were not reassuring to contemporaries, whose best evidence for the Emperor's intentions was drawn from his actions. These actions included proposals for international readjustment, often entailing some territorial bagatelle for France; two major wars before 1870, which by no stretch of even the French imagination could be considered defensive; the apparently boundless ambitions of the Mexican policy;[64] and continuous unsettling maneuvers, pronouncements, and

[60] *Ibid.*, p. 959

[61] Albert Pignaud, "La Politique extérieure du Second Empire," *Revue Historique*, CLV (Sept.-Oct., 1927), 42-43; G. Pagès, "La Politique extérieure de Napoléon III," *Bulletin of the International Committee of Historical Sciences*, V (Feb., 1933), 16, Pierre Renouvin, *Le XIXe Siècle, I. De 1815 a 1871*, Vol. V of *Histoire des relations internationales*, ed. P. Renouvin (Paris, 1954), pp. 269-270; Charles W. Hallberg, *Franz Joseph and Napoleon III, 1852-1864* (New York, 1955), pp. 23-24.

[62] Robert C. Binkley, *Realism and Nationalism, 1852-1871*, Vol. 16 of *The Rise of Modern Europe*, ed. W. L. Langer (New York, 1935), p. 260.

[63] E.g., Williams, "Louis Napoleon, A Tragedy of Good Intentions," p. 226; Case, *French Opinion . . . during the Second Empire*, p. vii; Simpson, *Louis Napoleon and the Recovery of France, p. x:* "Essentially he [Napoléon III] was an international figure; too good a citizen perhaps of Europe to be the ultimately successful ruler, of any one country in it." See also Luigi Salvatorelli "L'Europe de Napoléon III et l'Europe de Mazzini," *Revue historique*, CCXXIII (avril-juin, 1960), 275-286.

[64] The Mexican policy, which will not be examined here, has its defenders, e.g., Sencourt, *Napoleon III: The Modern Emperor*, 271-178; Guérard, *Napoleon III*, pp. 222-242; Barbier, *Outrances sur le Second Empire*, pp. 13-227.

projects which seemed to stem not from evident national requirements but from the Emperor's restless will.

Using information not readily available to Louis' contemporaries one can find a kind of consistency in his sincere belief that a revision of the unjust settlement of 1815 entailed, and without contradiction, the liberation of oppressed nationalities, the rightful extension of French territory and influence, and the reconstitution of a European polity. Most critics would now agree that the Emperor was sincere in his nationalities program, and that such policies as the weak, vulgar, and humiliating pursuit of compensations after 1866 were, in opposition to his deepest instincts, the reluctant responses to domestic pressures.[65]

To what extent Louis Napoleon's good intentions justify maladroit actions conducted under his authority is another question that can only be answered in the Emperor's favor if some force outside of the imperial establishment can be shown to have compelled the government to undertake erroneous policies. The defenders of the Empire have identified such a maleficent force in public opinion corrupted by an irresponsible opposition whose very existence depended upon Napoleon's good will.

The most thorough, effective and systematic work embodying such conclusions is Lynn Case's *French Opinion on War and Diplomacy during the Second Empire*. Case's careful analysis, based primarily on reports of the prefects and the procureurs généraux, shows that imperial policy during the springtime of the Empire's success was often carried out in spite of public opposition, but that during the last disastrous phase it was increasingly shaped by popular pressures. This was particularly striking in the case of the Emperor's program of army reform, blocked by a public which with equal zeal demanded bellicose foreign policy and cheap defense.[66] In the light of such behavior Case has no difficulty in casting up the balance of guilt:

Thus the responsibility for the dilution of the army bill ... falls directly upon French public opinion and its legislative representatives. This responsibility is all the heavier because at the same time that opinion was opposing the bill, it showed evidence of a universal belief in the inevitability of war with Prussia. ... The road to Sedan, unlike that to Hell, was not even paved with good intentions. And when the tragedy of defeat finally broke upon the land, the unrepentant people loaded all the blame upon the one man who, accepting captivity to save the lives of his handicapped soldiers, had long before exerted himself more than all the others to spare them that evil day.[67]

The force of this indictment falls not only upon mass opinion but upon a political opposition that was willing to accrue factional advantage by attacking the government both for unpopular policies and for the consequences of suspending them. Still, any judgment of responsibility must take into account the nature and personnel of a watered-down caesarism. One must distinguish between the Emperor, who was eager to pursue a rational policy of acceptance of German aspirations and a prudent policy of rearmament in the face of Prussian power, and both his enemies and his supporters who were willing to accept neither. As Albert Sorel observed,

[65] E.g., Taylor, *Struggle for Mastery in Europe*, pp. 173-177.
[66] Gordon Wright, "Public Opinion and Conscription in France 1866-1870," *Journal of Modern History*, XIV (March, 1942), 26-45.
[67] Case, *French Opinion ... during the Second Empire*, pp. 239-240.

But if the projects of Marshal Niel (for army reform) miscarried, the blame should not be placed exclusively on the orators of the opposition; these orators formed only a very limited minority in the *Corps Legislatif*, they had no influence on the government, and their speeches which were destined most of the time for the public, very rarely modified the opinions of the majority. This majority was composed of government candidates and it was it, in short, which thrust aside the Marshal's reforms or amended them so as to paralyze their effect. [EDITORS' TRANSLATION][68]

This observation has been reaffirmed by recent research.[69]

Even if the establishment had spoken with one voice on the reforms, which it did not, it could not present the public with clear alternatives because it tried to preserve an image of superior strength while soliciting remedies for relative weakness. The presentation of the official case between 1866 and 1870 scarcely contributed to a responsible and informed public evaluation of imperial programs.

These considerations do not lift the responsibility from an opposition that was willing to seek political advantage at the expense of national security, but they indicate the flaws of a system in which supreme responsibility for foreign and military policy was concentrated in the hands of the Emperor and in which the dilution of this responsibility in part reflected the conflicts within an irresponsible entourage. There is still force in Jaurès' observation that a regime praised for ability to override the caprices of the crowd and the tumult of the forum is not also to be justified because it succumbed to public caprice and emotion.[70]

This approach was rejected in principle and in closely reasoned detail by Case, who defended even the last stumbling parade into the trap of the Hohenzollern candidacy. His research into the public response at each stage of the crisis impelled him to revise earlier estimates that public opinion was for peace in 1870[71] These investigations suggested to Case that perhaps public opinion is inadequate to the formulation of foreign policy and that, indeed, given world realities it is problematical whether democracy can long survive in the present state system of international anarchy.[72]

This brings us back to the foundations of political value. If one does not choose to identify the concept of democracy with the momentary expression of the demos—if one conceives of democracy as a system of rules, processes and guarantees, including the right to form a meaningful opposition, then the aberrations of mass opinion in the short run do not constitute the ultimate test of democratic viability. Case praises the Empire for brushing aside political factions in order to combine authority with direct democracy, but it is precisely this caesarism which enforces an opportunism in relation to public opinion, not all of the time, for often the government flouted the public will, but only when the really difficult and embarrassing decisions had to be made. Then without the background of responsible opposition or continuous informed debate the system desperately

---

[68] Albert Sorel, *Histoire diplomatique de la guerre Franco-Allemande* (2 vols.; Paris, 1875), I, v-vi.

[69] Cf., Zeldin, *The Political System of Napoleon III*, p. 133; Guiral, *Prévost-Paradol*, pp. 483-484; Schnerb, *Rouher*, p. 200.

[70] Jaurès, *La Guerre franco-allemande*, p. 178.

[71] E.g., E. M. Carroll, "French Opinion on War with Prussia in 1870," *American Historical Review*, XXXI (July, 1926), 679-700.

[72] Case, *French Opinion . . . during the Second Empire*, pp. 275-277.

husbands its popularity and in effect places the security of the dynasty above the health of the state.[73] In the last years, anxiety regarding public opinion was expressed in terms of the overthrow of the regime, and quite rightly, because when such a regime is repudiated it does not go out of office, it goes out of existence. There was not the margin for error afforded to the notoriously unstable Third Republic which somehow maintained a coherent foreign policy for forty years and, unlike its predecessor, found it to be politically possible to retreat upon Paris and regroup to withstand a German invasion.

It is not the cult of success which makes foreign affairs so relevant to an evaluation of the Empire, although a regime whose actions were so often justified as expedient can only justify its expediencies by success. No French statesman could have contrived a policy to stay the inexorable German advance toward economic and military hegemony but, as de La Gorce justly observes, it is particularly in the realm of foreign affairs that the characteristic weaknesses of the imperial system persist, not in the manifestations of an authoritarian will, but in the old tendencies toward *"infatuation, incoherence and imprévoyance."*[74]

Admirers of the Second Empire sometimes regret the onerous legacy it had to accept from the First. The legend of dynamic imperialism, essentially so foreign to the gentle and visionary Louis Napoleon, forced him into ventures abroad that were eventually disastrous.[75] But there is an element of the testament fabricated at St. Helena which is fully consistent with the spirit of Louis Napoleon's regime. This is the tradition of mendacity, manifested in the first Napoleon's *Memoirs* as contempt for the truth and also apparent in the absence of intellectual courage at the core of the Second Empire. In the long run the regime was not characteristically brutal, nor consistently authoritarian, but meretricious. If the imperial system anticipated any aspect of the twentieth century, it is the tendency to conduct foreign affairs as a branch of domestic public relations and to beg many difficult alternatives of policy formulation by doublethink, self-deception, and cant.

[73] A similar phrase is applied by Guérard to the weaknesses of imperial leadership in his monograph on Napoleon III for the Great Lives in Brief series. This book presents the same general interpretation as his earlier work but is somewhat more critical of the last phase of the regime, particularly in relation to foreign policy. Guérard, *Napoleon III, a Great Life in Brief*, pp. 148, 187-191.

[74] De La Gorce, *Napoléon III et sa politique*, pp. 167-173.

[75] Williams, "Louis Napoleon. A Tragedy of Good Intentions," p. 220.

7 / Cavour and the Moderates: Creators of a United Italy or Saboteurs of Democratic Revolution?

Older historical literature, particularly in English, insisted upon the myth of a consensus in the creation of a united Italy: Count Camillo Benso di Cavour was the "brain," Guiseppe Mazzini the "heart," and Guisseppe Garibaldi the "sword" of the Risorgimento. They and their followers, willing or not, participated in a process destined to bring "Italy" into the concert of European nations.

The tragedy of the twenty-years interlude of fascism has led scholars to re-examine both the process and the results of the Italian unification. The British scholar, Denis Mack Smith, has re-emphasized the *conflict* between Cavour and Garibaldi.[1] In his championship of the latter, he has unleashed a bitter and still unresolved polemic. Shepard B. Clough and Salvatore Saladino frankly state that "the process of unification . . . was a triumph for the moderates and a source of despair for those federalists and republicans who could not reconcile themselves either to a unitary state under Piedmontese hegemony or to monarchical institutions."[2]

Even if we grant that conflict rather than consensus stood behind the creation of Italian unity, we must still judge the results. Was the Kingdom of Italy of 1861 the best polity that circumstances of the time would allow? Was it a secure base for further political and economic development? Or was it a compromise (however necessary), which made progress difficult and even facilitated the later preversion of fascism?

These are the questions which have provoked a most interesting polemic among post-war Italian historians. In the one camp are the radicals and Marxists who argue that current maladies of Italian political, social, and economic life are squarely rooted in the compromises and insufficiencies of Cavour's solution. In the other are most conservatives and those liberals who emphasize Cavour's and the moderates'

---

[1] *Cavour and Garibaldi 1860–A Study in Political Conflict* (Cambridge University Press, 1954).
[2] *A History of Modern Italy: Documents, Readings, and Commentary* (Columbia University Press, 1968), p. 63.

contribution to creating a modern state of high ideals under extremely adverse conditions.

The first selection in this section is taken from the notebooks of Antonio Gramsci, a founder of the Italian Communist Party and the chief inspiration for a whole generation of Italian Marxist scholars. Gramsci's analysis centers on the consequences which resulted from Cavour's alleged policy of excluding the masses, and particularly the peasants, from active participation in the Risorgimento.

The second selection is from the work of Rosario Romeo, one of the most effective liberal opponents of Italian Marxist historiography. His main thesis is that the political participation of peasants was neither possible nor desirable under the conditions of mid-nineteenth century Italy.

Portions of an article by one of the editors, John M. Cammett, provides the third selection, which is a summary of the issues raised by the debate. By and large, it is also a defense of the Gramscian position.

NEGLECTED AGRARIAN REVOLUTION

Antonio Gramsci

> . . . *Political Leadership in the Formation and Development of. . . the Modern State. . .*

The whole problem of the connection between the various political currents of the *Risorgimento*—that is to say, of their relationships with each other and with the homogeneous or the stratified social groups in the various historical sections of the national territory—reduces itself to these essential facts:

The moderates represented a social group that was relatively homogeneous. For that reason, their leadership underwent relatively slight modifications (and, in any case, they followed an organically progressive line of development). The so-called Action Party, on the other hand, did not rest specifically on any single historical class, and the oscillations that took place within its executive organs corresponded in the final analysis to the interests of the moderates. In other words, historically, the Action Party, was guided by the moderates. Thus the affirmation attributed to Victor Emmanuel II of having the Action Party "in his pocket," or something like that, is true for all practical purposes, and not simply because the Action Party was in fact led "indirectly" by Cavour and the King. . . .

For the Action Party to have become an autonomous force and, in the final analysis, to have succeeded at least in imprinting upon the *Risorgimento* movement a character that was more distinctly popular and democratic (more than this it perhaps could not do, in view of the fundamental premises of the movement itself), it should have countered the "empirical" activity of the moderates. . . with an organic program of government that reflected the essential demands of the popular masses, above all, of the peasants. It should have countered the "spontaneous" attraction exercised by the moderates with a resistance and an "organized," planned counteroffensive. . . .

Actually, the Action Party completely lacked a specific governmental program. More than anything else, it remained essentially in the service of the moderates as an organism for agitation and propaganda. The internal conflicts of the Action Party, the tremendous hatreds against Mazzini and his work that Mazzini aroused in the sturdiest Actionists (Garibaldi, Felice Orsini, and others) were caused by the absence of firm political leadership. The internal polemics were in large measure as abstract as the preaching of Mazzini had been. Yet one can draw useful historical lessons from them. (Of importance for everyone are the writings of [Carlo] Pisacane, who committed, however, irreparable political and military errors, such as opposing Garibaldi's military dictatorship in the Roman Republic.) The Action Party was intoxicated by the traditional rhetoric of Italian literature. It confused the cultural unity of the peninsula (a unity that was confined to a very narrow stratum of the population and was besmirched by the Vatican's cosmopolitanism) with a feeling of political and territorial unity on the part of the great popular masses, who actually stood quite apart from that cultural tradition and did not care about it, even when they knew of its existence. . . .

From these observations and analyses of several elements in Italian history after unification, one can form certain criteria for appreciating the contrasting positions of the moderates and the Action Party, and for discovering the diverse political "wisdom" of these two parties and of the various currents that fought for political and ideological leadership of the [Action Party]. In order to counter the moderates effectively, it is evident that the Action Party should have attached itself to the rural masses, especially in the south. It should have been "Jacobin" not only in external "form" and temperament, but above all in its economic and social program. Only by pushing forward in two directions could it have forestalled the consolidation of the various rural classes into a reactionary bloc, then being forged by legitimist and clerical intellectual cliques, and make room for a new liberal, national formation. [It should have pushed forward] (1) toward the peasants at the bottom, accepting their basic demands and making them an integral part of the new program of government; and (2) toward the intellectuals of the medium and lower strata, binding them together and insisting upon the themes that might interest them most. (Already the prospect of the formation of a new apparatus of government, with the possibility of employment therein, was a great attraction to them, if the prospect could be presented concretely on the basis of the aspirations of the rural population.)

The relationship between these two courses of action was dialectical and reciprocal. The experience of many countries—and above all that of France during the period of the great Revolution—shows that whenever the peasants act for "spontaneous" reasons, the intellectuals begin to waver. Conversely, if a group of intellectuals espouse a new program of specifically pro-peasant politics, they end by pulling along with them ever more important segments of the population. We can say, however, that in view of the dispersal and isolation of the rural population and the resulting difficulty of concentrating it in solid organizations, the movement must be initiated by means of intellectual groups. In general, however, it is the dialectical relationship between the two courses of action that must be kept in mind. One might add that it is almost impossible to create peasant parties in the strict sense of the term. The peasant party usually emerges only as a strong current of opinion, not in the well worked-out form of bureaucratic cadres. Nevertheless, the existence of even a skeletal organization is immensely useful, both in bringing about a certain solution to the leadership problem and in controlling intellectual groups and preventing caste interests from guiding them imperceptibly into new fields. . . .

The reasons why no Jacobin party was formed in Italy are to be sought in the economic field—that is, in the relative weakness of the Italian bourgeoisie and in Europe's different historical climate after 1815. Even though the Le Chapelier Law and the Law of the Maximum had limited the Jacobin program of seeking by force to reawaken the energies of the French popular masses so as to ally them with the bourgeoisie, the program still appeared in 1848 as a threatening "specter," and this fact was cleverly exploited by Austria and the old governments, even by Cavour—to say nothing of the pope. Perhaps because of subjective (though not objective) factors, the bourgeoisie could no longer extend its hegemony over as wide a range of common people [in Italy] as it had in France; nevertheless, activity among the peasantry was certainly always possible.

Relationship Between City and Countryside in the Risorgimento and National Structure

... Why did the Action Party fail to make an issue of the agrarian question in all its ramifications? The reason why the moderates did not is obvious. The terms of reference that the moderates assigned to the national problem necessitated a bloc of all rightist forces, including the great landed proprietors who would group themselves around the state and army of Piedmont. Austria's threat to resolve the agrarian question in favor of the peasants (a threat that had been carried out in Galicia against the Polish nobility, in favor of the Ruthenian peasants) threw dismay into the ranks of interested property owners in Italy and caused the wavering among the aristocrats. (The disorders of February 1853 in Milan and the paying of homage to [Emperor] Francis Joseph by Milan's most illustrious families occurred on the eve of the Belfiore atrocity.[1]) Moreover, the agrarian question paralyzed the Action Party itself, which on this subject thought the same way as the moderates, regarding only the aristocracy and property owners as "nationalists," not the millions of peasants. Only after February 1853 did Mazzini make any substantially democratic references (see his *Epistolario* [Correspondence] for that period), but he was incapable of giving a decisively radical slant to his abstract program. We should study too the political behavior of the *garibaldini* in Sicily in 1860, a political policy that was dictated by [Francesco] Crispi. The insurrectionary movements of the [Sicilian] peasants against the barons were pitilessly suppressed, and an anti-peasant National Guard was created. The repressive expedition of Nino Bixio in the Catania region where the insurrections were most violent was typical. Yet, even in the *Noterelle* [Diary] of G. C. Abba we find evidence that the agrarian question was the spring that was coiled to set the great masses into motion. It is enough to recall Abba's conversation with the monk who went to talk to the *garibaldini* right after their landing at Marsala.[2] And in several stories by G. Verga there is

---

[1] In March 1853 nine Italians were executed on the bastions of Belfiore in Mantau after being convicted of possession of anti-Austrian literature and raising money for an Italian revolt.— *Ed.*

[2] Gramsci's allusion is to the diary entry of May 22, 1860, by Giuseppe Cesare Abba, one of Garibaldi's Redshirts. Abba was flabbergasted by the social revolutionary comments of the friar. The monk intimated that if Garibaldi would launch a truly socioeconomic revolution and carry the Bible and cross before him, he would himself join forces with him. First published in 1880, Abba's *Noterelle* achieved widespread fame in Italy. It is now available in an English translation by E. R. Vincent as *The Diary of One of Garibaldi's Thousand* (London: Oxford University Press, 1962).—*Ed.*

picturesque evidence of this peasant unrest, which the National Guard stifled by means of terror and mass executions. This aspect of the expedition of the Thousand has never been studied and analyzed.

The failure to face up to the agrarian question led to the near impossibility of resolving the question of clericalism and of the pope's antiunification attitude. In this regard the moderates were much bolder than the Action Party. True, they did not distribute ecclesiastical holdings among the peasants. However, they used such holdings to create a new class of large and medium property owners who were linked to the new political order, and they did not hesitate to liquidate land holdings, even though these involved only property belonging to the Congregations. The Action Party was paralyzed in its attitude toward the peasantry, moreover, by illusory Mazzinian dreams of a religious Reformation—a goal that not only failed to interest the great mass of rural people but made them susceptible to reactionary moves against the new heretics. . . .

LIBERAL-CAPITALIST REBUTTAL
TO GRAMSCI'S THESIS

Rosario Romeo

[Italian] Marxist historiography during the past decade has concerned itself primarily with the history of the *Risorgimento* and the unified state. And this historiography is almost entirely focused on the noted thesis that the *Risorgimento* was an agrarian *rivoluzione mancata*— a thesis generally known as the "Gramsci thesis."

Attributing this thesis to Gramsci is a bit arbitrary and in part inexact. We mention this not to raise an abstract question as to its paternity—for in this respect the label may very well be adopted, as we certainly owe to Gramsci the most coherent and profound formulation of the thesis—but to point out an important element in it, an element that tends to be relegated to the background when it is attributed solely to Gramsci. In reality, the immediate post-World War II period saw the first explicit formulation of criticism of the bourgeoisie of the *Risorgimento* era for not broadening their national movement into a more consolidated democratic, bourgeois revolution that might also have mobilized the peasant masses for the purpose of overthrowing and eliminating the remnants of feudalism in the countryside. This criticism appeared in a noteworthy volume by [Emilio] Sereni. *Il capitalismo nelle campagne, 1860-1900* (Turin, 1947), which was written as part of a broader work in the years just before the outbreak of World War II.

Sereni's book did not find too favorable a reception among historians, perhaps because of the somewhat hasty manner in which it set forth information, its lack of original research, its excessively Marxist phraseology, and the error of some of its arguments (such as that on the financial policy of the *Destra*, [1] regarding which one should note the criticisms by [Federico] Chabod). Moreover, its rather undeniably

---

[1] The political right in Italy—the grouping to which Cavour belonged and which dominated Italian public life until 1876.—*Ed.*

schematic nature led to a somewhat oversimplified and rough antithesis between a typically feudal, aristocratic type of property and a bourgeois, capitalistic type of property—as if such noblemen as the Cavours, Jacinis, and Ricasolis did not represent in one way or another the most advanced aspects of capitalism in Italy. But in spite of all of this, Sereni's book remains the work of a scholar who is the secure master of Marxism's basic contentions regarding the way in which capitalism develops, and who in the light of such historical theory has carried out a serious effort to reinterpret the development of Italian society during the first forty years after unification. For this reason it is regrettable that few people have followed in Sereni's footsteps. It is precisely from the Marxian theory regarding capitalistic development that Sereni drew the conception of the agrarian revolution as a phenomenon that is historically linked to the complete victory of a bourgeois revolution. It is in the failure of such a revolution to occur during the *Risorgimento* that Sereni discerns the origin of the limitations and of grave contradictions that have existed in the social and political life of the unified state.

Gramsci, for his part, has further developed this same thesis, seeking to crown the economic and social doctrinairism of ordinary Marxist stamp with a perfected vision of the historical and political relationships that existed between the two principal forces of the *Risorgimento*. In Gramsci's writing appear also echoes of the debates that previous "revisionist-minded" historians sought to arouse among Italian scholarly circles. He ascribes the supremacy of the moderates to the fact that the Action Party was unable to carry out its own policy, in a coherently Jacobinic manner by incorporating into its program the social problems and goals of the peasants. And he frames this conception in a vision of Italian history that is dominated by the inability of the medieval Italian cities to resolve the conflict with the countryside that began to take shape after the first phase of the antifeudal alliance. The centuries of oppression in the countryside, the decline of creative ability, the failure of every political effort at unification (along with the closely connected cosmopolitanism of Italian culture and civilization) all hark back to this split, which thus remains at the root of the whole history of the country. For this reason, there is thoroughgoing political insistence on the need for an alliance of workers and peasants to produce a historical termination to an almost thousand-year-old problem in the history of the country and to provide a way to resolve its conflicts and basic problems.

It certainly cannot be said that this thesis has been discussed exhaustively. To be sure, almost all the Marxist historians of the *Risorgimento* have adopted it as their point of departure for a series of detailed investigations. Yet, so far as I know, no one has raised in adequate fashion the serious historical and methodological problems it contains. And this is the case despite the serious objections to it that were immediately raised. Some of our most authoritative historians—from [Benedetto] Croce and [Carlo] Antoni to [Federico] Chabod—have pointed out an error in Gramsci's position that is common to all the various revisionist interpretations of the *Risorgimento* since the time of [Alfredo] Oriani, [Mario] Missiroli, and [Piero] Gobetti—interpretations which are characterized by recourse to abstract moral and political idealism and which arbitrarily assume that what actually occurred ought to have occurred in a different fashion.

Along with this is the basic anachronism that this type of judgment did not arise out of the actual history of the time but rather out of much later problems that have presented themselves to the historian. Chabod has vigorously pointed out this anachronism on the part of Gramsci. He has emphasized the connection between

Gramsci's criticism of the *Risorgimento* and the practical problem that faced Italian socialists and communists after World War I when they tried to bring about an alliance between the urban working-class movement and the peasant masses who were largely controlled by the [Catholic-oriented] "white leagues."

On the other hand, it should be kept in mind that the Gramsci thesis was first formulated as a criticism of the Action Party on the level of historical and political coherency, and that it sought to emphasize the Action Party's inability to carry out its own battle in a revolution predicated on a Jacobinic alliance of the advanced bourgeoisie with the peasants—an alliance which alone would have permitted the Action Party to break away from the hegemony exercised by the moderates and achieve a "consequent" democratic revolution.

Basic to the entire thesis was the presupposition that there existed a peasant structure that could be mobilized for the purpose of a national and democratic revolution—that there existed an "objective" revolutionary possibility which the Italian Action Party, unlike the French Jacobins, was unable to bring into play but which nevertheless was very much in the picture. It is unnecessary to emphasize all the doubts and reservations that this notion of an "objective" structure existing apart from the awareness of the people of that era can arouse and does arouse among non-Marxist historians. But it is also true that if one wishes to take into account the unquestionable importance that the Gramsci thesis has assumed in the polemics pertaining to the *Risorgimento*, one must go beyond mere discussion of principles and seek to understand its author's thought in depth, within the framework of his own methodology—with the reservation that one may later try to translate the results of this analysis into an interpretation that possesses validity for intellectuals of different philosophical inspiration.

Thus apart from any general discussion of methodology, two basic questions should be raised with respect to the Gramsci thesis. The first relates to the real possibility of an agrarian revolution, to the actual existence, in other words, of an alternative course of action to that which the *Risorgimento* pursued. The second relates to the question whether such an alternative course would have produced an outcome somewhat more progressive than what actually resulted. The second question is no less important than the first, because Gramsci's criticism of the *Risorgimento* ruling class focuses precisely on the argument that the ruling class did not push to the limit all the possibilities for progress that were objectively present in the Italian situation; and especially because an accurate statement of the real problem of modern capitalistic development in Italy in the nineteenth century depends on a proper evaluation of the significance of the agrarian "revolution that was lacking" [*rivoluzione mancata*] .

Despite the ever longer list of peasant insurrections and disturbances that modern historians—not only Marxist writers—are preparing for us; despite the indubitable existence of widescale misery and privation in a large portion of the Italian countryside, and the widespread persistence of feudal remnants, especially in the south; despite the existence of a peasant population of more than fifteen million people in 1860, of whom the larger part were either poor peasants, hired day-laborers [*braccianti*] , or salaried workers [*salariati*] , and the proposals that hitherto had been suggested for mobilizing this mass of people against the old absolutistic regimes; despite all this, it seems undeniable that the presumed alternative course remained outside the sphere of practical historical and political action.

This was true not so much because of any tenaciously reactionary spirit [*sanfedismo*] in the countryside (for such a spirit might conceivably have been overcome by laying down guidelines for solution of the problem of land tenure) as because of the basic historical conditions in which the *Risorgimento* was destined to unfold. Rather, it seems certain that any agrarian and Jacobinic revolution in Italy would have provoked an anti-Italian coalition on the part of all the great powers of Europe, for the powers were interested in maintaining a conservative social order and held to a concept of civilization and of international relations that was deeply hostile to agrarian revolutionary activity. The problem of international relations in this respect has been vigorously emphasized by Chabod.

Even Gramsci asked the question (and he answered it negatively) whether it was possible in Italy to have a Jacobinic-type revolution in view of the fact that Italy had not yet achieved "international freedom of action," that France was still the traditionally dominant power in Europe, and that the climate of European opinion had changed so markedly since 1815. But in this respect his thinking seems particularly contorted, almost as though he were reluctant to accept all the consequences stemming from the difficulties that he posed:

Even though the Le Chapelier Law and the Law of the Maximum had limited the Jacobin program of seeking by force to reawaken the energies of the French popular masses so as to ally them with the bourgeoisie, the program still appeared in 1848 as a threatening "specter," and this fact was cleverly exploited by Austria and the old governments, even by Cavour—to say nothing of the pope. Perhaps because of subjective (though not objective) factors, the bourgeoisie could no longer extend its hegemony over as wide a range of common people [in Italy] as it had in France; nevertheless, activity among the peasantry was certainly always possible.[2]

Let us leave aside the "subjective" or "objective" character of the reasons which prevented an alliance of the bourgeoisie with the great popular masses throughout Europe in the nineteenth century, in the sense that Gramsci meant. (For in considering the "subjective" or "objective" character of the reasons we would have to raise once again the entire problem of the relationship between bourgeois liberalism and the proletarian movement during that period.) It remains a fact that in Italy's case, the hostility of all the great powers toward any agrarian uprising presented itself in a most "objective" fashion. It is therefore curious that one should affirm the possibility of "action among the peasants" after having denied the possibility of extending the bourgeoisie's domination over the wide strata of the populace— especially when it is clear that the two things are in reality only one, as it is impossible to shift the question to the urban strata of the populace, over whom the Action Party had largely succeeded in acquiring leadership.

Moreover, one should consider the extreme difficulty of transforming southern Italy (which, because of its relationship between town and country, stood at the center of the Gramsci thesis) into a country of rural democracy or small-scale property ownership after all we now know of the results of the census takings and tax assessments of the past century. (One should note that because of the flexibility of rules, those censuses eliminated in the zones in question the obstacle of land income chargeable to the cultivator.) Moreover, the experiences of the various governmental agencies for land reform have demonstrated to even the most obtuse

[2] Antonio Gramsci, *Il Risorgimento* (Turin: Giulio Einaudi Editore, 1949), pp. 87-88.

what large sums of capital and vast technical resources (which are of decisive importance in adapting, systematizing, and increasing land productivity, and which were nonexistent during the past century) are required to solve the problem even on a very limited scale. It is clear that we are discussing here precisely the creation of a rural democracy. For if one interprets the Gramsci thesis in the sense that it was an argument that the Action Party should have supported the peasants more openly in partitioning demesne lands or in revising ancient cut-throat contracts, one would not only distort Gramsci's explicit thought (which was based on a comparison of the Italian situtation with the agrarian policy of the French Jacobins), but one would empty it of all interest for our discussion, because it is evident that such a policy would have led either to a general uprising to seize the land, or to defeat, especially in the more backward zones where the old feudal structures would have survived. At most, it would have left but a few traces devoid of historical interest. . . .

Certainly the Gramsci thesis has a scope that extends well beyond the data of economics and class structure. It involves an interpretation of the entire history of Italy. For the Sardinian writer [Gramsci] the agrarian revolution was a great mechanism for resolving the deep-seated conflicts in the country's history, a powerful unifying instrument for all of Italian society, which would create a closer relationship between the State and the "national and popular" forces of cultured groups and society in general. Such a revolution, however, could not take place in the nineteenth century as a force hostile to the expansion of modern capitalistic relationships; it could take place only to the extent that it might be able to promote and even to identify itself with such capitalistic relationships (for certainly it could not make Italy into a country of peasants or of artisans in the way that was idealized by the *petit bourgeois* democrats of the early 1800s). Even in France, where the Revolution likewise laid the basis for a great democratic tradition and managed to bring the masses more intimately into the political life of the state than was the case in Italy, can one say that the agrarian revolution really achieved profound unity between city and countryside? The great revolutionary crises of the nineteenth century, in 1848 and in 1871, showed what a deep gulf separated the urban revolutionary masses from the tenaciously conservative small landowners who had come to the fore during the Great Revolution—and it was Marx himself who was among the first to underscore this fact. Doubtless in Italy too the gulf persisted and was no less deep. This is not surprising when we reflect that this gulf involved a problem that was a thousand years old, tenaciously rooted in the whole course of Italian history, and aggravated by the decadence and inertia that marked so many centuries of the history of our country—a problem that other more fortunate nations have resolved only by means of century-long processes. With good reason, therefore, we can doubt that even the revolution Gramsci espoused could have brought that solution.

Basically, the agrarian revolution assumed for Gramsci a value quite similar to the resolving and eschatological one that Marxism perceived in the proletarian revolution; and in its most intimate significance, in the position which it occupied in the feeling and spirit of Gramsci, it ended by identifying itself with this. This observation brings us back to the comments on historical methodology made by Croce, Antoni, and Chabod regarding the polemical and political nature of this theory, and hence its essentially antihistorical quality.

On another occasion we might take up Gramsci's specifically historical and political interpretation—namely, his assertion that the Action Party was substantially "directed" by the moderates, a statement which corresponds essentially to King Victor Emmanuel II's remark that he held the Action Party "in his pocket." In actual fact, the democratic alternative to the moderate solution was something that was quite real and politically feasible in 1860. Between August and September of that year the hypothesis of a march by Garibaldi on Rome in order to convene a constituent assembly there, with the further developments of a republican and democratic nature that this implied, seemed anything but impossible. And the results of Mack Smith's recent and very accurate work serve to confirm this thesis if they are rightly interpreted.

THE GRAMSCI-ROMEO DEBATE

John M. Cammett

. . . The issue of "present-mindedness" is central to the recent and most interesting controversy between Italian liberal and Marxist historians. Rosario Romeo, author of an important book on the Risorgimento in Sicily, began the polemic with the publication of two articles in *Nord e Sud* in 1956 and 1958. The articles later appeared as a book with the title *Risorgimento e capitalismo* (Bari: Laterza, 1959). Although the first part of the work was intended as a general survey of Italian Marxist historiography, its main burden—as well as that of the entire second part—was to refute Antonio Gramsci's interpretation of the Risorgimento. Romeo justifies this emphasis by asserting the almost "universal acceptance" on the part of Italian Marxists of "Gramsci's thesis on the Risorgimento" (p. 96).

According to Romeo, the core of Gramsci's thought on the Risorgimento lies in his criticism of its leaders, both moderate and democratic, for failing to carry through an agrarian revolution (*"una rivoluzione agraria mancata,"* cf. Romeo. pp. 19-21). Working on this assumption, Romeo then attempts to demonstrate that (1) Gramsci's thesis was motivated by his political position and not by "serene" historical examination; (2) his work was vitiated by his propensity for using the French Revolution as a model to demonstrate the inadequacy of the Italian Revolution; (3) his belief in the possibility of an agrarian revolution in the nineteenth century was wrong; (4) had such a revolution occurred, capitalist development would have been seriously delayed in Italy, a situation which Gramsci as a Marxist would have had to deplore.

Romeo believes that almost the entire corpus of Italian Marxist historical writing—not just Gramsci's—is permeated by unhistorical political attitudes. "Quite a few Italian historians," he writes, came to Marxism "under the combined action of complex motives, among which politically contingent passion and attitudes played a predominant role" (p. 94). Moreover, he sees political bias in the fact that Italian Marxist historiography has shown little interest in historical periods preceding the French Revolution and the Risorgimento. Gramsci's work too, he says, is to be understood as merely part of a whole "revisionist" tendency in Italian historiography (Smith would be included in this school) which stressed what the Risorgimento did *not* do rather than what it did. Romeo follows Benedetto Croce, Carlo Antoni, and Federico Chabod (pp. 20, 46) in charging that Gramsci "anachronistically" reflected the twentieth-century interests of the Italian

Communist Party in his stressing of the importance of the peasant movement and the Southern Question during the Risorgimento, in his underestimation of the role of the European powers in influencing the course of the Risorgimento, and even in his use of such terms as "national-popular (*nazionale-popolare*)," supposedly derived from the Russian term *narodnost* (p. 25, n.12).

Romeo has a particular aversion to Gramsci's purported tendency to use the French Revolution as a "model" for analyzing Italian history. The much greater industrial development of France invalidates such a comparison (p. 26). Romeo does not object to the comparative method for the study of revolutionary processes, though he tends to regard it as "arbitrary and incomplete." He does object strongly to the "assumption that French historical development is an 'exemplary' model for the creation of a modern bourgeois and capitalist country" (p. 44). From the economic and social point of view, he regards the "Prussian way" as "incomparably more energetic and expansive." Romeo follows Lenin in defining that "Prussian way" as a "compromise of the capitalistic bourgeosie with feudal elements" (p. 39) and recognizes that it is "undoubtedly less 'democratic' " (p. 40) than the French way. For this reason, Romeo attributes the tendency of Italian Marxists to exalt French history to a "certain Francophilia of our democratic thought" (p. 44). But Romeo goes much further. He asserts that Italy was fortunate in not following the pattern of the French Revolution, especially with regard to the agrarian revolution, since French industrial and agricultural development has been hindered precisely by the consequent changes in the relations of production in the countryside.

So far as Italy was concerned, Romeo flatly denies the possibility of an agrarian revolution in the nineteenth century, or indeed of the "effective existence" of any "alternative to the Risorgimento as it was concretely realized." Despite the innumerable peasant insurrections and the admitted existence of grinding rural poverty, an agrarian revolution would not have been tolerated by the great powers (p. 22). Although Romeo admits that Gramsci was aware of this very problem,[1] he nonetheless finds it contradictory that Gramsci could still assert the possibility of "an action on the peasants."[2]

Finally, Romeo thinks it most fortunate that an "agrarian revolution" did not occur in Italy. By employing the concept of "primitive accumulation" of capital, derived from Marx, and the principles of modern theory of economic development, Romeo attempts to show that an agrarian revolution would have raised the level of consumption of the peasant masses, then more than eighty percent of Italy's population, and would consequently have severely retarded the process of capital accumulation.

Italian agricultural production and productivity, according to Romeo, made great progress in the period 1861—1880. The increase in production was not transferred into greater rural consumption, but absorbed in the form of rents and profits, which allegedly formed the base for capital investment, especially for the "infrastructure" (public utilities and means of transportation and communication). Romeo does not deny the importance of high taxes and foreign investment in this process but insists that its real basis was the continued low level of consumption in the countryside accompanied by increased agricultural production. For him, neither the low consumption nor the higher productivity could have been maintained under the conditions of an "agricultural revolution." The peasants would have consumed

[1] *Cf.* Gramsci, *op. cit.,* p. 150.
[2] *Ibid.,* p. 88.

whatever meager increases they might have succeeded in wresting from the necessarily inefficient small units which a revolution would have created.

True, Romeo concedes that the agricultural crisis of the 1880's ended the flow of capital from the country to the city. By then, however, investments could be and were derived mainly from the profits of commerce and industry (p. 174). On the basis of calculations made by Gerschenkron and Clark, as well as the official *Indagine statistica sulla sviluppo del reddito nazionale dell'Italia dal 1861 al 1956,* Romeo optimistically concludes that Italian industrial development in the 1880's was "discreetly rapid: probably the most rapid in the history of the Italian industrial economy before the beginning of the new century" (p. 188). He urges us to keep in mind that "precisely because of the sacrifice imposed for so many decades on the countryside and the South, Italy, poor in territory and natural resources, was the only country in the Mediterranean area to succeed in creating a great industrial apparatus and a highly developed urban civilization" (p. 197).

The tone of the work is often harsh and condescending, a fact which goes far toward explaining the none-too-gentle response of Italian Marxists. Although the controversy is not yet finished, it is now possible to summarize the principal Marxian criticisms of Romeo's theses, as well as some observations made by other scholars.

Gramsci himself, as we have seen, was strongly opposed to "immediate and ideological, non-historical" interpretations of the Risorgimento.[3] Apart from the general question of how any history can be written without the stimulus of a present interest, it is nonetheless a fact that any history of the Risorgimento immediately excites political interests. Giorgio Candeloro, when writing of the conflict between the tendencies to exalt or to denigrate the Risorgimento, naturally urges the avoidance of either tendency, but further explains that these positions "have an ideological foundation which goes back to the Risorgimento itself and to the politico-social situation deriving from the events of a hundred years ago. Those events have preserved an "actuality" which continues to stimulate discussion of them in substantially political terms. . . above all because they gave birth to new problems (or a new face to old problems) which was central to the later history of Italy and which exist even today, albeit in some respects partly changed.[4] Thus, Candeloro concludes that any discussion of the Risorgimento must keep in mind the fundamental characteristics of both the Risorgimento and "united Italy and its social and economic development."

What is the case for the "political or ideological" character of Gramsci's work on the Risorgimento? Romeo's view rests fundamentally on the assertion that Gramsci's concern with the "agrarian question" reflects a political problem of twentieth-century Communism and is an "anachronism" when applied to the "concrete reality" (p. 20). of the Risorgimento. The question of the possibility and the desirability of an "agrarian revolution" will be taken up later. At this point, we must establish only whether agrarian reform was a consciously expressed need at the time of Italian unification. Was agrarian revolution only Gramsci's problem or also a problem of 1848 or 1860?[5]

---

[3] *Ibid.,* p. 55.
[4] "La nascita dello Stato unitario," *Studi storici,* I, 3 (April-June, 1960), p. 445.
[5] *Cf.* Gastone Manacorda in *Studi Gramsciani: Atti del convegno tenuto a Roma nei giorni 11-12 gennaio 1958* (Rome, 1958), p. 504.

Awareness of the need for agrarian revolution, however vaguely expressed, was certainly widespread among radicals during the Risorgimento. Apart from the views of Italian Jacobins (Buonarroti's communism, for example), during the Revolutionary and Napoleonic periods, the left-wing of the *Carbonari* (c. 1820) required its more advanced members to swear to "favor with all my forces and at the cost of my life the promulgation and the execution of the agrarian Law, without which there is no liberty since private property is an offense against the rights of humanity. . . .[6] There was also the social program of Carlo Bianco di St. Jorioz who, in a work significantly entitled *Della guerra nazionale d'insurrezione per bande applicata all'Italia* (Malta, 1830), urged that at the successful conclusion of the "national war of insurrection," the combatants receive "the domain lands and the private possessions of the princes and the enemies of liberty."[7] Though it is possible to dismiss such statements as nothing more than the expression of an insignificant "lunatic fringe," two recent works by Italian Marxists[8] have shown how important the question of an agrarian revolution had become by 1860 to a great many Italian democratic and socialistic figures in the Risorgimento. Finally, a principal reason for the support given to Garibaldi by the Sicilian peasantry was his promise to "divide up the large estates and distribute the land.[9] Very little came of this promise, it is true, and reference to these well-known ideas and facts may seem gratuitous. The point is merely that the question of "agrarian revolution" originated in the Risorgimento and not in the twentieth century. Almost immediately after the completion of national unity, the agricultural question became a major issue, not only for democrats but also for moderates, as the famous parliamentary investigation into agriculture demonstrates.

As Manacorda has shown, Gramsci's concern with the agrarian question (which is inseparable from the question of the South) is no more than the culmination of a specifically Italian tradition going back through Gaetano Salvemini and Antonio Labriola to Carlo Cattaneo. Even the idea of an alliance of southern peasantry and northern workers is not "Bolshevik" in origin since this very alliance had been called for by Salvemini as early as 1900.[10] This tradition culminates in Gramsci because only after World War I did it seem "concretely possible to overcome the social contradictions inherited from the Risorgimento.[11] To define Gramsci's place in the history of Italian social thought is no easy task; however, Romeo is quite wrong when—in his zeal to associate Gramsci with foreign sources—he dismisses the Communist leader's use of the term "national-popular" as a mere derivation from the Russian "narodnost." As far back as 1851, Vincenzo Gioberti had written, "A literature cannot be national if it is not popular,"[12] and in 1856, Ruggero Bonghi,

[6] *Cf.* the "Catechism of the Third Degree *Carbonaro*" in Carlo Francovich, *Idee sociali e organizzazione operaia nella prima meta dell' 800* (Milan, 1959), pp. 140-44. Francovich also reproduces the "Catechism of the Three Degrees of the Adelfia," another secret society widely diffused in north Italy during the Restoration. This document contains the phrase "Mishaps, vices, and crimes are born from the foolish division of land. Then peaceful equality disappeared, and greed for gold and power entered." (pp. 145-46.)

[7] As quoted in Candeloro, *Storia dell'Italia moderna*, II, p. 157.

[8] Franco Della Peruta, *I democratici e la rivoluzione italiana: Dibattiti ideali e contrasti politici all'indomani del 1848* (Milan, 1958) and Giuseppe Berti, *I democratici e l'iniziativa meridionale nel Risorgimento* (Milan, 1962).

[9] D. Mack Smith, *Garibaldi* (London, 1957), p. 96.

[10] Manacorda, *op. cit.*, p. 508.

[11] *Ibid.*, p. 509.

[12] *Cf.* Gramsci, *Il Risorgimento*, p. 145.

later a Minister of Public Instruction, wrote a work entitled *Perchè la letteratura italiana non sia popolare in Italia.*[13]

The French Revolution, too, according to Romeo unduly influenced Gramsci's view of the Risorgimento. Since social and economic conditions were entirely different in the two Latin countries, any comparison of their respective historical developments would have been gratuitous. Indeed, Gramsci did emphasize very strongly the failure of Italian revolutionists to develop a Jacobin-like program during the Risorgimento. But what precisely did Gramsci mean by "Jacobinism"? He used the term to describe not only a certain political temperament characterized by "extreme energy, decision and resolution"[14] but also a particular political program founded on an alliance of the urban bourgeoisie and the peasantry. The willingness and ability of the Jacobins to satisfy the essential demands of the peasants meant that "rural France accepted the hegemony of Paris," and the Jacobins were able to carry out much of that revolutionary program which resulted in the creation of the modern French state.

According to Gramsci this lack of Jacobinism in the Italian Risorgimento did most to determine the outcome of the movement. The retarded development of the Italian bourgeoisie, its semi-landed character, the traditional parasitism of Italian cities with regard to the rural areas, the "cosmopolitan non-national" functions which engaged so many Italian intellectuals (service in the papal bureaucracy and the age-old tradition of wandering Italian artists and musicians), the need for maintaining a high degree of unity among the national ruling groups in order to achieve independence, and, perhaps most important, the increasing conservatism of the European bourgeoisie as a whole after 1848, all prevented the democratic Party of Action from developing a coherent program of agrarian reform. That party, as the representative of the radical petty bourgeoisie—intellectuals, artisans, small entrepreneurs—as well as the exiguous urban proletariat, needed the mass support of the peasants, then about four-fifths of the population, in order to avoid being disintegrated by the moderates. The latter, which represented the bourgeoisie and those elements of the nobility whose economic activities were of a capitalistic nature (large landowners or tenants, industrial and commercial entrepreneurs) were much too powerful for the petty bourgeoisie alone.

On the other hand, the success of the moderates and the failure of the democrats to develop a Jacobin program established the fundamental character of the united Italian state: the result of a compromise between the old (the landed aristocracy) and the new (the commercial and industrial bourgeoisie). As Candeloro has concluded, Gramsci wished to show how, under such conditions as those indicated above, where essentially *political* problems like national independence and unity prevail, a bourgeois revolution in a limited form is possible without an alliance with the peasants and masses but through an alliance with the previous ruling class.[15]

Is Gramsci's use of the Jacobin idea as an instrument of research a valid one? Certainly not, if he meant to establish the French Revolution as an abstract model to which all other revolutions must conform. That Gramsci never intended this is shown by his dismissal of Giuseppe Ferrari (1811–1876), a federalist republican,

---

[13] *Cf.* Gramsci, *Letteratura e vita nazionale* (Turin, 1950), p. 89. In a long review of Romeo's book, Aurelio Macchioro points out that his grandmother used to refer to her lasagna as her "national-popular dish!" *Cf.* "Risorgimento, capitalismo e metodo storico," *Rivista storica del socialismo,* II, 7-8 (July-December, 1959), pp. 685-86.

[14] *Il Risorgimento,* p. 75.

[15] Candeloro, in *Studi Gramsciani, op. cit.,* p. 521.

because of his mechanical tendency to apply "French schemes" to Italian questions.[16]

Gramsci reasoned that in order to know what the Risorgimento was, it was also necessary to know what it was *not*. Through the "comparative method," it could be shown why Italian developments were *different* than the French. As a matter of fact, the comparison itself was an old tradition both in Italy and in Europe. In 1801, Vincenzo Cuoco published his *Saggio storico sulla rivoluzione napoletana del 1799* in which he developed the idea of "passive revolution," i.e., revolution from above or because of external pressures as contrasted with "active revolution" such as had occurred in France. In the 1860's, Alessandro Manzoni wrote on *La rivoluzione francese del 1789 a le rivoluzione italiana del 1859* in which the latter was defended as "legal" and the former attacked for its "violence." The method is even more fruitful today as is shown by Albert Soboul's recent essay on "Risorgimento et révolution bourgeoise."[17] Ironically enough, Romeo himself in another work makes a judgment which is almost identical to Gramsci's. In discussing why the Della Torre lords of Milan in the thirteenth century did not carry out a resolute anti-feudal struggle in the rural areas, Romeo concludes that the "lack of concrete support in the countryside, which they were unable or unwilling to find in the peasants, made effective control of the dominion much more difficult for the powerful city."[18] Another liberal, Giuseppe Talamo, seems equally unable to avoid a Gramscian point of view, this time in a discussion of the Risorgimento itself. With regard to the first constitutional ministry in Naples during the revolution of 1848, he says:

In the rural areas and in all the provinces in general the position of the constitutional ministry was very weak. The age-old question of the assignment of the common domains, arbitrarily occupied by the landowners, was not even discussed. This was undeniably to the advantage of the king who (as Spellanzon has written) would later be able to take advantage of the widespread discontent of the agricultural masses as an opposition to the political aspirations of the bourgeoisie.[19]

That Italian political leaders of every camp, from the Risorgimento to the present, have deplored the lack of change in agrarian relations of production is therefore easy to demonstrate. Romeo charges that Gramsci asserts the *possibility* of an agrarian revolution and makes it central to his "indictment" of the Risorgimento. Actually, the main point of Gramsci's work is to show why such a revolution did not occur in Italy. He demonstrates the reasons for the failure of the Party of Action[20] and those for the success of the moderates.[21]

---

[16] *Il Risorgimento*, p. 75. "Ferrari was unable to 'translate' French into Italian. . . ."
[17] *La Pensee*, 95 (Jan.-Feb., 1961), pp. 63-73.
[18] Romeo as quoted in Renato Zangheri, "La mancata rivoluzione agraria nel Risorgimento e i problemi economici del 'unita'," in *Studi Gramsciani, op. cit.*, p. 383, n.l.
[19] *Storia d'Italia* (Turin, 1959), III, p. 698.
[20] "If a Jacobin party was not formed in Italy, the reasons are to be sought in the economic field, that is in the relative weakness of the Italian bourgeoisie, and in the changed historical climate of Europe after 1815." *Il Risorgimento*, p. 87.
[21] The moderates represented a relatively homogeneous social group" (pp. 69-70) which permitted them gradually to "absorb elites from enemy groups. . . ." One example: "That the liberal movement succeeded in arousing a Catholic-liberal force and in bringing it about that Pius X himself, however temporarily, would take a stand for liberalism (which was enough to disintegrate the ideologico-political apparatus of Catholicism and destroy its faith in itself) was the political masterpiece of the Risorgimento" (p. 50).

Perhaps the only place in Gramsci's work unreservedly referring to a real possibility of enrolling the peasants in the national movement occurs when he accuses the Party of Action of not effecting an "action on the peasants [which] was certainly always possible."[22] But this vague charge comes after a discussion of the weakness of that very party. Elsewhere Gramsci explains very clearly why such a movement was not historically possible: "Did any of the conditions exist in Italy for a movement like that of the French Jacobins? For many centuries, France was a hegemonic nation: its international autonomy was very ample. For Italy, nothing of the kind: it had no international autonomy."[23] Agrarian revolution was not possible because of the relative strength of the moderates: Cavour and his party triumphed "because he represented the only correct politics of the era precisely because of the absence of valid and politically intelligent competitors."[24] An undistorted view of Gramsci's historiography forbids arbitrary selection of one element in his thought, be it the absence of Jacobinism or of agrarian revolution. In his own words, "The Risorgimento is a complex and contradictory historical movement which achieves wholeness by means of all its antithetical elements: its protagonists and antagonists, its struggles and the reciprocal modifications which those very struggles brought about, as well as the function of latent and passive forces such as the great agricultural masses, besides naturally the eminent function of international relations."[25]

This historical justification of the moderates does not prevent Gramsci from pointing out the same unfortunate results of their victory in the long run: The moderates "said they proposed the creation of a modern state in Italy and they produced a kind of bastard; they proposed the development of a broad and energetic ruling class and they did not succeed; [they proposed] the insertion of the people in the life of the state and they did not succeed. The poverty-stricken political life from 1870 to 1900, the elementary and endemic rebelliousness of the popular classes, the crude and belabored existence of a skeptical and lazy ruling class are the consequences of this deficiency. Another consequence is the international position of the new state, deprived of effective autonomy because it was undermined by the papacy and by the malevolent passivity of the great masses. Hence, the Rightwingers of the Risorgimento were really great demagogues. They made an instrument and an object of the people-nation by degrading it and therein lies the greatest and most contemptible demagoguery...."[26]

It is this complex and concrete view of the Risorgimento which brought a liberal like Aldo Berselli to the recognition that Gramsci cannot be included in the "general category of 'Risorgimental revisionism.' "[27] Similarly, A. William Salomone recently attacked revisionist tendencies in the historiography of the Risorgimento, but treated Gramsci's work itself with considerable respect.[28] Thus Romeo's charge of "present-mindedness" in Gramsci might better be applied to himself. Romeo

[22] *Il Risorgimento*, p. 88. *Cf.* Zangheri, *op. cit.*, p. 371.
[23] *Il Risorgimento*, p. 151.
[24] *Loc. cit.*
[25] *Ibid.*, p. 108.
[26] *Ibid.*, pp. 94—95.
[27] "Risorgimento e capitalismo," *Il Mulino*, 92 (1959), pp. 497—98.
[28] "The *Risorgimento* between Ideology and History: The Political Myth of *rivoluzione mancata*," *The American Historical Review* LXVIII, 1 (October, 1962), pp. 46-49. Although this writer believes that Salomone too has somewhat oversimplified Gramsci's thought, he is at least aware, unlike Romeo, of its complexities.

attempts to "idealize" the past, to demonstrate that what "really" happened did for the best and, indeed, could only have happened in that way. This is a very different matter from a disinterested examination of the past. As Macchioro has said, it may be dangerous to hypothesize another possible development in the past, but it is less dangerous than the tendency "to make what happened in the past not only the real history—which it is—but also ideal history."[29]

Must serious historical work give the stamp of approval to everything in the past? Gaetano Salvemini discusses this difficult problem beautifully in the following passage dealing with his apparently contradictory evaluation of Cavour's work:

The contradiction, I believe, disappears if we distinguish "historical" judgment from "political judgment." One can recognize "historically" that the Italian democratic parties produced an excessive number of inconclusive windbags, and that granted their incapacity and the objective conditions within which they worked, their defeats were not only inevitable but even deserved—however, one is not therefore obliged to condemn their ideals for all times and all places. One can recognize the superior political capacities of the conservatives in comparison with the democrats and still not pass over bag and baggage to the official historians of the conservative parties. ... As an "historian," I must see men as they were; as a "man of politics"—which is not the same thing as a "politician"—or as a "moralist" (to add a note of Crocean contempt), I do not remove my hat before accomplished facts, and if necessary, shall even take a stand for the defeated.[30]

Romeo, on the other hand, certainly does "take off his hat to accomplished facts." The actual course of Italian history is for him "the quickest and shortest road which history permitted for Italy to acquire the structure and characteristics proper to a modern country.[31] True, he cannot ignore the persisting ailments of the South, but these he regards as part of the process of "potentializing of the city at the expense of the country."[32] And even Southern backwardness is a " 'temporary condition (even if protracted for many decades), and destined to be reversed by the internal development of northern industrialism."[33] Quite apart from the question of how long a condition must persist before it ceases to be "temporary," recent statistics show that the regional contrast is increasing rather than decreasing. From this we may conclude that it is Romeo rather than Gramsci who imposes "abstract schemes" on historical development.[34] Capitalism is seen as a kind of providence which must be permitted to continue because it will eventually provide for all,[35] and any violence committed along this path is justified once the pieces have been picked up.

How much more sensible is Gramsci's approach:

The hegemony of the North would have been "normal" and historically beneficial if

---

[29] Op. cit. p. 512.

[30] Scritti sul Risorgimento (Milan, 1961), pp. 9-10, as quoted in Berti, op. cit., pp. 784-85.

[31] Romeo, p. 49.

[32] Ibid., p. 47.

[33] Loc. cit.

[34] Cf. Luciano Cafagna, "Intorno al 'revisionismo risorgimentale'," Società, XII, 6 (1956), p. 1033 and Dario Tosi, "Sulle forme iniziale di sviluppo economico e i loro effetti nel lungo periodo: l'agricoltura italiana e l'accumulazione capitalistica," Annali Feltrinelli, IV (1961), pp. 213-14.

[35] Cafagna, op. cit., p. 1033.

industrialization had had the capacity to widen its confines with a certain speed in order to incorporate new assimilated economic zones. Then this hegemony would have been the expression of a struggle between the old and the new, between the more productive and the less productive.... [However] it was not so. The hegemony was presented as permanent: the contrast was presented as a necessary historical condition for an indeterminate time—and therefore apparently "perpetual"—for the existence of nothern industry.[36]

Even Gerschenkron, in some ways sympathetic to Romeo, is annoyed by Romeo's tendency to justify every development in the Italian economy before 1890. He exaggerates the efficacy of governmental and banking policy, even going so far as to praise both those who maintained and those who abolished "forced currency," and justifies the predominance of small enterprise in Italian industry even though nineteenth-century economic history shows the decisive importance of larger enterprise in a rapid phase of development in a backward country.[37]

Romeo's defense of Italian economic development in the years from 1861 to 1887 has received as much attention from scholars as his critique of Gramscian historiography. His position is that the development of a modern capitalistic Italy came about precisely because there was no agrarian revolution. This thesis has been attacked on four principal grounds: (1) his conception of "primitive accumulation" of capital is mistaken; (2) his assumption of a direct relationship between the growth of small peasant property and an increase in consumption is unwarranted; (3) his belief that large landholdings are necessarily more progressive than small peasant holdings is often not true; (4) his data on the reasons and extent of economic growth in Italy and in relation to that of other countries are often misleading and exaggerated.

Romeo employs a Marxian-like concept of primitive accumulation to explain the problem of the formation of capital in the first two decades of Italian unity—"Marxian-like" but not Marxian, since Marx's analysis, which concentrated on the separation of the peasantry from the means of production and the increasing separation of agrarian from manufacturing activities, was limited to the *origins* of the capitalist system, especially in England. For Marx, this primitive or "original" accumulation extended over a very long period, from the sixteenth to the eighteenth centuries. Capitalist development took place at first mainly in the production of consumer goods (agricultural and textiles) and only with the industrial revolution was there a great increase in the production of the means of production. The whole process developed within the framework of an essentially closed economy, external factors being minimal in influence.[38]

The point is that for Marx "primitive accumulation" could occur only once, but Romeo believes that the main source of capital for the creation of the "infrastructure" was obtained in the same way as in the original process of accumulation, that is, by expropriating the peasantry, or more precisely by drastically limiting consumption in the countryside to permit a flow of capital to the cities. However, the problem of Italian industrialization is the problem of the

---

[36] *Il Risorgimento*, p. 210.

[37] Alexander Gerschenkron, "Rosario Romeo e l'accumulazione primitiva del capitale," *Rivista storica Italiana*, LXXI, 4 (1960), p. 584.

[38] *Cf.* Tosi, *op. cit.*, pp. 205-206, for a good summary of Marx's conception of primitive accumulation.

entry of a new country into capitalistic production. The formation of capital in such a situation requires consideration of a whole group of new factors, such as international capital investment and trade, technical progress, and the diffusion of ideas.[39]

Ironically, Romeo's idea that drastic limitation of rural consumption is the key to capital formation is much more applicable to the situation in backward countries with planned economies than to a country like Italy which functioned within the framework of world capitalism. In the former, "wage levels are stabilized in accordance with certain objectives, relations with other countries are reduced to a minimum, and tastes and preference of consumers are not much influenced from the outside."[40] This is not to say that rural consumption has not been drastically limited in capitalist or precapitalist countries too, but whether or not this is an effective way to achieve "primitive accumulation" under those circumstances is another matter.

Romeo of course does not deny the importance of foreign investment in Italy, but in his effort to justify the admitted exploitation of the peasantry, he tends to exaggerate both the quantity of potential capital extracted from the latter and the degree of efficacy of its employment. According to Luzzatto, more than one-third of Italian state bonds were held by foreigners; foreign investment in Italian transportation, industry and commerce was almost twice the amount the savings deposits in Italy in 1872-74; and Nitti states that "foreign capital in Italy had a prevailing importance; not only for the great number of state bonds held abroad but because all the great enterprises of trade, communications, and transportation were foreign or primarily foreign.[41] Then too, a considerable part of the funds obtained by the government through taxation of the peasantry was not used to create a "positive industrial movement," but dissipated to those holders of state bonds whom the non-Marxist Berselli calls "parasitic capitalists."[42] Another point overlooked by Romeo is the amount of capital which moved from *city to country*.[43] The great amount of land put on the market and the continued aspiration to hold land on the part of the Italian bourgeoisie, belie Romeo's assertion that "agrarian rents and profits gave rise to a current which freshened the whole urban economy."[44]

A most important hypothesis in Romeo's argument is his belief that an extension of small peasant property goes hand in hand with an increase in rural consumption. As Tosi has pointed out, Romeo supports this conviction with the Keynesian argument that a redistribution of land would enlarge the low-income group with respect to those of higher incomes. Since the former has a greater propensity to consume, the growth of savings would, therefore, decrease. Rather than accepting the judgment of twentieth-century thinkers, Tosi goes back to nineteenth-century economists for their views on the habits of rural classes. On the basis of a number

---

[39] *Ibid.*, p. 206. Because of these new conditions, Gerschenkron (*op. cit.*, pp. 579-80) believes that in recent time, the two phases of primitive accumulation and industrialization occur simultaneously in backward countries and that Romeo is wrong in separating them.

[40] *Ibid.*, pp. 207-208.

[41] Gino Luzzatto, *Storia economica dell'eta moderna e contemporanea* (Padua, 1955), II, p. 379 and F. S. Nitti, *Il capitale finanziario in Italia* (Bari, 1915), p. 17, both as quoted in Zangheri, *op. cit.*, p. 377.

[42] *Op. cit.*, p. 506.

[43] *Cf.* Cafagna, *op. cit.*, p. 1030.

[44] Romeo, p. 35.

of investigations carried out in various European countries around 1850, John Stuart Mill concluded that the peasantry, particularly in relation to the working class, was anything but prodigal. They typically deprived themselves of even simple pleasures in order to save for the morrow.[45] Tosi himself concludes that "parsimony is a typical behavior pattern of peasants." The resulting savings might, of course, be invested in economically useless ways such as usury, but the example of the French peasantry with its heavy investment in state and foreign bonds shows that such waste is not inevitable.

Similarly, the experience of the United States supports Gramsci's approach, not Romeo's. Possibly, the rapid westward movement of the free-farm economy of the Northern United States did attract labor and capital away from industry, but even if so, these losses were dramatically offset by the tremendous expansion of the rural market for textiles, farm equipment, and the like, and of the national demand for canals and railroads. The rapid development of the market provided a major impetus to American industrial development in the first half of the nineteenth century. The United States also had, and to some extent still has, a backward South. Until the Civil War of 1861-1865 the Southern slave states were dominated by huge slave plantations; the overwhelming majority of the rural population, in contrast to that of the free states, was poor—slaves, marginal producers, and "poor whites." American industry rose on the Northern free-farm economy, not on the plantation economy, which fettered industrial growth in the country as a whole and condemned the South to backwardness.

That division of the land is in itself anti-capitalist also seems axiomatic to Romeo. However, Tosi shows that in practically all of nineteenth-century Europe (except England), economists favored the broadening of peasant proprietorship as a means of perfecting the capitalist system.[46] At least up until the stage when technical progress requires a larger scale of enterprise, individual agricultural units on a modest scale can make great progress. "Factories in the field" are not necessary in order to practice crop rotation, employ new seeds, fertilizers, and draft animals, or to bring about land improvement, irrigation, and communications.[47] It may be argued that small owners could not afford even the capital necessary for such improvements as these; however, the aforementioned parliamentary investigation of agriculture revealed that most of the rural economy, regardless of the type of landownership, was of the "simple exploitative type," requiring only land and labor,[48] and that "landowners had little margin of profit for emergency reserves or for new capital to put back into the land.[49] In the nineteenth century at least, Italian peasant proprietors had several distinct advantages over the large estate of the *latifundia* type which predominated in the South. The former employed a greater variety of crops, thereby making better use of the land; labor was more frequently present on the farm; and the peasant owners had much greater incentive to work than those existing on a more precarious basis.[50]

---

[45] J. S. Mill, *Principi di economia politica* (Turin, 1953). Book VI, Chapter VI, quoted in Tosi, *op. cit.*, p. 209.

[46] *Ibid.*, p. 211.

[47] *Ibid.*, p. 214.

[48] *Cf. ibid.*, p. 216.

[49] Dennis Mack Smith, *Italy: A Modern History*, p. 149.

[50] Tosi, *op. cit.*, p. 221.

Finally, there is the problem of the accuracy of Romeo's statistics regarding the growth of the Italian economy in the twenty-year period which he selected. Fundamental to Romeo's thesis is his assertion that there was "marked progress in all the principal branches of [Italian] agrarian production" (p. 120). For if there were no such progress the contribution of Italian agriculture to primitive accumulation would necessarily have been insufficient to justify retention of the old system of land ownership. Yet Gerschenkron not only states that the amount of agricultural growth from 1861 to 1880 was probably not very high (averaging little more than two percent annually), but that the rate of investment and the interest on savings were relatively low compared to other countries in a similar stage, and that funds spent on public works were a small portion of the gross national product in 1861 and decreased until after 1880.[51] Gerschenkron concludes that economic change in this period was extremely small.[52]

Just as Romeo tends to underestimate the problem of demand and the function of the market in the process of industrialization, so too, in Gerschenkron's opinion, does he tend to overlook the inadequacies of Italian governmental and banking policy.[53] That the government might have played a more effective role in the transition to industrial capitalism is shown by the example of Japan where another "narrow bourgeois and conservative" revolution[54] was effected at almost the same time as the Risorgimento. There the government "relieved the magnates (daimyo) of their ancient debts to usurers, and ... transformed the capitalist-usurers ... into bearers of debentures redeemable by the nation. What only yesterday was valueless paper became capital with a modern function.[55] According to Paul Baran, who stresses the importance of the state in bringing about industrial capitalism, the Meiji government invested not only in railroads, shipbuilding and communications, but also in basic industries and production of machinery, guaranteed private investments, committed itself to purchasing goods and sold state-owned industries to capitalists at very low prices.[56] In the United States—as American historians generally recognize—capitalist development was spurred significantly by government aid, first in the form of funds provided by the state governments for internal improvements and then, after the Civil War, in the form of direct federal support for railroads. Very little of this was done by the Italian government. Much social injustice occurred in this process, but Romeo's whole point is to accept such injustice provided only that progress is made in the development of capitalism.

The results of the polemic have unquestionably demonstrated the inadequacy of Romeo's critique of Gramscian historiography and his view of the process of capital formation in Italy. Nevertheless, he has rendered a great service to Italian Marxist scholars by forcing them to avoid unhistorical condemnations of the past and to apply Gramsci's method and insights to the study of Italian history in a more concrete and creative way.

---

[51] *Op. cit.*, pp. 577-78. Investment in public works was, according to Romeo, a principal goal of the primitive accumulation of capital extracted from agriculture.

[52] *Op. cit.*, pp. 577-78.

[53] *Ibid.*, p. 581.

[54] The phrase is from Jean Jaurès with reference to the Risorgimento in *La Constituante* (Paris, 1904), p. 310 as quoted in Soboul, *op. cit.*, p. 65.

[55] H. K. Takahashi, "La place de la Révolution de Meiji dans l'histoire agraire de Japon," *Revue historique* (October-November, 1953), p. 252 n., as quoted in Paul A. Baran, *The Political Economy of Growth* (New York, 1957), p. 155, n.2.

[56] Baran, *op. cit.*, p. 157.

8 / Otto von Bismarck: "The Bismarck Problem"

Otto von Bismarck pushed through Germany's unification in little more than eight years after he became prime minister of Prussia in September 1862. His famous statement of that month before the budget committee of the *Landtag*, "The great questions of the time are not decided by speeches and majority resolutions—that was the great mistake of 1848 and 1849—but by blood and iron," has been described as Bismarck's theory of statecraft. And, in fact, the unification of Germany was consolidated by three wars: the Danish (1864), the Austrian or Seven Weeks War (1866), and the Franco-Prussian War (1870-71).

The speed and dimensions of Bismarck's achievement, however should not obscure the fact that it was accompanied by opposition. But, as the writer of one of the selections below reminds us, "nothing succeeds like success." After the Austrian War, the majority of the Liberals, who for four years had forced Bismarck into the embarrassing position of virtually governing without a parliament, were won over to his side. This last victory, coupled with considerations arising out of the Franco-Prussian War and its victorious conclusion, removed the last objections of the peoples and sovereigns of the various German states to a united Germany under Prussian leadership. It was on the motion of King Ludwig II of Bavaria, a country that had sided with Austria in 1866, that the crown of the German Empire was offered to William I of Prussia at Versailles in 1871.

Bismarck's dazzling success is reflected in the praise bestowed on him and William I in Heinrich von Sybel's monumental seven volume study *Die Begründung des deutschen Reiches durch Wilhelm I* (1889-94),[1] which was long the authoritative work on the 1848-1870 period in German history and was a source for many minor works by lesser authors, all pro-Bismarck and nationalist in tone. As the selections below explain, reappraisal began after World War I. The opening of German archives shed new light on the ramifications of *Realpolitik*. Moreover, Germany's defeat in 1918 meant that Bismarck's Reich had been a very impermanent one indeed. But before a truly liberal reappraisal of Bismarck could develop, the Nazi regime came to power, and the new analysis of Bismarck's policies ended. It was thus not until World War II that Erich Eyck, in exile in England, published in Switzerland his

---

[1] English translation: *Founding of the German Empire by William I, Based Chiefly Upon Prussian State Documents*, 7 vols. (New York: 1890-98).

Bismarck: Leben und Werk,[2] the first complete biography of Bismarck, and a critical appraisal of his life's work from a liberal point of view. It is, in a sense, the point of departure for each of the three selections below, which were written after it was published.

The first selection, by Professor Hans Rothfels of the University of Chicago, is a critique of Eyck's three-volume study which gives the reader a good idea of its salient points. Professor Rothfels is not so much critical of the content of Eyck's work—in fact he finds much that is good in it—as he is of the problems raised and unsolved by Eyck's liberal approach. Professor Rothfels feels that Eyck's underlying assumption, that German unity could have been attained "by other and less forceful means than those of Bismarck," overlooks some historical realities: the aggressive nationalism of German liberals (see chapter 2); the extent to which Bismarck actually "manipulated" history; the lack of Western sympathy "with the attempt at founding a 'good' German Reich, that is, on the liberal-democratic basis of 1848," and the strength of the East-West coalition threat.

The second selection by a German historian, Franz Schnabel, agrees with Rothfels' criticism of Eyck and gives us a further elaboration of the problem of liberal nationalism raised by Rothfels. Schnabel, however, advances the original conclusion that "Bismarck is the last great representative in the line of classic diplomats" beginning with the Venetian ambassadors. As such, he has little in common with the new nationalism of the nineteenth century, a point which seems proved by his lack of pan-Germanist sentiment after 1871. Bismarck, according to Schnabel, simply used nationalism, that is took it "into custody . . . subordinated it to the state conception and made it available for diplomatic craft." Schnabel does not try to excuse all of Bismarck's conduct, but by placing him in the tradition of seventeenth- and eighteenth-century state-builders. Schnabel does mitigate the criticism of Bismarck's methods found in Eyck's work.

In the third selection, Alfred von Martin, another German historian, agrees with Schnabel's emphasis on preBismarckian nationalism, but rejects his assertion that Bismarck was "the end-product of old-fashioned Cabinet diplomacy." Von Martin concurs with the writer of another German book on Bismarck who claims that Bismarck was a "revolutionary" in the Bonapartist sense of the word. A large part, however, of von Martin's short article is devoted to a warning against replacing the myth of the "good" Bismarck with that of the "bad" Bismarck. "In the final analysis," writes von Martin, "a people always has the government it deserves. . . . The examination of Bismarck ought to have led directly into necessary German self-criticism." Von Martin's essay is a good example of the intense soul-searching that German historians have carried out in the wake of World War II. And the three selections below, writing to one another or Eyck's book as they do, show the important and controversial part that "the Bismarck problem" has played in this process.

---

[2] A one volume abridged edition has been published in English. *Bismarck and the German Empire* (London: Allen and Unwin, 1950).

PROBLEMS OF A BISMARCK BIOGRAPHY

Hans Rothfels

Frederick Meinecke in his recent book on *The German Catastrophe*[1] quotes a Danish friend and historian as saying to him during the Hitler regime: "You know that I cannot love Bismarck, but in the present situation I must say: Bismarck belonged to *our world*." It would be easy to contrast this nicely balanced statement with innumerable others which, in the last years, indulged in indictments of the founder of the German Reich as a "Nazi forefather" or threw him into the line of descent which is supposed to lead from Frederick II's attack on Silesia in 1740 to Hitler's attack on Poland in 1939. Thus the myth of the "Iron Chancellor," of the man "in high dragoon's boots" revived and, amazingly enough, the Nazi trick of appropriating "Prussianism" as epitomized in the pageantry of the so-called "day of Potsdam," was given full credit by many of their very adversaries. But there were also the voices of those who, in a more careful and responsible way, tried to find out what links may possibly connect the beginnings with the end of the Prusso-German Reich or may point ahead from 1866 and 1871 or from 1879 to the potentialities of the Hitler regime. Meinecke's treatise is one of the finest examples of such conscientious scrutiny carried out by Germans themselves.[2] From whatever angle this question is raised the towering and baffling figure of Bismarck undoubtedly has won a new actuality. And it can easily be understood that in the recent crisis of statesmanship and particularly in view of the disaster which Germany brought upon herself and the world, attention turned back to the man who stands for decisive changes in the external setup as well as in the intellectual and moral, the political and social climate of nineteenth century Europe.

The Bismarck biography in three volumes by Erich Eyck, which was published in Zurich during the war,[3] gives to all such considerations a new basis and a sharp stimulus. It is in many respects a very timely book, or rather one that was long overdue. For in spite of the host of historians, German and non-German, who concentrated on Bismarck's era, his full life story has never been told before. There were, of course, many biographical sketches and essays, some popular and some scholarly, some adulatory and some hostile. But Erich Marcks, the only author who set out to write an all-embracing biography, stopped after completing one volume of Bismarck's youth, a subject which, in fact, proved better suited for the loving pen of an impressionist than the hard, ambiguous and often unpleasant facts of a great

---

[1] *Die deutsche Katrastrophe* (Ed. Brockhaus, Wiesbaden, 1946), p. 27.
[2] Another very impressive example of such a historiographic re-examination though pointing in a somewhat different direction, is Gerhard Ritter's *Geschichte als Bildungsmacht* (Stuttgart, Deutsche Verlagsanstalt, 1946). As to Bismarck, see pp. 46-50.
[3] (Eugen Rentsch Verlag, Erlenbach-Zuerich) vol. I (-1864), 679 pp., 1941 vol. II (1871), 630 pp., 1943; vol. III (1898), 687 pp., 1944.

political career. Neither the "Bismarck-orthodoxy" nor the opportunistic interpretation brought forth by the so-called *Realpolitik* nor the curious blend of both of these trends in the Wilhelmian era succeeded in producing a rounded-out biographical portrait. While the shadow thrown by the light was not neglected altogether, the general mood which prevailed among German historians of the early twentieth century was of an optimistic and harmonizing nature, little conducive to the appraisal of a "demonic" figure. Some political biographies of a limited scope were written from a more penetrating viewpoint: that by Martin Spahn (1915) from a conservative-Catholic, that by C. Grant Robertson (1919) from a liberal-English one. But like many other books they soon were dated.

This was due, in the first place, to the enormous outpouring of source material which occurred in the one and a half decades after the fall of imperial Germany. Moreover, the new sources offered ample evidence that the catchword of the "misunderstood Bismarck" had a much broader and much more fundamental meaning than O. Hammann, the aide of Bülow, who coined it, could ever have imagined. Not only an amazing number of facts appeared which were entirely new but also aspects came into the foreground which caused a change in emphasis and interpretation. While Bismarck's criticism of his bungling successors found a resounding echo and one borne out by incisive evidence, criticism turned to the basic features of his own life work. Was not the Reich of 1871 a foundation "against the ideas of the time" and therefore mortally ill from the beginning? Did not the shortcomings of the Wilhelmian era follow from the very methods of Bismarck's policy, from a will to, or a philosophy of power which first established the Reich with "blood and iron" and then arranged the balance of the constitution and the interplay of social forces essentially according to personal needs, from the suppression of independent characters and the cultivation of an autocratic spirit which denied to the Germans the opportunity of political education and deepened the submissiveness about which Bismarck himself was to complain so bitterly after 1890? These were questions, obvious from the experiences of the Western democratic world, which now entered the German way of thinking to an increasing extent.

But while the situation after 1918 forbade (or should have forbidden) any mere *laudatio temporis acti* it also became apparent that there was no better witness against all mirages of "splendid times" and all *Realpolitik* divested of any ideas—than Bismarck himself. He certainly had never been tempted to overrate what he achieved and he never indulged in the illusion that anything definite could be settled by mere power. Even in his years of revolutionary action there was the same attempt at checking irrational forces of which there is ample evidence in the documents of the years after 1871. Through the various phases of Bismarck's life, through the obvious changes in his objectives, some fundamental views could be traced which certainly stood against the "ideas of the time," particularly against the conception of the "nation-state," as prefigured in Western Europe and associated with democracy. It can be argued that his was a losing battle even in his own time. And the fact that the limited type of Bismarck's *Reich* (limited in scope, unity and intensity) eventually weathered war and defeat does not necessarily contradict such a statement. But in view of a rampant nationalism and biologism, of the emergence of the masses and many other consequences to which nineteenth century "liberalism" (rather than "Prussianism") had led, it was precisely Bismarck's nonconformity with his time upon which a good deal of attention was focussed.

These various impulses again did not succeed in bringing forth an adequate and balanced biography. Before they had been fully borne out and before the huge mass of new historical sources had been completely penetrated, there occurred the landslide of 1933. After that there was no chance of an independent and critical biography of Bismarck being written in Germany. Besides the well-known stifling effect of an official propaganda, which first "annexed" the "Iron Chancellor" and then let him linger on as a kind of larva in relation to the butterfly of the Third Reich, there was another less well known and yet very pertinent fact: eventually something like a ban was laid upon the very name and memory of Bismarck, the great "heterodox" figure of the recent German past.[4]

It was, therefore, only from outside Germany that a work could be written that had been conspicuous by absence for so long a time. And the explanation of this striking gap, while it reflects upon certain basic problems of a Bismarck biography, underlines also the highly important and significant achievement which Mr. Eyck's three volumes offer to the professional as well as to the general reader.

The book really fills the gap as far as the synthesizing of the widely dispersed fragments and sections of our knowledge is concerned. No aspect or phase has been neglected. From the viewpoint of an over-all coverage the task could not have been mastered more successfully. Likewise, the author's command of the source material is very comprehensive and in view of the difficult situation and of wartime conditions truly to be admired. So is his broad familiarity with research work previously done and with the huge monographic literature. Years of critical reading, of checking and rechecking must have gone into Mr. Eyck's book.

Of all this the author is far from making a pretentious show; references are kept to a bare minimum and placed at the end of the respective volumes. The text itself, at least in large parts, lives up to the sound traditions of narrative history, that is, the author knows how to tell the story and to tell it in an extremely interesting way. The style is smoothly flowing and colorful, sometimes it has a dramatic ring—not without descending, however, here and there into deplorable pitfalls of triviality and colloquialism.[5] This does not mean that the book tries to vie in any way with the easy belletristic type. It will hardly satisfy those needs and tastes to which Emil Ludwig has catered with such devastating effect. Instead of a cleverly got-up "psychognosis" which is so flattering to many readers, there prevails in Mr. Eyck's book a high sense of the historian's ethical responsibility, a very serious discussion of the political and social substance of Bismarck's life work as well as of its moral and philosophical implications.

It is also to the author's credit that some will like the diplomatic parts of the story best while others find them, at least in the first two volumes, too lengthy and too much loaded with detail. The wish has been expressed by one reviewer that the framework of society within which and upon which Bismarck acted might have

---

[4] Many evidences of this fact could be quoted. See, e.g., the remarks of the Princess Herbert v. Bismarck, who stated (Oct., 1938) that her father-in-law did not count for anything any more and that his name was systematically belittled." (Ulrich v. Hassel, *Vom Anderen Deutschland* (Atlantis Verlag, Zürich, 1946), p. 23). Hassel endorses this statement and also mentions in his diaries the fact that on occasion of the 50th anniversary of the death of Bismarck's wife it was forbidden to refer to the part which religion played in the Chancellor's matrimonial life.

[5] See such examples as: I, 92 (*"nicht mit ihr zu Rande kam"*) or III, 630 (*"wie sie dem Verfasser in seinen Kram passen"*).

been submitted to closer examination,[6] but most critics would agree that Mr. Eyck, in accordance with his whole approach, has given much more than the usual attention to Bismarck's domestic (if not actually his social) policies and the class elements involved: Bismarck's clash with, and his victory over, the liberal world being in fact a main and recurrent theme of the book. The more personal parts of the biography come into their own at the beginning and the end, but also with many interspersed scenes. There is a fine sense of balance in all that.

The same can be said, to a certain extent, of the author's attitude and concepts. He has his very definite opinions, of course, even a very definite thesis: the vindication of Bismarck's liberal opponents. But he does not throw his political philosophy upon the reader on every second page. He has enough of the primary interest in what happened rather than in what might have happened or ought to happen, in other words, he has enough of the historian's lifeblood to counterbalance the temptation of all too subjective speculation. In considerable parts of the work the reader is placed in a position to use his own judgment, he is called upon to read and to think before being faced with the author's conclusions.

This is perhaps a somewhat idealized picture of Mr. Eyck's book, to which the writer wants to pay as much tribute as he possibly can; certain reservations will have to be added. But in principle and against the background of so many examples of a different kind the author's "liberalism" stands out as genuine in as much as he makes a sincere effort to be fair before giving his verdict. There is something of a jurist's honesty in the book. As to the evaluation of Bismarck's personality we also find various viewpoints and standards applied, a procedure which avoids the danger of easy simplification. While Bismarck is repeatedly accused of brutality and cynicism, of faithlessness and of lacking a sense of justice, there is no slighting of those traits which simply do not fit the pattern of Queen Victoria's "wicked man." The author's suggestion that the German chancellor was "always peculiar and eminent in both good and bad," is at least non-partisan though obviously too smooth an explanation of his complexity. Thus in general Mr. Eyck tries to understand and to discriminate. In analyzing Bismarck's religiosity, for example (I, 43-54, 184-85, II, 503-504, III, 633-34) he shows a cautious and reverent hand. There is no trace of that enlightened arrogance which, in view of this problem, can not think of any other explanation than that of a diplomatic bargaining with God or a social mimicry. In summing up his portrait (III, 638), the author finds Bismarck one of the "great men" of world history: "...no figure to be loved, much less to be imitated but one to be studied—and with all critical reservations—to be admired." One may say that this "dualism of values" again is typically liberal, with politico-moral and aesthetic categories falling apart from one another.[7] Something of the peculiar nineteenth century cult of the genius still lingers on; it is Bismarck's virtuosity, his resourcefulness, his creativeness, his fascinating brilliance which commands a sort of private admiration. Whether or not one agrees with such

[6] See the interesting review by E. N. Anderson (*Journal of Central European Affairs*, April 1946, pp. 85-90), who also finds the "moral significance of the constitutional conflict" of the sixties slighted by the author. In contrast, it seems to this writer that in the framework of a biography the moral importance of the conflict has never before been emphasized so much and so legitimately.

[7] The same typical split appears when the *Gedanken und Erinnerungen*, first and with an untenable exaggeration, are denied any value as a historic source except that of creating a myth, and then, again with some exaggeration, are appraised as one "of the greater masterworks of world literature." (III, 630).

a balance sheet, it certainly does not expose the reader to any conventional pattern in black and white. Nor yet does it weaken the drive for a moral lesson which is likewise a traditional element of liberal historiography. Against the background of a broadminded appraisal of Bismarck's greatness, the thesis may appear all the more plausible that just because of his brilliant gifts he was able to turn German and European history from the right to the wrong track.

The seriousness of this thesis is not the least of the merits the book can claim. And if the accusation has a familiar ring it is derived not primarily from the usual anti-Prussian resentment, though much of it comes in, but rather from the same basic anxiety to which already two generations earlier a much profounder expression had been given by another and native historian from Switzerland. Mr. Eyck, however, does not agree with Jacob Burckhardt's verdict of the evil inherent in power as such, nor with the forebodings the wise man from Basel had about changing social conditions and the rising wave of mass civilization. The liberal historian, and this seems a decisive point, is outrightly optimistic in looking back upon the situation circa 1860. He draws his confidence obviously from certain principled views as well as from historic examples: from a great figure such as Gladstone, on whom he has written previously, and from those Prussian liberals who reconciled a sincere German patriotism, a desire for national greatness with a profound respect for justice and law, whether statutory or natural. These hopeful perspectives, however, the author sees shattered by Bismarck. His violation of the moral order was the cardinal sin which planted a poisonous germ in the structure of the new Reich and of Europe generally; he, therefore, paved the way for the final downfall of his lifework, for the corruption of the German character by undermining the principle of *justitia fundamentum regnorum.* This is, reduced to general terms, the basic theme of the book.

Before discussing some concrete aspects, in which the problem of politics and morality appeared in Bismarck's era, the intrinsic importance of the author's approach should be stressed. It cannot be waved aside with the conventional consideration that, after all, these are the ways of the world, that none of the great states has been created or maintained without Machiavellian means and that even in the midst of, and after, the most terrible experiences of a "dehumanized" policy, these ways of the world do not seem to be mended. Even those who, with Lord Acton, find Schiller's word: *Die Weltgeschichte ist das Weltgericht,* presumptuous, will readily admit the gravity of the problem and its special applicability to Bismarck's case. That he pursued his course almost singlehandedly (as it might appear), that he certainly counteracted almost all convictions of the time, German and non-German, conservative and liberal and perhaps even his own, that he placed policy, as he put it himself, on the "only sound basis of the egotistic interests of a great state" rather than on principles, that he stretched the constitution to the breaking point and interfered with justice, that he managed to have three wars as they suited his purposes, that he used and abused men, institutions and ideas for tactical ends, or even personal ends, and that he got away with it, i.e., that he reached his aims in spite of the greatest difficulties—all this had fateful implications. It seemed to prove the fallacy of any idealistic approach or rather it proved that nothing succeeds like success. When the Junker of Schoenhausen became Prussian Prime Minister in 1862, he was thoroughly hated; four years later, after Sadowa, the liberal historian Herman Baumgarten published his pamphlet: "Liberalism criticized by itself." It was a program that abandoned principles and gratefully absorbed the new forms of German life, a program that could have but an emasculating effect. At any rate the opportunity of cooperation on an equal footing, of aligning Prussia with western standards was over and would once more elapse in the late seventies. Not that opposition was silenced altogether, but with the great liberal movement exhausted and turning away from politics, an idealistic force was waning and the human level moved on the downward grade. In 1890 William II was told that if he displaced the bulky block of the "majordomo" he would find only "flattened worms" underneath. At the same time Herman Baumgarten in a dramatic reversal, spoke of the "great man who will bequeath to us great distress."

This is a note which stikes an even more responsive chord today than it did in the years after 1918. It concerns not only the decline in quality of German political conduct after Bismarck had gone or the self-centered and one-sided foundation of his work. More fundamentally the criticism points to the temptation to power for individuals and peoples, to the weakened sense of justice, to the arrest in civic maturity, to the glorification of expediency, to the contempt of humanitarian sentiments and moral scruples. However long and complex the way "from Bismarck to Hitler," the founder of the Reich certainly seems to stand for a "turn," or at least for legitimizing a "turn," the fateful climax of which has been only too manifest in our days.

The thesis of a disastrous "turn," however, has potentially a broader meaning than that referring in the main to moral categories. It is here, in the concrete historical matter, that the limits and some deficiencies, or even outright distortions come to the fore in the picture of "Bismarck seen by a liberal." The author, in his discussion of the sixties, does not exercise a radical criticism, such as has been sounded by other exiles in Switzerland. It is not the purpose of "national unification" as such but the Bismarckian means to this end which he rejects. In other words, he is a national liberal in the traditions of 1848 or rather of the Prussian progressive party. To him the "nation state" after the pattern of western Europe, including its democratic implications, is a natural aim for Germans just as much as for any other people. He does, therefore, not belong to the school of thought which recently and under the impact of totalitarianism has rediscovered such a man as Konstantin Frantz for the second time and sees in him (rather than in the advocates of the *Reichstaat* in Twesten, Gneist or Lasker) Bismarck's true antipode. Mr. Eyck has been blamed for this faulty perspective and half-way opposition,[8] for not realizing that the destiny of Germany and Europe was bound up with the revival (or survival) of a loose federation in the centre of the continent and that consequently, the real aberration was the *kleindeutsch* (or *grosspreussische*) solution as such, regardless of whether the means were those of "blood and iron" or of "moral conquest." This criticism is not quite just. There can be no doubt that Mr. Eyck combines or tries to combine, a sympathy with Prussian liberalism (and, of course, an aversion to the usual scapegoats: Junkers and military men) with a good deal of pro-Austrian feeling, with an approval of Bruck's "idealistic conception" of a Greater Germany (I, 202) and the last Habsburg attempt at reforming the German Confederation in 1863 (I, 519). But it is certainly true that he is no federalist in the central-European sense of the word and that any re-examination of Bismarck's historic role is incomplete which does not take this line of approach into account.

[8] See: Karl Thieme, *Das Schicksal der Deutschen* (Basel, Kobersche Verlagsbuchhandlung, 1945), pp. 104-107.

Whatever the bearing of the federalist thesis on the Reich of 1871—and some words will have to be said in that direction—it certainly touches upon fundamental problems of German history. Before coming back to that it may simply be stated that a revisionism which questions the nineteenth century idea of the "nation state" or its applicability to central Europe altogether, helps at least to clarify the horns of the dilemma with which Mr. Eyck is faced. In all his sincere liberalism he is obviously more "centralistic" than the man who is supposed to have started Germany the wrong way. Naturally he find Bismarck, the Prussian diplomat and "man of the state" lacking in "national motives" which he almost identifies with "ethical motives" (I, 578) though not so closely as Treitschke would have done. The author likewise seems to regret that Bismarck was not "attracted" by the idea to which E. M. Arndt in his song of the "German fatherland" had given so ringing an expression: "Good relations with the courts of Vienna and Petersburg were to him (Bismarck) more important than the fate of Austrian and Russian subjects of German tongue" (III, 29). With only a very slight change in verbal emphasis this could have been written by a Nazi critic of Bismarck just as well. In other words, the liberal and national position is not quite outside the danger line of certain accusations either.[9] And one wonders what severe judgment would be passed upon Bismarck today, if he had ever professed the same great-Prussian and annexationist aims which some liberals held (provided that Prussia turned "western") or if he had followed the centralistic and unitary policy which the liberal Crown Prince and the men around him advocated. As a matter of fact, some of the measures for which Mr. Eyck blames Bismarck are precisely those in which he came nearest, or made concessions to, liberal demands though he differed widely in motives. One may think of the annexation of Alsace-Lorraine or of the *Kulturkampf.* And it was no less a man than Gladstone who wrote in 1874: "Bismarck's ideas and methods are not ours; they spring out of other traditions, but my sympathies though they do not go with him, are more with him than against him. I cannot but say that the present doctrines of the Roman church destroy the title of her obedient members to the enjoyment of civil rights. . . ."[10]

These few remarks may suffice to indicate that the problem of the "turn" since the sixties and seventies had a much broader dimension and is much less specifically Bismarckian than it appears in the biography. They also point to a certain difficulty which runs through Mr. Eyck's book and ends up in a good deal of misinterpretation. From the moral and legal angle he cannot help having some sympathies with Prussian conservatives such as the Gerlachs, who certainly had principled views though he finds them, of course, reactionary. Among these views was the resolute rejection of the principle of nationality and its heathen consequences, a verdict which was shared in the sixties by Catholics, such as Lord Acton, and which was repeated by Konstantin Frantz in his book on federation in

---

[9] Since this was written the writer has read: L. B. Namier, *1848, the Revolution of the Intellectuals* (London, 1944). He will reply to this indictment of German liberalism in *Journal of Modern History* (September, 1947). But whatever Mr. Namier's exaggerations, he is certainly correct in stating that an aggressive nationalism "derives from the belauded Frankfort Parliament rather than from Bismarck and Prussianism." (*l.c.*, p. 33.) It can only be regretted that this insight seems to gain ground so belatedly. Not the slightest ripple of it has reached Mr. Eyck.

[10] P. Knaplund, *Letters from the Berlin Embassy (1871-85)* (Washington, 1944), p. 127. Mr. Eyck (III, 89, 163) mentions Gladstone's opposition to the Vatican decrees only in general terms.

1879. Mr. Eyck quotes with some approval Gerlach's thesis of 1850, that "the German nation had always ideals higher than the merely national idea" (I, 149). He finds in Bismarck nothing of these convictions but only the thought of future Prussian power. This dividing line is certainly correct though it appears overdrawn; it neglects Bismarck's turning away from a narrow Prussianism which made him a potential ally of the nationals without affecting his basic distrust of the principle of nationality. It was only along this road that Bismarck rose to statesmanship: by gradually emancipating himself from his conservative friends and accepting—with some limitations—the task which had been handed down from 1848. This, however, was a lengthy and complicated process, more painful than the author suggests (II, 186); it implied a soul struggle very much concerned with the problems of politics and morality, of revolution and legitimism. And it was a process which did not divorce Bismarck from fundamentally conservative views even during his most revolutionary period.

There is little echo of that in Mr. Eyck's biography. In fact, it must be difficult for him to appraise a man who appropriated national ends without sharing the underlying tenets and yet continued to have opinions which were not necessarily void of principles. The author's solution is typically "liberal" in as much as it overemphasizes the sovereignty of the "titanic" individual, his ability to handle and manipulate history at will. As mentioned before he pays a sort of aesthetic admiration to this virtuosity, and he is fair enough to see the other side in Bismarck which is not sheer will power: a personal tenderness, a poetic trait, his love of nature and music, his constant desire for retirement, his aversion to court life, to the cancerous growth of bureaucracy, to the *Racker Staat*, his ultimate insight into *vanitas vanitatum*. From a detached point of view there is something tragic about the man who in his old age confessed that policy had "devoured all other carps in his pond." To the author, however, this undercurrent is in the main the self-deception of a genius who is born to rule and knows it, who wants power in the first place for himself,[11] who pretends only to be loyal to his king and in fact speaks of him in the most abusive terms, who lies whenever it suits him and uses his unusual frankness[12] for the same purpose of deception, who hates and persecutes his opponents, both dead and alive, and identifies himself with his work to the extent that he may be able to destroy what he had created himself.

No doubt many and reliable evidences are available to bear out such a picture, though some gossip has also gone into it.[13] It is not necessary to insist upon retouching any details. But regarding the central point the fact cannot be omitted that Bismarck himself, though he profoundly influenced the course of events, was

---

[11] See I, 32, II, 242-43 (Sadowa was his victory; what fruits would it bear to *him?*), III, 381.

[12] The "obstinate veracity" of which John Motley spoke.

[13] Though the author does not fail to indicate the problematic character of some of his sources, the reader is constantly exposed to "the semper haeret aliquid." This is one of the reservations which has to be added to the appraisal of the fairness of the book. Also in the treatment of Bismarck's "grasping" nature, the documents regarding his double role as minister and as "subject" would be corrective and the book by Bismarck's head forester in Varzin (E. Westphal, *Bismarck als Gutsherr*, Leipzig, 1932) gives an entirely different picture. In the matter of the *Welfenfond* (II, 369-78) there is certainly every good reason for criticism, yet in fairness it may be added that it was not only used for press propaganda or for "bribing" Ludwig II (III, 553-555) but that part of the revenue went into public buildings and the improvement of the Northsea resort Nordeney, in order to continue or even increase payments formerly made by the dispossessed princes. (Bismarck, *Saemtliche Werke* VI, pp. 506, 553-554.)

not a liberal who thinks in emphatic terms about what the individual can do. Being certainly a master of surprising turns and endowed with the greatest flexibility, he confessed at the end of the Franco-German war, with a ring of sincerity: *fert unda nec regitur*. Even in his stormy beginnings it did not occur to him that history could be basically manipulated; and he tended, if changes had to be made, to cut them down as far as possible. He liked to take his figures of speech from the sphere of the peasant, the fisherman and the hunter who does not move unnecessarily, who always probes the ground before taking the step and who can wait. This attitude became all the more explicit as the years went by until Bismarck eventually confessed: "The statesman cannot create the stream of time, he can only navigate on it." Or to quote another word: "The statesman must try and reach for the hem upon hearing the garment of God rustling through events."

None of these evidences has been taken into account. Of course, they are autobiographic and do not tell the full story. But they cannot simply be discarded without the slightest reference—all the less so, since Bismarck's practical policy, even in the years before 1870, corroborates them to a large extent. There are, to be sure, many documents which show an amazing gift of prophecy on his part, which outline, more or less conditionally, the course he actually did take between 1863 and 1870. And if the story is built on this ground, it naturally appeals to the sense of the dramatic while at the same time bringing out, by implication, the arbitrariness of the means resorted to. Such is Mr. Eyck's technique throughout. But there are many other evidences, particularly among the recently published documents, which prove that Bismarck was far from a "one way policy" or from an early conception of a one and only solution by the sword. In this respect a good deal had already been learned by critical historians in many countries before Mr. Eyck wrote. As Dr. G. P. Gooch expressed it fifteen years ago: "The notion of the implacable Prussian sharpening the knife for the Austrian throat. . . fades away."[14] Mr. Eyck's discussion of this problem seems a drawback and rather strained (esp. II, 15-16). Neither the plan of the so-called "peaceful dualism" before 1866 nor that of a tripartite system in the years after Sadowa are considered on the basis of their respective merits. Nor are the documents fully and impartially used. To instance only one of the major gaps, there is an instruction of February 26, 1869 which Bismarck wrote to the Prussian minister in Munich:[15] "To me also it seems likely that the German unification will have to be promoted by forceful events. But to assume the role of provoking a catastrophe and the responsibility for choosing the right moment, this is quite a different proposition. An arbitrary and merely subjective interference with the course of history has always resulted only in beating off fruits which were not ripe. It seems to me obvious that German unity is at this moment not yet a ripe fruit." Bismarck added that if the years to come would proceed in the same way as they had done since the time of Fredrick the Great, and particularly since 1840 "we can look to the future with tranquility and leave the rest to our descendants." Or as he says in the concluding sentence: "We can advance the clock but the time does not move more quickly for that matter."

Whatever the tactical motives implied, this instruction certainly mirrors a genuine attitude which would be borne out by many other evidences. In fact, the aversion

[14] *Studies in Modern History* (1931), p. 241. Practically the same shift in evaluation (on the basis of new sources) was acknowledged by L.D. Steefel, one of the best American experts in the field of Bismarck research. See his bibliographical article in *Journal of Modern History*, vol. II, 1930.
[15] Bismarck: *Die Gesammelten Werke* (1931), vol. VI, b., p.2.

to "arbitrary and merely subjective interference with the course of history" was given expression by Bismarck time and time again. This does not mean that he did not interfere, when the moment came, nor that some of his decisions may not seriously be questioned. A good deal of criticism can be applied to the incorporation of Schleswig-Holstein which opened the way for extending Prussia, whereas Bismarck's restraint in 1866 rather calls for admiration. That the wisdom of re-annexing Alsace-Lorraine can be questioned goes without saying and it was questioned by Bismarck himself. He took the "lost provinces," as is well known, not for national reasons of history and language, upon which almost all liberals agreed, but for reasons of military security, of protection against a nation "which for 300 years has been in the habit of invading us." Or as the American minister in Berlin, the historian Bancroft, said precisely along the same line: "The main thing now is to protect Germany by better frontiers against aggressions from the West of which there has been such a great number during the last 300 years."

This brings the discussion back to Mr. Eyck's underlying assumption that the German national unity which he himself finds natural, would have been attainable by other and less forceful means than those of Bismarck. This is a hypothesis which, of course, can neither be proved nor repudiated. It can be said however, and in view of many "legends" it seems a matter of fairness to do so today, that there was little "western" sympathy with the attempt at founding a "good" German Reich, that is, one on the liberal-democratic basis of 1848. While Disraeli spoke of "the 50 mad professors at Frankfort," Palmerston felt alarmed by the development of a *"nation inconnu jusqu'ici au Foreign Office."* And Thiers later confessed that if he could have had his way in 1848 he would have extended the French frontiers to the Rhine and taken "the keys of Germany" into hand. When it eventually came to the half-liberal "policy of union" in 1850 it ended with a deadlock enforced by a Russo-Austrian ultimatum. Even Radowitz's very moderate aims would have to be carried out by arms. Nor was the diplomatic record of the "new era" in Prussia altogether promising. When the liberal policy of "moral conquest" was at its height in 1860, the *London Times* had this to say:[16] "Prussia is always leaning on somebody, always getting somebody to help her, never willing to help herself; always ready to deliberate, never to decide; present in Congresses, but absent in battles; speaking and writing, never for or against, but only on the question; ready to supply any amount of ideals or sentiments, but shy of anything that savors of the real or the actual. She has a large army, but notoriously one in no condition for fighting. She is profuse in circulars and notes, but has generally a little to say for both sides. No one counts her as a friend, no one dreads her as an enemy. How she became a great Power history tells us, why she remains so nobody can tell. . . . Prussia unaided could not keep the Rhine or the Vistula for a month from her ambitious neighbors."

Mr. Eyck has a rather optimistic view of these "ambitious neighbors," in particular of the French tradition of advancing to the East,[17] a view which was shared neither by the German socialists circa 1860 nor by the lauded Konstantin Frantz for that matter. It seems worthy of mentioning that the federalist thinker started from the very assumption of a double threat to *Mitteleuropa.*[18] He

---

[16] Quoted by R. J. Sontag, *Germany and England 1848-1894* (New York, 1938), p. 33.

[17] See his discussion of the "idealism" of Napoleon III and of Ranke's "pompous" reference to Louis XIV (II, 569).

[18] Particularly in his *Untersuchungen über das Europäische Gleichgewicht* (1859).

therefore advocated a universal system in the centre of the continent with a voluntary union of the historic states as its nucleus, a loose German and non-German federation, which Holland, Sweden, Denmark might join and England might protect. Such a system would guarantee peace by turning Russia's and France's ambitions to Asia and North Africa respectively. One may pay high tribute to this idealistic scheme and yet seriously doubt its chance of overcoming particularism by persuasion or achieving a British willingness to enter upon central European commitments and to sympathize with the economic perspectives of a great federative bloc (united by mutual preferences!). It is only in an entirely different situation, against the background of a post-Bismarckian development and with foreign powers ruling over Central Europe, that the federalist concept or rather that of a "Central European Switzerland" has gained a new meaning.

It would appear then that the consolidation of the weak centre of Europe presupposed other means than those suggested by Frantz and that the nucleus had to be created by diplomatic action rather than by a plea for sympathy or a moral appeal. Whether war was absolutely necessary may be doubted and certainly can not be demonstrated.[19] But it is definitely wrong to say that only the forceful foundation of the Reich of 1871 produced the *cauchemar des coalitions* as a sort of self-inflicted punishment. The conviction of a double threat was not of Bismarck's making. It had been widespread among the liberals of Germany around 1860 in the same sense as it was shared by Frantz. And it was the basis of Bismarck's diplomacy before 1870 just as much as afterwards it was simply a Central European fact. Only by a new distribution of power and a new security, in Bismarck's view, could the aim be reached (which he had in common with Frantz), of turning Russia's and France's ambitions "to Asia and North Africa respectively."

This criticism of some federalist illusions, however, should not prevent us from seeing that the pre- or supra-national and anti-centralistic elements in the structure of Bismarck's Reich came nearer to a basic federalism than is ordinarily realized. On this point Mr. Eyck's book falls particularly short of the mark. The fact that Bismarck stressed the institutional links between the old German Confederation and the new Reich, that he checked the Reichstag and its universal suffrage by the "anonymous-phalanx" of the federative council, that he kept the competence of the central organs within very narrow limits, that he resisted successfully a responsible Reichsministry—all this was, in the author's view, mere tactics and only meant to concentrate the real power in Prussia and, in the last analysis, in Bismarck's hands. There is truth in this interpretation, not a new one for that matter, but it is by far not the full truth or the most substantial part of it.[20] Again all evidences are omitted which refer to some of the underlying principles. It is certainly not uninteresting and beside the point to recall today such principles as Bismarck expressed in the Reichstag (April 16, 1869): ". . . In Germanic states one should not ask . . . what can be in common, how far can the great mouth of the commonwealth swallow the apple (*hineinbeissen in den Apfel*)—but rather one should ask: what must be absolutely in common." It seems safe to say that Bismarck, quite apart from other elements of his thought, was Junker enough to be anti-totalitarian in principle. More consideration should also be given to his plans to supplement the Reichstag by *staendische* organizations. Particularly in connection with the plan for

---

[19] Again this writer does not go as far as Mr. Namier does (see note 9).
[20] For Bismarck's system of "integration" the book of the jurist, R. Smend, *Verfassung und Verfassungsrecht* might have been consulted with usefulness.

compulsory insurance against accidents, he thought of a network of professional associations to be spread over the country.[21] This again implies anti-parliamentary tactics but also an insight into the dangerous process of social atomization. While in all this there was a federalist aspect domestically, the non-centralistic setup of the Reich had a broader meaning as a pattern of transition to other federative forms beyond the frontiers: Germany with her composite character might indicate, as Bismarck pointed out, a method by the use of which "Austria could reach a reconciliation of the political and material interests which exist between the Eastern frontiers of the Russians and the Bay of Cattaro."

These potentialities are often overlooked. They are certainly not seen by Mr. Eyck and he seems to be completely and rather naively unaware of the nationalist implications of a unitary and democratic German Reich in Central Europe or of Bruck's "Greater Germany." In contrast Bismarck's national state was no "nation state" proper; it included non-Germans (about 10%) and it did not include and ought not to have included all Germans. Jokingly Bismarck once said that, if the nine million contiguous Germans in Austria ever would try to join the Reich, he would wage war against them. In more serious words he admonished them that, instead of harking back, they should take the lead in evolving a multi-national combine in the South-East. The same restraint he observed towards the Germans in Russia, and he did so not only for diplomatic or opportunistic reasons. His so-called *étatisme* may have been a major limitation in some aspects of domestic policy; but what was opposition to democracy was at the same time opposition to nationalism. What was an attempt at checking "social atomism" was paralleled by a check on the trend towards a "national atomism" which would disintegrate Central Europe and end in a "war of races." That is why Bismarck opposed pangermanism no less than panslavism.

In this negative attitude—or rather in this conservative restraint—there was implied some positive appraisal of variety and multi-national forms of life. There was at least much more of it than liberal and federalist critics usually realize. The Crown Prince may have been thunderstuck when Bismarck, in 1870, admonished him to have his son learn the Polish language or when he added that all the Prussian rulers down to Frederick the Great had known it—and that he knew it himself. To the liberal biographer these remarks do not seem to have made any more sense than they probably made to the Crown Prince. Incidentally, Mr. Eyck does not speak of the anti-Polish "settlement law" of 1886 (*Ansiedlungsgesetz*) which ranks so high on the list of Prussian *hakatism*. As a matter of fact the settlement of German peasants in the eastern provinces was urged by the national liberals. Bismarck yielded to them but professed no sympathy with uprooting the Polish peasants or depriving them of their language. In his old age he spoke of the intermingling of peoples in the East as "riches willed by God." Whatever the shortcomings of his Polish policy he was certainly as remote from racialism and biologism as anyone could be.[22]

---

[21] Evidences for this in the writer's, *Theodor Lohmann und die Kampf jahre der staatlichen Sozialpolitik* (1927), pp. 63-64.

[22] The above interpretation of certain federalist trends in Bismarck's policy has been worked out by the writer in his *Bismarck und der Osten, Eine Studie zum Problem des deutschen Nationalstaats* (Leipzig, 1934). The study goes back to an address which was given in 1932 at the last pre-Nazi meeting of German historians and which ended with an attack on the "myth of the 20th century" (Rosenberg) as well as on that of the 19th century, i.e., the dogma of the "nation state." (The address is reprinted in the writer's: *Ostraum, Preussentum und*

I do not believe that these aspects have been left out on purpose. They may appear as residua of a little known old-Prussian "policy of nationalities" and simply not interesting from a Western liberal and national angle. But these omissions contribute toward making the third volume the least satisfactory. True, it contains also brilliant pages, particularly in the presentation of parliamentary history. And there is no doubt that the tactical motives of Bismarck, for example, the use of foreign policy for electioneering maneuvers come out more clearly than before. But again, and increasingly so, the tactical interpretation, while leading to a high appraisal of Bismarck's "virtuosity," misses many important points. It misses a full appreciation of the fact (which William L. Langer very well expressed as early as 1931) that Bismarck is the rare example of a European statesman who, after amazing successes, did not succumb to intoxication or the impelling drive which leads on. And it misses the basic views and experiences which are implied in this restraint, the opposition to ideological concepts (whether liberal or anglophile or pangerman) as well as to military trends, both of which would have caused an "unnecessary" war with Russia, the distinction between "questions of life" and "questions of mere interest," the aversion to a policy of prestige and uncontrolled emotions or to engagements which would follow from economic expansion. In these respects again Mr. Eyck's biography must be characterized as a definite drawback. In his book Bismarck's foreign policy after 1871 appears mainly in its undeniable complications; it seems artificially built up because little attention is given to its underlying principles: the support of the interests of all other European powers within a given sphere, and the basic view of Germany's saturation or her disinterestedness in any aggrandizement which forms the backbone of the system. In fact documents which show Bismarck's concept as a whole (for example the *Kissinger Diktat*) are omitted, and not a few among the others are seriously misread or outright misinterpreted.[23]

But the writer does not want this article to end on a note of professional controversy. There is more at stake than that. We may criticize Bismarck for many good reasons, for paving the way to some fatal trends of our days, but while doing so we cannot very well overlook the fundamental fact that Hitler, in almost every respect, did precisely what the founder of the Reich had refused to do. Many of those who were under the heel inside or outside Germany, had an appreciation of this fact. And thus the word of the Danish historian may be taken up once more as a summary which draws the essential frontier line: Bismarck certainly "belonged to our world," that is, to the anti-Hitlerian world. That this was not generally realized is in part the fault of Germans and German historians themselves. But it may be called a kind of saving grace that revival of genuine Bismarckian thought (as different from the old Bismarck orthodoxy) was one of the forces which went into

Reichgedanke (Leipzig, 1935), pp.65-93. If W. Roepke, *Die deutsche Frage* (2, A, 1945, p. 103 note), justly admires the courage of a German philologist who in 1940 (while writing on the Greek polis) declared the nation state to be only one political form among others, he seems to have overlooked that before, and still in the first years after 1933, there was a whole group of German writers and historians who openly assailed the general validity of the (western) dogma of the nation state and pleaded for a federative reconstruction of Central Europe with full autonomy for all the nations involved.

[23] This applies, e.g., to the Livadia episode, to the negotiations with Britain in 79, to the so-called "bogus document" of 84, to Bismarck's letter to Salisbury of 87, and to the Reinsurance Treaty. For all these matters and many others, consult William L. Langer's *European Alliances and Alignments* (1931), rather than Mr. Eyck's book.

the making of the German resistance against Hitler.[24] Specifically "Prussian" elements as far as they remained alive after the landslide of 1933 were also in the anti-Nazi camp. To state this is no longer a matter of any particular importance since these forces have been radically eliminated, but it seems to be a matter of historical justice.

THE BISMARCK PROBLEM

Franz Schnabel

* * *

The empire which Bismarck founded lasted half a century. When it fell, historians centred their interest upon the personality and life work of this man who, more than any other, put his own stamp upon the second half of the nineteenth century. What was written before 1918 on this great problem must now be considered for the most part obsolete. After the collapse of the German Empire and the monarchies in the middle and small German states, the archives were opened and a profusion of important, unknown documents brought to light. The events which took place in Germany between 1918 and 1945 were such, moreover, as to make men question what Bismarck did and said, what he was and what he wanted. Or, they made men change what he brought about. One after another all Bismarck's opponents have risen again; once more they have borne testimony against him. The multitude of those who in his lifetime heaped praise upon him, citing the success of his endeavours, were too hasty in their conclusions. Men had to learn from experience, like those before them, that only a much later age can pass final judgment on success in history—the Empire which began so brilliantly stood but for fifty years. There were times, to be sure, when Bismarck himself spoke with profound pessimism of the durability of his achievement. After his dismissal, domestic and foreign difficulties in fact continued to multiply. But dominant public opinion brushed aside any suggestion that the course along which Bismarck had directed German and European history was responsible for this state of affairs. The more painfully obvious were the shortcomings of his successors and the emperor under whom they served, the easier it seemed to bring forward the founder of the Reich in edifying contrast to them.

After the first catastrophe in 1918, however, the spiritual descendants of the earlier German liberalism and democrats took the field. They established Bismarck's responsibility for the predominance of the policy of "Blood and Iron." They voiced regret that ever since Bismarck the people and the parties had always played the role of followers or opposition, but not of participants in responsibility in the "authoritarian state" which bore the impress of the Prussian system. Bismarck was

---

[24] It happened by coincidence (though hardly, incidentally) that one of the leaders of anti-Nazi conspiracy, Ulrich v. Hassell, who was designated to be the Foreign Minister of the "Other Germany" (see note 4) paid a visit to Friedrichsruhe just 10 days before the fatal attempt of 20th of July 1944, for which he was to die on the gallows. The last entry in his diaries (*l.c.,* p.363) discusses two aspects of the problems with which this paper dealt: the distorted picture of Bismarck's "power policy" which was presented to the world and his true stature as one of the greatest and most moderate diplomats in history.

also criticized for having over-estimated the vitality of the Austro-Hungarian monarchy and neglected therefore to bring about *Anschluss*. Thereafter, as cupidity increasingly took the place of concern for the state and political life as such, as the masses ceased to think of the interests of the state, which guaranteed law and order, and should have provided their rational guide to action, as nationalism and neo-romanticism, literary scribblings (*Literatentum*) and theories of the "folk" (*Volk*) gained the upper hand, Bismarck's reputation began to decline correspondingly. Though once, in an exchange of opinions with Gottfried Kinkel,[1] he drew a distinction between his soul, the "soul of a diplomat," and the heart of the patriotic leader, the heart of a poet, men at that time began to draw closer again to the patriots of the period when unification was being prepared. They were extolled because they wished to unite all "folk comrades" (*Volksgenossen*) and "bring home" the *"disjecta membra"* into the empire for which they strove, and because they wished therefore to reorganize Europe upon the basis of folk membership (*Volkstrum*) and tongue. In this way, men knew, the old princely policy of territorial incorporations could be continued by a new, folkish policy of incorporations; but they did not gladly have their attention drawn to the fact that it was the doctrines of German romanticism which first really brought the nationalities of eastern Europe into movement. But, in the twentieth century, the national state conception reached a complete *reductio ad absurdum*; it brought incalculable disaster upon millions who were driven from their homes because of the language they spoke and the people to which they belonged. Not surprisingly, therefore, men found reason to reexamine critically the entire national state movement since 1815, which had resulted in endless disorder, two world wars, and catastrophe; nor was it surprising either that they called up again those opponents of Bismarck who combated his power-permeated concept of the state, his alliance with the German national state idea, and who condemned the division of Europe into national states and demanded a European federal structure.

Thus the age of Bismarck lies today concealed in profound obscurity. We do have the documents at hand, but interpreting them is difficult because, living in devastated lands, we find it hard to attain that lofty and far-off vantage point where the historian must take his stand. In earlier ages, when historical awareness had not yet been formed, men came quickly to their own aid in explaining things. Among us, too, resentment will bring about simplification. States and empires, it is said, decline for the same reasons by which they rise. Thus an effort has been made to find a single trace that goes from Bismarck to Hitler, from the "Iron Chancellor," the man in cavalry boots, to the National-Socialist policy of violence. But this means forgetting the popular and revolutionary forces which had been at work ever since 1815. To remember where we must seek in German history for the spiritual ancestors of modern demagogy, of explosive ideologies, of the extolling of violence, we need merely read the sentences written in 1833 by Heinrich Heine in which he drew the outlines of the future German revolution. At that time Lorenz Oken,[2] the philosopher of nature who has been lauded as the "great revolutionary," tried to start a movement of revolutionary enthusiasm among the youth in Germany and was expelled from the University of Jena, on Goethe's decision, as a "Catilinarian."

---

[1] Gottfried Kinkel (1815-82), German revolutionary poet, professor at Bonn; aided to escape (1850) from prison by Carl Schurz.

[2] Lorenz Oken (1779-1851), German scientist and philosopher, leading philosopher of nature of the romantic period.

As always, things were expected to take place faster than they actually occurred. But under the immediate impact of the Hambach Festival of 1832 which J. G. A. Wirth[3] organized, Heine felt so bold as to prophesy:

Kantians unwilling to hear of any piety in the phenomenal world either, ruthlessly upsetting the foundations of our European life, will make their appearance. Armed Fichteans unwilling to be hampered by aught in their fanatic wilfulness will take the stage. But most terrible of all will be the philosophers of nature, unleashing the daemonic forces of the German pantheism of yore and thus awakening that battle passion which fights not to win, but merely to fight. . . . To some extent, Christianity has mitigated that Germanic battle passion. But once the Cross is broken, then the clangour of that wildness of which the Nordic poets sing and speak so much will be heard again. . . . But when you hear such a crashing and clanging as was never before heard in the history of the world, then a drama will be played out in Germany, alongside which the French Revolution will seem but a harmless idyll. To be sure, things are still quiet among us; we do not as yet know whether the Crown Prince of Prussia or Dr. Wirth will come to power in Germany. But do not believe that one day to come these will appear upon the scene as the real actors. They are only the curs running about in the empty arena and snarling at each other, before the hour comes when the troop of gladiators enters who will fight for life and death. And that hour will come! The peoples will gather round Germany, as if seated upon the banks of an amphitheatre, to see the great battle-play.[4]

It must be admitted that in the procession of such antecedents there is no place for Bismarck. It is still our task to define his position in the history of Europe, and to determine what were the opportunities that were then open to him and to other positive forces in German history, as well. These were opportunities which he hampered or destroyed. During the last war a valuable start in this task was made by Erich Eyck. His three-volume biography of Bismarck was written and published outside of Germany. It is a work of high scholarly standing. Based upon knowledge of all the German and European sources, it is well written and to the point. It is, in fact, the first large, rounded biography of Bismarck. None the less, its description of Bismarck cannot be accepted as definitive. The discussion already under way over this important work must be continued; it can become fruitful and contribute to solving the problems which we still find in understanding Bismarck, the man, and his life work. We must frankly say that Eyck was able to write an imposing and easily understood work because he examined the play of opposing forces from a fixed position. But unfortunately, in taking this position, Eyck did not rise above the times. He stayed down amidst the embattled political parties. True, the author, thanks to his great skill as a writer, was able to leave the polemics of those strife-filled decades far behind him. Only a few presently current turns of phrase hinder the flow of the narrative here and there. The personal greatness of Bismarck is recognized, and the author, when he comes up against the weaknesses of Bismarck's foes, does not keep silence about them. But Eyck is convinced that the national-liberal movement of the sixties was on the right track, that it could really have established the German national state in conformity with its own ideals. Eyck

---

[3] Johann Georg August Wirth (1798-1848), German democratic leader; organizer of the Hambach Festival of revolutionary youth, May 27, 1832.

[4] Tempel ed. (Leipzig, n.d.), vii, pp. 424-26 (modified).

belongs among those opponents of Bismarck who may be called "German Whigs." They included persons in the highest reaches of society, including the royal family and the liberal princely courts. For the new Bismarck biographer, Gladstone is the lofty ideal of a statesman. Eyck, who lives in England, has written a fine monographic study on Gladstone. Bismarck, the great hater, held no other statesman of his time in such scorn as "the Grand Old Man" who let his policy be guided by humanitarian and even pacifist ideals, opposed the advance of imperialism, approached the Irish nationalist movement in an accommodating spirit, and extended the suffrage for the British parliament. According to Eyck, Bismarck's interference with the development of conditions for the rise of a statesman like Gladstone in Prussia and Germany was the source of all the evil to come for Germany and for Europe.

By now the reader will have realized that Eyck accepts without further ado the position that the isolated national state with centralized institutions was the only correct and possible solution of the "German question," the only one corresponding to the strivings of the German people for unity. He directs his criticism just at the methods which Bismarck employed. In Eyck's opinion, if Bismarck had given more consideration to the ideals of his liberal allies, the internal structure of the new Reich would have met the needs of that day better and would have been more durable as well. Moreover, it would have been possible to found the Reich without using the violent methods which Bismarck did. Eyck voices most profound regret that the new state was born with the flaw of lawbreaking and violence, and that German liberalism developed from a party of law and order into a service group of success worshipers.

Certainly, this is not a new train of thought. There were always at least a few liberal and democratic writers in Germany, during and after Bismarck's imperial chancellorship, who held firm to ideals of freedom and humanity, deplored their loss in Germany when it came under Prussian control, and therefore remained at all times critics of Bismarck. But they produced no major historical work. They were not able to distinguish and correctly to evaluate, upon the basis of detailed research, the various streams within the liberal and democratic movement. They had no importance compared with the specialists, from Sybel down to Erich Marcks, who did the valuable scholarly service of refuting the claims which the reigning monarch [William II] made on behalf of his grandfather [William I, "the Great"]; but these erstwhile leading historians took part in the movement of liberalism into Bismarck's camp, they defended it and found it to be in conformity with the needs of modern times. Eyck is the first person who has managed to put forward the position of the liberal opponents of Bismarck in a large, well-supported analysis. Since Eyck's work is becoming known in Germany at a time when, after a lapse of almost half a century, the spiritual and political ideas of Western European liberalism are again acceptable, there is a danger that the old myth, which justified and praised Bismarck as the "*Realpolitiker*" will now be replaced by a new historical myth. All the more must our thanks go to Eyck for his analysis, which affords us a reason for examining in a fundamental way the problems of Bismarck's achievements and establishing the facts in the matter.

Hans Rothfels, now of the University of Chicago, has set down in a far-reaching critique, "Problems of a Bismarck Biography," the principle points which must be made against Eyck's approach. Not only did he carry the analysis forward, he also greatly simplified it. The assumption that the goal which Bismarck and the liberals shared—the little-German (*kleindeutsch*) national state under Prussian leadership—could have been achieved without the methods employed by Bismarck, and that Bismarck brought the *kleindeutsch* Empire into ill repute by his methods, is one which cannot be proved. All the evidence we have supports the position that the powers accepted only unwillingly the formation of a new national state in the heart of Europe. Either, like Napoleon III, they wished for "compensations," or they were surprised by Bismarck's procedure and did not have time to prepare themselves spiritually and materially to counter it. All the virtuosity of Bismarck's manipulation of the rival powers, his skill in the handling of men and his daring as well, were required to achieve the goal. It was not alone the extension of Prussian power which the other states disliked. They did see with misgivings that the traditions of Frederick the Great had been taken up again, that the old policy of rounding-off the borders of Prussia and conquering new territories which at an earlier time had been directed against Saxony, now led to the annexation of Schleswig-Holstein and the kingdom of Hanover. But the programme of establishing a national state, which at the outset had nothing to do with the Prussian drive for expansion and a Frederician policy, gave the powers no less reason for anxiety and interference. Whether or not German nationalism became an ally of Bismarck, the liberals would have come into conflict with Europe. As early as the Hambach Festival of 1832, when most of the participants were wholly under the influence of the French revolutionary spirit and of Franco-German fraternization, the speakers could not refrain from rejecting France's claim to the left bank of the Rhine, and J. G. A. Wirth dared openly to express the view that the desired unification of Germany "very probably" would also have as a result the return of Alsace-Lorraine to the ancient homeland. The executive committee of the festival then eliminated this phrase from the official minutes, "in deference to the friendly French people," and there were many who took amiss the speaker's "slip." But the *"furor teutonicus"*—as the favorite catchword of the Bismarckian period ran—burned brightly precisely after 1859, and without Bismarck's intervention. The *kleindeutsch* patriots were scarcely ready to grant compensations to Napoleon III and to renounce the left bank of the Rhine. The German variety of nationalists in St. Paul's Church [where the National Assembly met in Frankfurt in 1848] had thrashed it all out! How many times had the verse *"So weit die deutsch Zunge klingt!"*[5] ('Where'er is heard the German tongue!) been reiterated within its walls, as the basis for far-reaching claims! Amid great applause a speaker in the National Assembly at Frankfurt declared that one could not draw the sword for the Germans in Schleswig and at the same time abandon South Tyrol. It became evident at St. Paul's Church that there were *irredenta* in many parts of Europe; the courts and governments of the powers agreed that to treat status as a people (*Volkstum*), nation and national state, as mutually equivalent expressions, was a "Germanism." They saw it as a great error which, as Ernest Renan expressed it in 1882, "if it came to dominate, would hurl Europe into immense wars and destroy its civilization." As a matter of fact, the governments feared the ideology of the German liberals and democrats more than the ambitions of the Prussian statesman. True the *kleindeutsch* programme was limited to strict boundaries, but once released and given wing by its first success, the movement would necessarily develop its latent tendencies and would then be able to make use of Bismarck's power

[5] A famous patriotic poem, *The German's Fatherland*, by Ernst Moritz Arndt.

methods. We need merely to recall the great interest which was given to the question of the "Germans in the outside world" at the festivals of gymnastic, rifle, singing and Schiller societies since 1840. After 1859 this element of national ambition kept emphatically to the front; even the *Kleindeutschen* could not remain free of it. It was expected in the European courts after 1871 that a period of pan-Germanic expansion would begin, and there was astonishment and a return to calm feelings when it was seen that such plans were far indeed from Bismarck's mind.

But the movement of folk groupings was the very force which, as soon as it could attain freedom for development, had to bring disorder and war upon Europe. Among the peoples of Europe, ambitious to make their own states, the belief in humanity and the solidarity of free nations, each developing along its own lines, did not prevent an embittered struggle from breaking out at once over the frontiers of provinces and folk groupings. Though still in vain, Robert Blum,[6] together with the leaders of the nationalities of eastern Europe, had already sought to bring about the dismemberment of the Habsburg Empire, in order to split away the Germans of Austria from all the other nationalities, bringing the Germans into a centralized unified Republic. This goal was not abandoned. Yet its achievement would have brought European chaos, as Metternich and Grillparzer in Vienna, the midpoint of many nations, had predicted. In our own day, we have experienced its terrible results. The beginnings of a secular nationalist "revivalist movement" were already quite strong in 1848. Blum, it is true, did not become the "leader and arouser of the people," and no one in Germany was called upon to play the role which was enacted in Hungary by Louis Kossuth; to a remarkable degree the German movement on behalf of a national state ran an anonymous course. Then Bismarck, having brought the liberals both into alliance and into subordination, took the rudder; thereafter there was no place for a patriotic leader like Gottfried Kinkel. Bismarck held fast to the traditions of the old statecraft, and thereby placed the German movement under the command of the state-centred conception. He maintained it in the form of a constitutional monarchy, in correspondence with the relationship of forces which existed within Germany after almost all German states had received such constitutions. The wars which he waged were in their own way wars for unification. They were not organized as people's wars, but were conducted in the strict forms laid down in the armies of the kings, and with strict, wholly political aims. We must always recall to our memories the sentence which proved such breadth of vision and which has received such frightening confirmation: "What ought to be placed in that part of Europe which is at present occupied by the Austro-Hungarian monarchy? New creations in this soil could only be of a revolutionary character."

This—and just this—was the decisive course of events. Bismarck thwarted not only the beginnings of a liberal and democratic movement, but he restrained the development of [Central] European nationalism in general, which for specific, historically verifiable reasons had arisen in close relationship with the liberal and constitutionalist conception, but, where it could develop, ended in dictatorship, the centralized unitary republic, and unlimited expansion. How Louis Kossuth, Mazzini and Daniele Manin were extolled in the democratic journals of bourgeois

---

[6] Robert Blum (1807-48), German political leader; head of Left at Frankfurt Assembly; executed (November 1848) by Austrians for part in Vienna uprising.

democracy, *Didaskalia* and *Gartenlaube*, although they were certainly not liberal and constitutionalist politicians; one wished to extend Hungary to the crest of the Carpathians, the other Italy to the Brenner frontier! Even Ferdinand Lassalle had entered upon a similar path, though he started from a different point of departure; he was a fervent patriot, and he would have favoured, in fact, a *grossdeutsch* socialist centralized republic. The extent to which the liberal upper bourgeoisie could construct a barrier from its own resources is very questionable. They could not bring forth, and could not desire, an arouser of the people. Into the gap stepped the statesman who had nothing in common with the dictators of the nationalist period, but had his origin in classic diplomacy and statecraft.

For historical science it is a question of assigning to Bismarck his correct place in the historical sequence, not of justifying him or "vindicating his honour." he had naught to do with the doctrines of folk and living space (*Lebensraum*), with the old imperial idea, or with what Eichendorff[7] so ironically called "modern patrioteering" (*moderne Vaterländerei*); the patriots and national heroes, as they arose everywhere in the wake of nationalism, were of different stamp. In his old age he permitted himself to take pleasure in popularity and noisy hero-worship, which were foreign to aristocratic times. But he did not owe his successes, certainly, to the "Third Estate" or to the masses, but rather to the mastery with which he controlled the rules of the older diplomacy. Actions and transactions involving the courts and states had been developed to a high level of science and art in the chancelleries of the Italian Renaissance and the absolute monarchy of the French type. European unity was smashed to bits upon this mosaic pattern of politics, and Machiavellianism came into practice. After the kings and their counsellors had brought this to pass, nationalism pushed them aside, took over and further developed their methods and works, and adapted them to the needs of the masses who were coming into prominence. The history of the rise and decline of classic diplomacy has still to be written, however rich the sources available for it; we have only fragments from the hands of experienced diplomatists. Bismarck is the last great representative in the line of classic diplomats, which begins with the famed Venetian ambassadors and the papal nuncios of the sixteenth century. He did not in any way create a new type, but rather acted out to the full an old and strong departmental tradition. Even in his time diplomacy was in the process of becoming a bureaucratized profession with a strict course of training and a caste-stratified pattern of promotion. When Junker Bismarck, then only the squire of Schönhausen, still on the lower rungs of his career as officer and jurist, entered their caste as an outsider, those who had served according to the rules were discontented. While he had deserved well of the crown in his service as a deputy, he had made his way into diplomacy by the detour of parliament. But he soon acquired the gentlemanly training of the international high society of Europe, to which stratum he belonged by origin and effort; his first assignment to Frankfurt as Prussian envoy to the Federal Diet gave him an opportunity to acquire experience and develop his abilities. His memoirs still give us today a direct impression of the way in which, in the style of the old diplomacy, he evaluated the forces at work in every situation which confronted him, and tested, and to some extent calculated through, all possible combinations one after another. Thus he was a "member of the guild" with Choiseul, Kaunitz, Talleyrand and Metternich, all of whom left us their memoirs;

[7] Joseph, Freiherr von Eichendorff (1788-1857), German romantic poet.

however different were the states and interests which they represented, politics was for each of them an exact science concerned with calculable magnitudes. We may let the question rest whether there is a difference of spiritual rank between Bismarck and his great predecessors, and it has been observed of his manner of negotiating that he had been in the habit of peddling his wool on the market square in Stettin. Talleyrand and Metternich, the bishop of the Gallican church and the Rhenish nobleman, had still absorbed the lofty intellectual culture of the *ancien régime*. But, in the last analysis, the East Elbian Junker had belonged to the exclusive student *Korps* at the University of Gottingen, educated himself in the world of society, and always maintained a French recess in his mind.

To be sure, Bismarck, as minister of a constitutional monarch, had to count no longer with potentates, courtiers and favorites. He had to play not only in the "concert of Europe," but also on the instrument of parliament as well. And here then was to be seen the limits beyond which the old classic diplomacy did not reach. The great transformation which was taking place in that period of the awakening of nationalism and its democratic concomitant, consisted precisely in the fact that it was no longer the governments which led the peoples, but the peoples which decided for the governments. Thereby an element was introduced into politics which escaped all calculation. So long as Bismarck had dealings only with the Tsar and Gorchakov, with the Empress and the ladies of the court, that is, with the great ones whom someone who knew people well could see through to some extent, his diplomatic art could hew to the old methods which earlier had been formed under the world dominance of mathematics and mechanics. But, with the rise of Panslavism, all calculations became uncertain. Bismarck took German nationalism into custody and utilized it, subordinated it to the state conception and made it available for diplomatic craft. It was a very unequal alliance which was concluded then—a true *societas leonina*, for the Prussian state received the lion's part; the nationalist movement had to permit limits to be drawn to its activity, with regard to domestic freedom as well as to "pan-German" tendencies. For the time being, Bismarck was the master; and the world in which he felt at home and moved with complete security was the grand world of the courts and aristocratic society. There he sought for the decisions, exactly as had been done in bygone times in the manner depicted in the historical writings of Ranke. Bismarck and Ranke, the contemporaries, belong together most intimately from this point of view as well, and everything, furthermore, which was common to them—the objective comprehension of reality, the conviction of the primacy of foreign policy, the doctrines of the power-state and the legitimacy of political action—came out of the school of the old diplomacy. Following the same pattern, Bismarck and Ranke both fundamentally looked upon the state from the top downwards, while the patriots saw it as their task in politics and science to judge public affairs from below, upon the basis of the rights and requirements of the people. This celebrated formulation, which fixes the difference between the enlightened-absolutist and the democratic conceptions of public life, was first coined by Arndt; Treitschke took it over from him and misunderstood it. Even in his later life Bismarck limited the labours of the statesman and the diplomat to governments and courts; he was always foreign to the newly developing diplomacy which had to devote its energies to the fatiguing tasks of directing large staffs and studying the peoples and the economic and social phenomena of distant lands. Bismarck was not equal to working in the new world of the popular forces which had come into movement—consider the fiasco of his domestic policy after 1871! In just the same way the historian Ranke did not judge correctly those parties in the past in which, alongside the diplomats and court theologians, primal forces from below forced their way. Bismarck never did learn, as Napoleon did, to flatter the crowd. He was gripped by narrow class prejudices as were other leading statesmen of his time. Hence he inaugurated his social policy principally for considerations of power politics and preferred such solutions as were, in his view, adapted to strengthening the state. Even when he desired, he was unable to negotiate with deputies and party leaders as skillfully as with ambassadors and ministers of other powers. He always looked upon Windthorst[8] as just the former minister of a defeated royal house who only sought revenge in gathering the Catholics around himself; he never even made the effort to achieve an understanding of the endeavour of the Catholic portion of the population to help shape the inner structure of the new Reich. And he made just as little effort to develop in August Bebel[9] and his party a willingness to co-operate upon the basis of even the slightest concession. There is no doubt that his narrow and unchanging horizon served to strengthen his national-liberal and conservative allies in their lack of understanding for the Christian and Social-Democratic labour movement.

Thus Bismarck is to be understood as a historical phenomenon only upon the basis of the old statecraft, with its lofty intellectuality and self-sufficiency, in which the people played no part. He created the German national state within the framework of the old state system and with the old methods; after him, it went into decline. One has to look at Hindenburg and Ludendorff and compare them to the earlier leaders of German destinies in order to realize that Germany used to live more decently. The charge has often been made, and is emphatically repeated by Eyck, that Bismarck took no care to provide for the new generation, and tolerated no independent persons of quality around him. His collaborator in St. Petersburg, Leopold von Schlözer, always called him "the Pasha." But yet it was rare for him to encounter in the government departments such fine and upstanding personalities as Schlözer himself; when he did meet them, he did not withhold his respect. Furthermore, not only in the chancelleries and governments, but in the other domains of life in the era of rising nationalism, with the entry of the masses into history, noble personalities were forced into the background behind robust and servile characters.

In the old classic diplomacy to which Bismarck belonged, it was true that the principles and methods which are included under the name of Machiavellianism had been in long use; it remains to be seen whether, in this respect, Bismarck acted without restraint to an unusual degree. Where it is required by reason of state, Machiavelli considers anything to be permissible. He recommends lying, breaking treaties, deceit, violence; one must be a lion and a fox at the same time, and success justifies the most outrageous villainy. But, on the other hand, as the sagacious and honourable Johann Jakob Moser[10] taught in the eighteenth century, the small state cannot build upon force; therefore it must build upon law and justice. But it is obvious that the "minor powers," when they became involved in the affairs of the world, have been most perfidious, while the great powers maintained their strong

---

[8] Ludwig Windthorst (1812-91), German political leader; minister of justice in Hanover (1851-53, 1862-65), leader of Centre Party in the German Reichstag after 1870.
[9] August Bebel (1840-1913), German political leader; founder and leader of German Social-Democratic Party.
[10] Johann Jakob Moser (1701-85), German juridical scholar and teacher.

positions and no longer had to pursue a shifty course. The Prussian state was the most recent and smallest of the powers. This is the explanation of many of the acts of treacherous behaviour which are to be found so frequently in the history of Prussian policy. But Talleyrand, too, who certainly had a great power behind him, was never squeamish, and in Bismarck's time Prussia was so great a military power that it did not need small expedients. But Bismarck always applied the methods of deceit or violence which seemed useful to him without meditating upon them. A statesman who saw his state as incomplete, he was moved by ambition to make it larger; moreover, the increase of power by all means was a personal necessity for him. He brought about three wars with complete deliberateness, as he frankly admitted afterwards. He dragged the King of Hanover into the war in order to drive him from his throne, confiscated his property in violation of an agreement, and then had parliament forbid him to make restitution. He concluded the Reinsurance treaty with Russia against Austria and carefully concealed this fact from his ally. It is not possible and not necessary to enumerate here all the misdeeds or improprieties of his foreign and domestic policy. Even at the time they were brought to light of day by those affected, and were vigorously discussed by contemporary public opinion; but when he was successful, his power became so great that all who were dependent by function or character, bowed their heads and worshipped his genius. It was an ill harbinger of things to come that these were the leading intellectuals; previously humanitarian or liberal in attitude, they wished to remain on top as time passed, whatever came to pass. Eyck has carefully brought out in the course of his narrative every instance of violation of law and justice, of violence, of unfair conduct of affairs on the part of Bismarck; we now know much more of what he did than contemporary polemists knew at the time. We possess for no other statesman, not even for Talleyrand, so elaborate a register of his sins. Bismarck had the additional misfortune of finding a historian who pursued the old sinner through every twist and turn of his career.

But, what is more, the picture of Bismarck was drawn even more unflatteringly because of his personal idiosyncrasies. Words exist to conceal ideas, went the celebrated paradox coined by Talleyrand. Such behaviour was not to Bismarck's taste. Though he was able to watch his step, he did not find it easy. He carried over into political controversy the coarse language he had used as a member of a student *Korps* at the university and as a reserve officer in the army. He never acquired the self-control which one learns in the chancellery of state or *salon* society. For him at least, parliament was not the best school at which to prepare for diplomacy. Furthermore, he tended to make his criticism too slashing. He took delight in witty conversation, which he spiced with the kind of merry tale and unexpected jest his adversaries would then turn against him. He did not scruple to speak his mind. He said openly that he would not be balked by trifles. Other cynical turns of phrase from his lips soon became public knowledge. Such cynicism, also, set his successors a bad example. His imitators mimicked his cynicism, but not his honourable traits. The time was not far off when the reigning monarch, in his overbearing arrogance, hardly cut the figure of a prince or nobleman. In a world of rapidly growing wealth and spendour, William II was more the *parvenu* than the aristocrat.

No one will deny, therfore, that Bismarck and William II introduced into politics the habit of acting harshly toward ostensible weakness, and the use of strong words, so that ever-larger sections of the German people were summarily stigmatized as enemies of the Reich. Such conduct was foreign to the despots in previous times, because they sat, lonely and silent, upon the thrones in their Escorials. To be sure, many a cynical, blunt remark ("a crime, but not a mistake") has come down to us from Napoleon, who was dependent upon the crowd. However, he too adapted very easily to the new opinions taking form among the people; what is more, he too failed. Like Hegel, the "Prussian" in philosophy, Bismarck inculcated in the German Empire the belief that one "shouldn't be squeamish" ["*Nicht viel Umstände zu machen*"]. The role which the Junkers from east of the Elbe were now called upon to perform was, perhaps, particularly appropriate to them. Every reformer, from Freiherr vom Stein down to the liberals of the pre-Bismarck period, was indeed convinced, of course, that Prussia would have to renew herself upon the basis of the forces and institutions of Rhenish and Westphalian Germany. As a matter of fact, despite Bismarck, the centre of gravity of the German national movement in the nineteenth century did lie in the West, where the Rhenish economic leaders were at home and democracy had roots in the life of the people. In northern Germany the liberal movement won influence only in the cities. In that area, the authentic Prussia of old, which was Bismarck's homeland, his methods were quickly adopted and imitated. Freiherr vom Stein and his collaborators had not worked wholly without success in Prussia; Berlin in the time of Schinkel,[11] and Königsberg in the time of Theodor von Schön, the Kantian and Prussian reformer,[12] gladly put a long distance between themselves and Frederick's Prussian system. But now, by Bismarck's example, anyone who had any power whatever to use found himself encouraged to act more abruptly. Only where constitutional courts were able to exercise effective control was there any safeguard against utter disregard of law and justice. This flouting of right under law was frankly proclaimed at the time in the form of the right of necessity, as was done in 1914 in the invasion of Belgium.

We may be surprised, therefore, that the leaders of the Prussian-German state adopted such methods when they had ceased to be customary among legitimate monarchies after Napoleon's fall. We must ascribe to Bismarck a large individual share in promoting this development. In Prussia itself professional diplomats looked amiss at these methods. Bismarck was, after all, not only an outsider, but a man out of the ordinary, from whom one could look for a *coup d'état*; he was, therefore, of the same ilk as the men of 18th Brumaire and 2nd December. We forget too easily how deep an impression was made by the reappearance of Bonapartism at a time when the nineteenth century was becoming more and more bourgeois, in an age of liberalism and belief in progress. It was a stupendous phenomenon which aroused misgivings lest the means and resources of liberal democracy prove inadequate in the difficult and hard time just beginning. If anything encouraged Bismarck to enter upon the path of violence, it was certainly the conduct of Prince Louis Napoleon. There is reason, furthermore, to investigate more deeply the extent to which he also felt encouraged by Cavour's example; the Piedmontese was a great "realist" who also drove many princes from their thrones and yet did not become dependent upon extremism. But, beyond doubt, many aspects of Bismarck's life work trace back to the French Second Empire. That is all just history now. It would be difficult to find threads which extended from that time into the twentieth century. The general character of Caesarism or dictatorship as such, exemplified in the Renaissance and once again brought into being by Napoleon I, was such a thread.

---

[11] Karl Friedrich Schinkel (1781-1841), German architect and painter, particularly active in Berlin.
[12] Theodor von Schön (1772-1856), Prussian statesman; took liberal role in East Prussia in war against Napoleon.

The twentieth century, on the contrary, did not find its exemplars in the great realists and proponents of reason of state, but rather in the theory and practice of violence as created by the nationalists of eastern Europe and Italy. Kossuth, Mazzini and Garibaldi mobilized the youth of their nations and led them in hosts, again and again, to destruction. They aroused men's instinctual passions. In general, they were demoniac in character for they adopted chimerical goals, used the most extreme methods, and remained relatively indifferent to success, which neither they nor their imitators met. Bismarck had no part in all their doings, not even when, in 1866, he entertained a plan to rouse up the Czechs and Magyars. Though he may have learned from Napoleon III, still we do not find in him any trace of admiration for the demoniac figure of Napoleon I. In his youth, he went through his "romantic" period; but, once the storms of youth were past, *déborder* became foreign to his nature. The traditional rules of conduct provided that in cases of extreme necessity one need not think twice about using any weapon at hand. If we wish to probe for the ultimate cause of all the processes which gave rise to Napoleon, to Bismarck and to the leaders of the nationalities, as well as to their methods and goals, we will become aware that, in general, these processes are rooted in modern humanity. It clearly was not at all the same thing when the old sovereign states used their machinery of power to define their interests, and when national sovereignty came into play. The sovereign nation, once it was swung into action, did not readily accept any limitation of its scope.

We cannot condemn these methods and accept their goals. Bismarck could attain his purposes only by such methods. How else could he have bound together the eastern and western halves of the Prussian monarchy, closing the gaps that lay between them? The King of Hanover acted cautiously and beyond criticism. He took his stand squarely on law and avoided taking any part in the conflict between the two big powers! In order to respect the rights of Hanover, Bismarck would have had to give up any hope of making the Prussian state a single territorial unit. But he wished the Prussian body politic to have one compact terrtory, which would enable it to prevail completely in the North German Confederation. When this was won, he turned at once to his next goal and established the German Empire. Prussia could have existed in it even if she did not have Hanover and Hesse. In any case, in spite of the federal organization of the state, which was inevitable at the time, the decisive fact remains that Bismarck did not free himself from the old political conception of the isolated, territorially-compact, state body. In this old classic policy, Machiavellianism, because it arose in fact out of the struggle of sovereign powers, was not something put in afterwards, but the principle of its very life. Though national sovereignty merely took the place of the princely sovereigns, it vastly intensified, as we know, the drive of Machiavellianism, extended it widely and made it all-inclusive.

We may correctly speak of Bismarck's being "misunderstood" nowadays in the sense that his work and activity have been viewed apart from their connexion with the previous system of states and its political conceptions. Bismarck's conduct was dictated by a line which traced back to Frederick the Great, Richelieu, Gustavus Adolphus and Maurice de Saxe. They all contributed to the destruction of Western unity, to the establishment of sovereign states, and to their mighty expansion by conquest, treaty-breaking and violence against the weak. For a long time, Bismarck merely put modern nationalism to his own uses. He was, first and foremost, the managing director of a state which played the role of a great power in the European state system of five great powers and many smaller powers; as yet, Prussia was not "saturated" within this state system. Once he said that Prussia wore too heavy armour for her small body. It is an image which corresponds to the old political thinking. Bismarck did not learn the new metaphors of nationalism. He was concerned with the interests of the state, with the state as a rational system of analysis and action. Hence he remained strange to the voluntarisms of the period of national states and democracy. The programme and slogans of nationalism—natural living space, historical borders, assimilation and national will—which derived in part from the French Revolution and for the rest from German romanticism, were widespread among the liberals in the sixties and seventies, and were already being fully acted upon among the eastern European peoples. Bismarck did not heed any of these slogans; he disregarded this programme. Even when he annexed Alsace and Lorraine, military considerations were paramount in his mind. He belonged to the system of states at it had been, when states looked out for themselves and wished to please only themselves, when the interests of the state were all that was at stake and the interests of the people were only of secondary concern. He brought two new great powers, Prussia-Germany and Sardinia-Italy into the old European state system. As a result, he transformed the "European concert." The forces which later put an axe to the entire historical state structure had been in being for a long time, and Bismarck had to reckon with them. But he still hoped to be able to bring them under control.

* * *

BISMARCK AND OURSELVES

Alfred von Martin

* * *

In the register of German sins there is a place for some of the history written in Germany—that produced by the Prussian school of historiography. From its inception it took a questionable attitude toward standards of objective criticism and hence toward scholarly method. As was to be expected, it did the most serious harm in works written for the general public. In this literature of edification, Bismarck, the great "folk hero" of Prussia, was apotheosized most uncritically. These works, nationalist, wholly secularist, and given over to Bismarck-worship, were put forward by a Protestantism turned political, that is, nationalist. In this literature, Bismarck's figure was placed beside that of Luther, the German, in the pantheon of that North German religion which Constantin Frantz once called "the religion of National-Liberalism."

The people wish to have their "great man." Their historians, too, like to say dramatically, "Men make history," but fail to ask what is the result of such history. The "great men" themselves, in rare moments of reflection, were more honest. Frederick II of Prussia once said frankly that "great men" were in the habit of making their peoples "very unhappy." On occasions Bismarck expressed wonder that "the greatest butchers of men are those most loved and admired." When Jakob Burckhardt, in his letters to Friedrich von Preen, comes to speak of Bismarck, he always calls him "the great man." Still this does not prevent Burckhardt, the humanist among historians in the German language, from remarking how "obnoxious" Bismarck's personality was to him. He knew that the morality of all "great men" in history was open to doubt. Yet not once did he carry this criticism through to its logical conclusion.

In Robert Saitschick's book,[1] we now have an impressive and informative work of Bismarck criticism, which yet is popularly written in the best sense of the word. It is the kind of book we have needed. In reading it, one gains the conviction that Bismarck's story is very much a part of the history of the German catastrophe, whose origins, therefore, go back long before Hitler. It is a worthwhile destruction of the Bismarck legend. It corrects the false picture of history upon which a good part of the German nationalist ideology was based. To be sure, this ideology is kept up to date in new guises. The most recent position of Bismarck apologetics is that his policy was an end-product of old-fashioned cabinet policy. It was an *étatist* policy "from above," in opposition to the revolutionary nationalism which forced its way up from below and served as a prelude to the power politics of the new twentieth century. They say that the old sorcerer, while using this nationalism, tamed it. According to this view, Bismarck was really sated after 1871, not just simply in the fashion of someone who wisely realizes that what has been devoured must first be digested, thst renewed robbery should not be risked immediately, but because Bismarck had reached the goal he had set himself in his previous policy. He still wanted it to be state, not national, policy. And we should probably add, because he trusted none of those who would have to take over the inheritance he passed on, to be able to do more, under the most favorable circumstances, than maintain what he had created. A self-made man has every reason to take for granted that his practical genius will not be transmitted by inheritance.

Is such an attitude really "conservative"? Saitschick correctly calls Bismarck the revolutionary (he was one, as Frederick William IV, the most un-Prussian of Prussian kings, had already accurately pointed out), the adherent of a Prussian "Bonapartism" which was "older than Bonaparte" himself (Bismarck had already thus characterized himself to Leopold von Gerlach, the conservative adjutant-general of the conservative king).

Even if statesmen, after 1789, and indeed after 1848, only continued the practice usual before 1789, that is, a policy—a policy of conquest, of course—which arose out of their lust for power, pure and simple, and their personal vanity, it was no longer the same. Since 1789 the voices of the people have also been heard on the European continent. The application of pure power politics in the era of the political collaboration of the nation would necessarily destroy "the forces supporting the state within the people itself," as Ludwig Bamberger, the liberal critic of Bismarck, remarked. Bamberger bears witness to the necessarily anti-conservative results of Bismarck's policy. It is playing with fire to arouse the revolutionary and nationalist passions of the people for political trickery.

Cui bono? Previously it was Frederick II who found shelter and concealment behind "service to the state." At least ideologically he was under the influence of the Enlightenment, though, in practice, to be sure, more under Machiavelli's. Meanwhile, idolatry of the state was made fashionable in intellectual society as well by Hegel, the Prussian state philosopher. But, on the other hand, Bismarck, like Frederick II before him, admitted openly, though not publicly, that vanity was the motive force of his powerful passions. He, too, sanctioned his political activity by ideological appeals to love of fatherland, but at the same time he looked upon men with cynical contempt. He was a born tyrant who wanted nothing from men but

[1] *Bismarck und das Schicksal des deutschen Volkes: Zur Psychologie und Geschichte der deutschen Frage* (Munich, 1948).

"subordination and discipline,[2] and indeed did not tolerate independent opinion, criticism or control by parliament. As a matter of fact he permitted only creatures around himself just as he could govern only with the assistance of a Press which he had made tractable by bribery. The Prussian Crown Prince and Princess, the future Emperor Frederick III and his wife, Victoria, were wholly justified when they called him an "evil" man, because he was "without principle" and was driven by a demoniacal will-to-power. Later, Bebel spoke of the pact which Bismarck made with "the devil" for the sake of contemptible political "advantage." On the eve of the war of 1866, August Reichensperger[3] meditated upon the recurring importance of arrogance in history, "from the fall of the Angel until our own day." In fact, Bismarck himself admitted to the Crown Prince at a later date, in November 1870, that he had already fixed upon his policy of war when he took office in 1862, but made no mention of it even to the king, until the "proper moment," of course. Thus he hoodwinked William I, though, to be sure, the king's sense of his Prussian political and military "honour" was always available for the *"suum cuique rapere"* (to rob each of his own), as Ludwig von Gerlach[4] realistically amplified the ideological device—*suum cuique* (to each his own)—of the Prussian kings. According to the sound judgment of the Crown Prince, Bismarck's entire policy was a frivolous game with the most sacred things." He embodied Machiavelli's *virtù*, which included *sceleratezza*; Bismarck himself felt that a Teutonic devil dwelled within him: the Germans, as a matter of fact, had not worshipped the sun, but the thunder and the lightning.

But the problem of historical guilt, properly speaking, is less concerned with individual motivations, however fascinating for the biographer, than with the objective results and consequences of political activity. It is significant, therefore, that the thoughtful, even among his faithful followers, like the historian Heinrich von Sybel, felt that Bismarck's work was very far from being a fulfilment of their wishes. Scarcely was his work ("performance," one might better say) completed in 1871 than there was a feeling of emptiness. "Now what?" they thought. Here we can already see the psychological pattern for the development out of psychic *horror vacui*, of a universally dangerous pan-Germanism. Bismarck himself in his old age caused bitter disappointment, indeed discouragement, for instance to young Count Harry Kessler, because he lacked awareness of any ultimate meaning of the universe.

Saitschick, for whom these psychological relationships do not arise, discusses in pragmatic terms, first, the seed which Bismarck sowed, and then, the harvest which inevitably grew. In this way he tries to prove that Bismarck's guilt was our "destiny." We question, in the first place, whether Bismarck was "destiny," in the sense that, had he not been there, "everything would have turned out differently." Then we doubt that we should thus thrust all our guilt upon this certainly portentous historical figure so that we ourselves appear blameless.

Viewed from without, the fateful moment of history was the year 1862. King William I was determined to abdicate on the issue of control of the army, but yielded to the persuasive power of Bismarck's energy, as he was to do so often thereafter. Had Frederick III taken over the government at that time, there would have been no "age of Bismarck." For, by then, at the time of the constitutional

---

[2] Sidney Whitman, *Errinerungen an Bismarck*, p. 238.
[3] August Reichensperger (1808-95), Prussian art historian and political leader, founder of the Centre Party in the German Reichstag.
[4] Ernst Ludwig von Gerlach (1795-1877), German publicist and statesman, one of the founders of the Conservative Party in Prussia.

conflict, the Crown Prince already saw so clearly, as he wrote in 1863, the "frightfully logical" road to "disaster" in Bismarck's policy of force, which openly trampled all law and justice, that he did not shrink from a conflict with his father.

Would the policy of "Blood and Iron" have been avoided by a government of Frederick III? or, in the sad, final analysis even if there had been no Bismarck, could things have turned out no differently than they did? Neither the German Confederation nor the supra-national atmosphere would have endured. The restoration system of 1815 was only a provisional interruption of the age of the revolution which continued to go forward, at least covertly, from 1789. Bismarck was only the man who, in Jakob Burckhardt's fine formulation, said *"Ipse faciam"* (I myself will do it). Certainly by setting the stone into motion he defined its path and chose the moment when it began to move. But, in any case, the stone was loose and it had to start rolling.

Saitschick rightly stresses that Bismarck's establishment of the Empire was "artificial" creation, a reversal, by means of true Prussian organization of the process of organic growth. But this course of events cannot simply be charged to the person of the organizer. So individualistic—that is, one-sided and unsociological—a method of historical analysis does not take into account that, however much one may deplore it, the development, in one way or another, from the organic and the federative, to the technically organized and centralized state of affairs belongs to the fundamental tendencies of modern times. Finally, we must still ask just how much even so "great" a man can do if the people do not join him sooner or later. Thus the National-Liberals, the predestined Bismarckian party, so to say, were those who accepted Bismarck's principle (which also had the historiographical sanction of Ranke) of the primacy of foreign policy over domestic policy, at least in those circumstances where the geopolitical situation of a country leaves it open to unremitting pressure from without. It was the National-Liberals who betrayed freedom to "unity," that is, to power. There had long existed as a popular current a liberal and centralist nationalism, which sang, "My fatherland must be greater!" and therefore created danger of "that dismemberment of the European community" which Saitschick sees as coming into existence for the first time only in Bismarck's era. Against Erich Eyck's liberal critique of Bismarck, Franz Schnabel has correctly emphasized how strong were the nationalist aspirations cherished even by the pre-Bismarckian German democratic movement. Heine already anticipated an unparalleled outburst of political radicalism as a result of the revolutionary development in Germany, first in religion, then in philosophy.

Fixing our attention upon a "great man," however grave the burden of his individual responsibility, diverts us too easily from the guilt manifestly shared by those who collectively went along with him. In the final analysis, a people always has the government it deserves. We should not, therefore, in all too simple fashion, replace previous customary glorification of the "great" man by accusations exclusively against the "evil" man. We are not divested of guilt because we have been influenced. For influence to work, someone must be open to it. Behind the endeavour to thrust all guilt upon Bismarck, and then upon Hitler, the old lack of civic consciousness and sense of responsibility, which was inculcated by the authoritarian state, none the less lies always concealed. We must ask ourselves how the German people came to give first Bismarck and then Hitler their opportunities. Indeed, how did they come to raise Bismarck and Hitler to idols? Because they have tended to worship force, because they consider every kind of inconsiderateness, especially in the military field and in domestic and foreign policy, to be proof of increased strength, so that the borderline of brutality becomes fluid; in short, because they are always impressed by the cavalryman's boot and a fist banged upon the table. The German people saw their ideal of power embodied in Bismarck. He was their great man. We ought to have a history of his fame, a history of the *Bismarck myth*, a critical history in which we would see ourselves depicted, as a mirror to hold up to ourselves, a mirror of the path of error by which we attained to ideals of such falsity. This is what we miss in Saitschick's book; he disregards this side of the problem, in the final analysis the most important one. The examination of Bismarck ought to have led directly into necessary German self-criticism.

Is it not highly suggestive that Bismarck himself felt that he was possessed of a "Teutonic" devil? Bamberger called Bismarck "the *barbare de génie.*" Straight through the soul and conscience of the Germans runs the uncertain frontier between the Christian West and barbarism, said Quariglia, the Italian anti-fascist, during the last war. What is worst is that so many among us have always been proud of our participation in barbarism, even before Hegel, then particularly after Nietzsche, and all the way down to Ernst Jünger. Barbarian or Christian? We ought to put that query to Bismarck, we must address it above all to every German. Unfortunately, Heinrich Heine was not far wrong when he expressed the opinion that Christianity had only thinly and temporarily tamed the barbarian instincts of the Germans. We must add as well the Prussian-German faculty for having simultaneously a private Christianity and a deliberately heathenish public policy which, as we saw, could call up old Thor or Donar. Ernst Troeltsch recounts that an ingenuous, but very serious Scottish pastor once declared to him, "I could not be a pastor in Germany. It just is not a Christian country." We should ask whether Bismarck's unscrupulous Machiavellianism would not have met more vigorous resistance if this had not been so.

Yet the glorification of war by Treitschke had been prepared by Hegel, and before him by the historian Luden. So we should not marvel that men of intellect, indeed jurists such as Rudolf von Ihering,[5] swarmed about the man of success and fell on their knees before him. The Prussian-German opposition to an international court of arbitration, after the period of Kant, the disqualification of desire for peace as weakness, corresponded to the fundamental defects of the German national character: the calamitous romanticism of force, and the tendency toward extreme solutions. Frederick William IV called German logical consistency the most wretched of all virtues; and Frederick III, while still a young man, said to his teacher, Ernst Curtius, that Prussian statesmen lacked the ability to give in.

Was there "another" Germany, better and wiser, besides Bismarck's Germany? There were, in any event, individual Germans who did not share his ideas and who foresaw the oncoming time of troubles, the era of destructive wars and the inevitable catastrophe. Paul de Lagarde[6] and Constantin Frantz are brought forward from time to time by Saitschick among Bismarck's contemporaries. Ludwig von Gerlach deserves no less a place. In general, the enemies of Bismarck ought to be portrayed together by someone—it would be a small German hall of fame. Yet they were never anything but solitary individuals, and their voices died away, almost unheard. To be sure, official policy and semi-official historiography deliberately did their best to bury them in silence. Thus they remained voices in the wilderness.

---

[5] Rudolf von Ibhering (1818-92), German jurist, famous for his *Geist des römischen Rechts* and *Der Zweck im Recht.*
[6] Paul de Lagarde (1827-91), German Orientalist and publicist.

Their warnings were in vain. For behind these Germans, among whom Crown Prince Frederick stood not among the last, there was no Germany they could represent. The hope of Germany rests, in spite of all, upon the possibility that such Germans may become representative of Germany. But no insight holds hope unless it makes us search into our own hearts.

* * *

9 / Disraeli and Gladstone: "Empirical Realism" Versus "Righteous Passion"

Benjamin Disraeli, Earl of Beaconsfield (1804-1881), and William Ewart Gladstone (1809-1898) had parliamentary careers which lasted more than forty and sixty years respectively. Disraeli was *de facto* and then actual head of the Conservative party over a period of thirty odd years; Gladstone led the Liberals for about the same length of time. Disraeli was prime minister twice; Gladstone, four times. In an abbreviated summary, D. C. Somervell wrote, "From 1865 to 1880 British politics was simply Disraeli versus Gladstone."[1] Somervell's remark well reflects the impact of these two personalities and their views upon their respective parties. Their record of service is extraordinary enough, but their domination of their parties has no subsequent parallel in British history, nor, for that matter, does their bitter but great duel in and out of Parliament.

Usually, appreciations of Disraeli have sought to strike a balance between his overseas empire-building and his role as the founder of "Tory Democracy"—that philosophy which envisioned a reconciliation between landed gentry and working classes, two groups presumed to be united by their opposition to the "new men," the industrialists and financiers of the liberal middle classes. Gladstone's legacy has generally been summarized as a commitment to the idea of "little England" in foreign policy and classical, liberal laissez-faire ideals in socio-economic policies. Gladstone argued for British cooperation with the Concert of Europe to handle international problems, but never supported policies which would deliberately diminish overseas British influence.

Between these two images of the two rivals and the actual policies each pursued, a contradictory and complex reality exists. Disraeli, in 1867, doubled the electorate in the Reform Bill and "dished the Whigs." In 1874 he returned to power on a platform promising a "rest at home" (regarding further social reform) and an emphasis on expanding overseas prestige. Nonetheless, this ministry (1874-1880) produced notable social legislation. During Gladstone's second ministry (1880-1885),

---

[1] D. C. Somervell, *Disraeli and Gladstone, A Duo-Biographical Sketch* (New York: Garden City Publishing Co., 1926), p. 310. In 1865 Palmerston died and Lord John Russell succeeded him as prime minister, but Gladstone was already established as the leading Liberal and became prime minister in 1868. In 1866 Russell resigned and his government was succeeded by the second Derby ministry (Conservative) in which Disraeli once again became the leader in the House of Commons.

Egypt was occupied despite Gladstone's misgivings. He could not bring himself to damage British prestige abroad.

In the first selection that follows, from Philip Magnus, *Gladstone, A Biography,* their respective duelling positions over foreign affairs are illustrated in their confrontation of 1876-8– caused by a major eruption of the Eastern Question. Besides the content of their differences, this section illuminates the divergent social bases to which each appealed, pointing to an often ignored relationship between class alliances and foreign policies.

Paul Smith's recent biography of Disraeli, from which the second selection is taken, is addressed to a political analysis of Tory Democracy and Disraeli's role as a founder of modern conservatism. Smith ignores the rhetoric of the youthful Disraeli's social visions, found mainly in his romantic novels, and focuses upon the real political alliances that the older constituency of the Tory party, the landed gentry, forged with the liberal middle class industrialists. Thus, Disraeli's real political work emerges as a combination of imperial successes and the "opening to the middle" –– a culmination of Sir Robert Peel's strategy developed in the earlier half of the century. Smith observes that even where Disraeli's social conscience in the form of popular Toryism played a role, "it was an ideal, an attitude, not a policy . . . calling for a regeneration, not a reconstruction of society." The excerpts from Smith's biography cover the period from the late sixties to 1880.

Despite the fundamental and often acrimonious split between the two leaders, are there any areas of mutual agreement which both accepted?

TALKING TURKEY

Philip Magnus

* * *

From those and other moody distractions, Gladstone was recalled by the extraordinary consequences of a peasants' revolt in Bosnia (part of the modern Yugoslavia) which then formed part of the Turkish Empire. The revolt which started in 1875 could not be suppressed. Aggressive Russian sympathy for the oppressed Southern Slavs clashed with British distrust of Russia and with Disraeli's desire to raise British prestige and to play a commanding role in Europe and the world. A great war was avoided by the narrowest of margins, and Gladstone, more furious than Achilles after the slaughter of Patroclus, returned to the political arena.

Early in 1876 it became clear that the flame of rebellion in the Balkans was spreading like a forest fire. The only political alliance on the Continent of Europe at that time was the League of the Three Emperors (Germany, Russia, and Austria) which proposed that the Turks should be coerced into granting better conditions to their Christian subjects. Disraeli rejected that proposal out of hand. He argued that it masked a conspiracy on the part of Russia and Austria to partition Turkey; and he sent a fleet to anchor off the Dardanelles as a warning to Russia. Joint intervention by the Great Powers was made difficult by that independent action; and the Turks, relying on British support as at the time of the Crimean War, were encouraged to adopt an intransigent attitude towards Russia.

The Three Emperors League was not hostile to Great Britain, but it saw no good reason why Great Britain should interfere in Eastern Europe. Disraeli, much influenced by considerations of prestige, had already, in pursuit of a colourful and active foreign and imperial policy, acquired control of the Suez Canal; and he was at that time forcing through Parliament a Bill to proclaim the Queen as Empress of India. The Queen herself was unhappily about to throw to the winds the wise restraint which she had hitherto shown. Influenced equally by distrust of Russia and dislike of Gladstone she became as violent a "Jingo" as any man or woman in the land.

In April, 1876, the Bulgarians revolted against the Sultan, and during May some 12,000 Bulgarian men, women, and children were massacred by Turkish irregular troops. The news gradually filtered through, and Disraeli was questioned about it in the House of Commons for the first time on 26 June. Two generations later, when the public had grown accustomed to horrors on an incomparably greater scale, British opinion might have been less deeply stirred. In 1876, however, statesmen were in a position to draw to almost any extent upon vast untapped reserves of moral indignation. Lord Derby, the Foreign Secretary, was profoundly moved by the "Bulgarian Horrors"; even the Queen was dismayed for a time by Disraeli's apparent sympathy with the Turks. Disraeli had little feeling for oppressed Christian peoples struggling to be free. He thought that the Turks would have done better to bribe than to massacre the rebels, and he was afraid lest the Russians should use the atrocities as an excuse for seizing Constantinople. From there they might have been in a position to threaten the new British naval base at Alexandria. He therefore affected to discount the atrocity stories, and he somewhat shocked public opinion by giving a flippant reply to W. E. Forster in the House on 10 July, 1876. The Prime Minister took leave to doubt whether "torture has been practised on a great scale among an oriental people who seldom, I believe, resort to torture, but generally terminate their connexion with culprits in a more expeditious manner."

Gladstone waited for nearly two months in a mood of very dangerous calm. He noted twenty years later that he had been "slow to observe the real leanings of the Prime Minister." As an ex-member of the Cabinet which had embarked upon the Crimean War in 1854, Gladstone felt a weight of personal responsibility towards the Christian minorities in the Balkans. The rights which Russia had formerly possessed to protect those minorities had been annulled after the Crimean War. The Treaty of Paris, 1856, had substituted a European guarantee of protection which the Powers had failed to enforce. Gladstone had a right, therefore, to claim that Great Britain was bound by international law to extend to the Christian minorities of the Turkish Empire the degree of succour and protection which Russia proposed to offer from motives which he optimistically held to be mainly Christian and humanitarian.

On 31 July, 1876, Gladstone asked Disraeli, in the House, to institute inquiries about the massacres. He urged that the Crimean War had substituted "a European conscience expressed by the collective guarantee and concerted action of the European Powers" for the rights which Russia had formerly possessed to intervene in Turkish affairs on behalf of the Christian minorities. He said that the only alternative to the "European Concert" was a "European convulsion." Disraeli retorted by dismissing exaggerated accounts of the atrocities as "coffeehouse babble." He said that it was futile at that late date "to enter into the politics of the Crimean War."

Thenceforward, as the crisis deepended and thrust every other issue into the shade, Disraeli's empirical realism was exposed to a constant and relentless flow of moral precepts from Gladstone. Disraeli, supported by the Queen, society, high finance, the most powerful section of the Press, and by what was left of the rough, happy, ignorant mass of merry England, took his stand on a rather narrow conception of British imperial and strategic interests. He identified those interests with the maintenance of Turkish integrity, and was only held back at the last moment from embarking on a war, which would have been as useless as the war in the Crimea, by a combination of ill-health, Cabinet dissensions, and popular discontent. When Disraeli discovered at Berlin that British prestige could be better secured by throwing over Turkish integrity, he did so without a qualm. He then received the credit for a settlement which embodied, not his ideas, but those of Lord Salisbury, Prince Bismarck, and Count Shuvalov.

Robustly opportunist as it was, Disraeli's policy throughout the crisis reflected the mood of the fashionable world. As Queen Sophie of Holland wrote on 7 September, 1876, to her intimate friend, Lady Derby: "I cannot feel any sympathy with Servians and Bulgarians, and think them as bad and cruel as their enemies." Disraeli tended to regard Turks and Christians as pawns in an exciting struggle which was being waged between Great Britain and Russia for a dominant position in the Mediterranean. To his mind, British interests were the sole test of policy, and in Gladstone's view, his interpretation of those interests excluded considerations of justice, or of humanity.

As the last round of the long duel between Gladstone and Disraeli opened, Gladstone, deriving his chief support from intellectuals, Nonconformists, and hosts of upright, God-fearing men and women many of whom had only recently been enfranchised, took his stand squarely on the moral issue. In that age his resolute insistence on that issue made his ultimate return to power inevitable. His greatest service, however, was his appreciation of the truth that the choice confronting Great Britain did not lie between support of Russia and support of Turkey. It lay between a continuance of Turkish misrule, and the adoption of the principle of national self-government in the Balkans. Gladstone constantly pointed out that the Balkan Christians were not seeking alliance with Russia, but delivery from oppression. He argued that, if Disraeli had his way, all the Christian peoples of the Near East would be driven into the arms of Russia.

Gladstone was far from being an unreserved champion of Russia. He sought to contain Russian expansion not by shoring up the decaying corpse of the Turkish Empire, but by calling into existence a string of independent Christian States from the Adriatic to the Aegean and the Black Sea. He did not want to allow Russia to become the sole champion of the principle of nationality in the Balkans; he repeatedly urged that the matter should be taken out of Russian hands and made a common European responsibility. Gladstone's approach to the problem was more realistic than Disraeli's. The future was on his side, as it had been also in the matter of the *Alabama* arbitration. Instead of identifying British interests with the integrity of Turkey, which could not, in the long run, be maintained, Gladstone identified them with the principle of nationality in the Balkans, and through that principle with the causes of Christian civilization, justice, and humanity.

Disraeli's attempt to discount the "Bulgarian Horrors" provoked an outbreak of protest meetings during the month of August, 1876, throughout Great Britain. That popular indignation gave Gladstone his opportunity to direct public opinion towards the end which he desired. He wrote calmly to Lord Granville on 7 August: "As a Party question this affords no despicable material, but there are much higher interests involved."

Gladstone was scandalized on 11 August when Disraeli, in the last speech which he made in the Commons before taking his seat in the Lords as Earl of Beaconsfield, argued that: "There is nothing to justify us in talking in such a vein of Turkey as has been, and is being, at this moment entertained. . . . What our duty is at this critical moment is to maintain the Empire of England."

Gladstone was about to talk to Turkey in a vein which succeeded in troubling momentarily, at any rate, the quietest waters of sophisticated apathy; on 29 August, after a consular report had been published which confirmed some of the worst details of the atrocities, he asked Lord Granville whether he would be shocked to hear that he proposed to write a pamphlet:

"Good ends can rarely be attained in politics without passion, and there is now, the first time for a good many years, a righteous passion."

Gladstone confided to his wife (5 September) that Granville had been lukewarm, but he added, "he could not persuade me to hold it back."

Gladstone at that moment was crippled by lumbago, but he wrote his pamphlet at white heat in four days. As he wrote, his mind was convulsed by the most violent earthquake which it had yet experienced. He laid aside a large bundle of notes, entitled *Future Retribution,* on which he had been working, labelling the wrapper: "From this I was called away to write on Bulgaria." On Monday, 4 September, 1876, his daughter Mary recorded: "Papa rushed off to London on Sunday night, pamphlet in hand, beyond anything agog over the Bulgarian horrors which pass description. The whole country is aflame—meetings all over the place."

Never had Gladstone's instinct for right-timing been more perfectly exemplified. *The Bulgarian Horrors and the Question of the East* was published by Murray on 6 September, and by the end of the month some 200,000 copies had been sold. Gladstone declared that the Turks "are, upon the whole, since the black day when they first entered Europe, the one great anti-human species of humanity." Disraeli had shamelessly condoned outrages so vile "that it passes the power of heart to conceive or of tongue and pen adequately to describe them." British and French blood and treasure, poured out like water during the Crimean War, had served only to afford the Turks this opportunity to indulge "abominable and bestial lusts" and to enact scenes "at which Hell itself might almost blush." Women and children had been violated, roasted, and impaled; no refinement of torture had been spared; and Gladstone concluded:

Let the Turks now carry away their abuses in the only possible manner, namely by carrying off themselves. Their Zaptiehs and their Mudirs, their Bimbashis and their Yuzbachis, their Kaimakams and their Pashas, one and all, bag and baggage, shall, I hope, clear out from the province they have desolated and profaned. This thorough riddance, this most blessed deliverance, is the only reparation we can make to the memory of those heaps on heaps of dead; to the violated purity alike of matron, of maiden, and of child. . . . There is not a criminal in a European gaol; there is not a cannibal in the South Sea Islands, whose indignation would not arise and overboil at the recital of that which has been done, which has too late been examined, but which remains unavenged; which has left behind all the foul and all the fierce passions that produced it, and which may again spring up in another murderous harvest, from the soil soaked and reeking with blood, and in the air tainted with every imaginable deed of crime and shame . . . No Government ever has so sinned; none has proved itself so incorrigible in sin or, which is the same, so impotent for reformation.

He called upon the Concert of Europe, which Disraeli had done his best to disrupt, "to afford relief to the overcharged emotion of a shuddering world."

Gladstone's overcharged emotion gained only a momentary respite as a result of the publication of that fulminating pamphlet. On 9 September he addressed a great open-air meeting of his constituents at Blackheath, in pouring rain. He said that he had lived long in public life, that he had witnessed "many vivid movements of the popular mind," but that he had never witnessed "one to compare with that which during the past fortnight has taken its commencement and which has swollen with such rapidity to the dimensions of a movement truly national." He said that the question at issue had "a breadth and a height and a depth that carries it far out of the lower region of party differences, and establishes it on grounds, not of political party, not even of mere English nationality, not of Christian faith, but on the largest and broadest ground of all—the ground of our common humanity." He called upon the Russians to drive the Turks out of Bulgaria:

I, for one, for the purposes of justice, am ready as an individual to give the right hand of friendship to Russia when her objects are just and righteous, and to say, in the name of God, "Go on and prosper!"

At Aylesbury, on 20 September, Disraeli accused Gladstone of using sublime sentiments for the furtherance of personal and party ends. He described him as worse than any Bulgarian horror, and was rebuked by *The Times* for bad taste. Gladstone was goaded almost beyond endurance by such language. Disraeli was toying with the idea of occupying the Dardanelles in order to forestall a Russian invasion of Turkey, and at the Guildhall, on 9 November, he not only made a bitter attack on Servia and Montenegro which had declared war on Turkey; he threatened Russia openly with war if she failed to stop the flow of "volunteers" into those countries. The language which Disraeli used inspired a famous music-hall refrain:

> *We don't want to fight, but by Jingo if we do,*
> *We've got the ships, we've got the men, we've got the money too!*

Gladstone described that provocation as "almost incredible." He told the Duke of Argyll that the Jews of the East had always hated the Christians, and that he could only suppose that Disraeli was motivated by that hatred. The Duke cordially agreed. He assured Gladstone that Disraeli's "Judaic feeling" was the only genuine motive left in his mind since Lady Beaconsfield's death, and that he would be willing to sacrifice everything to it. He made Gladstone read Disraeli's favourite novel, *Tancred* (1847), in which much of the action is laid in Palestine. The theme is the corruption of Western material civilization, and the author pleads for the establishment of a new Eastern Empire, under British suzerainty, which should be guided and inspired by the mystical genius of the Hebrew race.

Gladstone always denied that he had actually loathed Disraeli, but those who knew him best were agreed that at that time his sentiment towards his rival became that of black hatred. He read in *Tancred* how the hero was advised by an Eastern potentate to "magnetize" the British Queen. Tancred was told that all he need do was to use his "beautiful voice," to whisper "fine things" into her ear. Gladstone was alarmed by the constitutional dangers which might rise as a result of the ascendancy which Disraeli had acquired over the Queen. He would have been still more alarmed if he had known the full extent to which the Queen's views had become unbalanced; before long she was urging the Cabinet to go to war, and threatening to abdicate if it ignored her outbursts

Gladstone made no attempt to conceal his view that whatever had been objectionable in Lord Palmerston's policy had received a "tenfold development" in Disraeli. Immediately after Disraeli's death in April, 1881, Lord Acton, in a letter to Edward Burne-Jones (7 May, 1881), put Gladstone's opinion of his rival into words which "cannot be employed in public." He imagined Gladstone saying that he thought Disraeli's doctrine "false, but the man more false than his doctrine . . . that he demoralized public opinion, bargained with diseased appetites, stimulated passions, prejudices and selfish desires, that they might maintain his influence; that he weakened the Crown by approving its unconstitutional leanings, and the Constitution by offering any price for democratic popularity . . ." That was a moderate representation of Gladstone's opinion of Disraeli while the Eastern crisis lasted, and Disraeli reciprocated Gladstone's hatred. He gleefully told Lady Bradford (December, 1876) that the Queen really loathed Gladstone, and that she thought him mad. He told Lord Derby (October):

> Posterity will do justice to that unprincipled maniac, Gladstone—extraordinary mixture of envy, vindictiveness, hypocrisy, and superstition; and with one commanding characteristic—whether preaching, praying, speechifying, or scribbling—never a gentleman!

It was fortunate that the Conservatives and the Liberals were both divided among themselves at that time. Lord Salisbury, Lord Derby, and Lord Carnarvon all sympathized more than Disraeli did with the aspirations of the Christian peoples in the Balkans, and they managed to exert a restraining influence over their chief's pro-Turkish policy. On the Liberal side, Lord Granville and Lord Hartington both considered that Gladstone was being much too unguarded in his encouragement of Russia, and that he did not take sufficiently into account the difficulties in the way of bringing about self-government throughout the Balkans. Lord Hartington told Lord Granville (18 December, 1876) that if Gladstone went much further, *"nothing can prevent a break-up of the Party."*

Gladstone cared little about such risks, but his family was troubled. Lady Frederick Cavendish noted in her Journal (8 October, 1876) that "Uncle William" was too headstrong. He had rebuked Lord Frederick Cavendish for meeting Turkish diplomatic representatives at dinner, and had described them as untouchable "symbols of iniquity." Gladstone complained constantly that the upper classes had betrayed their responsibility: "When did the Upper Ten Thousand ever lead the attack in the cause of humanity? Their heads are always full of class interest and the main chance."

"Of one thing," Lady Frederick recorded, "I am as certain as I have been all my life—that there is no personal ambition, or any motive but love of justice and mercy (and utter disbelief in Dizzy, I allow) in his present course."

In fashionable circles, Gladstone was now so intensely unpopular that lying stories about his rescue work in the London streets by night were freely circulated, and his family treated with contempt a spate of anonymous letters. After the breakdown of a conference at Constantinople (8 December, 1876, to 20 January, 1877), the unparalleled vehemence with which Gladstone, taking to the platform, began slowly but inexorably to arouse the indignation of the British masses against Disraeli, excited animosities which were very slow to die down. The political atmosphere remained uncomfortably heated for years, with the result that, until Gladstone's final retirement, no important issue could be debated in a dispassionate mood. The tone of moral outrage which Gladstone used with complete sincerity in talking about Turkey between 1876 and 1880 was borrowed by his opponents and often used artificially during the succeeding decade when Ireland had replaced Turkey as the principal object of Party contention.

On 24 April, 1877, after long forbearance, Russia declared war on Turkey and started an all-out drive on Constantinople. Gladstone, who had noted in his diary (15 April) that he felt it "a holy duty" to write an article in praise of Montenegro for the *Nineteenth Century*, considered that Russia had good reason for her professed resolve to discharge single-handed a duty which the European Concert had shirked. The Cabinet as a whole exercised a restraining influence over the pro-Turkish ardour of the Prime Minister and the Queen; and the Government adopted a policy of conditional neutrality for so long as no threat developed to a specified list of vital British interests.

Lord Granville and Lord Hartington set themselves the task of restraining Gladstone's pro-Russian ardour. The views of some of the Liberal rank and file were expressed in a letter from Sir William Harcourt to Sir Charles Dilke (10 October, 1876): "Gladstone and Dizzy seem to cap one another in folly and imprudence, and I don't know which has made the greatest ass of himself."

The outbreak of the Russo-Turkish War divided public opinion on an issue of foreign policy more acutely than at any period since the French Revolution, and excitement was intense when Gladstone, against the wish of all his principal colleagues, gave notice that he would move five Resolutions in the Commons on 7 May, defining his policy in the Russo-Turkish War.

The first Resolution censured Turkey for failure to fulfil her treaty obligations; the second declared that the Turks had lost all claim to British moral or material support; the third recommended self-government in the Balkans; the fourth recommended that pressure should be brought to bear on Turkey by the Great Powers; the fifth recommended the first four Resolutions to Her Majesty's Government. As soon as Gladstone's intention was known, Disraeli's Cabinet, which had been in a ferment, rallied round its chief, while Lord Granville and Lord Hartington complained that Gladstone, after formally renouncing the leadership, was threatening to split the Liberal Party and to make their position impossible. Lady Frederick Cavendish, who loved her uncle very dearly, noted in her Journal (11-17 February, 1878) that her husband had been made ill with worry on account of the tension between his brother—Lord Hartington—and Gladstone:

They are 2 men so utterly unlike in disposition and mode of viewing things, and Uncle W. having been driven by the very nature of this great question to take a leading part (he has felt a special responsibility as the only surviving compos[1] statesman who conducted the Crimean War and was a party to the Treaty of Paris) has necessarily been prominent, though no longer leader ... I am come round to the conviction that he should either have continued to lead the Party, or withdrawn from Parliament altogether, or taken a Peerage. It is immensely to the credit of

[1] *Compos mentis,* or in possession of his faculties. Lady Frederick forgot Lord Granville and the Duke of Argyll.

both him and Cavendish[2] that they have pulled together at all, and is due to the perfect honesty and sense of duty of both.

Lord Hartington made it clear to the House on 7 May, 1877, that he was not willing to support Gladstone's third and fourth Resolutions, and that he considered them inopportune. Gladstone, in speaking to the first two only, admitted frankly that the disclosure of such differences of opinion "must have had a dissipating effect on the mind of the House." He argued that "we have improperly allowed the vindication of the great cause in the East to pass into the hands of a single Power"; and he pleaded that coercion should be applied to Turkey by a united Europe after the manner in which it had been applied in the 1820s, when Greece was struggling to be free:

But that was a policy that had no more the approval of what I may call the West End of London than the Christian cause has now. That portion of England does not express the true sentiments of England. Looking over all the great achievements that have made the last half century illustrious, not one of them would have been effected if the opinions of the West End of London had prevailed.

Gladstone rejoiced to proclaim "the knell of Turkish tyranny":

So far as human eye can judge it is about to be destroyed. The destruction may not come in the way or by the means that we should choose; but come this boon from what hands it may, it will be a noble boon, and as a noble boon will gladly be accepted by Christendom and the world.

A future Prime Minister, Arthur James Balfour, who was then aged twenty-nine and intimate with Gladstone's family, listened to that speech from a Government back bench. The House, when Gladstone began, was hostile and impatient, and at first members streamed out of the House. Then, as reports reached them that a major eruption was in progress, they poured back until the Chamber was crowded. Balfour said that he could never erase from his memory the impression which Gladstone's speech had made on his mind. As a feat of Parliamentary eloquence, endurance, and skill, he believed that it had never been equalled. In his diary Gladstone was content to record:

Such a sense of solitary struggle I never remember ... I rose on the main question nearly in despair ... I spoke 2½ hours, voice lasting well. House gradually came round ... Never did I feel weaker or more wormlike.

Replying to the debate on 14 May, Gladstone spoke with moderation. He described the Russian Emperor as "a Christian gentleman," and the Russians as a people "as capable of noble sentiments as any people in Europe." He said that if Russia succeeded, "as an Englishman I shall hide my head, but as a man I shall rejoice." Gladstone's Resolutions, which in fact constituted a plea for the coercion of Turkey, were lost by 253 to 354 votes. But for the loyalty of Lord Hartington it is likely that the figures would have been much more adverse, for contemporary estimates suggest that there were no more than sixty or seventy avowed coercionists in a House of 658.

Loyal as Lord Hartington was, he felt extremely uncomfortable. He wrote to Lord Granville (25 May, 1877):

[2] Lord Hartington.

Mr. G. says that he has never been able to comprehend the cause of the late split, and under those circumstances it seems to me very likely that it will occur again. . . . While we remain responsible for the management of the Party in Parliament, Mr. G. cannot expect that we should entirely subordinate our own opinions and judgement to his, and unless we do, it seems inevitable that one section of the Party will follow his lead, and the other ours. . . . I think that we have some right to ask Mr. G. to look at the facts, as they exist. . . . He does not cease to be the leader of the Party by merely saying that he will not be the leader. If, as he has done since the autumn, he takes the lead, he *is* the leader, and all that he can do is to disclaim (for I do not think that he can really divest himself of it) the responsibility which naturally attends upon leadership.

Lord Granville laid that letter before Gladstone without eliciting any response, but his tact helped to ease a delicate situation. He would have been consoled a little if he had known the extent to which Disraeli's Cabinet was torn by dissensions as the Russian armies advanced. In a letter to the Queen, dated 3 November, 1877, Disraeli outlined seven distinct shades of opinion in his Cabinet, from those who wanted immediate war with Russia to one member (Lord Derby) who stood for peace at any price.

The Turks put up a brave but hopeless resistance, and early in January, 1878, the Russians, after liberating the Balkans, surged almost up to the walls of Constantinople. In that month the excitement in Great Britain was quite as intense as at the time of Napoleon's escape from Elba. A storm of anti-Russian feeling swept England south of the Trent. It was impossible in London, and difficult elsewhere, for meetings to be held in favour of peace; and Gladstone, who had his windows in Harley Street smashed by a mob, was a constant object of hostile demonstrations and a liability to the police who were responsible for his safety. He was hustled on one occasion with Mrs. Gladstone, in the streets, and even hooted (12 April, 1878) by fellow-members in the lobby of the House of Commons. He noted in his diary (11 March):

Went to the Levée. The Princess [of Wales] for the first time received me drily. The Duke of Cambridge, black as thunder, did not even hold out his hand. Prince Christian could not but follow suit. This is not hard to bear.

Gladstone was anathematized by society, and deeply hurt on 11 January, 1878, when he was publicly described by the Duke of Sutherland, the son of his old confidante, Harriet, Duchess of Sutherland, as a Russian agent. Throughout the industrial North, however, and in Scotland, the masses had begun to hang upon every word he uttered, and to reverence him almost as a god.

On 24 January, 1878, the British Mediterranean fleet was ordered to sail through the Dardanelles to the Turkish capital. The orders were temporarily cancelled at the request of the Turks, who were anxious that the Russians should be given no excuse for breaking off negotiations for an armistice; but Gladstone was stung to fury by the provocation which Disraeli offered. Speaking at Oxford on 30 January he denounced the orders to the fleet as "an act of war, a breach of international law." He admitted that he had become an agitator, and said that he had been driven to it by Disraeli:

When you speak of the Government you mean Lord Beaconsfield. . . . Not one man in the Government has a tenth part of his tenacity of will and patient purpose. . . My purpose has been. . . to the best of my power for the last eighteen months, day and night, week by week, month by month, to counterwork as well as I could what I believe to be the purpose of Lord Beaconsfield.

Two days later, writing to Lady Bradford, Disraeli commented:

The mask has fallen, and instead of a pious Christian, we find a vindictive fiend who confesses he has for a year and a half been dodging and manoeuvring against an individual—because he was his successful rival.

On 1 February, 1878, an armistice was signed, and on 13 February orders were finally issued that the British Mediterranean fleet should sail through the Dardanelles into the Sea of Marmora. There was no opposition, but on 3 March, by the Treaty of San Stefano, which ended the Russo-Turkish War, Russia obtained far-reaching concessions from Turkey, including an outlet into the Mediterranean. Provision was made for the creation of a vast autonomous Bulgaria, which was to include Macedonia and to be under Russian tutelage. That and other provisions of the Treaty appeared unacceptable to the British Cabinet, and when the terms were made known on 22 March there was a panic on the Stock Exchange, and a shrill and prolonged public outcry.

Disraeli, who had indentified his country's interests with the maintenance of Turkish integrity, was greatly concerned about prestige. Gladstone repeatedly denounced prestige as a miserable delusion, but to it, in that crisis, Disraeli appeared willing to sacrifice much. If, however, he could avoid "losing face" he was as happy to retreat from his original position and to countenance a partition of Turkey, as he would have been to comply with the Queen's hysterical desire for a useless war with Russia if he could have induced his Cabinet to agree. Disraeli wished to make Great Britain the arbiter of Europe, and on 28 March Lord Derby resigned from the Foreign Office in protest against a decision to call out the reserves, and to move Indian troops through the Suez Canal to Malta. Lord Salisbury, who succeeded Lord Derby, pressed at once for a Conference in order to resolve the deadlock between Great Britain and Russia. A deepening trade depression in Great Britain, and Russian internal unrest, provided a stimulus to agreement, and after preliminary Anglo-Russian conversations in May, a conference opened at Berlin on 13 June, 1878, under the chairmanship of Bismarck, who saw no prospect of any advantage to Germany from a European war at that moment.

Disraeli and Lord Salisbury represented Great Britain at Berlin, and by 13 July a practical compromise was ready for signature. The swollen Bulgaria of San Stefano was split into three parts, of which one—Macedonia—was returned to Turkey without any guarantee of better government. In the main, however, the settlement was based on the abandonment of the principle of Turkish territorial integrity. Many wide provinces were amputated in order to satisfy the claims of Turkey's neighbours. By a separate Anglo-Turkish convention Great Britain received the island of Cyprus, and a pledge of good government was extorted from the Turks in return for a guarantee of the future territorial integrity of Turkey in Asia.

Crippled with gout, but beaming, and leaning on Salisbury's arm, Disraeli returned to London on 16 July saying that he brought "Peace with Honour." He received an unprecedented acclaim. The Queen wanted to make him a Duke, but he would only accept the Garter. In the Gladstone family the wish was expressed that he might be made Duke of Jericho and despatched to administer his duchy; and, Gladstone's first public reaction to his rival's apotheosis was silly, petulant, and ill-considered. Speaking at Southwark on 21 July, three days after Disraeli had defended the Berlin settlement in the House of Lords, Gladstone denounced it far too strongly. The country was overjoyed that the threat of imminent war had been removed, and the Treaty had much to recommend it. Gladstone's strongest abuse was reserved for the Cyprus convention, which he described as "insane ... an act of duplicity not surpassed and rarely equalled in the history of nations."

On 27 July, Disraeli delivered a crushing retort at a fashionable banquet at which he and Lord Salisbury were entertained in the Riding School at Knightsbridge. After making the sound point that the Crimean War could have been avoided by vigorous action before its outbreak, he said that Gladstone's talk about insanity could only have proceeded from "a sophisticated rhetorician inebriated with the exuberance of his own verbosity, and gifted with an egotistical imagination that can at all times command an interminable and inconsistent series of arguments to malign an opponent and to glorify himself."

The Times scolded Disraeli mildly the next day for his "curious little burst of irritation"; Gladstone made light of it to friends, saying that he could never, "condescend" to notice Disraeli "in a personal way" because there was no "foundation of good faith" or "anything serious or sincere in any of his utterances, however vehement." Disraeli was, however, determined on that occasion to score a personal point against Gladstone, if he could. On 29 July he complained to the House of Lords that he had been described by Gladstone as "a dangerous and even a devilish character," and that Gladstone was constantly employing offensive personal expressions about his conduct and character.

Gladstone felt it necessary to write to Disraeli on 30 July to ask for details. He began his letter "Dear Lord Beaconsfield," and begged that he might be supplied with a detailed list of the times and places at which he had used the offensive and personal expressions to which Disraeli had taken exception. Disraeli was now treading on air. He had angled for that opportunity to snub Gladstone, and he replied coldly, in the third person, on the same day, that the necessary researches would take time, and that he was busy.

The matter was carried no further. As Lord Granville told the Queen (24 April, 1880):

Lord Beaconsfield and Mr. Gladstone are men of extraordinary ability; they dislike each other more than is common among public men. Of no other politician would Lord Beaconsfield have said in public that his conduct was worse than the Bulgarian atrocities. He has a power of saying in two words that which drives a person of Mr. Gladstone's peculiar temperament into a great state of excitement.

Gladstone had learned slowly and very painfully the need for tolerance and compromise, but he was too simple, passionate, and high-minded to accept the world as it is. He never fully appreciated the limitations which are imposed by human nature upon all work that is performed by human hands and the process of achieving a modest degree of good by reconciling a host of selfish interests was always hateful to him. Edmund Burke, in a famous passage,[3] had deified "prudence and conformity to circumstances" as "the god of this lower world." Gladstone was always himself capable of both prudence and conformity, but in his opponents, and especially in Disraeli whose personality grated on him at almost every point, he was inclined to confound those qualities with depravity, and to treat them as tokens of the Beast in *Revelation.*

[3] Letter to the Sheriffs of Bristol 1777.

Disraeli's bluff had magnificently succeeded, but Lord Salisbury admitted some twenty years later that "the wrong horse" had been backed at Berlin. The country had been led to the brink of war, and if Disraeli's gamble had failed, his fame, which is unassailable in some other fields, would have been sadly tarnished. After throwing many provinces of Turkey to the wolves as well as to the lambs, Disraeli lacked the will, and the means, to carry to its logical conclusion the policy that he had been constrained to accept in place of his own. Cyprus had been acquired ostensibly as a base from which Great Britain would be in a position to implement what was virtually a single-handed guarantee of Turkish territorial integrity in Asia against further Russian aggression, in return for a promise of better government. That promise and guarantee proved unenforceable in face of Turkish resentment at her desertion by Great Britain. Russia's ambitions received a severe check, but she retained some of her conquests in Asia and in Europe. Only a British protectorate over Asia Minor, which was impossible; large-scale money grants, which were not forthcoming; or a truly popular Turkish revolution, for which the time was not then ripe, might have availed at that period to effect the regeneration of Turkey.

So great was the relief that war had been averted, that Disraeli's slogan, "Peace with Honour," delighted the British people. Together with the charming acquisition of Cyprus, it helped to conceal the fact that the Turkish problem in Europe had been solved to a great extent in the only possible way, by the adoption of the principle of self-government for oppressed national minorities. That was the principle which Gladstone had advocated throughout the crisis, and it was the opposite of the policy of maintaining intact the territorial integrity of Turkey which Disraeli had upheld until the last possible moment. Gladstone's hatred and distrust of Disraeli, and his delicate moral scruples about Cyprus, the acquisition of which was in many respects a brilliant coup, led him to do much less than justice to the merits of the Treaty of Berlin. It realized, at least in part, many of Gladstone's objects, and its substance was more important than the means by which it had been obtained. Gladstone had seen fit on a number of occasions to apologize publicly for his wish to make use of Russia in order to achieve his aims; his dismay at seeing those aims so unexpectedly realized by Disraeli, and the fierce language which he used, made him seem factious and inconsistent. Even the dubious arrangements about Turkey in Asia represented a fairly honest attempt in very difficult circumstances to secure reforms for which Gladstone had strongly pressed in European Turkey.

Despite the obloquy which he incurred in fashionable quarters, it is an astonishing tribute to the moral sway which Gladstone exerted over the masses whose material needs he never understood, that within eighteen months of Disraeli's apotheosis at Berlin, Gladstone should have succeeded in injecting into the minds of a majority of the British electors a potent dose of his intense, scorching conviction about the "infection" of Disraeli's personality, and the flagrant immorality of the policies which Disraeli had pursued. Thereafter, he never ceased to proclaim his faith in the political efficacy of what he called "righteous indignation," and the Queen, who thought him crazy, never forgave him. He stumped the country invoking the wrath of Heaven like some ancient Hebrew prophet; and at the General Election of 1880, when he enjoyed his finest hour, he was wafted back to Downing Street—against his innermost desire, as he was sometimes almost half inclined to believe—by the spirit of a nation which had never before been summoned from its depths by a call so heartfelt and so clear.

DISRAELI: FIRST MODERN CONSERVATIVE?

By Paul Smith

It is easy to see why Disraeli should so often be regarded as the prophet and founder of modern Conservatism, and the chief agent in the adaption of the party to the realities of a new era. At the beginning of his political career, he focused attention on social movements and their political implications, threw into sharp relief the dangers inherent in the division between the "two nations" of rich and poor, and insisted that the task of the Conservative or "national" party was to seek the reconciliation of classes and the stability of the social order through a timely consideration of popular welfare. In 1867, in what looked to many like conscious pursuit of his ideas of popular and national Toryism, he "educated" his followers into granting a largely increased share of electoral power to the working classes, turning the face of his party firmly towards the future; and in the following years he lent his approval to the development of the mass organisation needed to secure the party's advance under the new franchise. In 1872, putting before the party the three great objects which were long to form the basis of its creed, he coupled with the defence of the constitution and the maintenance of the empire the elevation of the condition of the people; and in his ministry of 1874–80, suiting actions to words, he presided over the most notable installment of social reform undertaken by any single government of the century. It is no wonder that it should be argued that it was Disraeli who secured the future of the Conservative party, by inducing it to accept and exploit the political implications of economic and social change, and in particular by reconciling it, between 1867 and 1880, to the conditions resulting from the political emergence of the working classes. For many modern Conservatives Disraeli stands as the originator of the concept of "Tory Democracy" by which they profess still to be inspired.

The development of "Disraelian" Conservatism between 1867 and 1880 thus appears as a vital factor in the making of the modern party. So, no doubt, it was. But the most cursory examination shows that the history of the Conservative party in the 'seventies and after cannot be written in terms of its adaptation to "Disraelian" ideas of popular appeal and social amelioration. As it emerged from the Disraelian era, the party bore only faintly the impress of Disraelian inspiration, and, despite Lord Randolph Churchill, the master's most potent contribution to its persona turned out to be imperialism, rather than the Tory Democracy with which his name is most commonly associated. The party of Salisbury and Balfour can hardly be described as Disraelian, still less the party of Bonar Law, Baldwin, and Neville Chamberlain. The basic theme in the evolution of modern Conservatism, it may be argued, is not *rapprochement* with the masses in the spirit of the Disraelian ideal, but the assimilation of the bourgeoisie, in whose image the modern party is so obviously cast—a process more in accordance with the policy of Peel than with the "democratic" Toryism attributed to Disraeli. Modern historians have not failed to notice that "though the myth of conservatism has been more often Disraelian, its practice has been almost uniformly Peelite," and that what emerged from the 'seventies and 'eighties was a "Peelite" rather than a "Disraelian" type of party.

It is sometimes held that 1886 was "the turning-point in the history of modern Conservatism," when Lord Randolph Churchill fell, and the Liberal split over Home Rule set in motion that influx into the Conservative party of "injured or apprehensive propertied interests in flight from the radicalism of the 'old man in a hurry' " which was to make it "the great bulwark of 'vested interests.' " Certainly 1886 has considerable importance, but the movement towards Conservatism of "injured or apprehensive propertied interests" and of the defensively-minded sections of the bourgeoisie was already appreciable in the 'seventies; and the achievement by the party of the alliance of landed with industrial and commercial property which Peel's policy had been directed to securing was in sight before Home Rule became a major political issue. There is reason to maintain that the very period which saw the efflorescence of "Disraelian" Conservatism was that which witnessed the fruiting of a line of policy closely comparable to the outlook and approach of Peel. It was precisely at the moment when Disraeli was inducing it to coquet with the working classes that the party was tending to consummate its relations with the urban bourgeoisie. The political practice of Disraeli himself seems on close examination to be largely "Peelite" in spirit.

The question of what was happening to the Conservative party between 1867 and 1880 requires more intensive study than it has hitherto received. It is necessary to ask how far the party's thought and practice were influenced by "Disraelian" ideas and orientated in a "Disraelian" direction, and how far, on the other hand, they took a course which might be more properly described as "neo-Peelite." The analysis of this problem should throw light on the nature of the process of adaptation to changing social conditions which Conservatism was undergoing, and thus assist in a clearer understanding of the evolution of the modern party.

A central feature of "Disraelian" Conservatism was social reform. Attention to the material needs of the masses was one of the basic means by which the Conservative party was to bring about class harmony, guarantee social stability, and secure support. Disraeli's stress on "the elevation of the condition of the people" is commonly regarded as one of his most important contributions to the development of his party, vital in enabling it to come to terms with the rising social and political power of the working classes and to sustain its appeal to the post-1867 electorate. The tradition of Conservative social reform which Disraeli did more than anyone to establish has been markedly useful to the modern party in its efforts to represent itself as the friend of the working man. Yet there is no detailed study of the role which social reform played in the thought and action of the Conservative party in the Disraelian era. The subject is worth investigation, not merely as being interesting in itself and in relation to the development of social policy and social legislation, but because it is important for the analysis of the real character of the Conservative metamorphosis in the late 'sixties and the 'seventies. By examining the place of social reform in the strategy of the parliamentary Conservative party, and scrutinising the attitudes which the party in practice adopted towards those social questions which primarily affected the condition of the working classes, in the years which separate the beginning of Lord Derby's third ministry in 1866 from the defeat of the Beaconsfield government in the general election of 1880, it should be possible to gauge more accurately how far Conservatism was moving in a "Disraelian" direction, and how far it was being shaped in other moulds, and thus to gain insight into the nature of its accommodation to social change. Such is the object of this work.

* * *

Disraeli's concept of Toryism was almost fully formed by 1846, and in essentials it never changed. The ideas which he propounded in 1835 in the *Vindication of the English Constitution in a Letter to a Noble and Learned Lord,* summarised in 1836 in *The Spirit of Whiggism,* and developed in 1844-5 in the novels *Coningsby* and *Sybil,* formed the basis of his expressed political outlook for the remainder of his career, and reappeared virtually unaltered in the famous speeches of 1867 and 1872. Upon them much of his fame rests.

Whether, or in what sense, he believed them has always been a matter of controversy. His best friends were never sure. It is a convention in England to regard politics as a matter of principle and conviction. Disraeli saw them primarily as the arena for the display of his remarkable talents. "We come here" he told Bright once at Westminster, "for fame!" His political ideas were not the motive force of his performance, but rather the costume which he wore in deference to the susceptibilities of his audience. A Jew, a quasi-intellectual, and a *littérateur,* standing by background and temperament outside the customary frame of British political life, he set himself not to assert a principle or attain an ideal, but to play the role of the romantic hero on the most unlikely of all stages, the floor of the House of Commons; and by wit, courage, and extraordinary force of will he succeeded. In order to take part in the game, he had to bow to its rules and adapt himself to the context in which he operated.

He conceives it right [Bright noted] to strive for a great career with such principles as are in vogue in his age and country—says the politics and principles to suit England must be of the "English type"....

But the traditional tenets and allegiances of English politics could have only limited meaning for him, and it is a question how far he took them seriously.

He was a detached and deeply sceptical man, who did not believe in much. His own ideas came less from the logical processes of the intellect than from the imagination; their status was not so much that of rational propositions, which might be true or untrue, as that of mental images, loosely related to reality, and designed for inspiration and for use, not for resistance to criticism. The power of human reason was, for Disraeli, severely limited. "Man," declared his *alter ego,* Sidonia, in *Coningsby,* "is only truly great when he acts from the passions; never irresistible but when he appeals to the imagination"; moreover, he is "made to adore and to obey," and needs not so much arguments for his understanding as images for his worship. Given their essentially nonrational character, it is not surprising that Disraeli's ideas should have been formulated with small regard for precision, coherence, and literal truth. Original and bizarre, brilliant and meretricious, fanciful and vulgar, mingling the true coin with the false, like the man himself, their value lies in insights, not in conclusions. They are a personal extravaganza, not an intellectual system. Their author "believed" in them as an artist in the artifact, not as a mathematician in the theorem. But they form a part of his public personality and of his political significance, and cannot be ignored.

Embarking on his political career in 1832-4, when Radicalism seemed to be on the upgrade, and social questions were coming into prominence, Disraeli had professed Radical and popular views, including a strong concern for the condition of the people. When the search for a seat in Parliament carried him into the Tory camp, he at once produced a version of Toryism which not merely accommodated these views but drew its distinctive character from them. The basis of his creed was his interpretation of English history since 1688 as essentially the story of the efforts of the Whig magnates to rivet a "Venetian" oligarchy upon an unwilling nation. The Reform Act of 1832 was represented as the latest step in this process, a Whig *coup d'état*, designed to facilitate the establishment of a centralising tyranny by enfranchising a class hostile to Crown, Lords, Church, and the landed interest, the institutions which alone could protect the national rights and liberties against Whig aggression. The undermining of the national institutions in the name of "liberalism" deprived the mass of the people of their main bulwarks against exploitation and oppression, and together with the growth of industrial and commercial wealth divorced from a sense of social obligation was largely responsible for the existence of the social problem, which threatened to rip apart the existing fabric of society. Disraeli was deeply impressed with the dangers inherent in the abandonment of the working classes to the vicissitudes of an industrial society governed by the tenets of individualism and political economy, and struck by the gulf between the "two nations" of rich and poor which he portrayed in *Sybil*, and the restoration of social cohesion was from the first among his major political themes.

The function of resisting Whig designs and reconciling the two nations was assigned in Disraeli's scheme of things to the landed aristocracy and gentry, the mainstay of England's "territorial constitution," and the obvious guarantors, together with Crown and Church, of the liberties and privileges of the people, whose "natural leaders" they supplied. It was in them that the masses must trust, not in their own movements. Theirs was the task of upholding "popular principles" against the selfish and irresponsible doctrines of Liberalism. It was the reaffirmation of the tenets of the society for which, in Disraeli's eyes, they stood, a hierarchical, paternalistic society, permeated by a sense of social responsibility, and held together by a universal nexus of rights and duties, that would secure the contentment and docility of the labouring classes. Disraeli did not really suppose that a return could be made to the medieval social order which Young England idealised, but he did advocate a revival of its imagined spirit.

The feudal system may have worn out [he wrote in maturity], but its main principle, that the tenure of property should be the fulfilment of duty, is the essence of good government.

It was for the Tory party, the political organ of the landed interest, to serve as the instrument of the nation's salvation. "The Tory party in this country," Disraeli insisted as soon as he had joined it, "is the national party; it is the really democratic party of England." It was necessary to recall it to its historic role of representing the nation and the people against the assaults of oligarchy, and to ensure

1st. That the real character and nature of Toryism should be generally and clearly comprehended: 2ndly. That Toryism should be divested of all those qualities which are adventitious and not essential, and which having been produced by the course of circumstances which are constantly changing, become in time obsolete, inconvenient, and by the dexterous misrepresentation of our opponents even odious: 3rdly. That the efficient organization of the party should be secured and maintained.

There, Disraeli liked to think, was the programme of his life's work.

Disraeli's "national" Toryism envisaged a mutually advantageous alliance between the party and the people, in which social paternalism would be traded for support of the established order. He agreed, he told the popular politician Charles Attwood, in 1840, that "an union between the Conservative party and the Radical masses offers the only means by which we can preserve the Empire. Their interests are identical; united they form the nation. . . .Recoiling from the idea that the corn law struggle would result in the transfer of power to the manufacturing class, he declared to the Commons, in February 1846, that instead of falling under "the thraldom of capital,"

. . . if we must find a new force to maintain the ancient throne and immemorial monarchy of England, I, for one, hope that we may find that novel power in the invigorating energies of an educated and enfranchised people.

The cement of the union between party and people was to be social reform, and in *Sybil* Disraeli offered the vision of the Toryism of Bolingbroke and Wyndham rising from the tomb "to bring back strength to the Crown, liberty to the subject, and to announce that power has only one duty—to secure the social welfare of the PEOPLE." Against the doctrines of political economists and "brutilitarians" he pitted the concept of the organic society, deriving its cohesion from the observance of mutual obligation, and ready to employ the force of government to promote the well-being of the masses.

The Disraelian version of Toryism as a strange mixture of insight and *opéra bouffe*. Its contact with reality was precarious: this was especially true of its analysis of the social situation and the possibilities it offered for a junction between the Tory party and the people. Its author never seriously attempted the task of rendering its romantic ideals into the concrete detail of policies and bills; such was not his forte. His advocacy of social reform was accompanied by no programme of measures; his criticism of the evil of allowing the dictates of individualist economics to override considerations of social welfare was not supplemented by the formulation of an alternative economic system upon which a social policy could be based. His practical contribution towards raising the condition of the people was not very extensive or assiduous: he voted for the repeal of the new poor law, spoke with some sympathy on Chartism., opposing excessive penalties for its leaders, and supported the ten-hours cause, but he did little more. Sharing the prejudices of his party against administrative centralisation, he joined in their hostility to important measures of social improvement which involve its growth, opposing, for instance, the Education Order of 1839 and the Public Health Act of 1848. Disraeli's popular Toryism, in short, was an idea, an attitude, not a policy, and what its progenitor was calling for was a regeneration, not a reconstruction, of society. Moreover, it had no sooner been fully formulated than circumstances compelled the muting of its expression.

It had provided a useful platform against Peel, but after 1846 it was no longer needed for this purpose and was becoming more of a liability than an asset. Transmuted from a back-bench *frondeur* into leader of the Conservative party in the Commons, Disraeli had to adjust himself to his new position. His hold on the party was, and for nearly twenty-five years was to remain, precarious, and he could not afford to risk it by stressing ideas which had no appeal for his chief, Stanley, and to which most of his followers were at best indifferent, at worst deeply hostile. Nor could he fail to realise, as the unrest of the 'forties gave way to the relative calm of the 'fifties, and social tensions relaxed, that the conditions on which the success of his brand of Toryism must depend were becoming rarer. There was little sacrifice involved in thrusting his popular doctrines into the background of his public persona. His attachment to his own ideas was shallow enough, as his conduct over the Mines Bill of 1850 neatly demonstrated. If Disraeli's professions of social concern were heartfelt, he should have supported this measure, vital to the welfare of the miners in providing for mines inspection. In fact, he opposed it at the request of one of the most tyrannical and inhumane coal-owners of the day, his friend Lord Londonderry, although, as he gaily told Lady Londonderry, "I know nothing about it!" That he was simultaneously renewing his support of the ten-hours cause does not remove the impression that five years after *Sybil* his practical zeal for "the social welfare of the PEOPLE" was not strong. From the Disraeli of the 'fifties no call to the junction of party and people and the pursuit of social reform could come.

The party was, in fact, tending increasingly in the 'fifties and early 'sixties to resume the course indicated by Peel and cultivate urban middle-class support. Electorally, it had no choice. Derby tried hard to broaden its base by bringing Gladstone and his fellow Peelites back, an effort which might have led eventually to a party reconstructed on Peelite principles with Gladstone at its head, and which perhaps only Gladstone's detestation of Disraeli prevented from succeeding. He did much, with Disraeli, to draw his followers away from the sterility of mere reaction and lead them back towards the mildly progressive Conservatism for which Peel had stood. At the beginning of his second ministry, in 1858, he recognised the necessity of meeting the demands of society by "judicious changes," and the 1858-9 government was sufficiently liberal in spirit (it even produced a Reform Bill) to cause mutterings among its supporters

Whatever his popular predilections of the 'forties, Disraeli fully concurred in the renewal of the effort to draw in the satisfied and defensive middle classes. No doubt his political thought, with its stress on the common interest and sympathies of Crown, aristocracy, and people, had tended to leave the bourgeoisie outside the pale, and even to represent it as a parcel of low Whigs and dissenters, whose spirit was inimical to that of the "nation." No doubt as a literary intellectual and a leader of the landed aristrocracy and gentry he looked down on bourgeois manners and pursuits. But he was too intelligent not to recognise (as in the portraits of the enterpreneurs Millbank and Trafford, in *Coningsby* and *Sybil,* and in the remark that "rightly understood, Manchester is as great a human exploit as Athens") the capacities and achievements of the industrial and commercial middle classes, and as a party leader avid for power he could not ignore the possibilities of incorporating them into a conservative alliance with land, in the manner of Peel.

Though Disraeli had made his fortune as Peel's executioner, it is doubtful how deep his hostility to Peel's general policy had been. Certainly there was a great difference in temper between his Toryism and Peelite Conservatism, with its lack of imagination and popular sympathies; but the philippics of 1844-6 owed as much to spleen at having been refused office by Peel in 1841, and to sheer ambition, as to divergence of political outlook. Disraeli's criticisms of Peel's Conservatism were rather nebulous, boiling down to the vague charge that it failed to assert genuine Tory principles, and it is noteworthy that in the very book, *Coningsby*, in which he gave them their most pungent expression, he approved, as a consonant with the Pittite tradition, the kind of adaptive, "liberal" approach which Liverpool's cabinet had pursued in the 'twenties, and for which Peel stood. He realised, like Peel, that substantial sections of the bourgeoisie had essentially conservative interests and could be induced to co-operate with the old aristocratic and landed classes in defending the established order, and if he laughed at the type of Peel's new Conservative Association, "with a banker for its chairman, and a brewer for its vice-president," he was far from despising the uses of bankers and brewers as auxiliaries of the aristocracy and gentry.

Disraeli saw clearly in the 'fifties and early 'sixties that if the Conservative party was to get out of minority and into power, it must resume the Peelite policy which he had wrecked in 1846 and render itself more palatable to urban middle-class taste. Protection had no sooner been jettisoned than he was embarking on his curious flirtation with Bright, discussing with his colleagues how to get at the urban vote, and stressing the identity of interest between town and country and the stake of the bourgeoisie in the maintenance of the national institutions. The second Derby ministry found him seeking anxiously to give the party a more "liberal" aspect and broaden its base. If he still sometimes recurred to the Toryism of "popular principles," upholding "the rights of the multitude," it was towards supplying the mildly progressive Peelite Conservatism which answered to the middle-class mood that his main practical effort was directed.

Bringing in the urban middle-class vote was uphill work. In a period of prosperity and low social tension, with the working classes quiescent and the Radical challenge unimpressive, there was little to drive the bourgeoisie into the Conservative party. The party's post-1846 image, despite the efforts of Derby and Disraeli, was too obscurantist, obstructive, and sectional to attract an electorate which, though conservative in temper, was concerned to have moderate progress. With the appeal exerted from the late 'fifties onwards by Palmerston, to many the soundest conservative in the country, it proved almost impossible to compete. There were, it is true, some signs by the 'sixties that the prospects for the Conservative party among the urban bourgeoisie were improving. Important elements of the middle classes, economically and socially satisfied, were taking up a defensive posture against the more radical tendencies of Liberalism, and against the advance of "democracy." Stanley told Disraeli in 1860 that the towns were full of "Conservative opinion, disguised as Moderate Liberalism," and it was only a matter of time before the disguise was thrown off. The Conservative party was beginning to show an appreciable representation of the industrial, commercial, and professional bourgeoisie in its ranks, with men like R. A. Cross, the barrister and country banker, who held Preston in 1857-62, the shipbuilder Laird, who represented his fief of Birkenhead from 1861, the Feildens and Hornbys, who led the party in Blackburn, each family providing a member for the borough in 1865, or Hugh Birley, W. R. Callender, junior, and J. W. Maclure, Conservative leaders in Manchester. There was reason to hope that this representation would eventually be reinforced by the accession of Palmerstonians such as the bookstall king, W. H. Smith, who in April 1865 was looking forward to the junction of Palmerston's and Derby's moderate adherents in a Liberal-Conservative party. But the fact remains that by 1865 the Conservatives had achieved only limited inroads among the urban middle-class voters, and their position in the towns was weak, sustained in too many cases by little more than "family tradition, social prestige, beer, corruption, and the Church".

The situation of the Conservative party in the mid-'sixties was, indeed, critical. It had failed to come to terms with urban and industrial Britain and its expanding social forces. It remained overwhelmingly the party of the landed and agricultural interest, deriving the great bulk of its parliamentary strength from the agricultural counties and small rural boroughs, and based primarily on southern and south-eastern England. Unable to attract the urban middle or working classes in large numbers, it could win few seats in the major centres of industry and population, and compared with its opponents could muster only a small representation of industrial and commercial interests on its benches. Though it was, of course, very far from monopolising the landed or excluding the manufacturing and commercial interest, which were in any case closely intertwined, the Liberal M.P. Hayter was not guilty of outrageous caricature, at least as regards the Conservatives, when in 1867 he spoke of the two great parties, "the one of which represented the agricultural, the other the manufacturing and commercial interests of our vast community."

The land was the only great interest from which the Conservative party drew real strength; and the relative economic and social weight of the land was slowly declining. The party was founded on a shrinking base; it stood for no emergent trend; there was no demand of the hour which it alone could fulfil. Its principles were implemented by its chief opponent: Derby was reduced to a tame support of Palmerston's regime, and it became hard to discern what the difference between Conservative and Liberal policy was. The only hope for the resurrection of the party's fortunes seemed to lie in the eventual disintegration of the opposing force. As Derby wrote despondently to Disraeli, after the Conservative setback in the general election of 1865,

. . . a purely Conservative Government is all but hopeless, until, upon Palmerston's death (for he will never resign), Gladstone tries his hand with a Radical Government and alarms the middle classes. Then there may come a reaction: but it will probably be too late for *my* time. . .

It was, in fact, Palmerston's death in October 1865 which gave the Conservatives a prospect of revival. The political situation was suddenly fluid. Russell and Gladstone were now free to pursue a policy of movement, and in particular to take up in earnest the question of parliamentary reform. A large extension of the franchise among the urban working class and a redistribution of seats in favour of the grossly under-represented manufacturing areas of the north and midlands became serious possibilities; these were the aims of the resurgent alliance between middle-class Radicalism and the working classes which Bright symbolised and inspired, and their imminent achievement threatened both the Conservative party and the world which it existed to preserve. Parliamentary reform, to the middle-class Radicals, was primarily a means of introducing into the fortress of the constitution a select contingent of working-class allies, and shifting the balance of representation towards urban and industrial Britain, in order that they might finally break down the grip of aristocracy, land, and Church and reform the country in their own image, doing what they had failed to do in 1832 and 1846. If they were allowed to carry it out in their own way, Conservatism risked being overwhelmed. But at the same time, the advance of Radicalism and "democracy" and the energy of Gladstone and Bright promised to reinvigorate the Conservative party by driving into its arms the Whigs and more moderate Liberals and the middle-class Palmerstonians. The Conservatives could hope to achieve at last a monopoly of conservatism, and to construct what Disraeli had called in August 1865 "an antirevolutionary party on a broad basis," fusing the defensive elements of the bourgeoisie with the landed interest in the great alliance of property which the Radical menace had enabled Peel to initiate a quarter of a century earlier.

Gladstone's introduction of a Reform Bill in 1866 thus opened a crucial phase for the Conservative party in its efforts to extend the socio-economic foundations of its support and extricate itself from a twenty-year minority The party's leaders were not committed against Reform in principle: they had always been careful to maintain their freedom of manoeuvre on the question, and had introduced a very restricted measure themselves in 1859. Disraeli, grasping that, since power followed the distribution of property, a wide franchise was perfectly compatible with government by a limited class, had little innate fear of an enlarged suffrage, and his strong warnings in 1859 and 1865 against the evils of democracy and the reduction of the £10 borough qualification were partly aimed at pleasing conservative middle-class sentiment. But, in the circumstances of 1866, it was inevitable that he and Derby should oppose Gladstone's bill. Their stand conformed to the feeling of the party, which certainly disliked and feared the idea of a substantially-widened franchise, and inclined to follow Viscount Cranborne (the future third Marquis of Salisbury) in seeing the Reform struggle as "a battle not of parties, but of classes" and "a portion of the great political struggle of our century—the struggle between property, be its amount small or great, and mere numbers." It was, however more a matter of tactics than of principle. Derby and Disraeli could not allow their opponents to alter the representative system on their own terms and to their own advantage, enfranchising just that class of workmen who might be expected to vote for Gladstone and Bright, but leaving a margin for further reductions whenever they should need an issue adapted to place the Conservative party in an obstructive and unpopular position; nor could they let slip the providential opportunity which Reform offered of breaking up the Liberals and winning over the satisfied and apprehensive middle classes.

Their policy quickly paid dividends. The Liberals were, indeed, disrupted. The air was full of projects of combination between the Conservatives and some of the Whigs in the first months of 1866, and in June the revolt of the Adullamites brought Russell's ministry down. The Queen summoned Derby to take office for the third time with a minority in the House of Commons. The moment seemed ripe for a Conservative-Whig fusion, but it failed to materialise, perhaps because Derby and Disraeli feared for their personal positions in a coalition, perhaps also because they wanted to avoid committing themselves too decidedly against Reform. Nonetheless, there was a good prospect that the new government would attract Whig support, and would be able to base itself solidly on the favour of the Palmerstonian middle classes. Derby made it clear in his ministerial statement on 9 July that he looked forward to a speedy political re-alignment in which the Conservative party would consolidate all the conservative forces in the nation in opposition to Radicalism and democracy:

. . . I do not [he said] conceal my hope—because I look to the real, and not the arbitrary distinctions of party—I do not conceal my earnest hope that the time is not far distant when there may be such a new arrangement of parties as to place on the one side those who are in favour of dangerous innovations and violations of the Constitution, and on the other side all those who, while they will not resist safe legislative progress, are determined to adhere to this Constitution and to those institutions under which this country has so long been loyal, prosperous, and happy.

It seemed in July 1866 that the Conservative party stood on the threshold of achieving the goal which Peel had failed to reach twenty years before, and refounding its fortunes on an alliance of landed and commercial property for the defence of the constitution and the social order. It was Peel's Liberal-Conservatism, drawing in the bourgeoisie, not Disraeli's faded popular Toryism, looking to the masses, that was to be the basis of its adaptation to social change.

The masses could not, however, be left out of Conservative calculations. No party which aspired to govern could, in the mid-'sixties, altogether ignore the growing social and political force of urban labour, to which the demand for Reform had begun to give focus and direction. If the Conservatives were to re-establish their fortunes on a stable and permanent foundation, it was essential that they should find means of cultivating support among the urban working men.

The gulf between the Conservative party and the urban working classes in 1866 was a wide one. As the party of land and agriculture, with little strength in the great towns and manufacturing regions, the Conservatives were largely out of touch with urban and industrial Britain and its inhabitants, and little attuned to its problems and needs. They had very slight appeal for the politically-conscious working men, who were generally found in close association with bourgeois Liberalism and Radicalism. Perhaps the only area in which they could claim substantial working-class support was Lancashire, and Lancashire working-class Conservatism was a special case, owing a good deal to Protestant and anti-Irish feeling, and to the association of Toryism in the 'thirties and 'forties with the operatives' struggle for factory reform and against the new poor law.

Nonetheless, it was not inconceivable that the Conservatives should extend their working-class support. It was here that social questions were likely to become of increasing importance in the party's stategy. Social improvement was almost the only card with which it could attempt to conciliate working-class opinion. Less closely identified than its opponents with the interests of the entrepreneurial class, and boasting some tradition of social concern, it might hope to show to advantage in compromising with the working men's economic and social demands and bettering their material condition. Even apart from their possible political uses, social questions were bound to impinge increasingly on its attention. They were becoming again, as they had been in the 'forties, part of the staple of politics, and neither party could any longer afford to neglect them. Much would depend in the future on Conservative ability to grapple effectively with social problems and safeguard the welfare of those whom they most directly touched.

The party's interest in, and grasp of, social problems was extremely limited. It had no shadow of a social policy: the conditions of mid-Victorian politics did not require it—or its opponents—to produce one. For nearly twenty years social questions had been in the background of politics; Conservatives had not been compelled to interest themselves in them, and in the mere twenty-six months of office which they had enjoyed since 1846 they had acquired little experience of them from the governmental viewpoint. They numbered in their ranks very few middle-class professional people of the type who were in the nineteenth century the driving force of social investigation and the formulation of social policy. They did not, except for a few individuals like Pakington or Adderley, spend much time thinking about social problems, and had small knowledge of them in their most acute manifestations in the great towns. As was natural with a party based on land and agriculture, what they did know and think about such problems derived largely from their practical experience of them in the countryside. The system of amateur administration by the local gentry, which still governed the countryside, and the social obligations attaching to land, compelled a degree of acquaintance with social questions, and helped often to nurture some sense of social responsibility. It was as magistrates, poor law guardians, and voluntary school managers and subscribers that many Conservatives formed their acquaintance with and views on social issues. The training was doubtless valuable, but the outlook it developed was seldom broad.

It is impossible to say that towards social problems in general and the question of the proper role of government and legislation in dealing with them there was any coherent or distinctive Conservative attitude. The antithesis occasionally drawn between a Liberal party wedded to *laisser-faire* capitalism and a Conservative party championing the paternal use of the authority of the state is a crude oversimplification. There was, indeed, an element of social paternalism in the outlook of the Conservative party, but with it mingled doubts about the state's power for good, misgivings as to the increase of centralisation and taxation, and reservations learned from the teachings of political economy, which seriously curtailed its force

The paternal, reformist Toryism of the 'thirties and 'forties, still remembered to the party's credit by the working men of the north, furnished a tradition of which Conservatism could make good propaganda use, but little of it was left by 1866, except, perhaps, in and around Manchester, where its spirit lived on in the hands of men like Birley, Callender, and Maclure. Oastler was dead, and of his leading colleagues only Ferrand remained politically active. Young England had become a historical curiosity, though in Manners, if not Disraeli, some of its ingenuous idealism survived. Shaftesbury still laboured prodigiously, but he stood largely outside party, and had small influence with his fellow Conservatives. The paternalist approach to social questions continued, however, to be discernible in the party. Its basis was generally a sense of duty towards the poor deriving from religion. With this mingled ordinary humanitarianism, and the consciousness of social obligation which Conservatives liked to think characterised the hierarchical rural world where most of them still had their roots. Such feelings might often issue in no more than private and local philanthropy. But coupled with fear of social upheaval if reform was not pursued, and sometimes with a tendency to welcome outlets for the venting of spite against the encroachments of industrial civilisation and its acolytes, they might generate support for the paternal intervention of the state on a national scale, to protect the social interests of its weaker members. While accepting that social improvement must depend ultimately on the elevation of the individual, a number of Conservatives felt that the minimum conditions for advance should be—perhaps could only be—secured by governmental action; and though attached to liberty, they understood that its enjoyment by the mass of the population might depend as much upon the presence as upon the absence of state interference in economic and social life, and that laws and regulations could be used, as Shaftesbury said, not to abridge "but to *enlarge* man's freedom; not to limit his rights, but to multiply his opportunities for enjoying them . . . ."

There was, however, much in the outlook of Conservatives to discourage social paternalism. The influence of religion by no means always favoured it: social evils might receive a kind of sanction from the idea of divine ordination, and the power of the state to achieve social amelioration might be discounted by those to whom the doctrine of original sin suggested that it was upon grace, not social reform, that the betterment of mankind must depend. The positive dangers of governmental interference in the social sphere, too, were very present in Conservative thinking. Viewing society as an organism, Conservatives were chary of disturbing what might be supposed to be its natural processes of growth. Social progress, they tended to feel, should come rather by internal evolution than by the artificial action of government, which was as likely to bring damage as benefit. There was very strong Conservative prejudice against the increase of centralised adminstration which commonly accompanied state intervention in social questions. Local self-government and independence appeared as an essential bulwark of civil liberty and a vital stimulant of those corporate virtues which formed the basis of the national character. Conservatives were determined to resist its erosion, especially in the countryside, where the landed classes had no intention of brooking any serious central challenge to the power which they had exercised since the Restoration. This localism, mingled with engrained respect for the rights of property, and coupled with the particularism of all kinds of special groups and interests, produced a Tory brand of *laisser-faire*, repulsing the interference of government in social matters, and seeking the motive force of social progress, if at all, in individual, corporate, and local initiative.

Nor was the mind of Conservatism unaffected by those objections to governmental social action deriving from political economy which are often listed among the stage properties of classical Liberalism. Conservatives in general looked at social problems in the 'sixties in the light of economic presuppositions identical with those of their opponents. They drew their basic economic ideas, as did Liberals, from the orthodox political economy of the day, built on the principles of individualism and free trade: there was, indeed, no other source available, for the tide of mid-Victorian prosperity seemed so convincing a proof of the validity of free trade economics as to give them a virtual monopoly of intellectual respectablility. Orthodox political economy—or rather that simplified, vulgarised, and slightly outdated version of it with which practical men usually worked—was by no means rigorously *laisser-fraire*, but its conclusion was commonly understood to be that the free pursuit of individual interest tended to result in the maximum of public wealth and welfare, and that consequently the interference of the state in economic and social life, while often necessary and inevitable, was generally best kept to a minimum. Conservatives, like Liberals, mostly accepted that governmental social action required jealous scrutiny lest it damage the economic foundations of national prosperity, and agreed that the ineluctable operation of economic laws made its usefulness in many areas highly doubtful.

In a society actuated by individualism, it was primarily from the striving of the individual that social improvement must come, and the overwhelming majority of Conservatives adhered staunchly to that natural corollary of orthodox political economy, the secular religion of self-help. The doctrine of self-help fitted in neatly with the stress on the overriding moral responsibility of the individual derived from religious sources, and the two together persuaded most Conservatives that the "condition of the people" question must be solved largely by the people themselves. Continence, sobriety, industry, and thrift, coupled with that grasp of the operation of economic laws which was often expected to be a by-product of the increase of elementary education, would enable the working classes to raise themselves, with only minimal external assistance. Where assistance was required, reliance was placed first on the action of voluntaryism, carefully controlled so as to reinforce the existing social system and avoid interference with its competitive mechanics. Only secondarily might the state be called upon, to supplement and aid—but never, except in extreme cases, supplant—individual and voluntary efforts.

The Conservative party of 1866 was, in fact, predisposed against rather than towards the extension of governmental intervention in social questions. It would be hard to say that its general ideas on the subject differed much from those of its opponents: certainly there was no obvious division between individualism and political economy on the one side and paternalism on the other. Conservatives were somewhat less dogmatic than many Liberals in their suspicion of state action—they had few Henry Fawcetts and Robert Lowes—and were sometimes quicker to understand that without such action the shibboleths of "free trade" and "freedom of contract" might produce a mockery of justice. Their approach was perhaps more empirical, their readiness to employ the force of government in cases where the need for it could be convincingly demonstrated was perhaps more pronounced. That is all that can be said.

Though constantly debated in general terms, the problem of the proper role of government and legislation in economic and social affairs was, of course, in the end, one of particular cases, and Conservative attitudes were shaped less by general ideas than by the relation of given problems to the interests which the party represented, the experience it embodied, and the prejudices it harboured. The party of the mid-'sixties inevitably looked at social questions primarily in the context of the rural and agricultural world with which it was so intimately linked. The Conservative reaction towards proposals of social reform was determined very largely by their prospective impact in the countryside. Sometimes this enlarged the party's capacity to support social reform: in particular it could relatively easily back measures for the regulation of urban labour, by which rural interests were scarcely affected. But more often the effect was cramping. In the fields of education, public health, and poor relief especially the party's bucolic preoccupations severely restricted its approach. Projects of improvement in all these spheres were frequently associated with the advance of centralisation and the increase of rates which the landed interest detested; in education, too, the position of squire and parson and the supply of juvenile agricultural labour were very much at stake.

The rating issue was so important as to deserve special mention, for it probably did as much to shape Conservative attitudes towards social improvement as any other factor. By 1866 the local taxation question was the major grievance of the landed interest, and the creation in that year of the Central Chamber of Agriculture gave its discontent a new focus of organisation. The agriculturalists resented not merely the level of the rates but their allegedly unfair incidence (they fell on real property alone) and the fact that they went largely to meet expenditure imposed by the central government for not strictly local objects. They differed as to what should be done—the establishment of representative county boards to control expenditure, government grants in aid, and the rating of personal property were the main proposals—but pending reform they were united in hostility to all measures threatening to increase rate burdens. Most of their parliamentary advocates were Conservatives. Disraeli had deliberately, in 1849-50, directed the party's attention to the local taxation question, in order to divert the landed interest from the hopeless cause of protection, and by 1866 his followers' preoccupation with it was so strong as seriously to constrict their outlook when social questions involving the rates were discussed.

It is clear from a brief survey of its main characteristics that the general attitude of the Conservative party towards social problems was not such as to encourage (or even permit) the cultivation of working-class sympathies by an extensive programme of social reforms. But there was no reason why, under the stimulus of political necessity, the party should not do something in the field of social improvement to recommend itself to working-class opinion. The question was how far cautious social measures would be adequate to advance the party's position with the working classes. The more independent and intelligent working men were pursuing not merely material betterment but higher social status, symbolised in 1866 by the franchise, which was desired partly as a means to securing material ends, but very largely as a token of acceptance into the national political community. The Conservatives would have to do something to satisfy this demand if they were to make serious inroads on working-class favour.

Some of them did grasp the importance of the working-class desire for status. In 1853, writing to Disraeli about the Lancashire strikes, Stanley had noted that what the operatives wanted was "social emancipation—a higher position—not merely increased pay." Shaftesbury said during the Reform debates of 1867:

It has occurred to me for a long time, and I am certain it is true, that we have in a great measure outgrown our institutions. There is an expansive force among the people. The advance of wealth, the increase of education, the capacity, or at least the ambition, that every man now feels to occupy a higher station than that in which he has been placed by Providence—all these things tend to make men dissatisfied with the institutions of the country, because they fancy themselves cribbed, cabined, and confined by the restrictions which these institutions impose.

But it was very doubtful how far the Conservative party could come to terms with the "expansive force among the people." To too many of its members the "masses" were still a separate, inferior, and dangerous species, to be kept at bay. Working-class aspirations were regarded less with sympathy than with apprehension. This was especially true of the demand for the extension of the franchise. Many Conservatives interpreted the knocking at the gates of the constitution not as a request for admission but as the prelude to a sack, and Shaftesbury and the acid Cranborne were agreed in feeling that the coming of "Democracy" would mean the end of liberty and the spoliation of property by indigence. In such a climate of fear and mistrust a real *rapprochement* between the Conservative party and the masses was bound to be difficult of achievement. The palliatives of social reform alone would not be enough. But such as they were, the party could not afford to neglect them in the effort to escape from its twenty-year minority and refound its power on a wide and lasting basis.

Conclusion

The study of the Conservative party's attitude to the major social problems bearing on the condition of the working classes between 1866 and 1880, and of the influences which affected it, provides some assistance in the important task of analysing the character of the adjustment which the party was making in these years to economic and social change, and in particular to the advance of urban and industrial civilisation and the growing power of the urban bourgeoisie and workers. The examination of the place of social reform in Conservative strategy and tactics helps to emphasise that despite the emergence of the mass electorate and the increasingly central role of social issues in politics, the main element in this adjustment was not any effort to create a party on "Disraelian" lines, closely linked to the people by the bonds of social paternalism, and preaching the tenets of "Tory Democracy"; it was the gradual coming to fruit of the course which Peel had pursued in the 'thirties and early 'forties, and Derby and Disraeli had tried to resume in the 'fifties, a course which aimed to draw the satisfied and defensive sections of the bourgeoisie into alliance with the land, in a party combining the defence of the constitution and the social order with the pursuit of cautious progress.

Paradoxically, it was the second Reform Act of 1867, at first sight the coup by which Disraeli committed his party to the pursuit of "Tory Democracy," that in the long run did most to establish the conditions necessary for the assimilation of the bourgeoisie. While it gave the urban working men a substantial instalment of political power, and the consideration of working-class interests vital to politicians, it intensified the pressures and fears which tended to drive elements of the middle classes into the Conservative party, as the only reliable agency of resistance to the advance of Radicalism and labour. The gradual polarisation of politics after the Palmerstonian truce, and the re-emergence of the social tensions on which Conservatism had fed in the 'thirties and 'forties, and whose anaesthesia through prosperity had done much to account for its weakness in the 'fifties and early 'sixties, acted increasingly towards giving the Conservative party what Palmerston had denied it, and what was essential for its electoral success, a near-monopoly of the conservative forces in the country, and hastened the coalescence of industrial and commercial with landed property in the "Peelite" alliance.

The result was that in the years after 1867, just when the enlargement of the franchise had made it vital for the Conservatives to build up working-class support and show their capacity and will to deal with the social questions which must in future be a major political theme, they were inhibited in their approach to the masses by the counter-attraction of a growing middle-class support, largely dependent on their potential as a bulwark against popular demands. It was impossible for them (even had they been willing) to adopt a very "popular" platform or to go very far in appealing to the working men in terms of their special interests as a class. Their main emphasis, as Disraeli saw clearly, had to be on the idea of the "national" party, demonstrating the community of class interests in the maintenance of existing institutions. This prevented them from seriously trying to fill the vacuum left by the inability of official Liberalism to give complete satisfaction to working-class claims and aspirations, and in particular meant that there could be no question of their exploiting social issues in the spirit of the paternalist and radical Toryism of the 'thirties and 'forties, with which their leader's name was associated. Conservative social reform, in the Disraelian era, had to be cautious and restrained.

The party's tactical necessitites corresponded, of course, to its natural inclinations. Very few Conservatives had any taste for appealing to the people at large, and genuine "Tory Democrats," like Gorst, were rare and unappreciated. For most, the essential problem was not how to take the newly enfranchised working men into partnership, but how best to reconcile the acknowledgement of their novel political influence with the maintenance of their economic and social subordination. As representatives of property, Conservatives were necessarily opposed to working-class claims which trenched upon what they held to be its rights, and to schemes of social improvement which did likewise. Most of the property, still, was landed, and it was very largely in relation to rural society that social questions were viewed, with generally narrowing effects. This was especially true of such vital matters as education, health, and poor relief, which had a direct impact upon the rural ratepayers, local autonomy, and the stability of the rural social order. If its bucolic (and predominantly southern) roots made it a little easier for the party to support, say, factory legislation, which hardly touched rural and agricultural interests, they rendered it in general difficult for it adequately to understand and come to grips with the social wants of the working classes in the great centres of industry and population in the midlands and north.

There was never any distinctive Conservative approach to social questions, though it would perhaps be true to say that the party was slightly more influenced by paternalism and slightly less by economic orthodoxy than the Liberals. On the general problem of the role of government and legislation in dealing with social matters, the Conservative attitude was always ill-defined, but with an engrained bias against the extension of central intervention and control unless a very good case could be shown for it. This bias tended to become deeper after 1867 had made real the prospect that ultimately the power and authority of government would be applied at the behest of the working classes, to give effect to their own interpretation of their own interests; and it was reinforced by the influx into the party of the conservative bourgeoisie, anxious to restrict the employment of the force of the state to satisfy the claims of the labouring population. Such paternalism as the Conservative party possessed could not be transposed into support for the collectivism which seemed to threaten as a consequence of the widened suffrage, and Conservative pronouncements on social problems became increasingly marked by adherence to the tenets of freedom and individualism commonly regarded as characteristic of classical liberalism. All this militated against any attempt to formulate a positive and coherent Conservative social policy. Such a policy, in any case, would have required an economic policy as its base: the Conservatives did not have an economic policy, or the intellectual resources and taste for schematic thought required to produce one.

In these circumstances, there was no possibility of the party's going far along the "Disraelian" road of popular appeal and social reform. Nor did Disraeli make very strenuous efforts to lead it in that direction. The popular Toryism of his youth had been in part a romantic extravaganza, in part a gesture against Peel, without much practical content, and after 1846 it was pushed into the background as he saw that the resumption of Peel's policy was the only viable course for the party. His coup of 1867 was not an attempt to reestablish the party's fortunes on the support of the masses, but a manoeuvre designed to break the Whig monopoly of the cause of constitutional progress, which the tactical situation forced him to carry further than he would have chosen. After Reform, he was conscious as much of the neccessary limits on the party's cultivation of working-class votes as of its importance. Not until 1872 did he seriously attempt to make political capital out of support for the improvement of the social condition of the people. Then, indeed, he elevated social reform into one of the principal objects of his party. But he followed this with no concrete initiative or plan, and the imperialism which he proclaimed at the same time was in the end to be a more potent influence. In power, in 1874, he had no specific projects of social advance, though the weight of his general approval of the measures which his colleagures devised was vital to the development of the ministry's reforming effort. It was not that Disraeli lacked a genuine predilection for social improvement, or a keen appreciation of its political uses, but he understood the need for caution to reconcile its pursuit with the interests and prejudices of his existing and potential followers of the propertied classes, and knew that the emphasis of the Conservative platform must lie rather on the furtherance of the common cause of all classes than on the special promotion of the welfare of one. Living in uneasy symbiosis with a party to which he was in many ways alien, at once its leader and its prisoner, he could not transform its character or reshape its thinking; he could only influence and modify its outlook and course He did not found modern Conservatism; indeed, in destroying Peel, he had retarded its main line of development, the absorption of the bourgeoisie, by some twenty years. What he did was to assist its gestation, and facilitate its achievement of some kind of *modus vivendi* with the working classes.

Given the built-in hindrances to Conservative social reform, it seems remarkable that the party contributed as much as it did in the social field in 1866-80. Even in the short minority ministry of 1866-8 something was done for factory reform, the sick poor, and the merchant seamen, and the government of 1874-80 was responsible for one of the most notable instalments of social reform of the century, conspicuously shaming its Liberal predecessors. To some extent, these achievements were the product of a deliberate intention to use social improvement as a means of gaining working-class favour. But very largely they were semi-enforced responses to problems which ministers could not ignore, shaped principally by the results of formal inquiry, the pressure of public opinion, and the promptings of the civil service. They implemented no programme and embodied no philosophy. Nearly all were cautious and limited, and some were weak and ineffectual in working. Only the labour laws of 1875 went substantially beyond what the immediate situation demanded, presumably—we have little evidence on the genesis of these two measures—because Disraeli thought that a generous settlement would definitively establish his party as the real friends of the working man. Taken as a whole, the measures of 1866-8 and 1874-80 form an impressive corpus of work by contemporary standards, but what they symbolise is less Conservative zeal for social reform than Conservative empiricism in the face of concrete problems.

How much good they did the party is open to argument. Coupled with the second Reform Act, they enabled it to claim that it had the true interests of the labouring classes at heart. It is inconceivable that this had no electoral effect, but doubtful whether it had a great deal. The Conservatives could always rely, after 1867, on a certain amount of working-class support from "deference" voters and from men who simply were, on general grounds, Conservative; there appears to be little evidence that this was markedly increased (though it was doubtless consolidated) by social reform. The appeal to national solidarity and patriotic pride, which Disraeli made a Conservative stock-in-trade, was probably more powerful than the promise of social improvement. Neither, in any case, succeeded in detaching the bulk of the working-class electors and the organised labour movement from Liberalism. A main reason for this (which in the end was to damage Liberalism also) was the failure to offer the working men enhanced social status. True, the Conservative party had given many of them the franchise, but it showed small inclination to follow out the implications of this step by paying genuine deference to their feelings and aspirations and giving them a significant role in its organisation and councils. The National Union exemplified the party's deficiencies in this respect: its existence was a recognition of the need to build up working-class Conservatism, but the indifference and even hostility of much of the party to its work showed in what a grudging spirit that need was approached. The gulf between the "two nations" was not bridged; too firm a sense resided in one of its qualitative difference from the other.

After the defeat of 1880 and the death of Disraeli, the themes of popular appeal and social reform were more at a discount than ever. The bulk of the Conservative party was content to rely for future revival on the alienation of the moderate middle-class voter by its opponents. There was, of course, Lord Randolph Churchill, with his Tory Democracy, pursuing the supposedly "Disraelian" tradition. But Churchillian Tory Democrat was a collection of postures and slogans, rather than a policy, whose main purpose was to serve as a vehicle for its author. To some extent, it was the gesture of a young cavalier aristocrat against the respectable, middle-aged, bourgeois Conservatism represented by men like "Marshall and Snelgrove," as Lord Randolph called Cross and W. H. Smith. "Marshall and Snelgrove" and their like, however, were coming increasingly to form the basis of the Conservative party, and Churchill's approach stood no chance against them.

Perhaps the only important effect of Lord Randolph's reassertion of "Disraelian" ideals was to retard a little his party's true course of development by alarming the moderate opinion that was moving to the Conservative side in recoil from Chamberlainite Radicalism. The bourgeoisie continued, however, to flow into the party in force, and their importance to it went on increasing. They brought it badly needed resources, at a moment when agricultural depression was weakening the strength of its traditional mainstay, the landed interest; and after the redistribution of 1885, with its recognition of the primacy of the urban and industrial areas and its single-member constituencies, they were in a position to bring it a larger number of seats. The Liberal split over Home Rule gave a considerable impetus to the middle-class movement towards Conservatism, but it only intensified a process that had been perceptible for at least twenty years and was already showing significant results.

Coming over Ireland, the Liberal schism gave the Conservatives Chamberlain, but such strength as he brought to the popular and reforming side of the party was more than counterbalanced by the accession of the Whigs and "Commercial Liberals," with their deep distaste for the expansion of state intervention for the welfare of the working classes. As politics crystallised increasingly along class lines, the Conservatives became more and more a union of propertied interests, embattled against organised labour and socialism, and largely wedded to the classical liberal tenets of individualism and free enterprise. The type of party Peel had tried to construct in the 'forties finally materialised in the 'eighties and 'nineties. It did not (electorally it could not) lose sight of the working man or of social reform, but the "Disraelian" themes were very subdued under Salisbury, Balfour, and Bonar Law. By the beginning of the twentieth century, there was a feeling among those who found inspiration still in Disraelian ideas that the soul of the party had been corrupted. In 1907 Gorst, soon to be a Liberal candidate, lamented the decline of Tory Democracy, and complained that the Conservative leaders had abandoned Disraeli's principles for the pursuit of class interest; and had become "the champions of vested interests and the protectors of monopoly and privilege."

The strain of Conservative social consciousness, however, did not die out, and it was stimulated by reflection on the causes of the disaster of 1906. There continued to be those who saw the necessity of grappling with social problems, if the party was to operate successfully in the age of the mass electorate; even those who carried on the tradition of Tory paternalism and favoured the social action of the state, agreeing with Lord Hugh Cecil that there was "no antithesis between Conservatism and Socialism." If no Conservative social policy emerged, and no economic policy on which one could be based (though the association of tariff reform with the cause of social improvement might have provided both), the activities of elements like the pre-1914 Social Reform Committee and the "Group" of 1918 kept open a vital channel through which Conservatism could attempt to reach the mass of the people. Even in the locust years between the wars the vein of social responsibility occasionally touched the surface: but for Hitler, it is for his efforts at social reform that we should remember Neville Chamberlain.

Modern Conservatism is essentially "Peelite" in its structure and outlook, and it became so partly under Disraeli's auspices. But its striking electoral success since 1867 would have been impossible without its capacity to command a significant working-class vote, and here it owes something to Disreali's sense of the necessity of accepting the enlargement of the political nation and making the social condition of the people one of the prime objects of the party's concern. Disraeli could not create, and did not really try to create, a "Disraelian" party, but he was able to introduce into the personality of Conservatism an element that assisted it in coming to terms with the rise of democracy and labour. He could not marry the party to the people, or fuse the "two nations," but he did much to ensure that between them there should be no complete and fatal divide.

IMPERIALISM

10 / The "New Imperialism"

The "new imperialism" is a term used to describe the extraordinary expansion of European rule over so-called backward peoples, which took place roughly from 1870 to the outbreak of World War I. We call it "new" because, in general, imperial systems are almost as old as history itself, and more particularly, because we can associate imperialism with the sixteenth, seventeenth and eighteenth centuries, when some European states carved out large empires for themselves in the New World or in the East. By the early decades of the nineteenth century, most of the New World colonies had won their independence and in addition a relative indifference to colonial expansion developed in Western Europe. The old empires in the New World had been, in a sense, projections—New Spain, New England, New France—of their mother country. Colonists there had settled in uninhabited or sparsely populated lands and had brought with them the institutions or traditions of their homeland.

By contrast the new imperialism was a movement in which small groups of Europeans sought to rule or to exploit relatively heavily populated areas in North Africa and Egypt, or densely populated areas in Asia, each with established institutions of their own—sovereign states, in some cases, that had entered into commercial or financial agreements with the European powers which took them over. Or, as in the case of tropical Africa and the desert regions, a whole subcontinent was divided up for what wealth or prestige it might bring without much hope of permanent European settlement.[1]

Other distinguishing features of the new imperialism were its extensiveness and the speed with which it was carried out. Not that these were intentional in the beginning. The British Empire is often described as having been created in "fits of absent-mindedness." But one wheel turned another, so that by the 1890's a competitive drive for empire was on between the Western European powers.[2] It

[1] South Africa and Algeria, with relatively extensive European settlement, could be called exceptions to the general pattern described in this paragraph. But while Britain acquired most of her South African possessions during the period of the new imperialism, she took them from what might be called a native, white population: the Boers, descendants of seventeenth-century Dutch settlers in the Cape Colony. The conquest of Algeria began in 1830; by 1870 there were three hundred thousand European settlers and a structure for colonization established there which had no counterpart in the subsequently acquired areas of the French Empire.
[2] As will be seen in the selections that follow, the United States, Japan, and Russia were also affected by imperialism, but their efforts cannot be placed in the same category as those of the European powers.

helped to sweep them into World War I, but even the war did not entirely halt the imperialist drive until France and Britain, not without some mutual recriminations and suspicion, had divided the Near Eastern parts of the defeated Ottoman Empire between them and acquired most of the former German-African colonies under the mandate system. Looking back on the course of little more than half a century, Parker T. Moon could observe in 1926 that:

Of ancient imperialism, of the empires of Alexander, of Cyrus, of Caesar, we have heard much and of Napoleon's spectacular exploits every schoolboy has read. But the realms conquered by military emperors of past ages were baubles, trifles compared with the far-flung dominions which have been won, more often with the pen than by the sword, in our own supposedly prosaic generation . . . .

Little as the general public may realize the fact, imperialism is the most impressive achievement and the most momentous world-problem of our age. Perhaps this statement should be thrust home. More than half of the world's land surface, and more than a billion human beings, are included in the colonies and "backward countries," dominated by a few imperialist nations.[3]

The problem that has occupied historians and others, and one which the three selections that follow treat, is the motivation of this imperial expansion. At the time many justifications for imperialism were given—control of raw materials and new markets, sometimes called neo-mercantilism, military security, outlets for surplus population, and the civilizing mission of "white man's burden."

Although there is some value in each of these explanations, none seemed sufficient to account for the gigantic scale of imperialist activity. A first and penetrating criticism of these justifications was made by the British economist, J. A. Hobson, in 1902 in *Imperialism, A Study.* Published during the heyday of Empire, Hobson's book caused an immediate sensation and has had a continuing influence on subsequent writings on the subject. Hobson was one of the first to point out that while imperialism benefitted only a few interests in the nation, it burdened the collectivity with a heavy cost.

This being the case, Hobson asked what were the motive forces of imperialism. There were many immediate causes, including such noneconomic forces as patriotism, adventure, the influence of the military, and so forth. Hobson also considered trade, but found it a negligible factor in comparison with the return from overseas investment. Thus he was led to conclude that investment and allied financial interests seeking an outlet outside the nation for surplus savings constituted the "economic taproot" of imperialism. The first selection gives the essence of this interpretation and Hobson's criticism of the process. The reader should remain alert to Hobson's prescription for better domestic utilization of the excess savings accumulated from capitalist production. In 1916, Lenin extended Hobson's "frankly pacifist and reformist" economic interpretation of imperialism to a general indictment of what he called "the highest stage of capitalism." Imperialism was a struggle of competing finance capitalist monopolies for the division of the world.

The second selection that follows here is a portion of D. K. Fieldhouse's essay reviewing leading twentieth century economic analyses of imperialism. Fieldhouse's denial of the validity of the general economic and neo-Marxian approaches is based on his belief that their use of evidence reflects a preconceived notion of what ought to be rather than what actually happened.

[3] Parker Thomas Moon, *Imperialism and World Politics* (New York: The Macmillan Co., 1926). p. 1.

A real and crucial connection between imperial, world power drives and the motor forces of economic expansion is the underlying assumption of Fritz Fischer's description of pre-1914 German developments, excerpted here in the third selection. Professor Fischer's book, *German War Aims in the First World War* became the center of a major historiographical and political controversy in Germany and elsewhere since its appearance in 1961. (See Chapter 11.) The selection included here, illustrating the close ties between the industrial financial establishment and the political-military decision makers of Wilhelmian Germany, argues, explicitly and implicitly, in favor of an economic interpretation of German overseas activity and world policy, including the fateful German-British rivalry preceding 1914. One example is the tie between the business community and the Navy League. Fischer maintains that the very dynamism of the German economy inspired its managers to adopt a parallel political notion, one which required continuous expansion around the globe as fitting and necessary for its impressive national economic miracle. One might object that this is as much a political or even "spiritual" interpretation of imperialism as it is economic. At the very least, however, Fischer does illustrate the interdependence of economic and political factors in the development of German imperialism.

THE ECONOMIC ASPECTS OF IMPERIALISM

T. A. Hobson

By far the most important economic factor in Imperialism is the influence relating to investments. The growing cosmopolitanism of capital has been the greatest economic change of recent generations. Every advanced industrial nation has been tending to place a larger share of its capital outside the limits of its own political area, in foreign countries, or in colonies, and to draw a growing income from this source.

No exact or even approximate estimate of the total amount of the income of the British nation derived from foreign investments is possible. We possess, however, in the income tax assessments an indirect measurement of certain large sections of investments, from which we can form some judgment as to the total size of the income from foreign and colonial sources, and the rate of its growth.

These returns give us a measure of the amount and growth of the investments effected by British citizens in foreign and colonial stocks of a public or semi-public character, including foreign and colonial public securities, railways, etc. The income from these sources is computed as follows:

	£
1884	33,829,124
1888	46,978,371
1892	54,728,770
1896	54,901,079
1900	60,266,886
1903	63,828,715

From this table it appears that the period of energetic Imperialism coincided with a remarkable growth in the income for foreign investments.

These figures, however, only give the foreign income which can be identified as such. The closer estimates made by Sir R. Giffen and others warrant the belief that the actual income derived from foreign and colonial investments amounted to not less than £100,000,000, the capital value of the same reaching a sum of about £2,000,000,000.

Income tax returns and other statistics descriptive of the growth of these investments indicate that the total amount of British investments abroad at the end of the nineteenth century cannot be set down at a lower figure than this. Considering that Sir R. Giffen regarded as "moderate" the estimate of £1,700,000,000 in 1892, the figure here named is probably below the truth.

Now, without placing any undue reliance upon these estimates, we cannot fail to recognise that in dealing with these foreign investments we are facing the most important factor in the economics of Imperialism. Whatever figures we take, two facts are evident. First, that the income derived as interest upon foreign investments enormously exceeded that derived as profits upon ordinary export and import trade. Secondly, that while our foreign and colonial trade, and presumably the income from it, were growing but slowly, the share of our import values representing income from foreign investments was growing very rapidly.

In a former chapter I pointed out how small a proportion of our national income appeared to be derived as profits from external trade. It seemed unintelligible that the enormous costs and risks of the new Imperialism should be undertaken for such small results in the shape of increase to external trade, especially when the size and character of the new markets acquired were taken into consideration. The statistics of foreign investments, however, shed clear light upon the economic forces which dominate our policy. While the manufacturing and trading classes make little out of their new markets, paying, if they knew it, much more in taxation than they get out of them in trade, it is quite otherwise with the investor.

It is not too much to say that the modern foreign policy of Great Britain has been primarily a struggle for profitable markets of investment. To a larger extent every year Great Britain has been becoming a nation living upon tribute from abroad, and the classes who enjoy this tribute have had an ever-increasing incentive to employ the public policy, the public purse, and the public force to extend the field of their private investments, and to safeguard and improve their existing investments. This is, perhaps, the most important fact in modern politics, and the obscurity in which it is wrapped has constituted the gravest danger to our State.

What was true of Great Britain was true likewise of France, Germany, the United States, and of all countries in which modern capitalism had placed large surplus savings in the hands of a plutocracy or of a thrifty middle class. A well-recognised distinction is drawn between creditor and debtor countries. Great Britain had been for some time by far the largest creditor country, and the policy by which the investing classes used the instrument of the State for private business purposes is most richly illustrated in the history of her wars and annexations. But France, Germany, and the United States were advancing fast along the same path. The nature of these imperialist operations is thus set forth by the Italian economist Loria:

"When a country which has contracted a debt is unable, on account of the slenderness of its income, to offer sufficient guarantee for the punctual payment of interest, what happens? Sometimes an out-and-out conquest of the debtor country follows. Thus France's attempted conquest of Mexico during the second empire was undertaken solely with the view of guaranteeing the interest of French citizens holding Mexican securities. But more frequently the insufficient guarantee of an international loan gives rise to the appointment of a financial commission by the creditor countries in order to protect their rights and guard the fate of their invested capital. The appointment of such a commission literally amounts in the end, however, to a veritable conquest. We have examples of this in Egypt, which has to all practical purposes become a British province, and in Tunis, which has in like manner become a dependency of France, who supplied the greater part of the loan. The Egyptian revolt against the foreign domination issuing from the debt came to nothing, as it met with invariable opposition from capitalistic combinations, and Tel-el-Kebir's success bought with money was the most brilliant victory wealth has ever obtained on the field of battle."[1]

But, though useful to explain certain economic facts, the terms "creditor" and "debtor," as applied to countries, obscure the most significant feature of this Imperialism. For though, as appears from the analysis given above, much, if not most, of the debts were "public," the credit was nearly always private, through sometimes, as in the case of Egypt, its owners succeeded in getting their Government to enter a most unprofitable partnership, guaranteeing the payment of the interest, but not sharing in it.

Aggressive Imperialism, which costs the taxpayer so dear, which is of so little value to the manufacturer and trader, which is fraught with such grave incalculable peril to the citizen, is a source of great gain to the investor who cannot find at home the profitable use he seeks for his capital, and insists that his Government should help him to profitable and secure investments abroad.

If, contemplating the enormous expenditure on armaments, the ruinous wars, the diplomatic audacity or knavery by which modern Governments seek to extend their territorial power, we put the plain, practical question, *Cui bono?* the first and most obvious answer is, the investor.

The annual income Great Britain derives from commissions on her whole foreign and colonial trade, import and export, was estimated by Sir R. Giffen[2] at £18,000,000 for 1899, taken at 2½ per cent., upon a turnover of £800,000,000. This is the whole that we are entitled to regard as profits on external trade. Considerable as this sum is, it cannot serve to yield an economic motive-power adequate to explain the dominance which business considerations exercise over our imperial policy. Only when we set beside it some £90,000,000 or £100,000,000, representing pure profit upon investment, do we understand whence the economic impulse to Imperialism is derived.

Investors who have put their money in foreign lands, upon terms which take full account of risks connected with the political conditions of the country, desire to use the resources of their Government to minimise these risks, and so to enhance the capital value and the interest of their private investments. The investing and speculative classes in general have also desired that Great Britain should take other foreign areas under her flag in order to secure new areas for profitable investments and speculation.

[1] Loria, *The Economic Foundations of Politics*, p. 273 (George Allen & Unwin).
[2] *Journal of the Statistical Society*, vol. xlii, p. 9.

If the special interest of the investor is liable to clash with the public interest and to induce a wrecking policy, still more dangerous is the special interest of the financier, the general dealer in investments. In large measure the rank and file of the investors are, both for business and for politics, the cat'spaws of the great financial houses, who use stocks and shares not so much as investments to yield them interest, but as material for speculation in the money market. In handling large masses of stocks and shares, in floating companies, in manipulating fluctuations of values, the magnates of the Bourse find their gain. These great businesses—banking, broking, bill discounting, loan floating, company promoting—form the central ganglion of international capitalism. United by the strongest bonds of organisation, always in closest and quickest touch with one another, situated in the very heart of the business capital of every State, controlled, so far as Europe is concerned, chiefly by men of a single and peculiar race, who have behind them many centuries of financial experience, they are in a unique position to manipulate the policy of nations. No great quick direction of capital is possible save by their consent and through their agency. Does any one seriously suppose that a great war could be undertaken by any European State, or a great State loan subscribed, if the house of Rothschild and its connexions set their face against it?

Every great political act involving a new flow of capital, or a large fluctuation in the values of existing investments, must receive the sanction and the practical aid of this little group of financial kings. These men, holding their realised wealth and their business capital, as they must, chiefly in stocks and bonds, have a double stake, first as investors, but secondly and chiefly as financial dealers. As investors, their political influence does not differ essentially from that of the smaller investors, except that they usually possess a practical control of the businesses in which they invest. As speculators or financial dealers they constitute, however, the gravest single factor in economics of Imperialism.

To create new public debts, to float new companies, and to cause constant considerable fluctuations of values are three conditions of their profitable business. Each condition carries them into politics, and throws them on the side of Imperialism.

The public financial arrangements for the Philippine war put several millions of dollars into the pockets of Mr. Pierpont Morgan and his friends; the China-Japan war, which saddled the Celestial Empire for the first time with a public debt, and the indemnity which she will pay to her European invaders in connexion with the recent conflict, bring grist to the financial mills in Europe; every railway or mining concession wrung from some reluctant foreign potentate means profitable business in raising capital and floating companies. A policy which rouses fears of aggression in Asiatic States, and which fans the rivalry of commercial nations in Europe, evokes vast expenditure on armaments, and ever-accumulating public debts, while the doubts and risks accruing from this policy promote that constant oscillation of values of securities which is so profitable to the skilled financier. There is not a war, a revolution, an anarchist assassination, or any other public shock, which is not gainful to these men; they are harpies who suck their gains from every new forced expenditure and every sudden disturbance of public credit. To the financiers "in the know" the Jameson raid was a most advantageous coup, as may be ascertained by a comparison of the "holdings" of these men before and after that event; the terrible sufferings of England and South Africa in the war, which was a sequel of the raid, has been a source of immense profit to the big financiers who have best held out against the uncalculated waste, and have recouped themselves by profitable war contracts and by "freezing out" the smaller interests in the Transvaal. These men are the only certain gainers from the war, and most of their gains are made out of the public losses of their adopted country or the private losses of their fellow-countrymen.

The policy of these men, it is true, does not necessarily make for war; where war would bring about too great and too permanent a damage to the substantial fabric of industry, which is the ultimate and essential basis of speculation, their influence is cast for peace, as in the dangerous quarrel between Great Britain and the United States regarding Venezuela. But every increase of public expenditure, every oscillation of public credit short of this collapse, every risky enterprise in which public resources can be made the pledge of private speculations, is profitable to the big money-lender and speculator.

The wealth of these houses, the scale of their operations, and their cosmopolitan organisation make them the prime determinants of imperial policy. They have the largest definite stake in the business of Imperialism, and the amplest means of forcing their will upon the policy of nations.

In view of the part which the non-economic factors of patriotism, adventure, military enterprise, political ambition, and philanthropy play in imperial expansion, it may appear that to impute to financiers so much power is to take a too narrowly economic view of history. And it is true that the motor-power of Imperialism is not chiefly financial: finance is rather the governor of the imperial engine, directing the energy and determining its work: it does not constitute the fuel of the engine, nor does it directly generate the power. Finance manipulates the patriotic forces which politicians, soldiers, philanthropists, and traders generate; the enthusiasm for expansion which issues from these sources, though strong and genuine, is irregular and blind; the financial interest has those qualities of concentration and clear-sighted calculation which are needed to set Imperialism to work. An ambitious statesman, a frontier soldier, an overzealous missionary, a pushing trader, may suggest or even initiate a step of imperial expansion, may assist in educating patriotic public opinion to the urgent need of some fresh advance, but the final determination rests with the financial power. The direct influence exercised by great financial houses in "high politics" is supported by the control which they exercise over the body of public opinion through the Press, which, in every "civilised" country, is becoming more and more their obedient instrument. While the specifically financial newspaper imposes "facts" and "opinions" on the business classes, the general body of the Press comes more and more under the conscious or unconscious domination of financiers. The case of the South African Press, whose agents and correspondents fanned the martial flames in this country, was one of open ownership on the part of South African financiers, and this policy of owning newspapers for the sake of manufacturing public opinion is common in the great European cities. In Berlin, Vienna, and Paris many of the influential newspapers have been held by financial houses, which used them, not primarily to make direct profits out of them, but in order to put into the public mind beliefs and sentiments which would influence public policy and thus affect the money market. In Great Britain this policy has not gone so far, but the alliance with finance grows closer every year, either by financiers purchasing a controlling share of newspapers, or by newspaper proprietors being tempted into finance. Apart from the financial Press, and financial ownership of the general Press, the City has notoriously exercised a subtle and abiding influence upon leading London newspapers, and through them upon the body of the provincial Press, while the entire dependence of the Press for its business profits upon its advertising columns has involved a peculiar reluctance to oppose the organised financial classes with whom rests the control of so much advertising business. Add to this the natural sympathy with a sensational policy which a cheap Press always manifests, and it becomes evident that the Press has been strongly biased towards Imperialism, and has lent itself with great facility to the suggestion of financial or political Imperialists who have desired to work up patriotism for some new piece of expansion.

Such is the array of distinctively economic forces making for Imperialism, a large loose group of trades and professions seeking profitable business and lucrative employment from the expansion of military and civil services, and from the expenditure on military operations, the opening up of new tracts of territory and trade with the same, and the provision of new capital which these operations require, all these finding their central guiding and directing force in the power of the general financier.

The play of these forces does not openly appear. They are essentially parasites upon patriotism, and they adapt themselves to its protecting colours. In the mouth of their representatives are noble phrases, expressive of their desire to extend the area of civilisation, to establish good government, promote Christianity, extirpate slavery, and elevate the lower races. Some of the business men who hold such language may entertain a genuine, though usually a vague, desire to accomplish these ends, but they are primarily engaged in business, and they are not unaware of the utility of the more unselfish forces in furthering their ends. Their true attitude of mind was expressed by Mr. Rhodes in his famous description of "Her Majesty's Flag" as "the greatest commercial asset in the world."[3]

* * *

...Overproduction in the sense of an excessive manufacturing plant, and surplus capital which could not find sound investments within the country, forced Great Britain, Germany, Holland, France to place larger and larger portions of their economic resources outside the area of their present political domain, and then stimulate a policy of political expansion so as to take in the new areas. The economic sources of this movement are laid bare by periodic trade-depressions due to an inability of producers to find adequate and profitable markets for what they can produce. The Majority Report of the Commission upon the Depression of Trade in 1885 put the matter in a nutshell. "That, owing to the nature of the times, the demand for our commodities does not increase at the same rate as formerly; that our capacity for production is consequently in excess of our requirements, and could be considerably increased at short notice; that this is due partly to the competition of the capital which is being steadily accumulated in the country." The Minority Report straightly imputed the condition of affairs to "over-production." Germany was in the early 1900's suffering severely from what is called a glut of capital and of manufacturing power: she had to have new markets; her Consuls all over the world were "hustling" for trade; trading settlements were forced upon Asia Minor; in East and West Africa, in China and elsewhere the German Empire was impelled to a policy of colonization and protectorates as outlets for German commercial energy.

---

[3] It will be observed that this, like not a few other words of revelation, has been doctored in the volume, *Cecil Rhodes: his Political Life and Speeches,* by "Vindex" (p. 823).

Every improvement of methods of production, every concentration of ownership and control, seems to accentuate the tendency. As one nation after another enters the machine economy and adopts advanced industrial methods, it becomes more difficult for its manufacturers, merchants, and financiers to dispose profitably of their economic resources, and they are tempted more and more to use their Governments in order to secure for their particular use some distant undeveloped country by annexation and protection.

The process, we may be told, is inevitable, and so it seems upon a superficial inspection. Everywhere appear excessive powers of production, excessive capital in search of investment. It is admitted by all business men that the growth of the powers of production in their country exceeds the growth in consumption, that more goods can be produced than can be sold at a profit, and that more capital exists than can find remunerative investment.

It is this economic condition of affairs that forms the taproot of Imperialism. If the consuming public in this country raised its standard of consumption to keep pace with every rise of productive powers, there could be no excess of goods or capital clamorous to use Imperialism in order to find markets: foreign trade would indeed exist, but there would be no difficulty in exchanging a small surplus of our manufactures for the food and raw material we annually absorbed, and all the savings that we made could find employment, if we chose, in home industries.

There is nothing inherently irrational in such a supposition. Whatever is, or can be, produced, can be consumed, for a claim upon it, as rent, profit, or wages, forms part of the real income of some member of the community, and he can consume it, or else exchange it for some other consumable with some one else who will consume it. With everything that is produced a consuming power is born. If then there are goods which cannot get consumed, or which cannot even get produced because it is evident they cannot get consumed, and if there is a quantity of capital and labour which cannot get full employment because its products cannot get consumed, the only possible explanation of this paradox is the refusal of owners of consuming power to apply that power in effective demand for commodities.

It is, of course, possible that an excess of producing power might exist in particular industries by misdirection, being engaged in certain manufactures, whereas it ought to have been engaged in agriculture or some other use. But no one can seriously contend that such misdirection explains the recurrent gluts and consequent depressions of modern industry, or that, when over-production is manifest in the leading manufactures, ample avenues are open for the surplus capital and labour in other industries. The general character of the excess of producing power is proved by the existence at such times of large bank stocks of idle money seeking any sort of profitable investment and finding none.

The root questions underlying the phenomena are clearly these: "Why is it that consumption fails to keep pace automatically in a community with power of production?" "Why does under-consumption or over-saving occur?" For it is evident that the consuming power, which, if exercised, would keep tense the reins of production, is in part withheld, or in other words is "saved" and stored up for investment. All saving for investment does not imply slackness of production; quite the contrary. Saving is economically justified, from the social standpoint, when the capital in which it takes material shape finds full employment in helping to produce commodities which, when produced, will be consumed. It is saving in excess of this amount that causes mischief, taking shape in surplus capital which is not needed to assist current consumption, and which either lies idle, or tries to oust existing capital from its employment, or else seeks speculative use abroad under the protection of the Government.

But it may be asked, "Why should there be any tendency to over-saving? Why should the owners of consuming power withhold a larger quantity for savings than can be serviceably employed?" Another way of putting the same question is this, "Why should not the pressure of present wants keep pace with every possibility of satisfying them?" The answer to these pertinent questions carries us to the broadest issue of the distribution of wealth. If a tendency to distribute income or consuming power according to needs were operative, it is evident that consumption would rise with every rise of producing power, for human needs are illimitable, and there could be no excess of saving. But is is quite otherwise in a state of economic society where distribution has no fixed relation to needs, but is determined by other conditions which assign to some people a consuming power vastly in excess of needs or possible uses, while others are destitute of consuming power enough to satisfy even the full demands of physical efficiency. The following illustration may serve to make the issue clear. "The volume of production has been constantly rising owing to the development of modern machinery. There are two main channels to carry off these products—one channel carrying off the product destined to be consumed by the workers, and the other channel carrying off the remainder to the rich. The workers' channel is in rockbound banks that cannot enlarge, owing to the competitive wage system preventing wages rising *pro rata* with increased efficiency. Wages are based upon cost of living, and not upon efficiency of labour. The miner in the poor mine gets the same wages per day as the miner in the adjoining rich mine. The owner of the rich mine gets the advantage—not his labourer. The channel which conveys the goods destined to supply the rich is itself divided into two streams. One stream carries off what the rich "spend" on themselves for the necessities and luxuries of life. The other is simply an "over-flow" stream carrying off their "savings." The channel for spending, i.e. the amount wasted by the rich in luxuries, may broaden somewhat, but owing to the small number of those rich enough to indulge in whims it can never be greatly enlarged, and at any rate it bears such a small proportion to the other channel that in no event can much hope of avoiding a flood of capital be hoped for from this division. The rich will never be so ingenious as to spend enough to prevent over-production. The great safety overflow channel which has been continously more and more widened and deepened to carry off the ever-increasing flood of new capital is that division of the stream which carried the savings of the rich, and this is not only suddenly found to be incapable of further enlargement, but actually seems to be in the process of being dammed up.[4]

Though this presentation over-accentuates the cleavage between rich and poor and over-states the weakness of the workers, it gives forcible and sound expression to a most important and ill-recognised economic truth. The "over-flow" stream of savings is of course fed not exclusively from the surplus income of "the rich"; the professional and industrial middle classes, and to some slight extent the workers, contribute. But the "flooding" is distinctly due to the automatic saving of the surplus income of rich men. This is of course particularly true of America, where multi-millionaires rise quickly and find themselves in possession of incomes far exceeding the demands of any craving that is known to them. To make the metaphor complete, the overflow stream must be represented as reentering the

[4] *The Significance of the Trust,* by H. G. Wilshire.

stream of production and seeking to empty there all the "savings" that it carries. Where competition remains free, the result is a chronic congestion of productive power and of production, forcing down home prices, wasting large sums in advertising and in pushing for orders, and periodically causing a crisis followed by a collapse, during which quantities of capital and labour lie unemployed and unremunerated. The prime object of the trust or other combine is to remedy this waste and loss by substituting regulation of output for reckless over-production. In achieving this it actually narrows or even dams up the old channels of investment, limiting the overflow stream to the exact amount required to maintain the normal current of output. But this rigid limitation of trade, though required for the separate economy of each trust, does not suit the trust-maker, who is driven to compensate for strictly regulated industry at home by cutting new foreign channels as outlets for his productive power and his excessive savings. Thus we reach the conclusion that Imperialism is the endeavour of the great controllers of industry to broaden the channel for the flow of their surplus wealth by seeking foreign markets and foreign investments to take off the goods and capital they cannot sell or use at home.

The fallacy of the supposed inevitability of imperial expansion as a necessary outlet for progressive industry is now manifest. It is not industrial progress that demands the opening up of new markets and areas of investment, but mal-distribution of consuming power which prevents the absorption of commodities and capital within the country. The over-saving which is the economic root of Imperialism is found by analysis to consist of rents, monopoly profits, and other unearned or excessive elements of income, which, not being earned by labour of head or hand, have no legitimate *raison d'être*. Having no natural relation to effort of production, they impel their recipients to no corresponding satisfaction of consumption: they form a surplus wealth, which, having no proper place in the normal economy of production and consumption, tends to accumulate as excessive savings. Let any turn in the tide of politico-economic forces divert from these owners their excess of income and make it flow, either to the workers in higher wages, or to the community in taxes, so that it will be spent instead of being saved, serving in either of these ways to swell the tide of consumption—there will be no need to fight for foreign markets or foreign areas of investment.

Many have carried their analysis so far as to realise the absurdity of spending half our financial resources in fighting to secure foreign markets at times when hungry mouths, ill-clad backs, ill-furnished houses indicate countless unsatisfied material wants among our own population. If we may take the careful statistics of Mr. Rowntree[5] for our guide, we shall be aware that more than one-fourth of the population of our towns is living at a standard which is below bare physical efficiency. If, by some economic readjustment, the products which flow from the surplus saving of the rich to swell the overflow streams could be diverted so as to raise the incomes and the standard of consumption of this inefficient fourth, there would be no need for pushful Imperialism, and the cause of social reform would have won its greatest victory.

It is not inherent in the nature of things that we should spend our natural resources on militarism, war, and risky, unscrupulous diplomacy, in order to find markets for our goods and surplus capital. An intelligent progressive community, based upon substantial equality of economic and educational opportunities, will

[5] *Poverty: A Study of Town Life.*

raise its standard of consumption to correspond with every increased power of production, and can find full employment for an unlimited quantity of capital and labour within the limits of the country which it occupies. Where the distribution of incomes is such as to enable all classes of the nation to convert their felt wants into an effective demand for commodities, there can be no over-production, no underemployment of capital and labour, and no necessity to fight for foreign markets.

The most convincing condemnation of the current economy is conveyed in the difficulty which producers everywhere experience in finding consumers for their products: a fact attested by the prodigious growth of classes of agents and middlemen, the multiplication of every sort of advertising, and the general increase of the distributive classes. Under a sound economy the pressure would be reversed: the growing wants of progressive societies would be a constant stimulus to the inventive and operative energies of producers, and would form a constant strain upon the powers of production. The simultaneous excess of all the factors of production, attested by frequently recurring periods of trade depression, is a most dramatic exhibition of the false economy of distribution. It does not imply a mere miscalculation in the application of productive power, or a brief temporary excess of that power; it manifests in an acute form an economic waste which is chronic and general thoughout the advanced industrial nations, a waste contained in the divorcement of the desire to consume and the power to consume.

If the apportionment of income were such as to evoke no excessive saving, full constant employment for capital and labour would be furnished at home. This, of course, does not imply that there would be no foreign trade. Goods that could not be produced at home, or produced as well or as cheaply, would still be purchased by ordinary process of international exchange, but here again the pressure would be the wholesome pressure of the consumer anxious to buy abroad what he could not buy at home, not the blind eagerness of the producer to use every force or trick of trade or politics to find markets for his "surplus" goods.

The struggle for markets, the greater eagerness of producers to sell than of consumers to buy, is the crowning proof of a false economy of distribution. Imperialism is the fruit of this false economy; "social reform" is its remedy. The primary purpose of "social reform," using the term in its economic signification, is to raise the wholesome standard of private and public consumption for a nation, so as to enable the nation to live up to its highest standard of production. Even those social reformers who aim directly at abolishing or reducing some bad form of consumption, as in the Temperance movement, generally recognise the necessity of substituting some better form of current consumption which is more educative and stimulative of other tastes, and will assist to raise the general standard of consumption.

There is no necessity to open up new foreign markets; the home markets are capable of indefinite expansion. Whatever is produced in England can be consumed in England, provided that the "income" or power to demand commodities, is properly distributed. This only appears untrue because of the unnatural and unwholesome specialisation to which this country has been subjected, based upon a bad distribution of economic resources, which has induced an overgrowth of certain manufacturing trades for the express purpose of effecting foreign sales. If the industrial revolution had taken place in an England founded upon equal access by all classes to land, education and legislation, specialisation in manufactures would not have gone so far (though more intelligent progress would have been made, by reason of a widening of the area of selection of inventive and organising talents); foreign trade would have been less important, though more steady; the standard of life for all portions of the population would have been high, and the present rate of national consumption would probably have given full, constant, remunerative employment to a far larger quantity of private and public capital than is now employed.[6] For the over-saving or wider consumption that is traced to excessive incomes of the rich is a suicidal economy, even from the exclusive standpoint of capital; for consumption alone vitalises capital and makes it capable of yielding profits. An economy that assigns to the "possessing" classes an excess of consuming power which they cannot use, and cannot convert into really serviceable capital, is a dog-in-the-manger policy. The social reforms which deprive the possessing classes of their surplus will not, therefore, inflict upon them the real injury they dread; they can only use this surplus by forcing on their country a wrecking policy of Imperialism. The only safety of nations lies in removing the unearned increments of income from the possessing classes, and adding them to the wage-income of the working classes or to the public income, in order that they may be spent in raising the standard of consumption.

Social reform bifurcates, according as reformers seek to achieve this end by raising wages or by increasing public taxation and expenditure. These courses are not essentially contradictory, but are rather complementary. Working-class movements aim, either by private co-operation or by political pressure on legislative and administrative government, at increasing the proportion of the national income which accrues to labour in the form of wages, pensions, compensation for injuries, etc. State Socialism aims at getting for the direct use of the whole society an increased share of the "social values" which arise from the closely and essentially co-operative work of an industrial society, taxing property and incomes so as to draw into the public exchequer for public expenditure the "unearned elements" of income, leaving to individual producers those incomes which are necessary to induce them to apply in the best way their economic energies, and to private enterprises those businesses which do not breed monopoly, and which the public need not or cannot undertake. These are not, indeed, the sole or perhaps the best avowed objects of social reform movements. But for the purposes of this analysis they form the kernel.

Trade Unionism and Socialism are thus the natural enemies of Imperialism, for they take away from the "imperialist" classes the surplus incomes which form the economic stimulus of Imperialism.

This does not pretend to be a final statement of the full relations of these forces. When we come to political analysis we shall perceive that the tendency of Imperialism is to crush Trade Unionism and to "nibble" at or parasitically exploit State Socialism. But, confining ourselves for the present to the narrowly economic setting, Trade Unionism and State Socialism may be regarded as complementary forces arrayed against Imperialism, in as far as, by diverting to working-class or

---

[6] The classical economists of England, forbidden by their theories of parsimony and of the growth of capital to entertain the notion of an indefinite expansion of home markets by reason of a constantly rising standard of national comfort, were early driven to countenance a doctrine of the necessity of finding external markets for the investment of capital. So J. S. Mill: "The expansion of capital would soon reach its ultimate boundary if the boundary itself did not continually open and leave more space" (*Political Economy*). And before him Ricardo (in a letter to Malthus): "If with every accumulation of capital we could take a piece of fresh fertile land to our island, profits would never fall."

public expenditure elements of income which would otherwise be surplus savings, they raise the general standard of home consumption and abate the pressure for foreign markets. Of course, if the increase of working-class income were wholly or chiefly "saved," not spent, or if the taxation of unearned incomes were utilised for the relief of other taxes borne by the possessing classes, no such result as we have described would follow. There is, however, no reason to anticipate this result from trade-union or socialistic measures. Though no sufficient natural stimulus exists to force the well-to-do classes to spend in further luxuries the surplus incomes which they save, every working-class family is subject to powerful stimuli of economic needs, and a reasonably governed State would regard as its prime duty the relief of the present poverty of public life by new forms of socially useful expenditure.

But we are not here concerned with what belongs to the practical issues of political and economic policy. It is the economic theory for which we claim acceptance—a theory which, if accurate, dispels the delusion that expansion of foreign trade, and therefore of empire, is a necessity of national life.

Regarded from the standpoint of economy of energy, the same "choice of life" confronts the nation as the individual. An individual may expend all his energy in acquiring external possessions, adding field to field, barn to barn, factory to factory—may "spread himself" over the widest area of property, amassing material wealth which is in some sense "himself" as containing the impress of his power and interest. He does this by specialising upon the lower acquisitive plane of interest at the cost of neglecting the cultivation of the higher qualities and interests of his nature. The antagonism is not indeed absolute. Aristotle has said, "We must first secure a livelihood and then practise virtue." Hence the pursuit of material property as a reasonable basis of physical comfort would be held true economy by the wisest men; but the absorption of time, energy, and interest upon such quantitative expansion at the necessary cost of starving the higher tastes and faculties is condemned as false economy. The same issue comes up in the business life of the individual: it is the question of intensive *versus* extensive cultivation A rude or ignorant farmer, where land is plentiful, is apt to spread his capital and labour over a large area, taking in new tracts and cultivating them poorly. A skilled, scientific farmer will study a smaller patch of land, cultivate it thoroughly, and utilise its diverse properties, adapting it to the special needs of his most remunerative markets. The same is true of other businesses; even where the economy of large-scale production is greatest there exists some limit beyond which the wise business man will not go, aware that in doing so he will risk by enfeebled management what he seems to gain by mechanical economies of production and market.

Everywhere the issue of quantitative *versus* qualitative growth comes up. This is the entire issue of empire. A people limited in number and energy and in the land they occupy have the choice of improving to the utmost the political and economic management of their own land, confining themselves to such accessions of territory as are justified by the most economical disposition of a growing population; or they may proceed, like the slovenly farmer, to spread their power and energy over the whole earth, tempted by the speculative value or the quick profits of some new market, or else by mere greed of territorial acquisition, and ignoring the political and economic wastes and risks involved by this imperial career. It must be clearly understood that this is essentially a choice of alternatives; a full simultaneous application of intensive and extensive cultivation is impossible. A nation may either, following the example of Denmark or Switzerland, put brains into agriculture, develop a finely varied system of public education, general and technical, apply the ripest science to its special manufacturing industries, and so support in progressive comfort and character a considerable population upon a strictly limited area; or it may, like Great Britain, neglect its agriculture, allowing its lands to go out of cultivation and its population to grow up in towns, fall behind other nations in its methods of education and in the capacity of adapting to its uses the latest scientific knowledge, in order that it may squander its pecuniary and military resources in forcing bad markets and finding speculative fields of investment in distant corners of the earth, adding millions of square miles and of unassimilable population to the area of the Empire.

The driving forces of class interest which stimulate and support this false economy we have explained. No remedy will serve which permits the future operation of these forces. It is idle to attack Imperialism or Militarism as political expedients or policies unless the axe is laid at the economic root of the tree, and the classes for whose interest Imperialism works are shorn of the surplus revenues which seek this outlet.

"IMPERIALISM": AN HISTORIOGRAPHICAL REVISION [1]

By D. K. Fieldhouse

It is now nearly sixty years since J. A. Hobson published *Imperialism: a Study*,[2] and thereby gave the word the connotation it still generally carries. His conception of the nature of "imperialism"[3] has, indeed, been almost universally accepted and, partly through the expository literature it has generated, may be said to have exercised a significant historical influence. Yet, for all its success, Hobson's argument has always been extremely vulnerable to criticism: and it is therefore surprising that those historians and economists who have argued effectively that his analysis is basically unsound should have received so little attention. The aim of the present article is to draw together some of the more important arguments that have been put forward for and against his thesis, and to suggest that, on balance, the noes have it.

Hobson's own claim to importance and originality lies simply in his having induced British, and subsequently world, opinion to accept his own special definition of the word imperialism. Professor Koebner has already examined the various meanings given to the word before 1902.[4] He has suggested that, as used in England, it had two general connotations in the 1890's, both of which were morally

---

[1] This essay arose out of reading the following recently published books: John Strachey, *The End of Empire* (London: Victor Gollanz Ltd. 1959. Pp. 351. 30s.); W. M. Macmillan, *The Road to Self-rule* (London, Faber and Faber. 1959. Pp. 296. 2 maps. 35s.); A. P. Thornton, *The Imperial Idea and its Enemies* (London: Macmillan & Co. Ltd. 1959. Pp. xiv + 370. 30s.); B. Semmel, *Imperialism and Social Reform* (London: George Allen & Unwin Ltd. 1969. Pp. 283. 28s.); H. Brunschwig, *Mythes et réalités de l'impérialisme colonial français* (Paris: Librairie Armand Colin. 1960. Pp. 205). The essay has benefited from being read by Miss M. Perham and A. F. McC. Madden.

[2] Published in 1902. References are to the third edition (1954).

[3] When used in Hobson's sense, the word will here be printed in inverted commas.

[4] R. Koebner, "The concept of Economic Imperialism," *Economic History Review*, 2nd ser. II, no. 1.

neutral. In one sense, it was being used of those who wished to prevent the existing British settlement colonies from seceding and becoming independent states, and was therefore a conservative factor. In another, and increasingly common, sense, it was being used to indicate an expansionist and "forward" attitude towards problems connected with the future control of the "uncivilized" parts of the world, such as Africa, the Middle East and the Pacific. Salisbury was, in this sense, regarded as an imperialist in accepting the need for Britain to share in the partition of East Africa. Gladstone, in opposing the acquisition of Uganda, was emphatically anti-imperialist, even though he had acquiesced in the need to gain some control over Egypt in 1882. In the eyes of the anti-imperialists the sin of expansionism lay in the waste of money it entailed on armaments, in the cost of colonial governments, and in the danger of international conflicts over intrinsically unimportant territories which it would be wiser to leave alone. As a rule no worse motive was attributed to the imperialists than "jingoism" or excessive concern with Britain's position as a great power.

But, between 1896 and 1902, imperialism, as a word, began to lose its innocence. Koebner has shown that events in South Africa, and particularly the Jameson Raid, gave rise to a suspicion that, here at least, the expansive urge was motivated by something other than a concern for national greatness, by what Harcourt called "stock-jobbing imperialism"—based on the interests of financiers. This was, of course, a special case, and a distinction remained between an honest, even if misguided, imperialism, and the debased variety to be seen on the Rand. Yet the idea now gained ground that South Africa might not, after all, be a special case, but might exhibit in an extreme form a factor inherent in all expansionism. By 1900 radical opinion had moved so far in this direction that the Fifth International Socialist Congress, taught probably by its English delegation, could resolve

. . . que le développement du capitalisme mène fatalement à l'expansion coloniale . . . : que la politique coloniale de la bourgeoisie n'a d'autre but que d'elargir les profits de la classe capitaliste et le maintien du système capitaliste. . . .[5]

Here, in a nutshell, was Hobson's doctrine of "imperialism." But it remained to be seen whether such a dogmatic interpretation would ever command a wide support: and it was essentially his achievement to ensure that, in his own non-Marxist form, it should become the generally accepted theory.

Hobson's *Imperialism* therefore came out at a time when British public opinion, disillusioned by the Boer war, was already profoundly suspicious about the motives behind recent imperial expansion. It was, in fact, a pamphlet for the times, rather than a serious study of the subject, and, like all pamphlets that achieve influence, it owed much of its success to the fact that it expressed a current idea with peculiar clarity, force and conviction. It arose immediately out of Hobson's visit to South Africa during the war, and derived from reports he sent back to *The Speaker,* which were published as a book in 1900 as *The War in South Africa, Its Causes and Effects.* Yet, paradoxically, Hobson was not primarily concerned with imperial problems: and *Imperialism* can only be properly understood on the basis that his interest, then and throughout his life, was with the social and economic problems of Britain. In a sense, this book was primarily a vehicle for publicizing the theory of "underconsumption," which he regarded as his main intellectual achievement, and which he expressed more fully in *The Evolution of Modern Capitalism,* and other

[5] Ibid. p.16.

works. In brief, the theory, which was an alternative to the Marxist concept of surplus value as an explanation of poverty, saw excessive investment by the capitalist, with its concomitant of underconsumption by the wage-earner, as the root cause of recurrent slumps, of low interest rates, and of permanent under-employment. Hobson thought there were only two answers to this problem. The correct one—which would also be the answer to the "condition of England question"—was to increase the buying power of the workers by giving them a higher share of the profits of industry. The wrong one, which was no answer to the social question, was to invest the surplus capital overseas, where it could earn a high interest rate, and thus sustain domestic rates of interest, without benefiting the British worker. And this, he held, was what Britain had been doing since at least the middle of the nineteenth century.

To this point the economic theory, though highly vulnerable, has no apparent relevance to the phenomenon of overseas expansion, that is, to imperialism. The key to Hobson's theory of "imperialism" lies in the connexion he makes between the two.

Overproduction in the sense of an excessive manufacturing plant, and surplus capital which could not find sound investments within the country, forced Great Britain, Germany, Holland, France to place larger and larger portions of their economic resources outside the area of their present political domain, and then stimulate a policy of political expansion so as to take in the new areas.[6]

Thus "imperialism," in the special sense used by Hobson, is an external symptom of a social malady in the metropolitan countries. Without this domestic pressure for investment overseas, there would be no effective impulse towards the acquisition of new colonies. Conversely, without colonies, capital would lack an outlet, and domestic rates of interest would sink. Thus the need to export capital and to make it politically secure overseas was what Mr. John Strachey has recently called the "prime mover for the modern imperialist process. . .".[7] And "imperialism," on this assumption, is not variously "sound" or "stock-jobbing"; but, without exception, results from the special economic interests of the capitalist, and is therefore "economic imperialism."

It is not proposed at this stage to examine Hobson's theory in detail: but some comment must be made on the logical value of the argument he uses to demonstrate the historical truth of this hypothesis. Does he, in fact, supply any evidence to support the claim that colonies were the product of a demand either for new investment opportunities, or for security for existing investments? He begins with a straightforward account of the expansion of the European empires since 1870, printing a list of territories acquired by Britain, which Lenin, and later Mr. Strachey, have reproduced. Then, in chapter two, he demonstrates that the expansion of the British empire had been of little apparent value to British trade; that trade with these recent acquisitions was the least valuable part of intra-imperial trade; and that British trade with all colonies was declining in relation to trade with the rest of the world.[8] Clearly, then "imperialism" was not good for trade. Nor was

---

[6] Hobson, p. 80.

[7] Strachey, *op. cit,* p. 123.

[8] Hobson based this conclusion on figures taken from Cd. 1761, p. 407, which are quoted in Hobson. p. 33. These were inaccurate. A. K. Cairncross *(Home and Foreign Investment 1870–1913,* Cambridge University Press, 1953), p. 189, shows that British exports

it good for emigration (which, in any case, he thought unnecessary), since these new tropical colonies were quite unsuited to white settlement.[9] And his conclusion was that

The Imperialism of the last six decades is clearly condemned as a business policy, in that at enormous expense it has procured a small, bad, unsafe increase of markets, and has jeopardised the entire wealth of the nation in arousing the strong resentment of other nations. . . .[10]

How then can a motive be found for this imperial expansion? The motive is to be seen if, alongside the list of territorial acquisitions, is placed a table showing the increase of British overseas investments in the same period.[11] It then becomes obvious that, during the period in which British possessions had increased by 4.754 m. square miles and by a population of 88 millions, British overseas investments had also increased enormously—from £144 m. to £1698 m. between 1862 and 1893 alone. Could there be any doubt that the two sets of figures were intimately connected as cause and effect? Hobson had no doubts about it: "It is not too much to say that the modern foreign policy of Great Britain has been primarily a struggle for profitable markets of investment."[12]

But it is immediately apparent that Hobson had in no sense proved that there was any connexion between the investments made overseas and the territory acquired contemporaneously. His table of investments[13] makes no differentiation between the areas in which investment had taken place, beyond such classifications as "Foreign," "Colonial," "U.S.A." and "Various," and, in fact, he assumes quite arbitrarily that the new colonies had attracted a high proportion of the investment called "Foreign" (i.e. before they were annexed) or "Colonial" (subsequent to annexation). This, it will be suggested below, is a basic fault of his theory of "imperialism." Indeed, to put the case bluntly, Hobson performed an intellectual conjuring trick. Convinced of the essential truth of his economic theory, he deceived the eye by the speed of his hand, creating the illusion that, of the two sets of statistics he held up, one was the cause of the other.

It is not possible here to consider the rest of Hobson's *Imperialism,* interesting though it is in relation to related controversies over protection, tariff reform and imperial unity. But two additional points in his main argument must be mentioned because they were intrinsic to his definition of the origins and nature of "imperialist" expansion.

The first of these concerns the relationship between the financial interest and other "imperialists," and is therefore crucial to his theory. He was aware that, contrary to his argument, the obvious driving force of British expansion since 1870 appeared to lie in the explorers, missionaries, engineers, patriotic pressure groups, and empire-minded politicians, all of whom had evident influence, and had demonstrable interests, other than those of investment, in territorial acquisitions.

to the empire increased from 24 per cent to 33.6 per cent of total British trade between 1870–2 and 1890–2, and imports from 21.9 per cent to 22.9 per cent in the same period. Both percentages continued to increase to 1910–12. But Hobson was right in saying that the new colonies contributed little to the increased volume of intra-imperial trade.

[9] Hobson, pp. 41–5.
[10] Hobson, p. 46.
[11] Hobson, p. 62.
[12] Hobson, p. 53.
[13] Hobson, p. 62.

And he was equally aware that if the impulse to expansion could be satisfactorily explained in the old-fashioned terms of their idealism, their ambition, or their concern with the status of Britain as a world power, rather than in terms of the self-interest of the capitalist, his own central thesis would collapse. It was therefore necessary that these men—the Lugards, the Milners, the Johnstons, and the Roseberys—should be shown to be mere puppets—the tools of "imperialism" rather than its authors. Hobson did this by falling back on what may be called the "faceless men" gambit:

Finance manipulates the patriotic forces which politicians, soldiers, philanthropists, and traders generate; the enthusiasm for expansion which issues from these sources, though strong and genuine, is irregular and blind; the financial interest has those qualities of concentration and clear-sighted calculation which are needed to set Imperialism to work. An ambitious statesman, a frontier soldier, an overzealous missionary, a pushing trader, may suggest or even initiate a step of imperial expansion, may assist in educating patriotic public opinion to the urgent need of some fresh advance, but the final determination rests with the financial power.[14]

In this ingenious way Hobson inverted the apparent relationship between the obvious "imperialists" and the investor. Instead of the financier being induced to invest in new possessions, with more or less enthusiasm, once political control had been imposed for other reasons, he becomes the essential influence in the take-over itself. Investment no longer follows the flag: it decides where it is profitable to plant it, and tells the government whether it is to follow the advice of men of action or of ideas in each particular case. Thus, "imperialism" can never be interpreted as the spontaneous expression of the idealism, the chauvinism or the mere energy of a nation. In its practical form it is the expression of the special interests of the financier behind the scenes, who decides whether it is worth his while to allow a dream to become a reality, and who alone will reap the benefits.

This assumption, which has been adopted by most subsequent supporters of Hobson's thesis, will be examined later.

The other essential point in the theory of "imperialism" is the suggestion that the possession of colonies by individual capitalist states results automatically in the exploitation of the indigenous peoples of Africa and Asia. In his long chapter "Imperialism and the Lower Races,"[15] which is in many ways one of the most undogmatic and constructive parts of the book, Hobson argued that exploitation, whether by appropriation of land, or by the use of cheap labour—forced or nominally free—in mines, farms and factories, had been a general feature of the colonies of all the European powers. Hobson, in the British humanitarian tradition, thought such exploitation to be both wrong and inexpedient. Economic development was good for undeveloped colonies and for the world as a whole. The danger lay in allowing the financiers to use the political power of the imperial authority for their own purposes; and the solution was for international control of colonies—the germ of the later mandate concept—and patience in allowing normal economic forces to give the natives an inducement to work freely in European enterprises. Sensible as his general attitude was, it is clear that Hobson had thus included in "imperialism" the suggestion that countries possessing colonies were

---

[14] Hobson, p. 59.
[15] Hobson, pp. 223–84.

almost certain to exploit them in their own interests; and this argument was to become a staple of later critics of "colonialism".

II

The theory of "imperialism" as it developed after the publication of Hobson's *Study* continued to be founded on the three main concepts outlined above. Yet, in examining its historiography, it is clear that it was Lenin, writing in 1916, rather than Hobson himself, who gave "imperialism" its dogmatic coherence and much of its eventual influence. It is therefore necessary to consider briefly the extent to which Lenin modified Hobson's ideas.[16]

The greatest difference lies in the first and most important part of the argument; that is, in the nature of the internal pressure in the capitalist countries which forces them to expand their colonial possessions. Hobson had explained this pressure in terms of "under-consumption": but Lenin naturally had a more orthodox theory to hand. Capitalism as a system was approaching the apocalypse Marx had foretold. Competitive capitalism had, in the late nineteenth century, been replaced by "monopoly capitalism," with its characteristic agencies, the cartels, trusts and tariffs. It was no longer dynamic, but anxious only to maintain its profit margins by more intensive exploitation of limited and protected markets. Moreover, the "finance-capitalists"—the banks and trusts—who now largely controlled capital itself, found that, under monopoly conditions, it was more profitable to employ surplus capital abroad than in domestic industry. At home, it could only increase production, lower prices, and raise wages. Abroad it could give a high interest return without any of these consequences. But, to gain the highest return from overseas investment it was desirable to have some political control over the territory in which the investment was made. This might be in the limited form of a "semi-colony," such as the Argentine. But only in the colony proper could really comprehensive economic and political controls be imposed which would give investments their highest return. The result had been the competition between the great powers to acquire new colonies after 1870, which would continue until the whole uncivilized world had come under imperial rule. Then would follow the inter-imperial wars for the redivision of the empires, leading to proletarian revolutions in the "imperialist" states, the creation of "socialist" states, and so, automatically, to the end of "imperialism."

How much, then, does Lenin's explanation of the force behind "imperialism" differ from that of Hobson? Fundamentally, only in this: that, whereas Hobson used his theory as evidence that social-democratic reform at home was necessary and possible to eliminate the evil of "under-consumption" and therefore make "imperialism" unnecessary, Lenin made "imperialism" the definition of an inherent and unavoidable stage in the growth of capitalist society which could not be "reformed." Hobson was a doctor prescribing a remedy, Lenin a prophet forecasting catastrophe.[17] But, while they disagreed as to the precise causes, both maintained

---

[16] V. I. Lenin, *Imperialism, the Highest Stage of Capitalism* (1916). References are to the Moscow edition of 1947. For the genesis of Lenin's ideas on the Marxist side see W. K. Hancock, *Survey of British Commonwealth Affairs,* vol. II, part I (1940). Appendix I, by W. H. B. Court, pp. 293–305.

[17] There are, of course, many other differences which cannot be considered here, e.g. Hobson ignored "semi-colonies", and thought of "finance" as operating in an essentially free-trade environment.

that there existed in the "capitalist" countries a tremendous pressure for overseas investment, and that this was the main factor in producing "imperialist" expansion after 1870.

On Hobson's second point—the control and influence exercised by "finance" over government and over the men who actually carved out the new empires—there is little difference between them. Lenin, if anything, went further, ignoring the theory that in a democratic country like Britain Hobson's "imperialists" found it necessary to corrupt public opinion through the press; and assuming, on the basis of Marxist theory and German experience, that the financial power of the banks and trusts was now so great that governments virtually did as they were told by the "finance-capitalist." Moreover, Lenin rejected entirely the possibility that the drive behind imperialism might have been the natural product of nationalism in international politics. To him as a Marxist such arguments were superficial. The only true explanation must lie in the fundamental economic environment which dictates political interests: and he castigates the unfortunate Kautsky on the grounds that he "detaches the politics of imperialism from its economics. . . ."[18] Economic factors are the root of all features of the "imperialist" state; and even Franco-German competition for Alsace-Lorraine exists "because an essential feature of imperialism is the rivalry between a number of great powers in the striving for hegemony, i.e. for the conquest of territory, not so much directly for themselves as to weaken the adversary and undermine *his* hegemony."[19] There is no room here for explaining the actions of governments in any terms other than of the economics of "imperialism."

On Hobson's third point, Lenin, had little explicit to say. As a Marxist he assumed it to be axiomatic that all workers were exploited by capital; so that a colony would differ from the metropolis only in the fact that the exploiting capitalist was an alien, and colonies merely added to the pool of labour from which he could extract "surplus value."

With the publication of Lenin's book it may be said that the concept of "imperialism" had reached its mature form; for, on points on which they differed, Lenin's interpretation has generally been the dominant one. The subsequent historiography of the subject on the "imperialist" side of the argument has tended to fall into two main categories—either glosses on the theory, or applications of it to the actual events of the period after 1870, and a few of the more important books in the English canon may be mentioned. First, in point of time, came Leonard Woolf's *Empire and Commerce in Africa* (1920) which was influential in British Labour Party thinking on the subject. P. T. Moon's *Imperialism and World Politics* (1928) used the theory to interpret the international politics of the age of "imperialism"; and in 1942 P. M. Sweezy restated Lenin's theory in relation to the central Marxist argument with considerable clarity and some minor modifications in *The Theory of Capitalist Development.* Finally, in 1959, Mr. John Strachey published *The End of Empire* which, as the most recent work of apologetics, deserves some comment as an honest and intelligent attempt to assess and defend the theory after the experience of half a century.

Like Professor Sweezy, Mr. Strachey is aware that the theory, as stated by Hobson and Lenin, had important limitations, of which the most obvious was that it related only to the period after 1870, and therefore offered no explanation of

[18] Lenin, p. 112.
[19] Lenin, p. 111.

earlier empires, or of developments since the First World War. It was Mr. Strachey's main aim to demonstrate that at least one concept of "imperialism"— that empire consists primarily in the exploitation of a dependent territory for the economic advantage of the metropolis — holds good for all empires at all times; and that it is the means, not the fact, of exploitation that varies. For the period after 1870 itself he thinks Hobson and Lenin were right in seeing "imperialism" as the external expression of the surplus capital of the European states; preferring Lenin's theory of "finance-capital" to Hobson's "under-consumption" as the basic factor. But he recognizes also that Lenin was less successful as a prophet, for he ignored the reformative capacity of political democracy to modify the structure of a capitalist society to such an extent as to make both "imperialism" and eventual revolution unnecessary. Much of the book consists of an attempt to apply the view that exploitation was the basic factor in the "imperialism" of the period after 1870 to other empires; and to suggest that the characteristic feature of each empire has been its own peculiar method of exploiting its dependencies. In the modern empires this was, as Hobson had said, to make wage-slaves of indigenous peoples by exporting capital to their countries, and forcing them to work within the capitalist economy, and he instances copper-mining in Rhodesia as a typical example. But other empires had their own characteristic methods. In India, the British began in the eighteenth century with mere plunder, which they later rationalized into the system of revenues exacted from Bengal, and replaced in the nineteenth century by the enforcement of the open door to British exports at the cost of ruining indigenous industries. Further back in time, Mr. Strachey suggests that the empires of the ancient world were based on the exploitation of slave labour—the original "surplus value": "Imperialism in its original form could almost be called enslavement applied externally . . . ."[20] The medieval European empires he calls "peasant empires"; and he thinks they were based on the "invention of a way in which men could be exploited without the cumbrous and difficult business of directly enslaving them."[21] After them came the mercantile empires, which ingeniously combined all known forms of exploitation—plunder (as in India or Mexico), enslavement for the silver mines and plantations, and trade on a one-sided basis with unsophisticated peoples.

Mr. Strachey's book covers far more ground than can be suggested here, and deserves a place in the "imperialist" canon both because of the ingenuity with which it attempts to give universality to the basic ideas of Hobson and Lenin, and because it shows the extent to which a confessed "revisionist" can adapt these ideas to the circumstances of the mid-twentieth century. But, without following his arguments further, it is necessary to turn to a critical examination of the central theory of "imperialism," and to alternative interpretations of the facts that first gave rise to it.

* * *

[20] Strachey, p. 322.
[21] Strachey, p. 327.

ECONOMIC EXPANSION AND WORLD POWER

Fritz Fischer

Germany's claim to world power was based on her consciousness of being a "young," growing and rising nation. Her population had risen from about 41 millions in 1871 to about 68 millions in 1915, while that of France, with a larger area, had remained almost stationary, reaching only 40 millions in 1915. Moreover, more than one-third of the population of Germany was under fifteen years of age, and this gave the national consciousness a dynamic element which further reinforced the demand for *Lebensraum,* markets and industrial expansion. Although emigration had been high (1.3 million persons emigrated between 1881 and 1890), the population figures for 1910 were nevertheless far more favourable than, for example, those of France: an excess of births over deaths of 800,000 (8.9 per 1,000 against 3.4 per 1,000 in France), while the expectation of life was increasing an infant mortality on the decline. With increasing industrialisation, internal migration was beginning to replace migration overseas and immigrants were beginning to come in from Austria, Italy, Russia, Poland and other European countries. Germany was developing more and more into a highly industrialised exporting country, and the problem of finding markets and raw materials to support her population was growing increasingly urgent. Industrialisation had concentrated the population in certain areas—the Ruhr, Saxony, Silesia, Berlin, the Rhine-Main area—and had within a few years totally transformed the face of the country; the numbers living in large towns had doubled and the occupational distribution of the population had changed radically.[1] This industrialisation and concentration of the population in a few centres had been accompanied by a shift from east to west, the results of which included a severe and growing shortage of agricultural labour in eastern Germany.

Wage and price levels were generally stable; slumps occurred, but the long-term economic trend was upward, and in spite of a chronic shortage of capital the national income was rising, as evidenced by rising real incomes and increased savings and investment.[2]

The increased wealth of all classes of society, combined with the stability of the currency, generated a feeling of security and strengthened the popular belief that continued growth would develop in an expansion which seemed almost predetermined by the laws of economics. Contemporaries pointed proudly to the national figures for imports and exports as proof of German's industrial

---

[1] In 1870, 50 percent of the population was employed in agriculture; in 1913 only 33 percent, against over 50 percent employed in commerce and industry.

[2] 21,500 million in 1896; 40,000 million in 1912. See the calculations in Karl Helfferich, *Deutschlands Volkswohlstand 1888–1913* (Berlin, 1913), pp. 92ff.

development; between 1887 and 1912 the former had risen by 243.8 percent (from 3,100 to 10,000 million marks), the latter by 185.4 percent (from 3,100 to 8,900 million).

The balance of trade had thus become unfavourable, and the restoration of a favourable balance had consequently become one of the essential tasks of German economic policy. No other country could show an increase in imports over this period comparable to Germany's 243 percent. Britain's figure was 108.7 percent, America's 136.9 percent, France's only 95 percent. On the other hand, the increase in American exports during the quarter century (208.6 percent) had exceeded Germany's. The total increase in foreign trade had, however, been far the highest in Germany (13,400 million marks, or 214.7 percent); America's figure was 173.3 percent, Britain's 113.1 percent, France's 98.1 percent.

There was, however, another factor of importance for Germany's world trading policy. In 1913 she was still leading in exchanges with the European states, but the direction of her trade had undergone a disquieting change since 1880. In that year 80 percent of her exports had gone to Britain, France and south-east Europe, and 77 percent had come from European countries. In 1913 the share of Europe in her imports and exports had gone down by 30 percent; overseas countries, the tropics and above all South America, were supplying an increasing proportion of her raw materials.

The world-wide activities of Germany's entrepreneurs were strongly supported by an official policy aptly described as one of "neo-mercantilism."[3] It had become axiomatic that the state should support economic enterprise, both at home and abroad; in nationalising the postal, telegraphic and railway services the state had already made itself into an important factor in Germany's economic life, and its social legislation, its protective tariff policy and its system of export premiums had laid the foundations of Germany's economic expansion, and therewith of the transformation of her economic structure. The foundation of a Reichsbank to act as a central clearing house for the German money market had made it possible for the state to collaborate with the private banks in supplying the country, short of capital as it was, with such ample resources that it was able to venture on big, politically important enterprises.

This advance was based on the expansion of the interlinked complex of the great iron, steel and mining industries. The production of coal, iron and steel in the great centres of the Ruhr, Lorraine and Upper Silesia had increased since the 1870s with a rapidity unparalleled elsewhere in Europe. The 5,000 million marks of the French war indemnity (which had begun the process), large orders for armaments, and above all the big expansion of communications within and beyond Germany's frontiers had enabled the Reich to increase its coal production by 800 percent, while England's had only doubled. At the same time German enterprise had entered the continental market in a big way; the mining industry, protected by the 1879 tariff, had now found secure outlets for its products in France, Belgium, Holland, Switzerland, Italy and Austria-Hungary. The growth of Germany's coal production, which was exceeded only by that of America (which rose in the quarter century before 1912 by 336.6 percent against Germany's 218.1 percent and Britain's 72.6 percent), was accompanied by an even more spectacular growth in her iron and steel

---

[3] Cf. Wilhelm Treue, *Wirtschafts und Sozialgeschichte Deutschlands im 19. Jahrhundert*, in Bruno Gebhardt, *Handbuch der deutschen Geschichte*, 8th ed. (Stuttgart, 1960), pp. 403 ff., heading *"Neumerkantilismus."*

production; the production of raw iron rose from 4.0 million tons in 1887 to 15.5, an increase of 387 percent. The figure for America was comparable (368.5 percent), but Britain—and that was the decisive thing in German eyes—was able in that time to raise her production of iron ore only by 30.6 percent from 7.6 to 10 million tons). The development of Germany's steel production was unparalleled anywhere in the world. Tomas's new processes and Siemens' and Martin's inventions enabled the production of steel to rise by 1,335 percent, from 0.9 million tons in 1886 to 13.6 millions. The estimated value of the production of Germany's mines (coal, ores and salt) rose from 700 million marks in 1886 to 2,000 million in 1912. At the same time Germany was becoming increasingly dependent on imports for her raw materials; these rose from 5.7 million marks in 1872 to 161.3 millions in 1910.

While the expansion of her heavy industry was the foundation on which the economic transformation of Germany rested, a number of entirely new industries also came into being: the chemical, electrical and optical industries and others. The new discoveries in aniline chemistry enabled the chemical industry, within a few decades, to outdistance all its European competitors; its exports in 1913 were of the value of some 125 million marks—an important item in Germany's trading figures. With its 150,000 employees, concentrated in a few mammoth enterprises, whose leading firms—Bayer, Hoechst and Ludwigshafen—had formed a cartel in 1904 (followed in 1916 by their fusion in I. G. Farben), the chemical industry was a typical example of the new, highly concentrated form of enterprise. The electrical industry was also concentrated in a few hands. Its connections with the big banks were particularly close. Equipped with patented inventions, less localised of its nature than heavy industry, it was by 1910 exporting to the tune of over 125 million marks and had a payroll of over 107,000 persons, most of them in Berlin. The optical industry, with 60 million marks, was smaller, but hardly inferior in the value of its production.

The textile industry, the only one to escape such high concentration, had maintained a steady growth since 1870. Its chief centres were Saxony, northern Bavaria, Württemberg and the lower Rhineland. The tendency towards intensification and mechanisation, characteristics of all German industry, was here particularly marked. While the number of persons employed in it hardly altered, its production rose tenfold in the quarter century: from 37,500 tons in 1878 to 370,000 in 1905.

The advance of the heavy and electrical industries would, however, not have been possible without the simultaneous development of communications and the rationalisation of trade and business, of which the concentration of the banks is the most striking example. In 1870 the German capital market was entirely in the hands of the private merchant bankers. By 1913 a complete change had come about; the world of German credit was dominated by the four "D Banks"—the Deutsche Bank, the Disconto-Gesellschaft, the Dresdner Bank and the Bank für Handel and Industrie, commonly called the Darmstädter Bank. On the eve of the World War these huge institutions, each of which was represented on the boards of the main industries, controlled 65 percent of the capital resources of all Germany's credit institutions, thus typifying the advanced degree of concentration which the German economy had achieved.[4]

[4] W. Strauss, *Die Konzentrationsbewegung im Deutschen Bankgewerbe* (Berlin, 1928), p. 18; H. Weber, *Der Bankplatz Berlin* (Cologne, 1957), pp. 47 ff.

Amalgamations, foundation of subsidiary branches and so on, had enabled the joint-stock banks, in partnership with the old private banking houses of Rothschild, Bleichröder, Warburg, etc., to go into business abroad. The Deutsche Bank, for example, financed the construction of the Anatolian Railway and the St. Gotthard road, and floated a number of issues in both North and South America. The great banks succeeded in establishing themselves securely in the main bourses and the chief centres of world trade—London, Paris, Brussels, New York, Vienna, and Madrid. By founding foreign subsidiaries, such as the Banca Generale Romana, the Brasilian Bank, the German East African Bank, the German-Asiatic Bank, etc., they secured the financing of the Otavi Mining and Railway company in South-West Africa, the Baghdad Railway in Asia Minor, the Shantung Railroad and Mining Company in China, the New Guinea Company, oil enterprises in Rumania and Iraq, the Tientsin-Puckow Railway and the Venezuela Railway. Combination between the banks enabled them to act as issuing houses for a large number of loans in Germany, both Reich and Federal, and also in Austria-Hungary, Turkey, Russia, Finland, Norway, Sweden, Italy, Switzerland, the Argentine, Brazil and China.

To free herself from dependence on British ships for moving the increasing volume of her merchandise, and to enable her to bring her exports, financed by her own capital, to their markets abroad without British middle-men, Germany had to have her own merchant marine. Its construction was accompanied by the expansion of the great ports of Bremen and Hamburg. Here, too, the trend towards concentration was apparent: in the Hapag and the Norddeutscher Lloyd, the biggest of many shipping companies which sprang into existence within a few years, Germany possessed for the first time merchant lines of international calibre.[5] They began their careers, and first grew rich, by carrying emigrants; when this traffic ebbed away, they turned their interest to regular passenger and freight services, for which the demand was growing as Germany's exports increasingly took the form of specialised finished products. Movement through the German ports had grown by 300 percent in 25 years, from 9.8 to 29.6 million tons incoming, and from 7.8 to 21.1 millions outgoing—figures which, it is true, still lagged far behind the British. The banks were also closely involved in the construction of the merchant fleet, as was a swiftly developing German dock industry (Howald, Blohm and Voss, Bremen Vulkan, Schichau-Danzig), which in its turn made possible the construction of a German navy.

The introduction of the 1879 tariff marked also the real beginning of the cartels; it was the protection of the new tariffs which made possible the creation of cartels capable of resisting both domestic and foreign competition. So the door was opened to a new type of entrepreneur, like Emil Kirdorf, who did not own the business managed by him, but was usually the "employee" of a new combine founded by one of the big banks. The ideal of these men was the systematic expansion of the giant concern as the most efficient economic form, and they therefore took advantage of every opportunity to combine the small mines and furnaces into productive, solid and profitable mixed enterprises, whose products were marketed by arrangement through syndicates. Men like Hugo Stinnes and August Thyssen, personally more ruthless and more familiar with the niceties of capital management than the older generation represented by Krupp, Stumm, Vögler and Röchling, built up their great combines on the "vertical" plan. The leading positions alike in heavy

[5] 1881, registered tonnage 1.8 million (nearly all sailing vessels); 1913, 3.1 million (all steam).

industry, in banking and in commerce came to be filled by men of essentially "patriotic" outlook. This new class, which largely moulded public opinion and exercised an increasing influence on government policy, was a characteristic phenomenon of the new Germany. The more it succeeded in introducing the principles of neo-mercantilism into German policy, the greater its influence became. Bankers such as Gwinner, Helfferich and Stauss (Deutsche Bank), Solmssen (Disconto-Gesellschaft), Nathan and Gutmann (Dresdner Bank), Rathenau (Berliner Handelsgesellschaft), Schinckel (Norddeutsche Bank) or Dernburg (Darmstädter Bank, afterwards Secretary of State in the Reich Colonial Office); industrialists such as Carl Friedrich von Siemens, Emil and Walther Rathenau (electric industry), Carl Duisberg (chemical industry), and the heavy industrialists mentioned above; the leading dock-owners, etc., etc., formed a group of entrepreneurs characteristic of the Germany of the day, whose assimilation with the older leading classes of society was facilitated by the ennoblement of many of them. The close relationship in which Ballin and Warburg stood to the Emperor is well known; no less significant was the position of a Gwinner, made a member of the *Herrenhaus* at the Emperor's own wish in recognition of his services in connection with the Baghdad Railway, or the intimate relationship in which, for example, Gwinner, Rathenau and Helfferich stood to Bethmann Hollweg.

Besides using their personal influence on many domestic issues—not least against the workers' associations—the employers combined in new pressure groups to influence foreign policy. Bueck and Roetger, the Secretaries of the heavy industrialists' powerful association, the Centralverband Deutscher Industrieller (General Federation of German Industrialists), Stresemann as a "syndic" of the Bund der Industriellen (Industrialists' Association), Voss as Secretary of the *Verein der Deutschen Berg und Eisenhüttenleute* (Union of German Mining and Ironworks Owners), Riesser as President of the Bankers' Association—to name only a few—exemplify the close connection which existed between business interests and government policy. A glance at the list of deputies in the Reichstag—even more, in the Prussian House of Deputies—belonging to the Conservative, Free Conservative, National Liberal and Zentrum parties will show how high a percentage of them were so intimately connected by business interest with agriculture, industry, commerce, etc., as to make a distinction between business and politics almost unreal (the officers of the business associations, for example, nearly always sat in parliament, usually as National Liberals).

The link between business and politics grew progressively closer in the opening years of the new century, as the basic political outlook of the leading industrialists, bankers and officers of the employers' associations came to conform more closely with that of the intellectual bourgeoisie, the higher bureaucracy and army and navy officers. The spiritual "nationalisation" of the German employer class, however, tended to aggravate political crises. Furthermore, Germany began to measure power by the yardstick of steel production, to regard Britain as an "ageing state," and to expect that the moulding of the future economic and political shape of the world would lie with the U.S.A. and Germany alone.

As early as 1900 George von Siemens, senior director of Germany's biggest bank, the Deutsche Bank, published in the *Nation* an article "On the National Importance of the Bourse," the significance of which as a programme was at once recognised, and its ideas endorsed, by leading bankers and industrialists. Arguing from the experience of the German money market on the London and Paris exchanges,

Siemens pleaded for the establishment of a strong German bourse. Should war break out, as he thought only too probable in view of the existing tension, Germany would need to place her economy on a footing of self-sufficiency, for which purpose a bourse was essential.

Economic calculation, emotions and straining after world power interacted mutually in a crescendo of crises and in controversies over Germany's claims and over what were felt to be the rights usurped by Britain, France or Russia in the Near or the Far East. Their outward and visible sign was the widespread support given to the Emperor's and Tirpitz's naval programme. The chorus was led by the Navy League *(Flottenverein)*. In its origin a purely business creation, founded by the *Centralverband Deutscher Industrieller,* whose first reaction to a naval programme was the thought that it would provide them with safe orders for years ahead, the League developed into the first great example of state-controlled propaganda.[6] The presidents of the Prussian provinces and the princes of the non-Prussian states were its patrons; its members included the senior bureaucracy and junior civil servants, such as teachers. Provincial and local school councils carried its ideas into every village; public opinion in return influenced the political parties. At least up to 1908 it was thus a "state association" which united industry and state service in devotion to the same patriotic cause. The retirement of the agitator in chief, General Keim, who had overstepped the limits envisaged by Tirpitz and given the campaign too much of an anti-government flavour, did not alter the League's character. The only result was that it now came under state control, being placed under the direction of the Reich Naval Office. General Keim became co-founder, with General Litzmann, and agitator in chief of the *Wehrverein* (Defence Association), a body founded in 1912 to call for expansion of the long neglected land forces on a scale equal to that now planned for the navy. The popular appeal of the *Wehrverein* soon exceeded that of the Navy League itself.

A German navy would, as the Navy League convinced the nation, protect German shipping, force Britain to regard Germany as an equal, a desirable ally and a friend, and thus become a symbol of Germany's claim to world power. At the same time it was one of the reasons for the hostility between Britain and Germany, although it would be an over-simplification to regard it as the only decisive factor in the relationship between the two countries. For the navy itself was unimaginable without the backing of Germany's economic power and without the pressure exercised by wide economic circles for a status of recognised partnership overseas and leadership in Europe. Often as the possibilities of worldwide expansion were discussed, they did not at that time really exist. And mutual consultation on plans—even governmental plans—relating to trade and business penetration was becoming regular: the discussions over Near and Far Eastern ores, oil and railways provide examples.

As the volume of Germany's production grew, the narrowness of the basis of her raw materials market became increasingly apparent, and as she penetrated more deeply into world markets, this narrowness became increasingly irksome. Devices such as the purchase of mines, obtaining concessions or shares in them, undercutting, and squeezing foreign rivals out of markets, enabled German interests to penetrate and establish themselves in the great minette field of Longwy-Briey and the iron ore deposits of Normandy. German industry reached out from Saxony across Bohemia

---

[6] Cf. Jonathon Sternberg.

and linked up the main industrial centre of Austria-Hungary with that of central Germany. At the same time, this penetration of German commerce into the still mainly agricultural economy of the Dual Monarchy made the latter increasingly dependent on German capital. And Austria-Hungary herself was only a bridge to south-eastern Europe, where German "commercialisation," as Conrad called it, steadily won ground against its Austro-Hungarian, French, British and Belgian competitors. The biggest of all the enterprises in this field was the Steaua Romana: here the big banks, led by the Disconto-Gesellschaft, succeeded in establishing an oil company, almost entirely financed by German capital, whose production was to go exclusively to continental consumers. This enterprise was to be linked with a consumers' organisation covering France, Belgium, Holland, Russia, Austria-Hungary and Germany, and to form a counterweight to the giant Standard Oil and Royal Dutch Shell companies. German industry, under the state-encouraged patronage of the great banks, participated in the construction of the Anatolian and Baghdad Railways and so paved the way to increasing investment in Turkey itself. In eastern and south-eastern Europe the chief advances were those made by the industry of Upper Silesia, which concentrated on these markets, as it could not venture overseas. At the same time, lack of native steel refineries drove heavy industry to penetrate the deposits of Krivoi Rog and Tchiaturi in the Ukraine and the Caucasus, and the banks tried to finance these plans through links with Russian banks—the more so since, in spite of French competition, big profits could be made out of Russia's need for armaments.

An economy organised on the most modern lines, regularly introducing every modern innovation and invention, fed by a network of technical academies organised exclusively to serve it, and manned by a disciplined, industrious and thrifty population—this was one side of the picture. In contrast to it, the organisation of the army, with a conservative leadership and methods which retarded not only democratisation but even the technical modernisation of its own weapons, constituted a glaring anachronism.[7]

Economic expansion was the basis of Germany's political world diplomacy, which vacillated in its methods between rapprochment and conciliation at one moment, aggressive insistence on Germany's claims the next, but never wavered in its ultimate objective, the expansion of Germany's power.

The Diplomacy of World Policy

Even in Bismarck's day, for all his elaborate system of alliances, there were signs that Germany's policy was leading her into isolation. She took the first step along this path when in 1879 she opted for alliance with that great question-mark, Austria-Hungary. In the 1880s it proved impossible to establish close relations with any one of the three other great powers, notwithstanding the achievement of a tolerable *modus vivendi* with Britain under Disraeli and Salisbury in spite of differences over colonial questions, and notwithstanding the reinsurance treaties

---

[7] The strength of the army was hardly raised up to 1912; machine guns were introduced late and in insufficient numbers, the intelligence service was too small; the air arm (unlike that of France) was neglected, even for reconnaisance purposes; motorisation was insufficient; the cavalry arm was too large; cavalry regiments were brigaded together with insufficient artillery, development of tanks and antitank weapons in the war was belated.

which, in the days of Gorchakov (1856–82) and Giers (1882–95), preserved a contractual relationship with Russia which, though rendered fragile by the increasing hostility of Russian public opinion, survived successive Balkan crises. This development was accentuated by the "new course" of the 1890s. First Russia was estranged, then Britain, and the Russo-French military alliance of 1893 wrought a radical change in Germany's position in Europe. From 1897 onward, the year in which Bülow became Foreign Secretary (from 1900 to 1909 he was Chancellor) and Tirpitz Secretary of State in the Reich Naval Office, Germany's pursuit of a "world policy" led straight to an isolation which was made inevitable by her over-insistence on the principle of a "free hand" and her over-assessment of her own strength.

The very first steps taken by her in the Far East, the lease of Kiaochow in 1897 and the attempt made in 1898, after first acquiring some of the Samoan islands, to establish a fortified base in the Philippines, led to sharp clashes with Britain, Russia, Japan and the U.S.A. Her Middle Eastern policy of these years was even more disquieting to Russia and Britain. Wilhelm II's tour and his speech in Damascus in November, 1898, in which he assumed the role of protector of three hundred million Mohammedans, were bound to sound like challenges to both Russia and Britain, with their numerous Mohammedan subjects; and they were in fact so taken, much more seriously than they had been meant. Similarly, the Baghdad Railway project, the concession for which was renewed in 1899, could not fail to rouse the mistrust of Britain and Russia. This mistrust was enhanced by Germany's attempts to establish coaling and trading stations in Aden, Yemen and on the south Persian coast, on the sea-route to India. Similarly, her efforts to secure concessions for borings for oil and irrigation works in Iraq trespassed on a zone of British interests. The threat to British and Russian interests presented by Germany's economic invasion of the Middle East seemed the more serious because in the same years Germany undertook the task of propping up Ottoman power, first delegating von der Goltz to reorganise the Turkish army (1886–95 and 1909–13) and then sending Liman von Sanders in the crisis of 1913.

The advance of German economic interests in the shipping, railways, ports and mines of East and South-West Africa, and particularly in the Boer Republic in the 1890s, led to friction with Britain: the "Kruger telegram" of 1896 was peculiarly resented. This worldwide search for acquisitions could not but lead to friction between Germany and the established powers of the world, but the immediate cause of her clash with Britain was her claim to possess her own battle fleet. The construction of this fleet cut across the feelers for an alliance which were put out between 1898 and 1901, and was one of the factors—Germany's over-rigid attitude towards the alliance being another (she believed that the differences between Britain and Russia were irreconcilable, and thought that she could steer a course between the two)—which made Britain decide finally after 1901 to seek other partners. Britain's immediate reaction was to assure herself of Japan through the alliance of 1902, proceeding to approaches to France in 1903 and the establishment of the Entente in 1904.

In this situation of growing isolation, the counter-moves undertaken by Germany showed that at least Holstein, the most influential member of the Foreign Ministry, and Schlieffen, Chief of the General Staff from 1892 to 1906, were ready, if necessary, to detach France from the Entente by force. When the Emperor and Bülow renounced the appeal to arms on which the Schlieffen Plan was based, they did so chiefly in the hope of being able to establish a continental bloc, consisting of Germany, Russia and France, by peaceful means; when the Emperor met the Tsar at

Bjoerkoë in July, 1905, he believed that he had achieved this aim. The measure of the excitement engendered in Germany by the Russian revolution, particularly the bloody repression of the workers' rising in Moscow in December, 1905, and by the war scare of that year, may be judged from the Emperor's famous New Year letter to Bülow, written in a sort of attempt to clear himself after his "flabby" attitude during the crisis. Making a characteristic nexus between domestic and foreign events, he instructed the Chancellor, "now that the Christmas candles have been re-lit": "Shoot down, behead and eliminate the Socialists first, if need be, by a blood-bath, then war abroad. But not before, and not à tempo."[8]

In this letter the Emperor was expressing what had been his pet idea since the end of the 1890s, that if she engaged in a major war, Germany must first conclude an alliance with Turkey and then revolutionise the Islamic world.

Disappointment over the course and results of the Algeciras Conference, which Germany had engineered in the hope of obtaining American support, caused her to determine never again to accept a conference as a method of resolving an international dispute. She had hoped to be able to play Britain and America off against one another at Algeciras. This hope proved illusory. Yet thereafter, up to the World War, German policy held fast to its old dogmas, entirely misinterpreting the effects of the events in the Philippines in 1898 (the clash between the American fleet and a German naval squadron); of the Venezuelan incident of 1902, when Britain and Germany carried through a joint blockade in defence of their interests (which American opinion resented more from Germany than Britain); and above all, of Britain's retreat from the West Indies in 1901, thanks to which America was able to make Colombia her satellite and to undertake the construction of the Panama Canal single-handed.

The Algeciras Conference revealed not only how few Germany's friends were, but how unreliable. Italy ranged herself on the side of the Entente, Austria's support was lukewarm. And just at this juncture "encirclement" became a reality. Defeated by Japan in the war of 1904–5 and shaken by revolution, Russia switched her attention from the Far East back to Europe. She was thereby brought increasingly into conflict with Austria-Hungary, and also with Germany, while at the same time an understanding between Britain and Russia became possible. A delimitation of their respective spheres of influence in Afghanistan, Tibet and Persia (this last amounting to a diplomatic partition of that country) led to the Anglo-Russian Entente of 1907, after which the Russo-French military alliance and the Anglo-French Entente hardened into the Triple Entente. One of the factors which attracted Russia to this rapprochement was the fear of German designs on the Baltic coast (which were in fact partly realised during the First World War), while for Britain it was another answer to Germany's attempts to gain a footing in Persia and India via Turkey.

The "encirclement" in turn brought Germany into increased dependence on the policy of her ally, Austria-Hungary. This dependence became evident in her reactions to Austria's policy in the Bosnian annexation crisis of 1908. Both the Chancellor, Bülow, and the Emperor (whom he had purposely kept in the dark until the last moment) at first disapproved strongly. The Emperor felt that "the Eastern policy which he had been following for twenty years" had been completely ruined, and that Britain had outbid him in support of Turkey. Bülow hoped that a strong and demonstrative stand by Germany would at once cover her Austrian ally and

---

[8] Cf. Bülow, *Denkwürdigkeiten*, Col. II (Berlin, 1930), p. 198.

keep the link with Turkey from snapping, and this hope proved justified, partly owing to Russia's reasonableness (although she drew closer than ever to her partners in the Entente), partly owing to the retreat of the Young Turk leaders, especially those in the army. Britain's popularity in Turkey soon passed, and the young German-trained officers accepted Germany's proposal of a financial indemnity for the cession of Bosnia-Herzegovina and responded again to Germany's advances.

Germany had been prepared—or so she had asserted—to enforce with arms a solution in the Balkans favourable to Austria-Hungary, rather than expose her ally to the danger of a humiliation à la Algeciras.

At the same time, Germany was trying to expand her continental power by diplomatic action, using Austria-Hungary as a bridge to Turkey. With the conclusion of the Franco-German colonial agreement of February 9, 1909, and the visit of the Tsar and Sazonov (Izvolski's successor as Foreign Minister) to Potsdam on November 3–4, 1910, her old goal of a constitutional bloc seemed on the point of realisation: the Tsar promised to loosen his ties with the Entente on the basis that Germany would similarly relax her links with Austria, and to withdraw the opposition which Russia had so long maintained to the construction of the Baghdad Railway; Germany in return recognised northern Persia as a Russian zone of influence and agreed to pay for the construction of branch lines running from the Baghdad Railway into Persia. The German-French agreement, which buried the Algeciras controversy in many respects, cleared Germany's path towards her goal of a large and continuous colonial empire.[9] But hopes of a continental understanding in east and west perished at Agadir in 1911 in the second Moroccan crisis, although Germany attempted to use the problems raised by France's advance in Morocco to bring about a continental bloc via the colonial problem.

The negotiations carried on in the summer of 1911 between Kiderlen-Wächter, Secretary of State in the Foreign Ministry, and the French Ambassador in Berlin, Jules Cambon, were at first directed towards reaching a delimitation of interests in Morocco itself; later, however, Kiderlen-Wächter's demand for the cession of the whole of the French Congo as "compensation" for Germany's désintéressement in Morocco, revealed one of the essential objectives of Germany's diplomacy: to acquire a continuous colonial empire in central Africa. Behind this stood the even more far-reaching ambition of breaking-up, or at least weakening, the Entente Cordiale by means of a Franco-German "settlement." Britain parried this danger by a public intervention in favour of France in the shape of Lloyd George's famous Mansion House speech, and by initiating with France military conversations of great importance; whereupon, in the autumn, Germany yielded and contented herself with the "prestige success" of an addition (of small intrinsic value) to her possessions in the Cameroons. Britain had saved France from the humiliation of a "settlement" with Germany involving French sacrifice which had threatened to undermine the solidarity of the Triple Entente and to replace the British policy of balance by a German Hegemony in Europe.

The strong reactions of public opinion to the crisis, the sharpness of the language used by statesmen, and above all the new prominence of the part played by the military, differentiated these later exchanges markedly from the transactions of the first years of German world policy. The German policy of "compensation," of those

---

[9] France received a free hand in North Morocco; Germany was left confined to South Morocco, but was to receive French help for the construction of a railway line from the Cameroons to East Africa across the French and Belgian Congos.

abrupt and seemingly endless demands which had so irritated all the powers except Germany's own allies and had done so much to draw them together against her—this was now at an end. Up to 1911 Germany had not succeeded in adopting Britain's policy of concluding compromises with her competitors, for she had equated moderation with an inferiority incompatible with the world power status which was her aim. Such a policy was inevitably rejected by a generation of politicians who had grown up in revolt against Bismarck's doctrine that Germany was a "saturated power," regarded the expansion of Germany as the supreme object of their policy, and were now occupying the leading positions in the imperial Chancellery, the Foreign Ministry and the Prussian ministries.

EUROPE IN THE
TWENTIETH CENTURY

11 / The Origins of World War I: A Survey and a Return to the Kriegsschuldfrage

The writing of the history of the causes of World War I begins with the war itself. The parallel development of nationalism and democracy during the second half of the nineteenth century meant, among other things, that now entire peoples instead of heads of state waged war. Thus within months of the outbreak of war in August 1914, the governments of all belligerents had placed before their parliaments and people and, not incidentally, the court of world opinion, collections of diplomatic documents so arranged as to show the perfidy of their enemies and the rightness of their cause.[1] As the war dragged on and costs and casualties soared, the unprecedented emphasis on the righteousness of this war was followed by an exceptional preoccupation with the *kriegsschuldfrage* ("war guilt" question)—a preoccupation that found its logical—or should we say illogical?—expression in the famous Clause 231 of the Treaty of Versailles:

The Allied and Associated Governments affirm, and Germany accepts, the responsibility of Germany and her allies for causing all the loss and damage to which the Allied and Associated Governments and their nationals have been subjected as a consequence of the war imposed upon them by the aggression of Germany and her allies.

The reaction of Germany to the Versailles Treaty and the war-guilt clause in particular are too well known to require elaboration. The point made here is that Socialist governments in Germany and Austria, exposed to the odium of signing the peace treaties, published in 1919 complete collections of documents from secret archives bearing on the crisis of July 1914. The Soviets had anticipated them in this. In 1917 they had begun to publish the secret treaties and other diplomatic documents of the Tsarist regime. The idea was to discredit the "imperialist" governments the Socialists had displaced, and whether or not they succeeded in this, they did succeed in showing that the question of war guilt was not the black and white one the Versailles Treaty had made it out to be.

The various collections of documents were widely read by interested parties in both the defeated and victorious nations. Several volumes of the German documents

---

[1] These were the *German White Book* (August 3), *British Blue Book* (August 6), *Russian Orange Book* (August 7), *Belgian Gray Book* (October), *Siberian Blue Book* (November), *French Yellow Book* (December), *Austrian Red Book* (February 1915).

were, in fact, translated into English in this country by the Carnegie Endowment for International Peace. The result, particularly in face of reticence on the part of France and Britain to make similar disclosures, was a flood of popular "revisionist" histories in which German responsibility for the outbreak of the war was minimized, chiefly at the expense of France and Russia.[2]

Scholars bided their time a little longer, however, until in 1926 the British government published all their documents relative to the July crisis. As a result, Sidney B. Fay, Bernadotte E. Schmitt, Luigi Albertini—among others—were able to publish their masterful studies. More recently, a great deal of additional evidence has appeared in the form of memoirs, collections of private papers, and new archival material.

In the following readings, two ways of examining the outbreak of the war are presented. The first, a broad overview which describes the tensions, forces, and misunderstandings that produced Europe's nervous breakdown in 1914, is drawn from Joachim Remak's recent survey, *The Origins of World War I*. Here the author discusses the variety of explanations for 1914—the state system, the alliance system, imperialism, European and world trouble spots, military and naval rivalries, economic conflicts, popular and national attitudes, the press, concluding with speculations on the general willingness to use war as a problem-solving mechanism.

In contrast to Remak's survey approach, the second reading, "The Outbreak of the First World War and German War Aims" by Imanuel Geiss, focuses on the history and historiography of the single, constantly intriguing question of the role of Germany. Geiss shares the perspective of a new, post-1945 generation of younger German scholars centering around the controversial work of Fritz Fischer[3] who have reopened the *kriegsschuldfrage*. Their perspective, by no means universally accepted in or out of Germany, charges the German policy makers of 1914 with a greater share of blame for the war than revisionist scholars of all national origins would allow.

[2] Probably the best written and most popular of these in this country was Harry Elmer Barnes, *Genesis of the World War: An Introduction to the Problem of War Guilt* (1926).
[3] Fritz Fischer, *Germany's Aims in the First World War* (New York: W. W. Norton & Co., 1967). Originally published as *Griff nach der Weltmacht* (Düsseldorf: Droste Verlag une Druckerei GmbH, 1961). For the English version, Professor Fischer reduced the size of his original text about one third.

EUROPE ON THE EVE: HOW DEEP THE TROUBLE?

Joachim Remak

According to one report (there was no Hansard then, and we rely on rumor) a member of the Polish *Sejm* once rose to stop the flow of an afternoon's particularly euphoric rhetoric. "Gentlemen," he said, "if everything is so good why is everything so bad?" If so much was right with pre-1914 Europe, how could a second-rate Balkan plot set off a first-rate catastrophe? Were there not, in truth, organic weaknesses that plagued Europe and lowered the continent's powers of resistance to a perilous degree?

What were the troubles, deeper than the immediate crisis, that affected Europe before 1914? We might do well to have at least a look at the principal diagnoses made by various writers: at the state system, at the system of alliances, at major sources of conflict both overseas and closer to the center, at the role of public opinion and the press, and finally at the acceptance of war as a means of policy.

A Matter of Political Organization: The National State

Some writers have suggested that one truly basic factor that made war an ever-present prospect in 1914 (as in 1814, as well as on the day that this is being read) was nothing less than the national state—a form of political organization accepted by a vast majority of its citizens as one of the immutable facts of life, no more subject to debate than, say, the sun's rising in the east. Actually, the argument for this point of view suggests, the national state was a relatively novel institution, replacing a feudal system in which differences of class, faith, guild, and estate had, on occasion, mattered far more than national dividing lines. The dangers already inherent in the sovereign state, which assumed most of its present characteristics in the age of absolutism of the seventeenth century, increased in the eighteenth and nineteenth centuries. For it was then that the people, as a whole, came of age politically, and the state was identified not primarily with its monarch but with the entire body politic. It was then, too, that nationalism tended to turn into a faith, replacing previous emotional, and sometimes formal, allegiances now dead.

An aspect of things that made this development especially explosive was that the limited kind of warfare that had characterized past ages was becoming a nostalgic memory—partly because of the advances of technology, but in even larger part, because it was no longer a case of Florence fighting Venice or of Tours having it out with Angoulême. Instead, it was one nation against another: all of France against all of Italy, with the concomitant release of hatreds and energies that had no equivalent in either the civic rivalries of the middle ages and the Renaissance, or in the comparatively civilized cabinet wars of the age of absolutism. National passions, organized or spontaneous, had entered the scene.

Even where these could be contained, something else that was very basic made for great peril. It was the permanent possibility of conflict between nations whose sovereignty was unrestricted. The sovereign state, that law unto itself, faced other sovereign states, and was, considering the propensities of independent entities, as likely as not to come into conflict with them. Yet there existed no organization that could intercede if violence should result from the pursuit of conflicting national interests. There was no higher, supranational authority that could be relied upon to arbitrate between nations bent on mutual destruction.

Where the beginnings of such an authority did exist, its powers were too circumscribed to be effective. The International Court of Arbitration at the Hague could act only if each one of the nations involved in some specific argument voluntarily agreed to submit the case to the Court's jurisdiction, and even then, the Court had no police powers with which to enforce its ruling. (This, incidentally, is a situation that continues unchanged to our day. The Court has changed its name, and been made a part of the United Nations, but its authority is precisely as limited as it was in the years preceding Sarajevo.) What Europe offered, in the phrase of G. Lowes Dickinson, British Liberal and pacifist, was the spectable of "international anarchy." The national state, unchecked as it was in the exercise of its sovereign power, except for self-restraint born of wisdom or fear, was set on the road to disaster. Trouble, if we accept this interpretation of events, lay deep indeed.

Poisonous Medicine? The Alliance System

What made the risks of international life even more terrifying was the system of alliances that had evolved by 1914. To a majority of powers, the answer to the international anarchy lay not in devising means to diminish national sovereignty, but in finding as many allies as they possibly could among the existing nation states. Faced as they felt they were by "reality," adding to their diplomatic strength by means of casting the widest conceivable net of alliances seemed very much preferable to waiting for Utopia. But should not Europe's statesmen have remembered Molière's words, from Le Malade Imaginaire, that "most men die of their medicines, not of their diseases"? Three major, and quite demonstrable, reasons would have seemed to indicate that, in this case at least, the cure was worse than the disease.

One was that Europe, after 1907 at the latest, was divided into two hostile camps: the Triple Alliance of Germany, Austria-Hungary, and Italy versus the Triple Entente of France, Russia, and Great Britain. Europe's six, then, had chosen sides years before any actual outbreak of hostilities, and in the process had decreased, and perhaps even destroyed, the space for diplomatic maneuvering that was (and is) essential for the preservation of peace.

The second and related point was that under the alliance system, as it then stood, minor powers were in a position to make very major decisions. Some rash action on the part of little Serbia could involve giant Russia in the consequences. Russia, in turn, might involve France. Or Austria-Hungary, with its entanglements in Southeastern Europe, could compel Germany to go to war over issues that were of no imaginable, or certainly of no direct, concern to Berlin. In short, any crisis, no matter how trivial by any reasonable and objective standards, carried the seeds of catastrophe. Given the facts of the alliance system, an offense to any one European nation might ultimately draw in that nation's ally, and then that ally's ally, or allies. The tail could wag a whole pack of dogs.

The third charge, and it is still a related one, was that nations at times were tempted to play a more reckless diplomatic game than they would have under different circumstances. Had they stood alone, their relative weakness might have served them as a continual reminder of the need for compromise and caution, but as it was, they could feel confident that their alliances would shield them from the worst results of their actions. Thus Russian ambitions in the Balkans, for instance, had been rather effectively held in check during an earlier period by the opposition of a number of other powers. But was it not natural that Russia, after the conclusion of the accords with Britain and France, should be inclined to pursue a much less circumspect policy, since in the event of a collision with Austria, or even with Austria plus Germany, St. Petersburg could count on the support of London and Paris? Thus Austria, for years, had been reluctant to pursue too irreconcilable a policy vis-à-vis Serbia. But, in 1909, as the Austro-German alliance hardened, the chief of the German general staff let his Austrian colleague know that if Austria should ever be compelled to march on Belgrade, and if Russia in such an event should come to Serbia's aid, Germany would be certain to go to war against Russia. It was a promise that Bismarck, with his far more skeptical view of alliances had never been willing to make; the idea that Austria might be encouraged to provoke Russia had terrified him. But now that Bismarck was dead and Austria could count on Germany's unquestioned aid, was it really very astonishing that she would act with such intransigence toward Belgrade in 1914?

This then, if we follow this particular argument, was the mood which the alliance system brought to Europe. And it brought it to a continent that was rent by national rivalries which had few precedents in past history.

Conflict Overseas: Imperialism

One such rivalry, or rather series of rivalries, took place overseas. The two-score years before Sarajevo were years of all but unparalleled imperialist activity. Not that imperialism was a new fact of European life. The practice, if not the term, had been quite as familiar to Ferdinand and Isabella as to Benjamin Disraeli. But imperialism seemed to have run its course. During the first three quarters of the nineteenth century, the powers of Europe were showing relatively little interest in acquiring any new territory beyond the confines of the continent. There was a good deal of economic imperialism, particularly on the part of Britain and France—in Latin America, in North Africa, in the Near East—but the outright acquisition of colonies tended to be regarded as an annoyance rather than an asset. The secession of the American colonies had been an object lesson to bear in mind.

In the 1870s, however, the attitude changed and changed abruptly. The powers were once again moving into Africa and Asia, and doing so with such energy and speed that by the time of Italy's Tripolitanian venture, the race was all but over. The end of Europe's overseas frontier had been reached. In the process, there had been acquired vast tracts of land and millions of new subjects. Africa, still largely uncharted in the 1880s, a generation later not only had some excellent maps, but roads and buildings, and hosts of white settlers as well.

The leader in the race was England, although other powers followed very closely. Nevertheless, it was the British who showed just how effectively one of the oldest of colonial powers could meet new opportunities, as they expanded into India, China, Persia, Egypt, the Southern part of Africa, until by 1914, one fifth of the world's land and one fourth of the world's population were under the rule of Britain—the world's largest Empire since Imperial Rome. Then there was France, her gains particularly impressive for a country that, in the wars of the eighteenth century, had lost most of the vast colonial holdings accumulated in the period between Henri IV and Louis XIV. The Third Republic now did as well as any Bourbon monarch ever had, establishing protectorates over Tunisia and Morocco and colonies in Western and Equatorial Africa, and taking control of Indo-China and Madagascar, of Tahiti and a number of other similarly tempting Pacific islands. It was a vast empire, and one whose population easily outnumbered that of the mother-country.

Then there were the powers new, or relatively new, to the colonial game: Germany, Italy, Belgium. In Germany's case, Bismarck's restraint was wearing off. Colonies, he had said, reminded him of the splendid furs some impoverished Polish noblemen wore with no shirt underneath. His successors felt differently about the matter. What they wanted were furs, not metaphors, and in their search they moved into East and Southwest Africa, farther north into Togoland and the Cameroons, and onto some Pacific islands as well. Italy, too, whose territory had only recently provided the scene for other nations' expansionist ambitions, turned from pursued into pursuer. The flag of Italy went up over Eritrea and the Somaliland, although an attempt to conquer the country bordering both, Abyssinia, ended in failure. At the battle of Adowa in 1896, the Abyssinians supplied the exception that proved the rule and startled the world with the news that Africans had beaten Europeans. But the Italians, as we saw, were to find another and happily feebler opponent in Turkey, and manage to incorporate Tripoli into their new empire. Belgium did even better as she acquired by purchase, rather than by battle, Congolese territory seventy-five times the size of Belgium proper—territory, moreover, that was appreciably richer in resources than Tripoli.

Finally, there were the two powers that, while either non-European or partly European only, still were very much part of the imperialist movement. One was the United States, which in this period annexed Hawaii, the Philippines, Cuba, Puerto Rico, and portions of Samoa, and made its presence felt on the Chinese mainland. The other power was Russia, whose imperialism largely followed the pre-1898 American pattern of expansion not so much overseas, as on her own continent. Like America's, Russia's aims were grand indeed. Russia was moving in the direction of the Middle East, or more specifically, toward Persia and Afghanistan, and toward the Far East, into Siberia, Korea, and the coastal regions of China.

It was, in sum, an unprecedented epoch of expansion. Of all the major powers, Austria-Hungary alone kept aloof, while Spain and Turkey, through lack of strength but not of desire, lost ground instead of gaining it.

What, however, was the connection between imperialism and war? The answer is that there were impressive arguments for maintaining that imperialism affected the policies of the European powers in several obvious, and ultimately disastrous, ways. There was, for instance, the new mood of violence that it helped to create. If ever one had daily proof of how might made right, imperialism provided it. Sweet were the uses of brute force: they had made the Queen of England Empress of India and created a new France beyond the seas. And it was violence that took place against the background of an often drab, dull, and tedious industrial society, thus making colonial wars seem all the more exciting and colorful.

As the great British historian and long-time Liberal member of Parliament, G. P. Gooch, wrote in 1902: "When we read on the bills: 'Boers sabred by moonlight,' we are supplied by a novel and striking image, which for a time relieves the monotony of life. The Romans clamored for *'panem et circenses.'* We have changed our religion and two thousand years have slipped by, but the cry is the same today." War, in an age where death was becoming mechanized as never before, was given an air of romance and glamor.

There was also another and even more concrete way in which imperialism could be said to have contributed to the destruction of the European order. It was that colonial ambitions required increased armaments. If one was to conquer the heathen—and be ready for possible trouble with some fellow missionaries as well, more money would have to be voted for arms, and so it was. The means as well as the spirit of violence were increasing. Very large amounts of effort went into the production of machineries of conquest. Very small amounts went into any real consideration of the consequences. In retrospect, we are startled by the recklessness with which the nations of Europe pursued their colonial dreams. In their greed, they appeared to be oblivious to the diplomatic repercussions of their Asian and African adventures. Thus, the 1880s and 1890s offered the almost constant spectacle of crises between England and Russia over who was to control Persia and Afghanistan. Thus, in the Pacific, Germany, England, and the United States would allow an inordinate amount of friction to develop between them over the precise delineation of interests on the island of Samoa; each nation's honor and survival, if one followed some of their respective spokesmen, were depending on the number of Polynesian palm trees it controlled. Thus, Germany and France, early in the new century, would twice go to the edge of war over the matter of spheres of influence in Morocco.

Lenin, looking on, thought it all very good news. Imperialism, he later wrote, was the final aberration of capitalism, the most fateful, perhaps, of capitalism's many inherent contradictions that would speed its end. How far from wrong was he, when we add to the sampling of near-wars the real wars that imperialism caused, from the Boer War to the Boxer Rebellion to the Russo-Japanese War of 1904-1905? Now it can be said that these wars were fairly remote in time and cause from World War I (an argument to which we will return later). But one aspect of imperialism that was not remote at all was the manner in which it poisoned relations between Germany and England. In the end, it would be the hostility between these two countries that would do as much as anything to transform a Balkan assassination into a world war.

Conflict at Home: Dardanelles to Alsace

Before dealing with the Anglo-German problem in any detail, however, it might be wise to cast a brief glance at Europe's basic trouble spots, *circa* 1914. For there existed some quite profound areas of friction between Russia and Turkey, between Russia and Austria, and between Germany and France, in addition to those between Germany and England. There existed others as well, of course; conflicts of interest are the daily bread of diplomacy. Yet it was on those four areas that the historians' attention has rightly concentrated. It was here that most of the explosives accumulated.

Russia's foreign policy, to start with the border region of Europe, was dominated, as it had been for two centuries, by the desire for access to the open seas and to the trade routes of the world. Specifically, this meant control of the Straits, and given the weakness of the Porte, the goal seemed worthier of pursuit than ever.

There was some irony in this, since by this time, the Straits were a matter of prestige rather than necessity to Russia. To quote George Kennan:

The regime of the straits that existed in the period prior to the war occasioned no difficulties for Russian commerce. And if one looks at the matter from the military standpoint, one can only say that this region, barring as it did the passage of foreign warships through the straits, was a positive advantage to a country which had lost most of its naval strength at Tsushima.[1]

Still, this *was* the aim Russia pursued, and it was a policy of great inherent risk. St. Petersburg was willing to take the risk because it had not quite adjusted to changed conditions; the habits of the past were more compelling than the realities

[1] George Kennan, "The Price We Paid for War," *The Atlantic* (October 1964), p. 51.

of the present. Besides, even where the statesmen's vision might be sharp and clear, there was the problem of Pan-Slav pressure.

Pan-Slavism, like official Russia's desire for the Straits, does not truly make a great deal of sense when looked at objectively in the second half of the twentieth century. To quote George Kennan again: "Membership in the Slavic branch of the human family is not really, as history has shown, a very important bond. Cultural and religious traditions, varying widely among the Slavic peoples, are more important as determinants of national policy, in the long run."[2]

Yet there it was. The actual number of dedicated Pan-Slavs in the Russian diplomatic service was relatively small; still, the sentiment and the pressures were there. No Russian foreign minister could entirely disregard them. And Pan-Slav pressures, combined with more traditional Russian foreign policy aims—the line dividing the two was a thin one in any event—placed a heavy burden not only on Russo-Turkish relations, but inevitably on Austro-Russian relations as well. The weakness of Turkey was an open invitation to both Russian and Austrian expansion in the Balkans, since none of the successor states to Turkey were viable enough to be wholly independent. True, statesmanship of a very superior order might have avoided or at least mitigated the resulting friction between the two great nations. If, on the one hand, the Austrians had acted with greater wisdom and restraint in 1908 and not faced the Russians with the choice between public humiliation and war, subsequent history might well have taken a happier course. So it might, on the other hand, if Russia had not involved herself quite so deeply in the affairs of Serbia, for what was at stake there was more than a competition for Balkan spoils. It was a question, rather, of national survival, since Belgrade, with Pan-Serb ideas of its own, posed a clear threat to the very existence of the Habsburg monarchy. But these are speculations. The fact was that both powers possessed foreign ministers of only quite ordinary and human ability and imagination, and that the pre-1914 Balkans provided another perennial trouble spot where crisis seemed normal and stability utopian, and where major powers were willing to take some terrible risks in the pursuit of gains that, from our vantage point at lease, seem wholly out of proportion to the price.

Then, closer to the center, there was the enmity that came between France and Germany. We can dispense with a long discussion of its roots; enough has been said about the conditions of the peace of Frankfurt. No more needs to be added here than to reiterate the fact that the French would not forget Alsace-Lorraine, and that a border region which should have been a bridge became a chasm. One of the reasons, for instance, for General Boulanger's vast popularity in the 1880s, and for his near success in destroying the Third Republic, was his supposed toughness toward the Germans:

> See him over there, he smiles as he goes by
> He has just set free Lorraine and All Alsace;

He had done nothing of the kind, nor did the duly constituted governments of France have the power to correct Frankfurt by diplomatic means. The Germans, for their part did not have the wisdom to do so, and so an unjust peace remained to divide two nations whose enmity was anything but eternal.

[2] Kennan, p. 51.

The Sources of Anglo-German Friction

The Germans did not even possess enough good sense to avoid policies that were bound to create friction with a nation from which no victor's peace kept them apart, that is, with Great Britain.

The causes, on the German side, went beyond any of the specific points at issue. Germany, under Wilhelm II, wished to be a great power. Why not, one might say. For Germany, exuberant in her new-found unity, possessed the population, the military strength, the industrial capacity, the vital energy, that go into the making of a great power. Why not, then? Mainly because Bismarck was gone and the conduct of Germany's foreign affairs rested in hands less steady than his. There was a very great deal of talk about Germany's might, about how Germany had been forgotten when the goods of this earth were distributed, about how Germany must trade the pursuit of limited objectives for that of *Weltpolitik*. There was very little clear thought, on the other hand, of what precisely it was that Germany wanted. How really does one translate *Weltpolitik*? "Global policy" perhaps, a term as hazy, and at the same time as ominous, as the original. The translator's difficulties are symptomatic.

The world, not surprisingly, was puzzled and concerned about the limits of Germany's ambitions. What were the Germans pursuing? Was it colonies, was it a new eminence on the continent, was it, perhaps, world domination? We know today that most foreign fears were groundless, and that no responsible German statesman before 1914 thought in terms of Napoleonic visions. At the time, the matter was less clear, as the Kaiser's far from subtle attempts to make Germany the equal of Great Britain, and above all, his ill-considered speeches allowed the impression to flourish that his country was a menace to peace, security, and a decent society. Many a German could also see the danger signs. Theodore Fontane, Germany's greatest nineteenth-century novelist, wrote to a friend:

You mention the speeches given by an exalted tongue, in which so much is said and even more is passed over in silence. I always lose my temper when I read them . . . . He has a million soldiers and wants to have a million battleships too. He dreams . . . of humiliating England. Germany is to be on top, in each and every thing. I rather like all this—I won't discuss right now whether it is clever or practical—and I would gladly follow him on his tightrope walk if only I could see the right sort of chalk under his feet and the proper balancing staff in his hands. But those are the things he does not have. What he wants, while it may not be impossible, is vastly dangerous, and his equipment is wrong and his means are insufficient.

Not all Germans were as cautious as Fontane. There had come into existence, simultaneously with Wilhelm's "New Course," the small but vocal group of Pan-Germans. Their specific aims were even more ill defined and fluid than those of Germany's official spokesmen. They talked of fusing such "Germanic" nations as Holland and Switzerland with the Reich. They dreamt dreams of incorporating, by political or economic union, regions reaching from Brussels in Bucharest into a German-dominated *Mitteleuropa*. They conjured up visions of a truly grand empire in Africa. The precise aims might change; the spirit remained the same. The Pan-Germans forever favored an aggressive and acquisitive approach to foreign policy; they were forever ready to engage in more tightrope walking, secure as they were in the knowledge that there were no ropes like German ropes and no nets like German nets.

The Pan-Germans were a minor group. They were less influential than their Pan-Slav counterparts in Russia, which was fair enough since their program was even more at variance with the world's realities. The largest membership they ever claimed at any given point was well under 25,000, and for the most part it was considerably smaller than that. Yet there existed several factors that made it difficult to deal with them as a mere fringe group. One was that among the members were a fair number of Reichstag deputies; in 1901, their most successful year, thirty-two Reichstag members were Pan-Germans. Another was the volume of the noise they made. A third was that the Kaiser's government, while not making Pan-German aims its own, failed to dissociate itself from their inanities with sufficient force. A fourth was that there were people beyond Germany's frontiers who were quite happy to make sure that the Pan-Germans received a wide hearing.

This applied, in particular, to Great Britain, where any indication of the existence of a German menace found some willing listeners. "It is of course true," noted a senior member of the British foreign office after reading a long dispatch on Pan-German activities, and making quite sure that it would reach the king, "that the Pan-German aspirations to dominion over the Low Countries and over the Adriatic are openly disavowed by all responsible people in Germany. But it would be foolish to doubt that if and when a favourable opportunity occurred for realizing such political aspirations in whole or part, the opportunity would be seized by the German Government with all its wonted energy."

The causes of this sort of suspicion, and of Anglo-German friction in general, were not all on one side of the channel, and on the British side, too, they transcended the individual points at issue. There were, on that side, factors that may make one appreciate why people as sensible and civilized and fond of many things British as Fontane was, wished the Kaiser luck in his policy toward England.

There was, for one thing, an amount of arrogance which exasperated people other than the Germans, too. God, to listen to some British speakers, had left the side of the bigger battalions where He had been in Frederick the Great's days, and permanently joined His cause with Britain's. There was, behind the arrogance, national expansion and power that had few parallels in history. It was, very likely, too much power, since the British Empire covered so much of the globe that just about any move on the part of just about any nation just about anywhere in the world could be considered a menace to either some part of the Empire or to its lines of communication. And the principal challenge to the Empire seemed to come from a nation too newly rich to abide by the rules laid down by British gentlemen, from the Kaiser's Germany. It was a threat to be resisted for moral as well as political reasons; one is back with the matter of arrogance. To quote Raymond Sontag:

Nearly all men, and groups of men, assume that what is good for them is good for the world, and that what is bad for them is bad for the world. Englishmen forgot their history and assumed that their supremacy resulted from the operation of a beneficent moral law. To challenge British supremacy was to challenge moral law. Could the Germans really be so wicked? Roughly speaking, the Conservatives believed that the Germans were capable of this crime; the Liberals were reluctant to entertain such a thought.[3]

That the Conservatives believed it might not have been too tragic, since it was two Liberal ministries, first that of Campbell-Bannerman and then that of Asquith, that held office after 1905. But among those who believed it were some of the permanent officials of the British foreign office as well. A passage written by one of them may serve to indicate their views; it may also illustrate the British attitudes just described. It comes from a memorandum written in 1907, by Sir Eyre Crowe, then the Senior Clerk of the Foreign Office. In a survey of Britain's relations with Germany and France, he had this to say as he came to discuss the matter of naval armaments:

The danger of a general combination against Britain's naval supremacy can in practice only be averted on condition that the national policy of the insular and naval state is so directed as to harmonize with the general desires and ideals common to all mankind.... Now the first interest of all countries is the preservation of national independence. It follows that England, more than any other non-insular Power, has a direct and positive interest in the maintenance of the independence of nations, and therefore must be the natural enemy of any country threatening the independence of the others, and the natural protector of the weaker communities.... It has been well said that every country, if it had the option, would, of course, prefer for itself the power of supremacy at sea, but that, this choice being excluded, it would rather see England hold that position than any other state.

But that happy state of affairs was in jeopardy, and the source of the threat was plain to Crowe:

A German maritime supremacy must be acknowledged to be incompatible with the existence of the British Empire, and even if that Empire disappeared, the union of the greatest military with the greatest naval power in one State would compel the world to combine for the riddance of such an incubus.[4]

Le style c'est l'homme. England, "the natural protector of the weaker communities." England, the chosen master of the seas. And why? Because "it has been well said" that this should be so. Because the possibility of any other nation's being supreme at sea was "being excluded." But by whom had it "been said"? By whom was it "being excluded"? How simple the problems of the world become in the passive tense. German naval supremacy? (A term which, when properly translated, should read "increased naval strength," since supremacy, even if the Germans had aimed at it, which they did not, would have been decades away.) It "must be acknowledged to be incompatible with the existence of the British Empire"—after all, that Empire was Germany's "natural enemy."

It was the voice of neither precision nor reason. When practicing diplomats begin to think of other powers in terms of natural enemies and of incubi, rather than in terms of nations with aims, interests, needs, and desires of their own—some

---

[3] Raymond J. Sontag, *European Diplomatic History, 1871-1932* (The Century Co., New York, 1933), p. 126.

[4] *British Documents on the Origins of the War, 1898-1914* (London, H. M. Stationery Office, 1928), III, Appendix A.

legitimate, some to be resisted—the end of meaningful discourse is in sight. Perhaps the one thing that "must be acknowledged" is that Germany was not the only country to miss a grand old man. Where was Disraeli? It is hard to visualize him tolerating a memorandum such as this. Sir Edward Grey, in whose hands the conduct of British foreign affairs now lay, not only tolerated it, but recommended it to the attention of the prime minister. Crowe's observations, he wrote, were "most valuable. The review of the present situation is both interesting and suggestive, and the connected account of the diplomatic incidents of past years is most helpful as a guide to policy." Grey was a man of great personal probity and attraction, yet, despite his long tenure of office (he served as under secretary for foreign affairs from 1892 to 1895, and as foreign secretary from 1905 to 1916) there was about him something of the air of the gifted amateur. Or, if that is too unkind a term, he strikes one as a statesman under whom expert advisers become makers of policy, and who, rather than shaping events, are all too easily controlled by circumstances.

Men who shape history are admittedly rare. Yet in the absence of genius, on the British as well as on the German side, the Anglo-German dispute continued unresolved. At least three specific problems and a matter of attitude combined to separate the two countries.

There was, in the first place, the economic rivalry between the two powers. The problem was not limited to England and Germany. Trade rivalries existed between a great many European states, and some writers have seen them as one of the truly basic problems aggravating European international relations before 1914. But Anglo-German competition probably was the sharpest of them all. German industrial growth, both in absolute terms and vis-à-vis England, had been phenomenal. In 1870, for instance, Germany had produced 169,000 metric tons of steel as against England's 286,000. In 1910, the figures read 13,698,000 for Germany and 6,374,000 for England. Not all figures were this spectacular; nevertheless, in coal production, Germany increased the yield by 800 percent between 1870 and 1914, England by 200 percent. In similar fashion, the Germans showed by their output of finished goods, particularly of chemicals and of electrical equipment, that while the industrial revolution had come late to their country, it had found a congenial home.

Statistics on exports were keeping pace with those on production. In 1871, for instance, German exports to the United States were well behind those of Great Britain; in 1898, they had nearly caught up; in 1913, they were nearly three times as high. In terms of total exports, Germany, while starting as a poor second indeed, by 1914 had become all but the equal of Britain. It was perfectly true that the world offered enough markets for both these industrial giants, yet the daily competition for sales tended to dramatize the conflict that existed in other fields as well. How was a British member of parliament to react when, during a foreign policy debate, he was to glance at his pencil and see the legend "Made in Germany"?

With trade rivalry went another problem, that of colonial friction. Too often, when the British wished to expand, whether it was in Africa or in the Pacific, there—or so at least it seemed to London—were the Germans, asking for "compensation." Nor would the British very easily forget the gratuitous insult of the Kruger dispatch. With the Germans in Southwest Africa now and in the Cameroons and in East Africa, unbidden and unwanted neighbors to Britain's domains, the memory was likely to remain fresh.

Why this German hunger for colonies, why the break with Bismarckian tradition? In part, German imperialism makes sense, even today. An expanding German industry was in need of markets and, to an even larger degree, in need of raw materials. Yet there is no absolute need to push forward the frontiers of empire in order to assure oneself of a proper supply of kapok from the Cameroons or of cloves from Zanzibar. Less aggressive ways of commerce may work equally well; certainly the Swiss have grown extraordinarily rich without acquiring a single colony. Switzerland, it can be replied, was a small power, Germany a very great one, which could not afford to rely on the good will of her potential enemies for the materials needed to sustain the nation's economy. Still, even when supposedly strategic economic needs are taken into account, there remains an element in Germany's colonial appetite that defies rational explanation. For economic blockades in time of peace tend to be as rare as they are ineffectual; nor was this contingency one that necessarily entered the minds of Germany's leaders. Trade flowed too freely in the years before 1914. It was rather that some Germans were getting intoxicated with their own slogans—of Germany's might, of keeping up with Great Britain, of needing a "place in the sun." Here, as elsewhere, there was much action for action's sake, and little thought about what the limits of Germany's ambitions should be.

Much of this also held true of the third issue that came between Germany and England, the naval race. "Our future," to recall the Kaiser's elegant phrase, "lies on the water." Deeds had followed his words. Under the leadership of Admiral von Tirpitz, Germany's all too energetic Secretary of the Navy from 1897 to 1916, the Germans proceeded to build a navy that was meant to be second only to that of Great Britain.

Some of the motives behind Tirpitz' program were rational enough. Both the expanding German Merchant Marine and the colonies that now flew the German flag deserved the protection of a German fleet. There may also have been an element of sense in the admiral's idea of the "risk navy." Let the German navy, argued Tirpitz, not aim at supremacy. That was a condition plainly beyond the country's potential. Let Germany's navy, however, be strong enough so that no other and superior naval power would think of attacking it for fear of the losses that such an attack might entail. Let it, in modern parlance, be a deterrent navy. Faced with such a navy, and here came the second, rather less solid part of Tirpitz' argument, the British would surely persuade themselves of the wisdom of reaching some political agreement with Germany.

This, as we know, was a miscalculation. It is not very often that nations can frighten each other into friendship, and the British reaction, not very surprisingly, was that of the clenched fist, and not of the outstretched hand. Not very surprisingly, for what did the Germans really have in mind when they embarked on Tirpitz' program; to what extent had they considered the consequences?

Historically, Germany was a land power with hardly any naval tradition. If one were to look at the new German battleships coming off the yards, one would be struck by how many of them were named after Prussian and German generals—Derfflinger, Moltke, Seydlitz, Goeben, Blücher—since there were simply not enough admirals to lend their names to the christenings. Obviously the British would be vitally concerned, even with people more balanced than Crowe in the foreign office, at the spectacle of Germany, the possessor of Europe's strongest army, setting about the creation of a major navy as well. The direct challenge to

Britain's control of the seas quite aside, it was too much power for any one country to hold.

Why, then, did the Germans go ahead, plain though the unfortunate effects of Tirpitz' ambitions on Anglo-German relations were? Why did the Kaiser continue to give the admiral his blessings; how could he tell his Chancellor, as late as the fall of 1913, that "England will come to us not in spite, but because of my Imperial Navy"? There was active here, one suspects, the same element that made the Germans proceed with equal disregard for caution in the colonial sphere: a burning desire to be recognized as Great Britain's equal, and with it, a suspicion that the desire was not likely ever to be fulfilled.

Out of place as the phrase may appear in a diplomatic narrative, there was a deep psychological bond as well as bar between Britain and Germany. What came into play here was a curious love-hate relationship, aggravated by some profound feelings of inferiority on the German side. It could be found in Wilhelm II, who delighted in seeing himself in a British admiral's uniform, who was proud of being half-English (his mother had been Queen Victoria's eldest daughter), who loved reading English books, and who spoke and wrote English with facility and pleasure, and who, at the same time, was worrying whether the British were taking him quite seriously, and behind whose nearly every move lurked fear of being secretly smiled at, of not being truly considered the equal of his cousin Edward and of Eton's best. It could be found among many educated Germans who sensed that no matter how much of Britain's tailoring, country clubs, parliamentary institutions, or orange marmalade they might imitate or import, they would never quite catch up with their cousins beyond the Channel; that they were newly rich but not yet newly wise; that they might be able to buy all the Harris tweed they wished, but that with all the cloth of the Hebrides, they would still lack the proper school tie.

Here is a passage from a German novel, *Peter Moor's Trip to Southwest*, by Gustav Frenssen, that may underline some of this. The book appeared in 1906 and was one of the year's best sellers. Its narrator and title hero is a good and simple fellow who has enlisted in the German marines and at the book's beginning is on his way to German Southwest Africa to fight in a campaign against a native rebellion. As his boat passes the Cliffs of Dover, he chances to overhear the following conversation between an officer in the medical corps and a deck lieutenant:

I heard the lieutenant say: "We sailors have different ideas about the British. . . .We meet them in all the world's ports and we know that they are the most reputable people of them all. There, behind those chalk cliffs, lives the first nation on earth: noble, wise in the ways of the world, brave, united, and rich. But we? For years past, we have had just one of their qualities, bravery. Slowly, now, we're gaining one more, wealth. But will we ever gain the rest? There now is the vital question." The words surprised me. But later, the old Africa hands I met also spoke with great respect about the British.[5]

Too often, the respect was not being returned. The "you are to love me!" approach is rarely effective. The Germans might have been well advised to drop the matter. How many foreigners, after all, did the British either love or respect? The Germans rarely paused to consider that the answer most likely was "none." An occasional exception was the Kaiser. "He is a thorough Englishman," he told

    [5] Gustav Frenssen, *Peter Moor's Fahrt nach Südwest* (G. Grote, Berlin, 1906), pp. 14-15.

Theodore Roosevelt when George V had succeeded Edward VII in 1910, "and hates all foreigners but I do not mind that as long as he does not hate Germans more than other foreigners." The insight did not last. Affection, as it so easily can, turned into hatred. Nor did the ethnic kinship that existed between the two nations stay the process. It certainly never acted as a substitute for missed alliance opportunities. On the contrary, it had a way of making things worse. Few feuds are as bitter as family feuds. In the end, when war came in 1914, one of the most wildly popular poems of the hour would be a "Song of Hate Against England," by a young and hitherto obscure German poet, Ernst Lissauer. Whom did the Germans really wish to see humbled? he asked. The French, whom they had battled in so many wars? No, not the French. "We love them not, we hate them not." The Russians, then, the ancient Slav antagonist of the Germans? No again. "We love them not, we hate them not"

> *What's the Frenchman to us, or the Russian foe*
> *We'll meet shot with shot, and blow with blow.*

No—"We all have but one foe, England":

> *Hate by water and hate by land*
> *Hate of the head and hate of the hand*
> *Hate of the hammer and hate of the crown*
> *Hate of seventy million choking down*
> *They love as one, they hate as one*
> *They all have but one foe: England*

A Matter of Publicity: The Press

The topic of Anglo-German friction has been stressed at such length because in a sense it was the ancient nursery rhyme's horseshoe nail. Without it, there might have been no *Entente Cordiale*, without that *Entente*, French support for Russia might have been less resolute; without that support, in turn, Russia might well have acted as a restraining influence on Serbia. For lack of an Anglo-German *détente*, in short, more than one kingdom would be lost.

What aggravated the points at issue between Germany and England even more was the publicity they received. The Germans not only had a navy, they also had a Navy League, and so did the British, and both these groups sponsored more speeches, books, pamphlets, and letters to the editor than was beneficial to the cause of peace. Nor was there any need to rely on special interest groups to worsen, or at times to create, international disputes; the press, with no particular prodding, did quite well enough at that.

The end of the nineteenth century had seen a new mass literacy, and with it, the creation of a mass-circulation press. The managers of that press were quick to learn that bad news sold more copies than good. "They have ceased to publish the 'Newgate Calendar' and 'The Pirate's Own Book,'" wrote Ralph Waldo Emerson, "since the family newspapers . . . have quite superseded them in the freshness as well as the horror of their records of crime." Emerson was angry, but was he exaggerating that much? "Boers sabred by moonlight." William Randolph Hearst was not the only magnate of the press to discover that crisis and war—stimulated, or even, with great ingenuity, created *ab ovo*—made fine circulation builders. Many a

European counterpart to Mr. Hearst would emulate him, exaggerating minor incidents into major crises, presenting another nation's new arms budget as a threat to his readers' survival, or converting the possession of some particular stretch of African jungle into a matter of national honor. The press, in sum, played a substantial part in accentuating international friction, and perhaps even in preparing a mood for war. To quote Sidney B. Fay:

Too often newspapers in all lands were inclined to inflame nationalistic feelings, misrepresent the situation in foreign countries, and suppress factors in favor of peace. . . . There is a vast literature on freedom of the press, censorship of the press, slander and libel, and the professional aspects of journalism, but there is very little sound writing on the relations of the press to governemntal control and on its influence in formenting national hatreds and war.[6]

The role of the press may be an aspect of Europe's pre-1914 troubles that stands in least need of further elaboration and illustration, even though some of the volumes Professor Fay had in mind still remain to be written. We are all quite familiar today with seeing those foreign statesmen whose policies or interests, at some given moment, run counter to ours, pictured as imbeciles, thieves, or megalomaniacs on the editorial pages or in our weekly news magazines. (The latter, perhaps, come closest to the pre-1914 European daily papers in their excess of opinion over fact.) Still, we may draw back a bit as we come across some of the offerings of the pre-war press.

There was the series of reports on Germany in London's mass-circulation *Daily Mail* in 1909, for instance, whose resonance was strong enough to lead to their being reprinted in pamphlet form. "Germany," the reader learned, "is deliberately preparing to destroy the British Empire." Nor was that the extent of Germany's ambition. "All of Europe is to be Teutonised. We are all to be drilled and schooled and uniformed and taxed by Prussian officials, and the Emperor William II is to rule us with a rod of iron." Britain could respond with nothing less than the creation of a larger navy and the introduction of compulsory military service. "Britain alone stands in the way of Germany's realization of world-power and domination."

The attitude was not restricted to that part of the press called "yellow" (as though that epithet was enough to discount its influence). Some years earlier, London's *Saturday Review*, a journal much smaller in circulation and normally far more literate in tone, had carried an article that suggested that in

. . . all parts of the earth, in every pursuit, in commerce, in manufacturing, in exploiting other races, the English and Germans jostle each other. . . . Were every German to be wiped out tomorrow, there is no English trade, no English pursuit that would not immediately expand. Were every Englishman to be wiped out to-morrow, the Germans would gain in proportion. Here is the first great racial struggle of the future: here are two growing nations pressing against each other, man to man all over the world. One or the other has to go; one or the other will go.

The proposed solution was even more simple and radical than that of the *Daily Mail*. Destroy the Germans! *"Germania esse delenda."*

---

[6] Sidney B. Fay, *The Origins of the World War* (Crowell-Collier and Macmillan, New York, 1930), I, 47-48.

For once, it is easy to sympathize with the Kaiser, who after reading the *Daily Mail* articles said, "They are all mad in England, and people seem to think that I am standing here with my battle axe behind my back ready to fall upon them at any moment." His point might have been even stronger had the German press, in its entirety, been that much more restrained. Instead, some of the notes that *Saturday Review* and *Daily Mail* had sounded were being returned from across the channel. Nor were a number of papers elsewhere on the continent reluctant to join in. There are a few more succinct comments on all this public venom than Humbert Wolfe's lines,

> No one can hope to bribe or twist
> Thank God the British journalist
> But seeing what the man will do
> Unbribed, there's no occasion to.

Arms and the Men: War as a Means of Policy

"Power without responsibility," Stanley Baldwin is reported to have said apropos of the press, "the privilege of the harlot throughout the centuries." The words were fairly mild if one considers the damage the press was capable of inflicting in an age in which war was still an acceptable means of policy, yet in which the physical nature of warfare was changing beyond the imagination of man.

Here lay another very basic trouble spot of pre-1914 Europe. No matter what was happening in the laboratories and on the military proving grounds, war, by implicit agreement among the nations remained the *ultima ratio regum*, the final argument of kings, the ultimate and permissible resort in disputes between sovereign states. In such an atmosphere, as Golo Mann has written:

... war, as a concept and an institution, is an important factor contributing to war itself. Why should not something assume real shape from time to time which in one's thoughts one considers quite normal, which forms the high point in the life of nations, which is the standard by which the affairs of state—in their ranks, values, and morals—tend to be measured.[7]

Yet how much wiser Europe would have been to search for other standards by which to measure the affairs of state. For what made the unbroken acceptance of Clausewitz' celebrated dictum of war as the continuation of policy by other means especially ominous was the changing nature of those other means. Weapons were becoming increasingly destructive, and there were too many of them. The years that reached from the Franco-Prussian War to Sarajevo were the years of the great arms race between the powers of Europe. Increased expenditures for armaments were motivated in part by steadily escalating technological improvements, in part by the desire to back conflicting national ambitions with sufficient force, in part by the need to keep each nation's military preparedness on a par with that of its potential enemies. No matter what the motives, the speed with which the race was run had few precedents. Here, then, are some of the basic statistics on the growth of

---

[7] Golo Mann, "Gute Vorsätze," *Der Monat* (August 1964). pp. 18-19.

European armaments in the period, expressed in terms of per capita expenditures as translated into dollars:

	1870	1914
Great Britain	$3.54	$8.23
France	2.92	7.07
Russia	1.28	3.44
Italy	1.38	3.16
Germany	1.28	8.19
Austria-Hungary	1.08	3.10

Although Great Britain continued to lead in absolute terms, by far the greatest single increase was made by Imperial Germany, and a more detailed breakdown will indicate that the rate of German armaments accelerated with particular speed in the years immediately preceding 1914. Yet, while the specific rate of increase might differ, there was no country which felt that in the pursuit of security and power, it could keep out of the arms race altogether. The irony was that power and security are elusive things, and in the end, no country felt much safer than before, since the *proportionate* distribution of arms remained very much what it had been to begin with. There was, on the contrary, good reason to feel less safe, since the line between defensive armaments and the readiness for aggression was all but impossible to define.

The nations might have tried to halt the trend had they been able to visualize the nature of a war fought with the weapons whose deadliness was being improved with ingenuity and skill. But most people thought of war in romantic terms, in terms of gallantry, devotion and comradeship, all qualities that would turn out to have comparatively little meaning in the face of the mass-produced slaughter for which the world was in fact preparing. A few of the experts knew better, but even they were wrong; for they thought in terms of quick, decisive campaigns and thus evaded contemplating the full discrepancy between the aims of twentieth-century warfare, on the one side, and its means, on the other. What no one foresaw was the kind of murderous yet indecisive warfare that would open in 1914. The generals played their war games and speculated, often with considerable intelligence, about the forms of future warfare, but not one among them envisaged what would take place between 1914 and 1918.

So the war games went on, and the statesmen did little to curb them. Here is a final aspect of the question "How Deep the Trouble?" that should at least be mentioned. Where were the inspired statesmen of early twentieth century Europe? Where were the men of power whose overriding desire was peace, and whose abilities matched their motives? They were dead. The nineteenth century had known them—Talleyrand and Metternich, Bismarck and Disraeli. The twentieth could only honor their memory.

But How Deep the Trouble? Some Conclusions

A formidable indictment, it seems. The national state and the alliance system, conflict overseas and conflict at home, a growing arsenal of arms and a press out for blood, an acceptance of war and a paucity of statesmanship. Was not a continent that permitted all these conditions to exist doomed in any event? At first glance, yes. At a second glance, we may begin to wonder; and at a third, the doubts will deepen.

For each and every point of danger mentioned, while real enough, had quite another side to it, too. The state system? But that was hardly new, and there neither was nor is any law stating that national sovereignty must automatically lead to war. Effectively, supranational forms of government have either been very rare—there was but one *Imperium Romanum*, and even in its case, an occasional fight was necessary to maintain peace—or quite illusory, such as the Holy Roman Empire, which in sober truth abounded with war. The national state, in short, was a reality and had been one for some centuries. Such a state, in the absence of a higher authority, could go to war; but it was equally free to remain at peace, and statesmanship, common sense, self-interest or fear were all powerful factors pointing to the desirability of the latter course.

The alliance system, then? Perhaps, if the alliances had actually been as binding and inflexible as some writers have made them out to be. But they were not. The British would consistently refuse a clear-cut promise to come to the assistance of France, let alone of Russia, in case of war. Every one of the alliances was quite specifically defensive in character, and as the Italians were to show, it was perfectly possible to change sides with impunity. In fact, instead of assailing a system that in essence was and is no more than the common pursuit of common interests (a difficult ambition to outlaw) might one not rather say that if only the alliances had been stronger, Europe would have been less troubled? To give but two specific illustrations, if, for instrance, the Austrians had been certain beyond a doubt that an attack on Serbia would be an attach on Russia, or if the Germans had been altogether convinced that to invade France would, undoubtedly, involve them in war with England, might not history have taken a happier course? (A matter of speculation? Yes. But it is the basic assumption on which the western alliance system since the end of the Second World War has rested.)

What, though, of imperialism? That its effects on Anglo-German relations were deplorable should need no further elaboration. However, it should be said that it made Anglo-Russian and Anglo-French relations fully as difficult. There was far more colonial rivalry between Britain and France, for instance, than between France and Germany—the Germans and the French, after all, had no Egyptian campaign of 1798 to fight over again—and the Anglo-Russian wrangling that went on over Persia alone was every bit as sharp as any Anglo-German conflict of interests in Africa. Yet for all their imperialist rivalries, England, Russia, and France would ultimately find an alliance both possible and profitable. That imperialism could accentuate trouble was evident. What was equally evident, however, was that it could, as the case of the relationship between the United States and Great Britain after 1898 showed, bring about the realization that the interests of two nations were best served by cooperation. Beyond this, one ought to say that the absence of colonial ambitions was, in at least one instance, a cause for regret. To quote A. J. P. Taylor, whose insights can be as perceptive as his fallacies can be mischievous: "All the Great Powers except Austria-Hungary found a safe channel for their exuberance in expansion outside Europe. They stumbled on this solution by chance, without foresight.[8]" If only it had been possible to deflect Austria's interests from the

[8] A. J. P. Taylor, *The Struggle for Mastery in Europe* (Oxford University Press, Oxford, 1954), p. 256.

Balkans to the South Seas, how much better that would have served the cause of European peace.

What of the more specific conflicts between the nations of Europe, the quarrels closer to home? Again, one hesitates to say that by themselves they doomed Europe in 1914. For surely one of the common denominators between the various issues that set Russia against Turkey, Austria against Russia, or France against Germany, was that none were worth a war. Russia might want the Straits, and want them badly, but given the opposition of Britain, France, and Austria, she was quite unwilling to risk an armed conflict over them. Austria might argue every inch of the way with Russia over Balkan spheres of influence, but the choice made was to let the diplomats and not the generals do the battling. France might seize every chance to change the verdict of Frankfurt, but it was every chance short of war. Whatever the period's equivalent of Henry IV's favorite city, it was worth a mass, but not the lives of one's countrymen. Or, to put the matter in another perspective, Russia, in the period that followed the First World War, faced territorial grievances infinitely worse than she, or for that matter, any other European nation confronted before 1914, *without* taking recourse to war to rectify them.

Besides, nothing is forever in diplomatic history. Russia and Austria, for instance, had lived through sustained periods of diplomatic harmony as well as of hostility; few powers had been closer partners than St. Petersburg and Vienna during the quarter century or so after the Napoleonic settlement. Circumstances had changed, but so they might again. There was no reason why alignments should not begin to shift once more, why partnership could not replace rivalry. This applied with equal force to Anglo-German relations. Again, none of the specific instances of friction mentioned were precisely trifling in nature, but neither were they irreparable. Trade rivalry there was, but there was also beginning to be an understanding on the peaceable division of the world's markets, with the British concentrating on trade with the Empire, the Germans on that with continental Europe. Besides, except in Marxist mythology, nations seldom go to war with each other to increase the ratio of their export trade. In theory, this is what should be happening. "War," if we follow the official *History of the Communist Party of the Soviet Union*, "is the inevitable concomitant of capitalism." But in reality, things were rather different. During the Algeciras crisis, for instance, the most determined advocates of a peaceable settlement were the representatives of the French and German coal industry, for they not only dreaded the price of war, they also were very much aware of the advantages which Franco-German cooperation would bring. When the final crisis came, as Bernadotte Schmitt has noted, "the loudest protests against war were made by the businessmen in Germany and Britain, who foresaw clearly what war would do to them."[9]

How much more serious, in the actual event, were naval and colonial rivalries? True, the Germans might have done well to make Falstaff's motto their own. Discretion would have been the better part of valor. But not all was bluster. Germans and Englishmen, as noted, had agreed, by quiet negotiation, rather than by public collision, on the division of the Portugese colonies. Some overall efforts to limit the naval race, such as that undertaken by Lord Haldane, then Secretary of War, during a mission to Berlin in 1912, ended in failure, but the two nations, by 1914, had managed to reach an informal understanding to construct new battleships

---

[9] Bernadotte E. Schmitt, *The Origins of the First World War* (Published for the Historical Association by Routledge and Kegan Paul, London, 1958), p. 5.

at a ratio of Britain's 16 to Germany's 10. There was no reason why more instances of accommodation could not follow—not even the psychological bar between the two nations. A look at some photographs of Edward VII enjoying a state visit plus family outing with his cousin Wilhelm may suggest that more than party manners or the anticipation of a good meal lay behind the smiles and the bonhommie. True, such periods of contentment might alternate with others of utter distemper, but that was hardly a problem that applied to Anglo-German relations alone.

The love-hate relationship, for one, between the United States and Great Britain paralleled it rather closely. It offered the same spectacle of the transaquatic cousins who would now detest and now embrace each other, of the American who would now lionize his British visitor and now delight in twisting his tail, of the Britisher who would now envy those Americans for their wealth and now think them vulgar for it, of the American who would now make fun of the broad "a" and now join the English-Speaking Union. Yet, there was, in this period, neither war nor the threat of war between these two powers. But that was different, one might say. National interests coincided, so it was easy enough to keep whatever antipathies existed from influencing the conduct of foreign policy. Perhaps so, but to repeat the truism: nothing is forever in diplomatic history. There was no immutable rule which stated that Britain and Germany could never again inhabit a world in which their interests would once more run parallel. Psychological barriers, by themselves, certainly were not deep enough to prevent such a state of affairs, if only for the simple reason that if a good many Britishers still tended to dislike the Germans, there were others who detested the French or Russians even more.

What about the press and its role, then? The case here is strong. Who would not wish that editors and publishers had never discovered the charms that lay in fomenting international trouble. Yet there existed a mass audience avid for precisely this sort of entertainment. To have asked the owners of the press to refrain from supplying what their readers wanted—and what their own prejudices as often as not made them want as well—would have been expecting a great deal more wisdom and self-restraint than is given to the vast majority of men. Nor could the press, by itself, quite start a war. "Remember the Maine" was a one-time coup, never to be repeated. That the press lent a special element of danger to the ordinary conduct of diplomacy was true, yet when all the evidence is considered, the influence of the press was subtantially smaller than its own spokesmen thought. The final decisions continued to remain with the prime minister and not the night editor.

But were not chauvinistic editorials twice as perilous in a society that continued to accept war as a means of policy, that daily added to its arsenal of arms, and that had not enough statesmen of vision to keep the warmakers in check? Again, one wonders. For it was, and is, easy enough to point to the dangers that flow from the acceptance of war; it is rather more difficult to say what might be done to prevent the dangers that were, or are, likely to result from the abandonment of war as a means of policy. Would a nation announcing that it would under no circumstances have recourse to war truly be furthering the cause of peace—its own or that of others? Yet an argument against war as the ultimate resort of kings which fails to suggest what else the king might resort to will have to carry relatively little conviction. On the contrary, in the eyes of both statesmen and public, were not the preparations for war a true insurance against a war's actually taking place? Vickers and Krupp were not really kept busy as they were turning out guns and shells because the men ordering these arms wished to use them against any live targets; rather each side wished to convince the other of their strength and seriousness of purpose, and hence of the unwiseness of deciding in favor of armed conflict. *Si vis pacem, para bellum.* Deterrence, by many another name, is rather a venerable concept. So is that of leading from strength. To quote Raymond Sontag: "Armed forces were not intended primarily for use in war; they were to bring victory without war by forcing rival states to give way without an armed encounter."[10]

But what if the available statesmanship did not match the weapons of destruction? After all, it takes keen eyesight and nimble feet to sense just where the brink ends and the precipice begins. How could matters have ended well at a time when Bethmann was sitting in Bismarck's chair, and Grey was holding the office once filled by Castlereagh? The answer—at times even rhetorical questions deserve an answer—was that matters very possibly could have ended well, for not only is genius customarily in short supply, but the statesmen of Europe were, with hardly an exception, if not inspired, at least competent and often quite shrewd men. So were many of the people serving under them, especially the diplomats in the field. As one looks at the dispatches of Paul or Jules Cambon, or of others for whose mention it has been hard to find room in a necessarily concise narrative—Marschall von Bieberstein on the German side, for instance, or Sir George Buchanan on the British—one is tempted to think of the era as at least the silver age of European diplomacy. And these were, again almost without exception, men genuinely committed to the cause of peace. Count Pourtalès, Germany's ambassador to St. Petersburg, openly wept when all had failed and, his hands shaking, he delivered his country's declaration of war to a Russian foreign minister who, in reply, embraced the representative of the power that Russia was now pledged to fight to the finish. Pourtalès' colleagues might do better at controlling their public displays of emotion, but they would feel as he did. The people, when the end came, were jubilant; the statesmen remained sober.

How deep, then, the trouble? Deep, but not fatal. War was possible in 1914—when is it not?—but it was not inevitable. An anatomy of many another year, whether 1874, 1884, 1894, 1904, or 1964, if undertaken as mercilessly as the inquest into 1914 necessarily is, may quite likely uncover troubles fully as profound as those of 1914.

We do not, for obvious reasons, undertake such inquests, but we may say that everything considered war was no more foreordained for 1914 than peace was for 1964. Too much was right with the world of 1914: the nations, on the whole, had learned to live with the differences that divided them; several of the outstanding points at issue between rival powers were being settled or mitigated; and as the changing relationship between Britain and France, France and Italy, or Russia and Britain had shown, nations that were very dissimilar in temper, ambitions, and historical memory were fully as capable of accommodation as they were of conflict. History is forever in flux. In time, the particular difficulties that beset Europe *circa* 1914 might well have vanished, changed, or looked rather insignificant when placed next to other and newer problems.

1939 is the exception and not the rule. It is rare that a power is truly bent on war, as Hitler's Germany then was. In 1914, that sort of will to war was absent, although error, miscalculation, and sheer accident were very much present. But let us, because they were present, and because the end result was catastrophe, not become too absorbed by a sweeping search for underlying causes. Let us avoid the fallacy of saying that because the First World War's consequences were so

[10] Raymond Sontag, *European Diplomatic History*, p. 146

momentous, its causes must of necessity have been equally significant. Captain Jenkins claimed to have had an ear cut off by some overly zealous Spanish guards in 1739, and England plunged into a war with Spain that lasted for two years. It was, Frederick the Great later admitted, his youth and "the satisfaction of seeing my name in the newspapers" which had in truth caused him to attack Maria Theresa in 1740 and to begin the long War of the Austrian Succession. Of course, other and deeper causes contributed to the origins of both of these wars, but so did these immediate reasons. Of course, there were many explosives about in early twentieth-century Europe—there seldom are not—but it still took a fire to light them, and certain quite unpredictable winds to fan the flames. We need, therefore, if we are to understand the war's origins, to turn to its direct source, the assassination of Archduke Franz Ferdinand of Austria-Este, and to the events that followed it.

THE OUTBREAK OF THE FIRST WORLD WAR AND GERMAN WAR AIMS

Imanuel Geiss

The Crisis of July 1914

German innocence — or at least relative innocence — for the outbreak of the 1914 war had for decades been something that could not be questioned in Germany. The function of this taboo varied according to the circumstances: in early August 1914 it was designed to impress both the SPD and Britain, in order to get the former into the war, and if possible to keep the latter out of it. During the war it was to convince neutrals and Germans alike of the righteousness of the Reich's cause. Immediately after the war, even the left-wing governments of 1918-19 clung in dealing with the Allies to the concept of German relative innocence, in the hope of getting a more lenient peace settlement. When they failed, later governments and public opinion in the Weimar Republic retreated from the relatively critical line of these earlier governments which, after all, had published the German documents and set up a Commission of Enquiry into the causes of Germany's defeat.

The Weimar Republic opened a sustained campaign against article 231 of the Versailles treaty; it hoped, by disputing Germany's responsibility for the war, to dismantle the treaty as a whole. The campaign had started at Versailles itself, where Bülow (later Secretary of State in the Auswärtiges Amt) mapped out and initiated the strategy. [1] In the Auswärtiges Amt a small sub-section, the Kriegsschuldreferat, inspired, directed, and financed the German innocence propaganda. Its chief instruments were two organizations, the Arbeitsausschuss Deutscher Verbände (ADV), and the Zentralstelle zur Erforschung der Kriegsschuldfrage. ADV, a federation of practically all reputable semi-political organizations, including the

---

[1] What follows is only a preliminary sketch of a very complicated story, based so far on the study of about half of the rich archival material of the Kriegsschuldreferat in the Political Archive of the Auswärtiges Amt at Bonn.

trade unions, looked after the general propaganda, while the Zentralstelle had to cover the scholarly aspects of the campaign.

The two organizations worked together, notwithstanding occasional rivalries and bickerings behind the scenes, and the Kriegsschuldreferat saw to the necessary finances and co-ordination. Each had a periodical, the more important one for the general historian being the Zentralstelle's *Kriegsschuldfrage*; for its launching it was possible to find money even in summer 1923, at the height of the inflation. The editor of *Kriegsschuldfrage* – later renamed *Berliner Monatshefte* – was Alfred von Wegerer, an ex-army officer. For tactical reasons he posed as an independent, but he was in fact employed by the Auswärtiges Amt, in a position ranking in salary and annual leave as a *Ministerialrat*. Both the budget and the literary activities of the Zentralstelle were controlled by the Kriegsschuldreferat, which in its turn gave Wegerer valuable information for pursuing the scholarly struggle against the "Kriegsschuldlüge."

A third, more subtle instrument consisted of a host of writers, none of them historians, engaged as part-time propagandists. For a moderate but regular monthly payment of a few hundred marks they wrote three or four articles a month in German dailies and/or periodicals on the war guilt question. The most prominent among them were Bernhard Schwertfeger, an ex-Colonel, and Hermann Lutz, a free-lance writer. The appearance of Lutz on the pay-roll of the Auswärtiges Amt is the more startling since, judging from his *Gutachten* for the work of the Commission of Enquiry,[2] he must have passed as an independent critic of the official line. A fourth means used was to subsidise publications which took the German line, although occasionally books with critical passages were allowed to pass in order not to arouse suspicions abroad. These publications ranged from *Die Grosse Politik* to insignificant pamphlets. The usual method was to buy a number of copies, often several hundred, in advance; these were afterwards sent to German missions abroad which distributed them free to key personalities in the respective countries. Many of the subsidised books were translations into German. (The Auswärtiges Amt subsidy was much sought after by German publishers, and it is quite possible that without the financial assistance of the Kriegsschuldreferat many a book might not have appeared.) Probably only a few foreign authors received more than this kind of subsidy: one, Boghitchevitch, living in Switzerland, was paid by the Auswärtiges Amt in gold francs, a difficult thing to manage in 1919. Most of the foreign authors supporting the German cause were probably unaware of the subsidy, though it is difficult to say how many would have minded if they had known.

The Kriegsschuldreferat decided which publications criticizing the German line were to be attacked, how, by whom, and when and where, or whether they should be simply ignored. This is what happened to a booklet by Walter Fabian, now editor of *Gewerkschaftliche Monatshefte*.[3] Similarly, it acted as internal censor for official or semi-official publications, in particular of the Untersuchungsausschuss, an effort in which it was partly supported by the latter's secretary-general, Eugen Fischer-Baling. Together, they prevented the publication of Hermann Kantorowicz's *Gutachten* for the Untersuchungsausschuss, although it was completed and set up in

---

[2] Hermann Lutz, *Die europäische Politik in der Julikrise 1914*. Das Werk des Untersuchungsausschusses, I. Reihe, Bd. II (Berlin, 1930).

[3] Walter Fabian, *Die Kriegsschuldfrage* (Leipzig, n.d. [1925]). The chapter on July 1914 was republished, unchanged, in August 1964; see W. Fabian, "So brach 1914 der Krieg aus," in *Gewerkschaftlicke Monatshefte*, vol. 15, no. 8.

type as early as 1927.[4] When, in 1932, the Untersuchungsausschuss wanted to publish five volumes of documents on German war aims, the Kriegsschuldreferat vetoed the proposal on the ground that the documents would prove to the whole world that German plans of conquest made nonsense of the German innocence campaign. Finally, the Kriegsschuldreferat prepared the many official statements of German chancellors and of President Hindenburg on the war guilt question during the Weimar period, statements which, perhaps more than anything else, helped to strengthen the taboo.

The campaign was the more effective since German historians lent it their great prestige. Most of them did not need official prompting but had only to follow their natural inclinations. Surprisingly enough, the contribution of professional German historians to a rational analysis of the causes of the war had been fairly slight. Most of the German campaigners were amateurs, and none of the few professionals who were prominently engaged (Hans Delbrück, Friedrich Thimme, Paul Herre, Erich Brandenburg, Richard Fester, Hans Rothfels, Hans Herzfeld) ever wrote anything comparable to the great works of Pierre Renouvin, Bernadotte E. Schmitt, or Luigi Albertini. The defense of the German cause was mostly left either to foreigners, such as Barnes or Fay, or to amateurs such as Wegerer or Lutz.[5]

How effective the German innocence campaign had been became clear after the second world war. To the rest of the world this had only proved German responsibility for the first. Not so in Germany. After a few years of confusion and hesitation, which produced some criticism by Friedrich Meinecke, most German historians swung back to the old line. They contended that Germany (or rather Hitler) was responsible for the second but not for the first. There was no fresh research or re-interpretation of the causes of 1914. Although a few modifications were introduced by Gerhard Ritter,[6] Wegerer's authority was never questioned[7]; Albertini's massive work was almost completely ignored. The German public remained dependent on the meagre fare offered by professional historians in articles, textbooks, and short chapters or sub-chapters in a number of more general works.

It is only against this background that one can understand the terrific outburst of excitement over Fritz Fischer's book,[8] which quickly became known as the "Fischer controversy." For Fischer not only questioned the taboo built up over five decades by successive political regimes in Germany; he also broke the monopoly of knowledge held by conservative or mildly conservative-liberal historians, in a historical problem which may well rank as one of the most complicated and bewildering in modern history. He did it just by picking up Albertini and reading the documents published since 1919.

[4] I hope to be able to publish this *Gutachten* in the near future.

[5] Pierre Renouvin, *Les origines immédiates de la guerre* (Paris, 1925); Bernadotte E. Schmitt, *The Coming of the War.* 2 vols. (New York, London, 1930); Luigi Albertini, *Le origini della guerra del 1914.* 3 vols. (Milan, 1942), English ed. *The Origins of the War of 1914.* 3 vols. (London, New York, Toronto, 1952/57); Harry E. Barnes, *The Genesis of the World War* (New York, 1927); Sydney B. Fay, *The Origins of the World War.* 2 vols. (New York, 1928); Alfred v. Wegerer, *Der Ausbruch des Weltkrieges 1914.* 2 vols. (Hamburg, 1939); for Lutz, see footnote 2.

[6] Gerhard Ritter, *Staatskunst und Kriegshandwerk,* 3 vols. (Munich, 1954-64), vol. 2, pp. 282-343.

[7] *Ibid.*, p. 386, n. 9. Karl-Dietrich Erdmann, "Die Zeit der Weltkriege," in: *Handbuch der deutschen Geschichte,* ed. Bruno Gebhardt, 8th ed. vol. iv (Stuttgart, 1961), p. 18.

[8] Fritz Fischer, *Griff nach der Weltmacht. Die Kriegszielpolitik des kaiserlichen Deutschland 1914/1918* (Düsseldorf, 1961), 3rd edition, 1964.

The leading German historians rushed angrily into print to denounce Fischer and closed ranks against the heretic. Vis-à-vis Fischer they all seemed to have forgotten their former squabbles and political disagreements. Erwin Hölzle from the right joined forces with Golo Mann, Ludwig Dehio, and Hans Herzfeld of the "left,"[9] while Gerhard Ritter from his centre position turned out to be Fischer's most persistent critic.[10] Taking real or imaginary defects as an excuse for condemning the effort as such, many concentrated their attacks on the chapter on July 1914. In the very year when their attacks reached an emotional climax in the shrill polemics of Michael Freund[11] and Giselher Wirsing,[12] the discussion took a turn for the better. After the initial formation of a united front against Fischer, three major groups emerged. One, led by Hans Rothfels, stuck to their traditional guns and said there was nothing to revise. A second, headed by Gerhard Ritter and Michael Freund, though criticizing the older German literature on July 1914 as "too apologetic" (Ritter) or even denouncing the traditional line as the "Unschuldslüge" (Freund), still maintained most of their old arguments.

A third group, represented by Egmont Zechlin and Karl-Dietrich Erdmann, have at least in part abandoned the old positions, although very discreetly and without giving any credit to Fischer. They now admit that Germany in July 1914 deliberately risked war, even with Britain, but they hedge this vital admission with a number of "explanations" which only tend to obscure the central issue. Zechlin argues that Bethmann Hollweg, when taking the plunge in July 1914, only wanted a limited, "rational" war in eighteenth-century style, not a ferocious world war.[13] In two recent articles he has moved even closer to the position of those who criticize the traditional line, so that the differences between him and the Fischer group, on that point at least, have now been reduced to a few subtle shades of interpretation. On the other hand, these slight divergences give even less warrant for Zechlin's (and others') view that Fischer is all wrong, since Zechlin now maintains that Bethmann Hollweg consciously took the risk of British intervention.[14] Erdmann gives a psychological portrait of the Chancellor, based mainly on the diary of Kurt Riezler, Bethmann Hollweg's close adviser, and stresses the Chancellor's subjective honesty, his rejection of world domination for Germany (which, unfortunately, Erdmann confuses with the alleged rejection of achieving the status of a world power).[15] Both harp on the rediscovered story of the proposed Anglo-Russian naval

[9] Hölzle in *Das Historisch-Politische Buch*, March 1962; pp. 65-9; Golo Mann in *Neue Zürcher Zeitung*, 28 April 1962; Dehio in *Der Monat*, February 1962; Herzfeld in *Vierteljahrshefte für Zeitgeschichte*, July 1963, pp. 224-45.

[10] Gerhard Ritter, "Griff zur Weltmacht?" in *Lübecker Nachrichten*, 20 May 1962; "Eine neue Kriegsschuldthese?" in *Historische Zeitschrift (HZ)* June 1962, pp. 646-68; *Staatskunst und Kriegshandwerk*, vol. 3 (Munich, 1964); *Der Erste Weltkrieg; Studien zum deutschen Geschichtsbild*. Schriftenreihe der Bundeszentrale für politische Bildung, no. 64 (Bonn, 1964); "Zur Fischer-Kontroverse," in *HZ;* June 1967, pp. 783-7.

[11] "Bethmann Hallweg, der Hitler des Jahers 1914?" in *Frankfurter Allgemeine Zeitung*, 28/29 March 1964.

[12] "...auch am Ersten Weltkrieg schuld?" in *Christ und Welt*, 8 May 1964; "Der Bauchredner," ibid., 10 July 1964.

[13] Egmont Zechlin, "Deutschland zwischen Kabinettskrieg und Wirtschaftskrieg. Politik und Kriegführung in den ersten Monaten des Weltkriegs 1914," in *HZ*, 199/2, p. 361 ff.

[14] E. Zechlin, "Bethmann Hollweg, Kriegsrisiko und SPD 1914," in *Der Monat*, January 1966; "Motive und Taktik der Reichsleitung 1914. Ein Nachtrag," ibid. February 1966.

[15] "Zur Beurteilung Bethmann Hollwegs," in *Geschichte in Wissenschaft und Unterricht*, September 1964, pp. 525-40.

convention. Still, Zechlin and Erdmann have introduced new tones into the debate and have made rational discussion possible. They set the final seal on the demolition of the traditional taboo.

Another myth has also to go for good — the myth of *Einkreisung*.[16] There was no "encirclement" of Germany by enemies waiting to attack and crush her. The partition of Europe and the world into two power blocks, with the Triple Entente on the one hand, the Triple Alliance on the other, was largely a result of German policy, of the German desire to raise the Reich from the status of a continental power to that of a world power. The Triple Alliance itself came into being as a purely continental arrangement in the years 1879-82, in order to keep France isolated, and the Franco-Russian Alliance of 1894, the nucleus of the Triple Entente, was the French means of escaping that isolation. It was only after Germany started on her ambitious and ill-fated career of becoming a full-fledged world power in her own right that the world situation changed radically. Britain, challenged by Germany's naval programme more than by her territorial claims, notably in Africa, abandoned her "splendid isolation" and sought alliances, first with Japan in 1902, then with France in 1904, and finally, in 1907, with Russia. What was — and to a certain extent still is — denounced in Germany as *Einkreisung*, amounted to the containment of German ambitions which ran counter to the interests of all other imperialist powers.

The concept of encirclement, however, played an important part immediately before the outbreak of war in 1914. In Germany the idea had become widespread that the only choice for the Reich was between rising to a full-fledged world power and stagnation. The German *Weltanschauung* saw only the unending struggle of all against all; this social-Darwinist concept was not limited to the lunatic fringe, but influenced even the most liberal spokesman of the Wilhelmian establishment, Riezler, Bethmann Hollweg's young protégé.[17] For him all nations had the desire for permanent expansion with world domination as the supreme goal. Since he looked upon any containment of German aspirations as a hostile act, Riezler's ideas, translated into official policy, were bound to make war unavoidable. Even Bethmann Hollweg thought in 1911 that war was necessary for the German people.[18]

The final logical conclusion was the idea of preventive war against those enemies who tried to block Germany's further rise. The traditional school in Germany always indignantly denied the existence of the preventive war concept even among the Prussian General Staff.[19] The prevailing spirit of militarism and social-Darwinism in Wilhelmian Germany made it, however, more than plausible. A new source, the private papers of Jagow, provides the missing link between Germany's pre-war *Weltpolitik* and the outbreak of war. At the end of May or early in June 1914 Moltke, Chief of the General Staff, asked Jagow, the German Secretary of State for Foreign Affairs, to start a preventive war as soon as possible,

---

[16] The best and most detailed study exploding the myth is the undeservedly forgotten book by Hermann Kantorowicz, *Der Geist der englischen Politik und das Gespenst der Einkreisung Deutschlands* (Berlin, 1929), in particular the last chapter.

[17] See Kurt Riezler, *Die Erforderlichkeit des Unmöglichen* (Munich, 1912), chap. vi; J.J. Ruedorffer (Riezler), *Grundzüge der Weltpolitik in der Gegenwart* (Stuttgart, 1914).

[18] K. D. Erdmann, *Zur Beurteilung Bethmann Hollwegs*, p. 534.

[19] A. v. Wegerer, *Ausbruch*, I. p. 355. G. Ritter, *Staatskunst und Kriegshandwerk*, vol. 2, p. 147.

because militarily the situation for Germany was constantly deteriorating. Jagow refused, pointing to the improvement in the German economic situation. But after the war he admitted that he was never *a limine* against the idea of preventive war — after all, Bismarck's wars had been preventive wars, according to Jagow — and that Moltke's words inspired him with confidence in military success when the crisis did come in July 1914.[20] Another recent find tallies with Jagow's point of view. In February 1918 ex-Chancellor Bethmann Hollweg, questioned privately by the liberal politician Conrad Haussmann, said: "Yes, My God, in a certain sense it was a preventive war. But when war was hanging above us, when it had to come in two years even more dangerously and more inescapably, and when the generals said, now it is still possible without defeat, but not in two years time. Yes, the generals!"[21]

Against that background the events after Sarajevo are easy to understand, for Sarajevo turned out to be hardly more than the cue for the Reich to rush into action, although Austria had to deal the first blow against Serbia. The Austrians, however, were originally divided in their counsels. Only the Chief of the General Staff, Conrad von Hötzendorf, pressed for immediate war against Serbia, supported by high officials in the Foreign Ministry and by most of the German press in Austria. Foreign Minister Berchtold, the Austrian and the Hungarian Prime Ministers, Stürgkh and Tisza, hesitated and were for less radical measures. But even Conrad realized that he could not wage war against Serbia without first making sure that Germany would cover Austria's rear against Russia.[22] Thus the real decision lay with Germany.

After Sarajevo Germany could not at once make up her mind which course to follow. The Auswärtiges Amt clearly saw the danger involved in Russia's trying to protect Serbia if Austria made war, namely, that a world war might result. This is why the Auswärtiges Amt from the first counselled moderation both to Austria and to Serbia. The German General Staff, on the other hand, was ready to welcome Sarajevo as the golden opportunity for risking a preventive war. In this situation it was the Kaiser's word that proved decisive. Wilhelm II was incensed at the murder, perhaps most because it attacked his cherished monarchist principle. When he received the report of Tschirschky, the German ambassador to Vienna, of 30 June, telling of his moderating counsels to the Austrians, the Kaiser commented in his usual wild manner and provided the specious slogan "Now or never!" which turned out to be the guiding star of German diplomacy in the crisis of July 1914.

On 5 July, Count Hoyos came to Berlin, bringing with him two documents on Austrian policy towards the Balkans. The Austrian ambassador, Szogyeny, handed them to the Kaiser at a special audience at the Potsdam Palace, in which he apparently used fairly warlike language, although the documents of his own government spoke of war, if at all, only by implication. After initial hesitation, Wilhelm II promised German support to the Dual Monarchy, whatever Austria did.

[20] Nachlass Jagow, vol. viii; Politische Aufsätze. Politisches Archiv des Auswärtiges Amts, Bonn. The relevant document has meanwhile been published by E. Zechlin in *Der Monat*, February 1966.

[21] Wolfgang Steglich, *Die Friedenspolitik der Mittelmächte*, vol. I (Wiesbaden, 1964), p. 418, n. 3.

[22] To save space, references to well-known documents have been omitted. All the relevant material mentioned can be found, arranged in chronological order, in my *Fulikrise und Kriegsausbruch 1914. Eine Dokumentensammlung* (2 vols. Hannover, 1963/64), and in a condensed pocket-book version. *Fuli 1914. Die eüropaische Krise und der Ausbruch des Ersten Weltkriegs* (Munich, 1965).

His promise soon came to be called the German *carte blanche* to Austria. But the Kaiser was not satisfied with giving his ally a free hand against Serbia. He urged Vienna, which apparently had not made up its mind, to make war on Serbia, and that as soon as possible. Bethmann Hollweg and the Emperor's other civilian and military advisers duly endorsed these imperial decisions.

When Bethmann returned to Hohenfinow, he told Riezler what had happened at Potsdam. From what Riezler recorded in his by now famous diary, it appears that the Chancellor was not only fully aware of the possible consequences when taking his "leap into the dark" — war with Britain, i.e. world war — but that already at that stage his first objective seems to have been war with Russia and France; a diplomatic victory — France dropping Russia, Russia dropping Serbia — would have been accepted only as a second best.[23]

Impressed by the German stand, Berchtold swung round in favour of Conrad's line. His colleagues in the Cabinet followed suit, last of all Tisza, and so did Emperor Francis Joseph. Preparations were made in Vienna and Berlin for the *coup* against Serbia: it was decided to confront Serbia with an ultimatum which would be designed to be unacceptable as soon as the French president Poincaré and his prime minister Viviani had finished their state visit to Russia. That was to be on 23 July.

Meanwhile, the Austrian and German governments did everything to create a peaceful impression. The two emperors enjoyed their usual summer holidays, as did the leading generals of the Central Powers. But they returned to their respective capitals before or just after the ultimatum was handed over at Belgrade. Austria kept the German government informed of her intentions through the normal diplomatic channels, while the German government pressed Austria to start the action against Serbia as soon as possible. Privately the Germans aired serious misgivings at the lack of energy Austria displayed, and the Auswärtiges Amt suspected her of being unhappy about Germany's urgency. These suspicions were not unfounded: the Austrians had waited to make a decision until the German declaration of 5 July, but even then they moved slowly. According to Austrian plans, mobilization would begin after the rupture of diplomatic relations with Serbia, but it was originally intended to delay the actual declaration of war and the opening of hostilities until mobilization was completed, i.e., until approximately 12 August. The Wilhelmstrasse, however, deemed such delay absolutely intolerable. It was quick to see that the powers might intervene diplomatically during the interval to save Serbia from humiliation. As the German government was bent on preventing any mediation, it spurred Vienna on, as soon as it learned of the Austrian time-table, to declare war on Serbia immediately after the rupture with Belgrade and to open hostilities at once. On 25 July, Jagow told Szogyeny that the German government

...takes it for granted that upon eventual negative reply from Serbia, our declaration of war will follow immediately, joined to military operations. Any delay in beginning warlike preparations is regarded here as a great danger in respect of intervention of other powers. We are urgently advised to go ahead at once and confront the world with a *fait accompli*.

On the other hand, Jagow justified his refusal to pass on British proposals of mediation to Vienna by the alleged fear that Vienna might react by rushing things

---

[23] K. D. Erdmann, *Zur Beurteilung*, p. 536.

and confronting the world with a *fait accompli.* Yet when Austria, giving way to German pressure, did declare war immediately, the German Secretary of State told the British Ambassador, Sir Edward Goschen, that now the very thing had happened he had always warned against: namely, Austria rushing things as an answer to proposals of mediation.

German pressure on Vienna to declare war on Serbia without delay had an immediate and telling effect: on 26 July, Berchtold, who had been wavering and who tended to be timid rather than aggressive, adopted the German idea, and in this he was vigorously supported by Tschirschky. Conrad, however, was far from happy. Although usually thought of as the most warlike on the side of the Central Powers,[24] he would have preferred to stick to the original time table, but he gave in, and the Austrian government decided on an early declaration of war. On 27 July the final decision was taken to declare war the following day.

Now the German government had accomplished one of its short-term aims: Austria had confronted the world with a *fait accompli* in the form of an early declaration of war against Serbia, which was bound to undermine all attempts at mediation between Austria and Serbia. The following day, 29 July, the Austrians rushed things even more, again following German advice, when they started the bombardment of Belgrade.[25] The immediate effect was catastrophic: the Russians took the bombardment of Belgrade as the beginning of military operations against Serbia, as it was meant to be. They had, on 28 July, already ordered partial mobilization against Austria in order to deter her from actual warfare against Serbia. Now the Russian generals, thinking war with Austria and Germany imminent, successfully pressed for immediate general mobilization, since Russian mobilization was known to be far slower than Austrian or German. The Tsar ordered a halt to general mobilization and a return to partial mobilization after the receipt of a telegram from Wilhelm II late in the evening of 29 July, but the next afternoon the generals and the foreign minister Sazonov renewed their pressure on him. Nicholas gave way and Russian general mobilization was ordered for a second time on 30 July, at 6 p.m.

The German government rushed things also in two more respects: on 27 July Jagow had assured Jules Cambon and Sir Horace Rumbold, the British chargé d'affaires in Berlin, that Germany would not mobilize so long as Russia mobilized only in the south, against Austria. Two days later, however, the Auswärtiges Amt received a lengthy memorandum from General Moltke, whose arguments boiled down to an insistence on German general mobilization. Again the Auswärtiges Amt followed the lead of the generals. After 30 July, Berlin demanded the cancellation of Russian mobilization not only against Germany, but also against Austria, and that demand was expressly included both in the German ultimatum to Russia on 31 July and in the declaration of war of 1 August. When the French ambassador reminded Jagow of his words only a few days earlier, Jagow apparently shrugged his shoulders and replied that the generals wanted to have it that way, and that his words had, after all, not been a binding statement.

---

[24] As shown recently in G. Ritter, *Staatskunst,* vol. 2, p. 282.

[25] The German government was informed of Austrian preparations to shell Belgrade through a report by the German military attaché at Vienna, Count Kageneck, of 18 July: *Politisches Archiv des Auswärtiges Amts, Der Weltkrieg* (vol. 2). Kageneck's report is one of the documents not included in the German documents; it was published for the first time in *Julikrise* (137).

The second point was at least as serious: while the Entente powers tried desperately to prevent a local war, in order to avert a continental and world war, by making a whole series of proposals of mediation,[26] the German government not only flatly rejected them or passed them on to Vienna without giving them support, but also stifled the only initiative from the German side which might have saved the general peace. This time, the initiative had come from the Kaiser. Wilhelm had returned from his sailing holiday in Norway after learning of the Austrian suspension of diplomatic relations with Serbia on 25 July. He arrived at Potsdam on the 27th. Early the following morning he read the Serbian answer to Austria's ultimatum. Like nearly everybody else in Europe outside Germany and Austria, the Kaiser was impressed by Serbia's answer, which had conceded practically everything except one point, and made only a few reservations. Suddenly all his warlike sentiments vanished and he minuted:

... a brilliant achievement in a time-limit of only 48 hours! It is more than one could have expected! A great moral success for Vienna; but with it all reason for war is gone and Giesl ought to have quietly stayed on in Belgrade! After that I should never have ordered mobilization.

He immediately ordered the Auswärtiges Amt to draft a note for Vienna, telling the Austrians that they should accept the Serbian answer. To satisfy the army, and at the same time as a guarantee for what the Serbians had conceded, the Kaiser suggested that Austria should content herself with occupying Belgrade only and negotiate with the Serbians about the remaining reservations.

Apparently the Auswärtiges Amt took fright at their sovereign's weakness. The moment that had come during both Moroccan crises threatened to come again: that the Kaiser would lose his nerve and beat the retreat. This time, however, Bethmann Hollweg and the Auswärtiges Amt did not listen to their sovereign as they had done on 5 July. The Chancellor despatched the instructions to Tschirschky on the evening of 28 July, i.e., after he had learned that Austria had declared war on Serbia. Furthermore, he distorted the Kaiser's argument by omitting the crucial sentence that war was now no longer necessary. The occupation of Belgrade was not meant to be, in Bethmann's words, a safeguard for the implementation of Serbian concessions, but a means to enforce Serbia's total acceptance of the Austrian ultimatum. Finally, the Chancellor added a comment which was sure to defeat any conciliatory effect of his démarche, if any chance of this had remained.[27]

In these circumstances, the démarche, when executed by Tschirschky, had no effect whatsoever, nor did a later British proposal along similar lines.

When developments had gone so far, Bethmann Hollweg undertook his most important move, the bid for British neutrality. On 29 July he had despatched the ultimatum to Belgium to the German minister in Brussels. The violation of Belgian neutrality made it vital for Germany that at least British acquiescence be secured. During the evening of 29 July, Bethmann, returning from talks with the Kaiser and his military advisers at Potsdam, summoned the British ambassador. The Chancellor asked for England's neutrality in return for the promise that Germany would not annex French or Belgian territory. The reaction of the Foreign Office was scathing, as is borne out by Crowe's comment.

---

[26] In particular the suggestion to extend the time limit for answering the ultimatum and the British proposal to hold a four-power conference in London.
[27] Albertini, op. cit., II, p. 456 ff.

A British answer to the German demand was no longer needed, for, just after Goschen left the Chancellor, a telegram from London arrived: Lichnowsky reported Grey's warning that Britain would not remain neutral if France were involved in a continental war. Now Grey − at last − had spoken in such a way that even the German Chancellor had to abandon his cherished hope of British neutrality, which would have meant certain victory for Germany in the imminent continental war. Bethmann Hollweg was dumbfounded, for he saw clearly the consequences of Grey's warning − a world war which Germany could hardly win. In his panic, he tried to salvage what seemed possible. He now pressed the Austrians in all sincerity to modify their stand, but did not go so far as to advise the Austrians to drop the whole idea of war against Serbia. He only pleaded with them to accept the British version of the "halt-in-Belgrade" proposal and to open conversations with the Russians. In such conversations the Austrians were to repeat their promise not to annex Serbian territory, a pledge which, as the Chancellor knew quite well, was regarded by Russia as insufficient. Bethmann made his proposals in the vague hope that by shifting the blame to Russia the British might stay out after all. At the same time he wanted to persuade the German public, especially the social-democrats, to follow his policy by demonstrating his peaceful intentions. The Chancellor did not want to put an end to the local war, which had just seen its second day; what he wanted was to improve Germany's position in a major conflict.

Bethmann Hollweg failed in his first objective; he succeeded in his second only too well. The social-democrats supported the German war effort, and the Russians are still blamed in Germany today for having started the war. For this same reason − to shift the blame to Russia − Bethmann also resisted the pressure of the General Staff who pleaded for immediate German mobilization. The Chancellor urged that Russia be allowed to mobilize first against Germany, since, as he put it, he could not pursue military and political actions at the same time. In other words, he could not simultaneously put the blame on Russia and order German mobilization before Russian general mobilization.

On 29 July, the German generals still appreciated Bethmann Hollweg's policy. But during the 30th they became impatient. In the evening, about two hours after Russian general mobilization had been definitely ordered, they told the Chancellor that he had to make up his mind about German mobilization immediately. The Chancellor won a delay until noon next day, but there was little doubt which way the decision was meant to go. Bethmann Hollweg agreed, in the hope that the Russians might order general mobilization beforehand. During the morning of 31 July the Germans waited for the news of Russian general mobilization as their cue to rush into military action themselves. Luckily enough for Bethmann Hollweg and generations of German historians, Sazonov lost his nerve and had, in fact, already ordered Russian general mobilization.

At 11 a.m. Bethmann, Moltke, and Falkenhayn met again, anxiously waiting for news from Russia with only one hour left before the deadline they had set themselves. At five minutes to twelve a telegram from Pourtalès, the German ambassador to St Petersburg, was handed to them. It confirmed the rumours that Russian general mobilization had been ordered. Now they could order German mobilization with what they thought a clear conscience. Immediately after the receipt of the telegram the state of threatening war, the phase of military operations which immediately preceded general mobilization, was declared in Germany. The same afternoon, two ultimata went off − one to Russia demanding that she stop all military preparations not only against Germany but also against Austria, the other to France, asking about the stand France would take in a war between Germany and Russia. At the same time the Auswärtiges Amt prepared the declarations of war on both countries. Thus war had become inevitable, even more so since German general mobilization, according to the famous Schlieffen plan, meant opening hostilities against neutral Belgium a few days after mobilization had actually started.

After noon on 31 July, therefore, the catastrophe could no longer be averted. On 1 August, Germany ordered general mobilization, at the same hour as France. In the evening of that day, Germany declared war on Russia. An hour before, a curious and revealing incident had occurred. A telegram from Lichnowsky arrived suggesting that Britain might remain neutral if Germany were not to attack France. The Kaiser and his military, naval, and political advisers were happy, since their tough line during the July crisis seemed to be paying off after all. Only Moltke demurred. He was shocked by the idea of having to change his plan, and even feared that Russia might drop out as well. Late in the evening another telegram from London arrived, making the true position clear.

The French answer was evasive in form but firm in content: France would not forsake her ally. At the same time, France tried desperately to secure British support. The Russians, the French, and Crowe in the Foreign Office, urged Grey to make Britain's stand quite clear, that she would not remain neutral in a continental war. Grey had warned Germany before, but his language had not been straightforward enough to destroy German illusions. When Grey made the British policy unmistakably clear, even to the German Chancellor, it was too late.

How much Germany up to the last hour still hoped for British neutrality can be seen by the invention of a whole series of alleged border incidents, some of which were so crudely presented that outside Germany nobody believed them. They were part of the German manoeuvre to put the blame this time on France and to impress Britain. The German invasion of Belgium, however, removed the last hesitations: Britain sent an ultimatum to Germany demanding the immediate withdrawal of German troops from Belgium. When Germany refused, Britain entered the war automatically after the time-limit of the ultimatum had expired, i.e., at 11 p.m. Greenwich time on 4 August.

In trying to assess the shares of responsibility for the war two basic distinctions have to be made: on the one hand between the three stages of war connected with its outbreak: local war (Austria v. Serbia), continental war (Austria and Germany v. Russia and France), and world war (Britain joining the continental war). On the other hand, one has to distinguish between the will to start any of those three stages of war and the fact of merely causing them.

Since the world war developed out of a local war, then of continental war, the major share for causing it lies with that power which willed the local and/or continental war. That power was clearly Germany. She did not will the world war, as is borne out by her hopes of keeping out Britain, but she did urge Austria to make war on Serbia. Even if Austria had started the local war completely on her own — which, of course, she had not — Germany's share would still be bigger than Austria's, since a German veto could have effectively prevented it. Germany, furthermore, was the only power which had no objection to the continental war. So long as Britain kept out, she was confident of winning a war against Russia and France. Germany did nothing to prevent continental war, even at the risk of a world war, a risk which her government had seen from the beginning.

Austria, of course, wanted the local war, after — with German prodding — she had made up her mind, but feared a continental war. In fact, she hoped that Germany, by supporting her diplomatically, might frighten Russia into inaction.

Russia, France, and Britain tried to avert continental war. Their main argument for mediation between Serbia and Austria was precisely that to prevent the local war would be the best means of averting continental war. On the other hand, they contributed to the outbreak, each in her own way: Russia by committing the technical blunder of providing the cue for German mobilization, instead of waiting until Germany had mobilized. The French attitude was almost entirely correct; her only fault was that she could not hold back her Russian ally from precipitate general mobilization. Britain might have made her stand clear beyond any doubt much earlier, since this might have been a way of restraining Germany, although it is doubtful whether this would have altered the course of events to any appreciable degree. The share of the Entente powers is much smaller than Germany's, for it consisted mainly in reacting — not always in the best manner! — to German action.

Looking back on the events from the mid-sixties, the outbreak of the first world war looks like the original example of faulty brinkmanship, of rapid escalation in a period of history when the mechanisms of alliances and mobilization schedules could still work unchecked by fear of the absolute weapon and the absolute destruction its use would bring in what would now be the third world war.

12 / The Treaty of Versailles: A Carthaginian Peace?

Whereas the revisionism outlined in Chapter 2 was directed at the Versailles Treaty's war-guilt clause, John Maynard Keynes's *The Economic Consequences of the Peace* (1919) condemned the peace settlement in general and its economic clauses in particular. According to Keynes, the Peace Conference at Paris was a "morass" where a "Carthaginian peace" prevailed over Wilson's idealistic Fourteen Points. The reparations that the treaty called for were beyond Germany's capacity to pay and insured a troubled economic, political, and social future for Europe.

Although his *General Theory* was yet to be written, John Maynard Keynes (later Baron Keynes of Tilton) was already an economist widely known in academic circles when the war broke out. Except for a brief period of public service in the India Office, he had been lecturer in economics at King's College, Cambridge, where he had assumed an important position as editor of *The Economic Journal* in 1913. In 1915 he was attached to the British Treasury. In 1918, he was chairman of the International Financial Delegates in armistice negotiations with Germany; in 1919, deputy for the chancellor of the exchequer on the Supreme Economic Council and official representative of the British Treasury at the Paris Peace Conference. He resigned from these last two posts on June 7, 1919 and, in a few months, wrote *The Economic Consequences of the Peace.*

The sincerity implicit in Keynes's resignation, the moral passion and brilliance with which he denounced the treaty, and the authority of his position as economist and representative at the Peace Conference gained the widest possible audience for his book. It was, of course, the subject of immediate controversy. Keynes's biting descriptions of the conference and its leaders angered some; others criticized the book's political chapters or else found it politically inopportune. But very few challenged Keynes's prophecies or conclusions about the economic aspects of the treaty, and as postwar developments seemed to confirm them, the earlier criticism was silenced.

R. F. Harrod, Keynes's biographer, has answered the often-made charge that *The Economic Consequences of the Peace* bolstered American isolationism. He replies that, in such a case, one would have "to specify precisely how but for the book, the situation would have developed differently."[1] The same answer could be made to the additional charge that the book encouraged Allied disunity and apathy in the enforcement of the Peace Treaty. But to the extent that writings influence public attitudes, it must be admitted that *The Economic Consequences of the Peace* played a most important part in shaping public opinion about the Versailles Treaty.[2]

At all events, it was not until 1946 and another world war that Keynes's book found a serious challenge in *The Carthaginian Peace or The Economic Consequences of Mr. Keynes,* by Étienne Mantoux. Mantoux's work had the advantage of historical perspective, but although his book contains moving passages, it is not polemical. It is a scholarly book which hits hard at Keynes's arguments. At the same time, as its author intended, there are no blows "aimed below the belt."

Étienne Mantoux, after graduating from the University of Paris and the *Ecóle des Sciences Politiques,* attended the London School of Economics in 1935-36, where he attracted the attention and friendship of such figures as Harold Laski and Friedrich Hayek. *The Carthaginian Peace* was written in English on a Rockefeller fellowship at the Institute for Advanced Study in Princeton. On its completion early in 1943, the young author joined the Free French Forces in England. In the last weeks of the war Étienne Mantoux died in action in Germany. A brilliant career was thus ended prematurely.

The first selection below, from *The Economic Consequences of the Peace,* gives the essential points of Keynes's position. Although Mantoux's *Carthaginian Peace* attempts a point by point rebuttal of Keynes, our second selection from it concentrates on the reparations question which is at the core of the argument and forms an important chapter in the economic history of Germany between World Wars I and II.

THE CASE AGAINST THE VERSAILLES TREATY

John Maynard Keynes

In those parts of the Treaty with which I am here concerned, the lead was taken by the French, in the sense that it was generally they who made in the first instance the most definite and the most extreme proposals. This was partly a matter of tactics. When the final result is expected to be a compromise, it is often prudent to start from an extreme position; and the French anticipated at the outset—like most other persons—a double process of compromise first of all to suit the ideas of their allies and associates, and secondly in the course of the Peace Conference proper with the Germans themselves. These tactics were justified by the event. Clemenceau gained a reputation for moderation with his colleagues in Council

---

[1] R. F. Harrod, *The Life of John Maynard Keynes* (London; Macmillan & Co., Ltd., 1951), p. 282. It was the actual "course of events culminating in the fiasco of the Ruhr invasion that swayed America . . . The book did little more than give pleasure to them (the Americans) by confirming their worst suspicions."

[2] "By 1924 the book had been translated into eleven languages and its various editions had run into some 140,000 copies . . . . It had been read, in the opinion of Sir William Beveridge, 'by—at a moderate computation—half a million people who never read an economic work before and probably will not read one again.' " Étienne Mantoux, *The Carthaginian Peace* (London: Oxford University Press, 1946), p. 6.

by sometimes throwing over with an air of intellectual impartiality the more extreme proposals of his ministers; and much went through where the American and British critics were naturally a little ignorant of the true point at issue, or where too persistent criticism by France's allies put them in a position which they felt as invidious, of always appearing to take the enemy's part and to argue his case. Where, therefore, British and American interests were not seriously involved their criticism grew slack, and some provisions were thus passed which the French themselves did not take very seriously, and for which the eleventh-hour decision to allow no discussion with the Germans removed the opportunity of remedy.

But, apart from tactics, the French had a policy. Although Clemenceau might curtly abandon the claims of a Klotz or a Loucheur, or close his eyes with an air of fatigue when French interests were no longer involved in the discussion, he knew which points were vital, and these he abated little. In so far as the main economic lines of the Treaty represent an intellectual idea, it is the idea of France and of Clemenceau.

* * *

He felt about France what Pericles felt of Athens—unique value in her, nothing else mattering; but his theory of politics was Bismarck's. He had one illusion—France; and one disillusion—mankind, including Frenchmen, and his colleagues not least. His principles for the peace can be expressed simply. In the first place, he was a foremost believer in the view of German psychology that the German understands and can understand nothing but intimidation, that he is without generosity or remorse in negotiation, that there is no advantage he will not take of you, and no extent to which he will not demean himself for profit, that he is without honor, pride, or mercy. Therefore you must never negotiate with a German or conciliate him; you must dictate to him. On no other terms will he respect you, or will you prevent him from cheating you. But it is doubtful how far he thought these characteristics peculiar to Germany, or whether his candid view of some other nations was fundamentally different. His philosophy had, therefore, no place for "sentimentality" in international relations. Nations are real things. of whom you love one and feel for the rest indifference—or hatred. The glory of the nation you love is a desirable end—but generally to be obtained at your neighbor's expense. The politics of power are inevitable, and there is nothing very new to learn about this war or the end it was fought for; England had destroyed, as in each preceding century, a trade rival; a mighty chapter had been closed in the secular struggle between the glories of Germany and of France. Prudence required some measure of lip service to the "ideals" of foolish Americans and hypocritical Englishmen; but it would be stupid to believe that there is much room in the world, as it really is, for such affairs as the League of Nations or any sense in the principle of self-determination except as an ingenious formula for rearranging the balance of power in one's own interests.

* * *

According to this vision of the future, European history is to be a perpetual prizefight, of which France has won this round but of which this round is certainly not the last. From the belief that essentially the old order does not change, being based on human nature which is always the same, and from a consequent skepticism of all that class of doctrine which the League of Nations stands for, the policy of France and of Clemenceau followed logically. For a Peace of magnanimity or of fair and equal treatment, based on such "ideology" as the Fourteen Points of the President [Wilson], could only have the effect of shortening the interval of Germany's recovery and hastening the day when she will once again hurl at France her greater numbers and her superior resources and technical skill. Hence the necessity of "guarantees"; and each guarantee that was taken, by increasing irritation and thus the probability of a subsequent *Revanche* by Germany, made necessary yet further provisions to crush. Thus as soon as this view of the world is adopted and the other discarded, a demand for a Carthaginian Peace is inevitable, to the full extent of the momentary power to impose it. For Clemenceau made no pretense of considering himself bound by the Fourteen Points and left chiefly to others such concoctions as were necessary from time to time to save the scruples or the face of the President.

* * *

Two rival schemes for the future polity of the world took the field,—the Fourteen Points of the President, and the Carthaginian Peace of M. Clemenceau. Yet only one of these was entitled to take the field; for the enemy had not surrendered unconditionally, but on agreed terms as to the general character of the Peace.

This aspect of what happened cannot, unfortunately, be passed over with a word, for in the minds of many Englishmen at least it has been a subject of very great misapprehension. Many persons believe that the Armistice Terms constituted the first Contract concluded between the Allied and Associated Powers and the German Government, and that we entered the Conference with our hands free, except so far as these Armistice Terms might bind us. This was not the case. To make the position plain, it is necessary briefly to review the history of the negotiations which began with the German Note of October 5, 1918, and concluded with President Wilson's Note of November 5, 1918.

On October 5, 1918, the German Government addressed a brief Note to the President accepting the Fourteen Points and asking for Peace negotiations. The President's reply of October 8 asked if he was to understand definitely that the German Government accepted "the terms laid down" in the Fourteen Points and in subsequent Addresses and "that its object in entering into discussion would be only to agree upon the practical details of their application." He added that the evacuation of invaded territory must be a prior condition of an Armistice. On October 12 the German Government returned an unconditional affirmative to these questions;—"its object in entering into discussions would be only to agree upon practical details of the application of these terms." On October 14, having received this affirmative answer, the President made a further communication to make clear the points: (1) that the details of the Armistice would have to be left to the military advisers of the United States and the Allies, and must provide absolutely against the possibility of Germany's resuming hostilities; (2) that submarine warfare must cease if these conversations were to continue; and (3) that he required further guarantees of the representative character of the Government with which he was dealing. On October 20 Germany accepted points (1) and (2), and pointed out, as regards (3), that she now had a Constitution and a Government dependent for its authority on the Reichstag. On October 23 the President announced that, "having received the solemn and explicit assurance of the German Government that it unreservedly accepts the terms of peace laid down in his Address to the Congress of the United States on January 8, 1918 (the Fourteen Points), and the principles of settlement enunciated in his subsequent Addresses, particularly the Address of September 27,[1] and that it is ready to discuss the details of their application," he has communicated the above correspondence to the Governments of the Allied Powers "with the suggestion that, if these Governments are disposed to effect peace upon the terms and principles indicated," they will ask their military advisers to draw up Armistice Terms of such a character as to "ensure to the Associated Governments the unrestricted power to safeguard and enforce the details of the peace to which the German Government has agreed." At the end of this Note the President hinted more openly than in that of October 14 at the abdication of the Kaiser. This completes the preliminary negotiations to which the President alone was a party, acting without the Governments of the Allied Powers.

On November 5, 1918, the President transmitted to Germany the reply he had received from the Governments associated with him, and added that Marshal Foch had been authorized to communicate the terms of an armistice to properly accredited representatives. In this reply the Allied Governments, "subject to the qualifications which follow, declare their willingness to make peace with the Government of Germany on the terms of peace laid down in the President's Address to Congress of January 8, 1918, and the principles of settlement enunciated in his subsequent Addresses." The qualifications in question were two in number. The first related to the Freedom of the Seas, as to which they "reserved to themselves complete freedom." The second related to Reparation and ran as follows:—"Further, in the conditions of peace laid down in his Address to Congress on the 8th January, 1918, the President declared that invaded territories must be restored as well as evacuated and made free. The Allied Governments feel that no doubt ought to be allowed to exist as to what this provision implies. By it they understand that compensation will be made by Germany for all damage done to the civilian population of the Allies and to their property by the aggression of Germany by land, by sea, and from the air."

The nature of the Contract between Germany and the Allies resulting from this exchange of documents is plain and unequivocal. The terms of the peace are to be in accordance with the Addresses of the President, and the purpose of the Peace Conference is "to discuss the details of their application." The circumstances of the Contract were of an unusually solemn and binding character; for one of the conditions of it was that Germany should agree to Armistice Terms which were to be such as would leave her helpless. Germany having rendered herself helpless in reliance on the Contract, the honor of the Allies was peculiarly involved in fulfilling their part and, if there were ambiguities, in not using their position to take advantage of them.

* * *

[1] Perhaps the most important points made in these Addresses which serve Keynes's argument and which the quotes along with others are: February 11, 1918 before Congress, "There shall be no annexations, no contributions, no punitive damages"; September 27, 1918 in New York City, "The impartial justice meted out must involve no discrimination between those to whom we wish to be just and those to whom we do not wish to be just. . . . No special or separate interest of any single nation or group of nations can be made the basis of any part of the settlement which is not consistent with the common interest of all." [EDITORS' NOTE.]

This wise and magnanimous program for the world had passed on November 5, 1918, beyond the region of idealism and aspiration, and had become part of a solemn contract to which all the Great Powers of the world had put their signature. But it was lost, nevertheless, in the morass of Paris;—the spirit of it altogether, the letter in parts ignored and in other parts distorted.

* * *

The categories of damage in respect of which the Allies were entitled to ask for Reparation are governed by the relevant passages in President Wilson's Fourteen Points of January 8, 1918, as modified by the Allied Governments in their qualifying Note, the text of which the President formally communicated to the German Government as the basis of peace on November 5, 1918. These passages have been quoted in full at the beginning of Chapter IV. That is to say, "compensation will be made by Germany for all damage done to the civilian population of the Allies and to their property by the aggression of Germany by land, by sea, and from the air." The limiting quality of this sentence is reinforced by the passage in the President's speech before Congress on February 11, 1918 (the terms of this speech being an express part of the contract with the enemy), that there shall be "no contributions" and "no punitive damages."

It has sometimes been argued that the preamble to paragraph 19[2] of the Armistice Terms, to the effect "that any future claims and demands of the Allies and the United States of America remain unaffected," wiped out all precedent conditions, and left the Allies free to make whatever demands they chose. But it is not possible to maintain that this casual protective phrase, to which no one at the time attached any particular importance, did away with all the formal communications which passed between the President and the German Government as to the basis of the Terms of Peace during the days preceding the Armistice, abolished the Fourteen Points, and converted the German acceptance of the Armistice Terms into unconditional surrender, so far as it affects the Financial Clauses. It is merely the usual phrase of the draftsman, who, about to rehearse a list of certain claims, wishes to guard himself from the implication that such list is exhaustive. In any case, this contention is disposed of by the Allied reply to the German observations on the first draft of the Treaty, where it is admitted that the terms of the Reparation Chapter must be governed by the President's Note of November 5.

Assuming then that the terms of this Note are binding, we are left to elucidate the precise force of the phrase—"all damage done to the civilian population of the Allies and to their property by the aggression of Germany by land, by sea, and from the air." Few sentences in history have given so much work to the sophists and the lawyers, as we shall see in the next section of this chapter, as this

---

[2] "With reservation that any future claims and demands of the Allies and the United States of America remain unaffected, the following financial conditions are required: Reparation for damage done. Whilst Armistice lasts, no public securities shall be removed by the enemy which can serve as a pledge to the Allies for recovery or reparation of war losses. Immediate restitution of cash deposit in National Bank of Belgium, and, in general, immediate return of all documents, of specie, stock, shares, paper money, together with plant for issue thereof, touching public or private interests in invaded countries. Restitution of Russian and Roumanian gold yielded to Germany or taken by that Power. This gold to be delivered in trust to the Allies until signature of peace."

apparently simple and unambiguous statement. Some have not scrupled to argue that it covers the entire cost of the war; for, they point out, the entire cost of the war has to be met by taxation, and such taxation is "damaging to the civilian population." They admit that the phrase is cumbrous, and that it would have been simpler to have said "all loss and expenditure of whatever description"; and they allow that the apparent emphasis on damage to the persons and property of *civilians* is unfortunate; but errors of draftsmanship should not, in their opinion, shut off the Allies from the rights inherent in victors.

But there are not only the limitations of the phrase in its natural meaning and the emphasis on civilian damages as distinct from military expenditure generally; it must also be remembered that the context of the term is in elucidation of the meaning of the term "restoration" in the President's Fourteen Points. The Fourteen Points provide for damage in invaded territory—Belgium, France, Roumania, Serbia, and Montenegro (Italy being unaccountably omitted)—but they do not cover losses at sea by submarine, bombardments from the sea (as at Scarborough), or damage done by air raids. It was to repair these omissions, which involved losses to the life and property of civilians not really distinguishable in kind from those effected in occupied territory, that the Supreme Council of the Allies in Paris proposed to President Wilson their qualifications. At that time—the last days of October, 1918—I do not believe that any responsible statesman had in mind the exaction from Germany of an indemnity for the general costs of the war. They sought only to make it clear (a point of considerable importance to Great Britain) that reparation for damage done to non-combatants and their property was not limited to invaded territory (as it would have been by the Fourteen Points unqualified), but applied equally to *all* such damage, whether "by land, by sea, or from the air." It was only at a later stage that a general popular demand for an indemnity, covering the full costs of the war, made it politically desirable to practice dishonesty and to try to discover in the written word what was not there.

What damages, then, can be claimed from the enemy on a strict interpretation of our engagements?

* * *

We are finally left with the following—

Belgium	$ 2,500,000,000[3]
France	4,000,000,000
Great Britain	2,850,000,000
Other Allies	1,250,000,000
Total	$10,600,000,000

I need not impress on the reader that there is much guesswork in the above, and the figure for France in particular is likely to be criticized. But I feel some

---

[3] Assuming that in her case $1,250,000,000 are included for the general expenses of the war defrayed out of loans made to Belgium by her allies.

confidence that the *general magnitude,* as distinct from the precise figures, is not hopelessly erroneous; and this may be expressed by the statement that a claim against Germany, based on the interpretation of the pre-Armistice engagements of the Allied Powers which is adopted above, would assuredly be found to exceed $8,000,000,000 and to fall short of $15,000,000,000.

This is the amount of the claim which we were entitled to present to the enemy. For reasons which will appear more fully later on, I believe that it would have been a wise and just act to have asked the German Government at the Peace Negotiations to agree to a sum of $10,000,000,000 in final settlement, without further examination of particulars. This would have provided an immediate and certain solution, and would have required from Germany a sum, which, if she were granted certain indulgences, it might not have proved entirely impossible for her to pay. This sum should have been divided up amongst the Allies themselves on a basis of need and general equity.

But the question was not settled on its merits.

* * *

I cannot here describe the endless controversy and intrigue between the Allies themselves, which at last after some months culminated in the presentation to Germany of the Reparation Chapter in its final form. There can have been few negotiations in history so contorted, so miserable, so utterly unsatisfactory to all parties. I doubt if any one who took much part in that debate can look back on it without shame. I must be content with an analysis of the elements of the final compromise which is known to all the world.

The main point to be settled was, of course, that of the items for which Germany could fairly be asked to make payment. Mr. Lloyd George's election pledge to the effect that the Allies were *entitled* to demand from Germany the entire costs of the war was from the outset clearly untenable; or rather, to put it more impartially, it was clear that to persuade the President of the conformity of this demand with our pre-Armistice engagements was beyond the powers of the most plausible. The actual compromise finally reached is to be read as follows in the paragraphs of the Treaty as it has been published to the world.

Article 231 reads: "The Allied and Associated Governments affirm and Germany accepts the responsibility of Germany and her allies for causing all the loss and damage to which the Allied and Associated Governments and their nationals have been subjected as a consequence of the war imposed upon them by the aggression of Germany and her allies." This is a well and carefully drafted Article; for the President could read it as statement of admission on Germany's part of *moral* responsibility for bringing about the war, while the Prime Minister could explain it as an admission of *financial* liability for the general costs of the war. Article 232 continues: "The Allied and Associated Governments recognize that the resources of Germany are not adequate, after taking into account permanent diminutions of such resources which will result from other provisions of the present Treaty, to make complete reparation for all such loss and damage." The President could comfort himself that this was no more than a statement of undoubted fact, and that to recognize that Germany *cannot* pay a certain claim does not imply that she is *liable* to pay the claim; but the Prime Minister could point out that in the context it emphasizes to the reader the assumption of Germany's theoretic liability asserted in the preceding Article. Article 232 proceeds: "The Allied and Associated Governments, however, require, and Germany undertakes, that *she will make compensation for all damage done to the civilian population of the Allied and Associated Powers and to their property* during the period of the belligerency of each as an Allied or Associated Power against Germany *by such aggression by land, by sea, and from the air,* and in general all damage as defined in Annex I. hereto."[4] The words italicized being practically a quotation from the pre-Armistice conditions, satisfied the scruples of the President, while the addition of the words "and in general all damage as defined in Annex I. hereto" gave the Prime Minister a chance in Annex I.

So far, however, all this is only a matter of words, of virtuosity in draftsmanship, which does no one any harm, and which probably seemed much more important at the time than it ever will again between now and Judgment Day. For substance we must turn to Annex I.

A great part of Annex I. is in strict conformity with the pre-Armistice conditions, or, at any rate, does not strain them beyond what is fairly arguable. Paragraph 1 claims damage done for injury to the persons of civilians, or, in the case of death, to their dependents, as a direct consequence of acts of war; Paragraph 2, for acts of cruelty, violence or maltreatment on the part of the enemy towards civilian victims; Paragraph 3, for enemy acts injurious to health or capacity to work or to honor towards civilians in occupied or invaded territory; Paragraph 8, for forced labor exacted by the enemy from civilians; Paragraph 9, for damage done to property "with the exception of naval and military works or materials" as a direct consequence of hostilities; and Paragraph 10, for fines and levies imposed by the enemy upon the civilian population. All these demands are just and in conformity with the Allies' rights.

Paragraph 4, which claims for "damage caused by any kind of maltreatment of prisoners of war," is more doubtful on the strict letter, but may be justifiable under the Hague Convention and involves a very small sum.

In Paragraphs 5, 6, and 7, however, an issue of immensely greater significance is involved. These paragraphs assert a claim for the amount of the Separation and similar Allowances granted during the war by the Allied Governments to the families of mobilized persons, and for the amount of the pensions and compensations in respect of the injury or death of combatants payable by these Governments now and hereafter. Financially this adds to the Bill, as we shall see below, a very large amount, indeed about twice as much again as all the other claims added together.

The reader will readily apprehend what a plausible case can be made out for the inclusion of these items of damage, if only on sentimental grounds. It can be pointed out, first of all, that from the point of view of general fairness it is monstrous that a woman whose house is destroyed should be entitled to claim from the enemy whilst a woman whose husband is killed on the field of battle should not be so entitled; or that a farmer deprived of his farm should claim but that a woman deprived of the earning power of her husband should not claim. In fact the case for including Pensions and Separation Allowances largely depends on exploiting the rather *arbitrary* character of the criterion laid down in the pre-Armistice conditions.

---

[4] A further paragraph claims the war costs of Belgium "in accordance with Germany's pledges, already given, as to complete restoration for Belgium."

Of all the losses caused by war some bear more heavily on individuals and some are more evenly distributed over the community as a whole; but by means of compensations granted by the Government many of the former are in fact converted into the latter. The most logical criterion for a limited claim, falling short of the entire costs of the war, would have been in respect of enemy acts contrary to International engagements or the recognized practices of warfare. But this also would have been very difficult to apply and unduly unfavorable to French interests as compared with Belgium (whose neutrality Germany had guaranteed) and Great Britain (the chief sufferer from illicit acts of submarines).

In any case the appeals to sentiment and fairness outlined above are hollow; for it makes no difference to the recipient of a separation allowance or a pension whether the State which pays them receives compensation on this or on another head, and a recovery by the State out of indemnity receipts is just as much in relief of the general taxpayer as a contribution towards the general costs of the war would have been. But the main consideration is that it was too late to consider whether the pre-Armistice conditions were prefectly judicious and logical or to amend them; the only question at issue was whether these conditions were not in fact limited to such classes of direct damage to civilians and their property as are set forth in Paragraphs 1, 2, 3, 8, 9, and 10 of Annex I. If words have any meaning, or engagements any force, we had no more right to claim for those war expenses of the State, which arose out of Pensions and Separation Allowances, than for any other of the general costs of the war. And who is prepared to argue in detail that we were entitled to demand the latter?

What had really happened was a compromise between the Prime Minister's pledge to the British electorate to claim the entire costs of the war and the pledge to the contrary which the Allies had given to Germany at the Armistice. The Prime Minister could claim that although he had not secured the entire costs of the war, he had nevertheless secured an important contribution towards them, that he had always qualified his promises by the limited condition of Germany's capacity to pay, and that the bill as now presented more than exhausted this capacity as estimated by the more sober authorities. The President, on the other hand, had secured a formula, which was not too obvious a breach of faith, and had avoided a quarrel with his Associates on an issue where the appeals to sentiment and passion would all have been against him, in the event of its being made a matter of open popular controversy. In view of the Prime Minister's election pledges, the President could hardly hope to get him to abandon them in their entirety without a struggle in public; and the cry of pensions would have had an overwhelming popular appeal in all countries. Once more the Prime Minister had shown himself a political tactician of a high order.

A further point of great difficulty may be readily perceived between the lines of the Treaty. It fixes no definite sum as representing Germany's liability. This feature has been the subject of very general criticism,—that it is equally inconvenient to Germany and to the Allies themselves that she should not know what she has to pay or they what they are to receive. The method, apparently contemplated by the Treaty, of arriving at the final result over a period of many months by an addition of hundreds of thousands of individual claims for damage to land, farm buildings, and chickens, is evidently impracticable; and the reasonable course would have been for both parties to compound for a round sum without examination of details. If this round sum had been named in the Treaty, the settlement would have been placed on a more business-like basis.

But this was impossible for two reasons. Two different kinds of false statements had been widely promulgated, one as to Germany's capacity to pay, the other as to the amount of the Allies' just claims in respect of the devastated areas. The fixing of either of these figures presented a dilemma. A figure for Germany's prospective capacity to pay, not too much in excess of the estimates of most candid and well-informed authorities, would have fallen hopelessly far short of popular expectations both in England and in France. On the other hand, a definitive figure for damage done which would not disastrously disappoint the expectations which had been raised in France and Belgium might have been incapable of substantiation under challenge,[5] and open to damaging criticism on the part of the Germans, who were believed to have been prudent enough to accumulate considerable evidence as to the extent of their own misdoings.

By far the safest course for the politicians was, therefore, to mention no figure at all; and from this necessity a great deal of the complication of the Reparation Chapter essentially springs.

The reader may be interested, however, to have my estimate of the claim which can in fact be substantiated under Annex I. of the Reparation Chapter. In the first section of this chapter I have already guessed the claims other than those for Pensions and Separation Allowances at $15,000,000,000 (to take the extreme upper limit of my estimate). The claim for Pensions and Separation Allowances under Annex I. is not to be based on the *actual* cost of these compensations to the Governments concerned, but is to be a computed figure calculated on the basis of the scales in force in France at the date of the Treaty's coming into operation. This method avoids the invidious course of valuing an American or a British life at a higher figure than a French or an Italian. The French rate for Pensions and Allowances is at an intermediate rate, not so high as the American or British, but above the Italian, the Belgian, or the Serbian. The only data required for the calculation are the actual French rates and the numbers of men mobilized and of the casualties in each class of the various Allied Armies. None of these figures are available in detail, but enough is known of the general level of allowances, of the numbers involved, and of the casualties suffered to allow of an estimate which may not be *very wide* of the mark. My guess as to the amount to be added in respect of Pensions and Allowances is as follows:

British Empire	$ 7,000,000,000[6]
France	12,000,000,000[6]
Italy	2,500,000,000
Others (including United States)	3,500,000,000
Total	$25,000,000,000

[5] The challenge of the other Allies, as well as of the enemy, had to be met; for in view of the limited resources of the latter, the other Allies had perhaps a greater interest than the enemy in seeing that no one of their number established an excessive claim.

[6] M. Klotz has estimated the French claims on this head at $15,000,000,000 (75 milliard francs, made up of 13 milliard for allowances, 60 for pensions, and 2 for widows). If this figure is correct, the others should probably be scaled up also.

I feel much more confidence in the approximate accuracy of the total figure[7] than in its division between the different claimants. The reader will observe that in any case the addition of Pensions and Allowances enormously increases the aggregate claim, raising it indeed by nearly double. Adding this figure to the estimate under other heads, we have a total claim against Germany of $40,000,000,000.[8] I believe that this figure is fully high enough, and that the actual result may fall somewhat short of it.[9]

* * *

On the 13th May, 1919, Count Brockdorff-Rantzau addressed to the Peace Conference of the Allied and Associated Powers the Report of the German Economic Commission charged with the study of the effect of the conditions of Peace on the situation of the German population. "In the course of the last two generations," they reported, "Germany has become transformed from an agricultural State to an industrial State. So long as she was an agricultural State, Germany could feed forty million inhabitants. As an industrial State she could insure the means of subsistence for a population of sixty-seven millions; and in 1913 the importation of foodstuffs amounted, in round figures, to twelve million tons. Before the war a total of fifteen million persons in Germany provided for their existence by foreign trade, navigation, and the use, directly or indirectly, of foreign raw material." After rehearsing the main relevant provisions of the Peace Treaty the report continues: "After this diminution of her products, after the economic depression resulting from the loss of her colonies, her merchant fleet and her foreign investments, Germany will not be in a position to import from abroad an adequate quantity of raw material. An enormous part of German industry will, therefore, be condemned inevitably to destruction. The need of importing foodstuffs will increase considerably at the same time that the possibility of satisfying this demand is as greatly diminished. In a very short time, therefore, Germany will not be in a position to give bread and work to her numerous millions of inhabitants, who are prevented from earning their livelihood by navigation and trade. These persons should emigrate, but this is a material impossibility, all the more because many countries and the most important ones will oppose any German immigration. To put the Peace conditions into execution would logically involve, therefore, the loss of several millions of persons in Germany. This catastrophe would not be long in coming about, seeing that the health of the population has been broken down during the War by the Blockade, and during the Armistice by the aggravation of the Blockade of famine. No help, however great, or over however long a period it were

---

[7] That is to say, I claim for the aggregate figure an accuracy within 25 per cent.

[8] In his speech of September 5, 1919, addressed to the French Chamber, M. Klotz estimated the total Allied claims against Germany under the Treaty at $75,000,000,000, which would accumulate at interest until 1921, and be paid off thereafter by 34 annual instalments of about $5,000,000,000 each, of which France would receive about $2,750,000,000 annually. "The general effect of the statement (that France would receive from Germany this annual payment) proved," it is reported, "appreciably encouraging to the country as a whole, and was immediately reflected in the improved tone of the Bourse and throughout the business world in France." So long as such statements can be accepted in Paris without protest, there can be no financial or economic future for France, and a catastrophe of disillusion is not far distant.

[9] As a matter of subjective judgment, I estimate for this figure an accuracy of 10 per cent in deficiency and 20 per cent in excess, i.e. that the result will lie between $32,000,000,000 and $44,000,000,000.

continued, could prevent these deaths *en masse*." "We do not know, and indeed we doubt," the report concludes, "whether the Delegates of the Allied and Associated Powers realize the inevitable consequences which will take place if Germany, an industrial State, very thickly populated, closely bound up with the economic system of the world, and under the necessity of importing enormous quantities of raw material and foodstuffs, suddenly finds herself pushed back to the phase of her development, which corresponds to her economic condition and the numbers of her population as they were half a century ago. Those who sign this Treaty will sign the death sentence of many millions of German men, women and children."

I know of no adequate answer to these words. The indictment is at least as true of the Austrian, as of the German, settlement. This is the fundamental problem in front of us, before which questions of territorial adjustment and the balance of European power are insignificant. Some of the catastrophes of past history, which have thrown back human progress for centuries, have been due to the reactions following on the sudden termination, whether in the course of nature or by the act of man, of temporarily favorable conditions which have permitted the growth of population beyond what could be provided for when the favorable conditions were at an end.

* * *

In proposing a modification of the Reparation terms, I have considered them so far only in relation to Germany. But fairness requires that so great a reduction in the amount should be accompanied by a readjustment of its apportionment between the Allies themselves. The professions which our statesmen made on every platform during the war, as well as other considerations, surely require that the areas damaged by the enemy's invasion should receive a priority of compensation. While this was one of the ultimate objects for which we said we were fighting, we never included the recovery of separation allowances amongst our war aims. I suggest, therefore, that we should by our acts prove ourselves sincere and trustworthy, and that accordingly Great Britain should waive altogether her claims for cash payment in favor of Belgium, Serbia, and France. The whole of the payments made by Germany would then be subject to the prior charge of repairing the material injury done to those countries and provinces which suffered actual invasion by the enemy; and I believe that the sum of $7,500,000,000 thus available would be adequate to cover entirely the actual costs of restoration. Further, it is only by a complete subordination of her own claims for cash compensation that Great Britain can ask with clean hands for a revision of the Treaty and clear her honor from the breach of faith for which she bears the main responsibility, as a result of the policy to which the General Election of 1918 pledged her representatives.

With the Reparation problem thus cleared up it would be possible to bring forward with a better grace and more hope of success two other financial proposals, each of which involves an appeal to the generosity of the United States.

The first is for the entire cancellation of Inter-Ally indebtedness (that is to say, indebtedness between the Governments of the Allied and Associated countries) incurred for the purposes of the war. This proposal, which has been put forward already in certain quarters, is one which I believe to be absolutely essential to the future prosperity of the world. It would be an act of far-seeing statesmanship for the United Kingdom and the United States, the two Powers chiefly concerned, to adopt it.

* * *

Failing such a settlement as is now proposed, the war will have ended with a network of heavy tribute payable from one Ally to another. The total amount of this tribute is even likely to exceed the amount obtainable from the enemy; and the war will have ended with the intolerable result of the Allies paying indemnities to one another instead of receiving them from the enemy.

For this reason the question of Inter-Allied indebtedness is closely bound up with the intense popular feeling amongst the European Allies on the question of indemnities,—a feeling which is based, not on any reasonable calculation of what Germany can, in fact, pay, but on a well-founded appreciation of the unbearable financial situation in which these countries will find themselves unless she pays. Take Italy as an extreme example. If Italy can reasonably be expected to pay $4,000,000,000, surely Germany can and ought to pay an immeasurably higher figure. Or if it is decided (as it must be) that Austria can pay next to nothing, is it not an intolerable conclusion that Italy should be loaded with a crushing tribute, while Austria escapes? Or, to put it slightly differently, how can Italy be expected to submit to payment of this great sum and see Czecho-Slovakia pay little or nothing? At the other end of the scale there is the United Kingdom. Here the financial position is different, since to ask us to pay $4,000,000,000 is a very different proposition from asking Italy to pay it. But the sentiment is much the same. If we have to be satisfied without full compensation from Germany, how bitter will be the protests against paying it to the United States. We, it will be said, have to be content with a claim against the bankrupt estates of Germany, France, Italy, and Russia, whereas the United States has secured a first mortgage upon us. The case of France is at least as overwhelming. She can barely secure from Germany the full measure of the destruction of her countryside. Yet victorious France must pay her friends and Allies more than four times the indemnity which in the defeat of 1870 she paid Germany. The hand of Bismarck was light compared with that of an Ally or of an Associate. A settlement of Inter-Ally indebtedness is, therefore, an indispensable preliminary to the peoples of the Allied countries facing, with other than a maddened and exasperated heart, the inevitable truth about the prospects of an indemnity from the enemy.

It might be an exaggeration to say that it is impossible for the European Allies to pay the capital and interest due from them on these debts, but to make them do so would certainly be to impose a crushing burden. They may be expected, therefore, to make constant attempts to evade or escape payment, and these attempts will be a constant source of international friction and ill-will for many years to come. A debtor nation does not love its creditor, and it is fruitless to expect feelings of goodwill from France, Italy, and Russia towards this country or towards America, if their future development is stifled for many years to come by the annual tribute which they must pay us. There will be a great incentive to them to seek their friends in other directions, and any future rupture of peaceable relations will always carry with it the enormous advantage of escaping the payment of external debts. If, on the other hand, these great debts are forgiven, a stimulus will be given to the solidarity and true friendliness of the nations lately associated.

The existence of the great war debts is a menace to financial stability everywhere. There is no European country in which repudiation may not soon become an important political issue. In the case of internal debt, however, there are interested parties on both sides, and the question is one of the internal distribution of wealth.

With external debts this is not so, and the creditor nations may soon find their interest inconveniently bound up with the maintenance of a particular type of government or economic organization in the debtor countries. Entangling alliances or entangling leagues are nothing to the entanglements of cash owing.

The final consideration influencing the reader's attitude to this proposal must, however, depend on his view as to the future place in the world's progress of the vast paper entanglements which are our legacy from war finance both at home and abroad. The war has ended with every one owing everyone else immense sums of money. Germany owes a large sum to the Allies; the Allies owe a large sum to Great Britain; and Great Britain owes a large sum to the United States. The holders of war loan in every country are owed a large sum by the State; and the State in its turn in owed a large sum by these and other taxpayers. The whole position is in the highest degree artificial, misleading, and vexatious, We shall never be able to move again, unless we can free our limbs from these paper shackles. A general bonfire is so great a necessity that unless we can make of it an orderly and good-tempered affair in which no serious injustice is done to any one, it will, when it comes at last, grow into a conflagration that may destroy much else as well.

THE QUESTION OF REPARATIONS

Étienne Mantoux

Why, then it will now be asked, was it so difficult to secure the enforcement of Reparations? Did not the following years confirm the prediction that "the claims against Germany were impossible of payment," and that "the economic solidarity of Europe was so close that to enforce these terms might ruin every one"?

A brief reconsideration of Reparation payments should supply the answer.[1] The history of Reparations divides itself into three distinct chapters. From 1920 to 1924, the execution of the Treaty was in the hands of the Reparation Commission. From 1924 to 1930, Reparations were governed by the Dawes Plan. From 1930 to 1931 they were governed by the Young Plan, then suspended, and finally cancelled altogether in 1932.

1. *The Reparation Commission.* The Treaty had prescribed that a Commission would fix the total amount of the Reparation debt. It was then to draw up a schedule of payments and to control its execution over a period of thirty years, which could be prolonged if necessary.

The German delegation protested vehemently against this scheme. "German democracy is thus annihilated at the very moment when the German people were about to build it up after a severe struggle. . . . The Commission, which is to have its permanent headquarters outside Germany, will possess incomparably greater rights than the German Emperor ever possessed; the German people under its regime would remain for decades shorn of all rights, and deprived, to a far greater extent

---

[1] The facts of the Reparation story are entirely of a public character and ought to be known to the whole world. But the merit belongs to Mr. G. Borsky and to Lord Vansittart for having recently rescued them from a limbo of uneasy silence. (*The Greatest Swindle in the World*, New Europe Publishing Company, London, 1942. See also Lord Vansittart: *Lessons of My Life*, London, 1943.)

than any people in the days of absolutism, of any independence of action, of any individual aspiration in its economic or even in its ethical progress. These comments," added Mr. Keynes, after having analysed at length the functions of the Commission, "were hardly an exaggeration."[2]

Yet the Allied Reply had had little difficulty in doing justice to them. "The observations of the German delegation," said the Note of 16 June, "present a view of this Commission so distorted and so inexact that it is difficult to believe that the clauses of the Treaty have been calmly or carefully examined. It is not an engine of oppression or a device for interfering with German sovereignty. It has no forces at its command. It has no executive powers within the territory of Germany; it cannot, as is suggested, direct or control the educational or other systems of the country. Its business is to ask what is to be paid; to satisfy itself that Germany can pay; and to report to the Powers, whose delegation it is, in case Germany makes default. . . ." "This," wrote Mr. Keynes, "is not a candid statement of the scope and authority of the Reparation Commission." And he went on to explain how the terms of the Treaty could open the way to an interpretation much wider than that assumed in the Allied Reply. What he omitted to say was that in a reply by the Conference's Committee on Reparation to a request from the German delegation for further elucidation, it had been stated that the Allied Reply of 16 June would have binding force as interpretation of the Articles on Reparation.[3] Candid or not candid, the interpretation given in the Note was therefore an authoritative one, and was invoked as such before the Commission later on.[4]

Now if it were true that the Commission "was to possess incomparably greater rights than the German Emperor ever possessed," etc., etc., how strange that Mr. Keynes, when he came to demonstrate that Germany could not meet the coal demands of the Treaty, should have suggested that the powers of the German Government would probably be inadequate to restore the length of the working day in the mining industry to its former figure of eight hours![5] If the German Government could not, surely the Commission, with its exorbitant powers, could? Thus on the one hand we were told that the Commission would be "in many different particulars the arbiter of Germany's economic life";[6] but on the other we were warned not to expect that the German miners could work more than seven hours a day.

The truth is that time and again the Commission had been instructed to spare the social, economic, and financial structure of Germany. It was to return to Germany

---

[2] *E.C.P.*, p. 201. [Economic Consequence of the Peace: London and New York, 1920—EDITORS' NOTE]

[3] This reply had been approved by the Council of Four. (Miller, vol. xix, p. 287.)

[4] Let it be added that the discussions which had taken place in the Council of Four over the drafting of that section confirm this restrictive interpretation of the Commision's powers. Thus Mr. Lloyd George thought that the original drafting of the paragraph that enabled the Commission to demand payment "in the form of properties, chattels, commodities, business rights," etc., etc., was "too stiff." "It would give the Commission power practically to take any property or material to which it took a fancy." President Wilson agreed. "What he wanted was to avoid even the appearance of a forced Brest-Litovsk Treaty." So the provision was modified accordingly. (Burnett, op. cit., vol. I, pp. 1000 ff.) Such instances could be multiplied. If my guess is right, this particular meeting (27 April) must have been precisely the one described by Mr. Keynes in his famous second chapter. Perhaps his mind was too deeply engaged in a contemplation of Clemenceau's shoe-buckles to pay attention to such details.

[5] *E.C.P.*, p. 83.

[6] *E.C.P.*, p. 200.

out of her payments before 1921 the sums necessary to meet "such supplies of food and raw materials as may be judged by the Governments of the Allied and Associated Powers to be essential to enable her to meet her obligations" (Article 235.) In considering the Allied claims, it was to give the German Government a just opportunity to be heard, though not to take part in the Commission's decisions. (Annex II, part 10.) It was required to hear, if the German Government so desired, evidence and arguments on the part of Germany on any question connected with her capacity to pay. And in periodically estimating this capacity, the Commission was to satisfy itself that in general, the German scheme of taxation was "fully as heavy proportionately as that of any of the Powers represented on the Commission."[7] In other words, the charges supported by Germany were to be *at least* equal to those supported by the Allies—but it was not specified that they should be greater. So *this* was the measure of the burden imposed upon Germany! *This* was "the policy of reducing Germany to servitude for a generation"! Let us now see how it was actually carried into effect.

The period which starts with the coming into force of the Treaty and ends with the adoption of the Dawes Plan subdivides itself into three intervals. The first ends with the acceptance by Germany of the Schedule of Payments of May 1921. The second with the occupation of the Ruhr in January 1923. The third with the application of the Dawes Plan in 1924.

In January 1920 the Reparation Commission entered upon its tasks. Its first mission was to secure, in execution of Article 235, a payment of 20 milliard marks before 1 May 1921. "The payment," said this Article, "should be made in such instalments and in such manner (whether in gold, commodities, ships or otherwise) as the Commission may fix." In order to show how the Treaty gave to the Commission "dictatorial powers over all German property of every description whatever,"[8] Mr. Keynes had placed upon it the most extreme interpretation. "They can under this Article," he wrote, "point to any specific business, enterprise, or property, whether within or outside Germany, and demand its surrender. . . . For example, they could pick out—as presumably they will as soon as they are established—the fine and powerful German enterprise in South America known as the *Deutsch Ueberseeische Elektrizitätsgesellschaft* (the D.U.E.G.), and dispose of it to the Allied interests. The clause is unequivocal and all-embracing."[9]

One of the first acts of the Commission was to ascertain the extent of its own powers under Article 235. There is no indication that it even considered the possibility of disposing of all kinds of German property whatsoever. All it did was to debate whether the foreign securities in the possession of German nationals (apart from those that were already specifically affected by the Treaty) could be demanded. Four legal experts answered in the affirmative. The American expert, Mr. Hugh A. Bayne, entered a dissenting opinion. One of the most convincing arguments adduced in its support was a reference to a passage in the Allied Reply of 16 June 1919. "Outside the Empire," said the Note, "the Allied and Associated Powers have

---

[7] The discussion of this clause by the Council of Four on 23 April shows that their intention was to enable the Commission to relieve Germany, if it was thought proper, once it was established that taxation was proportionately as heavy as in the most heavily taxed country represented on the Commission, but not before. This principle was so obviously just that it was embodied five years later in the Dawes Plan, which Mr. Keynes, as we shall see, described at first as "an honourable document."

[8] *E.C.P.*, p. 71.

[9] *E.C.P.*, pp. 71-2.

abstained from claiming the transfer of German property and interests in the neutral countries." This, wrote Mr. Bayne, settled the meaning of the Treaty, and would render it improper to contend that "under Article 235 the Reparation Commission has the power to compel the surrender of German interests in neutral countries."[10]

"The difference of opinion disclosed in the legal service," adds the Commission's report, "was reproduced in the Commission itself." And as under the Treaty unanimity was necessary for interpretation of the Treaty's text, the Commission could not demand these securities.[11]

So the fate of the D.U.E.G., which had inspired Mr. Keynes with such doleful forebodings, was undisturbed. And it happened, incidentally, that the use to which its assets were put did not turn out to be exactly in furtherance of Allied interests. The company was thoroughly reorganized in 1920; its most important installations in South America were transferred to a new firm, the Hispano-American Electric Company, founded by a certain number of Spanish banks. The preferred stock and all the bonds were then refunded to the holders in paper marks; and 120,000 new shares were attributed, as a commission, to the founders of the new company. Their value, amounting to more than 120 million gold marks, represented so much capital exported from Germany under the nose of her creditors.

To return to the Commission: all that it could do was to inform Germany that it was necessary for her to use all "neutral securities" in the possession of the Government or of her nationals in payment for the indispensable food supplies and raw materials to which Article 235 entitled her; and to declare that it would consent to no sum of money being deducted from the 20 milliard gold marks to pay for these supplies unless the German Government was immediately to take all steps necessary to acquire the securities in question and apply them to meeting Germany's requirements.[12] As for the rest of the 20 milliards, Germany was left literally to raise the money in her own way. All that the Commission did was to address a letter to the German Government requesting to be informed as soon as possible of how it proposed to carry out Article 235.

There is no record, in the published documents of the Commission, of any reply to this letter. Meanwhile, Germany had not yet paid to the Commission one single cent in cash.[13] But in January 1921 the German Government submitted to the Commission a memorandum purporting to demonstrate that the value of deliveries in kind effected since the Armistice amounted already to more than 20 milliard marks. The Commission replied that a number of the items involved were not liquid or capable of being made liquid in the near future; that it made all reservations on the evaluation of the other items; and that the final account under Article 235 could not, in these conditions, fail to reveal a deficit of at least 12 milliard marks. On 14 March the German Government answered, maintaining its former position. The Commission persisted. It reminded Germany that she had to pay the balance

[10] Reparation Commission, V, *Report on the Work of the Reparations Commission from 1920 to 1922*, p. 187.
[11] *Ibid.*, p. 13.
[12] Reparation Commission, IV, *Statement of Germany's Obligations*, p. 14. Even though these securities were not delivered, yet 3.8 milliard marks were deducted from the 20 milliard debt in order to pay for Germany's food and raw material supplies.
[13] Apart from the 3.8 milliards spent by Germany for her own supplies. The only cash payments made to the Commission prior to May 1921 amounted to some 84 million marks (£4.2 million) and came not from Germany, but from France and Denmark, as credits for the value of property ceded under the Treaty. (Reparation Commission, IV, *Statement of Germany's Obligations*, pp. 5 ff.)

before 1 May; and that she must pay before 25 March *at the latest without fail* (things had come to a point where the Reparation Commission did not refrain even from the use of italics!) a first instalment of one milliard gold marks. After a further exchange of letters, unbrightened by any cash payments, the poor Commission found that "there was nothing left but to notify the Allied Governments formally that Germany was in default in respect of her obligations under Article 235 of the Treaty to the extent of at least 12 milliard gold marks."[14]

Thus did the first task of the Commission come to an end.

It met with more success in the second, which was the fixing of Germany's total obligations. On 27 April 1921 the Commission made it known, as we have seen, that the total liability came to 132 milliard marks,[15,16] in accordance with Mr. Keynes's calculations; and the Supreme Council of the Allies worked out a Schedule of Payments which was accepted a few days later by Germany, after an ultimatum including the threat to occupy the Ruhr valley had been sent by the Supreme Council.

The provisions of the Schedule of Payments fell into three parts: (1) a delivery of bonds in three portions, A, B, and C, the details of which are now of little interest as they were never carried into any practical effect (it would be unfair not to mention Mr. Keynes's remark at the time, that these details were "not likely ... to be operative, and need not be taken very seriously"[17]; (2) the constitution for the supervision of Germany's payments of a Committee of Guarantees to which were assigned, said Mr. Keynes, "the various wide and indefinite powers accorded by the Treaty of Peace to the Reparation Commission";[18] Germany's payments were, in addition, regulated by special provisions. She was to pay each year 2 milliard marks plus a sum equivalent to 26 per cent of the value of her exports, or alternatively an equivalent amount as fixed in accordance with any other index proposed by Germany and accepted by the Commission. Payments were to be made by quarterly instalments, but one milliard was to be paid within the first 25 days. "The probable burden of the new settlement in the near future," wrote Mr. Keynes, is probably not much more than half that of the Treaty."[19] But although it provided a transition from "foolish expectations," it could not be more than "a temporising measure" which was bound to need amendment."[20] Some time between February and August 1922 Germany will succumb to an inevitable default. This is the maximum extent of our breathing space.'"[21]

The reader shall be spared a detailed account of the harassing epistolary tournament that followed between the imploring Reparation Commission and the dodging German Government. With the aid of short-term foreign credits, the first milliard prescribed by the Schedule was duly paid in August 1921. (This was the first *cash* payment made for Reparation since the Treaty had come into force.) The Committee of Guarantees, after a visit to Berlin, found little that was encouraging

[14] Reparation Commission, IV, *Statement of Germany's Obligations,* p. 23.
[15] In the course of the discussions, the German Government had submitted estimates of 7.3 milliards for damages to France and 2 milliards to Belgium.
[16] $33,000,000,000. [EDITORS' NOTE]
[17] R.T., p. 60 [*Revision of the Treaty, Being a Sequel to the Economic Consequences of the Peace,* London, 1922—EDITORS' NOTE]
[18] R.T., p. 62; this comment was made in spite of the express provision to the effect that the Committee was "not authorised to interfere in German administration."
[19] R.T., p. 65.
[20] R.T., p. 67.
[21] R.T., p. 71.

to report. Although the German Government complained that the difficulty was to collect foreign bills for the external payments, the exportation of private capital continued practically unchecked. Public expenditure and budget deficits were increasing. Germany's "food policy, which could be justified immediately after the raising of the blockade, has been continued on a large scale and still figures in the budget for several milliards."[22] And the Committee expressed fears that the German Government might declare that it was unable to make the next payments.

Nevertheless, In November 1921, Germany paid another instalment of 500 million marks. But the following month, in reply to a letter from the Commission entreating them to take the necessary steps for the next instalment, the German Government declared that it would be unable to pay it, and, for the first time, officially requested a moratorium.

Greatly annoyed, the Commission expressed "its surprise" that the German Government should not even have mentioned a time limit to the extension requested, or an indication of the security proposed in the meantime; nevertheless, a provisional postponement was soon granted. This was confirmed a little later, after the Conference of Cannes had reduced Germany's obligations for 1922 to a total of some 2.2 milliard marks. As a condition of the postponement, Germany was asked to undertake a thorough reorganization of her finances, under the supervision of the Commission.

This decision was greeted in Germany with an outburst of indignation. The principle of supervision, claimed Chancellor Wirth in a bitter speech, was imcompatible with the right of self-determination or with the honour of a nation. A reply to this effect was accordingly dispatched to the Commission.[23]

The Commission noted "with surprise and regret" that its proposals were rejected. But while it still insisted on the necessity of increased taxation, it hastened to reassure the German Government that as far as supervision was concerned, its disquietude was quite unjustified. The German Government accepted the Commission's apology and noted with satisfaction that there existed no intention of trespassing upon Germany's sovereignty. And so monetary inflation, tax evasion, public expenditure, and capital flight continued as fast as ever; and in July 1922 the German Government asked for a complete postponement for the rest of the year, adding, by the way, that the Allies had better not expect any payments in 1923, or in 1924 either.

Thus Mr. Keynes's prediction of "inevitable default" was, in a way, verified.

On 31 August the unhappy Commission saved its face. It announced that it would accept German Treasury bills for the next instalments, and Germany was thus freed of all cash payments for the rest of the year.

Greatly encouraged, the German Government now decided that the time had come for positive demands. In November 1922 it insisted that Germany should be relieved of all Reparation payments for the next three or four years, with a view to stabilizing the mark; in return, it declared itself ready to issue internal and foreign loans, as soon as an improvement in the mark exchange should have restored Germany's credit.

M. Poincaré, the French Premier, who, as is well known, had no sense of humour, was not amused. At a Conference held in London, he announced his intention to

---

[22] Reparation Commission, III, *Official Documents*, p. 38.
[23] See Carl Bergmann: *The History of Reparations,* 1927, p. 121. According to this authority, the speech in question had been drafted by Rathenau.

occupy the Ruhr if the German defaults were to continue. On 26 December the Commission was asked by its chairman, M. Barthou, on behalf of the French delegation, to declare Germany in default on deliveries of timber. Sir John Bradbury admitted that the delivery had not been made, but he questioned whether this delay constituted a "default" as contemplated by paragraph 17 of Annex II. "Since," he concluded, "in the tenth year of the war, Troy fell to the stratagem of the wooden horse, history recorded no similar use of timber. The situation was at present somewhat different; it was the fifth year of the peace, and the city under attack was not Troy, but Essen."[24] By a vote of three to one, Germany was declared in default of her obligations under the Treaty.

Another Conference met at Paris. Mr. Bonar Law, the British Prime Minister, proposed a plan whereby Germany's debt would be reduced to 50 milliard marks; M. Poincaré declared that this scheme would destroy the Treaty of Versailles. Mr. Bonar Law answered that to insist upon the application of the Treaty was destroying Germany's credit. No agreement could be reached. On 4 January the Conference adjourned. On 9 January the Reparation Commission, by a vote of three to one, declared Germany in voluntary default in respect to coal deliveries. On 11 January French and Belgian troops occupied the Ruhr district, and Germany ceased all Reparation deliveries.

The occupation of the Ruhr met with sharp disapproval in Great Britain, where the general belief was that no useful purpose could be served by applying military coercion to enforce demands which were economically "impossible." In France, while there was a good deal of opposition to Mr. Poincaré's venture, it was still generally believed that Germany was not incapable, but unwilling to pay. The deadlock continued throughout the year, in spite of active diplomatic correspondence between the two Governments.

In Germany, wrath was naturally widespread. A policy of "passive resistance," marked by strikes and sabotage, was actively organized by the industrialists and the Government. This attitude brought a series of conflicts with the occupying authorities, and led to coercive measures, including the expulsion of a large number of recalcitrants into non-occupied Germany. Economic life in the Ruhr district was disorganized until a Franco-Belgian engineering mission (the "MICUM") took over control of transport and production. In September 1923 the German Government abandoned the policy of passive resistance, and came to an agreement with the MICUM for the resumption of production and of certain deliveries in kind.

The limited material yield that was brought by the occupation of the Ruhr has often been taken as the proof that "force can settle nothing" in economic affairs. The experience of Europe after 1939 has perhaps taught us differently; for it is irrelevant to argue that the German "New Order" "failed" in the face of the resistance of the peoples of Europe. It is true that if these people had not resisted, Germany's task would have been easier; but when the "New Order" failed it was because Germany was met by superior force, and the severity of the efforts necessary to bring about this defeat is the measure of the success with which Germany used force to "settle" her dominion over Europe. If the occupation of the Ruhr was only partly successful, it was because the coercive policy carried out by France was, compared to Germany's "New Order," an evidently half-hearted one, and also because no unity between the Allies had been achieved. Had this unity existed, not even the *application* of force would have been necessary.

[24] Reparation Commission, v, *The History of Reparations,* 1927, p. 253.

It is also generally alleged that the occupation of the Ruhr, as the culmination of a period of reckless efforts to enforce the Treaty of Versailles, precipitated the final annihilation of the mark and the "collapse" of the German economy. This afforded complete proof, in the eyes of the public, of Mr. Keynes's claim that the Reparation demands were impracticable, and that any attempt to enforce them would end in ruining Germany and the whole of Europe.

The depreciation of the German mark has often been ascribed to the adverse effect of Reparation payments upon Germany's exchanges. It cannot be denied that even in the absence of internal inflation, the strain placed upon the balance of payments by the remittance of large sums abroad would, under a paper standard, have affected the exchange rate. But in the first place, this external depreciation would not in itself have depressed the internal purchasing power of the mark, if a continuous increase in the volume of the currency had not been taking place simultaneously, and it would have stopped after a new position of equilibrium had been reached. External depreciation could have gone far, no doubt, if the payments had been large; yet it cannot be seriously maintained that the payment of *less than 2 milliard marks,* which was all that Germany ever paid in cash between 1919 and the end of 1923, could have had this effect.[25]

The Reparation charges added to the budgetary deficit which it was the purpose of inflation to cover; in this sense, Reparations did contribute to the German inflation. But compared to other expenses, the Reparation charges were small. Before the signing of the Treaty, the deficit amounted already to some 10 milliard gold marks; from 1920 to 1923, the deficits totalled some 18.7 milliards; while all expenses under the Treaty represented 6.5 milliards.[26] As was the case in all belligerent countries, monetary inflation had started during the war; in October 1918 the volume of fiduciary circulation was nearly four and a half times as large as in 1914. After 1919 the mark depreciated continuously. When all Reparation cash payments ceased in July 1922, the rate was about 500 to the dollar. It was after that period, and particularly in 1923, when the German Government was financing "passive resistance" by a massive issue of notes, that the mark depreciated until in November 1923 the rate was 4,200,000,000,000 to the dollar. The currency was then stabilized at the rate of 1,000,000,000,000 paper marks for 1 "rentenmark." Thus, the German inflation, which had started before Reparation payments had begun, reached its wildest proportions after they had ceased.

The depreciation of the mark was essentially due to inflation, a malady from which all countries in Europe suffered as a consequence of the War, and the evil effects of which had been brilliantly exposed by Mr. Keynes.[27] The victors were not immune from it; the value of the German mark was reduced by more than 99.9 per cent, but the value of the French franc was finally reduced by more than 80 per cent. Thus inflation could take place even in the absence of Reparations. If, on the other hand, Reparations had been paid to the full, inflation could still have been avoided. After 1933 Germany was able to finance a much heavier public

---

[25] Deliveries in kind, being unpaid-for exports, no doubt also affected the balance of payments, even though they involved no foreign exchange operations; but if the balance of payments was then heavily passive, it was because imports into Germany continued unchecked—which would not have happened if the ordinary effects of transfer depreciation had alone operated and which shows that Germany's needs in foodstuffs and raw materials were not denied satisfaction.

[26] See C. Bresciani-Turroni: *The Economics of Inflation,* London, 1937, p. 93.

[27] *E.C.P.,* pp. 220 ff.

expenditure without any considerable depreciation of her currency, by means of an energetic policy of taxation, forced loans, and exchange control. Similar measures could have prevented inflation in Germany after 1919. The stabilization of the mark was achieved with great success in 1923, *during the period of the Ruhr occupation.* It could have been achieved no less easily before that time if the German Government had been ready to put a stop to the issue of notes.

This being said, the annihilation of the mark was undoubtedly a catastrophe; the German middle classes were beggared, and the resulting social instability had much to do with the success of National Socialism in later years. But while inflation affected the distribution of wealth, it did not destroy national wealth as a whole. Even if it is reckoned that, in spite of the increase in capital represented by the progress of industrial equipment during that period, the capital structure of Germany was put out of equilibrium, it is clear that Germany was not seriously impoverished by inflation. We often hear of the "collapse" of the German economy. What is meant by a "collapse" is at best questionable. The collapse of a bank, of a commercial firm, even of the finances of a state—all these have a very definite significance, as the holders of German bonds found to their own cost. But as long as the physical resources of a nation are not impaired, it is idle, even in the case of the gravest disturbances of economic life, to speak of the "collapse" of the national economy. One year after the extinction of the mark, the real income of the German people was already 97 per cent of what it had been in 1913, and the value of their savings was about three times as large as Mr. Keynes's maximum estimate of their capacity to pay. To what particular category of "collapse," then, belongs that which is followed by immediate prosperity?

2. *The Dawes Plan.* In December 1922, Secretary of State Hughes had suggested that if statesmen could not agree, the task of working out a solution should be given to financial experts of different countries, and that he did not doubt that Americans would be willing to serve on such a commission. The proposal was renewed by President Coolidge in October 1923. And in November the Reparation Commission announced that it had decided to create two Committees of experts, "in order to consider, in accordance with the provisions of Article 234 of the Treaty of Versailles, the resources and capacity of Germany." One would examine "the means of balancing the budget and the measures taken to stabilize the currency"; the other, "the means of estimating the amount of exported capital and of bringing it back to Germany."

The two Committees submitted their reports in April 1924. The first Committee, constituted under the genial chairmanship of General Charles G. Dawes, proposed that the German currency be stabilized on a gold basis, and made known the amount of the charges which it considered compatible with the balancing of the budget. In the first two years, the annuities should be respectively of 1,000 million and 1,220 million marks; in a transitional period, they were to rise to 1,200 and 1,750 millions; in the fifth year there would be a "standard" payment of 2,500 millions, and thereafter the payments could be increased according to an index reflecting the variations of Germany's prosperity. The plan, as we have seen, retained the principle that Germany's fiscal charges should be commensurate with those of her creditors. Its execution was to be supervised by an organization of trustees (for the German railways, for certain industrial debentures, and certain controlled revenues), under the authority of an Agent General for Reparation Payments.

The most original feature of the plan was the solution given to the transfer problem. "There is," said the report, "an important difference between Germany's capacity to pay taxes, and Germany's capacity to transfer wealth abroad." Accordingly, a transfer committee was to obviate the dangers to currency stability arising from excessive remittances; the annuities were to be paid in marks by the German Government to the Agent General's account at the Reichsbank, and the Committee, composed of "five persons skilled in matters relating to foreign exchange and finance," was to decide how much could be transferred without endangering the currency. The Dawes Committee also recommended that a loan of 800 million marks be granted to Germany for the purpose of establishing the Bank of Issue and the currency system on a new basis.

The Dawes Report has generally been considered as a remarkable document, and such, at first, was the opinion of Mr. Keynes. "Germany," he wrote, "can scarcely expect better terms than these. . . . If the plan is worked with skill and good faith, it seems to protect Germany from the dangers of oppression and ruin. . . . The Report is the finest contribution hitherto to this impossible problem. It breathes a new spirit and is conceived in a new vein. . . . Though it compromises with the impossible and even contemplates the impossible, it never prescribes the impossible. This façade and these designs may never be realized in an edifice raised up in the light of day. But it is an honourable document and opens a new chapter.[28] The merit of the plan, in his eyes, was that even if the demands made upon Germany were to reveal themselves as excessive, the necessary safeguards were provided within the plan itself "in the event of optimistic forecasts going wrong."

The proposals of the Dawes Report were embodied in the agreements signed a few months later between Germany and her creditors. This time Germany was acting under no ultimatum and the agreement was freely concluded. But in the meantime, for some unexplained reason, the opinion of Mr. Keynes had changed. In the first place, the plan did not, in spite of the loan, allow Germany the respite she needed for the replenishment of her working capital. In the second place, "the Dawes plan pretends to erect a system which is not compatible with civilization or with human nature. It sets up foreign control over the Banking, the Transport, and the Fiscal Systems of Germany, the object of which will be to extract from the German people the last drop of sweat. . . . No reparations will ever be obtained from Germany except such moderate sums, well within her powers, as she will voluntarily pay. The Dawes Scheme pretends to attempt more than this. Therefore it will fail."[29]

The Dawes Plan worked to perfection. During the following five years, the annuities were paid regularly and transferred to the creditors without any difficulty. But then a new factor had come into play: Germany's massive and continuous foreign borrowings.

As soon as the mark had definitely been stabilized in 1924 foreign capital began to pour into Germany. Between 1924 and 1930, the importation of long-term capital amounted to more than 9 milliard Reichsmarks, and the short-term credits

[28] "The Experts' Reports. I. The Dawes Report," *The Nation and Athenaeum,* 12 April 1924, pp. 40-1.
[29] "The Dawes Scheme and the German Loan," *The Nation and Athenaeum,* 4 October 1924. Mr. Keynes did not believe that the machinery of control had been conceived in a spirit of oppression, but rather to perfect the demonstration that "when the breakdown comes, every possible precaution had been taken, and that the breakdown was, therefore, due to nothing else but the inherent impossibility of the task which had been set."

to some 12 milliards. To these sums must be added direct investments in real property, German securities, etc. It was reported in December 1931 that according to the figures submitted by the German authorities, the total foreign capital in Germany amounted to nearly 30 milliard marks.[30] This sum, however, does not represent the *net* inflow of capital, as a certain amount of capital was also exported out of Germany at the same time. It was calculated in August 1931 that the net influx between 1924 and 1930 amounted to some 18 milliards.[31] This corresponds fairly closely to the estimate which has been given above[32] of the total debits of the German balance of payments during that period; it explains why this balance, at a time when Germany was paying Reparations, was constantly *passive*. In other words, the net importation of foreign capital by Germany during the period of the Dawes Plan was more than twice the amount of her Reparation payments, and the gross importation was more than three times that amount.

It is for this reason that the transfer safeguards provided by the Dawes Plan were never put into operation; there was always a considerable excess of foreign exchange at the disposal of the German Government, and the stability of the mark was never endangered. But, at the same time, the effect of the borrowings meant that the ultimate problem of German payments was being postponed. Reparations were being paid, literally, with the money of foreign investors, not with the savings and taxes of the German people.

It is not surprising, therefore, that Germany showed such signs of prosperity during that period. We have already noted the progress of her national income. The relative charge represented by Reparation payments is given below:

Year	National Income (Milliards)	Reparation Payments (Milliards)	Per cent
1925	59.9	1.1	1.8
1926	62.6	1.3	2.1
1927	70.7	1.8	2.5
1928	75.4	1.8	2.4
1929	75.9	2.5	3.3
1930	70.2	1.6	2.3

Thus, the heaviest burden imposed upon Germany by the Dawes Plan represented 3.3 per cent of her national income. Such was the scheme that was "to extract from the German people the last drop of sweat."

It is unnecessary to dwell at any length on the increase of Germany's wealth during that period. The signs were obvious to every visitor, and they persisted even after the depression of 1929-33.[33] It was estimated in 1930 that the total value of new building in Germany since 1924 amounted to more than 40 milliard

[30] Report of the Young Plan Advisory Committee. (See *The Economist,* Supplement, 2 January 1932.)

[31] See C. R. S. Harris: *Germany's Foreign Indebtedness,* London, 1935, pp. 8-9.

[32] *Supra,* p. 119.

[33] "You could search far and wide through Berlin's sea of houses or Hamburg's huge harbour district, but you could never find a slum or anything approaching one," wrote an American journalist, relating the impressions of his arrival in 1936. (Howard K. Smith: *Last Train from Berlin,* New York, 1942, p. 9.) This could not have been due to the housing policy of the National Socialists, who had been there for only three years, but to a legacy from the palmy days of the Weimar Republic—that, is from the Versailles period.

marks—more than five times the amount of Reparations paid during that period.[34] At the same time, consumption increased continuously, and by 1926 Mr. Keynes was of the opinion that the German worker had already "very nearly recovered his pre-war real wages."[35]

That the real problem was thus being postponed was repeatedly stressed by Mr. Keynes. "Reparations and Interallied Debts," he wrote in 1926, "are being mainly settled in paper and not in goods. The United States lends money to Germany. Germany transfers its equivalent to the Allies, the Allies pay it back to the United States Government. Nothing real passes—no one is a penny the worse."[36] But what would happen when the foreign loans ceased? That was the question; and, for this reason, it is true that the German payments under the Dawes Plan were not in themselves a proof that the system was workable. But it is enough, as we have already observed, to consider the net amount of capital imports *into* Germany during that period to see that large tranfers could be effected without injury either to the capital-exporting or to the capital-importing country; for Germany did not, during that period, complain that the inflow of capital might "disturb" the balance of her economy. On the contrary: when the long-term loans ceased in 1929, she continued to borrow at short term and throughout the following crisis she was constantly asking for more.

3. *The Young Plan and the End of Reparations.* The Dawes Plan had been conceived as a provisional settlement. It had left untouched the question of Germany's total liability, which remained in principle that fixed by the Schedule of 1921, a total which the Dawes annuities would never have been sufficient to discharge. In 1929 the creditors assembled again, and after a series of negotiations that led to agreements at The Hague, adopted the plan of a new Committee of Experts presided over by Mr. Owen D. Young.

The Young Plan was to be the final solution of the Reparation problem. Germany's obligations were again considerably reduced. Although the plan provided only for annual payments and did not expressly fix the capital value of the debt, the present value of the fifty-nine annuities provided for was about 37 milliard marks; the annuities, which were to be paid until 1938, varied in amount with time, and totalled 121 milliards. Another original feature of the plan was that the system of transfer protection was modified: Germany was to find the foreign exchange herself, but a fraction of the annuity (the "conditional" fraction) could be postponed if circumstances required it. On the other hand, a new German loan was to be issued, this time of 1,200 million marks. The Reparation Commission, which had faded into oblivion since 1924, was finally suppressed, and all payments were to be made through the new Bank of International Settlements, to which were assigned the administration and the "commercialization" of Germany's debt in future.

The Young Plan was short-lived. While it was being discussed, the Great Depression had already begun. It grew in violence in 1930 and 1931. Prices fell, production slowed down, unemployment increased throughout the whole world. In Germany these effects were particularly severe. By the end of 1931 the index of

---

[34] Estimate of the Institut für Konjunkturforschung. See *Report of the Agent General for Reparation Payments,* 21 May 1930, p. 284.

[35] "Germany's Coming Problem: The Prospect of the Second Dawes Year," *The Nation and Athenaeum,* 6 February, 1926, p. 636.

[36] *The Nation and Athenaeum,* 11 September 1926.

industrial production had fallen from 100 to 66—in other words one-third of the industrial life of Germany had stopped. Unemployment (including part-time) rose to a figure of 5 million. In May 1931 the financial crisis had been precipitated by the failure of the Austrian Credit Anstalt. The withdrawal of foreign credits took alarming proportions, and in 1931 the balance of payments was suddenly reversed, showing a net surplus of 2.3 milliard marks. By June, the Reichsbank was facing withdrawals at the rate of 200 million a week, and the Stock Exchange deteriorated rapidly. On 29 June President Hoover issued his proposal for a one-year moratorium of all Reparations and inter-Allied debts. After somewhat difficult negotiations (for France, who had been told, after so many successive abatements, that the Young Plan was *positively* the last settlement, and that the unconditional part of the annuity could never be postponed, would not easily consent to a new revision which boded ill for the future) the moratorium was accepted by all parties. Reparation payments were suspended. They were never resumed.

It appeared, therefore, that once Germany ceased to receive foreign loans, the crisis became inevitable. The reversal of the balance of payments certainly did not point to any "stickiness"; but although this process was by no means *impossible*, it was so violent as to provoke a catastrophe to Germany's national economy—and even to the whole financial world; so that in the eyes of the public, the forebodings of Mr. Keynes were once again "confirmed."

There is no doubt that, in view of the gravity of the financial crisis, the postponement of Reparation payments could be justified. Yet the notion that the crisis of 1931 was caused mainly by Reparation payments, or that it indicated that such payments would be *impossible* in future, will hardly bear examination.

The crisis of 1931 was essentially a "run" on the German banks, and to a large extent a run away from them. The strain brought upon the financial system and the balance of payments was not only due to the withdrawal of foreign credits, but also to the massive flight of German private capital. In August 1931 the amount of German assets abroad was estimated at more than 9 milliards,[37] and additional exports of short-term capital had taken place on a large scale in the course of the crisis. Compared with this figure, or even with a fraction of it, the 800 million paid for Reparations in the first half of 1931 do not suggest that they were the major factor of the crisis. If a strict exchange control had been established by the German Government, the strain on the balance of payments would not have been so heavy. But the measures taken at that time—even the increase in the bank rate—were quite insufficient. German capital was allowed to flee abroad, and it found there a refuge from whence it was later safely repatriated (at least in part), for no obstacles were placed by the countries of refuge to their return. On the other hand, all foreign credits in Germany were "frozen"; no more withdrawals could take place, and the stability of the mark was thus assured. Taken earlier, such measures would have stopped the flight of capital. Exchange control was used with some success after 1933 to build up Germany's war economy; but the German Government's reluctance to use this method merely to allow the payment of Reparations to continue was entirely understandable.

That the financial system was, for a short time, brought to a standstill was no evidence of the economic "collapse" of the country. Financial crises have been known to all times, and the moratorium of 1931 was hardly different in kind, if

[37] Estimate of the Wiggin Committee.

not in degree, from the methods used by the City of London to surmount the periodical crises of the nineteenth century. It was hardly different from the measures taken in the United States in March 1933, when all the banks were closed by Governmental order, and the gold standard suspended. Economic recovery followed more or less quickly in all cases. The Young Plan's Special Advisory Committee, which had been summoned in December 1931 to recommend the measures to be taken, had been well inspired when it had observed that "nothwithstanding the exceptional character of the present crisis, there is no instance in economic history of a crisis, no matter how great, which was not followed by periods of stability and prosperity. . . . In past years, Germany has built up an immense and powerful economic equipment, capable of yielding a great return. The restriction of markets and the fall of prices have prevented her from utilizing this equipment to the full. The activity of her factories is now necessarily reduced, but although it is impossible to fix a date for the recovery of stability which is still threatened to-day, it is none the less certain that this stability will ultimately be restored with the help of the measures suggested. . . ."

To argue from the crisis to the final impossibility of Reparation payments, therefore, would be "the humbug of finance" at its best.

It is unnecessary to describe here the negotiations which led, in July 1932, to the Lausanne agreements. Reparations were finally cancelled. Germany agreed to deliver to the Bank of International Settlements bonds for a total of 3 milliard marks, not to be issued before three years; any amount remaining unsold to be cancelled after fifteen years. Should any of my readers be interested in this type of investment, I feel confident that the Bank will be pleased to sell him—while there is still time—as many bonds as he desires, up to 3 milliard marks, with the special compliments of Dr. Hjalmar Schacht.

Thus did Reparations come to an end. An examination of how much Germany did actually pay will constitute a fitting epilogue to their melancholy story.

4. *The Reparation Account.* According to the books of the Reparation Commission, the total of Germany's payments, from 1918 to 1931, amounted to some 21 milliard marks; the German Government, on the other hand, asserted in a communiqué of 1932 that Germany had paid some 68 milliards. The details of these accounts can be conveniently summarized as follows:[38]

		Reparation Commission	German Government
		(Million Marks)	
I.	Payments made between 11 November 1918 and 31 August 1924	9,637.8	42,059.0
II.	Payments under the Dawes Plan	7,553.2	7,993.0
III.	Payments under the Young Plan	2,800.0	3,103.0
IV.	Other Payments	778.9	14,608.0
	Total	20,769.9	67,763.0[39]

[38] For further details, see *Le Temps*, 13 February 1932; M. Antonucci: *Le Bilan des Réparations et la Crise Mondiale*, Paris, 1935, pp. 424 ff; Borsky, op. cit., p. 45.

[39] The totals represent approximately $5,250,000,000 and $17,000,000,000, respectively. [EDITORS' NOTE]

Germany therefore claimed that she paid more than three times the amount credited to her in the books of the Reparation Commission. How can such a fantastic divergence be explained? Was it not evident, it was argued, that even after taking into account a certain amount of exaggeration on the part of Germany, the Reparation Commission, which represented Allied creditors and could not be a really impartial body, erred on the side of its own interests?

Let us examine the nature of these divergences. In the case of payments made under the Dawes and Young Plans, the difference is small, but deserves special mention: it represents the value of the service on the Dawes and Young loans. In other words, the German Government, after having first used the proceeds of the loans for the initial Reparation payments (or for the stabilization of its currency) entered again the interest on these loans as Reparation charges.

The main difference is accounted for by the other payments. In the first place, the German Government entered a certain number of items which the Reparation Commission did not even retain. Thus, it entered as a Reparation delivery the value of German ships seized during the War. It entered under "destruction of war material" a sum of 8.5 milliards, which included the scuttling of the fleet at Scapa Flow. It entered 1.2 milliards, the value of the work performed by German prisoners of war—but did not enter on the debit side the work done by many more Allied prisoners and by civilians deported into Germany during the War. The cost of "industrial disarmament" (?) was also entered as 3.5 milliards. It is only to be wondered that the whole of Germany's War costs were not included as Reparation payments.

The remaining and most important divergence is found in the payments made between the Armistice and the coming into force of the Dawes Plan. As these were made almost exclusively in kind (there is no substantial divergence over cash payments, which amounted in all to some 1.7 milliards), there arose a difficult problem of valuation. The endless disputes to which this problem gave birth provide in the writer's opinion, one of the strongest possible arguments against the system of payments in kind, and they rank among the best examples of the dangers attending any system of exchange which attempts to do without the lubricant of money. It is possible and even probable that the real value of these deliveries to the Allies was in several cases inferior to the sacrifice they represented to the German economy, and we have already concurred, in that respect, with the criticisms addressed by Mr. Keynes to the clauses of the Treaty dealing with German private property. But even when this factor is taken into account, the facts of Germany's exaggeration are still patent.

Thus, the value of the merchant fleet was estimated by the Reparation Commission at 711.5 million marks, and by the German Government at 3,436 millions. It would appear that even the Commission's figure was an over-estimate; for Helfferich had valued the entire merchant fleet before 1914 at one milliard marks, and only half of this tonnage was delivered under Versailles. It may be added that the German Government paid as compensation to shipowners in Germany a sum even smaller (550 million marks) than the credit given by the Reparation Commission. This did not prevent the German merchant fleet increasing by 2,800,000 tons in the next two years.

Again, the item of public property in the ceded territories was valued by the German Government at more than three times the estimate of the Reparation Commission (9,670 against 2,780 millions). The case of the Saar mines is particularly interesting. They had been estimated by Helfferich at 300 million marks before the War; the Commission entered the same estimate, the German Government a figure of 1,018 millions; but after the Saar plebiscite, the German Government, which, under the Treaty, was to pay back in gold the value of the mines to the French Government, offered a sum of 900 million francs—or about 150 million marks—and this sum was, of course, accepted. Such examples could be multiplied.[40] In the absence of any further proof to the contrary, we are therefore, I believe, justified in adopting Mr. Borsky's conclusion that the statement of the Reparation Commission was on the whole an accurate one, and that the German estimates "were not merely characteristic exaggeration, but also an attempt to render the whole scheme ridiculous in the eyes of the world and thus to hoodwink its critical faculty."[41] This attempt was entirely successful.

It is therefore interesting to consider what was the real burden supported by Germany during this period. We have already seen that, after 1924, Germany borrowed some 30 milliard marks abroad. But this is not all. Before 1923, a vast quantity of German bank notes and balances were bought by foreigners, at a time when the German exchange was rapidly deteriorating, in the ingenuous expectation that the mark would some day recover to par. It was estimated in 1924 that Germany had profited by the sale of mark credits and notes by an amount of from 7.6 to 8.7 milliard marks. "What Germany has appeared to pay in Reparations," observed Mr. Keynes at the time, "is nearly equal to what the foreign world has subscribed in return for worthless marks. . . . A million foreigners, we are told, have acquired bank balances in Germany, and each of these accounts has cost its owner on the average about £ 400. It is these lively gentlemen who have paid the bill so far."[42] Not a single cent, therefore, had really been paid by Germany before 1924. There remain the loans made to Germany after that date. The quasi-totality of these investments was lost in consequence of German defaults, more or less propped up by bank moratoria, standstill agreements, exchange clearings, and other such contrivances, all powerfully assisted by the running accompaniment of Dr. Schacht's suave exhortations:[43]

> *"I weep for you," the doctor said,*
> *"I deeply sympathize."*

---

[40] They will be found, with many instructive details, in Mr. Borsky's study, quoted above. See also, M. Antonucci, op. cit., pp. 424 ff. For a German source, see Heinecke.: *No More Reparations.*, 1932, pp. 23-6.

[41] Borsky, op. cit., p. 53. H. G. Moulton and C. E. McGuire, who made in 1923 an interesting analysis of the valuation problem, came to the conclusion that the Reparation Commission's estimates were too low (though not so low as the German Government pretended) and that the value of Germany's losses (as distinct from the value to the Allies of Germany's payments) between 1918 and 1923 amounted to 25,791 million marks. (See their *Germany's Capacity to Pay,* New York, 1923.) This figure was adopted by Mr. Keynes at that period. ("How Much has Germany Paid?" *The Nation and Athenaeum,* 27 October 1923.) In the absence of detailed justification from the accounts concerned for every item, however, there is no reason to accept this figure rather than that of the Commission.

[42] "The Experts' Reports. II. The McKenna Report"; *The Nation and Athenaeum,* 19 April 1924, p. 77.

[43] "I have the greatest compassion," said Dr. Schacht on 29 October 1934, "for the foreign holders of German bonds who, believing what they were told in their countries, thought they were making a good investment by subscribing to German loans, and are now compelled to forgo interest. Nevertheless, I cannot see any way to help them, except by telling them: one can pay one's debts only when one is making money."

But Germany swallowed up "those of the largest size," and interest was paid in shells, bombs, bullets, torpedoes—and other "sinking" funds.

Thus a total of some 35 to 38 milliard marks had been received by Germany from abroad between 1920 and 1931, as against the 21 milliards she had paid for Reparation.[44] Such was Germany's burden after the Treaty of Versailles.

The Politics of Reparation

Mr. Keynes had predicted that the Reparation clauses could never be carried out. They never were. This outcome has earned him the glory of a prophet. It is perhaps fair that others should have some share of these laurels. Foch, for instance, had expressed his own opinion to M. Klotz in no equivocal terms: "With the Treaty you have just signed, sir," he said, "you can expect with certainty to be paid in monkey tricks." Neither was Foch alone, in France or elsewhere, in harbouring such misgivings.

Following events, as we have seen, confirmed several of the Marshal's presentiments. It would appear there here, too, his apprehensions were correct. Reparations were not outside the range of economic *possibility*. Had they been literally enforced, they would no doubt have put the screw on Germany up to the topmost pitch. For having suggested that Germany be *squeezed til the pips squeaked*, Sir Eric Geddes was exposed by Mr. Keynes to the superciliousness of a pharisaical posterity; it is too often forgotten that the man whose efficiency and drive had overcome, in the face of administrative prejudice, some of the deadliest "bottlenecks" of the war, and who himself had made Britain's own pips squeak in the process, was probably entitled to view the limits of financial possibility in a more sanguine light than many others. In fact, a large part of what appeared to increase the burden to such heavy proportions consisted in the provisions relating to interest, and the Treaty had given sufficient powers to the Commission to reduce the rate according to circumstances; Clemenceau himself had conceded that the Allies might have to forgo interest altogether. Reparations were not paid because Germany, as was quite natural, did not want to pay them, and—which was perhaps not *quite* so natural—the Allies showed themselves incapable or unwilling to take jointly the necessary measures which could have made Germany pay.

The whole question, therefore, boiled down to political expediency.

Now expediency, political or otherwise, is not a negligible factor in human affairs, and there would have been nothing dishonourable in taking account of it squarely in the making of the Peace. Thus, when the Draft Treaty came up for final reconsideration, it was to expediency that Mr. Lloyd George, at the meeting of the Imperial Cabinet, had explicitly drawn the attention of his colleagues. The terms imposed, he said, "must be expedient as well as just. Justice was a question which the Germans were at liberty to raise, but expediency was a matter for the Allies to consider and not the Germans...."[45] And almost at the same time, Mr. Hoover was raising the question at the meeting of the American delegation.

"*Mr. Hoover:* Apart from all questions of justice, how far does the question of expediency come in?"

---

[44] If we adopt the figure of Moulton and McGuire for the 1918-23 period, the total paid would come to a little more than 37 milliards.

[45] Lloyd George: *The Truth about the Peace Treaties*, vol. I, p. 701.

"President Wilson: In order to get them to sign, do you mean?

"Mr. Hoover: In order to get them to sign. It strikes me that that is a more important thing than the question of justice or injustice, because the weighing of justice and injustice in these times is pretty difficult.

"President Wilson: Yes, nobody can be sure they have made a just decision. But don't you think that if we regard the treaty as just, the argument of expediency ought not to govern, because, after all we must not give up what we fought for? We might have to fight for it again.

"Mr. Hoover: But we look at expediency in many lights. It may be necessary to change the terms of the reparation in view of getting something, rather than to lose all. And it is not a question of justice; justice would require, as I see it, that they pay everything they have got or hope to get. But in order to obtain something, it may be expedient to do this, that and the other."[46]

Expediency, therefore, could have been understood as requiring that Reparation demands should not be too heavy. In such a case, Mr. Keynes had shown a strong sense of political expediency in 1919. Yet, strangely enough, the criticism most frequently levelled against his book in early days was that it lacked all sense of political necessity. But, later on, it was his critics who were to be chaffed for their subservience to political opportunism and their disregard of economic laws. "One may," wrote Lord Stamp, several years afterwards, "distinguish political from economic wisdom by saying that the latter will and must ultimately prevail, but that it is too hard and unpalatable for a world that will not 'come off' its wishes until relentlessly pulled by the force of events. It may be political 'wisdom' to flatter the public mind with slightly weaker and weaker doses of what it likes and slightly stronger and stronger doses of what it will have to get used to. ... If that be the sense of political wisdom, then Mr. Keynes's book wholly lacked it."[47] Clearly "political necessity" could have more than one meaning.

I have endeavoured, for my part, to show that the demands of the Treaty of Versailles were not economically impossible. Whether they were *politically practicable* is of course another question. It could be contended that the economic and financial achievements of wartime were no longer obtainable in peacetime; that it was *politically impossible* for the Allies to enforce these demands upon the German people. We have seen, for instance, that Mr. Keynes did not believe that the German Government would have the power to increase the length of the working day. He feared, in 1919, that excessive demands might provoke revolution in Central Europe. He explicitly declared that there were cases where "particular claims, however well founded in sentiment or in justice, must yield to sovereign expediency."[48] And he claimed, a few years later, that neither the collection of War Debts nor the enforcement of Reparations was "serious politics" in the long run.[49]

The Economic Consequences of the Peace, therefore, did not "wholly lack" a sense of "political wisdom." It was probably impolitic to run the risk of incurring Germany's resentment if one was not prepared to take the consequences. It was certainly impolitic to overlook the indisputable fact that Germany's nuisance value

[46] Baker, vol. III, p. 501.

[47] Sir Josiah Stamp: "The Economic Consequences of the Peace," *Foreign Affairs,* October 1934, p. 106.

[48] *E.C.P.,* p. 89.

[49] *R.T.,* p. 165.

was greater than that of her victims. But then it is hard to see how this political wisdom on the international plane was very different, in moral essence, from (say) the subservience of politicians to the wrath of their electorates. It was only much later that "realism" was frankly invoked to justify the "appeasement" of Germany. But then Mr. Keynes protested that it was "to fraternize with what is vile."

In 1919, the Allied and Associated Powers, rightly or wrongly, had not believed that to compromise with justice would be an act of political wisdom. "Justice," they said in their Reply to the German delegation, " is the only possible basis for the settlement of the account of this terrible war. Justice is what the German delegation asks for and says that Germany has been promised. Justice is what Germany shall have. But it must be justice for all. There must be justice for the dead and wounded and for those who have been orphaned and bereaved that Europe might be freed from Prussian despotism. There must be justice for the peoples who now stagger under war debts which exceed £ 30,000,000,000 that liberty might be saved. There must be justice for those millions whose homes and land, ships and property German savagery has spoliated and destroyed.

"That is why the Allied and Associated Powers have insisted as a cardinal feature of the Treaty that Germany must undertake to made reparation to the uttermost of her power; for reparation for wrongs inflicted is of the essence of justice. . . . Somebody must suffer for the consequences of the war. Is it to be Germany, or only the peoples she has wronged?

"Not to do justice to all concerned would only leave the world open to fresh calamities. If the German people themselves, or any other nation, are to be deterred from following the footsteps of Prussia, if mankind is to be lifted out of the belief that war for selfish ends is legitimate to any State, if the old era is to be left behind and nations as well as individuals are to be brought beneath the reign of law, even if there is to be an early reconciliation and *appeasement*,[50] it will be because those responsible for concluding the war have had the courage to see that justice is not deflected for the sake of convenient peace."

But Mr. Keynes was not satisfied. "I cannot," he wrote, "leave this subject as though its just treatment wholly depended either on our own pledges or on economic facts. The policy of reducing Germany to servitude for a generation, of degrading the lives of millions of human beings, and of depriving a whole nation of happiness should be abhorrent and detestable—abhorrent and detestable, even if it were possible, even if it enriched ourselves, even if it did not sow the decay of the whole civilised life of Europe. Some preach it in the name of Justice. In the great events of man's history, in the unwinding of the complex fate of nations Justice is not so simple. And if it were, nations are not authorised, by religion or by natural morals, to visit on the children of their enemies the misdoings of parents or of rulers."[51] Amen. But what was to be *the alternative?* Could Mr. Keynes tell us *how* the innocent was to be saved? *Delicta majorum immeritus lues.* . . . What happened was that the misdoings of a nation were visited on the children of its victims.

* * *

As the years went by, Mr. Keynes was able to follow in some detail the fulfilment of his own prophecies, and to draw, from time to time, the attention of the public

[50] Italics mine.
[51] *E.C.P.*, pp. 209-10.

to the process. "So far," he wrote in 1921, "the forecasts, which I was rash enough to make 18 months ago, have been borne out by the event." First, the claims against Germany had been evaluated by the Reparation Commission at a total lying between the two limits of his own estimates. Second, "the Treaty provided for certain specific deliveries from Germany prior to May 1, 1921, and these were estimated in Paris at a prospective value of £1,000 million. I criticized this," continued Mr. Keynes, "and put the value at a maximum between 330 and 430 million; this was exclusive of current deliveries of coal," which now proved broadly correct. Thirdly, he had predicted that Germany's total output of coal would fall at least as low as 100,000,000 tons; this was exactly the figure for the year 1920. Lastly, the prediction that there would be a two-thirds majority for Germany in Upper Silesia was also confirmed by the plebiscite.[52]

We have already had occasion to acknowledge the correctness of Mr. Keynes's estimate of Germany's final liability. So far, so good. The next item calls for some reservations. Article 235 of the Treaty, as we have seen, had prescribed a payment of 20 milliard marks (£1,000 million) before 1 May 1921. The Treaty had also, quite independently, provided for certain specific deliveries, the value of which was to be credited to Germany in the discharge of that initial sum. But nowhere was it provided that these deliveries would cover it completely; on the contrary, one of the very features to which Mr. Keynes had taken the strongest exception was that the payment of the 20 milliard marks could be requested by the Reparation Commission "in such manner as they may fix, whether in gold, ships, securities or otherwise," implying thereby that the specific deliveries mentioned elsewhere would probably not be sufficient to cover that initial payment. As we have seen, the Commission did not even take the necessary steps to secure this payment; thus the foreign securities of Germany, for instance, which ranked at £100 to £250 million in Mr. Keynes's 1919 estimate of £330 to £430 million[53] were not even demanded. It was therefore most irrelevant to take the figure of £400 million published by the Commission in 1921, which represented the value of *all* the deliveries made by Germany up to that date, as comparable with the £330–430 million calculated in 1919 by Mr. Keynes of certain assets, some of which were never delivered.

The third forecast was not so very accurate either. The figure of 100 million tons mentioned in 1919 related to output exclusive of lost territory and of consumption at the mines.[54] The 100 million tons produced in 1920 were, as Mr. Keynes had indicated, inclusive of consumption at the mines; but he did not indicate so clearly that they were exclusive of *all* Upper Silesian territory. Now in 1920 partition had not yet taken place, and Germany's total coal output was then 131 million tons. But even if the loss of Polish Upper Silesia was reckoned, the total output, exclusive of lost territorities, was not 100, but 107.5 millions, since a substantial part of Upper Silesia was to be retained by Germany in the end. Perhaps I labour the point; but if Mr. Keynes had thought it worth while to draw the public's notice to this particular piece of prophecy, he might at least have got his figures right, the more so as his fourth forecast related to the Upper Silesian plebiscite, the result of which was to leave part of the district to Germany. While this prediction, again was correct, it was not one that pointed to any economic impossibility in the

[52] Letter to *The Times*, London, 2 May 1921.
[53] *E.C.P.*, pp. 168, 171.
[54] *E.C.P.*, p. 83.

enforcement of the Treaty, but to a possibility which the Treaty in the very provision for the plebiscite, had precisely taken into account—while Mr. Keynes's argument about this part of the Treaty had assumed that the whole of Upper Silesia would be lost, and indicated that to the extent that this assumption proved erroneous, "the conclusions must be modified."[55]

"All my other forecasts," Mr. Keynes had added, "still lie in the future." The future having now receded into past, we are to-day in a position to verify the full extent of their fulfilment.

In *The Economic Consequences of the Peace*, Mr. Keynes predicted that the Treaty, if it was carried into effect, "must impair yet further, when it might have restored, the delicate, complicated organisation, already shaken and broken by war, through which alone the European peoples can employ themselves and live."[56] Europe would be threatened with "a long, silent process of semi-starvation, and of a gradual, steady lowering of the standards of life and comfort."[57] Ten years after the Treaty, European production was well above its pre-war level, and European standards of living had never been higher.[58]

He predicted that the iron output of Europe would decline as a consequence of the Treaty.[59] In the ten years that followed the Treaty, the iron output of Europe, which had fallen considerably during the War, increased almost continuously.[60] In 1929, Europe produced 10 per cent more iron that in the record year 1913, and would no doubt have produced still more had not the producers combined to restrict output for fear of injuring prices by overproduction.

He predicted that the iron and steel output of Germany would diminish.[61] By 1927, Germany produced nearly 30 per cent more iron and 38 per cent more steel than in the record year 1913, within the same territorial limits.[62]

He predicted that the efficiency of the German coal-mining industry lowered by the War, would remain low as a consequence of the Peace.[63] By 1925, the efficiency of labour, which had dropped seriously in the meantime, was already higher, in the Ruhr coal industries, than in 1913; in 1927 it was higher by nearly 20 per cent; and in 1929 by more than 30 per cent.[64]

---

[55] *E.C.P.*, p. 78 n.
[56] *E.C.P.*, pp. 1-2.
[57] *E.C.P.*, p. 277.
[58] The general index of European production compiled by the Berlin Institut für Konjunkturforschung (Sonderheft No. 31, 1933, p. 66) shows that European production (U.S.S.R. excluded) had regained its pre-war level around 1925 and was above that level by 20 per cent in 1929.
[59] *E.C.P.*, p. 91.
[60] With one exception, in 1921. The output of pig-iron and ferro-alloys in Europe (U.S.S.R. excluded) was as follows (000,000 tons):

1909-13	1913	1920	1921	1922	1923	1924	1925	1926	1927	1928	1929
39.2	45.7	22.5	18.7	25.9	25.9	33.2	36.5	35.2	45.6	45.4	50.3

[61] *E.C.P.* pp. 89-92.
[62] See Reichs-Kredit-Gesellschaft, *Germany's Economic Development in the Second Half of the Year 1930*, Berlin, 1931, p. 6.
[63] *E.C.P.*, p. 92.
[64] Reichs-Kredit-Gesellschaft, op. cit., p. 15. Output per underground labourer was 1,161 kilogr. in 1931; in 1920 (after a reduction in working hours from 8 or 9 to 7 or 7½) output was 830 kilogr.; in 1921, 809 kilogr., and increased constantly after 1924, reaching 1,558 kilogr. in 1929.

He predicted that a pre-war level of output could not be expected in the German coal industry.[65] In 1920, 1921, and 1922, coal output was well above the average level of the five years preceding the war, within the same territorial limits. It fell sharply in 1923, and was slightly below pre-war average in 1924. It was above that average in 1925; and in 1926, it was already higher than in the record year 1913.[66]

He predicted that Germany "cannot export coal in the near future, ... if she is to continue as an industrial nation."[67] In the first year following the Treaty, Germany exported (net) 15 million tons of coal; and in 1926 she exported (net) 35 million tons, or *twice* the amount of the average (1909-13) pre-war exports of *all* her pre-war territories.[68]

He predicted that the German mercantile marine "cannot be restored for many years to come on a scale adequate to meet the requirements of her own commerce."[69] The total German tonnage was a little above 5 millions in 1913. It was reduced in 1920 to 673,000; but in 1924 it already approached 3 million tons; in 1930 it was well above 4 million, and German liners were the wonder of the transatlantic world.

He predicted that "after what she has suffered in the war and by the Peace," Germany's annual savings would "fall far short of what they were before."[70] The monthly increase in German savings bank deposits was 84 million in 1913; in 1925 it had become 103 million; and in 1928 it was nearly 210 million.[71]

He predicted that Germany's annual surplus would be reduced to less than 2 milliard marks.[72] In 1925, the net accumulation of domestic capital was at 6.4 milliards, and in 1927 at 7.5 milliards.[73]

He predicted that in the next thirty years, Germany could not possibly be expected to pay more than 2 milliard marks a year in Reparation. In the six years preceding September 1939, Germany, by Hitler's showing, had spent each year on rearmament alone about seven times as much.[74]

Here, if not before, the reader's patience comes to an end. What point can there be in all this pedantic splitting of statistical hairs? Will any amount of figures detract from the broad fact that the German people were thrown by the Treaty of Versailles into misery and despair, and that Mr. Keynes's apprehensions were very much more than confirmed?

In 1919 Mr. Keynes had quoted at length a Note addressed by Count Brockdorff-Rantzau to the Supreme Council, in which the Consequences of the Peace were duly outlined. After the diminution of products due to territorial losses, "after the economic depression resulting from the loss of her colonies, her merchant fleet and her foreign investments, Germany will not be in a position to import from abroad an adequate quantity of raw material. An enormous part of German industry

---

[65] *E.C.P.*, p. 83.
[66] *Supra*, p. 86.
[67] *E.C.P.*, p. 84.
[68] *Supra*, p. 86.
[69] *E.C.P.*, p. 61.
[70] *E.C.P.*, p. 191.
[71] Reichs-Kredit-Gesellschaft, *Germany's Economic Development in the First Half of the Year 1931*, p. 27.

[72] *E.C.P.*, p. 192.
[73] *Supra*, p. 116.
[74] There is, of course, nothing new about these facts. Several of them were pointed out by a witty and clairvoyant observer, R. C. Long (*The Mythology of Reparations*, London, 1928, pp. 103-4).

will, therefore, be condemned inevitably to destruction. The need of importing foodstuffs will increase considerably at the same time that the possibility of satisfying this demand is as greatly diminished. In a very short time, therefore, Germany will not be in a position to give bread and work to her numerous millions of inhabitants, who are prevented from earning their livelihood by navigation and trade. These persons should emigrate, but this is a material impossibility, all the more because many countries and the most important ones will oppose any German immigration. To put the Peace conditions into execution would logically involve, therefore, the loss of several millions of persons in Germany. . . . No help, however great, or over however long a period it were continued, could prevent these deaths *en masse*. . . . Those who sign this Treaty will sign the death sentence of many millions of German men, women and children." "I know," added Mr. Keynes, "of no adequate answer to these words."[75]

Yet there *had* been an answer. It had been sent, a few days later, by Clemenceau in the name of the Supreme Council. "This report," it said, "appears . . . to contain a very inadequate presentation of the facts of the case, to be marked in parts by great exaggeration, and to ignore the fundamental considerations arising both out of the incidence and the results of the War, which explain and justify the terms that it is sought to impose." The total population of Germany, the note went on, would be reduced by about six million persons in the non-German territories which it was proposed to transfer. "It is the needs of this reduced aggregate that we are called upon to consider." The note insisted that there was nothing in the Treaty to prevent either the continued production of commodities in the areas lost by Germany or their importation into Germany as before. "On the contrary, the free admission of the products of the Eastern districts is provided for during a period of three years. . . ."[76] The German Note complained repeatedly of the necessity to import certain products from abroad in future. "It is not understood why Germany should be supposed to suffer from conditions to which other countries contentedly submit. It would appear a fundamental fallacy that the political control of a country is necessary in order to procure a reasonable share of its products. Such a proposition finds no foundation in economic law or in history. . . . There is not the slightest reason to believe that a population is destined to be permanently disabled because it will be called upon in future to trade across its frontiers instead of producing what it requires from within. A country can both become and continue to be a great manufacturing country without producing the raw materials of its main industries. . . . There is no reason whatever why Germany, under the new conditions, would not build up for herself a position both of stability and prosperity in the European world."[77]

But perhaps Mr. Keynes did not think this was an *adequate* answer.

---

[75] *E.C.P.,* pp. 214-15.

[76] This part of the Note referred to the Eastern districts, but the same could, as we have seen, have been said of the other lost territories.

[77] Full text of the Note in Burnett, vol. II, Doc. 366, pp. 27-31. Curiously enough, this opinion was being shared, and expressed, almost at the same moment, by General Groener, then Head of the German Army. "The aim we must now, in my opinion, set before ourselves," he told a meeting of officers, "is to hold the 60 million Germans firmly together in one single State, as far as possible a centralized State. . . . When we have attained this, a great deal will have been gained. And if we then go on to steadily working, . . . then I do not see why we should not forge ahead again, especially in the economic field. . . ." (Quoted in K. F. Nowak, *Versailles*, London, 1928, pp. 280-1.)

Twenty-one years later, the German Army was entering Paris. With steady stride they came, the sturdy youths, marching along the streets of the half-deserted city to the tunes that had carried them across Europe. "Erika . . . Heidi, heido . . . Wir fahren gegen England." . . . Here were the "starved and crippled" children of 1919. They would soon be scouring across the steppes of Russia, the sands of Libya, the skies of London and of Crete, the waters of the broad Atlantic. . . . At the sight of them, the Parisian housewives broke out in angry stupefaction: "And we were told they were starving!"

Who knows an adequate answer to *these* words?

13 / Fascism

The search for an explanation and theory of fascism has produced a great variety of contradictory answers, especially in very recent years. From the end of World War II to the early 1960's scarcely a single work appeared in English on the nature and theory of fascism. True, the literature on Nazi Germany was fairly extensive and a few books on Italy under fascism had been published, but none of them really came to terms with the special problem of fascism as such. Then in 1963, Ernst Nolte's *Der Faschismus in Seiner Epoche*[1] appeared in Germany while Eugen Weber was completing his brief study of the *Varieties of Fascism* (Anvil Book, 1964). Both were comparative studies. The German title of Nolte's work is especially significant because it indicates his belief that fascism was a product of the general historical conditions of the twentieth century up to World War II.

Since 1966 ten or more important works have appeared which apply the comparative method to the study of fascism. True enough, there are very great differences and not a few contradictions between the many more or less fascistic movements and regimes. As Ernst Nolte argues: "the pupils of Fourier and St. Simon were not without reason bitter enemies. Yet there is no question but that a fundamental kinship existed. And just as the historian must protest the exclusion from socialism of all those who do not acknowledge the idea of a phalanstery, so he must object to the narrowing *a limine* of the concept of Fascism merely on account of isolated distinguishing marks."

Fruits of this recent spate of studies are the following observations which may serve as handy definitions of fascism in general. Naturally, they must be used with caution. Ernst Nolte, in the above cited work, concluded that "Fascism is anti-Marxism which seeks to destroy the enemy by the evolvement of a radically opposed and yet, related, ideology and by the use of almost identical and yet, typically modified methods, always, however, within the unyielding framework of national self-assertion and autonomy." John Weiss in *The Fascist Tradition: Radical Right-Wing Extremism in Modern Europe* (Harper & Row, 1967), asserts that fascism is a convenient term to describe certain movements hostile to liberal and socialist values and institutions. The movements, composed of traditional conservatives become *fascist* when they are combined with an effort to gain mass support and with a decision to use extreme violence and sophisticated methods of thought control.

[1] English translation, *Three Faces of Facscism* (Holt, Rinehart & Winston, 1966)

Two scholars, Wolfgang Sauer and Barrington Moore, Jr., have centered their analysis on the nature of the crisis which may lead to fascism. Wolfgang Sauer, in his "National Socialism: Totalitarianism or Fascism?" *(American Historical Review,* December, 1967) rejects Naziism as a merely German form of social disease. National socialism, he says, is also "fascism," that is, one national variety of a more general "mass movement with a character and aim of its own, indicating a major crisis in liberal democracy and capitalism." Sauer finds the heart of this crisis in the "industrialization process." Thus, fascism "can be defined as a revolt of those who lost—directly or indirectly, temporarily or permanently—by industrialization." The main losers were the various elements of the *Mittelstand* including peasants, small businessmen, artisans, many white collar workers, the lower levels of the professions, and the military. Certain upper class losers such as the aristocracy, the large landowners, and the high bureaucrats tended to react to the crisis in old-fashioned counter-revolutionary ways, but were nevertheless "potential allies of fascist regimes." In his *Social Origins of Dictatorship and Democracy,* Barrington Moore similarly stresses, and in much greater detail, the nexus between rapid social and economic change and fascism: the latter "is a product of both the intrusion of capitalism into the rural economy and of strains arising in the post-competitve phase of capitalist industry."

The first selection is the previously mentioned essay by Wolfgang Sauer, a professor at the University of California, Berkeley. Sauer urges a return to a socio-economic interpretation of fascism, albeit a "non-Marxist" one. What were the cultural and social conditions which encourgaged the development of fascism?

The second selection is from David Schoenbaum, *Hitler's Social Revolution: Class and Status in Nazi Germany 1933-1939.* Schoenbaum is less interested in the causes of fascism than its results.

All fascist movements claim to be revolutionary. National socialism was no exception. Did the Nazis in fact bring social revolution to Germany? Schoenbaum concludes that they did, but to a lesser degree and in different ways than they had originally intended.

NATIONAL SOCIALISM: TOTALITARIANISM OR FASCISM?

Wolfgang Sauer*

It is only two decades since National Socialism has left the scene, and yet the literature dealing with it is already immense. The fifty-year rule, never much respected by historians, has been quickly ignored in the face of so provoking a subject. This was all the more easy since, in this case, no Cerberus guarded the gates of the archives. Never before in the history of historiography did the documentary record of events become accessible to historians so quickly and comprehensively.

---

*Mr. Sauer, a professor at the University of California, Berkeley, wrote Part III of Karl Dietrich Bracher *et al., Die nationalsozialistische Machtergreifung: Studien zur Errichtung des totalitären Herrschaftssystems in Deutschland* (2d ed., Cologne, 1962). This article is an enlarged version of a paper presented to the Conference Group for Central European History at the Annual Meeting of the American Historical Association, San Francisco, California, December 28, 1965.

One of the thought-provoking effects of this state of affairs is that historians suddenly have begun to wonder whether this surfeit of documents may not be, as one of them put it in a recent review, "a source of confusion rather than clarification.[1]

One way to avoid confusion is to define clearly the concepts and theories used in interpreting Nazism and to evaluate them in terms of the available evidence. Such an enterprise may seem all the more urgent since well-established concepts have become questionable in recent years. The following discussion attempts to clarify the problem. It first surveys past efforts of interpretation, then reviews present studies in this field, and, finally, develops some suggestions for further interpretive analyses.

The study of Nazism has so far traversed three periods with the two turning points being the outbreak of the Second World War and the start of the cold war.[2] In the first period, prior to 1939, scholars tended to explain National Socialism in terms of fascism. Adolf Hitler seemed merely a German variant of Benito Mussolini, and both appeared, during the Great Depression and the popular front, to be but varieties of the agony of capitalism. Many writers were strongly influenced by socialist thought and, what is more, by socialist hopes. They sensed a profound revolutionary change in their time and interpreted it in terms of Marx's prophecies of the coming of the classless society. From this point of view, the rise of fascism in many parts of Europe appeared as a desperate last effort of monopoly capitalists to reassert their control over the masses against the tide of socialism, using the stick of terror and the carrot of pseudo socialism. Fascism, in this view, was understood as a mere manipulation by big business. The outstanding example of this approach was Franz L. Neumann's *Behemoth* with its emphasis on social and economic analysis.[3]

Historiography proper started with the Second World War. Under the impact of the war situation and in view of a growing awareness among social scientists of the differences between Nazism and other forms of fascism, authors tended to interpret the former as a Germanism, that is, some particularly German form of social diesease. Studies focused, consequently, on the historical roots of Nazism and analyzed them especially in terms of intellectual history. The tendency of scholars in this field to stress logical sequences in historical developments may have contributed to the well-known deterministic interpretation of German history. A. J. P. Taylor's *Course of German History*[4] is characteristic of this determinism, though Taylor did not emphasize intellectual history. German responses after 1945 varied from the apologetic tone of Gerhard Ritter to the searching analysis of Friedrich Meinecke and the universal view of Ludwig Dehio.[5]

---

[1] Walter Laqueur, "Nazism and the Nazis: On the Difficulties of Discovering the Whole Truth," *Encounter,* XXII (Apr. 1964), 41.

[2] For an earlier bibliographical survey, see Andrew G. Whiteside, "The Nature and Origins of National Socialism." *Journal of Central European Affairs* XVII (No. 1, 1957-58), 48-73.

[3] Franz, L. Neumann, *Behemoth: The Structure and Practice of National Socialism* (2d ed., New York, 1944).

[4] A. J. P. Taylor, *The Course of German History* (London 1945; 2d ed. New York 1962).

[5] Gerhard Ritter, *Europa und die deutsche Frage* (Munich, 1948), *Das deutsche Problem: Grundfragen deutschen Staatslebens gestern und heute* (new rev. ed., Munich 1962); Friedrich Meinecke, *Die deutsche Katastrophe* (Wiesbaden, 1946), tr. as *The German Catastrophe* (Boston, 1963); Ludwig Dehio, *Gleichgewicht und Hegemonie* (Krefeld, 1948), tr. as *The Precarious Balance* (New York, 1965).

In the third period, starting with the cold war, the prevalent interpretation was that of totalitarianism. Nazism now appeared as but one form of a more general disease of modern society similar to Communism. Socialist hopes had yielded to deep pessimism in light of such staggering and embarrassing experiences as World War II, the rule of Stalinism in Russia and in Eastern Europe, and the rise of mass society, automation, and managerial bureaucracy in the West. Instead of the end of capitalism, the end of civilization seemed to loom ahead. Characteristic is the change in the attitude of Neumann, who referred, in the early 1950's, to Sigmund Freud's idea that "conflicts deepen with the process of civilization, for . . . the increasing technical progress which in itself ought to make possible a greater measure of instinct gratification, fails to do so."[6] What was true of former Marxists was no less true of conservatives. To writers such as Hannah Arendt, Carl Joachim Friedrich, and Jacob L. Talmon,[7] totalitarianism appeared more or less a kind of suicide of civilization, a dialectical reversal by which progress turned against itself. Their studies stressed the omnipotence and the monolithic structure of totalitarian regimes and analyzed them in terms of the relationships between ideology and terror and between elites and masses.

It should be noted, however, that this survey deals with shifts in emphasis among interpretations and not with the replacement of one interpretation by another. Actually, the theories of fascism, Germanism, and totalitarianism coexisted to a degree from the outset.[8] In addition, a fourth interpretation that has emerged since the war defines Nazism as but a modern variant of classical tyranny. Held mainly by British historians, this view rejects the thesis advanced by Friedrich and others that totalitarian dictatorship is an entirely new phenomenon, unprecedented in history; the British school stresses, instead, historical continuity. In this regard it approaches the thesis of Dehio, who interpreted Nazism as the last link in a long chain of European struggles for hegemony. The case of tyranny has been most powerfully argued by Alan Bullock in his biography of Hitler, but similar views have been held both by Hugh Trevor-Roper, who compared what he called Hitler's court to the late Roman monarchy, and by Taylor, who recently argued that Hitler was but a traditional statesman.[9] The discontinuity thesis has been rejected, interestingly enough, also for Communism. Karl Wittfogel, for example, has maintained that a continuity runs from Oriental despotism to modern Communist totalitarianism in Russia and China.[10]

These historicist interpretations in terms of classical tyranny or Oriental despotism have so far been what might be called a minority opinion. Yet they should be noted the more carefully since the totalitarianism approach has generally begun to lose ground since the end of the 1950's. Khrushchev's anti-Stalinist and coexistence

[6] Franz L. Neumann, *The Democratic and the Authoritarian State* (Glencoe, Ill., 1957), 273.

[7] Hannah Arendt, *The Origins of Totalitarianism* (2d, enlarged ed., Cleveland 1958); Carl J. Friedrich and Zbigniew K. Brzezinski, *Totalitarian Dictatorship and Autocracy* (Cambridge, Mass. 1956); Jacob L. Talmon, *The Origins of Totalitarian Democracy* (London, 1952).

[8] The shifts in emphasis can clearly be observed if one rearranges the works quoted in Whiteside, "Nature and Origins of National Socialism," according to date of publication.

[9] Alan Bullock, *Hitler: A Study in Tyranny* (rev. ed., New York, 1960); Hugh R. Trevor-Roper, *The Last Days of Hitler* (London 1947); A. J. P. Taylor, *The Origins of the Second World War* (London, 1961).

[10] Karl A. Wittfogel, *Oriental Despotism: A Comparative Study of Total Power* (New Haven, Conn., 1957).

policies, the conflict between Russian and Chinese Communism, and a growing awareness in the West that industrial society might eventually produce mass prosperity rather than deadly conflict—all these developments militated against the apocalyptic visions of the totalitarianism theory. In addition, scholars had meanwhile begun to penetrate the mountains of documentary material and had gained a closer view of the historical realities of the Third *Reich*. These realities proved to be quite different from the monolithic image of totalitarianism. If we compare, for example, the view of Nazi rule as it emerges from Friedrich's studies to that which appears in Robert Koehl's article on "Feudal Aspects of National Socialism,"[11] we might wonder whether the two authors are talking about the same subject.

An unfortunate effect of using the totalitarianism approach is the emergence of a striking imbalance in covering the field of Nazi history. While we have an abundance of studies on the Nazi terror system, on military and war history, and on the history of the resistance, we know little or nothing about the problems of Nazi domestic politics and social history after 1934. The feuds within and between the bureaucracy and the party, the organization and social composition of the party and most of its affiliated organizations, the Nazi economic policy, particularly the Four-Year Plan, the effects of this policy and of the war on German society, and the attitude of various social groups, particularly of the workers, toward the Nazi government are subjects of major importance that are neglected to a surprising degree by studies of Nazism.[12] Even in the case of Nazi ideology, we know more about its roots and about its propaganda system[13] than about its structure and its functional role in the social system.

Such evidence seems clearly to suggest that a revision of the existing conceptual framework is needed. To be sure, the totalitarianism theory cannot be dismissed entirely. Modern dictatorships have undoubtedly developed new characteristics, and totalitarianism is certainly one of them. It is, however, hardly as important as the totalitarianism theory has maintained. The theory of Germanism has been abandoned already as a possible alternative; William Shirer's attempt to revive it was a popular rather than a scholarly success.[14] The question as to why Nazism rose just in Germany certainly remains, but scholars seem generally to agree that the understanding of the problem needs a wider horizon than a mere national perspective can provide.

Recent writings even show a tendency to conceive the responsibility for the Nazi atrocities in a broader way than before. This problem has caused three of the most passionate debates in recent years: the controversies over Arendt's comment on Adolph Eichmann, over Rolf Hochhuth's criticism of Pope Pius XII, and over

[11] Robert Koehl, "Feudal Aspects of National Socialism," *American Political Science Review*, LIV. (Dec. 1960), 921-33.

[12] For some recent studies indicating a change, see note 19, below. One of the neglected topics is the story of rescuers of Jews. Research in this field has recently been organized by Rabbi Harold M. Schulweis in the Institute for the Righteous Acts, Oakland, California. For an earlier attempt see Kurt R. Grossmann, *Die unbesungenen Helden: Menschen in Deutschlands dunkelsten Tagen* (Berlin, 1957).

[13] The most recent contributions are Zbyneck A.B. Zeman, *Nazi Propaganda* (Oxford Eng., 1964), and Ernest K. Bramsted, *Goebbels and National Socialist Propaganda, 1925-1945* (East Lansing, Mich., 1965). Haio Holborn, "Origins and Political Character of Nazi Ideology," *Political Science Quarterly*, LXXIX (Dec. 1964), 542-54, gives valuable suggestions for a comprehensive analysis. Specifically, the press is treated by Oron J. Hale, *The Captive Press in the Third Reich* (Princeton, N. J., 1964).

[14] William L. Shirer, *The Rise and Fall of the Third Reich* (New York, 1960).

Taylor's new *coup de main* on the established thesis regarding the origins of the Second World War.[15] Historiography has gained from these debates mainly by the stimulation they provided. Books like Raul Hilberg's *The Destruction of the European Jews* and Ernst-Wolfgang Böckenförde's critical article on German Catholicism in 1933[16] had dealt even earlier with similar problems. Taylor's book, however, raises a major historiographical problem that deserves brief discussion here.

Taylor's thesis is professedly an attempt to anticipate a revision of historical opinion, which he believes will eventually occur as it did after World War I. But the idea of revision arose after 1918 from original research rather than from a consideration of what future historians might say. Taylor's results are not, however, too convincing in terms of research. His thesis seems to be, therefore, but an attempt to escape a condition that is at least uncommon, if not unprecedented, in historiography. In Nazism, the historian faces a phenomenon that leaves him no way but rejection, whatever his individual position. There is literally no voice worth considering that disagrees on this matter, and it is probably not accidental that Taylor felt the stress of the situation most strongly.[17] Does not such fundamental rejection imply a fundamental lack of understanding? And if we do not understand, how can we write history? The term "understanding" has, certainly, an ambivalent meaning; we can reject and still "understand." And yet, our intellectual, and psychological, capacities reach, in the case of Nazism, a border undreamed of by Wilhelm Dilthey. We can work out explanatory theories, but, if we face the facts directly, all explanations appear weak.

Thus, the attempt to write the history of Nazism confronts the historian with an apparently unsolvable dilemma and raises the question of what historical understanding and historical objectivity may mean in the face of Nazism. One of the merits of the totalitarianism theory was that it took care of this condition; from this point of view, one might be tempted to define it as a scoholarly formulation of our lack of understanding.

Is there a better way to conceal our weakness? Among the established concepts one remains: fascism. To be sure, the theory of fascism has also suffered severely from both the politics of and the historical studies on Nazism. This concerned, however, the Marxist-Leninist interpretation of fascism, and it may be worthwhile to ask if this interpretation is the only possible one. Attempts have indeed been made recently to repair the damaged tool for use. Some outstanding examples are Seymour Lipset's *Political Man,* which contains a comprehensive study of fascism on the basis of election analyses; Iring Fetscher's article on *Faschismus and Nationalsozialismus,* in which the author explicitly aims at a refutation of the Marxist concept of fascism; Eugen Weber's works on the *Action Française* and the European Right; and Ernst Nolte's volume *Der Faschismus in seiner Epoche* of which an English translation has meanwhile appeared. Mention must also be made in this context of Arthur Schweitzer's *Big Business in the Third Reich* in which the author attempts, unsuccessfully, I believe, to fuse elements of Max Weber's and

---

[15] Hannah Arendt, *Eichmann in Jerusalem: A Report on the Banality of Evil* (New York, 1963); Rolf Hochhuth, *Der Stellvertreter* (Hamburg, 1963) tr. as *The Deputy* (New York, 1964); Taylor, *Origins of the Second World War.*

[16] Raul Hilberg, *The Destruction of the European Jews* (Chicago, 1961); Ernst-Wolfgang Böckenförde, "Der deutsche Katholizismus im Jahre 1933," *Hochland, LIII* (No. 3, 1961), 215-30.

[17] For a historiographical analysis of Taylor's work, see Edward B. Segel, "A. J. P. Taylor and History," *Review of Politics, XXVI* (Oct. 1964), 531-46.

Marxist theories.[18] These works constitute, as a whole and despite differences in approach and position, the first serious attempt to develop a workable, non-Marxist concept of fascism. Their results are less conclusive regarding the relationship between fascism and totalitarianism; this issue needs further clarification. A shift in emphasis toward an interpretation in terms of fascism is, nevertheless, unmistakable. In this context it is notable that works like William S. Allen's study of Nazi rule in a northern German town, Schweitzer's study, and Alan S. Milward's brilliant book on *The German Economy at War*[19] show a disposition of historians to turn to the neglected topics of Nazi history. In the case of Schweitzer the turn is obviously related to the fascism approach; his book continues the earlier analysis of Neumann. Allen and Milward, by contrast, seem to have chosen their subjects without major theoretical considerations.[20] But whatever the reasons for this turn, the tendency expressed in all of these works seems to be the most characteristic development in recent studies of Nazism.

Leaving aside the mainly empirical studies of Allen and Milward, we may ask what image of fascism emerges from these works. A summary is naturally difficult in view of the differences in individual positions, and yet there are two closely related points of agreement. First, the authors agree that fascism is not, as the Marxist interpretation holds, merely a manipulation by monopoly capitalists: it is a mass movement with a character and aim of its own, indicating a major crisis in liberal democracy and capitalism. Whether or not this crisis is temporary remains controversial. Second, it is now established beyond doubt that the lower middle classes, both rural and urban, were at least one of the major social components of fascist movements.

There are also many divergences and discrepancies, however. Some confusion exists regarding the distinction between fascist movements and fascist regimes. Fetscher's analysis shows that fascist movements can ally, in view of their basic opportunism, with a wide variety of other groups; Schweitzer has exemplified this in the case of Nazism.[21] Consequently, there may be a marked difference between the original, relatively homogeneous fascist movements prior to the seizure of power and what emerges as fascist regimes after that event. This leads to the equally important problem of the relationships between fascist movements and their allies. For example, Lipset's interesting definition of fascism as the extremism of the

[18] Seymour M. Lipset, *Political Man* (New York, 1960), Chap. v; Iring Fetscher, "Faschismus und Nationalsozialismus: Zur Kritik des sowjetmarxistischen Faschimusbegriffs," *Politische Viertelighrsschrift, III* (Mar. 1962), 42-63; Eugen Weber, *Action Française* (Stanford, Calif., 1962); *The European Right: A Historical Profile,* ed. Hans Rogger and Eugen Weber (Berekley, Calif., 1964); Eugen Weber, *Varieties of Fascism* (Princeton, N. J., 1964); Ernst Nolte, *Der Faschismus in seiner Epoche* (Munich, 1963), tr. as *Three Faces of Fascism* (New York, 1966); Arthur Schweitzer, *Big Business in the Third Reich* (Bloomington, Ind., 1964).

[19] William S. Allen, *The Nazi Seizure of Power: The Experience of a Single German Town. 1930-1935* (Chicago, 1965); Alan S. Milward, *The German Economy at War* (London, 1965). Since the completion of this article in May 1966, further studies have been published confirming this trend and covering many of the hitherto neglected subjects.

[20] Allen tends, in fact, to use the totalitarianism concept, but his results disprove largely his thesis that Nazi rule led to an "atomization" of society. (See, e.g., Allen, *Nazi Seizure of Power,* 278.)

[21] Schweitzer, *Big Business,* distinguishes two periods in the Nazi rule: "partial Fascism" with alliances between fascism and other groups until 1936 and "full Fascism" after this date. The thesis is basically correct (see page 419, below), though Schweitzer is too rigid on several points. (Cf. Carl Landauer's criticism, *Journal of Economic History, XXV* [1965], 293-95.)

liberal Center, in contrast to Right-wing extremism and Left-wing extremism (Communism), does not sufficiently explain why fascist regimes were frequently built on alliances with conservatives while alliances with Communists never materialized. Which social groups, then, were likely to become allies of fascist movements, and what functional role did these alliances play in the structure of the individual fascist regimes?

Other questions concern the social composition and the revolutionary aims of the movements. On the first question, most authors limit their analysis to the lower middle class and the problems of its definition. This is, indeed, an important issue since the concept of the lower middle class still needs clarification, both in itself and in relation to the varieties of fascist supporters. Historical evidence shows that support of fascism may not be confined to the classical elements of the lower middle class *(Mittelstand* – peasants, artisans, small businessmen, and so forth), but may extend to a wide variety of groups in the large field between the workers on the one hand and big business, the aristocracy, and the top levels of bureaucracy on the other. This evidence agrees, interestingly enough, with Leo Baeck's statement that it was among the workers, the aristocracy, and the upper strata of the civil servants that the Jews found strongest support against persecution in Germany.[22]

Important as such an analysis is, however, it is still incomplete; it neglects the military element as a major social component of fascist movements. The military is apparently still not a category for social analysts. Among the authors quoted, only Fetscher recognizes its importance to fascism. It may even be said that a distinct interest group was formed within the fascist mixture by what might be called the military desperadoes, veterans of the First World War and the postwar struggles, who had not been reintegrated into either the civilian society or the armed forces. In an age of mass armies they were a sizable minority. Having become primitive warriors in four years and more of struggles, they sought to return into the arms of the mother army and to reform it according to their own model. Their conflict with society was, hence, not mainly economic, though this factor certainly was not absent. The main conflict was that between militarism and pacifism. In a time when the League of Nations appealed to the widespread war-weariness and the rising pacifism of the masses, the military desperadoes fought, not only for their own survival, but for the survival of soldiery in general.

The desperadoes were, thus, natural participants in the fascist revolution, but they did not merge entirely in the movement. Both in Italy and Germany the social differentiation was reflected in varying degrees in organizational differentiations between the party and the militia or the *Sturmabteilung* (SA), respectively. This indicates that the conflict over militarism re-emerged in varied form within the fascist movements. What was a conflict of principles in the relationship between the military desperadoes and society was a conflict of preferences in the fascist movements. The lower-middle-class groups and the military desperadoes considered each other as tools. The lower-middle-class members regarded the military desperadoes as a weapon to force their way into government; the military desperadoes hoped that the lower-middle-class members would provide the mass basis without which they could not expect to rule.

After the seizure of power the smoldering conflict within the fascist movements had to be resolved if the fascist regimes were to last. In Germany the conflict was

---

[22] *Das Dritte Reich und die Juden,* ed. Leon Poliakov and Josef Wulf (Berlin, 1955), 439.

terminated by Hitler when, in June 1934, he crushed the Röhm "revolt" which was, as I should like to maintain against Hermann Mau and others, predominantly a movement of the military desperadoes.[23] To be sure, the SA contained in its rank and file large parts of the lower-middle-class Nazi supporters, but Ernst Röhm had ousted their representative in the leadership of the SA Chief of Staff Otto Wagener, immediately after he assumed office in 1931.[24] Röhm was, and always remained, the leader of the military desperadoes, and he defended their interests in 1934. He may have received some lower-middle-class support, so that his opposition might appear, consequently, as an embryonic revolt of the movement against Hitler's alliance with big business and the *Reichswehr*. Yet Röhm's opposition was aimed as much against the Nazi party as against Hitler, and his victory would invariably have led to a conflict with, and possibly a defeat of, the lower-middle-class forces. They were not better off with Hitler, however; the party won against Röhm, but lost against Hitler (and, *nota bene,* Heinrich Himmler and Hjalmar Schacht). Hitler's victory prevented the pending conflict within the movement from breaking through the facade of the *Volksgemeinschaft,* and rearmament "resolved" the conflict by securing occupations both for all types of business and for the desperadoes. It may be added that basically the same situation existed in Italy, though things were somewhat different, and, above all, less radical, there. One wonders whether Mussolini's imperialist adventure in Abyssinia did not play a role equivalent to Hitler's crushing of the Röhm revolt.[25]

The control fascist regimes achieved over the dynamism of their movements creates doubts concerning the revolutionary character of fascist movements. There is virtual agreement among scholars that fascist movements contained, contrary to the Marxist thesis, a true revolutionary potential. This seems to conflict, however, with the noted opportunism of these movements. Rudolf Heberle's well-known study on the Schleswig-Holstein peasants, recently republished in its unabridged German form,[26] first revealed this point, and Lipset has now been able to generalize Heberle's results. A look at the fascist regimes in operation, moreover, would show that, whatever the revolutionary potential of the movements, the revolutionary results were meager.

How can this problem be resolved? May an answer be found by setting fascism in a wider historical framework? This is the way Nolte approaches his subject, but his answer is suggestive rather than conclusive. He advances the thesis that fascism was a revolt against the universal process of secularization, democratization, and international integration in the modern era. When this process reached its critical stage in the period of the two world wars, those elements in the culture that were

[23] Hermann Mau, "Die 'zweite Revolution'–der 30. Juni 1934," *Vierteljahrshefte für Zeitgeschichte,* I (Apr. 1953), 121. Cf. my analysis of the SA and the Röhm crisis in Karl Dietrich Bracher *et al., Die nationalsozialistische Machtergreifung: Studien zur Errichtung des totalitären Herrschaftssystems in Deutschland* (2d ed., Cologne, 1962), 829-966. In the present article, I have tried to supplement the political analysis of my earlier study by adding a social dimension.

[24] Cf. Bracher *et al., Nationalsozialistische Machtergreifung,* 882-83.

[25] See Gaetano Salvemini, *Under the Axe of Fascism* (New York, 1936), 391. Salvemini's suggestion of a comparison between Mussolini's Abyssinian war and Hitler's Röhm purge has so far not been taken up by historians.

[26] Rudolf Heberle, *Landbevölkerung und Nationalsozialismus: Eine soziologische Untersuchung der politischen Willensbildung in Schleswig-Holstein 1918 bis 1932* (Stuttgart, 1963), tr. as *From Democracy to Nazism: A Regional Case Study on Political Parties in Germany* (Baton Rouge, La., 1945).

doomed to perish revolted, according to Nolte, with increasing radicalism and decreasing rationality, or, in national terms, from the French *Action Française* through Italian Fascism to German National Socialism. On the last, most radical stage, fascism turned, Nolte argues, into a resistance against what he calls the "transcendence." He does not succeed, however, in clarifying this point sufficiently.

Nolte's thesis is not new in terms of facts. Its originality lies in assigning a metaphysical dimension to the fascist revolt and definitely attaching this revolt to a historical period. Fascism, Nolte suggests, is dead. This is, on the one hand, a more optimistic variation of the totalitarianism analysis; on the other hand, he tries to ascribe a historical meaning to fascism, which would provide a starting point for historical understanding. Much of this remains abstract and vague, however—mere *Ideengeschichte*. If the modernization process was universal, was fascist revolt also universal? If so, why does Nolte deal only with France, Italy, and Germany? If not, why did the fascist revolt occur only in these (and some other) countries? And what was the cause for differentiation? Why was this revolt most radical in Germany? Or, to put the question in a sociological rather than a national form, which social groups provided the mass basis of fascism, and why were just these groups antimodernist in their orientation? Why did the antimodernist fascist revolt frequently foster industrialization? And, finally, what exactly does "transcendence" mean, and by which concrete means did the fascist resistance against it manifest itself?

Nolte's neglect of these questions can be attributed primarily to his method, which he calls "phenomenological" and which he conceives as an attempt to return to G. W. F. Hegel's integration of philosophy and history.[27] This attempt is, however, problematical. Hegel's striking success in synthesizing philosophy and history depended on his dialectical "logic"; Nolte's method is not dialectical. Nor does Nolte develop an alternative. He has not succeeded, therefore, in invalidating Leopold von Ranke's argument against Hegel that philosophy in itself does not produce a method for the analysis and organization of empirical facts. Philosophy alone was, indeed, not sufficient for Nolte; his phenomenological method turns out, under scrutiny, to be essentially Dilthey's good, old method of empathy, supplemented by some fragmentary social-scientific concepts formed *ad hoc* to satisfy immediate needs.

To be sure, Nolte makes this method operative by confining his study mainly to an interpretation of the ideas of the fascist leaders—Charles Maurras, Mussolini, Hitler—and he achieves much in this way, especially with regard to psychological and ideological analysis. Such a biographical approach is too narrow, however, to support Nolte's generalizations. What is true of the fascist leaders is not necessarily true of the masses of their followers. Their attitudes and motivation can be recognized only by a social analysis that includes economic factors. Nolte would perhaps respond to such a suggestion with as much contempt as he shows for the use of the concept of industrialization.[28] What does his concept of "practical transcendence" mean, however, if not that economic factors have adopted in modern societies a significance that transcends their "materialistic" meaning? And if this is true, how can we expect to gain meaningful results about modern societies without taking these factors into account? Nolte's method, in fact, seems to conflict heavily with his concept of "practical transcendence."

[27] Nolte, *Der Faschismus,* 516-17.
[28] *Ibid.,* 541.

This must raise some doubts about the origin of Nolte's thesis of fascism as an antimodernist revolt. Indeed, he seems to have obtained his thesis, not through his biographical analyses, but rather through an analysis of Maurras's ideas. Nolte's decision, not too plausible at first glance, to raise the *Action Française* to a prominent position in the history of the origins of fascism, has actually, methodological rather than historical reasons. The *Action Française* is important to Nolte because Maurras succeeded in building an intellectual bridge between the counterrevolutionary tradition and fascism, thereby establishing a unified concept of antimodernism that Nolte found apparently suggestive as an analytical concept for his own study. His chapter on the *Action Française* is, thus, actually a part of his methodological introduction.

The conclusion that Nolte arrived at his thesis in a methodologically irregular way does not necessarily imply that the thesis is wrong. It does imply, however, that he has not proven his case. Fascism and counterrevolution are actually different social phenomena, the latter being the earlier position of a part of what has been defined here as the allies of fascism. Fascism had its own independent antecedents: pseudo revolutionaries like Father Jahn and the anti-Semites of the 1880's and 1890's (as examples in Germany.[29] To be sure, counterrevolution showed a combination of revolutionary and reactionary elements similar to fascism, but it was a revolution from above while fascism is a revolution from below. The discussion of Maurras by Nolte explains, therefore, the possibility of the fascist-conservative alliance, but it does not explain fascism. Nor does Nolte provide a satisfying answer to the question of the origins of fascism, especially in the German case. Nolte's chapters on pre-1914 Germany and Austria are in fact among the weakest in his book, though this is owing partly to Nolte's general weakness in historical knowledge.

These criticisms do not, however, detract from the value of the book, which is a major step forward in the study of fascism. If verified, Nolte's hypothesis can offer, for example, an explanation for the fascist tendencies in the military; its metaphysical implications might, in addition, open a way to understand certain aspects in the relationship between the churches and fascism. Nolte might indeed have achieved his aim of developing a comprehensive theory of fascism had it not been for his mistaken conception of the relationship of philosophy and history and his refusal to consider the socioeconomic aspects of the problem.

The task is, then, to provide the non-Marxist theory of fascism with a socioeconomic dimension; more precisely, the task is to bring the earlier attempts of this kind up to date. Some contributors to the discussion in the 1930's have already laid important foundations for a socioeconomic theory of fascism.[30] We have only to adjust these foundations to today's advanced stage of practical experience,

[29] The German anti-Semitic movement around 1900 has attracted, understandably enough, much attention in recent years. It is important to note, however, that it was only a part of a broader trend that extended to France (the Dreyfus affair, Edouard Drumont) and Austria (Karl Lueger and the Christian-Social party). As a whole, it has not yet been sufficiently investigated: Nolte *(Der Faschismus)* and Weber *(Action Française)* focus on France while Peter G. J. Pulzer, *The Rise of Political Anti-Semitism in Germany and Austria* (New York, 1964), disregards France.

[30] Harold D. Lasswell, "The Psychology of Hitlerism," *Political Quarterly* (No. 4, 1933), 373-84; David J. Saposs, "The Role of the Middle Class in Social Development: Fascism, Populism, Communism, Socialism," in *Economic Essays in Honor of Wesley Clair Mitchell, Presented to Him by His Former Students on the Occasion of His 60th Birthday* (New York, 1935); Talcott Parsons, "Some Sociological Aspects of the Fascist Movement," (1941), reprinted in Talcott Parsons, *Essays in Sociological Theory* (Glencoe, Ill., 1954).

historical research, and theoretical thought. With regard to theory the most important recent contribution probably comes from economic historians who have worked out, on the basis of the experiences of both the Great Depression and the underdeveloped countries, a non-Marxist concept of economic development that is highly suggestive to the analysis of fascism.

The attempt to use this concept for the interpretation of fascism poses, of course, certain problems. The Marxist trap of economic determinism is but a minor difficulty. Apart from the fact that the difference between causes and conditions in social developments has meanwhile become sufficiently familiar to social scientists, it must also be stressed that the main purpose in using, here, an economic theory for a historical analysis is merely a heuristic one. In addition, the "theory of economic growth" is, in the last analysis, not strictly an economic theory. It is rather a historical synthesis of the process of industrialization on the basis of a socioeconomic analysis. Consequently, it already implies that the relationship between social and economic factors is a reversible one. In applying this theory to the interpretation of fascism, we merely shift the perspective without abandoning reversibility.

A more important problem arises because we have to face, as usual, several conflicting formulations of that theory. Only those formulations that focus on continental European conditions, however, are useful to the analysis of fascism. This reduces the number of alternatives to two: the models of Alexander Gerschenkron and W. W. Rostow.[31] If we analyze the results of these two theories with regard to the social context of industrialization, we find that they are complementary. Gerschenkron's theory of "relative backwardness" provides a model of historical differentiation missing in Rostow's "stage" theory, and the latter offers a model for periodization not developed by Gerschenkron.

The critical problem is the development of a model for the advanced period of the industrialization process. Gerschenkron's model of relative backwardness cannot be directly extended to it since it deals with the starting conditions, while Rostow's definition as a stage of "high mass consumption" is still unsatisfactory.[32] Rostow hits, certainly, the essential point: that industry if it exceeds a certain limit of growth, must turn to mass production. He is also aware that private mass consumption is not the only possible response. Rostow's idea, however, that societies on the stage of mass production have a choice between high mass consumption and national political expansion (or, between private mass consumption and mass consumption by the state), does not entirely agree with the historical evidence. There is certainly an element of choice in the situation; yet it may well be that there are also constraints working against a choice. They may be owing to the consequences of relative backwardness, or to differential national developments and resulting international tensions and crises such as war. Rostow

---

[31] Alexander Gerschenkron, *Economic Backwardness in Historical Perspective* (Cambridge, Mass., 1962), esp. 1-51, 353–64; W. W. Rostow, *The Stages of Economic Growth* (Cambridge, Eng., 1959); *The Economics of Take-off into Sustained Growth*, ed. id. (London, 1963). Cf. the review by Henry Rosovsky, "The Take-off into Sustained Controversy," *Journal of Economic History*, XXV (1965), 271-75.

[32] Rosovsky, "The Take-off," 274-75, proposes to replace the concept of "stage" by that of the "long swing." This might, however, deprive the concept of growth of its meaning and would necessitate, therefore, a decision on whether the idea of growth should be abandoned altogether or whether the idea of swing must be adjusted to that of growth. In the latter case, the concept of stage might prove indispensable as a complement.

neglects the impact of national economic growth on international relations and vice versa; this seems to be, in fact, the major weakness of his theory. If we analyze twentieth-century history from this point of view, we do indeed find a period of world crises (World War I, the Great Depression, World War II) spreading between Rostow's stages of industrial maturity and high mass consumption.

In terms of a theory of economic growth revised in this way, fascism can be defined as a revolt of those who lost—directly or indirectly, temporarily or permanently—by industrialization. Fascism is a revolt of the *déclassés*. The workers and industrialists do not fall under this definition; it applies mainly to most of the lower middle class as defined above. They indeed suffered, or feared they would suffer, from industrialization—peasants who opposed the urbanizing aspects of industrialism; small businessmen and those engaged in the traditional crafts and trades that opposed mechanization or concentration; white-collar workers (at least as long as they felt the loss of economic independence); lower levels of the professions, especially the teaching profession, which opposed changing social values; and so forth. Also, the military joins here, with opposition against the industrialization of war, which tended to destroy traditional modes of warfare and which by its increasing destructiveness intensified pacifism and antimilitarism. On the other hand, groups like the aristocracy, the large landlords, the higher bureaucrats, and so on, who lost also by industrialization, generally did not turn to fascism. In continuing the counterrevolutionary position, they defended hierarchical society and abhorred, therefore, the egalitarian elements in fascism. In exact distinction, then, fascist movements represented the reaction of the lower-class losers, while the upper-class losers tended to react in a nonfascist way, but were potential allies of fascist regimes.

Such an analysis seems to be a way of explaining the intriguing paradox of a revolutionary mass movement whose goals were antirevolutionary in the classical sense. As a movement of losers, it turned against technological progress and economic growth; it tried to stop or even to reverse the trend toward industrialization and to return to the earlier, "natural" ways of life. In this respect the movement was reactionary, but, as a movement of the lower classes, its means were necessarily revolutionary. In defining fascism as a revolt of losers, we can also understand better both fascist atavism and fascist opportunism. Since the process of industrialization as a whole is irresistible, the existence of civilization is inextricably bound to it. Fascist revolt against industrialization must, therefore, eventually turn against civilization too. This was most evident in Germany, where Nazism developed into full fledged neobarbarism, but it is also true of the other fascist movements, though for various reasons neobarbarism remained, there, more or less underdeveloped. Such a definition of fascism as a neobarbaric revolt against civilization seems to describe in more concrete terms what Nolte calls the resistance against the "transcendence."

The same condition led to fascist opportunism. Since fascists acted, as losers, essentially from a position of weakness, they were compelled, in spite of their tendency toward violence, to compromise with their environment, even with their industrial enemy. This accounts for the contradiction that fascist regimes often fostered industrialization and yet insisted, ultimately, upon setting the clock back. The dialectic that resulted from this condition led eventually to a point at which the movement assumed suicidal proportions. Industrialization was sought in order to destroy industrial society, but since there was no alternative to industrial society, the fascist regime must eventually destroy itself. This was the situation of Nazism. The Nazis built an industrial machinery to murder the Jews, but once in operation the machine would have had to continue and would have ruined, indirectly at least, first the remnants of civilized society and then the fascist regime. Industrialization of mass murder was, thus, the only logical answer Nazism had to the problems of industrial society.

The analysis of fascism in terms of economic growth also offers a way to define more précisely the fallacy in the Marxist-Leninist concept of fascism. The fallacy lies in that Marxism blurs the distinction between early commercial and late industrial capitalism. Fascism indicated a conflict within capitalism, between traditional forms of commercialism and the modern form of industrialism. The fact that the former had survived in the twentieth century only on the lower levels of the middle classes accounted for the social locus of fascism. It is true, therefore, that fascism was capitalist by nature; it is not true that it was industrial. It is also true that fascist regimes often were manipulated in varying ways and degrees, but the share of industrialists in manipulation was rather small. Fetscher shows convincingly that the share was indeed larger in industrially underdeveloped Italy than it was in industrially advanced Germany.

On the other hand, the difference between fascism and Bolshevism appears, in light of this analysis, more fundamental than the totalitarianism analysis would admit. Neither V. I. Lenin nor Joseph Stalin wished to turn the clock back; they not merely wished to move ahead, but they wished to jump ahead. The Bolshevik revolution had many elements of a development revolution not unlike those now under way in the underdeveloped countries. One of the striking differences between the two systems appears in the role of the leaders. The social and political order of Bolshevism is relatively independent from the leadership; it is, so to speak, more objective. Fascist regimes, by contrast, are almost identical with their leaders; no fascist regime has so far survived its leader. This is why Bullock's interpretation of Hitler in terms of traditional tyranny has some bearing. The limits of this approach would become evident, I believe, if scholars could be persuaded to balance their interest in Hitler's secret utterances and political and military scheming by also stressing his role as a public speaker. The Nazi mass rallies with their immediate, ecstatic communication between leader and followers were, indeed, what might be called a momentary materialization of the Nazi utopia, at least so far as the "Nordic race" was concerned.[33]

Finally, it is plain from an analysis in terms of economic growth that the degree of radicalization must somehow be related to the degree of industrialization. The more highly industrialized a society, the more violent the reaction of the losers. Thus Germany stood at the top, Italy lagged behind, and Spain and others were at the bottom. In Germany, fascism gained sufficient momentum to oust its allies. By

---

[33] This is one of the reasons why the lack of a collection of Hitler's speeches, as complete as technically possible, is one of the most serious obstacles to a successful study of Nazism. Such a collection is indispensable not only for a biography of Hitler (How can we expect to understand a man whose political career was built to such an extent on success as a public speaker if we have no means to analyze him in this role?), but still more for the analysis of the Nazi ideology. Only if we approach the Nazi ideology through a dynamic analysis will we be able to solve the methodological dilemma of dealing rationally with Nazi irrationalism and with whether the Nazi ideology had substance or was merely a tactical function. To this effect we must follow the course of Hitler's thought and its response to the successive political changes, and this can be done only by following him through his speeches.

the dismissal of Schacht, Werner von Blomberg, Werner von Fritsch, and Konstantin von Neurath in 1937-1938, the Nazis assumed control over the economy, the army, and the diplomacy, those exact three positions that their conservative allies of January 30, 1933, had deemed it most important to maintain.[34] In Italy a fairly stable balance was sustained between the movement and its various allies until the latter, relying on the monarchy and assisted by Fascism's defeat in war, finally ousted the Fascists. In Spain, a borderline case, the allies assumed control from the outset and never abandoned it. Similar observations can be made with the many cases of pre-, proto-, and pseudofascist regimes in Central, Eastern, and Southeastern Europe.

The thesis of the parallel growth of industrialization and fascist radicalization seems to conflict, however, with the evidence of some highly industrialized societies such as France and England where fascist opposition never gained much momentum. The problem can be solved only by adding a broader historical analysis involving the specific national, social, and cultural traditions that industrialization encountered in individual societies. It is perhaps not accidental that the industrialization process ran relatively smoothly in West European nations whose political rise concurred with the rise of modern civilization since the late Middle Ages. Fascist opposition, by contrast, was strongest in the Mediterranean and Central European regions where the premodern traditions of the ancient Roman and the medieval German and Turkish Empires persisted. The religious division between Protestantism and Catholicism may also have some relevance: one remembers both Max Weber's thesis on the correlation of Protestantism and capitalism and the recent controversy on the attitude of Pope Pius XII toward Fascism and Nazism. In other words, fascism emerged where preindustrial traditions were both strongest and most alien to industrialism and, hence, where the rise of the latter caused a major break with the past and substantial losses to the nonindustrial classes.

This definition is still incomplete, however, since it does not tell why fascism emerged rather simultaneously throughout Europe though the countries affected were on different levels of economic growth. We face here the question of the "epoch" of fascism, raised but not answered by Nolte. The general conditions of fascism as defined above existed, after all, earlier. In Germany, for example, lower-middle-class opposition against industrialization had already emerged in the mid-nineteenth century and accompanied economic growth in varying degrees through all its stages.[35] Why did it not turn into fascism prior to 1914, though it did so on parallel stages of growth in Italy and Spain after the First World War? At this point the importance of the military element for the analysis of fascism becomes apparent again: Only after total war had militarized European societies and had created large military interests were the conditions required for fascism complete.[36] The First World War had tremendously strengthened industrialization in

---

[34] The focus of present studies on the spectacular Blomberg-Fritsch affair has blurred the comprehensive character and the importance of the change in 1937-1938.

[35] Already Marx observed the antimodernist attitude of the petty bourgeoisie, though he partly misinterpreted it. The anti-Semitic movement at the end of the century was indicative of the growing radicalization of lower-middle-class opposition. (See Hans Rosenberg, *Grosse Depression und Bismarckzeit* [Berlin, 1966]; for France, see André Siégfried, *Tableau politique de la France de l'ouest sous la troisième république* [Paris, 1913], 413; cf. Lipset, *Political Man,* 131-32.)

[36] The *Vaterlandspartei,* organized in 1917 by military and agrarian groups (Alfred von Tirpitz; Wolfgang Kapp) in Germany to support imperialist warfare, was, significantly

technical terms, but it had diverted it from production to destruction. After the war the victorious nations of the West managed, on the whole, to stabilize industrial society and to return to production, but the defeated nations and those industrially underdeveloped found it extremely difficult to follow the same course. When they met with economic crises, many of them abandoned whatever advance they had made toward democracy and turned to fascism.

This breakdown occurred roughly along the social and cultural lines defined above. If we examine the geographical distribution of fascist regimes in Europe between the two world wars, we find that they emerged mainly in three areas: the Mediterranean coast; the regions of Central, Eastern, and Southeastern Europe; and Germany. In the first area, the original and highly developed Mediterranean urban and commercial civilization that reached back to antiquity faced destruction by the invasion of industrialism as released or accelerated by World War I. Defeat, either imagined as in the case of Italy or real as in the case of Spain at the hands of Abd-el-Krim at Anual in 1921, played an additional role. In the second area, an old feudal civilization struggled with the problems arising out of sudden liberation from Habsburg or tsarist dominations as well as from competition with both Western industrialism and Eastern Bolshevism. Both regions were predominantly Catholic. In the third area, a technologically fully developed industrial society clashed violently with the stubborn resistance of surviving remnants of preindustrial forms of society over who was to pay for defeat and economic crises. Catholicism played, here, a dual and partly contradictory role. On the one hand, it seems to have influenced indirectly Nazism as such top Nazi leaders as Hitler, Himmler, and Goebbels were Catholic by origin, and the Vatican was quick to compromise with the Hitler regime. On the other hand, the vast majority of the Catholic population was relatively immune to Nazi temptations. Significantly enough, Protestantism also split, though along somewhat different lines.

These differentiations suggest a division into three subtypes of fascism: the Mediterranean as the "original" one; the various and not too long-lived regimes in Central, Eastern, and Southeastern Europe as a mixed, or not full-fledged, variation; and German Nazism as a special form.

The "epoch" of fascism starts, thus, with the aftermath of the First World War, but when does it end? Eugen Weber and Lipset agree with many scholars who believe that there is no epoch of fascism, that fascism is a general condition of modern society contingent upon crises in liberal democracy.[37] This is certainly indisputable as far as fascist attitudes and movements are concerned; it is quite another problem, however, whether fascist regimes will emerge again. This emergence seems unlikely for two reasons. First, the socioeconomic development in the highly industrialized societies of the West generally rules out the re-emergence of the historical condition of fascism—a disarrangement of society in which the rise of large masses of déclassés coincides with the rise of a sizable group of military

---

enough, the first prefascist mass movement. The foundation of the Nazi party later followed the same pattern: Hitler acted originally as an agent of the Munich headquarters of the *Reichswehr*. In addition, Anton Drexler, the founder of the first nucleus of the Nazi party, was a member of the *Vaterlandspartei*. Both the *Reichswehr* officers in Munich and Drexler aimed at overcoming what they felt was the major shortcoming of the *Vaterlandspartei*: it had no appeal to the workers. (Among recent accounts, see Günther Franz-Willing, *Die Hitlerbewegung* [Hamburg, 1962], I.)

[37] Weber, *Varieties of Fascism*, 3; Lipset, *Political Man*, Chap. v.

desperadoes. There are no longer economic losers of industrialization, at least not on a mass scale, and Charles de Gaulle's victory over the rebellious French military shows that military desperadoes alone will not get very far.[38] In addition, the horrible experience of neobarbarism puts a heavy burden on all attempts at imitation. If the success of fascism under modern, Western conditions is unlikely, there remain, theoretically, the underdeveloped countries as possible breeding grounds of fascism. Yet it is doubtful whether opposition against industrialization will assume there the form of fascism since these countries lack the specific traditions of the ancient and medieval civilizations that conditioned the antimodernist revolt in Europe. The second reason working against fascist regimes is, thus, that fascism is inseparable from its Central and South European conditions; it is, in fact, one of the products of the dialectical movement of European civilization.

Some remarks on specific characteristics of Nazism and its German origins may be added as a conclusion to this discussion of fascism. The specialty of the German case may be seen, in light of this analysis, in that Germany was the only highly industrialized society in which a fascist regime emerged. Some authors have tried to explain this by pointing to the dominant role the state played in German industrialization. Yet Gerschenkron has convincingly shown that a relatively strong role of the state is a general characteristic of industrialization under conditions of "relative backwardness." We must look, therefore, for other causes, and it seems that they can be found in social rather than in political conditions of industrialization. A comparison with developments in France and Russia shows that the state in these countries changed its social basis by revolutionary means either prior to or during the process of industrialization; in Germany, however, preindustrial social traditions proved so strong and so flexible that they maintained influence on, if not control over, the state up to and beyond the stage of what Rostow calls industrial maturity.[39] The ambivalent social structure that resulted from this twisted process was so fragile that it broke apart under the impact of the series of severe crises from World War I to the Great Depression.

One of the conditions that complicated German industrialization may be seen in the fact that Wilhelm von Humboldt's reform of the German educational system favored, at the very moment when Germany began to industrialize, an aesthetic-aristocratic idea of culture over an idea of civilization compatible with industrialism. The tensions resulting from this divergence are reflected in German nineteenth-century intellectual history and its complex relationship to the intellectual roots of Nazism. Fritz Stern and George L. Mosse, among others, have recently made important contributions to this subject.[40] Mosse has taken up the issue of the *Völkisch* ideology and has convincingly shown how deeply it had penetrated into German society already prior to 1914. In focusing on the *Völkisch* ideology alone, Mosse has, however, by-passed what appears to be the real problem. Parallel to the rise of the *Völkisch* ideology, Germany experienced one of the greatest intellectual flowerings in its history during the first three decades of this

---

[38] It would be different in case of large-scale war which might, of course, drastically change present social conditions.

[39] I have tried to analyze this particular aspect in "Das Problem des deutschen Nationalstaates," rev. ed. in *Moderne deutsche Sozialgeschichte,* ed. Hans-Ulrich Wehler (Cologne, 1966), 407-36.

[40] Fritz Stern, *The Politics of Cultural Despair: A Study in the Rise of the Germanic Ideology* (Berkeley, Calif., 1961); George L. Mosse, *The Crisis of German Ideology: Intellectual Origins of the Third Reich* (New York, 1964).

century. In many cases it reached the level of the classical period around 1800, and it certainly surpassed it in breadth.[41] The real question is, then, why this parallelism occurred and why the *Völkisch* ideology eventually triumphed. As far as intellectual history is concerned, there was, in fact, no gradual decline toward Nazism; there was a clear rupture in 1933.

Stern's study is less ambitious and more penetrating. Its results might lend some support to Nolte's thesis of metaphysical despair, but they are valuable especially because they draw attention to the crisis of self-confidence in the academic establishment. This seems to correspond to Allen's findings that indicate a deep and violent resentment on the "grass root" level of the Nazi party against the "educated" classes,[42] and both studies together may hint at some reasons for the triumph of the *Völkisch* ideology analyzed by Mosse. Synthesized in this way, the results of the three authors may draw attention to one of the unduly neglected class divisions in Germany: between the educated and the uneducated. In the classical country of *Bildung* where the professor held and still holds one of the top positions in public prestige, such a division was highly important in itself. It became still more important, even in a political sense, when the aristocracy partially adopted during the nineteenth century the bourgeois ideal of *Bildung*. Most telling in this respect is the rise of the idea of the army as a "school of the nation," indicating that even the Prussian army felt advised after 1848 to engage in a competition for education with the bourgeoisie.[43] The civil bureaucracy had already adopted the educational ideal earlier; now, the military and part of the aristocracy followed in an attempt to maintain their position and to provide for the cooptation of "suitable" bourgeois elements.

In view of these facts, the hypothesis seems to arise that the division between the educated and uneducated may have developed in the nineteenth century into the true dividing line between the ruling oligarchy and its subjects. If this is true, subjects seeking emancipation had two ways to respond: either forming a subculture or resorting to barbarism. The first was the solution of the socialist labor movement; the second was the way of the Nazis, and it was the true revolutionary way. Evidence suggests that Hitler's prestige with the masses did not rest exclusively on economic and foreign policy successes; it also appears to have been supported by the fact that Hitler succeeded again and again in defeating and humiliating the members of the old oligarchy. Hitler's frequent invectives against this class in his

---

[41] It is indeed surprising to what extent a split in our knowledge of this period has developed. The general facts are known: in the sciences—Max Weber, Max Scheler, Karl Mannheim, Ernst Troeltsch, Friedrich Meinecke, Max Planck, Albert Einstein, and so forth; in literature—Thomas and Heinrich Mann, Bertold Brecht, the expressionists, the *Weltbühne*, and others, plus Austrians such as Franz Werfel, Robert Musil, Karl Kraus, R. M. Rilke, and Franz Kafka; in the dramatic arts—Max Reimann, Leopold Jessner, and similar names; in the visual arts—the *Bauhaus*, music, films, and dance must also be mentioned. Berlin was, in the 1920's and early 1930's a major center of European intellectual life. And yet in our conception of this period of German intellectual history the notion prevails that there were few but nationalists and racists in Germany. A well-balanced intellectual history of the Weimar Republic is, thus, still painfully needed for the study of modern Germany.

[42] Allen, *Nazi Seizure of Power*, 279-80.

[43] Reinhard Höhn, *Die Armee als Erziehungsschule der Nation: Das Ende einer Idee* (Bad Harzburg, 1963). Another aspect of these attempts at adjustment is treated by Hans Rosenberg, "Die Pseudo-Demokratisierung der Rittergutsbesitzerklasse," in *Zur Geschichte und Problematik der Demokratie: Festgabe für Hans Herzfeld*, ed. Wilhelm Berges and Carl Hinrichs (Berlin, 1958), 459-86, reprinted in *Moderne deutsche Sozialgeschichte*, ed. Wehler, 287-308.

speeches are usually explained as motivated merely by his own personal resentments. The motive may well have been more sophisticated, however. Such considerations must lead to the perplexing question of whether the Nazi movement did involve some elements of a completion, terribly distorted indeed, of Germany's age-old unfinished revolution. This would open some new perspectives on the resistance movement, and it would perhaps explain the intriguing fact that the Nazi regime, in contrast to the Hohenzollern monarchy in 1918 and to the Fascist regime in Italy in 1943-1944, was not overthrown by a mass upheaval from within. The question cannot be answered here, but it is crucial. The answer will determine not only our understanding of the nature of Nazism in terms of the problem of fascism, but also our interpretation of Nazism as an element in German history.

THE THIRD REICH, SOCIAL OPPORTUNITY AND SOCIETY

David Schoenbaum

... Franz Neumann's thesis that "National Socialist social policy consists in the acceptance and strengthening of the prevailing class character of German society,"[1] that the Third Reich represented, as before, the domination of the generals, the Junkers, and the industrialists with an admixture of Nazis, is a generally accurate reflection of the basic social situation, but doubly misleading. It is misleading in its suggestion of conscious purpose, its confusion of expediency with moral approval. It is still more misleading in its neglect of the dynamism characteristic of all Nazi policy, which revolutionized the role and influence of institutions and individuals with little reference to their size or titles.[2] What was involved was a revolution of class and a revolution of status at the same time. Two tendencies again interacted. On the one hand, the imperialist dynamics of the Third Reich, its eugenics and anti-intellectualism notwithstanding, sustained the position of the intellectual and the technician. National Socialism accelerated the already considerable mobility of German industrial society, creating at least an atmosphere of opportunity, and often enough, real evidence of it. Actual opportunity was limited in school and university, but neither of these was exactly a key institution

---

[1] Franz Neumann, *Behemoth,* New York, 1942, p. 367.

[2] Irrespective of their striking similarities, a striking difference between Hitlerism and Stalinism is the near absence of purges in the former. The purge of June 1934 is remarkable as an exception. Failure or differences of opinion with Hitler led not to show trials, exile or execution, but at worst to private life in the case of Schacht or the Nazi version of an old Bolshevik like Feder; in the case of others, Frank, Rosenberg or Goering, it led to continued or even augmented titles and honors. At the same time, it seemed a characteristic of both states that actual influence could well be in inverse proportion to size—though the Labor Front might again be an exception. Thus, in the Third Reich, Party influence declined as the Party increased, and in the SS, as total membership grew, power was continually concentrated in one subdivision after another.. Cf. Hannah Arendt, *The Origins of Totalitarianism,* New York, 1958, p. 403; Karl O. Paetel, "Geschichte and Soziologie der SS," *Vierteljahreshefte für Zeitgeschichte,* 1954, pp. 1 ff.

in Nazi society. But it was real enough in the military, the economy, and even the civil service, the institutions that held Nazi society together.[3]

The status revolution, that accompanied this, was not a matter of elitism, even in the form of technocracy, but the triumph of egalitarianism, the reward and consummation of the Volksbewegung that had brought Hitler to power. The triumph of the down-and-out's, of the "armed Bohemians," did not necessarily mean that they ruled the state, or in the special case of the SS, committed murder in a Volksgemeinschaft with princes and graduate lawyers. What it did mean was that they represented it, that a man without diploma, family, or independent economic position laid cornerstones, greeted foreign visitors at the station, shook the hands of graduates, and claimed the royal box at the theatre. This symbolic role represented real social opportunity for those who enjoyed it, opportunity that neither Weimar nor the Empire had offered them. Like a super Elks Club, the Third Reich pampered the familiar human weakness for distinction on a scale probably without precedent. As early as 1935, the party listed over 200,000 "representatives of authority" (Hoheitsträger). Functionaries of various satellites like the corporatist groups, professional and welfare organizations, totaled nearly 1½ million, not including the representatives of still embryonic institutions like the Hitler Youth or the SS.[4] This, in the form of jobs, medals, uniforms, irrespective of authority, was status distribution in the grand manner, personal identification for thousands with the brave new world Hitler offered them. If it produced no elite, if it, in fact, precluded one, it nonetheless contributed to the general image of an open society.

The parents of a former pupil who had recently fallen in action expressed thanks to the commander of an Adolf Hitler School "for the splendid hours that our Hellmut was allowed to spend at the highest school of the Reich as a simple miner's son, something we could not have afforded to offer him ourselves.[5] Their letter tells at least as much about the Party academies, and by extension about opportunity in Nazi society, as any number of demonstrations of their practical failures.

The Third Reich and Society

The Third Reich proved that a house divided against itself *can* stand, provided, at least, that the occupants have no alternative place to go and that the landlord pays attention to the wallpaper, if not to the walls.

The German house was no less divided in 1939 or 1945 than it was in 1933 when Hitler took possession of it. The Gemeinschaft invoked by Nazi ideology struck

---

[3] Cf. Shirer, op. cit., p. 218. "Did a mike interview with General Ernst Udet tonight. . . . Udet . . . is something of a phenomenon. A professional pilot, who only a few years ago was so broke he toured America as a stunt flier, performing often in a full-dress suit and a top hat, he is now responsible for the designing and production of Germany's war planes. Though he never had any business experience, he has proved a genius at his job, . . . I could not help thinking tonight that a man like Udet would never be entrusted with such a job in America. He would be considered 'lacking in business experience.' Also, businessmen, if they knew of his somewhat bohemian life, would hesitate to trust him with responsibility. And yet in this crazy Nazi system he has done a phenomenal job." Udet, the hero of Carl Zuckmayer's 1946 play *"Des Teufels General,"* later committed suicide in despair with Hitler's policies.

[4] *Partei-Statistik,* Vol. II, p. 17; Vol. III, p. 14.

[5] "Schüler des Führers," Richthefte für Adolf-Hitler-Schüler, December 1944, p. 20, Archive of Institut für Zeitgeschichte 1720/55.

genuinely resonant notes in the hearts of a population desperate for authority and sick unto death of conflict. But real Gemeinschaft was no closer to realization in practice at the end of Nazi rule than it was at the beginning. With all good will, German society was finally united only in a negative community of fear, sacrifice, and ruin. The elimination of class conflict, the Third Reich's major social boast from 1935 on, was at best a half truth. Beneath the cover of Nazi ideology, the historic social groups continued their conflicts like men wrestling under a blanket.[6] Beneath the surface of apparent economic recovery, none of the basic problems of German society had been solved; a more equitable relationship had not been found between capital and labor, between big business and small business, or between industry and agriculture. The problems had at best been postponed, in the case of agriculture even exacerbated.

The division of the Nazi house was built into the Party program. National Socialism was to turn the clocks back, to make the German-speaking world safe for small business, small farmers, and small-towners. The goal was not only political but social revisionism, revision of the tyranny of big industry, big cities, big unions, big banks; and at the same time a revision of Versailles. But the simultaneous revision of Versailles and of the twentieth—not to say the nineteenth—century, *in* the twentieth century, was an attempt to square the circle. Revision of Versailles, in Nazi dimensions, involved at the very least the threat of force. But the threat of force in an industrial age presupposes industry, and there is, as Nazi society conclusively proved, no industry without an industrial society.

The result was an inevitable rapprochement, at first with the industrialists, the generals, the diplomats, and the civil servants, whom the Nazi movement was expected to destroy; not, as should be obvious, because they were admired, but because they were necessary.[7] Then came the inevitable rapprochement with labor, without which there is no industrial society, a rapprochement born of industrial recovery and full employment and sustained with both concessions and ideology. The effective common denominators were the values traditionally called "national"—the efficient administration of the State, the expansion of the economy, the growth of the military establishment, and beyond these, the extension of German markets and frontiers. But the effective lever was the legitimacy and the threat of a mass movement that Hitler had, and that the industrialists, generals, diplomats, and civil servants did not have, and knew they did not have.

Papen's intrigues, Hindenburg's senility, and the hubris of the nationalist Right too contributed to Hitler's success. But the basic justification of Hitler's appointment was that authoritarian government under Papen, who had scorned mass support, and under Schleicher, who had failed to find it, had reached a dead end. If the decision to yield power to this particular mass movement was a fatal illusion, the decision to yield power to a mass movement at all was, in its way, a moment of truth. It was also only a step from here to the conclusive demoralization of the industrialists, the intimidation of the generals, and the capitulation of the civil

---

[6] According to a contemporary joke, A tells B that "in Britain and America the plutocrats are still in control."
"What are ours then?" B replies. "Cratopluts?"
[7] Hitler himself admitted this. "When I look at the intellectual classes here in Germay . . . ," he told the press. "But we need them. Otherwise, I don't know, we could wipe them out or something. But unfortunately we need them." Speech of 10 November 1938, in Domarus, op. cit., pp. 957f.

service that followed.[8] What had not happened in 1918 happened in 1933. Nazi *élan* had its complement in the shattered self-confidence of the old social elites. Like the figures in an animated cartoon, they had gone over a cliff in 1918, still running though nothing was beneath them. This time they recognized the abyss and fell. With them fell the institutions of German middle-class society—the parties, the universities, and the churches.

But while Hitler opened the door on a vacuum, it was one he could only partially fill. Filling it entirely presupposed the necessary administrative, economic, and military skills that his following basically lacked; it meant the collaboration of those who had themselves created the vacuum. To this they agreed, paving the road to hell with rationalizations of self-interest and national interest, positivist legality, hopes for the best, and hopes of avoiding the worst. What Hitler offered them was what they thought they wanted anyway. What he threatened them with was the achievement of these aims without their help. This characteristic dialectic of "national" ends and mass means was the basis of a new synthesis, the carrot-and-stick principle that was the de facto constitutional premise of the Third Reich.

But this too had paradoxical implications. Its success depended on the assumption that the movement was there as a deterrent and not an object of use. The practical consequence in this case was the schizophrenia typical of Nazi society. So far as could be seen, everything had changed and nothing had changed. Revolution was both imminent and indefinitely suspended. Industry enjoyed record profits, the generals appeared to be unchallenged, and Meissner, for example, who had once sat in Ebert's office and Hindenburg's, now sat in Hitler's. Yet industry made concessions not even demanded of it by a revolutionary SPD, the Army capitulated to a civilian administration like no other Army in German history, and the Reich was represented by a set of "new men" compared to whom the revolutionaries of 1792 appear in retrospect like representatives of the *ancien régime*—abroad by a one-time wine salesman, at home by a neurotic ex-corporal who had failed in the pursuit of everything but power.

What held things together was a combination of ideology and social dynamics on a foundation of charisma and terror. As time went on, even ideology became increasingly unnecessary, particularly for a younger generation of true believers.[9] Behind the entire system was an apparently total lack of alternatives. The official social goals were neither revoked nor seriously pursued, but indefinitely suspended. Symptomatically, Drexler's pamphlet of 1919, like Rosenberg's and Feder's commentaries on the Party program, was still being published in the late 1930s, long after the authors had subsided into one or another form of oblivion. What mattered was faith, and faith was rewarded. In the last analysis, anything could be rationalized with a reference not to Versailles but to 1932. Industrial production did go up, unemployment did go down, Austrians, Sudeten Germans, and Memellanders did come *heim ins Reich* (home to the Reich), foreign diplomats did capitulate, and foreign armies surrendered. Did it matter that the department stores

---

[8] A revealing illustration of their attitude is Speer's account at Nuremberg of overhearing a group of miners in early 1945 declare their still unbroken faith in Hitler. This made such an impression on him that he dropped plans for an attempt on Hitler's life. Cf. Trevor-Roper, op. cit., pp. 89—91.

[9] Cf. Rauschning, *Die Revolution des Nihilismus,* Zurich-New York, 1938, p. 34; Haffner, op. cit., pp. 79ff..

survived and that big business grew bigger? The Communists, the Jews, and ultimately the war itself were the explanation and the apology. Utopia was suspended for the duration. But if Feder and Darré disappeared, their petit-bourgeois fantasies marched on, all evidences of social reality notwithstanding.

The SS and the Labor Front, the Third Reich's most successful institutional innovations, demonstrate the impact of social necessity on ideological orientation. From beginning to end, Himmler preached "racial" elitism, presided—as he saw it—over a new knightly order, dreamed of feudal domains, new gods, a state of nature. At the same time, his policy precluded anything of the sort. Institutional survival in an industrial society requires administrators, not knights; diplomas, not blue eyes. Himmler consequently recruited administrators and diplomas. The success of his organization itself depended on its abstention from the very ideology it represented and in which at least some of its members really believed. In turn, the SS' success derived from its accommodation to a society its members were sworn to destroy. Only this initial accommodation, the organizational basis of administrators and diplomas, permitted the subsequent recruitment of knights and blue eyes at all. The Ordensideologie (the ideology of a knightly order), to the extent it was ever realized, was necessarily realized in the social vacuum of the occupied Eastern territories, not in Germany.

By comparison, Ley's Ordensburgen, which nominally practiced Ordensideologie at home, which recruited not frustrated officers, civil servants, and doctors, but "ganze Kerle," ("all good fellows," by general agreement, another expression for yokels) vegetated in every sense, including the geographical, on the margins of Nazi society. So did the Hitler Youth with its uncomprehending complaints about the consistently bad results of its own consistently executed selection policy for the Adolf Hitler Schools. Both cases demonstrate the limits imposed even by the Third Reich on careers for the untalented.

If the SS was the bridge that carried the old social elites into the heart of the Third Reich, it was the Labor Front that carried the plebs. In the case of the Labor Front, success was not a result of administrative talent or particular organizational solidarity, but more or less automatic. The premise of mass support in a society resolved and compelled to be industrial made concessions from the regime inevitable. The full employment produced by total industrial mobilization then made concessions from employers inevitable too. In both cases, concessions derived from the decision to reverse Versailles, irrespective of, even despite, the interests and intentions of the respective partners. The lesson might be that an industrial society cannot exist without a labor movement. If one does not exist, it has to be invented.

What is striking in both the case of the SS and the Labor Front is the reorientation of support without any equivalent change of ideology, a paradox based on the adaptability of its supporters as well as adaptability of the ideology. In the years before 1933, the SS had lived in the shadow of the SA. The NSBO, predecessor of the Labor Front, had existed in the shadow of the Party and an electorate of irate shopkeepers, small businessmen, and small farmers and their Nazified pressure groups and front organizations. The ascent of the SS and the Labor Front after 1933 was matched by the decline of the SA and the Party. This meant a fundamental shift in the sociological basis of Nazi support. But there was no consequent redefinition of Nazi goals. A movement carried to power by the outsiders of Weimar society was now carried beyond it by the earlier insiders—at least passively. Labor and Bildungsbürgetum (educated middle class) alike surrendered to the stronger battalions by joining them.

This process helps to account for the remarkable durability of Nazi society despite the centrifugal forces it created. In the context of both ideological mobilization and industrial recovery, every social group was integrated, almost overnight, into the new system. The immediate dissatisfactions were wiped out. The unemployed returned to work, the economic curve went up, the farm price index held firm. The new dissatisfactions, to the extent they were perceived at all, were rationalized and sublimated in a system whose very fluidity promised eventual solution to those with enough faith and hard enough elbows. Success promised more success, and war obviated the need for producing it. In the meanwhile, as a kind of advance payment on success, there were opportunities for the taking—by those with talent and those without it, those with education and those without it, those with money and those without it.

The conflicts that might have arisen from extended reflection on the limits of such successes and the reality of such opportunities were resolved by the genuine conceptual difficulties the new situation presented. In the Third Reich, relative approximation of class and status came to an end. Discontent presupposes its recognition. The disillusion induced by one's awareness of his own importance or unimportance presupposes that one is aware of it—or at least is made aware of it by one's neighbors. This was next to impossible in the wonderland of Hitler Germany where there were no longer reliable indications of what was up and what was down. How important was a minister, a diplomat, a Party functionary, a Labor Front functionary, a Hitler Youth leader, a member of an Ordensburg? The question was unanswerable.

A few examples indicate the problems involved in trying to answer it. Since the publication of *Mein Kampf,* Hitler had regularly and consistently declared his unambiguous contempt for the businessmen, diplomats, civil servants, and university graduates of official German society. There was no reason to doubt his sincerity. Deviations were never total but always qualified. Each audience was distinguished from "the others," an honorable exception to a general rule. Even at his most conciliatory, as in the famous Industry Club speech in Düsseldorf in 1932, Hitler left no doubt of his real position, tactfully but unmistakably reminding his audience of its share in the disaster of 1918, and leaving no doubt that business in the Third Reich was never again to achieve primacy over politics.[10]

In an expansive moment in 1940, according to Rosenberg, Hitler spoke "very negatively of the civil service," to which a liaison officer of the Foreign Minister "smilingly" asked whether the Foreign Ministry might be an exception. "It is a remarkable thing," Hitler replied, "that in every operetta the diplomats are portrayed as stupid (doof). This is no coincidence. The father of several sons let the

---

[10] Domarus, op. cit., pp. 72f. The first charge alone, coming from a man who maintained that his entire life had been changed by the disaster of 1918, was equivalent to condemning the audience to outer darkness. But the proposition of the primacy of politics was doubly revealing. "In Germany too the power state (Machtstaat) created the basic premises of later economic prosperity," Hitler declared, to which members of his audience replied, "Sehr richtig!" This episode reveals not only how Hitler felt about the businessmen in front of him. Their assent also gives some idea of why he felt that way, some idea of the real limits of German capitalism. Even if one could imagine Roosevelt making a comparable statement to a comparable American business audience at the same time, can one imagine a similar response from them?

most efficient take over the estate or something equally sensible. The one who was not all there was sent into the diplomatic service."[11]

But what did all this say about businessmen, about the civil servants or the diplomats, all of whom continued to exist as before? Was it a coincidence that even among the new diplomats there was a von Jagow and a von Killinger? What was the German on the street, whether pro-Nazi or anti-Nazi, to conclude about the status of diplomats or about diplomats as a class? What, considering the labyrinthine diplomatic practices of the Third Reich, was in fact the status of diplomats? What, in the main, were its diplomats as a class?

The same problems arose in the anarchic relations of Party and State. For Frick, Guertner, Ribbentrop, promotion to ministerial rank meant a loss, not a gain, in influence. Compared with their old Party offices, promotion to Governor General of Poland for Frank, to Reichsminister for the Eastern Territories for Rosenberg, "did not signify the climax but the end of their National Socialist careers."[12] On the other hand, to cite two contrary examples, this was not true for Goebbels or for Goering, appointed to ministerial rank in 1933, or for Himmler in 1944. What did this say about the status of ministers and Party officials? Hitler's ministers like Papen's tended to be university graduates, doctors, high civil servants.[13] What did this say about Hitler's government compared with Papen's as a matter of class?

The answers depended on the observer. For the conservative observer, the old guard was the guarantor of continuity, of the historical state that demanded his confidence and his patriotism. For the radical observer, Hitler himself was the guarantor of change, of the new State that demanded his confidence and his patriotism. For even if the old guard was still on top,[14] Hitler himself, the corporal and "building worker," was at the very summit. In an economy primed in the meantime with armaments appropriations and building contracts, a society burgeoning with new offices and new opportunities, further reflection could be avoided where objective analysis was in any case impossible. In an extreme case—again the SS—members had the opportunity of humiliating doctors, professors, and judges while being led by doctors, professors, and judges.

In the resultant collision of ideological and industrial revolution, traditional class structure broke down, and with it the traditional structure of political action. If no social group did well in the Third Reich, no social group did badly—or so badly that its discontent was not compensated by the contentment of another group. Labor's defeat was business' triumph, agriculture's frustrations labor's relief, small business' misfortunes the consumer's reward, the consumer's aggravation agriculture's compensation. *Kraft durch Freude* was supplemented by *Kraft durch Schadenfreude*. At the same time, at any given moment, some businessmen did well enough, some farmers did well enough, some workers did well enough, to distinguish their interests, their stake in the new regime, from that of their sociological fellows. The classless reality of the Third Reich was mirrored by its opponents, the historically unique coalition of aristocrats, civil servants, clergymen of both Christian churches, and trade unionists who joined forces in 1944 in a final desperate attempt to bring it down.

[11] Rosenberg, *Politisches Tagebuch,* op. cit., p. 134.
[12] Hannah Arendt, op. cit., p. 404.
[13] Nor were Nazis with doctorates, even the most aggressively egalitarian of them like Ley and Goebbels, inhibited about appearing in public with their titles.
[14] According to a typical contemporary joke, "NSBO=*Noch sind die Bonzen oben.*"

The net result was not so much a dual state of Nazi politics and capitalist economics as a dual society in which the status of both groups and individuals moved independently of their old objective underpinnings. There was no new class, still less a new elite. There was at best a new set of classes, a set of mutually competitive elites. It was a world that defied the laws of social gravity without replacing them. The average citizen, passive or participant, lived in a world of traditional relationships, forces, and status, and a Nazi world where the addition of a uniform or a lapel pin could immediately invalidate them.[15] The conflicts of "real" world and "Nazi" world were then reproduced in every kind of combination and permutation. The Wehrmacht rejected the SA; the SA despised the SS; SA and SS deeply resented the Party; SA, SS, and Party resented the power of the incumbent civil service. Everyone seems to have joined in common contempt for the "golden pheasants" of Ley's Ordensburgen. The reports of SS sergeants beating up the graduates of Napolas,[16] of the muffled conflict between generations within the ranks of the Party bureaucracy,[17] indicate lines of division not only between but within institutions. Mutual recognition was the product not of consensus but of quasi-diplomatic negotiations between quasi-sovereignties like the Labor Front and the industrialists at Leipzig in 1935, between the Hitler Youth and the Labor Front, the Hitler Youth and the Party or SS, or between any of them, as in the case of the Four Year Plan, and the relevant branches of the civil service.

The synthesis was a world of frustration and exaltation. But above all it was a world of general perplexity in which, even before the war, "Nazi" and "German" merged indistinctly but inseparably, and the Volksgemeinschaft of official ideology acquired a bizarre reality. In a society accustomed to identify political conflict with class conflict, conflict—in the sense that it had hitherto resulted in organization and action—seemed to have disappeared altogether. Instead, it reproduced itself in forms so diverse that their only common denominator seems in retrospect to have been the near universality with which they were misunderstood. In a world where the purge of 30 June 1934, for example, meant not the end but the transitional phase of a revolution and where an informed and intelligent foreigner could maintain plausibly in 1937, shortly before the second—if bloodless—purge, that the conservative forces were now regaining control of German society,[18] the contemporary, observer and participant alike, was without a map. Reluctant to return to the original entrance, he not surprisingly plunged ever deeper into a forest he found ever harder to describe. It is revealing that the most profound analysis of the Third Reich in the context of the social history of the preceding century, Thomas Mann's *Doktor Faustus*, was a novel, written by a man who never set foot in the Third Reich at all.

[15] An example of this in practice can be found in an order of Hess's. "Just as high-ranking Party functionaries, in the performance of their military service, have no right to claim a commission on the basis of their Party rank, Party members who happen to hold high positions in the State or to have spent years in the Wehrmacht have no reason, on that account, to lay claim to comparable Party offices, let alone to get them." *Anordnungen des Stellvertreters des Führers* 36/36 of 3 March 1936, op. cit. Cf. Arendt, op. cit., p. 399: "The inhabitant of Hitler's Third Reich lived not only under the simultaneous and often conflicting authorities of competing powers, such as the civil services, the Party, the SA, and the SS; he could never be sure and he was never explicitly told whose authority he was supposed to place above all others. He had to develop a kind of sixth sense to know at a given moment whom to obey and whom to disregard."

[16] Cf. Ch. VIII.

[17] Cf. Ch. VII.

[18] Stephen H. Roberts, *The House That Hitler Built*, London, 1937, pp. 359ff.

The social consequences of this ultimate disorientation were correspondingly paradoxical. A consistent extension of German history, the Third Reich consistently perpetuated the historic discrepancy between objective social reality and its interpretation. Objective social reality, the measurable statistical consequences of National Socialism, was the very opposite of what Hitler had presumably promised and what the majority of his followers had expected him to fulfill. In 1939 the cities were larger, not smaller; the concentration of capital greater than before; the rural population reduced, not increased; women not at the fireside but in the office and the factory; the inequality of income and property distribution more, not less conspicuous; industry's share of the gross national product up and agriculture's down, while industrial labor had it relatively good and small business increasingly bad. The East Elbian estates continued to be run by the gentry, the civil service by doctors, and the Army by generals whose names began with "von." Not surprisingly, the history of the Third Reich is a story of frustration, cynicism, and resignation, the history of an apparently betrayed revolution whose one-time supporters, Otto Strasser, Rauschning, Feder, and Rosenberg, one after the other, denounced it as vehemently as its opponents.

Interpreted social reality, on the other hand, reflected a society united like no other in recent German history, a society of opportunities for young and old, classes and masses, a society that was New Deal and good old days at the same time. Like no world since 1914, it was a world of career civil servants and authoritarian paternalism, a world of national purpose and achievement where the Army was once again "the school of the nation." It was no less a world where officers and men ate the same meals and conversed "as men to men."[19]

"Formerly when I went to the theatre with my wife," a prison camp guard told Hans Habe, "there was always trouble. We got a seat in the twentieth row. But Huber, our chief accountant, and his wife were in the tenth row. And afterward all hell broke loose. Why can the Hubers afford the tenth row and not ourselves? Nowadays, six nights a week, all the seats in the theatre cost the same. First come, first served. Sometimes the Hubers sit in the tenth row, and we sit in the twentieth. But my wife knows that's because the Hubers live nearer the theatre."[20]

"For the first time in my life," a Marburg Gymnasium teacher told Milton Mayer after the war, "I was really the peer of men who, in the Kaiser time and in the Weimar time, had always belonged to classes lower or higher than my own, men whom one had always looked down on or up to, but never at.... National Socialism broke down that separation, that class distinction. Democracy—such democracy as we had had—didn't do it, and is not doing it now."[21]

The interpreted social reality, in turn, had its own objective reality where a Prince of Schaumburg-Lippe served as Goebbels' adjutant and a Prince of Hesse answered Goering's telephone; where Prussian marshals saluted an Austrian corporal;[22] where a bourgeois Berlin school girl, fleeing the stuffiness of her German Nationalist home in search of "working youth," sought it in a career in the Hitler Youth and the Labor Service;[23] and an audience of Göttingen law students told a bemused von

[19] Cf. Shirer, op. cit., pp. 213, 345.

[20] Hans Habe, A Thousand Shall Fall, London, 1942, p. 217.

[21] Milton Mayer, They Thought They Were Free, Chicago, 1955, p. 105.

[22] "... welche Abdikation des Marschallstabes vor dem Tornister." Karl Kraus, Die dritte Walpurgisnacht, Munich, 1955, p. 83.

[23] Maschmann, op. cit., p. 25. The Hitler Youth, in 1933 when she joined it, was a particularly unlikely place to find what she was looking for. What makes the story important is that a girl from such a background was looking for this at all.

Salomon, "We don't want a state, we want a Volksgemeinschaft."[24]

It is axiomatic that very few of the participants in this world were seriously alienated from the "real" world, let alone clinically abnormal.[25] Sadists, paranoids, ne'er-do-wells, represented the smallest of minorities, and a minority that tended to be eliminated, not concentrated, from 1933 on.[26] Of the Nuremberg defendants, only two, Hess and Streicher, could be regarded as clinically abnormal, and both were men who had failed in Nazi society rather than succeeded.[27] In both cases, real insanity had proved to be a professional obstacle, not an advantage. The rest, not mad but, in Riesman's phrase, "other-directed" men, were the real executors of the Third Reich, in Hannah Arendt's expression "banal" in their evil, the "normal" representatives of a pathological society.

The basic problem was not political or economic, but social, the problem of an arrested bourgeois-industrial society, convinced by its guilt feelings and its impotence of its own superfluousness, and prepared to destroy itself with the means of the very bourgeois-industrial society it aimed to destroy. The "conservative" motives of so many of the ostensible revolutionaries make the Third Reich a novelty among revolutions since 1789, but a revolution nonetheless, united by a community of enemies and supported by representatives of every social group. Destruction alone was a common goal after all others—"Beamtenstaat" and Volksgemeinschaft, "back to the land" and back to the boundaries of 1918, the salvation of private property and the achievement of "national socialism"—had eliminated one another in a process of mutual cancellation. In the end, with the achievement of each partial goal, the destruction of unions and aristocracy, of Jews, of the Rights of Man and of bourgeois society, destruction was all that was left.

"The insensate hate which presided over and directed this enterprise," writes Rousset, "derived from the specter of all the frustrations, of all the mean, deceived aspirations, of all the envy and despair engendered by the extraordinary decomposition of the German middle classes between the wars. To pretend to discover in these the atavisms of a race is to echo the mentality of the SS. With each economic catastrophe, with each financial blow, the structure of German society collapsed. Nothing remained but an extraordinary nudity composed of impotent rage and criminal malice, thirsting for vengeance."[28]

In a simultaneous revolution of their situation and their awareness of it, the pillars of society—the Junkers, the industrialists, the Bildungsbürgerstum—joined forces with their own enemies to pull down the roof that had hitherto sheltered them. Goebbels invoked the splendid egalitarianism of the bombs falling around him, the total social revolution of total war.[29] His invocation was not only the appropriate elegy of the Third Reich but the elegy of a whole German society.

---

[24] Salomon, op. cit., p. 249.

[25] Cf. Bayles, op. cit., pp. 180f.

[26] Many concentration camp survivors report that it was only the earliest generation of SA guards that tortured prisoners for pleasure. The SS guards who followed them tended rather to be "businesslike." Cf. Arendt, op. cit., p. 454.

[27] Cf. G. M. Gilbert, Nuremberg Diary, New York, 1947.

[28] David Rousset, L'Univers Concentrationnaire, Paris, 1946, pp. 114f.

[29] Cf. Trevor-Roper, op. cit., p. 57. "The bomb terror spares the dwellings of neither rich nor poor; before the labour offices of total war the last class barriers have had to go down."

14 / Stalin and the Soviet Union: The Fulfillment or Perversion of Marxism-Leninism?

In 1967, the fiftieth anniversary of the Russian Revolution took place. No one denied the importance of the revolution; hence, there appeared a great many publications varying from uncritical acclaim to equally uncritical rejection of this half century of Soviet experience.

In all this literature a few themes stand out in great prominence. One is the problem of the *continuity* of Soviet history. Is the Soviet Union of 1967 the legitimate heir or the negation of the Russian Revolution of 1917? Does Soviet history consist of a series of senseless and bloody upheavals or is today's "collective leadership" the logical result of a series of historical stages summarized in the names of Khrushchev, Stalin, and Lenin? To what extent is the Soviet Union the realization or the perversion of Marxian socialist values? The late Isaac Deutscher entitled his last book *The Unfinished Revolution* (Oxford University Press, 1967) to indicate his belief that the Soviet Union was still far from completing the building of socialism.

There is general recognition that the "era of Stalin" and especially the years from 1929 to 1940 are crucial to our interpretation of the whole Soviet experience. Was Stalin a faithful executor or a perverter of Lenin's ideas? Nikolay Valentinov, a revolutionary émigré who died in Paris in 1964, insisted that "a straight well-bulldozed road leads" from Lenin's *Materialism and Emperio-Criticism* "to the official philosophy backed by the G.P.U.–N.K.V.D.–M.G.B."[1] On the other hand, Moshe Lewin, a Polish émigré writer, asserts that Lenin, acting in concert with Trotsky and others, would have been able to bring Soviet Russia through a less tragic, more rational and, for the cause of socialism, less compromising path" than Stalinism.[2]

The second selection is by the late J. P. Nettl, author of a much acclaimed biography of Rosa Luxemburg. His is a survey of the economic and political life of the Soviet Union for the late 1920's to 1940. Nettl clearly emphasizes the break in

[1] *Encounters with Lenin* (Oxford University Press, 1968), p. 260.
[2] *Lenin's Last Struggle* (New York: Pantheon Books, 1968), pp. 139-40.

continuity of Stalinism with the Bolshevik tradition. Politically, this is best seen in Stalin's doctrine of "objective treachery" where, by mere edict, a life-long communist could become a traitor to the working class. Economically, the discontinuity is even more marked in the ruthless drive toward collectivization and industrialization. Nettl is generally skeptical of the economic results. He agrees that in some respects they are impressive but that much the same might have been attained through the continuation of Lenin's less drastic methods. The key element in Stalin's Five-Year Plans was the absolute priority given to heavy industry. This raises a point which is not yet resolved: Would another kind of industrialization, however successful statistically, have prepared the Soviet economy adequately to resist the Nazi onslaught?

The first selection is the work of Leonard Schapiro, Professor of Political Science at the London School of Economics and author of *The Communist Party of the Soviet Union* (Random House, 1960). Schapiro is clearly on the side of those who accept a fundamental continuity between Lenin and Stalin. He does concede that there was "a certain ambivalence in Lenin's views" toward the end of his life; however, the principal basis for Stalin's dictatorship, the "monopolistic Party in its monolithic form," was inherited from Lenin.

INDUSTRIALIZATION IN THE SOVIET UNION, 1929-1940

J. P. Nettl

The Bolsheviks' second, industrial revolution began in 1928. It was this which ultimately gave the Soviet Union its modern character, the basic image and the various associations implied by the term Soviet Communism. In one sense this second revolution completed the work of Lenin and the old Bolsheviks. Where they had superimposed a new philosophy, a new instrument of rule and a new group of leaders on an ancient predominantly peasant society, Stalin and his new Bolsheviks reached right down into every cranny of conservatism with their plans of steel and concrete and their foreshortened but irresistible Marxist pedagogy. By the time Stalin died the Soviet Union had been completely transformed—not only as an international entity but as a society.

Yet the industrial revolution also involved a sharp break with Bolshevik tradition. Hitherto there had always been a clear contrast between the Party and the rest of society, between the Soviet Union and the capitalist world. "We" and "they" had been marked off from each other by discontinuities and conflicts which Marxists had learnt to recognize as instinctively as they told night from day. Indeed, they had been taught to maintain the distinction as sacred. Now these frontiers were to shift and to dissolve; people became capitalists or representatives of capitalist interests by edict, because Stalin and the leadership said so. The doctrine of objective treachery came to mean that you could spend a lifetime in the cause of communism, and yet be objectively bourgeois—a traitor. This applied not only to individuals, but also to classes. The *kulaks* were transformed almost overnight from a tolerated necessity to a hostile class which must be destroyed at once. Writers who criticized or merely abstained from praising Bolshevik achievements; workers who grumbled openly; Party members who dissented or merely confused yesterday's truth with today's heresy; finally leaders who disagreed (or had disagreed) with Stalin openly or potentially—all were cast into the same fatal mould of class enemies and bourgeois traitors. Bolsheviks had always conducted their polemics in hard language, following a tradition dating back long beyond Marx to 1793. But when Stalin, in one of his homely phrases, referred to "dogs returning to their own dung" it was not only an earthy epithet but a reduction to subhumanity—and could well be a mandate for liquidation.

It all started so gradually, almost by accident. The government of the Soviet Union, the leadership of Party and Comintern—for all important purposes one and the same body of men—seemed, at the beginning of 1928, to be as firmly wedded to the economic and social guidelines of NEP as ever: state control of the commanding heights of the economy, small capitalist accumulation everywhere else.

The opposition in the party to NEP and "socialism in one country" had either been expelled or had capitulated—and now humbly sought readmission at the bottom like discards in a game of poker. The strongest advocates of the continuation of NEP, Bukharin and Rykov, were firmly in the saddle. Some people believed that these men would at last be able to rid themselves of their uncomfortable ally Stalin, the General Secretary, acclaimed at Party Congresses for always representing the majority—hence correct—line, but surely no match for so many experienced and clever men. Everything seemed set for at least a few more years of peace and quiet inside the Party, at home as well as abroad. Yet by the summer of 1928 a full-scale campaign against the *kulaks* was getting under way, and Stalin was moving against his right-wing allies in the Politburo. The towns were short of food once more. According to Stalin, the government purchases of grain fell two million tons below what was needed. Emergency measures were called for and these, as always, were legitimized by a simple slogan summing up the political line: "The *kulaks* are disrupting Soviet economic policy." So they had to be squeezed.

The campaign began in May, at first in the context of improving grain deliveries, if necessary by pressure. "It would be folly," said Stalin, "to think of expropriating the *kulaks*." But by the end of the year collectivization was already in full swing. All over the Soviet Union, Party workers from the big cities, flushed from their desks and with only the most rudimentary instructions, found themselves in the countryside, first pleading with, then bullying and finally forcing the peasants willy-nilly into the new collectives. It was like the raids on the farms in 1919 and 1920, but this time under the banner of Leninism and not merely as a means of alleviating an overwhelming food crisis in the midst of civil war. The hope that the operation could be converted into a self-generating class struggle in the country, by raising the poor and landless peasants against their richer neighbours, turned out to be illusory. In general, village solidarity proved too strong and the temporary Commissars had to rely on volunteers from the towns, policemen and above all the military, to enforce collectivization and the demanded supply of grain. "We must smash the *kulaks*, eliminate them as a class. . . . We must strike at the *kulaks* so hard that they will never rise to their feet again," Stalin thundered encouragingly from the Kremlin.

Seen from that austere bastion, collectivization might perhaps appear as a process of revolutionary fervour. Certainly it was a statistical transformation. Within two years over half of all Soviet agricultural production had been turned from private farming to co-operative and state farming. But seen from below by those involved it was primarily a heartbreaking story of futile peasant resistance, of large-scale slaughter of animals and, in many cases, desperate starvation. A few peasants were willing to give the new collectives a try; the majority joined because they had to or starve. A statistical revolution had certainly been achieved, but the problem of agricultural production was not solved. It was to be a running sore on the glossy surface of Soviet economic growth, mutinously erupting to trouble Stalin and his successors.

Why was it done? Those historians who like to think of Stalin as a demigod brooding over a totally subservient society have pictured him ruminating in the Kremlin as early as 1927 on what steps should be taken to bring about the Great Society. Others, more strictly chronological in their approach, see a very close connection between the destruction of Stalin's right-wing allies and the adoption of left-wing measures. According to this canon, collectivization in the Soviet Union was a handy means of getting rid of unwanted colleagues at the top, every colleague being a potential rival for power. Contemporary Russian historians, especially those who write official history, generally tend to describe collectivization and the industrialization drive of the first Five Year Plan as a necessary and logical step in the development of the Soviet Union, its timing governed by the termination of the historical usefulness of NEP. Finally, unrepentant opponents of Bolshevism and the Soviet Union emphasize not only the human tragedy and the brutal bureaucratic dictatorship which caused it, but its pointlessness; the NEP growth rate in industry and agriculture could, with some foreign help and investment, have reached the required levels without force or a Five Year Plan. Probably each of these explanations has some measure of truth. Those who like their history spiced with irony find a sort of monstrous satisfaction in Stalin's adoption of what was essentially the policy advocated by Trotsky, Preobrazhensky and Sokolnikov immediately after he had removed them from positions of power. The relationship between the adoption of a new policy and the destruction of those who first advocated it appears indeed to be one of the features of Soviet history. Certainly their earlier advocacy of forced industrialization did the left no good, for Stalin hit out at left and right from 1929 onwards with equal vigour and finished up a few years later by circling the triangle: left and right were pronounced to be indistinguishable, identical, a matter of personal idiosyncrasy of phrase. And certainly there was a real connection between the new policy in the countryside and the elimination of suspected opponents in the Party. At least such a connection was pointed up by Stalin when an extensive purge of Party members took place in the spring of 1928. Abroad, the failures of Soviet diplomacy in Europe and communist activity in the Far East cried out for a successful diversion at home. Seldom had Soviet foreign policy been at such a low ebb as at the end of 1927, with the virtual destruction of the Chinese communists by their former allies, the Kuomintang, Great Britain's rupture of diplomatic relations in May 1928, finally the assassination of the Soviet Ambassador to Warsaw on 7 June—the first attack on a Soviet diplomat abroad for some years. World revolution was not only at a standstill but in full retreat. Socialism needed some glamour in its one home country to compensate for its tarnished image abroad.

All these factors played a part. But the most important one has not yet been listed. The year 1928 also witnessed the first of the Five Year Plans, the instrument by which the Soviet Union was to become a predominantly industrial power. To achieve the required growth of industry, four basic conditions had to be met. First, the availability of natural resources. Here the Soviet Union was most abundantly supplied, at least potentially. Secondly, a population structure producing a relative surplus in the crucial category between twenty and forty-five years was required. This existed in the USSR; neither famine nor the war period of 1914–21 had seriously altered the basic demographic trend of very high fertility and rather high mortality (though the peak in births took place during the NEP period, providing the maximum reservoir of youth for the Second World War and the subsequent reconstruction). Hence the Soviet Union in the 1930s had a relatively lower burden of old people to carry than probably any other country in Europe. At the same time the ideological pressure to equate men and women in work load and professional opportunities also had a sound demographic basis, for between the ages twenty to forty-five the estimated ratio of men to women was abnormally low—90:100.

The other two conditions were more directly controllable. Extra food would have to be available to support the growing population in the industrial towns, largely made up of peasants moving from the land to form the new labour force. And the final condition was the formation of extra capital for investment. Every second-year student of economics—and every politician in developing countries—knows that without surplus agricultural supplies and capital for investment, no major efforts at industrialization can succeed. Such surpluses exist in the form of money savings, and/or an agricultural surplus currently being exported or capable of creation through more intensive exploitation of under-utilized resources. Alternatively, surpluses have to be created artificially by squeezing consumption. In the Soviet Union there were no obvious surpluses or spare capacity on any large scale. In calling for an intense drive against the *kulaks,* Stalin spoke of immense hoards of food, but these soon proved either laughable or illusory, just as they had in the lean years of War Communism. Nonetheless, with the vast majority of the population living on the land, a food surplus could conceivably be squeezed out by force—providing that the same peasant, viewed as a consumer, could be forced to make do with far less. Henceforward the propaganda pictures of well-fed peasants sitting on tractors in the midst of glowing ears of corn emanated from one or two show collectives in so far as they were not studio portraits. In the vast majority of *kolkhozy* those who produced the food often did not have enough to eat, especially when the harvest was average or less.

There was also little surplus of capital available for investment in industry; this, too, the agricultural sector had to provide. The major part of the industrialization drive was thus financed, directly or indirectly, by the difference between the food prices charged to the urban consumer and the return to the peasant. The only way to maintain this disequilibrium was by rigid control of production and distribution—and by force, or at least the threat of it. As the purges of the 1930s got under way, an enormous reserve army of forced labour was created, which also played its part in the process of accumulation by working for almost nothing.

The collectivization drive and the first Five Year Plan coincided more or less in time. We do not know whether one led directly to the other, and if so which. The main political interest from 1928 to the beginning of 1930 was focused on collectivization, with the result that the percentage of collectives to total farm holdings rose from 4 percent in the middle of 1929 to 58 percent by the end of March 1930, when they contained 60 percent of the rural population of the Soviet Union. From the end of 1929 onwards industrialization and the first Five Year Plan began to take first place in the preoccupations of the rulers of the Soviet Union. In fact the government became worried by the reports of the destruction of livestock and the general disorganization in the countryside. It called a halt to collectivization. On 2 March 1930 Stalin claimed that the campaign had caused people to become dizzy with success; now they must sober up. All along he had insisted on regarding collectivization in public as a voluntary process—with just a little push here and there. The excesses to which he now admitted were caused by "stupid and reactionary" elements who wrongly wished to produce collectivization by force. But within six months the percentage of collective farms had dropped substantially as the peasants left the collectives almost as quickly as they had been made to enter them. So the drive was renewed with quieter determination, and collectivization went ahead from then on until by 1934 almost three-quarters of all farms had been collectivized. Nature took a hand and compounded the man-made tragedy; the depletion of livestock by deliberate slaughter and the destruction of grain and seed through disorganization and neglect contributed substantially to the appalling famine of 1932. Even the best agricultural areas of the Ukraine suffered; in the marginal areas the peasants starved, fled and died in tens of thousands. Famines in Russia are like hurricanes in the Caribbean, a recurrent disaster built into the life-cycle and consciousness of the population. But the famine of 1932 became a Soviet legend of horror, just as the simultaneous industrial depression in the West is still the cautionary basis of our industrial folklore. Nonetheless the squeeze and the Five Year Plan based on it were not relaxed. Agricultural production fell substantially in the early period of collectivization, but the quota of compulsory food deliveries to the state were maintained almost intact—"the first commandment," as Stalin called it. The difference was made up in the kitchens and hearths of the collective households.

Little of this was allowed to penetrate into the official cognizance of the town-dweller, himself now preoccupied with the long assault on the new industrial heights of the *piatiletka*, the Five Year Plan—unless he chose to listen to the groundswell of rumour, the lamentations of country friends or relations. Many of the first generation of urban dwellers were socially still embedded in the village from which they had come, a common phenomenon of early urbanization. The new industrial towns in the Ukraine, on the Volga and in Siberia, especially the areas of forced resettlement, were at first populated by uprooted peasants barely leavened with urban Party volunteers—the beginning of the great move East which characterized the Stalin period. Here resentment was strong if inchoate, and the Party kept the strictest vigil. In the big cities of western Russia the process of finally divorcing towns from country, implicit in the sharp Bolshevik class differentiation between workers and peasants, was carried to its final stage by the twin policies of collectivization and the Five Year Plans. The Communist Party had been and continued to be an urban party, the efforts to broaden it feeble and spasmodic; the country was left to sink into an oblivion fitfully illuminated by an occasional flurry of statistics. Without some support in the towns, peasant discontent could find no focus of opposition. The press sang only the praises of the enormous upswing in industrial production, and kept mute about the agricultural failures. Officially, at any rate, collectivization followed the pattern which Stalin had tried to lay down: a sharpened class struggle in the countryside, guided by the Party, in the course of which the smaller peasants and landless labourers successfully asserted themselves against the *kulaks*. *Kulaks* soon ceased to be any distinct class or group; all those who resisted collectivization were *kulaks*.

Collectivization and the initiation of the Five Year Plan must obviously be considered as one and the same social phenomenon, even if the order of individual decisions suggests a more complex connection. In the next few years the achievements of the Five Year Plan provided the main content of news in the Soviet Union. Production statistics became the thought and life of Soviet society. For foreign communists and sympathizers the cautious self-regarding foreign policy of the Soviet Union, and the macabre horrors of the great purges to come, could be made intellectually bearable only by off-setting them against the industrial attainments of socialist Russia. The domestic stress on economic development was readily echoed by sympathizers everywhere, to explain the disappointing and, for many, downright reactionary, features of Stalinism, its cruelty and its apparently blind unpredictability. Rapid industrial development became the main goal of Soviet society, its attainments a blanket justification for everything else. The nascent *ouvrièrisme* which had emerged so clearly in leadership styles from the Fifteenth Congress at the end of 1927 onwards now became the desired style at all levels of Party life. The final victims were the intellectuals, for whom a world of production figures in percentages could hardly be a creative environment. Since for most people figures are cold and unlovely things, the spirit of the 1930s in the Soviet Union was epitomized in popular culture by spectacular examples of production—the Dnepropetrovsk Dam and, perhaps most memorable of all, the Moscow Underground. No traffic analyst looking for a means of relieving pressure on surface transport would have plumped for this particular investment in a metropolis where automobiles were few, yet the "Metro" came to epitomize heroic achievement in the face of physical and technical odds. All the decisions, down to relatively minute technical problems, were made by the Party rather than by the engineers. Given a willingness to work regardless of hours, and unshaken faith in the human capacity to triumph over any environment, no task was too great for the activists of the Communist Party if the will was there. This approach to the solution of technical and economic problems, known as *sturmovshchina,* governed official Soviet attitudes to production for several decades. It also set norms which all were enjoined to follow.

The real importance of the second revolution of 1928–30 was not so much in what it achieved, as in the radical change in the manner of achieving it. Figures for overall industrial production do not in fact show any marked increase between the NEP period and that of the first two Five Year Plans (though the rate of growth increased by about 2 to 3 percent in the first few years); agricultural production actually declined for a time.[1] The second revolution as such can hardly be deduced from gross production figures at all. It was in the emphasis on *what* should be produced that the great change made its impact—the stress on heavy industry at the expense of consumer goods which was to be a prime feature of Soviet economics for the next twenty-five years. More important still, perhaps, was the change in outlook. Henceforward politics and economics were to be fused into one, and not divorced as they had been during NEP. Every political decision seemed to be shaped to a single end—more production, and still more. Marx had derided capitalist society

---

[1] Statistics in the USSR for a long time presented a special problem, since they were intended to convey a minimum of accurate information to potential critics and a maximum of propaganda for supporters. Accordingly the analysis of Soviet industrial and agricultural statistics is itself a major academic exercise. Figures in this book have been selected from a wide range of possible alternatives as being the most informative in the view of the author. Recent Soviet statistics are of course a considerable improvement over those put out under Stalin.

as an inhuman engine for the production of profit: "Accumulate, accumulate: that is Moses and all the Prophets." Yet nowhere in any capitalist society was the entire weight of propaganda directed quite so firmly and self-consciously towards the end of capital accumulation as in the Soviet Union under Stalin. We shall meet this paradox again: precisely those features which Marx had characterized as typical of "high" capitalism, and which he had condemned accordingly, reached their official apotheosis in the Soviet Union, legitimized only by the destruction of the private capitalist as a class and his replacement by "the workers' state." The motor of investment in capitalist development had usually been the agricultural surplus; in Soviet Russia this principle was pushed to its logical conclusion in that the agricultural "surplus" was simply provided more or less by force. Finally the state and its institutional apparatus, whose destruction had been the first task of Bolshevik revolution, were strengthened beyond all measure in the Soviet Union of Joseph Stalin, and provided the cutting edge of "the dictatorship of the proletariat." The point in emphasizing this is not to convict communists of hypocrisy and insincerity (which are unmarketable commodities in politics anyway) but to show that self-conscious and rapid industrialization has a logic of its own to which ideologies and philosophies—capitalist and communist alike—have necessarily to be tailored.

In effect the second revolution transformed the whole of the Soviet Union into a single enormous firm. The management of the economy merged with the government of the country: managing director Stalin, the Politburo his board, and everyone else managers, technicians, public-relations men and workmen. The plan figures of 1929 had been merely indicators of what production levels were desirable, as was the practice during NEP; they now became overnight a legal norm—by statute. This did not make the figures any more attainable; it took many years of hard struggle and the dismantling of an already outdated Stalinism before the technique of planning could finally be made to accommodate economic criteria of balance and preference instead of a set of behavioural rules which incessantly spurred and threatened. Many competent economists have devoted much time to exposing the irrationality of Soviet industrial plans, as well as measuring (on the basis of insufficient and often highly inaccurate figures) reality against expectation and propaganda. In a sense all this is beside the point. What mattered was the obsession with *more.* At the level of production of the USSR in the late 1920s there could hardly be a serious danger of over-production in physical terms, and the problem of balance was solved, at least for the next decade, by the concentration on heavy industry as a first priority. So everything was ploughed back into more production. The bottlenecks came mainly in distribution, and these were tackled, if not always solved, by the institutionalization of permanent crisis. Almost overnight the Soviet Union became "plan conscious"; as children learn the Ten Commandments in Christian countries, so Soviet children learned the importance of fulfilling plans.

This involved a cultural and social revolution as much as an economic one. For the sake of production some very fundamental tenets of Bolshevism were sacrificed. The basically egalitarian approach to economic and social rewards, which had been a distinctive feature under Lenin and had been retained in the state sector of agriculture and industry even during NEP, was now abandoned. Inequality had not only to exist but to be seen to exist. Military ranks were once again introduced into the Red Army in 1936, when it was reconverted into a standing force, and with formal ranks came the more ornate courtesies and visible differentiation that go under the name of military discipline. But of course the resulting social rewards were quite distinct from the hierarchy of political power. The effective authority of commanders was reduced by the system of political commissars (*politruky*). A tense competition between commander and political officer developed which Stalin deliberately refused to resolve; apart from an inevitable but temporary relaxation during the war it was only in the 1950s that the military commanders finally obtained a clear decision on their own primacy in all matters pertaining to military discipline and control.

Planned as they were, prices had to give expression to the social priorities of the planners—both in artificially cheapening strategic materials and supplies, and in inhibiting comsumption at the retail end. The inequalities of the price system therefore reflected, at least officially, the priorities of the government rather than the scarcity expression of the market—a special and not always rational form of inequality. The whole system of consumer supplies was, however, partially removed from the influence of the pricing system altogether. In times of crying shortage, special shops sold superior food and clothing to the privileged and the deserving—not against payment of money but against proof of status. Above all Stalin fulminated against wage levelling, and stressed the importance of rewarding workers in accordance with what they produced—a piecework mentality of an extreme kind. In 1935 a coal-miner called Stakhanov, under the full glare of publicity, succeeded with two assistants in producing 102 tons of anthracite in a work shift of five and three-quarter hours at the Irmino Coal Mine in the Ukraine. Stakhanovism had arrived: the perpetual pressure to overfulfil work norms and plans, with rewards of public esteem and material benefits in money and kind for success, and public condemnation or punishment for failure. Within a few months similar records were reported from many other industries. In spite of its unpopularity—during the mid 1930s shock-workers ran the risk of being killed by their workmates—the Stakhanovite campaign was never abandoned during Stalin's life, and was even copied in some of the People's Democracies in eastern Europe after the war. It may seem a heavy-footed, even absurd approach today, but it dominated the attitude to work of an entire Soviet generation.

Secondary and deeper effects soon made themselves felt. The Lenin period of freedom and experimentation was over, not only in the Party but in every sphere of life. The debates of the 1920s about the proper representation of Party ideals in literature now gave way to direction from above, and the professional organization of writers with its link to the Party was transformed into an institution through which the Party could exercise tight control over literary production. We may ask whether forced industrialization, with its built-in pressures for conformity and commitment, can ever co-exist with an atmosphere of free criticism and comment; Stalin and his colleagues certainly did not believe this to be the case. In the course of his authoritative definition of Marxism-Leninism, artists, scientists and even architects had their tasks minutely allocated. Literature had to be solid and earthy and concern itself with the objective problems of socialist construction rather than idealist speculations about human nature. Painting had also to represent the ideal of socialist construction—this is the period of endless canvases of happy people working on building sites or on farms. Industrial art of a sophisticated kind is a perfectly feasible form of expression, as artists like Lissitzky showed; but direction on the subject-matter was not enough, content and form were specified as well.

Both writing and art had to have pedagogical as well as highly representational qualities. The buildings of the period were grandiose, old-fashioned and heavy in exterior and internal design.

Nor did this incorporation of intellectual activity into the Stalinist version of an industrial society stop at the immediately expressive arts. The writing of history was examined critically according to the new criteria. Party history was already being re-written to suit the current political situation from 1930 onwards; after 1932 Stalin's pronouncements on the past as an integral part of the present became the stuff of Soviet historiography. Henceforward footnotes and references were not designed to do anything but give a scientific appearance to these proceedings—the writings of Lenin and Stalin became the main sources of all Party history. World history as a whole was put through the same mincing machine. The class struggle became the main component of history since the Neolithic Age. Science also was classified into Marxist and bourgeois concepts. Lysenko and the environmental school of biologists triumphed on political rather than experimental grounds—inhibiting advances in research for two decades. Even exact sciences like mathematics were analysed according to ideological content, and mathematical concepts were subjected to the "correct" critical analysis. In the fields of both art and science the strait-jacket was laced tight; only physics and chemistry escaped unscathed in their basic approaches. The arts have not fully recovered to this day. The sciences lived off capital by concentrating largely on problems of application and technology for twenty years, and only the enormous revival of basic research less inhibited by ideological considerations after Stalin's death refurbished the partially depleted intellectual capital of Soviet science.

These developments should not be viewed as mere narrow-mindedness. We have seen that in the 1920s the fundamental question of a proletarian culture had been posed and answered mainly in the negative in accordance with Lenin's own strongly felt views. Stalin did not specifically subscribe to any notion of a proletarian culture, but he did believe that culture was a secondary consequence of the social environment. This was being visibly changed, and the control of and interference with free expression were designed to align the arts and sciences with the concrete phenomena of the new industrial society—a process of the firmest integration. There was accordingly a basic logic in this proceeding. Its failure, as Lenin in a sense foresaw, was due partly to the fact that science and art relate not only to the social processes of any one society, but form an international system of their own; unless the Soviet Union really could be hermetically sealed for many generations, this international system could not wholly be broken. More important, the relationship between social life and its intellectual reflection is not a simple step-by-step process but a complex and long-term one. No one can predict accurately the precise way in which cultural and intellectual changes will reflect those of society. The attempt, therefore, to integrate these two spheres merely resulted in the impoverishment of scientific and intellectual achievement: the substitution of photography for art, of technology for science—an impoverishment which Soviet scientists and writers were to feel all the more acutely when they had to chance once more to "compare" themselves.

Yet, the very impoverishment of quality seemed to make possible the vast increase in quantity, or at least the widest diffusion of a basic minimum. By reducing history, philosophy and science to a series of over-simple paradoxes, Stalin made them comprehensible to levels of society which hitherto had been quite untouched by them. Anyone reading today the famous *Short Course in the History of the Communist Party of the Soviet Union,* anonymously published but strongly influenced if not indeed written by Stalin, is struck at once by its falsifications, its simplifications and turgidness of style. Yet this was the book that hundreds of thousands of Party workers and agitators in the Soviet Union and abroad learned by rote, and which formed the basis of their approach to Marxism and its history. They in turn reproduced its heavy-footed simplicities to millions of listeners forcibly collected in study groups and Party cells. In judging its quality we should therefore bear in mind not what it represents as history, but its enormous success as a simple pedagogical instrument, the font of baptism through which the complex ideas of Marxism were sprinkled over a whole society. Not since the Bible has any single text had the same impact. In the absence of challenge, and with the irresistible push of authority behind it, the *Short Course* became the most important document of the Stalinist era.

Meanwhile "socialism in one country" was to be applied literally and universally—and socialism for the moment meant industrialization. Everything that was conducive to higher production was stressed and supported. During the first flush of free thinking the institution of marriage had been left to the individual's private proclivities; in the 1920s divorce and abortions were easily obtained (at least as far as facilities allowed). Now the sanctity of marriage began once more to be officially reaffirmed, divorce became more difficult and in 1936 abortions were made illegal. The struggle against religion was no longer left primarily to Party agitation; the limited revival of overt religion during NEP was now met by the full force of Soviet law. The decree of 7 April 1929 forbade the Orthodox Church to own property or to teach. Only local Soviets could license a building for purposes of worship on a temporary basis. Some 2,000 monasteries and many more churches were closed during the two years 1929-30, and the new towns often contained no churches at all.

The educational experiments of the 1920s at first received an enthusiastic further lease of life with the challenge of the new industrialization policy. Learning by doing, the Complex and Project Methods, and even the Dalton Plan seemed to acquire new relevance. But from 1931 a new and strictly conservative trend was initiated from the top. Experiments were quietly abandoned, and classrooms became disciplined centres for turning out the necessary army of conventionally qualified workers and technicians. Teachers were restored to full authority in their domain. Even equality of opportunity came to mean something different. Access to educational opportunity had been opened to the children of workers and, to a lesser extent, peasants, but the selection of those able to go on to higher education was henceforward increasingly based on the ability to excel in examinations. The education authorities went back to prescribing curricula in the minutest detail, as in Tsarist times, tailoring the educational system to serve the recruiting needs of the vast Soviet "firm," not those of an experimental society in revolution. The technicians and scientists of whom Khrushchev was to be so proud in the 1950s were mostly selected and trained in the schools of Stalin.

But the second revolution succeeded where the first had really failed. Liberation by example and by cultural prescription had not been enough. Only by destroying the very basis of the old society and providing a universal infrastructure of literacy, by controlled mobilization into a social environment dominated by crude perspectives of production, could the basis of a new society be created. But no one could foresee the shape of the new. Perhaps it was this deliberate unwillingness to gaze into the future—to make the present seem as though it embraced both past and future, as though there would never be anything but this present—that actually made the future possible.

What was life like for ordinary people in the 1930s? The answer must be: grim and grey. If you were not a Party member for whom the present was made luminous by the logic of historical necessity and the conviction of being on the side of the future, if you were not a manager, technician or shock-worker with special privileges, the pressures must at times have seemed well-nigh intolerable. At the bottom of the process of industrialization, life is hard under any system, but even more so when all the basic received certainties of life—religion, friendship, tradition—were being questioned and changed at the same time. The myth of the good times under Lenin and NEP grew up in this period, particularly in the countryside. Some people even thought nostalgically of pre-war Russia, though of course they did not dare to say so. This was above all a period of dislocation, of movement into new regions and towns. Housing was in desperately short supply, and not high on the order of official priorities. Around many of the major cities of the Soviet Union, both in the old industrial Russia of the west and in the new towns in the centre and east, there grew a ring of improvised dwellings, often no more than holes in the ground, in which whole families crowded together. The provision of an adequate apartment was in fact one of the rewards for deserving workers and technicians, and therefore a major incentive. The hours of work were long. When they were over, social and political obligations started: meetings of factory groups or cells, trade union meetings and other activities in which Party and government plans were explained and—in an increasingly formalized manner—discussed. Informal social life virtually disappeared from the Soviet Union, for by the time all obligations of formal society had been discharged, only one's immediate family could enjoy the little energy and time that was left. Nevertheless, in spite of the fact that almost all women worked, and that the state assumed ever greater responsibilities for children, the family was the residual beneficiary; even more than in western Europe family ties were actually strengthened in this period. For every son who denounced his father to the police or the schoolteacher during the purges, a thousand failed to do so. The only successful splitters of the family in this era were the Nazis in Germany.

In general the Party was everywhere. Behind it, once the great purges began, stood the Secret Police. You learnt to trust no one. The naturally open nature of the Russians, to whom long and inconclusive conversations about the problems of life, and the offer of intimate confidences to almost complete strangers, were a normal part of life, gradually became enclosed in the new official culture of silence. The class enemy, one was constantly reminded, lurked everywhere, waiting and watching. With household names like Trotsky, Zinoviev and Bukharin suddenly revealed as bourgeois agents, English spies, whom could you trust? Did not Stalin call for incessant vigilance, which made surveillance of your neighbour a social duty? Whatever else the purges did, they taught the Russians the need for extreme reserve.

In the countryside things were worse, though for different reasons. The economic discrimination against agriculture made itself felt on all levels. The Communist Party made little headway among the collective farmers. Recreation, medical services, education hardly existed except on posters. The idiocy of rural life (Marx's phrase) found a grimmer realization in the Soviet Union. The depletion of the human and cultural as well as economic resources of the countryside in favour of the new industrial towns was only made worse by the absolute refusal of the leadership to acknowledge it—even though official policy was directly responsible.

Any objective evaluation of the Soviet standard of living during these years must take into account the substantial benefits supplied by the state to sections of the population who had hitherto been almost completely deprived. During the period of industrialization, there was an enormous expansion of medical and health services. Already by 1940 there were more doctors per thousand of population than in the United States, Britain, Germany or France. The system of polyclinics, whatever its medical pros and cons, certainly made access to facilities more readily available to greater numbers of people—especially since some of the sociological inhibitions which prevent people from visiting doctors were largely removed. It was in this period that relatively general sick-pay benefits were instituted, though an attempt to reduce the excessive labour turnover in the late 1930s tied these to a minimum period of service in any one enterprise. Sport became professionalized. Footballers, athletes, and above all chess players (the Russian national game *par excellence)* were induced to treat their performance as part of their plan fulfilment. Outstanding excellence was equivalent to the achievements of the shock-worker in industry. More important, however, was the popularization of these events in terms of mass participation. The commitment to the performance of teams and individuals, which still marks the Soviet Union today, is thus a compound of the natural loyalties of most *aficionados* for their favourite performers with the identification of support for sporting performance as a social duty.

The system of paid holidays also dates from the mid-1930s. Naturally the facilities in no way expanded as rapidly as the demand, but the principle had at any rate been established, and was to survive as a sheet-anchor of the Soviet approach to labour problems. It is significant that recent investigations into comparative job satisfaction in the Soviet Union, on the one hand, and the United States and the West on the other, show clearly how important a part of the general attitude to work paid and organized holidays have become, and above all to what extent this institution is regarded as a fundamental and original aspect of Soviet life.

The first decade of industrialization thus witnessed substantial hardships—though not without some very basic benefits, the results of which were only to be reaped a generation later. Parallel to these official benefits were the informal mechanisms with which the Soviet citizen learnt to defend himself against excessive demands and controls. These were the result of the failure of even the best of plans to provide for every eventuality, but in fact they "humanized" the system and made it possible to function and live in it. *Blat,* the unofficial lubrication of the wheels of production and supply through hoarding, supplementary private purchase and bribery, was in some ways "higher than Stalin"—as the saying went. Managers of factories, caught in the trap between fulfilling plans that were sometimes unattainable through miscalculation or supply breakdowns (and would, if achieved, almost inevitably bring higher norms for the next year), and failure, which could mean severe punishment, learnt to circumvent the official channels of material distribution. They also hoarded material in short supply, which they did not declare in their returns of material balances—figures on which the whole edifice of planning depended. Such materials could only be obtained unofficially. To supply them a small army of fixers or *tolkachy* grew up, who handled the whole delicate business. Since government and Party insisted during the heyday of planning on laying down the precise amounts of each product which individual farms were expected to deliver—as though the very earth itself could be made amenable to the planners' will—collective farms were sometimes obliged to purchase at higher prices in the open market such amounts of grain and other produce as were needed to fulfil their delivery quotas. The farms had no mechanical equipment of their own, for the collectivized peasant could not be trusted with such valuables. Tractors and other machines were supplied by hire arrangements with state-owned Machine and Tractor Stations, whose job it also was to keep an eye on the honesty and efficiency of the farmers. Since peasants were not paid wages, but received a share of the total collective farm profit divided into so many labour days per member of the farm, they went short if the farm failed to make a surplus. This was no rare occurrence—especially in the marginal farming areas in the centre and south of the Soviet Union. Controlled, supervised and squeezed as farmers were, the job of collective farm chairman was not an enviable one, and it often proved difficult to find suitable candidates. Many of those who undertook the job were not attracted by the challenge but rather by the chance to exercise power or extortion, to squeeze the farm still further for their own and their cronies' benefit.

Probably the most important single factor of relief for the peasant was the existence of the private plot within the framework of the collective. A collective farm differed from a state farm in that it was legally regarded as the property of the members, rather than of the whole society represented by the state. This was of course of no advantage to the participants. Quite the contrary, it was a means of discriminating against them as compared to the state farmer or *sovkhoznik*. But the collective farmer did retain small peripheral plots of land in and around the new collective farms. Though the time spent on these for his own benefit, and the disposal of the produce, were strictly controlled by law, in practice these private plots afforded the *kolkhoznik* the only straw of private incentive. It was almost impossible to check accurately the division of his time between the private plot and the collective as a whole—especially in the many cases where the farm chairman and other local authorities connived at the neglect of the farm for the private plot in return for "contributions." The removal of private plots was threatened at various times, but overall the system has survived—at times proliferating to such an extent that after the Second World War a quite disproportionate amount of food was produced privately.

The ability of the individual to bypass the endless regulations depended ultimately on the collaboration of others. There gradually developed throughout the Soviet Union a system of *quid pro quo,* through which one eye was shut to the misdeeds of others in return for a reciprocity of blindness—a system known as "family relationships." In a sense this system follows logically from the enormous apparatus of control built up during these years, in which everyone in a job or office from the lowly farmer to the highest official had somebody watching over him. These relationships were primarily based on the Party. In the provinces particularly the secretary of the local Soviet Executive Committee, the secretary of the Party Committee, the representative of the Procuracy (local law enforcement) and the representative of the police collaborated with managers, collective farm chairmen and other interested parties in a well-organized chain of mutual protection. The same type of relationship operated even in individual ministries at the centre. The Party was well aware of this, and for the next twenty years eternal vigilance against such secondary "families" was preached in the newspapers and at Party meetings. The systematic purge in the Stalin period may partly be explained as the only means available to break these informal ties. While it is not suggested that the first purges were in any sense due to such considerations, the vicious spiral of more control, more evasion, more supervision and still more evasion, could in the last resort be broken only by undermining all sense of security in personal relationships based on mutual interests. Mutual protection is a bureaucratic phenomenon in all societies. With the existence of a supreme and irremovable Communist Party as a fundamental part of the system, and the exacting demands it made upon the system's members, the institutionalization of such relationships became almost inevitable—and purges, or the threat of purges, the only way of somehow limiting them. It can therefore be argued that the Soviet system, as it developed in these years, threatened to block all known channels of change. Revolutionary fervour was certainly not enough; normal processes of turnover had atrophied with the reduction of elections to a mere formality. Only the institutionalization of insecurity could provide a safeguard. Even today, with terror largely dismantled, the basic insecurity as a built-in system of Soviet administration and Party life partly remains.

To us and our contemporaries in the Soviet Union today, preoccupied with welfare and rising standards of living, these times must in retrospect seem grim indeed. What was achieved? Let the unadorned figures speak once more. In general the year 1928, just prior to the first Five Year Plan, showed a level of industrial production very similar to the Russia of 1913 (adjusted for loss of territories after 1918). The enormous ravages of six years of foreign and civil war had been made good at last. By 1940 Soviet industrial output had trebled. The annual growth rate in these twelve years was almost 9 percent per annum, compared to present British growth rates of less than 3 percent. The beginning of Soviet industrialization, and the period of the first Five Year Plan, coincided with the great depression in other parts of the world, when output in the United States fell by almost a third. By 1940 the Soviet Union was a major industrial power. Yet at the same time the rate of growth, impressive as it appeared, was not significantly higher than during the recovery period of NEP from 1921 to 1927. We are therefore faced with two obvious questions, only one of which historians have really tried to answer. This concerns the means chosen to achieve full-scale industrialization in the Soviet Union. Could NEP have been continued and still have attained the levels of industrial output and the growth rates of the Stalin period? Not surprisingly historians divide ideologically over this question. Pointing to the growth rates of NEP, many Western economists and historians maintain that the system was "taking off" in any event. The partial market factors of "limited" socialism under NEP might have allocated resources more rationally, they say; there would have been more consumer goods, and a more efficient use of resources. Soviet historians naturally take a contrary view. Only the absolute priority for basic industries made possible the further growth rates of the post-Second World War period, and the attainment of the superior technological sophistication of the present day. Moreover they consider the question itself largely absurd. Socialism requires this order of priorities, the transformation of the economy from individual small-scale procedures to collective and integrated large-scale production. This problem had already been discussed in the early 1920s. Only fully controlled industrialization justifies planning; and *vice versa*—only full-scale planning can solve the problems of socialist industrialization.

This leads to the second question: why was the process of industrialization in this form begun in 1928? Was it a purposeful execution of a rational and deliberate decision, or did it just happen? It is still not possible to answer this question with any real authority, but I think that within the context of a desire to accelerate production and tighten the planning process, Soviet industrialization was to a considerable extent self-generated, feeding on itself politically and economically just as collectivization had done. However much Stalin covered his actions with explanations of historical and logical inevitability, he was a far less acute theorist and thinker than Lenin. His explanations were always retrospective rather than programmatic. The squeeze on the *kulaks* may have started as an attempt to obtain grain, but once the class-war justification for it had been articulated, a more fundamental solution to the problem developed mainly under its own steam, and this self-reinforcement was fed back up the line into the political process to become official policy. Similarly the dramatic switch from indicative planning to a full command economy became self-generating, with official explanations and justification hurrying alongside. Once the process was under way, the Soviet leaders embraced it wholeheartedly. The vision of a long next step towards socialism and finally communism opened out in the early 1930s, and transformed a series of particular policies into a fundamental philosophy.

There was one field especially to which Stalin had devoted a great deal of time and effort—Party manipulation and control. Both collectivization and the first Five Year Plan meant a greatly strengthened role for the Party, which was wholly in line with the wishes and intentions of the communist leaders. In the course of the economic upheaval the Party was to become formally integrated into Soviet life at every level—except in the agricultural countryside—in a way which hitherto had been impossible. By the time things had settled down after the purges and just before the Second World War, the Party was installed literally everywhere. Those who controlled the Party really controlled the Soviet Union rather than merely ruling it.

The great purges from 1934 to 1938 seem to be in flagrant contradiction to the demands of forced industrialization. If the Party was to lead society in its enormous production drive, it would surely need to be cohesive and united. But there are always two approaches to cohesion and unity: consensus or discipline, persuasion or terror. Stalin chose the latter alternative. Society and Party were galvanized simultaneously. Terror was applied to production. Its threat was a spur to fulfilment, and its victims were often reintegrated into the bottom of the production process as slave labourers who consumed only a fraction of what they produced—the ideal form of surplus accumulation. How then to galvanize the Party? Hitherto the struggle among the leadership in the late 1920s had had relatively little effect on the middle and lower Party levels. By 1929 the simple and gross condemnation of Trotskyism had worked its way right through, and following on the leaders the lower echelons were being purged as well—no longer because they were unsuitable, but because they were deviationists. By the mid-1930s recantation of error no longer made re-admission possible. Between 1928 and 1933 industrialization brought an influx of new recruits; the Party grew from one and a half to three and a half million members and candidates. But the numbers declined again sharply during the continuous purge of the next three years, and this time the mass purge preceded that of the elite. By the beginning of 1937 numbers were down to just below two million. The purge had got out of hand. From then on there was again to be an excess of recruitment over evictions. Most important, the character of the Party was completely changed during these years; it became on average substantially younger, and though the proportion of workers or sons of workers was still overwhelming, they were themselves increasingly members of the new intelligentsia, the product of Soviet schools and Komsomol.

The idea of different norms for Party and society, of keeping the two distinct through hierarchically connected at the top, had been fundamental to Lenin's thinking. He envisaged that the period of amalgamation between Party and society would be a gradual and very long-term process. Stalin decided to shorten it; in the process Lenin's conception of the amalgamation procedure was radically changed. In the course of four years he eliminated a large part of Lenin's old Bolsheviks, the leadership of the foreign Communist Parties (physically if they happened to be in the Soviet Union, by eviction if not), and finally a nameless host of more or less innocent people who were caught up in the vortex of destruction. By the time it was over, the Communist Party of the Soviet Union had become a monolithic and disciplined instrument of control. But instead of being the vanguard of society, distinct and self-conscious, the Party had become a social and political elite, with all positions of importance and power in its hand. The non-Party specialist, engineer, professor or lawyer had effectively ceased to exist in any position of importance.

Though the channels of discussion and participation in the Party became replaced by mere ritual, new channels of social mobility were opened up instead. With the destruction of a whole generation of old Bolsheviks, whose main experience had been the clandestine political life before 1917 and the pioneering spirit of the early years, a new generation moved into positions of power, to whom these early years were sacred legends rather than actual adult experiences. These were people to whom concern about basic problems was unfamiliar and therefore secondary, who accepted the industrializing perspectives of the Stalinist leadership as a part of their life, and whose activism was revolutionary not so much in a political as in an economic sense. Though solid Party members all, whose whole *raison d'être* was encapsulated within the Communist Party, they viewed their privileged position increasingly as connected with specific know-how in different fields. Instead of debating the first principles of Marxism, they applied Stalin's interpretation of Marxism-Leninism to production, planning, military strategy and management. Most of them were not technicians in the ordinary sense (though a few were), but rather politicians whose politics consisted of the ability to move rapidly from one technical sector to the other. They were political professionals specializing in management. Each of them saw himself as the beneficiary as well as the expression of the historical wisdom residing in the Party as a collective. But they regarded membership of the Party in terms of something they possessed rather than something which they created. Khrushchev was typical of these men. Beneath and below them there was to grow up yet another generation of *real* technicians, silently awaiting their turn—but this comes later.

At the approach of the 1930s, Stalin, Bukharin, Rykov and Tomsky were uneasily expressing their conflicting views about collectivization and Party policy behind closed doors. If Bukharin and his friends opposed the principles of collectivization and the first Five Year Plan, they certainly were not going to create the same open split for which they had condemned Trotsky and Zinoviev. Nonetheless Stalin moved firmly against them. The Party men who had supported the General Secretary at the Fourteenth and Fifteenth Congresses, the loyal Central Committee and purged Politburo, now supported him again. It was Stalin's particular expertise to draw arbitrary lines across overlapping shades of opinion; Bukharin, Rykov and Tomsky had to go, Kalinin remained untouched. By the end of 1929 all three had been removed from their top posts in the Soviet state and the Comintern. Bukharin was expelled from the Politburo; his vague *pourparlers* with the previously routed "left" were loudly denounced as yet another attempt to form an opposition block—the Party crime that had become unforgivable. Bukharin now began to realize what so many other Bolsheviks would yet discover: Stalin, the grey, silent and inscrutable bureaucrat, who had always appeared as the very embodiment of a self-effacing Party official, was in fact an unprincipled intriguer who subordinated everything to his appetite for power. "Whenever necessary he will from one moment to the next change his theories in order to get rid of someone. He will strangle us all."

Stalin now had an absolutely reliable majority on the Central Committee, the Orgburo and the Politburo—not merely allies but direct and often dependent supporters. The Sixteenth Congress in July 1930 enthusiastically supported his call for unremitting struggle against right-wing opportunism. Organizations at lower levels, who had voted with the opposition, were dissolved or purged. The collectivization drive was at its height—and so was resistance to it; opposition within the Party suggested all too clearly and directly an alliance with the recalcitrant class enemies of the regime.

We do not know exactly when police terror as such really began. Khrushchev, in his anti-Stalin speech at the Twentieth Congress in 1956, cited documents to show that in Stalin's view the purges of 1936 came four years too late. Nor can we assess the attitude of the Politburo, in effect the ruling institution of the Soviet Union. It is at least possible that some of those who had backed Stalin solidly against the more individualistic and enterprising intellectuals might still have baulked in private at the use of this ultimate weapon indiscriminately and generally against the Party as a whole. One effect of the industrialization drive, with its emphasis on rigid obedience and loyalty, was that many former Mensheviks who had joined the Bolsheviks after 1917 and had been left to occupy important posts were now flushed out again as an "objective" danger to security. Those former Mensheviks who wanted to survive had to distinguish themselves by their superlatives in Stalin's service. Vyshinsky was one of them—the gruesome and unlovely Fouquier-Tinville of the great trials, to whom fell the task of prosecuting and annihilating men far more distinguished than himself. In March 1931 a group of Mensheviks, including the eminent economist Groman and the historian Sukhanov, were sentenced to long terms of imprisonment for treason. Riazanov, perhaps the most distinguished Marxist scholar in Russia and former head of the Marx-Lenin Institute, certainly a Bolshevik of independent mind, was implicated and evicted from the Party: he was to be one of the first to perish in the purges. From 1933 onwards the purges of the Party were no longer carried out by regular Party organs like the Control Commission or the Central Committee, but by a group of new Party men like Ezhov whose career was the NKVD, the Commissariat or Department of the Interior. This organization in July 1934 integrated the secret police (GPU), which in the 1920s had replaced the Cheka.

At the time, these events seemed no more than an unusually heavy and prolonged squall. At the Seventeenth Party Congress in early February 1934 it looked for a moment as though the worst excesses of collectivization were over and industrialization safely on its way. This congress of the victors had about it some of the air of reconciliation and mutual satisfaction. Even condemned oppositionists like Bukharin, Zinoviev and Kamenev, who had been savagely attacked at previous Congresses, were now able to appear and speak in an atmosphere of apparent good will. The idea of mass trials, terror and death was unthinkable, fantastic.

Ten months later, on 1 December 1934, Kirov, a rising member of the Politburo and head of the Leningrad Organization, was murdered by a young communist called Nikolaev. This was at once labelled as the joint work of the opposition—all of them lumped amorphously together for purposes of condemnation. In fact it may have been the single and unsponsored action of an individual. Possibily Stalin had a hand in it: at least in 1956 Khrushchev was to hint strongly at Stalin's complicity. It may be, as one commentator has alleged, that the relaxation and apparent harmony in Party affairs between 1932 and 1934, and the reintegration of the former oppositionists, was due to Kirov's "new line," according to which the oppositionists had been punished enough and the industrialization drive now required Party harmony. With support for Kirov coming from within Stalin's own Central Committee Stalin was faced with both a restriction on his own freedom of action and a possible alternative leadership. The assassination of Kirov was thus extremely convenient for Stalin, ridding him of a powerful opponent and giving grounds for the liquidation of the oppositionists. The great purges followed directly from this event. It became "the basis for all the mass acts of abuse aginst socialist legality," in Khrushchev's words. During many of the fabricated cases the accused were charged with the preparation of terrorist acts. This deprived them of any possibility that their cases might be re-examined though they stated before the court that their confessions had been secured by force, and in some cases even managed to disprove the detailed evidence against them in a convincing manner. By the time Nikolaev and his alleged accomplices had been executed their activities were being publicly linked with Zinoviev. At the beginning of 1935 charges were laid against Zinoviev and Kamenev: they were sentenced to imprisonment. For the first time the law was used openly against Lenin's peers and colleagues. In January 1935 Kuibyshev died suddenly; in June 1936 Maxim Gorky, Lenin's friend and the revolution's best-known writer, also died. The then police chief, Yagoda, initiator of the mechanism of the purges and himself a later victim, was to be accused in due course of having poisoned them. In any case these deaths removed two of the last potential public obstacles of conscience to the full fury of the great purges.

Just as the purges were getting under way a new Soviet constitution was being worked out. All through 1936 Stalin, Bukharin and Radek co-operated with many other future victors and victims in producing a draft of what was proclaimed, at the meeting of the Supreme Soviet of 5 December 1936, to be the freest constitution in the world. Designed to embody fully planned state ownership of industry and collective farming as the twin bases of Soviet society, the constitution guaranteed solid liberties to the citizen, rights of independent decision-making and even secession to the Federal Republics. For the first time in Soviet constitutional history, the Party was formally mentioned—as "containing the most active and politically conscious citizens . . . the vanguard of the working people in their struggle to build a socialist system . . . and the leading core of all organizations . . . both public and of the state." Stalin himself described it as "the only completely democratic constitution in the world. Its international significance is without parallel." But the heavy irony of the timing of this charter of Bolshevik democracy emanates from a sense of right and wrong peculiar to our present time; for many Soviet citizens, and particularly for foreign sympathizers in the new left-wing Popular Front against Fascism, this well-publicized document helped above all to make the great trials and purges plausible. In such an atmosphere of triumph and achievement, with Stalin (in the words of *Pravda*) "the genius of the new age, the wisest man of the epoch," was there not bound to be something in these charges against the major accused, however monstrous they sounded? Did not the defendants admit to almost all the accusations against them? Above all, was the Soviet Union not somehow generically different from the rest of mankind, so that normal judgments of right and wrong did not apply?

By the end of 1936 a wave of arrests with and without subsequent trial was swamping the Soviet Union. The most distinguished old Bolsheviks were being arraigned and executed in batches. Perhaps a formal trial was the only concession to their rank; for every one of these, hundreds and thousands of people simply disappeared into the prisons and labour camps of the secret police and thence all too often to the grave. No one really knew how it had all started, and certainly no one knew how it was going to end. Safety of a very uncertain kind lay in denouncing others, and so the gruesome immolation went on for two years. The record, like all records of such enormity, loses its impact by the sheer quantity of well-known men who died: in August 1936 the trial of Zinoviev, Kamenev and fourteen others on capital charges, in September 1936 the suicide of Tomsky, in January 1937 the suicide of Ordzhonikidze, hitherto one of Stalin's closest collaborators (according to Khrushchev once more, he was forced to shoot himself). In June 1937 the secret trial and execution of Tukhachevsky with a galaxy of the most senior Red Army commanders—German spies all. In March 1938 the trial of Bukharin, Rykov, Yagoda and eighteen others on capital charges. Each time the arch-villain was Trotsky, grinning behind the scenes and manipulating corrupt Bolsheviks into their treacherous practices. By the time the last trial had taken place even the solid Stalinist majority of the Central Committee of 1934 had been almost wholly liquidated; the leadership of the army, of the Komsomol, and of every other major institution of the Soviet Union had been turned upside-down.

Then, quite suddenly, the fury of the terror died down to a dreadful whisper. As in the case of collectivization, the purge was rotting away the foundations of those very sectors of society which it had meant to cleanse and strengthen. The Party hierarchy was running out of replacements. In January 1938 the new Central Committee met and issued a stern warning against excesses. It was time to make an end. By December 1938 Ezhov, whose name has become notorious in Russia through the word *"Ezhovshchina* by which the great purges are usually referred to, had quietly disappeared. The men now around Stalin, with a few exceptions, were relatively unknown: Molotov, Zhdanov, Khrushchev and Beria, Kaganovich and Mikoyan. The aftermath of the purges was in fact truly Thermidorean: the liquidation of the secret police, a purge of the purgers. In the meantime, however, the prison population, especially of the labour camps, had swollen to the size and importance of a state within a state, and went on making its contribution to socialist accumulation. People began to wonder if the growth rate and the whole system could in fact survive without them, whether the real reason for the purges was not the need for a cheap supply of non-consuming labour.

After five years, in March 1939, a new Party Congress assembled at last, the eighteenth. The new leaders could review the purges as a necessary attack on counter-revolution, open and disguised, and take stock of its consequences. They decided to admit that there had been excesses; it fell to Zhdanov to berate the assembled delegates on this account. At the same time the class struggle which allegedly had necessitated all this was still not resolved: "Many of the real enemies remain unscathed." The delegates agreed and applauded the reams of figures, the cost of so many lives, as a necessary price for the continued advance of all the main economic indicators. In spite of Zhdanov's cautionary warning against self-satisfaction there was certainly a hope that the terror had now perhaps served its function and would never happen again. But when Stalin himself announced to the Congress that the Soviet Union was now stronger than it had ever been, he almost certainly did not realize how soon its strength, indeed its very existence, would be challenged by the onslaught of Nazi Germany. Whatever the delegates at the Eighteenth Congress thought about the future—and who dared any longer to speculate too closely upon it?—the idea that within twenty-seven months the nation would be fighting for its very existence, not against internal opposition, but against the German invader, can hardly have occurred to them. Even if there had been such a danger, Stalin was sure to know and guard against it.

THE BASIS AND DEVELOPMENT
OF THE SOVIET POLITY

Leonard Schapiro

The Soviet state came into existence in November 1917 as the result of a revolutionary seizure of power. The Bolsheviks claimed then, as their successors still maintain, that they were creating a society of an entirely new kind, the like of which has never been known before, and that the result in no way resembled anything that had ever existed before. It is not necessary at this point to comment on this traditional view. The uncommitted historian will perhaps be more concerned to look for the main elements which went into the composition of the new state, and these can, I think, be summarized under three headings.

There is first the theoretical element, since no one can deny that the Bolsheviks were, at any rate in part, motivated by strongly ideological considerations. There was secondly the traditional element. Whatever the Bolsheviks may have said about themselves, their revolutionary seizure of power took place within Russian history and within the orbit of Russian traditions and it was inevitable that some specifically Russian features should have left their mark on what emerged. And then, thirdly, as in every revolution there were the fortuitous and unpredictable happenings, and these form the necessary third element in our analysis of the origins of the Soviet policy.

Under the heading of the theoretical element, one might list three components: There is first of all Marxism; and within Marxism in particular the broad identification of state and society, the view that society and the state must become co-extensive to such a degree that the state ceases to be something independent of society, and society in turn absorbs all the functions and activities of the state. I should also list as one of the fundamental features of Marxist doctrine, though perhaps associated more with Engels than with Marx, the belief that society, until it has been transformed into a socialist society, cannot provide real freedom for the individual; the individual will always be subject to exploitation by the dominant bourgeois class which will prevent his exercise of real freedom and will leave him only formal freedom. There is also the component of Marxism which takes the dynamic, forward looking view of human society. Society is moving toward a goal and therefore the individual or the present generation must, if necessary, be sacrificed to the benefit of all, or to the benefit of the future, in order to achieve that great destiny which history has in store for mankind.

Next, there is the Bolshevik adaptation of Marxism. This consists mainly of the two essential elements which Lenin added to the theories of Marx—no doubt with the Russian situation in mind. There is first of all, of course, the elitism, the reliance on the Party, on organization, the realization that without a determined organization nothing can be achieved, and so forth. But I think there is something else as well. There is a kind of hard "Bazarovism" about Lenin, a kind of assertion of the need to put an end to the sentimentality, the vacillations, the intellectual cerebrations, which characterized the Russsian intelligentsia. In Lenin's terms it would be "anti-Oblomovism." One could argue that in making the Russian intellectual more tough, more fit for his revolutionary task, more ruthless, Lenin at the same time destroyed the features which had made his nobility and self-sacrifice the center of so much admiration. But I think this transformation of the Russian *intelligent* was as essential an addition to Leninism as Lenin's insistence on Party leadership and Party organization.

There is also a third feature of this general element. However much Bolshevism may have neglected or may have transformed the Social Democratic tradition, however much Lenin may have scoffed at and derided the Social Democratic tradition of freedom of speech for the working class, nevertheless something of this tradition of freedom remained which even Lenin could not destroy. In the early years, after all, the Party was a very mixed company. The first serious purge took place only in 1921. Until then the Party remained a conglomeration of socialists of many colors who had hastily joined the victorious Bolshevik group. Something of the old libertarian tradition lingered on until rooted out by Stalin.

So much for the theoretical element. Let us look at the traditional element. Now of course it is a commonplace to argue that in a country in which there has been so long a tradition of autocracy the chances of one dictatorship replacing another were always very high. I should go rather farther than that. I think the habit of autocracy had persisted in Russia in spite of the interlude of the constitutional period and the even shorter interlude of the Provisional Government. On the one hand Lenin was probably the only Social Democrat to recognize the need in Russian conditions to capture and use the central autocratic power. He was, as is known, relatively indifferent to the soviets, which he was prepared to support or discard as opportunity required, and much of his talk of democracy and mass support has to be taken with a very large grain of salt. In this respect Lenin was very different not only from the Mensheviks but from many of his followers—as events very soon after the Bolshevik coming to power were to show. Conversely, the one institution which might have replaced the autocracy as a viable center of legitimate authority, the Duma, had signally failed. The whole of its existence was not a failure, on the contrary it had some very remarkable achievements to its credit. But at the crucial time, when the unexpected revolution broke out in March, the Duma failed to take over and to become the center of authority and very soon lost the position which it might conceivably have been able to win in the imagination of the population. The Provisional Government, as it were, operated in a vacuum, with the Petrograd Soviet increasingly occupying the place in popular imagination that might legitimately have been won by the Duma had circumstances been otherwise. Whatever the reason, within this vacuum the Bolshevik restoration of the one institution which had a traditional and accepted reason for its existence, the monarchy, in the new guise of Lenin and his Council of People's Commissars, was a fairly easy step.

Another tradition, however, was equally decisive in shaping the nature of the new state. This was the traditional revolutionary fear of counterrevolution. This was based on the experience of Europe, the defeat, as the revolutionaries saw it, of the French Revolution and more recently in revolutionary imagination the defeat of the revolutions of 1848 and the suppression of the Paris commune. We need not consider the rights and wrongs of this tradition, nor indeed how far the traditional fear, even if valid for West European conditions, had very much application in Russian conditions. But it was very strongly felt indeed by revolutionaries from the extreme right to the extreme left. It colored all Boshevik policy from the start. But what was more important, during the rule of the Provisional Government it had strongly colored the policy of that government. The Provisional Government lived in the belief that the revolution was in danger and had to be safeguarded. That these fears were grossly exaggerated may very well have been the case, but they did much to hamper the Provisional Government in its attempts to establish the kind of authority which might have given it a chance to survive. Notable of course was the episode of Kornilov's rising, when the reaction of the Provisional Government to a threat of which the magnitude was enormously inflamed by their own imagination led directly to the rise and triumph of the Bolsheviks. I should also add that the emergence within the Bolshevik faction, at the very earliest stages, of a powerful terror organization to deal with its enemies was also a part of this tradition.

And lastly what might be called the fortuitous, the accidental element, the concatenation of circumstances which do not appear to have been foreseen or planned, but which nevertheless closely affected the course of events. One could list many such circumstances connected with the foundation of the Soviet state, but two in particular seem to have been of outstanding importance. The first was the divergence, quarrel even, between Lenin and Trotsky on the course which the revolution should take during the last days before the seizure of power by the Bolsheviks. Lenin was primarily insistent on speed. To wait, for example, for the meeting of the Second Congress of Soviets was according to Lenin nothing short of madness. Trotsky on the other hand, who unlike Lenin was on the spot in Petrograd, saw the importance of linking what was essentially a military coup d'état to the democratic facade of the soviets. He was therefore insistent that the seizure of power should coincide with the meeting of the Second Congress of Soviets which in fact took place on November 7, 1917 (October 25, Old Style). The actual seizure of power by the Red Guards took place shortly before the opening of the congress, but in the result, either by accident or by design, the seizure of power could be portrayed as a seizure of power by the soviets in the name of the people. The whole future democratic facade was therefore made possible by this brilliant tactical move of Trotsky's.

The second fortuitous circumstance was the mistake of the Mensheviks and the Social Revolutionaries in leaving the Second Congress of Soviets. The majority of them stumped out in protest against the military coup d'état by the Bolsheviks. Now protests are all very well in democratic societies where they can affect an electorate, but they were totally useless in the conditions then prevailing. The Bolsheviks voted themselves into power with the almost unanimous support of those who stayed behind. This was probably not a decisive factor, but it made it easier for Lenin to begin to build up the kind of monopoly of power which had been his aim from the first. The importance of this tactical victory may have been quite considerable, if one recollects that at that time the general view, even among rank-and-file Bolsheviks, was that the proper course was rule by the soviets, which meant rule by all the left-wing parties and not only by the Bolsheviks.

The Foundations Laid

During the period from November 1917 until April 1921 the Bolsheviks, having established themselves in sole power after a short and unsuccessful coalition with the Left Social-Revolutionaries, consolidated their precarious hold over the country. A policy of terror toward political opponents was a foregone conclusion, as some of Lenin's critics inside the Bolshevik faction had foreseen. It is indeed obvious that a minority party can establish itself in sole power only by methods of terror. The machinery of terror already existed in rudimentary form before the October Revolution, in the shape of the security organization within the Military Revolutionary Council, which the Bolsheviks of the Petrograd Soviet dominated on the eve of their seizure of power. There was, however, no fully consistent or worked out policy toward politcal opponents, so far as can be discovered, when the Bolsheviks came to power. The result was a policy which was never fully consistent and which took shape empirically largely under the impact of events.

So far as bourgeois opponents were concerned, that is to say center and right-wing opponents, there was never any question that these would be treated as enemies and rendered harmless. This was a matter on which there was no dissension in the Party, and Lenin's policy won almost unchallenged support from his colleagues. This was indeed an essential part of the revolutionary tradition which all Social Democrats, both Bolshevik and Menshevik, were prepared to accept. The position was quite different as regards the repression of socialist opponents, the Mensheviks and the Social Revolutionaries. Here the attitude of the Bolsheviks was ambivalent. That is not say that Lenin himself had any serious qualms in the matter, but in the early years of power even Lenin could not go against the revolutionary tradition which accepted the right of all left-wing parties to a voice in the affairs of the new revolutionary state. The great majority of Bolshevik deputies to the Second Congress of Soviets in November 1917 had expressed, in answer to questionnaires submitted to them, their conviction that government should be shared by all left-wing parties. The notion of a complete monopoly of power still lay ahead.

The period up to the end of 1920 illustrates this ambivalent attitude. Both Mensheviks And Social Revolutionaries were continuously harried, arrested, released, rearrested on trumped up charges, forcibly expelled from soviets to which they were elected, and the like. But, except for a short period in 1918, they were not officially outlawed. Of course, the trend toward the establishment of a Bolshevik monopoly was already pretty obvious after the dispersal of the Constituent Assembly and after the violent break up of the coalition with the Left Social-Revolutionaries in July 1918. But advice by Lenin to the Communists of the city of Yelets offered shortly after the July revolt illustrates the way in which even Lenin had to take account of the tradition of tolerance toward socialist opponents in the Social Democratic movement. The Communists of Yelets had pursued the usual practice of hounding and persecuting the Left Social-Revolutionaries who were still entitled to sit in the local soviet to which they had been elected. The Yelets Communists sought Lenin's advice on the matter, and he replied as follows:

It is a pity that you have not arrested them [the Left Social-Revolutionaries] as is being done everywhere. It is essential to oust all Social Revolutionaries from responsible posts... we cannot of course, give you written authorization to arrest Social Revolutionaries, but if you drive them out of Soviet organs, if you arrest them and expose them before the workers and peasants and if you destroy their influence before the peasantry (if they have any) you will be doing good revolutionary work, and we in the center... will only praise you for it.

There was one matter in which there was full agreement in the Party. This was the question of dissent inside the Party by Party members. Subsequent events suggest that this tradition may not have been entirely welcome to Lenin, but there are no indications until 1920 or 1921 that he was able to do very much about it. It must be remembered that the Party had grown very rapidly and was no longer the small band of carefully disciplined and purged followers which Lenin had built up before the revolution. Throughout the period until 1921, dissent in the Party was free, criticism was unrestrained, and debate was fast and furious. The subsequent opponents of Stalin were to look back on this period with nostalgia and to claim, somewhat inaccurately in view of Lenin's policy before the revolution, that this represented the true Bolshevik tradition. It was however a fact that during these years Lenin retained his authority in the Party not by forcible measures against his colleagues nor by repression of criticism, but by his powers of persuasion and by the logic of his case. It was in this way that he succeeded in winning over the party in 1918 against the views of the Left Communists, and in establishing the main outlines of his policy in the succeeding years.

The real break in policy came at the end of 1920 and the beginning of 1921, and took place in response to certain definite trends within the Party. The elimination of other socialists and the suppression of dissent in the Party is explained by Bolshevik and pro-Bolshevik historians as having been due to the emergency of the situation and the need to deal with enemies of the revolution. This is a very much oversimplified explanation, which is improbable if only for the reason that Socialist opponents, and in particular the Mensheviks, were tolerated throughout the Civil War when one might have expected, had there been any truth in the official explanation, their elimination as a threat to security; they were only finally suppressed after the virtual end of the Civil War in November 1920. One of the main reasons for the decision to eliminate the Mensheviks and Social Revolutionaries from the political scene, and to put an end to the very limited tolerance which had been extended to them hitherto, was the growing effectiveness of their criticism and the increase of their popularity. Menshevik criticism of Bolshevik repressive measures and of the growing intolerance of dissent was beginning to find considerable response in the trade unions and among workers generally. This was very much in contrast to the very low ebb of Menshevik popularity in 1917 and 1918. The Social Revolutionaries were in turn becoming the spokesmen of the wave of peasant discontent with the repressive policy of procurement and with communism generally, which was beginning to break out into violence on a big scale. Moreover, the Mensheviks had for some time before 1921 been advocating the essential features of what was to become Lenin's New

Economic Policy. Once Lenin decided to make this break, it was essential for him to begin by eliminating his critics—unless he was prepared to take them into a coalition government.

Similarly, the virtual end of dissent inside the Communist Party, which was imposed at the Tenth Party Congress in March of 1921, has often been explained in terms of the emergency of the situation. The outbreak of the Kronstadt revolt and the wave of strikes in Petrograd certainly lend some justification to the view that this was a panic measure dictated by fear. But again it is doubtful if this is the whole story. By 1920 Lenin was facing a considerable crisis in the party in the form of syndicalist demands by the trade-union Communnists who wanted more freedom of action and more extensive control over industry than the Bolshevik authoritarian and centralistic tradition could conceivably have tolerated. Again, it was in 1920 and early in 1921 that the disciplined central machinery of the party was forged. This was in part an improvisation resulting from a number of fortutious circumstances. But the revival of what was so essential a feature of Lenin's political faith had a more immediate and practical cause: the thread of localism, the demand of Communists in the local soviets for greater initiative, even leading at times to questioning the need for Party leadership at all, except in the ideological sphere. One can imagine Lenin's reaction to this!

It is obvious that the policy established at the Tenth Party Congress, of central control and the virtual elimination of all dissent within the Party, was in tune with the whole of Lenin's pre-revolutionary thought as it developed in the last months of his exile in 1899. It is also true that there is a certain ambivalence in Lenin's views at this period which suggest that he may have wavered before deciding to create a monolithic party. Assertions were frequently made after 1921 that this was only a temporary solution which never represented Lenin's permanent policy. It is impossible to give a final answer on this, because Lenin only had about a year's work ahead of him and was not even in full control of affairs during this year. Moreover it can be said that if the measures of March 1921 were dictated by the emergency, then the emergency remained in full force so long as Lenin stayed at the helm. On the other hand, there is no doubt that there are elements of a totalitarian attitude in all Lenin's thought, beginning with *What Is to be Done.* There is further the strong element of utopianism in Lenin, as expressed in *State and Revolution,* which envisages a return to a kind of primitive city-state ideal, in which cooperation on a voluntary basis by all will take the place of government. Obviously, the realization of such utopian dreams can only be attempted by means of considerable force. There is moreover Lenin's consistent refusal to recognize the supremacy of the law or the separation of powers; also his faith in the predominance of the Party in all spheres of activity. Finally, one must recognize the progressive retrenchment by Lenin of the hope of the withering away of the state which was so boldly proclaimed in *State and Revolution* as about to begin immediately after the revolution. By 1921 Lenin was envisaging forty to fifty years of dictatorship, even if, as he believed, this dictatorship would take place in relaxed economic conditions, under which voluntary cooperation, especially by the peasants, in socialist schemes would take place progressively as evidence accumulated that socialism offered the best way of life. The question of Lenin's intentions must remain one of the unsolved problems of Soviet history. Of his policy as it developed in the hands of his successors, however, there is no doubt.

The Rise of Stalin: 1922—36

Two main aspects of the first period of Stalin's rise to power, after he became General Secretary in 1922, affected the nature of the Soviet state. First of all, the consolidation of the dominance over the country of the monopolistic Party in its monolithic form. This Stalin had inherited from Lenin: the Party which brooked no rivals, and the Party which had set up iron discipline in its own ranks.

The first clear assertion of Party supremacy was the role which the highly centralized Party was destined to play in the ostensibly federal structure embodied in the first Constitution of the Soviet Union. This constitution provided for a federal structure of union republics with wide autonomy, including the quite exceptional and quite unrealistic right of secession. But the debates at the Party congress in 1923 showed quite clearly, as indeed some of the Communist critics who were still bold enough to challenge Stalin were able to point out, that any autonomy granted by the constitution in the sphere of the state machinery was going to be totally unrealistic so long as the highly centralized Party predominated. This feature of Soviet federalism remains as prominent today as it was in 1923. True, at different periods, and particularly during the first phase of Khruschev's rule, the union republics attained greater autonomy in certain spheres than they had ever enjoyed before. But then as today, republican autonomy was tolerated autonomy which the centralized "All Union" Party can always withdraw or circumvent.

The second aspect of this consolidation of the Party stranglehold during the first period of Stalin's rise to power was the elaborate development of the Party apparatus. Building on the foundations which had been evolved in 1920 and 1921, Stalin enlarged the apparatus and perfected its hold and control over individual Party members. The instruments of discipline were considerably strengthened, and by 1925 if not before the whole process of election of Party officials and of deputies to Party meetings was completely controlled by the Secretariat. It is, of course, common knowledge that this enabled Stalin with relative ease to defeat Trotsky and his other political opponents.

The third feature of this period was the rise of the police—the G.P.U. and later the O.G.P.U. The security organs dated from November 1917, but their use against the Party was generally avoided in the early years. The first prominent case of the direct intervention of the police in a Party affair was the trial in 1923 of Sultan-Galiev, the national Tartar communist leader. By the time the struggle with Trotsky and his supporters was reaching its height in 1926 and 1927, the police had become a normal instrument of action against opponents.

It is plain that in all these instances the debt Stalin owed to Lenin was great, even though the manner in which Stalin used the apparatus with which Lenin had provided him was very different from the way in which Lenin might have used it. No doubt also a large element in the development of Stalin's power was personal ambition. Lenin was ambitious in the sense that he was confident in his own rightness and therefore intolerant of all opposition to his views, but unlike Stalin Lenin did no seek his own personal aggrandizement. However, it would be wrong, in my view, to attribute Stalin's method of achieving control over the country solely to personal ambition. Stalin did not enjoy moral authority in the Party or the respect or even legitimacy which Lenin enjoyed as revolutionary leader. Therefore, insofar as the Soviet system demanded the presence of one authoritative leader, as I think was the case, there was no way other than violence open to Stalin to assert that authority. With the experience of fifty years of this type of rule we can confidently assert that the whole idea of a monolithic party is nonsense. Indeed, voices are being heard even in the ranks of the Party apparatus in the Soviet Union today to the effect that dissent and difference of opinion are healthy phenomena and that unanimity cannot be expected in any assembly of thinking human beings. It is not unreasonable to suppose that Lenin would at any rate have tempered violence with some attempt to conciliate the pluralistic forces which survived within the Communist Party for many years. But this path was not open to Stalin, and was indeed totally alien to his character.

Stalin's second main contribution to the nature of the Soviet state was his "third revolution": the enforced collectivization and rapid industrialization following upon the elimination of the right opposition headed by Bukharin. Of course, this momentous turn in Soviet policy can be explained, no doubt ought to be explained in part, in terms of economic necessity. It can again be argued that for a man like Stalin, who had already made so many enemies as General Secretary, there was no way other than terror to accomplish this economic revolution. But we must remember that the economic policy had a very definite political objective. This consisted mainly in the desire to eliminate possible opponents, who belonged to the earlier period of revolutionary history and who were therefore not prepared to accept Stalin as their undisputed leader. It is also possible, as often asserted by Soviet and pro-Soviet historians, that there was a genuine fear in 1928 or 1929 of peasant sabotage. I have never been strongly convinced by the evidence of this, but it is possible that Stalin was.

It is notable that throughout this period Stalin was unable to assert the kind of total control which appears to have been his object when he launched the terror in mid-1936. From the mysterious murder of Kirov on December 1, 1934 until mid-1936, much still remains obscure. But it seems a fair inference that Stalin was faced with the possibility of a revolt within the Party centered around Kirov, and that he was playing a very careful political game in order to deal with potential enemies. While playing for time, he skillfully exploited the fear within the Party that a violent change of leadership could precipitate the downfall of the whole regime. He was also very skillful in appearing to conciliate the more moderate elements, the former right-wing leaders who were allowed to return to some position of tolerated existence after the Seventeenth Party Congress in 1934. The whole farce of the ostensibly democratic constitution of 1936, drafted by a group of oppositionists headed by Bukharin and promulgated in the very midst of the terror, is one illustration of this conciliatory policy. Another was the toleration in 1936 of a discussion which took place in the Legal Institute, headed by Pashukanis, which aimed at liberalizing and humanizing the draconic Soviet criminal system. Here again Pashukanis was allowed to conduct his debate almost up to the moment in 1937 when the police swooped down upon him.

There was a certain inexorable logic about the use of Stalin's terror machine. True, his enemies were of his own creation. But, having created them, he was faced with the prospect that if he did not eliminate them they would eliminate him. These enemies were both the Old Bolsheviks who did not recognize his authority and the moderates of the N.E.P. period, the Leninists, as they saw themselves, headed by Bukharin, who believed that Lenin's policy of a long period of cooperation and relaxation of the class struggle was the right one.

The imposition of totalitarian control by Lenin and Stalin, in their different ways, required nearly twenty years, from 1917 until 1936. Throughout that time resistance in one form or another, both within the Party, and outside it, was never absent from the Soviet scene. If the accounts that have reached us are correct, then the last opposition within the Central Committee was only broken at the end of 1936 or the beginning of 1937. It is often asserted that the Soviet regime found ready acceptance among a population which had no sense of democracy and little ability to defend its freedom. It is probably true that the opposition displayed little skill in defending itself. But the suggestion that the Russian people suffered from some peculiar fatality which destined them for despotism will not stand up. It is only necessary to recall that the much more politically developed Germans were subjugated by Hitler in fourteen months in contrast to the nineteen or twenty years required by the Communists to achieve the same result in Russia.

Personal Despotism: 1936—53

The period of terror from 1936 to 1938 entirely transformed the Soviet system. Before the terror Stalin ruled through his monopolistic and monolithic party, after the terror the despotism was much more personal. I have never been convinced that Stalin's policy of terror was the policy of a madman or that it lacked a basic, inherent logic of its own. It can of course be argued that anyone who is prepared to sacrifice millions of lives in order to achieve his ends can scarcely be regarded as fully sane. But there is a pattern about Stalin's policy during the terror and a certain inherent logic in the whole process which does not suggest the action of a madman. In the first place, the elimination of those fantastic percentages of Party members and members of the bureaucracy seemed to serve a very definite plan, which was indeed recognized by Stalin himself at the Eighteenth Party Congress in 1939. What he achieved was a total social transformation of the ruling apparatus, and the replacement of Party and government officials, whose dependence on Stalin was not total in the sense that they had revolutionary records of their own, by henchmen whose sole loyalty was to Stalin, to whom they owed everything. Moreover the process by which tens if not hundreds of thousands rose to prominence on the corpses of their superiors whom they had denounced bound these men to Stalin in a link of common guilt. This common guilt made them more inclined to be circumspect in their actions and speech and created, in the phrase of Professor Fainsod, "a system of institutionalized suspicion," or to use a phrase which was current during and after the period of terror, and indeed still is, "the generation of those who had been frightened once and for all."

But there was also an inherent logic in the extent of the terror. Once you start on a policy of this kind, it must extend to all sections of society. No republic and no branch of the service, be it police, Party, state apparatus, or army, could be allowed to survive unscathed. Terror had to be extended to all so that dreams of revenge might be stilled, as Stalin hoped, forever. It may be that after the war he felt that memories of the thirties no longer inspired fear in the new generation which was beginning to knock at the door. Theories that toward the end of his life Stalin was contemplating another mammoth purge thus acquire a certain degree of conviction. It may indeed be that if you govern by terror you have to be prepared to repeat the dose at intervals.

The most notable feature of Stalin's second period of rule was the setting up of a much more elaborate democratic facade than had hitherto been the case. For example, the Party as part of the Soviet system of government had not even been mentioned in the constitution of the R.S.F.S.R. of 1918 or the first All-Union Constitution. In the Stalin Constitution of 1936 the Party is openly acclaimed as the leading core of all institutions. The whole machinery of government was also transformed in the sense that the unwieldy All-Union Congress of Soviets which was totally unsuited to be a legislature was replaced by the more compact Supreme Soviet with its Presidium and its two chambers. True, this Supreme Soviet has never played any part as a real legislative body. But it was part of Stalin's style of government to create the appearance of normal, democratic governmental institutions. Moreover, the new Soviet no longer harked back to the traditional soviets of Lenin's day which were specifically designed to unite executive and legislature and proclaimed with pride their novel and ostensibly totally democratic and popular nature. The Soviet Union was now endowed with an orthodox bicameral legislature, with secret elections based on universal and equal franchise. The cabinet, the Council of People's Commissars, later the Council of Ministers, was nominally responsible to the Supreme Soviet. This highly centralized executive and policy-making ministerial body was designed to run the entire nationalized industry of the country, and its scope of operation was very much extended.

In addition the constitution proclaimed fundamental civil rights. True, analysis of this constitution shows that in many instances the civil rights are not guaranteed even on paper in a way which would be of very much use if the relevant paragraphs should ever be tested in the courts. For example, freedom of speech, assembly, and the like are only guaranteed, even on paper, in the interests of strengthening the socialist system, and it was obvious that the Party alone, or Stalin himself, was going to be the final arbiter as to what did and did not "strengthen the socialist system." In any case, the question was academic because the one thing that the Soviet Constitution lacked was any provision for judicial review, or any other means by which the citizen could test the actions of the government before any independent tribunal. Nevertheless the constitution was quite sufficient to take in a great deal of quite enlightened opinion outside Russia, and may still take in some people today. No doubt, in the atmosphere of the Popular Front Era which then prevailed, the bemusing of foreign opinion, and particularly foreign Socialist opinion, was one of the main objects of the Stalin Constitution. But I do not think it was the sole object. It was part of the method of Stalin's rule to recognize the importance of a facade even if he had no intention of letting it become more than a facade. The constitution in force today is virtually identical with the one promulgated by Stalin. There is no more provision today for judicial review than there was in 1936. The nature of the guarantees is as limited as it was in 1936. Nevertheless, the very existence of the document is an important element in Soviet life in the sense that the inconsistency between constitution and daily practice is a constant stimulus to criticism and opposition. We repeatedly hear nowadays of protests to the Soviet authorities, from within the churches, particularly the Baptist movement, from intellectuals and so forth, in which violation of the constitution is criticized.

All this would suggest that Stalin intended to set up a democratic facade behind which the Party would in fact exercise the real power. Had this been the case it would have been little more than a continuation in rather more elaborate form of the principle of rule devised by Lenin in 1917. Paradoxically, however, this was very far from being the case. The Party under Stalin remained monolithic but not monopolistic. There was no longer a monopoly of rule by the Party, but a monopoly of rule by Stalin. In exercising this personal rule, Stalin naturally relied on the Party as one instrument of control. But however important, it was only one of several instruments. He relied additionally on the police, on the government apparatus, and even to some extent on the army. Each of these pillars of rule was used as required, and it cannot really be said of the second period of Stalin's reign that any one pillar was at all times clearly superior to another. Each was terrorized, streamlined, and thoroughly subordinated to the personal despotism which Stalin exercised over the whole country; but none could be singled out as supreme. This became particularly evident during the war, when Party and government apparatus became to a very large extent fused, and one or other was used interchangeably according to the needs of the moment. This was also evident after the war when at different periods in the later years of Stalin's rule it very often became impossible to determine whether the Party apparatus was more important or the government apparatus. At times the one appeared more influential and at different times the other. Indeed, some competent students of the Soviet scene have suggest that Malenkov, when presumably forced to choose between the two offices which he held after Stalin's death, Chairman of the Council of Ministers and Secretary of the Party, chose the former in the mistaken belief that the government apparatus was going to be the more influential in the future.

Of course Stalin's personal despotism was not exercised by one man alone. The hub of his rule lay in his private secretariat or Secret Department of the Central Committee, which was the center of authority, at any rate after 1936. It is very significant that this private secretariat has never been identified since his death and it is virtually certain that it no longer exists. Equally important were the personal agents who carried out Stalin's behests. Vyshinsky, the Chief Procurator, was one such agent and there were a number of others, all of whom met their death or at any rate disappeared very soon after Stalin's death. There is no reason to doubt Khrushchev's description in his speech in closed session to the Twentieth Party Congress in 1956 of how Stalin did not convene the Politburo, but operated through special meetings of two or three Party leaders. Plenary meetings of the Central Committee, let alone Party congresses, were likewise very infrequent. In short, Stalin created a personal despotism to which the entire bureaucratic machine both of the Party and of the government was in the last resort subordinate.

It was a notable feature of this regime of Stalin's that industry and agriculture, indeed the entire state bureaucracy, was controlled through a complex network of informers and police agents. But the police were not operating as an independent agency, and, as became evident in 1938, were themselves subject to purging and decimation as much as any of the other instruments of control. Stalin destroyed the whole polity, such as it was and such as it had been built up by Lenin, and replaced it by a system in which he held all the reins of power and in which there was no obstacle to his personal rule so long as he could control the few devoted agents whom he required to pass on his orders.

This seems of considerable relevance for our understanding of totalitarian systems in general. Insofar as "totalitarian system" implies control by a ruler or ruling elite of all institutions and the suppression of every conceivable kind of pluralism, no one could seriously dispute that Stalin's regime was totalitarian. But this totalitarian regime was maintained for years without the need for a monopolistic party. A number of authors have argued that the single party enjoying a monopoly of power is an essential feature of a totalitarian regime. The Soviet experience during the second phase of Stalin's rule certainly seems to throw considerable doubt on this particular hypothesis.

It was natural enough that this flouting of the Party—for it was little less than that—by Stalin should have created considerable resentment and anticipation in the minds of the members of the Party apparatus in particular, and indeed in the ranks of the Party as a whole. This must have been particularly true in view of the enormous growth from an elite to a mass Party during the war and the years immediately following the war. This had involved the influx of a new generation of younger men without much influence, but nevertheless men to whom an appeal to the traditions of the Party could still be made. It was therefore only to be expected that Stalin's death would be followed by an attempt to restore the Party to its former predominance, to its monopoly position in fact, and that the man who succeeded in doing so could get off to a good start in terms of support from that section of Soviet society where the biggest vested interest and the strongest tradition of rule was to be found. It was Khrushchev who understood the importance of this factor and introduced an entirely new relation between Party and state. . . .

15 / The Origins of World War II:
A Controversial Interpretation

In 1961, A. J. P. Taylor, one of the leading British historians, published *The Origins of the Second World War*. In the first chapter of his book, he referred to his subject as a "forgotten problem," pointing out that the important work on the origins of World War II was done soon after the war ended,[1] and that it echoed views held during the war or even before it had begun. Now, more than twenty years later, Taylor notes that these same views are generally held as an explanation of the events leading up to September 1939, a marked contrast to the revisionism which followed the end of World War I (see Chapter II).

Taylor admits there are reasons for this, but adds that "it seems unlikely that historians a hundred years hence will look at these events exactly as men did in 1939."[2] The task that Taylor sets himself is "to tell the story as it may appear to some future historian working from the records."

The result may be to demonstrate how much historians miss or misunderstand. We must go on writing history all the same. Like my imaginary successor, I have often had to confess ignorance. I have also found that the record, considered in detachment, often pushed me towards interpretations different from those which men (including myself) gave at the time. This has not weighed with me one way or the other. I am concerned to understand what happened, not to vindicate or condemn. I was an anti-appeaser from the day that Hitler came to power; and no doubt should be again under similar circumstances. But the point has no relevance in the writing of history. In retrospect though many were guilty, none was innocent. The purpose of political activity is to provide peace and prosperity; and in this every statesman failed, for whatever reason. This is a story without heroes; and perhaps even without villains.[3]

The main points of Taylor's thesis may be described as follows. The war that broke out in 1939 was not premeditated. It was the result of diplomatic blunders on both sides. Although Hitler changed much in Germany to the point of

---

[1] Works by authors named by Taylor are Maurice Paumont, *La faillite de la paix, 1918-1939*, 3rd ed. (1950); Sir Lewis B. Namier, *Diplomatic Prelude, 1938-1939* (1948); John W. Wheeler-Bennett, *Munich: Prologue to Tragedy* (1948); Elizabeth Wiskemann, *The Rome-Berlin Axis: A History of the Relations Between Hitler and Mussolini* (1949).

[2] A. J. P. Taylor, *The Origins of the Second World War*, p. 9.

[3] *Ibid.*, pp. 16-17.

destroying freedom and the law, his foreign policy was simply that of his predecessors since 1919—freeing Germany from the restrictions of the Versailles Treaty and making her the greatest power in Europe from her "natural weight." Hitler's foreign policy was not systematic.[4] He waited for opportunities rather than initiating them, as was the case with Austria and Czechoslovakia. He carried on a war of nerves—bluff, violent talk and threats to use force. But the foreign policy of France and Britain also rested ultimately on force, although they hoped not to have to use it.

Hitler had no territorial grievances against France and Britain; he accepted the Versailles settlement in the West. He did have territorial and other grievances in the East; specifically Danzig (Gdańsk), and more generally a restoration of the Brest-Litovsk settlement which Versailles had undone.[5] To quote Taylor, "Hitler probably intended a great war of conquest against Soviet Russia so far as he had any conscious design; it is unlikely that he intended the actual war against Great Britain and France which broke out in 1939."[6] But "the statesmen of western Europe moved in a moral and intellectual fog—sometimes deceived by the dictators, sometimes deceiving themselves, often deceiving their own public,"[7] and so Great Britain and France dithering between resistance and appeasement "helped to make war more likely."[8]

The above summary does not do full justice to Taylor's account of events, but it should, at least, give the reader an idea of how far Taylor's interpretation departs from the more orthodox explanations. Taylor's views have not gone unchallenged. In fact, they have started the most spectacular controversy in recent British historiography, where Taylor's foremost opponent has been Hugh Trevor-Roper, another distinguished British historian.[9] The two men have exchanged criticism, some of it quite bitter, in *Encounter* magazine and in a television debate.[10] Other historians have joined in, and the last word has probably not yet been had.

The character of Hitler has dogged Taylor's interpretation; many critics are offended by the detachment with which Taylor views Hitler as a diplomatist. Can foreign policy be so dissociated from domestic policy and the character of its author? Here Taylor stands fast on the validity of his method. He has professed his abhorrence many times of Hitler's crimes, but he feels they are not related to—indeed, consideration of them would obscure—a study of the negotiations that went on in the chancelleries of Europe. If these negotiations were not in large part

---

[4] It is a cardinal point with Taylor that "systems are created by historians. . . . Statesmen are too absorbed by events to follow a pre-conceived plan" p. 69.

[5] Such a restoration need not have affected the sovereignty of Poland or the Baltic states although it would have drawn them in the German orbit. If it meant carrying out the Treaty to the letter, however, it would have made a German satellite out of the Ukraine, an obvious act of aggression against the Soviet Union.

[6] Taylor, *op. cit.*, p. 103. "He was as much dismayed on 3 September 1939 as Bethmann had been on 4 August 1914."
According to the much-quoted Hossbach Memorandum, 1943 was the date for Hitler's war. Taylor tends to discount the Hossbach Memorandum as a real statement of Hitler's plans. It was featured as an important piece of evidence at the Nuremberg Trials.

[7] *Ibid.*, p. 107.

[8] Preface to American edition, p. ix.

[9] Trevor-Roper is Regius Professor of Modern History at Oxford and the author of *The Last Days of Hitler* (London: 1947), 3rd ed. 1956.

[10] See H. R. Trevor-Roper, "A. J. P. Taylor, Hitler, and the War," *Encounter* (July 1961), pp. 88-96; A. J. P. Taylor, "How to Quote." *Encounter* (September 1961), pp. 72-73; H. R. Trevor-Roper, "A Reply," *Ibid.*, pp. 73-74.

gentlemanly, they were at least conducted according to "the textbooks of diplomacy."

A more specific criticism of Taylor is his tendency to discount Hitler's ambitions for world conquest as expressed in *Mein Kampf* and other documents. Taylor makes the point several times in *The Origins of the Second World War* that when Hitler talked it was often for effects quite different than those which, from his words, would seem to be the apparent ones. Taylor writes, "it is an elementary part of historical discipline to ask of a document not only what is in it, but why it came into existence."[11] Whether one can impute too much from such a method is perhaps an open question, if one considers the alternative as accepting documents at their face value. But it is, nevertheless, a question that Taylor's critics have pointedly asked.

Another question revolves around what may be called Taylor's philosophy of history. We have noted his contention that the war was a mistake, "the result of diplomatic blunders on both sides," and that his story is one "without heroes" or "perhaps even without villains." If one reads Taylor right, statesmen are dominated by circumstances rather than vice versa. Their field of action is restricted by the realties of the situation. The realities of the situation after World War I were that the war had left Germany defeated and exhausted, but that Versailles had left her united and, potentially, in terms of manpower and resources, the strongest state on the continent. Thus the area in which German diplomacy inevitably moved was the realization of this potential, while that of Great Britain and France aimed at the conciliation of Germany. The two allied powers hoped that Czechoslovakia and Poland would contain German expansion. But these creations of Versailles, as it turned out, were poor substitutes for the dismembered Austro-Hungarian Empire and a Russia now forced out of a European role. French and British diplomacy was only further restricted by the circumstances of its alliance with the eastern buffer states.

Trevor-Roper has thus been led to interpret Taylor's philosophy as one where "the real determinants of history . . . are objective situations and human blunders."

Objective situations consist of the realities of power; human intelligence is best employed in recognizing these realities and allowing events to conform with them; but as human intelligence seldom prevails in politics, the realities have to assert themselves, at greater human cost, through the mess caused by human blunders. . . . Do statesmen really never make history?[12]

Such then are the important questions raised by *The Origins of the Second World War*. From the first selection that follows, the reader may be able to answer some of them to his own satisfaction. "War for Danzig," the last chapter of Taylor's interesting and provocative study, is a masterfully written account of the dilemmas of the statesmen and the tortuous negotiations that preceded the German attack on Poland on September 1, 1939 and the declaration of war on Germany by Great Britain and France two days later.

In the second selection, a critical review by Zygmunt Kulak questions the basic philosophy and method as well as the interpretation of specific crises used by Taylor. Kulak's thrust suggests that the limitations of diplomatic history, a story constructed mainly from secret papers, and abstracted from the total spirit of the

[11] Taylor, *op. cit.*, p. 133. For Taylor's opinion on *Mein Kampf* and *Table Talk*, p. 69; on the Hossbach Memorandum, pp. 131-134.
[12] Trevor-Roper, *Encounter* (July 1961), p. 90.

epoch, may outweigh its benefits. In handling the Danzig (Gdańsk) issue, the reviewer wonders whether, by 1939, anyone in Europe believed that Hitler would have been appeased by possession of that city and the Polish Corridor.

WAR FOR DANZIG

A. J. P. Taylor

The crisis of August 1939 which led to the second World war was, ostensibly at any rate, a dispute over Danzig. This dispute was formulated in the last days of March, when Germany made demands concerning Danzig and the Corridor, and the Poles rejected them. From that moment everyone expected Danzig to be the next great topic of international conflict. Yet, in strange contrast to earlier crises, there were no negotiations over Danzig, no attempts to discover a solution; not even attempts to screw up the tension. This paradoxical calm was partly caused by the local situation at Danzig. Here both Germany and Poland had an impregnable position so long as they did not move; a step by either would start the avalanche. Hence there could be none of the manoeuvres and bargaining which had marked the Czechoslovak crisis. The Sudeten Nazis, like the Austrians before them, built up the tension gradually without guidance from Hitler. In Danzig the tension was already complete; and Hitler, so far as he did anything, held the local Nazis back. They had already won Danzig internally; the Senate of the Free City was firmly under control. But Hitler could not take advantage of this situation. If the Danzig Nazis openly defied the treaty-settlement by voting for incorporation into Germany, the Poles would be free to intervene with the approval of their Western allies; and this intervention would be effective. For Danzig was cut off from East Prussia, the only neighbouring German territory, by the unbridged Vistula; while the Poles controlled three railways and seven roads leading into it. There could be no half-hearted German aid to Danzig, only a full-blown war; and Hitler would be ready for such a war only when his military preparations matured at the end of August.

Until then Danzig lay at Poland's mercy. But the Poles, too, could not turn this position to their advantage. Though they had alliances with Great Britain and France, they had failed to secure any firm promise of support over Danzig itself; indeed they knew that both their allies sympathised with the German case. They could retain the favour of their allies only by hanging back and waiting for the "clear threat" to Polish independence. It had to appear that action was forced on them; and in Danzig it never was. Under similar circumstances, Hitler's previous antagonists, Schuschnigg and Benes, had sought desperately for a way of escape, endlessly devising compromises which might avert the threatened crisis. The Poles faced the approaching crisis imperturbably, confident that Hitler would be exposed as an aggressor and that the justified grievances of Danzig would then be forgotten. They would not respond to Nazi provocation; but equally they ignored the pleas for concession which came to them from the West.

On the larger field of grand policy also, both Hitler and the Poles held rigid positions in the war of nerves. After 26 March Hitler did not again formulate demands concerning Danzig until the day before war broke out. This was not surprising; it was his usual method. So he had waited for offers from Schuschnigg over Austria; so he had waited for offers from Benes, from Chamberlain, finally from the conference at Munich over Czechoslovakia. Then he did not wait in vain. Did he appreciate that this time no offer would come from the Poles? It seems so from the record. On 3 April he issued instructions that preparations for an attack on Poland "must be made in such a way that the operation can be carried out at any time as from 1 September 1939."[1] But a further directive a week later explained that these preparations were purely precautionary, "should Poland change her policy ... and adopt a threatening attitude towards Germany."[2] On 23 May, however, he spoke with less reserve to a gathering of generals: "There will be war. Our task is to isolate Poland.... It must not come to a simultaneous showdown with the West."[3] This sounds clear enough. But Hitler's real plans are not so easily detected. He had talked just as bravely about war against Czechoslovakia in 1938; yet then, almost certainly, he was playing for victory in the war of nerves. Now, too, preparations had to be made for war whether he were planning to win by war or diplomacy. When Hitler talked to his generals, he talked for effect, not to reveal the workings of his mind. He knew that the generals disliked and distrusted him; he knew that some of them had planned to overthrow him in September 1938; probably he knew that they were constantly sounding the alarm at the British and French embassies. He wanted to impress the generals and, at the same time, to frighten them. Hence on 23 May he talked not only of war against Poland, which he may have seriously intended; but even of a great war against the Western Powers, which was undoubtedly not part of his plan. Hitler's calculation worked: no sooner was the conference of 23 May ended than the generals, from Goering downward, were imploring the Western Powers to bring Poland to reason while there was still time.

Hitler's later behaviour suggests that he had not made up his mind as decisively as he indicated on 23 May. To the very last minute he was battering away for the Polish offer which never came. Maybe he did not expect the Polish nerve to break of itself; but he expected the Western Powers to do the breaking for him, as they had done predominantly with Benes in 1938. He did not foresee exactly how the nerve of the Western Powers would crumble or precisely what effect this would have on the Poles. Nor was it of much moment to him whether the Poles then gave way without war or were left to be destroyed in isolation; the results would be the same either way. On the larger point—the crumbling of Western nerve—he never doubted. There are also indications that, as the summer wore on, he began to foresee how this would come about. A collapse of the Anglo-Franco-Soviet negotiations would, he thought, do the trick. Hitler's confidence that these negotiations would fail is an extraordinary feature even in this extraordinary story. How could he be so sure? Why did he make little effort to approach Russia and assert that the Russians would come over to his side of themselves? Had he secret means of information, never to be traced by historians—some agent in Whitehall or at the Kremlin, perhaps a direct line to Stalin himself? Was it profound social analysis—a realisation that *bourgeois* statesmen and Communists would not find terms of mutual understanding? Maybe; we have no means of knowing. Probably it was simply the gambler's invariable conviction that his hunch must be

[1] Directive by Keitel, 3 April 1939. *German Foreign Policy*, series D. vi. No. 149.
[2] Directive by Hitler, 11 April 1939. *Ibid*. No. 185.
[3] Minutes of conference, 23 May 1939. *Ibid*. No. 433.

right—otherwise, after all, he would not play. A casual phrase reveals more of Hitler's policy than all the grandiloquent talk to generals. On 29 August, Goering, anxious for a compromise, said: "It is time to stop this *va banque.*" Hitler replied: "It is the only call I ever make."[4]

It was Hitler's misfortune (and not his alone) to encounter in the Poles political gamblers of the same school. *Va banque* was not merely the only call they made; it was the only call they could possibly make if they were to maintain their illusory position as an independent Great Power. Sober statesmen would have surrendered at discretion when they contemplated the dangers threatening Poland and the inadequacy of her means. Germany, powerful and aggressive, was on one side; Soviet Russia, potentially hostile on the other; and in the distance, two unwilling allies, eager to compromise with Hitler and geographically unable to give effective aid. The Poles had to depend on such resources as they possessed themselves; and had not even developed these efficiently. Less than half the men of military age had received military training; fewer still could hope for equipment. Czechoslovakia, the year before, with not much more than a third of Poland's population, had a larger trained manpower; and the Czechs were armed with modern weapons into the bargain. Of these the Poles had virtually none: some 250 first-line aeroplanes of antiquated type, one tank battalion also not up to date. Under such circumstances what could the Poles do except dismiss Hitler's threats as bluff? It was obvious that any move by them must involve concession; therefore they made none. After all, standing still is the best policy for anyone who favours the *status quo,* perhaps the only one. Poland's Western allies were of course an additional reason for her diplomatic immobility; it was obvious that Great Britain and France would give way over Danzig, if the Poles once opened the door to negotiation. Therefore they kept it closed. "Munich" cast a long shadow. Hitler waited for it to happen again; Beck took warning from the fate of Benes.

Germany and Poland held rigid positions. The three Western Powers—Italy, as well as Great Britain and France—shrank from raising the question of Danzig for the opposite reason: because their positions were so soft. All three were convinced that Danzig was not worth a war; all three were agreed that it should return to Germany, with safeguards for Polish trade. But all three recognised that Poland would not give way without a fight and that Hitler would not postpone Danzig until a more peaceful moment. Italy was committed to Germany by the Pact of Steel, Great Britain and France were committed to Poland. None of the three wanted to fight over Danzig; neither of the two principals would yield. The only course therefore was to ignore the question of Danzig and to hope that the others would ignore it also. The three Western Powers did their best to wish Danzig out of existence:

> As I was going up the stair,
> I met a man who wasn't there.
> He wasn't there again today.
> I do so wish he'd go away.

This was the spirit of European diplomacy in the summer of 1939. Danzig was not there; and if all the Powers wished hard enough it would go away.

When August arrived, it became clear that Danzig had not gone away. The local Nazis stepped up their provocations to the Poles; the Poles responded with

---

[4] Weizsäcker, *Erinnerungen,* 258.

challenging firmness. Reports of German troop movements grew stronger; and this time the rumours were well founded. Hitler, it was expected, would act soon. But how? and, still more important, when? This was the vital question in both the Czech and Polish crises. On each occasion the Western Powers assumed that Hitler would explode the crisis in public, at the Nazi party rally in Nuremberg. On each occasion this assumption was mistaken; but in the Czech crisis the Western Powers erred on the right side, in the Polish crisis on the wrong one. In 1938 the party rally was held on 12 September; Hitler's military plans were set only for 1 October, and therefore "appeasement" had an unexpected fortnight in which to operate. In 1939 the party rally was fixed for the first week in September; this time Hitler had decided to achieve success beforehand. At the "Rally of Peace," he would announce victory, not prepare for it. No one could have guessed that the German military plans were timed for 1 September. The date—like 1 October in the previous year—was not chosen on any rational ground, meteorological or other, despite assertions to the contrary by most later writers it was arrived at, as such dates usually are, by sticking a pin in the calendar. The margin for negotiation was narrow in any case; the diplomatic plans of the Western Powers misfired partly because the margin was about a week narrower than they thought.

At the beginning of August, the Western Powers were still marking time, in the hope that their undefined relations with the Soviet Union would deter Hitler. Others were less confident. A procession of visitors to Berchtesgaden tried to gauge Hitler's intentions. Perhaps the probings first made him decide what these were. The Hungarians led the field. On 24 July Teleki, the Hungarian prime minister, wrote two letters to Hitler. In one he promised "that in the event of a general conflict Hungary will make her policy conform to the policy of the Axis"; but in the other, "Hungary could not, on moral grounds, be in a position to take armed action against Poland."[5] On 8 August Csáky, the Hungarian foreign minister, received at Berchtesgaden a ruthless answer. Hitler did not want Hungarian assistance. But "Poland presents no military problem to us. . . . It is to be hoped that Poland will still see reason at the last minute. . . . Otherwise not only the Polish army but also the Polish state will be destroyeed. . . . France and Britain will not be able to prevent us from doing this." Csáky stammered, apologised, and withdrew Teleki's letters, "as unfortunately, they had apparently been misunderstood."[6]

Three days later it was the turn of Burckhardt, the League High Commissioner at Danzig. Hitler was again bellicose: "I shall strike like lightning with the full force of a mechanised army, of which the Poles have no conception." But he also showed signs of conciliation: "if the Poles leave Danzig absolutely calm . . . then I can wait." He made it clear what he would wait for. He would still be content with the terms which he demanded on 26 March—"unfortunately that is definitely ruled out by the Poles." Then, more generally, "I want nothing from the West . . . But I must have a free hand in the East. . . . I want to live in peace with England and to conclude a definite pact; to guarantee all the English possessions in the world and to collaborate."[7] With both Csáky and Burckhardt, Hitler was clearly talking for effect—bellicose at one moment, conciliatory at the next. It was exactly the tactic of the previous year. Why not now? If his talk of peace was play-acting, so also was

[5] Memorandum by Weizsäcker, 24 July 1939. *German Foreign Policy*, series D. vi. No. 712.

[6] Memorandum by Erdmannsdorff, 8 Aug. 1939. *Ibid*. No. 784.

[7] Minute by Makins, 14 Aug. 1939. *British Foreign Policy*, third series. vi. No. 659.

his talk of war. Which would become real depended on events, not on any resolution taken by Hitler beforehand.

On 12 August a more important visitor appeared: Ciano, the Italian foreign minister. The Italians had been full of fight so long as war seemed a long way off; they grew anxious when reports accumulated that war was approaching. Italy was exhausted by her prolonged intervention in Spain—perhaps the only significant effect of the Spanish civil war. Her reserves of gold and raw materials were run down; her rearmament with modern weapons had hardly begun. She could be ready for war only in 1942; and even this was an imaginary date which merely meant "in some distant future." On 7 July Mussolini said to the British ambassador: "Tell Chamberlain that if England fought on the Polish side over Danzig, Italy would fight on that of Germany."[8] A fortnight later he swung round, and asked for a meeting with Hitler on the Brenner. He proposed to insist that war must be avoided, and that Hitler could get all he wanted at an international conference. The Germans first waved the meeting away; then said that one should be held solely to discuss the coming attack on Poland. Maybe Mussolini distrusted his ability to stand up to Hitler; at any rate he decided to send Ciano instead. Mussolini's instructions were clear: "We must avoid a conflict with Poland, since it will be impossible to localise it, and a general war would be disastrous for everybody."[9] Ciano spoke up firmly when he met Hitler on 12 August, but his remarks were swept aside. Hitler announced that he proposed to attack Poland unless he got complete satisfaction by the end of August; "He was absolutely certain that the Western democracies . . . would shrink from a general war"; the whole operation would be over by 15 October. This was more precise than any previous statement by Hitler; yet doubt remains. He knew that anything he said to the Italians would be passed on to the Western Powers; and he was concerned to shake their nerve, not to reveal his real plans to Mussolini.

An odd little episode showed what these plans were. While Ciano was talking to Hitler, "the Führer was handed a telegram from Moscow." Ciano was told what was in it: "The Russians agreed to a German political negotiator being sent to Moscow." According to Ciano, "The Russians asked for the sending to Moscow of a German plenipotentiary who would negotiate a pact of friendship."[10] No such telegram has been found in the German archives; and none can ever have existed. For the Russians agreed to the sending of a German negotiator only on 19 August, not on 12 August.[11] Of course Stalin may have communicated his decision to Hitler, by some hidden means, a week before he made it. But this is a fantastic hypothesis, for which all evidence is lacking. It is far more probably that the telegram was a fabrication, designed to impress Ciano and to quieten his doubts. Yet, though a

---

[8] Loraine to Halifax, 7 July 1939. *Ibid.* No. 261.
[9] *Ciano's Diary 1939-1943*, p. 123.
[10] Conversation between Hitler and Ciano, 12 Aug. 1939. *German Foreign Policy*, series D. vii. No. 43; *I documenti diplomatici italiani*, eighth series. xiii. No. 4.
[11] It is now universally admitted that there was no telegram from Moscow on 12 August. But it is often suggested that agreement to the visit of a German negotiator was given by the agency of Astakov, the Soviet chargé d'affaires in Berlin. This also is untrue. Astakov merely said that "the Soviets were interested in a discussion of individual questions." He did not mention a pact of friendship; and "he left the matter open as to who was expected in Moscow to conduct the conversations, whether the Ambassador or someone else." *German Foreign Policy*, series D. vii. No. 50. Astakov was probably acting on his own initiative, as he had often done before. In any case, there is no evidence that the information was passed on to Hitler.

fabrication, it was not without foundation. This foundation was Hitler's "hunch"—his conviction that what he wanted to happen would happen. His second sight had never failed him so far. This time he was staking everything on it, certain in advance that the Anglo-Franco-Soviet negotiations would break down and that then the Western Powers would collapse also.

On 12 August the Anglo-Franco-Soviet negotiations had not broken down. They were actually being resumed. The British and French military missions had at last arrived in Moscow. The French had been told by Daladier to get a military convention as quickly as possible. The British, on the other hand, were instructed to "go very slowly" until a political agreement was reached (though discussions for this had been suspended on 27 July until a military convention was made): "Agreement on the many points raised may take months to achieve."[12] The British government, in fact, were not interested in solid military cooperation with Soviet Russia; they merely wanted to chalk a Red bogey on the wall, in the hope that this would keep Hitler quiet. But, when the talks started, the British spokesmen soon found themselves being bustled by the French and by Voroshilov, the Soviet leader, into serious discussion. British and French plans for war were described in detail; the resources of the two countries somewhat generously catalogued. On 14 August the Soviet turn came. Voroshilov then asked, "Can the Red Army move across North Poland . . . and across Galicia in order to make contact with the enemy? Will Soviet troops be allowed to cross Rumanian territory."[13] It was the decisive question. The British and French could not answer. The talks ran to a standstill; on 17 August they were adjourned, never to be seriously resumed.

Why did the Russians ask this question so ruthlessly and so abruptly? Was it merely to have an excuse for negotiating with Hitler? Perhaps. But the question was a real one which had to be asked—and answered. Poland and Rumania had presented insuperable obstacles against any Soviet action in 1938. These obstacles had to be overcome if Soviet Russia were to act now as an equal partner; and only the Western Powers could overcome them. The question raised the old dispute of principle in a new form. The Western Powers wanted the Soviet Union as a convenient auxiliary; the Russians were determined to be recognised as principals. There was also a difference of strategical outlook which has been less noticed. Great Britain and France still thought in terms of the Western front during the first World war. They therefore exaggerated the strength of defensive positions. The military mission had been told: if Germany attacked in the West, even through Holland and Belgium, "sooner or later, this front would be stabilised." In the East, Poland and Rumania would slow down a German advance; with Russian supplies they might stop it altogether.[14] In any case the Red Army would have plenty of time to build up lines of defense after the war had started. Then everyone would remain securely entrenched until Germany collapsed under pressure of a blockade. Holding these views, the Western Powers could see in the Russian demand to advance through Poland only a political manoeuvre; the Russians, they thought, wished to humiliate Poland or perhaps even to destroy her political independence.

---

[12] Instructions to the British Military Mission, Aug. 1939. *British Foreign Policy,* third series. vi. Appendix v.

[13] Minutes of meeting, 14 Aug. 1939. *Ibid.* vii. Appendix ii.

[14] Instructions to Military Mission, Aug. 1939. *British Foreign Policy,* third series. vi. Appendix v, para. 83.

No one can tell whether the Russians had such designs. But it is clear that they had different strategical conceptions which were enough in themselves to explain their demands. The Russians started from their experiences in the civil wars and wars of intervention, not from the preceding World war. Here cavalry offensives had everywhere carried the day. Moreover, as Communists, they automatically favoured a strategical doctrine more dynamic and revolutionary than that held in the decadent capitalist West. The Russians held that cavalry offensives, now in mechanised form, were irresistible, or rather they could be resisted only by similar offensives at some other part of the front. It was their intention, in case of war, to fling armoured columns into Germany, regardless of German attacks elsewhere. This remained their intention even in 1941; and they were prevented from putting it into operation only by the fact that Hitler attacked them before they were ready. Their doctrine was, in fact, mistaken, though not more so than that of the Western Powers; and in 1941 Hitler's surprise attack saved them from a disaster which might have been beyond remedy. These later experiences are irrelevant to the diplomacy of 1939. Then the Russians asked to go through Poland because they believed, however mistakenly, that this was the only way to win a war. Political aims may have existed as well; but they were subordinate to genuine military needs.

The British and French governments did not appreciate these Soviet calculations; but they realised that the unwelcome question would have to be answered, now that it had been asked. Both turned, though without much hope, to Warsaw. The British still used political arguments: "Agreement with the Soviet Union would be calculated to deter Hitler from war." If negotiations broke down, "Russia might either share the spoils with Germany . . . or constitute the chief menace when the war was over."[15] Beck gave an equally political answer: agreement to the passage of Russian troops across Poland, far from deterring Hitler, "would lead to an immediate declaration of war on the part of Germany."[16] Both political arguments made sense; both were irrelevant to the military situation. The French thought in more practical terms. They were only concerned to get the Red Army involved in conflict with Hitler, and did not mind if this were done at the expense of Poland. Left to themselves they would gladly have jettisoned Poland if they could have won Soviet co-operation in exchange. London forbade any such threat; therefore the French had still to attempt persuasion. Bonnet thought he saw a way out. The Russians insisted on an agreement for military collaboration with the Poles before war started; the Poles would accept Soviet aid only when the war had begun. Hence Bonnet argued that a moment had arrived which still seemed like peace to the Russians but like war to the Poles. The manoeuvre failed. Beck was obdurate: "It is a new partition of Poland that we are being asked to sign." On 21 August the French lost patience. They decided to ignore the Polish refusal and to go ahead, hoping to commit the Poles willy-nilly. Doumenc, the head of the military mission in Moscow, was instructed to give "an affirmative answer in principle" to the Russian question; and he was to "negotiate and sign whatever arrangement might best serve the common interest, subject to the final approval of the French Government." The British refused to be associated with this move, though they did not protest against it.

In any case, the chance of a Soviet alliance, if it ever existed, had now been lost. On 14 August, a few hours after Voroshilov had raised his fateful question,

---

[15] Halifax to Kennard, 17 Aug., 20 Aug. 1939. *British Foreign Policy*, third series. vii. No. 38, 39, 91.
[16] Kennard to Halifax, 18 Aug. 1939. *Ibid.* No. 52.

Ribbentrop drafted a telegram to Schulenberg, his ambassador in Moscow: "There exist no real conflicts of interests between Germany and Russia.... There is no question between the Baltic Sea and the Black Sea which cannot be settled to the complete satisfaction of both parties." Ribbentrop was prepared to come to Moscow there "to lay the foundations for a final settlement of German-Russian relations."[17] This message was the first real move in German-Soviet relations. Until then they had been stagnant; the discussions between subordinates, of which so much was to be made later by Western writers, were no more than soundings, inspired by regrets for the vanished intimacy of Rapallo. Now Hitler was at last taking the initiative. Why did he do so at this precise moment? Was it supreme political skill, a second sight which told him that the military talks would reach deadlock two days after they started? Was the coincidence of Voroshilov's question and Ribbentrop's approach arranged secretly between Stalin and Hitler in advance? Did some unknown agent in the Kremlin tell Hitler that the right moment had arrived? Or was the coincidence pure chance? Hitler had first blurted out his plan of breaking Anglo-French nerve by an agreement with Soviet Russia when he boasted untruly to Ciano of an invitation from Moscow on 12 August, and so stilled Italian fears. Perhaps Hitler only devised this strategy consciously at the moment of boasting. After all, he was always the man of daring improvisations; he made lightning decisions, and then presented them as the result of long-term policy. Ribbentrop remained at Berchtesgaden until 13 August. He returned to Berlin on 14 August. This was therefore the first day when the message to Moscow could have been sent. Probably chance is the correct answer; but this is one of the problems which we shall never be able to solve.

Schulenberg delivered Ribbentrop's message on 15 August. Molotov refused to be hurried. Though he received the message "with greatest interest," he thought negotiations would take some time. He asked: "How were the German Government disposed towards the idea of a non-aggression pact with the Soviet Union?"[18] The answer came back within less than twenty-four hours: Germany offered not only a non-aggression pact, but a joint guarantee of the Baltic States and mediation between Soviet Russia and Japan. The essential thing was the visit by Ribbentrop.[19] The Russians still kept the way open on both sides. On 17 August Voroshilov told the British and French military missions that there was no point in a further meeting until they could answer his question about Poland; however, after some prodding, he agreed to meet again on 21 August. At almost exactly the same time Molotov told Schulenberg that the improvement in Soviet-German relations would be a long business. First there must be a commercial agreement; next a pact of non-aggression. Then perhaps they could think about a visit from Ribbentrop; but the Soviet government "preferred to do practical work without fuss."[20]

On 18 August Ribbentrop knocked harder than ever at the Soviet door. Relations must be clarified at once "so as not to be taken by surprise by the outbreak of a German-Polish conflict."[21] Once more Molotov hesitated. Ribbentrop's visit "could not be fixed even approximately." Within half an hour, Schulenberg was called back

[17] Ribbentrop to Schulenberg, 14 Aug. 1939. *German Foreign Policy,* series D. vii. No. 56.

[18] Schulenberg to Ribbentrop, 16 Aug. 1939. *Ibid.* No. 70.
[19] Ribbentrop to Schulenberg, 16 Aug. 1939. *German Foreign Policy,* series D. vii. No. 75.

[20] Schulenberg to Ribbentrop, 18 Aug. 1939. *Ibid.* No. 105.
[21] Ribbentrop to Schulenberg, 18 Aug. 1939. *Ibid.* No. 113.

to the Kremlin; Ribbentrop, he was told, could come a week later.[22] There is no means of knowing what brought this sudden decision. Schulenberg thought that Stalin had intervened personally; but this was a guess, like all others made later. The Soviet invitation was not soon enough for Hitler; he wanted Ribbentrop to be received at once. This may have been simply the impatience which always followed his prolonged hesitations. Perhaps there is a deeper explanation. 26 August would be soon enough if Hitler merely aimed to clear the way for an attack on Poland on 1 September. It was not soon enough to give him time for two operations: first breaking the nerve of the Western Powers by an agreement with Soviet Russia; then breaking the nerve of the Poles with the assistance of the Western Powers. Hence Hitler's urgency strongly suggests that he was aiming at another "Munich," not at war.

At any rate, Hitler now acted without a diplomatic intermediary. On 20 August he sent a personal message to Stalin, agreeing to all the Soviet demands and asking that Ribbentrop should be received at once.[23] The message was a milestone in world history; it marked the moment when Soviet Russia returned to Europe as a Great Power. No European statesman had ever addressed Stalin directly before. Western leaders had treated him as though he were a remote, and ineffectual, Bey of Bokhara. Now Hitler recognised him as the ruler of a great state. Stalin is supposed to have been immune to personal feelings; Hitler's approach must have flattered him all the same. The moment of decision had arrived. On 20 August the commercial treaty between Soviet Russia and Germany was settled; the first Soviet condition had been fulfilled. On the morning of 21 August Voroshilov met the two military missions. They had nothing to report; and the meeting adjourned *sine die*. At 5 p.m. Stalin agreed that Ribbentrop could come to Moscow at once—on 23 August. The news was announced that same night in Berlin, and on the following day in Moscow. The French still tried to save something. On 22 August Doumenc saw Voroshilov on his own. On Daladier's instructions, he offered to agree to the Soviet demand without waiting for a reply from the Poles. Voroshilov rejected the offer: "We do not want Poland to boast that she has refused our aid—which we have no intention of forcing her to accept."[24] The Anglo-Franco-Soviet negotiations were at an end. On the following day, 23 August, the French finally wheedled out of the Poles a grudging formula. The French might say to the Russians: "We have acquired the certainty that in the event of common action against a German aggression collaboration between Poland and the U.S.S.R. is not excluded (or: is possible)."[25] The formula was never placed before the Russians. In any case it was fraudulent. Beck agreed to it only when he knew that Ribbentrop was in Moscow and that there was no danger of Soviet aid to Poland. Nor did this dismay him. He still believed that an independent Poland had more chance of reaching agreement with Hitler. Soviet Russia, he thought, was withdrawing from Europe; and that was good news for the Poles. "It is now Ribbentrop's turn," he said complacently, "to experience Soviet bad faith."[26]

Ribbentrop did not think so. He came to Moscow to reach agreement; and he

[22] Schulenberg to Ribbentrop, 19 Aug. 1939. *Ibid*. No. 132.

[23] Ribbentrop to Schulenberg, 20 Aug. 1939. *German Foreign Policy*, series D. vii. No. 142.

[24] Conversation between Voroshilov and Doumenc, 22 Aug. 1939. *British Foreign Policy*, third series. vii. Appendix ii. No. 10.

[25] Kennard to Halifax, 23 Aug. 1939. *Ibid*. No. 176.

[26] Noël, *L'agression allemande*, 424.

succeeded immediately. The public Pact, signed on 23 August, provided for mutual non-aggression. A secret protocol excluded Germany from the Baltic states and from the eastern parts of Poland—the territory east of the Curzon line which was inhabited by Ukrainians and White Russians. This was, after all, what the Russians had sought to obtain from the Western Powers. The Nazi-Soviet pact was only another way of doing it: not so good a way, but better than none. The settlement of Brest-Litovsk was at last undone, with the consent of Germany, instead of with the backing of the Western Powers. It was no doubt disgraceful that Soviet Russia should make any agreement with the leading Fascist state; but this reproach came ill from the statesmen who went to Munich and who were then sustained in their own countries by great majorities. The Russians, in fact, did only what the Western statesmen had hoped to do; and Western bitterness was the bitterness of disappointment, mixed with anger that professions of Communism were no more sincere than their own professions of democracy. The pact contained none of the fulsome expressions of friendship which Chamberlain had put into the Anglo-German declaration on the day after the Munich conference. Indeed Stalin rejected any such expressions: "The Soviet Government could not suddenly present to the public German-Soviet assurances of friendship after they had been covered with buckets of filth by the Nazi Government for six years."

The pact was neither an alliance nor an agreement for the partition of Poland. Munich had been a true alliance for partition: the British and French dictated partition to the Czechs. The Soviet government undertook no such action against the Poles. They merely promised to remain neutral, which is what the Poles had always asked them to do and which Western policy implied also. More than this, the agreement was in the last resort anti-German: it limited the German advance eastwards in case of war, as Winston Churchill emphasised in a speech at Manchester immediately after the end of the Polish campaign. In August the Russians were not thinking in terms of war. They assumed, like Hitler, that the Western Powers would not fight without a Soviet alliance. Poland would be compelled to yield; and, with the Polish obstacle out of the way, defensive alliance with the West might then be achieved on more equal terms. Alternatively, if the Poles remained defiant, they would fight alone; and in that case they would be driven to accept Soviet assistance after all. These calculations were falsified by the actual outcome: a war in which both Poland and the Western Powers took part. Even this was a success for the Soviet leaders: it warded off what they had most dreaded—a united capitalist attack on Soviet Russia. But it was not the intention of Soviet policy; the events of 1 September and 3 September could not be foreseen on 23 August. Both Hitler and Stalin imagined that they had prevented war, not brought it on. Hitler thought the he would score another Munich over Poland; Stalin that he had at any rate escaped an unequal war in the present, and perhaps even avoided it altogether.

However one spins the crystal and tries to look into the future from the point of view of 23 August 1939, it is difficult to see what other course Soviet Russia could have followed. The Soviet apprehensions of a European alliance against Russia were exaggerated, though not groundless. But, quite apart from this—given the Polish refusal of Soviet aid, given too the British policy of drawing out negotiations in Moscow without seriously striving for a conclusion—neutrality, with or without a formal pact, was the most that Soviet diplomacy could attain; and limitation of German gains in Poland and the Baltic was the inducement which made a formal pact attractive. The policy was right according to the textbooks of diplomacy. It contained all the same a grave blunder: by concluding a written agreement, the

Soviet statesmen, like Western statesmen before them, slipped into the delusion that Hitler would keep his word. Stalin obviously had doubts. At the moment of parting with Ribbentrop he said: "The Soviet Government take the new Pact very seriously. He could guarantee on his word of honour that the Soviet Union would not betray its partner." There was a clear implication: "Do thou likewise." All the same Stalin obviously thought that the pact had value, not only as an immediate manoeuvre, but over a long period. This is curious, but not unusual. Men, themselves without scruple, often complain when they are cheated by others.

At any rate the bomb had exploded. Hitler was radiant, confident that he had pulled off the decisive stroke. On 22 August he entertained his leading generals to the wildest of his speeches: "Close your hearts to pity. Act brutally." This rigmarole was not a serious directive for action—no formal record was kept. Hitler was glorying in his own skill. Tucked away in the speech was a hard core: "Now the probability is great that the West will not intervene."[27] As well, Hitler was talking for effect. A report of the speech reached the British embassy almost at once;[28] whether intentionally or not, the so-called German "resistance" did Hitler's work for him. On 23 August Hitler took a further step. He fixed the attack on Poland for 4.40 a.m. on 26 August. This, too, was play-acting to impress the generals and, through them, the Western Powers. The German time-table could operate only from 1 September. Before then an attack on Poland was possible only if she had already surrendered. But technical considerations no longer seemed to matter: the Nazi-Soviet pact was assumed to have cleared the way for a diplomatic collapse on the part of the Western Powers.

The French almost came up to Hitler's expectations—or down to them. Bonnet had always been eager to desert the Poles. He resented the way in which they had behaved during the Czech crisis; he accepted the German case over Danzig; he had no faith in the Polish army. The Russians, Bonnet argued, claimed that they could not fight against Germany without a common frontier; a German conquest of Poland would provide one, and the Franco-Soviet Pact could then be revived to real effect. On 23 August, when Ribbentrop's journey to Moscow became known, Bonnet asked Daladier to summon the Committee of National Defence. There he hinted at his policy: "Should we blindly apply our alliance with Poland? Would it be better, on the contrary, to push Warsaw into a compromise? We could thus gain time to complete our equipment, increase our military strength, and improve our diplomatic position, so as to be able to resist Germany more effectively if she turned against France later." But Bonnet was no fighter, even for peace. He left the decision to others. The generals would not confess France's military weakness, for which they were responsible; perhaps they did not even appreciate it. Gamelin declared that the French army was "ready" (whatever that might mean); he further said that Poland would hold out until the spring and that by then the Western front would be impregnable.[29] No one raised the question whether it was possible actually to aid the Poles. Obviously those present all assumed that the French army would merely man the Maginot line, despite Gamelin's promise to the Poles of an offensive. There was no discussion of policy, no proposal to warn the Poles of their

[27] Memorandum of speech by Hitler, 22 Aug. 1939. *German Foreign Policy*, series D. vii. No. 192 and 193.
[28] Ogilvie-Forbes to Kirkpatrick, 25 Aug. 1939. *British Foreign Policy*, third series, vii. No. 314.
[29] Bonnet, *Fin d'une Europe*, 303-4.

danger. The Poles were left free to resist Hitler or to compromise with him, just as they chose. Even more remarkable, there was no approach to the British, no Anglo-French meeting of ministers such as had marked the Czech crisis. The British, too, were left free to resist Hitler or to compromise, without any information as to French wishes or French strength. Yet the British decision would commit France. The French would either abdicate finally in eastern Europe or would carry, almost alone, the burden of a great European war, entirely according to which London preferred. There was silence towards the British, silence towards the Poles, almost silence towards the Germans. Daladier sent a letter of warning to Hitler. Otherwise French statesmen did nothing throughout the week which determined, for many years, the fate of France.

This was a strange passivity, but not stranger than the French policy during previous years. The French did not know which way to turn. They would not deliberately abandon the settlement of 1919; and yet sensed that they were incapable of maintaining it. They had behaved like this over German rearmament. They refused to allow it, yet could find no way of preventing it. It was the same over Austria: "No" was repeated until the Anschluss happened. Czechoslovakia would have seen the same story again, had it not been for British prompting. Then the British urged surrender, and the French acquiesced. Now no word come from the British; and Daladier, the most representative of French politicians, relapsed into sullen resistance. The French cared no more for Danzig than they had done for the German-speaking territories of Czechoslovakia; but they would not themselves destroy what they once had made. They wanted to make an end one way or the other. "Il faut en finir" was the universal French mood in 1939. They had no idea what the end would be. Hardly any Frenchmen foresaw military defeat; victory over Germany seemed equally remote. There is some slight evidence that the French secret service exaggerated the opposition inside Germany. But there was no rational calculation behind the decision of 23 August. The French were at a loss what to do; they therefore decided to let things happen.

Decision thus rested exclusively with the British government. Their policy, too, seemed in ruins; the Anglo-Soviet alliance was gone beyond recall. This was a basic misunderstanding of the British position—indeed a misunderstanding which did as much as anything else to cause the second World war. Alliance with Soviet Russia was the policy of the Opposition—the policy of Labour, of Winston Churchill, and of Lloyd George. It was they who insisted that resistance to Hitler was possible only if Soviet Russia were on the Allied side. The government did not share this view. They never attached practical value to the Soviet alliance; and they drifted into negotiations unwillingly, driven on by agitation in Parliament and in the country. They were relieved when negotiations broke down; delighted to be able to say, "We told you so," to their critics; and freed from an embarrassment. The Conservative back-benchers went further. Many of them had favoured Hitler as a bulwark against Bolshevism; now he became, in their eyes, a traitor to the cause of Western civilisation. At the same time as the Conservatives swung against Hitler, Labour turned, with almost equal bitterness, against Stalin; resolved to show that they, at any rate, were sincere in their anti-Fascism, even if it meant supporting Chamberlain. On any rational calculation, the Nazi-Soviet Pact ought to have discouraged the British people. Lloyd George was almost alone in making this calculation. Otherwise the Pact produced a resolution such as the British had not shown for twenty years. On 22 August, to universal applause, the Cabinet determined to stand by their obligation to Poland.

There was no discussion how this obligation could be fulfilled; indeed there was no way of fulfilling it. Military advisers were not called in except to consider the civil defences of London. The British government still thought in terms of policy, not of action. Their policy remained unchanged: on the one hand, firm warnings to Hitler that he would face general war if he attacked Poland; on the other, equally steady assurances that he would receive concessions if he acted peacefully. They were resolved on this policy. Hence they did not consult the French whether war were practicable, nor enquire of the Poles what concessions could be made. Indeed they were determined on concessions over the Poles' heads, if Hitler were reasonable. The British government still agreed with Hitler in regard to Danzig. But even now the question of Danzig was not formally raised. Hitler waited for offers which could be screwed up; the British waited for claims which could be scaled down. Whichever made the first move would lose; hence neither made it. The British government found a middle way: they would warn Hitler against war and, at the same time, hint at the rewards which peace would bring him. Their original intention had been to send a special emissary—not Chamberlain this time, but perhaps Field Marshal Lord Ironside. In the hurry consequent on the Nazi-Soviet pact, this was impossible. The message had to be delivered by the ambassador, Nevile Henderson, who flew to Berchtesgaden on 23 August.

It was an unfortunate choice. Henderson no doubt tried to speak firmly, but his heart was not in it. With consistency worthy of a better cause, he remained convinced that the Poles were in the wrong. He wanted them to be forced to give way, as the Czechs had been forced to give way the year before. A few days previously he wrote to a friend in the Foreign Office: "History will judge the Press generally to have been the principal cause of the war.... Of all Germans, believe it or not, Hitler is the most moderate so far as Danzig and the Corridor are concerned.... We could not say Boo to Benes last year till we were on the abyss of war. And we can't say Boo to Beck now."[30] He certainly failed to say Boo to Hitler. Though he loyally delivered the British message, he still paraded British conciliation. He told Hitler, quite truly: "The proof of Chamberlain's friendship was to be found in the fact that he had refused to have Churchill in the Cabinet"; and he said further that the hostile attitude in Great Britain was the work of Jews and enemies of the Nazis, which was exactly what Hitler thought himself.[31] Faced with such a half-hearted opponent, Hitler bullied and stormed. When Henderson left the room, Hitler slapped his thigh and said: "Chamberlain will not survive that conversation; his Cabinet will fall to-night."[32] Henderson responded as Hitler intended. Immediately on his return to Berlin, he wrote to Halifax: "I have held from the beginning that the Poles were utterly foolish and unwise"; and again: "I personally no longer see any hope of avoiding war unless the Polish Ambassador is instructed to apply today or at the latest tomorrow for personal interview with Hitler."[33]

In England, however, events did not come up to Hitler's expectation. Quite the reverse. Parliament met on 24 August, and unanimously applauded what it supposed

[30] Henderson to Strang, 16 Aug. 1939. *British Foreign Policy,* third series. vii. No. 37.

[31] Memorandum by Loesch, 24 Aug. 1939. *German Foreign Policy,* series D. vii. No. 200.

[32] Weizsäcker, *Erinnerungen,* 252.

[33] Henderson to Halifax, 24 Aug. 1939. *British Foreign Policy,* third series. vii. No. 257 and 241.

to be the government's firm stand. Hitler began to have doubts: evidently more was needed to extract from the British government the concessions on which he still counted. On 24 August Hitler flew to Berlin. On his instructions, Goering called in the Swede Dahlerus, and sent him off to London with an unofficial appeal for British mediation. This was an ingenious trap: if the British refused, Hitler could claim that he had never made a move; if they yielded, they would be compelled to put pressure on Poland. The same evening Hitler held a meeting with Goering, Ribbentrop, and the principal generals. Should they go on with the attack on Poland, now due to begin within thirty-six hours? Hitler declared that he would make a further attempt to detach the Western Powers from their Polish allies. The attempt took the form of a "last offer," communicated to Henderson shortly after noon on 25 August. Germany, Hitler declared, was determined "to abolish the Macedonian conditions on her eastern frontier." The problems of Danzig and the Corridor must be solved—though he still did not say how. Once these problems were out of the way, Germany would make "a large, comprehensive offer"; she would guarantee the British Empire, accept an agreed limitation of armaments, and renew the assurance that her frontier in the west was final.[34] Henderson was impressed, as usual. Hitler, he reported, spoke "with great earnestness and apparent sincerity."[35] Later writers have all dismissed Hitler's offer as fraudulent; and so in a sense it was. The immediate object was to isolate Poland. Yet the offer also represented Hitler's permanent policy: though he wanted a free hand to destroy conditions in the east which enlightened Western opinion had also pronounced intolerable, he had no ambitions directed against Great Britain and France.

But what could Hitler hope to achieve by this offer in the circumstances of the moment? Henderson promised to fly to London on the morning of 26 August; and by then the attack on Poland presumably would have begun. Was Hitler merely talking for the record—to clear himself in the eyes of posterity or even of his own conscience? Or had he forgotten his time-table, unable to realise that orders, once given, will be ultimately carried out? The latter seems the more likely explanation. Throughout the afternoon of 25 August, Hitler raged round the Chancellery, uncertain what to do. At 3 p.m. he ordered that the attack on Poland should be carried out. Three hours later Attolico, the Italian ambassador, arrived with a message from Mussolini: though Italy stood by Germany unconditionally, she could not "intervene militarily," unless Germany at once supplied all her needs in war material; and these, when the list came, were—in Ciano's words—"enough to kill a bull if a bull could read." Mussolini had acted the strong man till the last moment; now, with war apparently imminent, he ran away. Immediately after this blow came another. Ribbentrop reported that the formal alliance between Great Britain and Poland had just been signed in London. Hitler summoned Keitel, his chief-of-staff: "Stop everything at once, fetch Brauchitsch [the commander-in-chief] immediately. I need time for negotiations." The new orders went out shortly after 7 p.m. The premature offensive was as precipitately cancelled.

Here was another mysterious episode. Why did Hitler pull back at the last moment? Did he lose his nerve? Did the two events of Mussolini's neutrality and the Anglo-Polish alliance really take him by surprise? He himself, with the normal propensity of statesmen to put the blame on others, at once complained that it was all the fault of Mussolini: news of the Italian decision not to fight had stiffened the

[34] Henderson to Halifax, 25 Aug. 1939. *Ibid.* No. 283.
[35] Henderson to Halifax, 25 Aug. 1939. *Ibid.* No. 284.

British just when they were on the point of surrender. This was nonsense. The British did not know of Mussolini's decision when they signed the alliance with Poland, though they could make a good guess at it. Nor was the alliance timed for its effect at that particular moment. Its conclusion had been held up during the negotiations with Soviet Russia; once these failed, there was no reason for further postponement, and the British signed it as soon as formalities could be completed. They were unaware that Hitler had fixed on 25 August as the day of crisis. They were thinking in terms of the first week in September; just as Hitler had long thought in terms of 1 September. Probably this is the explanation of his apparent hesitation on 25 August. Advancing the offensive to that date was a "try-on," an extra call rather like his exaggerated obstinacy at Godesberg the previous year. Quite apart from the diplomatic events of 25 August, there were good military reasons for reverting to the original date. On 25 August the Western frontier of Germany was still virtually undefended. Perhaps thereafter Hitler faced the fact that some sort of war with the Western Powers was in the offing. But it is more likely that he spoke the truth to Keitel: he needed time for negotiation.

The British, too, were intent on negotiation. The signing of the Anglo-Polish alliance was a preliminary to this, not a firm decision for war. There is clear evidence that the British did not take the alliance all that seriously. Their draft had been designed to fit in with an Anglo-Soviet alliance, now vanished. In the hugger-mugger which followed the Nazi-Soviet pact, clauses from a Polish draft were included as well; and one of these contained the pledge which the British had hitherto evaded—a full extension of the alliance to cover Danzig. Yet almost at the moment of signing the alliance, a member of the foreign office drafted "possible counter-proposals to Herr Hitler" which postulated that Danzig should have "the right to determine its political allegiance," subject to the recognition of Poland's economic rights;[36] and Halifax himself told the Polish ambassador that "the Polish Government would make a great mistake if they sought to adopt a position in which discussion of peaceful modifications of the status of Danzig was ruled out."[37] Thus the British government and Hitler were close to agreement on how the crisis should end and the Poles were out of step. The problem however was not how negotiations should end, but how they should begin; and for this no solution was found.

Preliminaries for a negotiation proceeded furiously between 26 August and 29 August: the British hinting at what they would offer, Hitler at what he would demand. Both sides hesitated to go over the brink into actual negotiations. There was further confusion in that these soundings were conducted on two levels. Nevile Henderson acted as official intermediary; Dahlerus shuttled between Berlin and London even more assiduously. He flew to London on 25 August and back to Berlin on 26 August; to London and back on 27 August; and the same again on 30 August. In Berlin he saw Goering and sometimes Hitler; in London he was received with every precaution of secrecy, and saw Chamberlain and Halifax. The British might insist that their remarks to Dahlerus were "off the record"; Hitler was bound to feel all the same that a second Munich was being prepared for him. He may have been genuinely taken aback by the signature of the Anglo-Polish alliance; this effect was lost as Henderson and Dahlerus multiplied their exertions. Yet at the same time

[36] Memorandum by Makins, 25 Aug. 1939. *British Foreign Policy*, third series. vii. No. 307.

[37] Halifax to Kennard, 25 Aug. 1939. *Ibid.* No. 309.

the British, listening to Dahlerus, imagined that their position was improving. A member of the foreign office commented on the activities of Dahlerus: "This shows that the German Government are wobbling. . . . Whilst we may and should be conciliatory in form, we should be absolutely firm in substance. . . . The latest indications are that we have an unexpectedly strong hand." This minute bears the further comment: "Seen by S. of S. who says he quite agrees with it."[38] With extreme ingenuity Halifax even believed that a second Munich would discredit Hitler, not the British government. He wrote: "When we speak of Munich we must remember the change that has supervened since then in the attitude and strength of this country, and in many other directions—Italy—and let us hope Japan—etc. And if Hitler is led to accept a moderate solution now, it is perhaps not altogether wishful thinking to believe that his position will suffer a certain diminution within Germany."[39]

Thus the two sides circled round each other like wrestlers seeking advantage before the clinch. The British offered to arrange direct negotiations between Germany and Poland if Hitler would promise to behave peacefully; Hitler replied that there would be no war if he got his way over Danzig. Later writers have argued that Hitler's reply was dishonest; that he was concerned to isolate Poland, not to avoid war. This may well be true. But the offer by the British government was dishonest also: there was no chance of extracting concessions from the Poles once the danger of war was removed, and the British knew it. In the previous year Benes had appealed for British support. They had implied that he might secure it if he were conciliatory enough; and he had swallowed the bait. Now the British were already committed—their hands tied not so much by their formal alliance with Poland, as by the resolution of British public opinion. They could not dictate concessions to the Poles; they could not allow Hitler to dictate them. Yet there would be no concessions unless someone did the dictating. On 23 August Sir Horace Wilson, acting on Chamberlain's behalf, saw Kennedy, the American ambassador. After the conversation, Kennedy telephoned the State Department: "The British wanted one thing of us and one thing only, namely that we put pressure on the Poles. They felt that they could not, given their obligations, do anything of this sort but that we could."[40] President Roosevelt rejected this idea out of hand. Chamberlain—again according to Kennedy—then lost all hope: "He says the futility of it all is the thing that is frightful; after all, they cannot save the Poles; they can merely carry on a war of revenge that will mean the destruction of all Europe."[41]

The deadlock lasted until 29 August. Then it was broken by Hitler. He was in the weaker position, though the British did not know it. There was not much time left before 1 September for him to pull off diplomatic success. At 7:15 p.m. he made to Henderson a formal offer and a formal demand: he would negotiate directly with Poland if a Polish plenipotentiary arrived in Berlin the following day. This was a retreat from the position Hitler had rigorously asserted since 26 March—that he would never again deal directly with the Poles. Though Henderson complained that

[38] Minute to Kirkpatrick, 27 Aug. 1939. *British Foreign Policy*, third series, vii. No. 397.

[39] Minute by Halifax on Henderson to Halifax, 29 Aug. 1939. *Ibid.* No. 455.

[40] *Moffat Papers 1919-43* (1956), 253. Cordell Hull supplies Wilson's name. *Memoirs*, i. 662.

[41] Kennedy to Hull, 23 Aug. 1939. *Foreign Relations of the United States*, 1939. Vol. I. General.

the demand was perilously near an ultimatum, he was eager to accept it; it constituted in his opinion the "sole chance of preventing war." Henderson pressed the demand on his own government; he urged the French government to advise an immediate visit by Beck; he was most insistent of all with the Polish ambassador Lipski.[42] Lipski took no notice—apparently he did not even report Hitler's demand to Warsaw. The French government responded as clearly in the opposite direction—they told Beck to go to Berlin at once. But the decision rested with the British government. Here was the proposal which they had always wanted and which they had repeatedly hinted at to Hitler: direct negotiations between Poland and Germany. Hitler had now done his part; but they could not do theirs. They had the gravest doubt whether the Poles would thus present themselves in Berlin at Hitler's behest. Kennedy reported Chamberlain's feeling to Washington: "Frankly he is more worried about getting the Poles to be reasonable than the Germans."[43] The British gnawed over the problem throughout 30 August. Finally they hit on a sort of solution. They passed Hitler's demand on to Warsaw at 12:25 a.m. on 31 August—that is to say, twenty-five minutes after the German ultimatum, if such it were, had expired. The British had been correct in their apprehension of Polish obstinacy. Beck, when informed of Hitler's demand, at once replied: "If invited to Berlin he would of course not go, as he had no intention of being treated like President Hacha."[44] Thus the British, by acting too late, could still claim that they had offered something which they knew they could not deliver: a Polish plenipotentiary in Berlin.

Hitler had not anticipated this. He had expected that negotiations would start; and he then intended them to break down on Polish obstinacy. On his instructions detailed demands were at last prepared. These were principally the immediate return of Danzig, and a plebiscite in the Corridor[45]—the very terms which the British and French governments had themselves long favoured. But, failing a Polish plenipotentiary, the Germans had difficulty in making their terms known. At midnight on 30 August Henderson brought to Ribbentrop the news that a Polish plenipotentiary was not coming that day. Ribbentrop had only the rough draft of the proposed German terms, scribbled over with Hitler's emendations. It was not in a condition to be shown to Henderson; and Ribbentrop had instructions from Hitler not to do so. He therefore read the terms over slowly. Later a myth grew up that he had "gabbled" them, deliberately cheating Henderson with terms that were only for show. In fact Henderson got the gist clearly, and was impressed. Taken at their face value, he thought, they were "not unreasonable." On his return to the British embassy, he summoned Lipski at 2 a.m., and urged him to seek an interview with Ribbentrop at once. Lipski took no notice, and went back to bed.

The Germans were now anxious that their terms had not gone properly on record with Henderson. They once more employed Dahlerus as an allegedly unofficial emissary. Goering, claiming to be acting in defiance of Hitler, showed the terms to

---

[42] Henderson to Halifax, 29 Aug., 30 Aug. 1939. *British Foreign Policy,* third series, vii. No. 493, 510.

[43] Kennedy to Hull, 30 Aug. 1939. *Foreign Relations of the United States, 1939.* Vol. I. General.

[44] Kennard to Halifax, 31 Aug. 1939. *British Foreign Policy,* third series. vii. No. 575.

[45] Schmidt, circular dispatch, 30 Aug. 1939. *German Foreign Policy,* series D. vii. No. 458.

Dahlerus, who in turn telephoned them to the British embassy about 4 a.m. Since Goering knew that all telephone conversations were monitored by at least three government agencies (one of them his own), his defiance of Hitler was of course a fiction. The next morning Goering abandoned it. Dahlerus was given a copy of the German terms, and took it round to the British embassy. Henderson again summoned Lipski, who refused to come. Dahlerus and Ogilvie-Forbes, the British counsellor of embassy, were dispatched to see Lipski. He remained unmoved. He refused to look at the German terms. When Dahlerus was out of the room, Lipski protested against introducing this intermediary, and said: "He would stake his reputation that German morale was breaking and that the present regime would soon crack.... This German offer was a trap. It was also a sign of weakness on the part of the Germans."[46] In a further effort to break through the crust of obstinacy, Dahlerus telephoned to Horace Wilson in London. The German terms, he said, were "extremely liberal"; it was "obvious to us [Dahlerus? Goering? Henderson?] that the Poles were obstructing the possibilities of a negotiation." Wilson realised that the Germans were listening-in; he told Dahlerus to shut up and put down the receiver.[47]

The precaution came too late. Every move of the last few hours had been as public as if it had been announced in the newspapers. The telephone calls between Henderson and Lipski, and between Dahlerus and Henderson, the comings and goings between the British and Polish embassies—all these were known to the Germans. They were undoubtedly known to Hitler. What conclusion could he possibly draw? Only the conclusion that he had succeeded in driving a wedge between Poland and her Western allies. This was true in regard to the French government. It was true in regard to Henderson. He wrote late on 31 August: "On German offer war would be completely unjustifiable.... Polish Government should announce tomorrow, in the light of German proposals which have now been made public, their intention to send a Plenipotentiary to discuss in general terms these proposals."[48] Hitler was not to know that Henderson no longer carried the weight in London which he had carried the year before. But even the British government were losing patience with the Poles. Late on the night of 31 August Halifax telegraphed to Warsaw: "I do not see why the Polish Government should feel difficulty about authorising Polish Ambassador to accept a document from the German Government."[49] Given another twenty-four hours, and the breach would be wide open. But Hitler had not got the twenty-four hours. He was the prisoner of his own time-table. With his generals watching sceptically, he could not again call off the attack of Poland unless he had something solid to show; and this was still denied him by the Poles. The breach between Poland and her allies gave him a chance. He had to gamble on it.

At 12.40 p.m. on 31 August Hitler decided that the attack should proceed. At 1 p.m. Lipski telephoned, asking for an interview with Ribbentrop. The Germans, who had intercepted his instructions, knew that he had been told not to enter into "any concrete negotiations." At 3 p.m. Weizsäcker telephoned Lipski to ask whether he was coming as a plenipotentiary. Lipski replied: "No, in his capacity as an

[46] Henderson to Halifax, 31 Aug. 1939. *British Foreign Policy,* third series. vii. No. 597.

[47] Minute by Cadogan, 31 Aug. 1939. *British Foreign Policy,* third series. vii. No. 589.

[48] Henderson to Halifax, 1 Sept. 1939. *Ibid.* No. 631
[49] Halifax to Kennard, 1 Sept. 1939. *Ibid.* No. 632.

ambassador." This was enough for Hitler. The Poles, it seemed, were remaining obstinate; he could go forward to the gamble of isolating them in war. At 4 p.m. the orders for war were confirmed. At 6.30 p.m. Lipski at last saw Ribbentrop. Lipski said that his government were "favourably considering" the British proposal for direct Polish-German negotiations. Ribbentrop asked whether he was a plenipotentiary. Lipski again answered No. Ribbentrop did not communicate the German terms; if he had tried to do so, Lipski would have refused to receive them. Thus ended the only direct contact between Germany and Poland since 26 March. The Poles had kept their nerve unbroken to the last moment. At 4.45 a.m. on the following morning the German attack on Poland began. At 6 a.m. German aeroplanes bombed Warsaw.

Here was a clear *casus foederis* for both Great Britain and France. Their ally had been wantonly attacked; it only remained for them to declare war on the aggressor. Nothing of the kind happened. Both governments addressed a pained remonstrance to Hitler, warning him that they would have to go to war unless he desisted. Meanwhile they waited for something to turn up; and something did. On 31 August Mussolini, carefully following the precedent of the previous year, proposed a European conference: it should meet on 5 September and should survey all causes of European conflict, with the precondition that Danzig should return to Germany in advance. The two Western governments were favourable to the proposal when it first reached them. But Mussolini had got his timing wrong. In 1938 he had three days in which to avert war; in 1939 less than twenty-four hours, and this was not enough. By 1 September, when the Western governments replied to Mussolini, they had to postulate that fighting must first stop in Poland. Nor was this all. While Bonnet was enthusiastic for Mussolini's proposal, in Great Britain public opinion took charge. The House of Commons was restive when Chamberlain explained that Germany had merely been "warned"; it expected something more solid next day. Halifax, swinging as usual with the national mood, insisted that the conference could be held only if Germany withdrew from all Polish territory. The Italians knew that it was hopeless to place such a demand before Hitler; they dropped the conference without further effort.

Yet both the British and French governments, the French especially, went on believing in a conference which had vanished before it was born. Hitler had initially replied to Mussolini that, if invited to a conference, he would give his answer at mid-day on 3 September. Therefore Bonnet, and Chamberlain with him, strove desperately to postpone a declaration of war until after that time, even though the Italians no longer intended to invite Hitler or anyone else. Bonnet conjured up the excuse that the French military wanted the delay in order to carry through mobilisation, undisturbed by German air attack (which, they knew, would not occur anyway—the German air force was fully employed in Poland). Chamberlain conjured up no excuse except that the French wanted delay and that it was always difficult to work with allies. In the evening of 2 September he was still entertaining the House of Commons with hypothetical negotiations: "If the German Government should agree to withdraw their forces then His Majesty's Government would be willing to regard the position as being the same as it was before the German forces crossed the Polish frontier. That is to say, the way would be open to discussion between the German and Polish Governments on the matters at issue." This was too much even for loyal Conservatives. Leo Amery called to Arthur Greenwood, acting leader of the Opposition: "Speak for England," a task of which Chamberlain was incapable. Ministers, led by Halifax, warned Chamberlain that the government would fall unless it sent an ultimatum to Hitler before the House met again. Chamberlain gave way. The objections of the French were overruled. The British ultimatum was delivered to the Germans at 9 a.m. on 3 September. It expired at 11 a.m., and a state of war followed. When Bonnet learnt that the British were going to war in any case, his overriding anxiety was to catch up with them. The time of the French ultimatum was advanced, despite the supposed objections of the General Staff: it was delivered at noon on 3 September and expired at 5 p.m. In this curious way the French who had preached resistance to Germany for twenty years appeared to be dragged into war by the British who had for twenty years preached conciliation. Both countries went to war for that part of the peace settlement which they had long regarded as least defensible. Hitler may have projected a great war all along; yet it seems from the record that he became involved in war through launching on 29 August a diplomatic manoeuvre which he ought to have launched on 28 August.

Such were the origins of the second World war, or rather of the war between the three Western Powers over the settlement of Versailles; a war which had been implicit since the moment when the first war ended. Men will long debate whether this renewed war could have been averted by greater firmness or by greater conciliation; and no answer will be found to these hypothetical speculations. Maybe either would have succeeded, if consistently followed; the mixture of the two, practised by the British government, was the most likely to fail. These questions now seem infinitely remote. Though Hitler blundered in supposing that the two Western Powers would not go to war at all, his expectation that they would not go to war seriously turned out to be correct. Great Britain and France did nothing to help the Poles, and little to help themselves. The European struggle which began in 1918 when the German armistice delegates presented themselves before Foch in the railway-carriage at Rethondes, ended in 1940 when the French armistice delegates presented themselves before Hitler in the same carriage. There was a "new order" in Europe; it was dominated by Germany.

The British people resolved to defy Hitler, though they lacked the strength to undo his work. He himself came to their aid. His success depended on the isolation of Europe from the rest of the world. He gratuitously destroyed the source of this success. In 1941 he attacked Soviet Russia and declared war on the United States, two World Powers who asked only to be left alone. In this way a real World war began. We still live in its shadow. The war which broke out in 1939 has become a matter of historical curiosity.

A. J. P. TAYLOR AND THE ORIGINS
OF WORLD WAR II

Zygmundt Kulak

It is very rarely that a historical work has aroused so much lively discussion as the book[1] by A. J. P. Taylor, Professor of history at Magdalene College, Oxford. This was because, in this book, Taylor revised the previous views

[1] A. J. P. TAYLOR, *Die Ursprünge des zweiten Welkrieges*, Sigbert Mohn Verlay, Gütersloh 1962, pp. 383.

of international historiography as regards the causes of the outbreak of the Second
World War and interpreted these causes in his own, new way. Taylor gives his
reasons for having revised the views held so far. He says that only a few of the
explanations of the causes of the outbreak of the First World War published in
August 1914 could be uncritically accepted twenty years after it began. On the
other hand, twenty years after the Second World War, almost all the explanations of
the causes of its outbreak formulated in September 1939 have been accepted
without reservations. All the outstanding historians in whose works we seek
elucidation of the reasons for the outbreak of the Second World War – Namier,
Wheeler-Bennet and Wiskemann in Great Britain and Beaumont in France – express
views formulated during the war or even earlier. In other words, Taylor suggests
that all the evaluations of the causes of the Second World War made so far have
been subjective because the historians were emotionally engaged in the course of
events they have described. Thus, they wrote history *cum ira et studio*. But Taylor
does not hold them responsible for this state of affairs, since he considers that this
is a typical shortcoming and practically unavoidable in works on contemporary
history. For contemporary history deals with events which are evaluated while still
fresh in the mind, under the impressions of the moment, the assumption being that
the reader will show understanding for this type of evaluation because that same
reader also adopts an emotional attitude towards the events described. Thus it can
be seen that Taylor's judgement on contemporary history is very severe and reminds
one of the view once disseminated by malicious Mediaevalists, that research on
contemporary history is synonymous with looking at a picture with one's nose
pressed against it. Taylor also negates the very possibility of a scientific elaboration
of contemporary history, simply because an historian must approach the subject of
his research from the proper chronological distance. Only when he can present the
events of contemporary history with the same objectiveness as he would present
events from the period of the Investiture Dispute or the period of the Civil War in
Britain can one speak of a scientific and objective study of events. And, in Taylor's
opinion, this objective distance already exists in relation to the Second World War,
which is no longer contemporary history, but simply history. So it is only now that
the proper conditions have come into being to enable a new and fully scientific
study of the causes of the Second World War and an elucidation of those causes. In
this way, Taylor lightly dismisses all the scientific works written so far on the
subject of the causes of the Second World War, saying that there is no sense in
repeating these evaluations because it is very unlikely that in another hundred years
historians will evaluate these events in the same way as their predecessors of 1939.
That is why it is better for the historian (Taylor was undoubtedly thinking of
himself) to attempt to make such an evaluation as will be formulated in the future
than to repeat what has been said in the past.

It should be stressed at once that the assumptions of the British historian are
risky from the scientific point of view, for how are we to know how historians will
evaluate the events of the Second World War a hundred years hence? In addition,
Taylor over-estimates the importance of what he calls chronological distance. The
results of a historian's studies depend less on the distance dividing him from the
subject of his research, than, first and foremost, on ability to apply the proper
methods of research. There are known cases in the history of historiography, in
which the historian, however great his chronological distance from the subject of
research, reached very subjective and even completely erroneous conclusions

consequent on applying erroneous methods of research. The problem of interpretation is much more complicated and goes far beyond the question of so-called distance.

The evaluation of the causes of the Second World War made by the British historian questions the whole of international historiography on this subject. Thus, in Taylor's opinion, the Second World War was not caused by Hitler, nor was it planned by him, but was only the result of the bungling of the diplomats of both sides, who failed completely in discharge of their responsibilities. If Hitler, Chamberlain and Beck had been better diplomats, the outbreak of the Second World War could — according to Taylor — have been avoided by the conclusion of a Polish-German agreement under pressure from Great Britain. Taylor maintains that this could very easily have been achieved since Hitler was aiming at an alliance with Poland and not her destruction (p. 270). But the problem of Gdańsk stood in the way of Polish-German cooperation and it was only for this reason that Hitler wanted to remove this problem. The most amazing thing is that Taylor presents the Polish-German dispute as though its only cause was the problem of Gdańsk and the Corridor, and that it was not a matter of a first step towards conquering Poland and then the whole of Eastern Europe. If, in fact, Hitler's aims were only Gdańsk and the Corridor, there is no doubt that the same pressure would have been put on Poland by Great Britain and France to force her to make concessions to Hitler as was put on Czechoslovakia in the Sudeten crisis.

From the point of view of the political interests of Great Britain, the most important thing was not the problem of Gdańsk and the Corridor — for the German claims to these territories were at first very favourably regarded in London, a fact that Taylor rightly points out — but the question of whether Hitler could be trusted in his statement of his political aims. Contrary to Taylor's present statements, from the moment Czechoslovakia was occupied in March 1939, nobody believed that the territorial appetite of Nazi Germany was limited to Gdańsk and the Corridor. And the further growth of the power of the Nazi Reich was regarded in London as a danger which threatened also Great Britain (the historical course of events later showed how right these anticipations were); hence efforts were made to prevent Hitler's further expansion by guaranteeing Poland's western frontier and the signing of an alliance with Poland. In the end, when the need arose to fulfill the commitments of that alliance, war was declared on Hitler. Thus, it is difficult to take seriously Taylor's statement that Hitler had been involved on a war just because he only began on August 29th the political manoeuvre, he should have started on August 28th (p. 354). Here, the British historian has in mind the move aimed at isolating Poland from Great Britain and strengthening the influence of these in favour of the policy of appeasement in London. However, Taylor does admit that Hitler wanted to force through his demands on Poland at all costs — even the cost of a small "local" war, which in the face of the guarantee given by Great Britain, must of necessity turn into a great war. The probability of such a development of events did exist and in spite of this Hitler took the risk and thus took upon himself the responsibility for the further development of the situation, a fact which it is difficult to justify. But Taylor does justify him by saying that Hitler wanted to attain his object not by means of war, or if that proved unavoidable, by only a small war which would be hardly more than a diplomatic move. Hitler had not planned or prepared for a bigger and longer war. Taylor justifies this statement by pointing to the position of Germany as regards armaments in 1939. This argument, far from supporting his thesis, rather disproves it. For how can one explain the fact that after less than a year, Germany was able to conquer not only Poland, but also France, Belgium and Holland and to occupy Denmark and Norway? Such arbitrary interpretations are to be found in abundance in Taylor's book. For instance, we are told that the annexation of Austria was initiated by Franz Papen to save his personal prestige, and not by Hitler. And the crisis of March 1938 itself, which ended with the annexation of Austria, was provoked by Chancellor Schuschnigg and not Hitler. The Third Reich was—in Taylor's opinion—completely unprepared for this undertaking, both in the military and the diplomatic sense. Thus, if we are to believe the British historian, the thesis that the annexation of Austria was a deliberate move prepared long before and was Hitler's first step towards hegemony in Europe is but a fairy tale (p. 197). Even Taylor finds it difficult to be consistent in his distorted interpretation of historical facts, for on page 111 he admits that Nazi Germany was a threat to Austria and that Austrian Nazis received money and arms from the Reich, while the Munich radio station incited them to the putsch. At the same time, he quotes an excerpt from the memorandum of Bernhard von Bulow, Secretary of State at the *Auswärtiges Amt,* containing a statement by Hitler to the effect that he was ready to postpone the question of Austria for some years but that he could not assure Mussolini that he had no interest as regards that country.

Taylor gives a similar presentation of the Czechoslovak crisis, which in his opinion, was automatically put on the agenda. It was as though this crisis had been specially created for Hitler and all he did was to take advantage of it. And again, Hitler had not set up the Henlein movement. The movement had been waiting for him and was eager to go into action. Here Taylor gives proof of his lack of knowledge of the role of the German national minorities in realizing Hitler's plans in Czechoslovakia and Poland. For it is well known that Hitler was not long in subordinating the German minorities in Czechoslovakia and Poland to his plans and that they became completely devoted instruments in the realization of his political aims. Suffice it to recall the role played by the Sudeten Germans in the Czechoslovak crisis and the Germans living in Poland in the Polish-German crisis, to draw the proper conclusions as to the way the Nazi regime took advantage of the German minorities to realize its expansionist plans. In Austria, the role of the German national minority was played by Austrian Nazis. In the west, the role of the German minorities in the realization of Hitler's plans to conquer central and eastern Europe is underestimated, and this is evident not only in Taylor's book. This is because neither Czechoslovak nor Polish historians have attempted a thorough scientific study of this problem and presentation of their theses to their colleagues in the West. The occupation of Czechoslovakia in March 1939 was, according to Taylor, also unintended. In fact, it was only a bi-product of the development of the situation in Slovakia and was directed more against the Hungarians than it was against the Czechs (sic!). The Slovaks, we are told, were supported by the Nazi regime for their own sake, without any side considerations. Taylor justifies this thesis with the statement that the frequently heard view that Hitler wanted to use Slovakia as a spring-board to the Ukraine is quite groundless, for Slovakia did not border on the Ukraine. But did not the occupation of Czechoslovakia and the creation of a Slovak state completely dependent on the Third Reich increase German domination in central and eastern Europe? Was it not an important step forward on the way to carrying out the plans to conquer the whole of eastern Europe? But for Taylor, all the above mentioned events have no causal association, since he is of the opinion that Hitler had no aggressive plans worked out in advance and only limited himself to skilfully turning all situations to his own advantage. The British historian maintains that politicians and statesmen are too absorbed in the development of current events to be able to act according to a plan worked out in advance. Plans, we are told, are created *post factum* by historians. Thus we have the statement that the real authors of the plans attributed to Hitler are such British historians as Trevor-Roper, Wiskemann or Bullock. Nevertheless, Taylor does admit that there are certain grounds for formulating such views, which he calls speculations.

But Taylor comes up against certain difficulties owing to the fact that his theses are contradicted by many important documents which prove that Hitler constantly stressed and justified the absolute necessity of acquiring living space to the East by means of war. Taylor gets out of these difficulties in a very facile manner simply by rejecting all documents which contradict his theses, saying that Hitler's statements were an expression of his day-dreams and visions and could not therefore have any real connection with reality. Thus, Taylor rejects as source material *Mein Kampf, Hitler's Table Talk: 1941–1944,* and also his last will and testament written by Martin Bormann in the Berlin bunker in February 1945. True, Taylor rejected *Mein Kampf* as source material but this did not prevent him from quoting from it when it suited him. But not all documents indicting his theses could be rejected, and consequently Taylor interprets them in his own way, the most glaring example of this being his interpretation of the document known as Hossbach's protocol. It is known that at the conference held on November 5th, 1937, Hitler first revealed his aggressive plans to the commanders of the various arms, the Minister of War and the Minister of Foreign Affairs. At that time, those plans were concentrated on Austria and, above all, on Czechoslovakia. The account of that meeting is precisely the previously mentioned Hossbach's protocol. Hitler then envisaged the circumstances which would enable him to realize his plans. None of the circumstances envisaged by Hitler materialized, and on this basis, Taylor puts forward the unambigous suggestion that Hossbach's protocol was not a plan of Hitler's foreign policy since Hitler did not limit himself to the situations envisaged at the conference in the realization of his intentions. Does Taylor really think that a politician like Hitler would limit the realization of his plans to a previously envisaged situation and would not realize them at all costs? For Hitler said many times that in realizing the aim one has set oneself, all available means and methods should be used, "beginning with diplomatic skill and ending with skill in warfare." This should have been remembered in interpreting such an important document as Hossbach's protocol. But for Taylor, Hitler's plans, revealed at the conference referred to, were "day-dreams" having no real connection with reality. In Taylor's opinion, the conference held on November 5th, 1937, was but an internal-political manoeuvre, the aim of which was to win over the highest military commanders and gain their support for the further expansion of the armaments programme and in this way to isolate Schacht, who opposed that programme. Taylor over-estimates Schacht's opposition as an obstacle to the realization of the Nazi armaments programme. For it is known that even at that time Göring was responsible for the entire economic policy and the realization of the armaments programme as "General Plenipotentiary for the Four-Year Plan." No less unacceptable is Taylor's interpretation of the changes made by Hitler on February 2nd, 1938, when he dismissed: Neurath, Minister of Foreign Affairs; Blomberg, Minister of War; and General Fritsch,

Commander-in-Chief of the Land Forces. These changes were—in Taylor's opinion—made to divert attention from Schacht's dismissal. Meanwhile, it is known that Neurath, Fritsch and Blomberg were not one hundred percent supporters of the Nazi regime and in addition had been so bold as to express their reservations concerning Hitler's aggressive plans — a boldness which was the most important reason for their dismissal. For Hitler could not tolerate in leading political and military posts people who did not want to carry out his plans of conquest blindly. Taylor did not wish to see this causal connection since it would have contradicted his thesis that Hitler was not aiming at war and was not preparing for it. It is probably for the same reasons that Taylor omitted to mention one of the most important documents, which absolutely and unambigously belies his thesis — Hitler's memorandum on the Four-Year Plan. In this memorandum Hitler stated literally: "The following tasks must be carried out: (1) In four years the German army must be ready for combat. (2) In four years the German economy must be ready for war." But Taylor preferred not to refer to that document, for he could not very well say that Hitler mobilized the whole economy for war purely for tactical reasons — as he took the liberty of saying in reference to the conference of May 23rd, 1939, when Hitler openly admitted that his aim was war. Hitler's order of August 23rd, 1939, setting the date of the attack on Poland as August 26th, was — in Taylor's opinion — issued only to make an impression on his generals and, through them, on the western powers with which the generals were in contact as members of the anti-Nazi opposition.

Taylor's interpretation must inevitably lead to conclusions of a methodological nature. His book is an example of the fact that limiting research exclusively to the history of diplomacy, where the course of events is — as a rule — very rapid and most of such events are dictated by tactical considerations aimed at concealing the real aims and misleading the opponent, can easily lead to absurd conclusions. If, however, Taylor had extended his studies to include economic problems, where the development process is much slower and where tactical considerations hardly play any role, he would surely have noticed that Hitler's economic policy in its absolute drive towards autarchy was aimed at war mobilization. Also, the scope of armaments, as was shown in the book published by Burkhart Mueller-Hillebrand, for many years an officer of the organizational department of the General Staff of the German Land Forces, was designed with war in mind from the very beginning.

But Taylor preferred to limit himself to juggling with diplomatic documents, so as to back up at all costs his previously conceived revision of old views concerning the causes of the Second World War. In this way, Taylor did bad service to the science of history; he undermined confidence in it as a scientific discipline. Taylor's irresponsible interpretation has also brought fatal political results in its wake. Taylor's book was greeted by many Nazis in western Germany with enthusiasm, despite the fact that this British historian had not been very popular with them in view of his realistic attitude towards the German problem and the frontier on the Oder and Neisse. They breathed a sigh of relief because at last they had found a well known historian who had attempted to relieve their Führer of the responsibility for the outbreak of the Second World War. So it is not surprising that Taylor's book was such a success in western Germany that its first edition was sold out within twelve days and second and third editions appeared soon after. Nor was this not all. Such periodicals as "Nation Europa," "Deutsche Hochschullehrer Zeitung" and "National Zeitung und Soldaten Zeitung," which express the views of former Nazis, introduced a new division in the whole of the historiography devoted to the Second World War. In their opinion, all previous works on this subject were *Geschichtsklitterung* and *Lügenpropaganda* and only with the publication of Taylor's work had real and reliable scientific research, what they called *Wahrheits-forschung,* been started. This evaluation does not change the fact that experts in western Germany unambiguously rejected the main theses of the Oxford historian.

Taylor had evidently envisaged the political effects his book would have in western Germany; therefore he added an afterword to the German edition, in which he calls on the Germans to abandon revisionism since, once started, it cannot be held back, becoming more and more violent with the passing of time. Thus, he enjoins the Germans to accept the present situation in Europe, contrary to their fathers who did not want to accept the order of things established in 1919, with the results that we all know. The unification of Germany, if it were at all possible, would lead to the revision of the frontier on the Oder and Neisse. This, in turn, would lead to demands for the whole of Silesia, as a result of which even the 1919 frontier would be questioned. Gdańsk and the Corridor would again become a bone of contention, as would Sudetenland. In the end, a strong Germany would not be satisfied until it got the Ukraine and had introduced a "new order" in Europe. That is why Taylor appeals to the Germans to avoid revisionism from the very beginning and not to cherish any illusions that they would be able to stop half-way. Taylor says that the German nation supported Hitler and thus brought upon themselves a great deal of suffering, but they brought even greater suffering on other nations. Lands in which Germans once lived are no longer inhabited by them. There are no longer Germans outside the frontiers of Germany. Taylor points out that despite this the majority of Germans are flourishing. If one considers what sufferings the Germans inflicted on other nations, this is an amazingly magnanimous act on the part of the victors. We are ready, says Taylor, to forget the past, but the Germans must forget it too. They must forget the whole of their past and be satisfied with the present conditions, which are really very tolerable. We must all make a contribution to future peace.

Accept the frontier on the Oder and Neisse as being permanently and finally regulated. Learn to say Wroclaw instead of Breslau. If you look back on what the Germans did to other European nations in Hitler's time, this demand is not too great.

And with this Taylor ends his appeal to the Germans. It would most certainly have been much more effective if it were not for the arguments which preceded it.

16 / The Problem of Twentieth Century Revolutions

The study of revolution is surely one of the fastest growing fields in the historical profession. The frequency of revolution in our century is only the most obvious explanation. Equally important is a growing uncertainty concerning the nature and causes of revolution itself. Exactly what do we mean conceptually when we refer to the Russian, Chinese, or Cuban revolutions? What are the fundamental similarities and differences in these experiences? Then too, older assumptions such as the intimate relationship of poverty and revolution are no longer regarded as axiomatic. Today we speak of "revolutions of rising expectations."

Fortunately, historians are not alone in their study of the problem of revolution. In recent years, anthropologists, economists, psychologists, sociologists, and other social scientists have been hard at work on this question. As Lawrence Stone points out, historians should approach this material with caution. Much of the literature of the social sciences in this field consists of "ingenious feats of verbal juggling in an esoteric language, performed around the totem pole of an abstract model, surrounded as far as the eye can see by the arid wastes of terminological definitions and mathematical formulae." Nevertheless, historians cannot ignore this work since the social scientists are asking questions and asserting hypotheses which have already enriched our knowledge of the process of revolution.

In the first selection, Stone critically analyzes several recent "theories of revolution" developed by the social sciences. His reservations are far-reaching but he closes with the hope that "social scientists can supply a corrective to the antiquarian fact-grubbing to which historians are so prone."

In the second selection, Barrington Moore, Jr., author of an important work of comparative social history,[1] presents some thoughts on the social role of the peasants, the most important revolutionary class in the twentieth century. Moore finds the key to the structure of many modern states in the social role of the peasantry. Where the latter has been able to carry out a revolutionary break with the past, either parliamentary democracy or communism becomes triumphant (England, France, Russia, China). Where it has been repressed, and when accompanied by rapid industrialization, fascism wins (Germany, Italy, Japan). Even

[1] *Social Origins of Dictatorship and Democracy: Lord and Peasant in the Making of the Modern World*. (Boston: Beacon Press, 1966).

more controversial is Moore's pessimism regarding the role of American democracy towards the world's peasant masses.

There is a major implicit assumption in Moore's argument, one that he makes clear elsewhere: "There has never been any such thing as a long-term revolutionary mass movement in an urban environment."[2] For Moore, revolutions occur only under conditions of underdevelopment. The events of May-June, 1968 in France, student upheavals and "urban crises" throughout the world, have led some to re-evaluate this judgment. A young American sociologist, Martin Nicolaus, claims real "socialist" revolutions can in fact occur only under conditions of advanced capitalism. This is a well-known thesis of Karl Marx. Appropriately, therefore, Nicolaus returns to the work of the father of "scientific" socialism. Not, however, to *Das Kapital*, but to the little known work, *Grundrisse der Kritik der Politische Okonomie (Rohentwurf)—Fundamental Traits of the Critique of Political Economy* (Rough Draft). Only a few pages of the work have appeared in English. Nicolaus shows, however, that it was the product of fifteen years of ecomonic research, "the best years of Marx's life." Furthermore, he claims that the *Grundrisse* is "the only work in which [Marx's] theory of capitalism from the origins to the breakdown was sketched out in its entirety.

Skepticism of many readers regarding these claims is understandable. Yet it is astonishing that in the *Grundrisse* and perhaps only there, Marx predicts many of the developments of a mature capitalist society including a rising level of consumption of the working classes and a constant increase of the middle classes. One might say that Marx was proposing a theory of the "absolute enrichment" of the working and middle classes as the essential condition for a truly "socialist" revolution.

[2] "Revolution in America?" *The New York Review of Books*, XII, 2 (January 30,

THEORIES OF REVOLUTION *

Lawrence Stone

In attacking the problem of revolution, as most others of major significance in history, we historians should think twice before we spurn the help offered by our colleagues in the social sciences, who have, as it happens, been particularly active in the last few years in theorizing about the typology, causes, and evolutionary patterns of this particular phenomenon. The purpose of this article is not to advance any new hypothesis, but to provide a summary view and critical examination of the work that has been going on.

The first necessity in any inquiry is a careful definition of terms: what is, and what is not, a revolution? According to one view, it is change, effected by the use of violence, in government, and/or regime, and/or society.[1] By *society* is meant the consciousness and the mechanics of communal solidarity, which may be tribal, peasant, kinship, na-

1969), 8.

* I am grateful to Professors Cyril E. Black, Arno J. Mayer, and John W. Shy for some very helpful criticisms of this article.

[1] Chalmers Johnson, *Revolution and the Social System*, Hoover Institution Studies 3 (Stanford 1964).

tional, and so on; by *regime* is meant the constitutional structure—democracy, oligarchy, monarchy; and by *government* is meant specific political and administrative institutions. Violence, it should be noted, is not the same as force; it is force used with unnecessary intensity, unpredictably, and usually destructively.[2] This definition of revolution is a very broad one, and two historians of the French Revolution, Crane Briton and Louis Gottschalk, would prefer to restrict the use of the word to the major political and social upheavals with which they are familiar, the "Great Revolutions" as George S. Pettee calls them.[3]

Even the wider definition allows the historian to distinguish between the seizure of power that leads to a major restructuring of government or society and the replacement of the former elite by a new one and the coup d'état involving no more than a change of ruling personnel by violence or threat of violence. This latter is the norm in Latin America, where it occurred thirty-one times in the ten years 1945-1955. Merle Kling has arrived at a suggestive explanation of this Latin American phenomenon of chronic political instability, limited but frequent use of violence, and almost complete lack of social or institutional change. He argues that ownership of the principle economic resources, both agricultural and mineral, is concentrated in the hands of a tiny, very stable, elite of enormously wealthy monoculture landlords and mining capitalists. This elite is all-powerful and cannot be attacked by opposition groups within the country; externally, however, it is dependent on foreign interests for its markets and its capital. In this colonial situation of a foreign-supported closed plutocracy, the main avenue of rapid upward social mobility for nonmembers of the elite leads, via the army, to the capture of the government machine, which is the only accessible source of wealth and power.

This political instabilty is permitted by the elite on the condition that its own interests are undisturbed. Instability, limited violence, and the absence of social or institutional change are therefore all the product of the contradiction between the realities of a colonial economy run by a plutocracy and the facade of political sovereignty—between the real, stable power of the economic elite and the nominal, unstable control of politicians and generals.[4]

The looser definition of revolution thus suits both historians of major social change and historians of the palace coup. It does, however, raise certain difficulties. Firstly, there is a wide range of changes of government by violence which are neither a mere substitution of personalities in positions of power nor a prelude to the restructuring of society; secondly, conservative counterrevolutions become almost impossible to fit into the model; and lastly, it remains hard to distinguish between colonial wars, civil wars, and social revolution.

To avoid these difficulties, an alternative formulation has recently been put forward by a group of social scientists working mainly at Princeton. They have dropped the word "revolution" altogether and put "internal war" in its place.[5] This

---

[2] Sheldon S. Wolin, "Violence and the Western Political Tradition," *American Journal of Orthopsychiatry*, XXXIII (January 1963), 15-28.

[3] Brinton, *The Anatomy of Revolution* (New York 1938); Gottschalk, "Causes of Revolution," *American Journal of Sociology*, L (July 1944), 1-8; Pettee, *The Process of Revolution* (New York 1938).

[4] "Toward a Theory of Power and Political Instability in Latin America," *Western Political Quarterly*, IX (1956).

[5] Harry Eckstein, ed., *Internal War* (New York 1964), and "On the Etiology of Internal War," *History and Theory*, IV, No. 2 (1965), 133-63. I am grateful to Mr. Eckstein for allowing me to read this article before publication.

is defined as any attempt to alter state policy, rulers, or institutions by the use of violence, in societies where violent competition is not the norm and where well-defined institutional patterns exist.[6] This concept seems to be a logical consequence of the preoccupation of sociologists in recent years with a model of society in a stable, self-regulating state of perpetual equipoise. In this utopian world of universal harmony, all forms of violent conflict are anomalies, to be treated alike as pathological disorders of a similar species. This is a model which, although it has its uses for analytical purposes, bears little relation to the reality familiar to the historian. It looks to a society without change, with universal consensus on values, with complete social harmony, and isolated from external threats; no approximation to such a society has ever been seen. An alternative model, which postulates that all societies are in a condition of multiple and perpetual tension held in check by social norms, ideological beliefs, and state sanctions, accords better with historical fact, as some sociologists are now beginning to realize.[7]

The first objection to the all-embracing formula of internal war is that, by covering all forms of physical conflict from strikes and terrorism to civil war, it isolates the use of violence from the normal processes of societal adjustment. Though some of the users of the term express their awareness that the use of violence for political ends is a fairly common occurrence, the definition they have established in fact excludes all times and places where it *is* common. It thus cuts out most societies the world has ever known, including Western Europe in the Middle Ages and Latin America today. Secondly, it isolates one particular means, physical violence, from the political ends that it is designed to serve. Clausewitz's famous definition of external war is equally applicable to internal war, civil war, or revolution: "War is not only a political act, but a real political instrument; a continuation of political transactions, an accomplishment of them by different means. That which remains peculiar to war relates only to the peculiar nature of its means."[8]

It is perfectly true that any means by which society exercises pressure or control, whether it is administrative organization, constitutional law, economic interest, or physical force, can be a fruitful field of study in its own right, so long as its students remain aware that they are looking at only one part of a larger whole. It is also true that there is something peculiar about violence, if only because of man's highly ambivalent attitude towards the killing of his own species. Somehow, he regards physical force as different in kind from, say, economic exploitation or psychological manipulation as a means of exercising power over others. But this distinction is not one of much concern to the historian of revolution, in which violence is a normal and natural occurrence. The concept of internal war is too broad in its comprehension of all types of violence from civil wars to strikes, too

[6] The formula has been used by a historian, Peter Paret, in *Internal War and Pacification: The Vendee, 1793-96* (Princeton 1961).

[7] Barrington Moore, "The Strategy of the Social Sciences," in his *Political Power and Social Theory* (Cambridge, Mass., 1958); Ralph Dahrendorf, "Out of Utopia: Toward a Reorientation of Sociological Analysis," *American Journal of Sociology*, LXIV (September 1958), 115-27; C. Wright Mills, *The Sociological Imagination* (New York 1959); Wilbert E. Moore, *Social Change* (Englewood Cliffs 1963). It should be noted that both the equilibrium and the conflict views of society have very respectable ancestries. The equilibrium model goes back to Rousseau—or perhaps Aquinas; the conflict model to Hobbes, Hegel, and Marx.

[8] Quoted in Edward Mead Earle, ed., *Makers of Modern Strategy* (Princeton 1943), 104-5.

narrow in its restriction to normally nonviolent societies, too limited in its concern with one of many means, too arbitrary in its separation of this means from the ends in view, and too little concerned with the complex roots of social unrest to be of much practical value to him.

The most fruitful typology of revolution is that of Chalmers Johnson, set out in a pamphlet that deserves to be widely read.[9] He sees six types, identified by the targets selected for attack, whether the government personnel, the political regime, or the community as a social unit; by the nature of the carriers of revolution, whether a mass or an elite; and particularly by the goals and the ideologies, whether reformist, eschatological, nostalgic, nation-forming, elitist, or nationalist. The first type, the *Jacquerie*, is a spontaneous mass peasant rising, usually carried out in the name of the traditional authorities, Church and King, and with the limited aims of purging the local or national elites. Examples are the Peasant Revolt of 1381, Ket's Rebellion of 1549, and the Pugachev rebellion in Russia in 1773-1775. The second type, the *Millenarian Rebellion*, is similar to the first but with the added feature of a utopian dream, inspired by a living messiah. This type can be found at all times, in all parts of the world, from the Florentine revoltion led by Savonarola in 1494, to the Anabaptist Rebellion in Münster led by John Mathijs and John Beukels in 1533-1535, to the Sioux Ghost-Dance Rebellion inspired by the Paiute prophet Wovoka in 1890. It has attracted a good deal of attention from historians in recent years, partly because the career of Hitler offered overwhelming proof of the enormous historical significance of a charismatic leader, and partly because of a growing interest in the ideas of Max Weber.[10] The third type is the *Anarchistic Rebellion*, the nostalgic reaction to progressive change, involving a romantic idealization of the old order: the Pilgrimage of Grace and the Vendée are examples.

The fourth is that very rare phenomenon, the *Jacobin Communist Revolution*. This has been defined as "a sweeping fundamental change in political organization, social structure, economic property control and the predominant myth of a social order, thus indicating a major break in the continuity of development."[11] This type of revolution can occur only in a highly centralized state with good communications and a large capital city, and its target is government, regime, and society—the lot. The result is likely to be the creation of a new national consciousness under centralized, military authority, and the erection of a more rational, and hence more efficient, social and bureaucratic order on the ruins of the old ramshackle structure of privilege, nepotism, and corruption.

The fifth type is the *Conspiratorial Coup d'État*, the planned work of a tiny elite fired by an oligarchic, sectarian ideology. This qualifies as a revolutionary type only if it in fact anticipates mass movement and inaugurates social change—for example the Nasser revolution in Egypt or the Castro revolution in Cuba; it is thus clearly distinguished from the palace revolt, assassination, dynastic succession-conflict, strike, banditry, and other forms of violence, which are all subsumed under the "internal war" rubric.

[9] *Revolution and the Social System.*
[10] N. R. C. Cohn, *Pursuit of the Millennium* (New York 1961); Eric J. Hobsbawm, *Primitive Rebels* (Manchester 1959); S.L. Thrupp, *Millennial Dreams in Action*, Supplement II, Comparative Studies in Society and History (The Hague 1962); A.J.F. Köbben, "Prophetic Movements as an Expression of Social Protest," *Internationales Archiv für Ethnographie*, XLIX, No. 1 (1960), 117-64.
[11] Sigmund Neumann, quoted in Chalmers, 2.

Finally, there is the *Militarized Mass Insurrection,* a new phenomenon of the twentieth century in that it is a deliberately planned mass revolutionary war, guided by a dedicated elite. The outcome of guerrilla warfare is determined by political attitudes, not military strategy or matériel, for the rebels are wholly dependent on broad popular support. In all cases on record, the ideology that attracts the mass following has been a combination of xenophobic nationalism and Marxism, with by far the greater stress on the former. This type of struggle has occurred in Yugoslavia, China, Algeria, and Vietnam.

Although, like any schematization of the historical process, this sixfold typology is concerned with ideal types, although in practice individual revolutions may sometimes display characteristics of several different types, the fact remains that this is much the most satisfactory classification we have so far; it is one that working historians can recognize and use with profit. The one obvious criticism is semantic, an objection to the use of the phrase "Jacobin Communist Revolution." Some of Johnson's examples are Communist, such as the Russian or Chinese Revolutions; others are Jacobin but not Communist, such as the French Revolution or the Turkish Revolution of 1908-1922. It would be better to revert to Pettee's category of "Great Revolutions," and treat Communist revolutions as a subcategory, one type, but not the only type, of modernizing revolutionary process.

Given this classification and definition of revolution, what are its root causes? Here everyone is agreed in making a sharp distinction between long-run, underlying causes—the preconditions, which create a potentially explosive situation and can be analyzed on a comparative basis—and immediate, incidental factors—the precipitants, which trigger the outbreak and which may be nonrecurrent, personal, and fortuitous. This effectively disposes of the objections of those historians whose antipathy to conceptual schematization takes the naïve form of asserting the uniqueness of each historical event.

One of the first in the field of model-building was Crane Brinton, who, as long ago as 1938, put forward a series of uniformities common to the four great Western Revolutions: English, French, American, and Russian. These included an economically advancing society, growing class and status antagonisms, an alienated intelligentsia, a psychologically insecure and politically inept ruling class, and a governmental financial crisis.[12]

The subjectivity, ambiguity, and partial self-contradiction of this and other analyses of the causes of specific revolutions—for example the French Revolution—have been cruelly shown up by Harry Eckstein.[13] He has pointed out that commonly adduced hypotheses run the spectrum of particular conditions, moving from the intellectual (inadequate political socialization, conflicting social myths, a corrosive social philosophy, alienation of the intellectuals) to the economic (increasing poverty, rapid growth, imbalance between production and distribution, long-term growth plus short-term recession) to the social (resentment due to restricted elite circulation, confusion due to excessive elite recruitment, anomie due to excessive social mobility, conflict due to the rise of new social classes) to the political (bad government, divided government, weak government, oppressive government). Finally there are explanations on the level of general process, such as rapid social change, erratic social change, or a lack of harmony between the state

[12] *Anatomy of Revolution.*
[13] "On the Etiology of Internal War."

structure and society, the rulers and the ruled. None of these explanations are invalid in themselves, but they are often difficult or impossible to reconcile one with the other, and are so diverse in their range and variety as to be virtually impossible to fit into an ordered analytical framework. What, then, is to be done?

Fundamental to all analyses, whether by historians like Brinton and Gottschalk or by political scientists like Johnson and Eckstein, is the recognition of a lack of harmony between the social system on the one hand and the political system on the other. This situation Johnson calls *dysfunction*, a word derived from the structural-functional equilibrium model of the sociologists. This dysfunction may have many causes, some of which are merely cyclical, such as may develop because of personal weaknesses in hereditary kingships or single-party regimes. In these cases, the revolution will not take on serious proportions, and will limit itself to attacks on the governing institutions, leaving regime and society intact. In most cases, however, including all those of real importance, the dysfunction is the result of some new and developing process, as a result of which certain social subsystems find themselves in a condition of relative deprivation. Rapid economic growth, imperial conquest, new metaphysical beliefs, and important technological changes are the four commonest factors involved, in that order. If the process of change is sufficiently slow and sufficiently moderate, the dysfunction may not rise to dangerous levels. Alternatively, the elite may adjust to the new situation with sufficient rapidity and skill to ride out the storm and retain popular confidence. But if the change is both rapid and profound, it may cause the sense of deprivation, alienation, anomie to spread into many sectors of society at once, causing what Johnson calls multiple dysfunction, which may be all but incurable within the existing political system.

In either case the second vital element in creating a revolutionary situation is the condition and attitude of the entrenched elite, a factor on which Eckstein rightly lays great stress. The elite may lose its manipulative skill, or its military superiority, or its self-confidence, or its cohesion; it may become estranged from the nonelite, or overwhelmed by a financial crisis; it may be incompetent, or weak, or brutal. Any combination of two or more of these features will be dangerous. What is ultimately fatal, however, is the compounding of its errors by intransigence. If it fails to anticipate the need for reform, if it blocks all peaceful, constitutional means of social adjustment, then it unites the various deprived elements in single-minded opposition to it, and drives them down the narrow road to violence. It is this process of polarization into two coherent groups or alliances of what are naturally and normally a series of fractional and shifting tensions and conflicts within a society that both Peter Amman and Wilbert Moore see as the essential preliminary to the outbreak of a Jacobin Revolution.[14] To conclude, therefore, revolution becomes *possible* when a condition of multiple dysfunction meets an intransigent elite: just such a conjunction occurred in the decades immediately before the English, the French, and the Russian Revolutions.

Revolution only becomes *probable* (Johnson might say "certain"), however, if certain special factors intervene: the "precipitants" or "accelerators." Of these, the three most common are the emergence of an inspired leader or prophet; the formation of a secret, military, revolutionary organization; and the crushing defeat of the armed forces in foreign war. This last is of critical importance since it not

[14] Amman, "Revolution: A Redefinition," *Political Science Quarterly*, LXXVII (1962).

only shatters the prestige of the ruling elite, but also undermines the morale and discipline of the soldiers and thus opens the way to the violent overthrow of the existing government.

The first defect of Johnson's model is that it concentrates too much on objective structural conditions, and attempts to relate conditions directly to action. In fact, however, as Eckstein points out, there is no such direct relationship; historians can point to similar activity arising from different conditions, and different activity arising from similar conditions. Standing between objective reality and action are subjective human attitudes. A behaviorist approach such as Brinton's, which lays equal stress on such things as anomie, alienation of the intellectuals, frustrated popular aspirations, elite estrangement, and loss of elite self-confidence, is more likely to produce a satisfactory historical explanation than is one that sticks to the objective social reality. Secondly, Johnson leaves too little play for the operation of the unique and the personal. He seems to regard his accelerators as automatic triggers, ignoring the area of unpredictable personal choice that is always left to the ruling elite and to the revolutionary leaders, even in a situation of multiple dysfunction exacerbated by an accelerator. Revolution is never inevitable—or rather the only evidence of its inevitability is that it actually happens. Consequently the only way to prove this point is to indulge in just the kind of hypothetical argument that historians prudently try to avoid. But it is still just possible that modernization may take place in Morocco and India without revolution. The modernization and industrialization of Germany and Britain took place without revolution in the nineteenth century (though it can be argued that in the latter case the process was slow by twentieth-century standards, and that, as is now becoming all too apparent, the modernization was far from complete). Some think that a potentially revolutionary situation in the United States in the 1930's was avoided by political action.

Lastly it is difficult to fit into the Johnson model the fact that political actions taken to remedy dysfunction often themselves precipitate change. This produces the paradoxical hypothesis that measures designed to restore equilibrium in fact upset equilibrium. Because he begins with his structural-functional equilibrium model, Johnson is a victim of the fallacy of intended consequences. As often as not in history it is the *unintended* consequences that really matter: to mention but one example, it was Louis XVI's belated and half-hearted attempts at reform that provoked the aristocratic reaction, which in turn opened the way to the bourgeois, the peasant, and the sans-culotte revolutions. Finally the dysfunction concept is not altogether easy to handle in a concrete historical case. If societies are regarded as being in a constant state of multiple tension, then some degree of dysfunction is always present. Some group is always in a state of relative deprivation due to the inevitable process of social change.

Recognition of this fact leads Eckstein to point out the importance of forces working *against* revolution. Historians, particularly those formed in the Western liberal tradition, are reluctant to admit that ruthless, efficient repression—as opposed to bumbling, half-hearted repression—involving the physical destruction of leading revolutionaries and effective control of the media of communication, can crush incipient revolutionary movements. Repression is particularly effective when governments know what to look for, when they have before their eyes the unfortunate example of other governments overthrown by revolutionaries elsewhere. Reaction, in fact, is just as infectious as revolution. Moreover diversion of energy and attention to successful—as opposed to unsuccessful—foreign war can ward off serious internal trouble. Quietist—as opposed to activist—religious movements may serve as the opiate of the people, as Halévy suggested about Methodism in England. Bread and circuses may distract popular attention. Timely—as opposed to untimely—political concessions may win over moderate opinion and isolate the extremists.

Basing himself on this suggestive analysis, Eckstein produces a paradigm for universal application. He see four positive variables—elite inefficiency, disorienting social process, subversion, and available rebel facilities—and four negative variables—diversionary mechanisms, available incumbent facilities, adjustive mechanism, and effective repression. Each type of internal war, and each step of each type, can, he suggests, be explained in terms of these eight variables. While this may be true, it is fair to point out that some of the variables are themselves the product of more deep-seated factors, others mere questions of executive action that may be determined by the accidents of personality. Disruptive social process is a profound cause; elite inefficiency a behavior pattern; effective repression a function of will; facilities the by-product of geography. One objection to the Eckstein paradigm is therefore that it embraces different levels of explanation and fails to maintain the fundamental distinction between preconditions and precipitants. Secondly, it concentrates on the factors working for or against the successful manipulation of violence rather than on the underlying factors working to produce a revolutionary potential. This is because the paradigm is intended to apply to all forms of internal war rather than to revolution proper, and because all that the various forms of internal war have in common is the use of violence. It is impossible to tell how serious these criticisms are until the paradigm has been applied to a particular historical revolution. Only then will its value become apparent.

If we take the behaviorist approach, then a primary cause of revolutions is the emergence of an obsessive revolutionary mentality. But how closely does this relate to the objective material circumstances themselves? In every revolutionary situation one finds a group of men—fanatics, extremists, zealots—so convinced of their own righteousness and of the urgent need to create a new Jerusalem on earth (whether formally religious or secular in inspiration is irrelevant) that they are prepared to smash through the normal restraints of habit, custom, and convention. Such men were the seventeenth-century English Puritans, the eighteenth-century French Jacobins, the twentieth-century Russian Bolsheviks. But what makes such men is far from certain. What generates such ruthlessness in curbing evil, such passion for discipline and order? Rapid social mobility, both horizontal and vertical, and particularly urbanization, certainly produces a sense of rootlessness and anxiety. In highly stratified societies, even some of the newly-risen elements may find themselves under stress.[15] While some of the *arrivistes* are happily absorbed in their new strata, others remain uneasy and resentful. If they are snubbed and rebuffed by the older members of the status group to which they aspire by reason of their new wealth and position, they are likely to become acutely conscious of their social inferiority, and may be driven either to adopt a pose *plus royaliste que le Roi* or to dream of destroying the whole social order. In the latter case they may try to allay their sense of insecurity by imposing their norms and values by force upon society at large. This is especially the case if there is available a moralistic ideology like

---

[15] Emile Durkheim, *Suicide* (Glencoe 1951), 246-54; A. B. Hollingshead, R. Ellis, and E. Kirby, "Social Mobility and Mental Illness," *American Sociological Review*, XIX (1954).

Puritanism or Marxism to which they can attach themselves, and which provides them with unshakable confidence is their own rectitude.

But why does the individual react in this particular way rather than another? Some would argue that the character of the revolutionary is formed by sudden ideoligical conversion in adolescence or early adult life (to Puritanism, Jacobinism, or Bolshevism) as a refuge from this anxiety state.[16] What is not acceptable is the fashionable conservative cliché that the revolutionary and the reformer are merely the chance product of unfortunate psychological difficulties in childhood. It is possible that this is the mechanism by which such feelings are generated, though there is increasing evidence of the continued plasticity of human character until at any rate post-adolescence. The main objection to this theory is that it fails to explain why these particular attitudes become common only in certain classes and age groups at certain times and in certain places. This failure strongly suggests that the cause of this state of mind lies not in the personal maladjustment of the individuals or their parents, but in the social conditions that created that maladjustment. Talcott Parsons treats disaffection or "alienation" as a generalized phenomenon that may manifest itself in crime, alcoholism, drug addiction, daytime fantasies, religious enthusiasm, or serious political agitation. To use Robert Merton's formulation, Ritualism and Retreatism are two possible psychological escape-routes; Innovation and Rebellion two others.[17]

Even if we accept this behaviorist approach (which I do), the fact remains that many of the underlying causes both of the alienation of the revolutionaries and of the weakness of the incumbent elite are economic in origin; and it is in this area that some interesting work has centered. In particular a fresh look has been taken at the contradictory models of Marx and de Tocqueville, the one claiming that popular revolution is a product of increasing misery, the other that it is a product of increasing prosperity.

Two economists, Sir Arthur Lewis and Mancur Olson, have pointed out that because of their basic social stability, both preindustrial and highly industrialized societies are relatively free from revolutionary disturbance.[18] In the former societies, people accept with little question the accepted rights and obligations of family, class and caste. Misery, oppression, and social injustice are passively endured as inevitable features of life on earth. It is in societies experiencing rapid economic growth that the trouble usually occurs. Lewis, who is thinking mostly about the newly emerging countries, primarily of Africa, regards the sense of frustration that leads to revolution as a consequence of the dislocation of the old status patterns by the emergence of four new classes—the proletariat, the capitalist employers, the urban commercial and professional middle class, and the professional politicians—and of the disturbance of the old income patterns by the sporadic and patchy impact of economic growth, which creates new wealth and new poverty in close and conspicuous juxtaposition. Both phenomena he regards as merely transitional, since in a country fully developed economically there are strong

[16] Michael L. Walzer, "Puritanism as a Revolutionary Ideology," *History and Theory*, III, No. 1 (1963), 59-90.

[17] Parsons, *The Social System* (Glencoe 1951); Merton, *Social Theory and Social Structure* (Glencoe 1957), chap. 4.

[18] W. Arthur Lewis, "Commonwealth Address," in *Conference Across a Continent* (Toronto 1963), 46-60; Olson, "Rapid Growth as a Destabilizing Force," *Journal of Economic History*, XXIII (December 1963), 529-52. I am grateful to Mr. Olson for drawing my attention to Sir Arthur Lewis's article, and for some helpful suggestions.

tendencies toward the elimination of inequalities of opportunity, income, and status.

This model matches fairly well the only detailed analysis of a historical revolution in which a conscious effort has been made to apply modern sociological methods. In his recent study of the Vendée, Charles Tilly argues that a counterrevolutionary situation was the consequence of special tensions created by the immediate juxtaposition of, on one hand, parish clergy closely identified with the local communities, great absentee landlords, and old-fashioned subsistence farming, and, on the other, a large-scale textile industry on the putting-out system and increasing bourgeois competition.[19] Though the book is flawed by a tendency to take a ponderous sociological hammer to crack a simple little historical nut, it is nonetheless a suggestive example of the application of new hypotheses and techniques to historical material.

Olson has independently developed a more elaborate version of the Lewis theory. He argues that revolutionaries are déclassé and freed from the social bonds of family, profession, village or manor; and that these individuals are the product of rapid economic growth, which creates both *nouveaux riches* and *nouveaux pauvres*. The former, usually middle-class and urban artisans, are better off economically, but are disoriented, rootless, and restless; the latter may be workers whose wages have failed to keep pace with inflation, workers in technologically outdated and therefore declining industries, or the unemployed in a society in which the old cushions of the extended family and the village have gone, and in which the new cushion of social security has not yet been created. The initial growth phase may well cause a decline in the standard of living of the majority because of the need for relatively enormous forced savings for reinvestment. The result is a revolution caused by the widening gap between expectations—social and political for the new rich, economic for the new poor—and the realities of everyday life.

A sociologist, James C. Davis, agrees with Olson that the fundamental impetus toward a revolutionary situation is generated by rapid economic growth but he associates such growth with a generally rising rather than a generally falling standard of living, and argues that the moment of potential revolution is reached only when the long-term phase of growth is followed by a short-term phase of economic stagnation or decline.[20] The result of this "J-curve," as he calls it, is that steadily soaring expectations, newly created by the period of growth, shoot further and further ahead of actual satisfaction of needs. Successful revolution is the work neither of the destitute nor of the well-satisfied, but of those whose actual situation is improving less rapidly than they expect.

These economic models have much in common, and their differences can be explained by the fact that Lewis and Olson are primarily concerned with the long-term economic forces creating instability, and Davis with the short-term economic factors that may precipitate a crisis. Moreover their analyses apply to different kinds of economic growth, of which three have recently been identified by W. W. Rostow and Barry Supple: there is the expansion of production in a pre-industrial society, which may not cause any important technoligical, ideological, social, or political change; there is the phase of rapid growth, involving major changes of every kind; and there is the sustained trend toward technological

[19] *The Vendée* (Cambridge, Mass., 1964).

[20] "Toward a Theory of Revolution," *American Sociological Review*, XXVII (February 1962), 1-19, esp. the graph on p. 6.

maturity.[21] Historians have been quick to see that these models, particularly that of Rostow, can be applied only to a limited number of historical cases. The trouble is not so much that in any specific case the phases—particularly the last two—tend to merge into one another, but that changes in the various sectors occur at irregular and unexpected places on the time-scale in different societies. Insofar as there is any validity in the division of the stages of growth into these three basic types, the revolutionary model of Olson and Lewis is confined to the second; that of Davis is applicable to all three.

The Davis model fits the history of Western Europe quite well, for it looks as if in conditions of extreme institutional and ideological rigidity the first type of economic growth may produce frustrations of a very serious kind. Revolutions broke out all over Europe in the 1640's, twenty years after a secular growth phase had come to an end.[22] C. E. Labrousse has demonstrated the existence of a similar economic recession in France from 1778,[23] and from 1914 the Russian economy was dislocated by the war effort after many years of rapid growth. Whatever its limitations in any particular situation, the J-curve of actual satisfaction of needs is an analytical tool that historians can usefully bear in mind as they probe the violent social upheavals of the past.

As de Tocqueville pointed out, this formula of advance followed by retreat is equally applicable to other sectors. Trouble arises if a phase of liberal governmental concessions is followed by a phase of political repression; a phase of fairly open recruitment channels into the elite followed by a phase of aristocratic reaction and a closing of ranks; a phase of weakening status barriers by a phase of reassertion of privilege. The J-curve is applicable to other than purely economic satisfactions, and the apex of the curve is the point at which underlying causes, the preconditions, merge with immediate factors, the precipitants. The recipe for revolution is thus the creation of new expectations by economic improvement and some social and political reforms, followed by economic recession, governmental reaction, and aristocratic resurgence, which widen the gap between expectations and reality.

All these attempts to relate dysfunction to relative changes in economic prosperity and aspirations are hampered by two things, of which the first is the extreme difficulty in ascertaining the facts. It is never easy to discover precisely what is happening to the distribution of wealth in a given society. Even now, even in highly developed Western societies with massive bureaucratic controls and quantities of statistical data, there is no agreement about the facts. Some years ago it was confidently believed that in both Britain and the United States incomes were being levelled, and that extremes of both wealth and poverty were being steadily eliminated. Today, no one quite knows what is happening in either country.[24] And if this is true now, still more is it true of societies in the past about which the information is fragmentary and unreliable.

Secondly, even if they can be clearly demonstrated, economic trends are only one part of the problem. Historians are increasingly realizing that the psychological

[21] Rostow, *The Stages of Economic Growth* (Cambridge, Mass., 1960); Supple, *The Experience of Economic Growth* (New York 1963) 11-12.

[22] Hobsbawm, "The Crisis of the Seventeenth Century," in T. H. Aston, ed., *Crisis in Europe, 1560-1660* (London 1965), 5-58.

[23] *La Crise de l'Économie française á la fin de l'Ancien Régime et au début de la Révolution* (Paris 1944).

[24] Gabriel Kolko, *Wealth and Power in America* (New York 1962); Richard M. Titmuss, *Income Distribution and Social Change* (London 1962).

responses to changes in wealth and power are not only not precisely related to, but are politically more significant than, the material changes themselves. As Marx himself realized at one stage, dissatisfaction with the status quo is not determined by absolute realities but by relative expectations. "Our desires and pleasures spring from society; we measure them, therefore, by society, and not be the objects which serve for their satisfaction. Because they are of a social nature, they are of a relative nature."[25]   Frustration may possibly result from a rise and subsequent relapse in real income. But it is perhaps more likely to be caused by a rise in aspirations that outstrips the rise in real income; or by a rise in the *relative* economic position in society of the group in question, followed by a period in which its real income continues to grow, but less fast than that of other groups around it. Alternatively it may represent a rise and then decline of status, largely unrelated to real income; or if status and real income are related, it may be inversely. For example, social scientists seeking to explain the rise of the radical right in the United States in the early 1950's and again in the early 1960's attribute it to a combination of great economic prosperity and an aggravated sense of insecurity of status.[26] Whether or not this is a general formula for right-wing rather than left-wing revolutionary movements is not yet clear.

Moreover the problem is further complicated by an extension of the reference-group theory.[27] Human satisfaction is related not to existing conditions but to the condition of a social group against which the individual measures his situation. In an age of mass communications and the wide distribution of cheap radio receivers even among the impoverished illiterate of the world, knowledge of high consumption standards elsewhere spreads rapidly, and as a result the reference group may be in another, more highly developed, country or even continent. Under these circumstances, revolutionary conditions may be created before industialization has got properly under way.

The last area in which some new theoretical work has been done is in the formulation of hypotheses about the social stages of a "Great Revolution." One of the best attacks on this problem was made by Crane Brinton, who was thinking primarily about the French Revolution, but who extended his comparisons to the three other major Western revolutionary movements. He saw the first phase as dominated by moderate bourgeois elements; their supersession by the radicals; a reign of terror; a Thermidorian reaction; and the establishment of strong central authority under military rule to consolidate the limited gains of the revolution. In terms of mass psychology he compared revolution with a fever that rises in intensity, affecting nearly all parts of the body politic, and then dies away.

A much cruder and more elementary model has been advanced by an historian of the revolutions of 1848, Peter Amman.[28] He sees the modern state as an institution holding a monopoly of physical force, administration, and justice over a wide area, a monopoly dependent more on habits of obedience than on powers of coercion. Revolution may therefore be defined as a breakdown of the monopoly due to a failure of these habits of obedience. It begins with the emergence of two or more foci of power, and ends with the elimination of all but one. Amman includes the possibility of "suspended revolution," with the existence of two or more foci not yet in violent conflict.

[25] Davis, 5, quoting Marx, *Selected Works in Two Volumes* (Moscow 1955), 1, 947.
[26] Daniel Bell, ed., *The Radical Right* (Garden City 1963).
[27] Merton, chap. 9.
[28] "Revolution: A Redefinition."

This model admittedly avoids some of the difficulties raised by more elaborate classifications of revolution: how to distinguish a coup d'état from a revolution; how to define the degrees of social change; how to accomodate the conservative counterrevolution, and so on. It certainly offers some explanation of the progress of revolution from stage to stage as the various power blocs that emerge on the overthrow of the incumbent regime are progressively eliminated; and it explains why the greater the public participation in the revolution, the wider the break with the habits of obedience, and therefore the slower the restoration of order and centralized authority. But it throws the baby out with the bathwater. It is impossible to fit any decentralized traditional society, or any modern federal society, into the model. Moreover, even where it might be applicable, it offers no framework for analyzing the roots of revolution, no pointers for indentifying the foci of power, no means of distinguishing between the various revolutionary types, and its notion of "suspended revolution" is little more than verbal evasion.

Though it is set out in a somewhat confused, overelaborate, and unnecessarily abstract form, the most convincing description of the social stages of revolution is that outlined by Rex D. Hopper.[29] He sees four stages. The first is characterized by indiscriminate, uncoordinated mass unrest and dissatisfaction, the result of dim recognition that traditional values no longer satisfy current aspirations. The next stage sees this vague unease beginning to coalesce into organized opposition with defined goals, an important characteristic being a shift of allegiance by the intellectuals from the incumbents to the dissidents, the advancement of an "evil men" theory, and its abandonment in favor of an "evil institutions" theory. At this stage there emerge two types of leaders: the prophet, who sketches the shape of the new utopia upon which men's hopes can focus, and the reformer, working methodically toward specific goals. The third, the formal stage, sees the beginning of the revolution proper. Motives and objectives are clarified, organization is built up, a statesman leader emerges. Then conflicts between the left and the right of the revolutionary movement become acute, and the radicals take over from the moderates. The fourth and last stage sees the legalization of the revolution. It is a product of psychological exhaustion as the reforming drive burns itself out, moral enthusiasm wanes, and economic distress increases. The administrators take over, strong central government is established, and society is reconstructed on lines that embody substantial elements of the old system. The result falls far short of the utopian aspirations of the early leaders, but it succeeds in meshing aspirations with values by partly modifying both, and so allows the reconstruction of a firm social order.

Some of the writings of contemporary social scientists are ingenious feats of verbal juggling in an esoteric language, performed around the totem pole of an abstract model, surrounded as far as the eye can see by the arid wastes of terminological definitions and mathematical formulae. Small wonder the historian finds it hard to digest the gritty diet of this neo-scholasticism, as it has been aptly called. The more historically-minded of the social scientists, however, have a great deal to offer. The history of history, as well as of science, shows that advances depend partly on the accumulation of factual information, but rather more on the formulation of hypotheses that reveal the hidden relationships and common properties of apparently distinct phenomena. Social scientists can supply a corrective to the antiquarian fact-grubbing to which historians are so prone; they

[29] "The Revolutionary Process," *Social Forces*, XXVIII (March 1950), 270-79.

can direct attention to problems of general relevance, and away from the sterile triviality of so much historical research. They can ask new questions and suggest new ways of looking at old ones. They can supply new categories, and as a result may suggest new ideas.[30]

[30] See Werner J. Cahnman and Alvin Boskoff, eds., *Sociology and History: Theory and Research* (New York 1964); H. Stuart Hughes, "The Historian and the Social Scientist," *American Historical Review*, LXVI, No. 1 (1960), 20-46; A. Cobban, "History and Sociology," *Historical Studies*, III (1961), 1-8; M.G. Smith, "History and Social Anthropology," *Journal of the Royal Anthropological Institute*, XCII (1962); K.V. Thomas, "History and Anthropology," *Past and Present*, No. 24 (April 1963), 3-18.

THE UNKNOWN MARX

Martin Nicolaus

What Is the Fundamental Contraction?

The various steps by which Marx builds his fundamental insight that capitalist production involves a category radically different from mere commodity exchange into the fully fledged theory of capitalist accumulation which he later presents in *Capital* need not arrest us here. Exploitation proceeds "behind the back of the exchange-process"; that is the basic insight which marks his penetration beyond the critique of bourgeois society as a market society. We may proceed now to examine to what extent the text of the *Grundrisse* justifies the sweeping claims made for Marx's new scientific achievements in his 1859 Preface. In particular we will be interested in knowing whether the *Grundrisse* provides further elucidation of the famous passage in the Preface about *revolution:* "At a certain stage of their development, the material forces of production in society come into conflict with the existing relations of production, or—what is only a legal expression of the same thing—with the property relations within which they had been at work before. From forms which developed the forces of production, these relations now turn into their fetters. Then comes the period of social revolution."[1]

While there are echoes of this passage in some of the earlier works as well as on one occasion in *Capital*,[2] they remain on a level of generality so high as to be virtually useless. Above all, it is never made clear exactly what is meant to be included under the rubric of "forces of production" or "relations of production." Are we to understand "material forces of production" as meaning merely the technological apparatus, and "relations of production" as the political-legal system? In other words, is the phrase "material forces" only another way of saying

[1] W13:9 and *Selected Works I*, p. 363.
[2] W4:181 and *Poverty of Philosophy*, p. 174; *Manifesto*, E5:467 and *Selected Works*, I, p. 39; *Capital* I, W23:791 and *Capital* I, London and New York, p. 763.

"infrastructure" and does "relations" mean "superstructure"? What precisely do these terms refer to?

The basic clue for the deciphering of what Marx had in mind with the phrase "relations of production"—to begin with this half of the dichotomy—is already provided in the *Preface* itself. Marx writes that legal-political forms such as property relations are not these "relations of production" in themselves, but are merely an *expression* of these relations. From this starting point, the text of the *Grundrisse* can be seen as an extensive and detailed commentary on the nature of these "relations." For what else is the chapter on money? Here Marx demonstrates, as we have seen, that money in bourgeois society is no mere natural object, but rather the objectified form of the basic *social relation* within which capitalist production takes place. Money is the social bond which links the otherwise isolated producers and consumers within capitalist society together, and which forms the starting and ending points of the process of accumulation. The social relation which lies at the basis of all capitalist legal and political relations, and of which the latter are mere expressions—as Marx shows in the chapter on money—is the exchange-relation. It is the social imperative that neither production nor consumption can take place without the mediation of exchange-value; or, in other words, that the capitalist must not only extract surplus value but must also realize surplus value by converting the surplus product into money, and that the indivudual must not only have a need for consumer goods, but must also possess the money to purchase them. Far from being immutable natural laws, these twin imperatives are characterized by Marx as historically produced social relations specific to the capitalist form of production.

As for the other side of the dichotomy, it is easy to be misled by the word "material" in the phrase "material forces of production." Indeed, the German original *(materielle Produktivkrafte)* could as well be translated as "forces of material production," and it is clear in any case that the term "material" for Marx did not refer merely to the physical attributes of mass, volume, and location. A machine is always a material thing, but whether it is utilized in a productive capacity, whether or not it becomes a force of production, depends on the social organization of the productive process, as Marx goes to great lengths to point out in the *Grundrisse*.[3] The forces of production are themselves a social and historical product, and the productive process is a social process for Marx. It is necessary to emphasize this point in order to make clear that the important role which Marx assigns to the development of the material production forces under capitalism does not make Marx a technological determinist. Quite the opposite is the case; it is not technology which compels the capitalist to accumulate, but the necessity to accumulate which compels him to develop the powers of technology. The basis of the process of accumulation, of the process through which the forces of production gain in power, is the extraction of surplus value from labour-power. The force of production is the force of exploitation.

It is apparent, then, that the dichotomy formulated by Marx in the *Preface* is identical to the dichotomy between the two distinct processes which Marx identifies as basic to capitalist production in the *Grundrisse:* on the one hand, production consists of an act of exchange, and on the other, it consists of an act which is the opposite of exchange. On the one hand, production is an ordinary exchange of

[3] *Grundrisse*, pp. 169, 216, 579, etc, and R:89-90.

equivalents, on the other, it is a forcible appropriation of the worker's world-creating power. It is a social system in which the worker, as seller, and the capitalist, as purchaser, are juridically equal and free contracting parties; and it is at the same time a social system of slavery and exploitation. At the beginning and at the end of the productive process lies the social imperative of exchange-values, yet from beginning to end the productive process must yield surplus values. The exchange of equivalents is the fundamental social relation of production, yet the extraction of nonequivalents is the fundamental force of production. This contradiction, inherent in the process of capitalist production, is the source of the conflicts which Marx expected to bring about the period of social revolution.

The Road to Revolution

The problem of precisely how this contradiction can be expected to lead to the breakdown of the capitalist system is one which has plagued students of Marx for at least half a century. The volumes of *Capital* provide no very clear answer. This deficiency is at the root of the "breakdown controversy" which agitated German Social Democracy and which continues intermittently to flare even today. Veritable rivers of ink have been spent in an effort to fill up this gap in Marx's theoretical system. Yet this gap is present not because the problem was insoluble for Marx, not because he saw no answer, but because the conclusions he had reached in the *Grundrisse* lay buried and inaccessible to scholars until 20 years after the First World War. *Capital* is a work which proceeds slowly and carefully from pure forms of economic relationships step by step toward a closer approximation of economic-historic reality; nothing is prejudged and no new theories are introduced until the basis for them has been prepared. At that rate, it is easily conceivable that several more volumes of *Capital* would have been necessary before Marx could catch up with the point he had reached in the outline of his system in the *Grundrisse*. *Capital* is painfully unfinished, like a mystery novel which ends before the plot is unravelled. But the *Grundrisse* contains the author's plot-outline as a whole.

From the very beginning, the economics of the *Grundrisse* are more ambitious and more directly relevant to the problem of the capitalist breakdown than the economics of the extant portions of *Capital*. In the latter work, Marx relegates the relationship between persons and commodities (the utility relation) to a realm with which he is not then concerned, and he accepts the level of consumer needs which prevails in the economic system as a historical given which receives little further analysis.[4] In general, he takes consumption for granted, and concentrates his investigation on the how, instead of on the whether, of surplus realization. In the *Grundrisse*, however, he begins with the general assertion that the process of production, historically considered, creates not only the object of consumption but also the consumer need and the style of consumption.[5] He specifically criticizes Ricardo for consigning the problem of utility to the extra-economic sphere, and states that the relation between the consumer and the commodity, because this relation is a product of production, belongs squarely within the proper purview of political economy.[6] That he is aware not only of the qualitative but also of the quantitative aspects of the problem of consumption is apparent from excerpts such

[4] *Capital I*, W23:49-50 (Section One, Chapter One, page one).

[5] *Grundrisse*, pp. 13-18 and R:14-18.

[6] *Ibid.*, pp. 178-179n., 226-27, 763.

as this: "Incidentally, . . . although every capitalist demands that his workers should save, he means only *his own* workers, because they relate to him as workers; and by no means does this apply to the remainder of the workers, because these relate to him as consumers. In spite of all the pious talk of frugality he therefore searches for all possible ways of stimulating them to consume, by making his commodities more attractive, by filling their ears with babble about new needs *(neue Bedürfnisse ihnen anzuschwatzen).* It is precisely this side of the relationship between capital and labour which is an essential civilizing force, and on which the historic justification—but also the contemporary power—of capital is based."[7]

These general remarks are then set aside with a reminder to himself that "this relationship of production and consumption must be developed later.[8] A hundred pages later on the problem is taken up again. After a critique of Ricardo's neglect of the problem of consumption, and of Sismondi's utopian panaceas against overproduction, Marx formulates the inherent contradiction of capitalism as a "contradiction between production and realization" of surplus value. "To begin with, there is a limit to production, not to production in general, but to production founded on capital. . . . It suffices to show at this point that capital contains a *specific* barrier to production—which contradicts its general tendency to break all barriers to production—in order to expose the basis of *overproduction,* the fundamental contradiction of developed capitalism." As is apparent from the lines which follow immediately, Marx does not mean by "overproduction" simply excess inventory"; rather, he means excess productive power more generally.

"These inherent limits necessarily coincide with the nature of capital, with its essential determinants. These necessary limits are:

"1. *necessary labour* as limit to the exchange-value of living labour-power, of the wages of the industrial population;

"2. *surplus value* as limit to surplus labour-time; and, in relation to relative surplus labour-time, as limit to the development of the productive forces;

"3. what is the same thing, the *transformation into money,* into exchange value, as such, as a limit to production; or: exchange based on value, or value based on exchange, as limit to production. This is again

"4. the same thing as *restriction of the production of use-values* by exchange-value; or: the fact that real wealth must take on a *specific* form distinct from itself, absolutely not identical with it, in order to become an object of production at all."[9]

While a proper analysis of the implications of these rather cryptic theses would require a book, it is immediately apparent that these four "limits" represent no more than different aspects of the contradiction between "forces of production" and "social relations of production." The task of maintaining the enormous powers of surplus-value extraction within the limits set by the necessity of converting this surplus value into exchange value becomes increasingly difficult as the capitalist system moves into its developed stages. In practical terms, these four "limits" could be formulated as four related, but mutually contradictory political-economic alternatives between which the capitalist system must choose, but cannot afford to

---

[7] *Ibid.,* p. 198 and R:71.

[8] *Ibid.*

[9] *Ibid.,* pp. 318-19. A five-element model of a closed capitalist system, from which Marx deduces the impossibility of expanded reproduction due to the impossibility of realization, appears on pp. 336-47. More on realization on pp. 438-442 (R:174-176) and elsewhere.

choose: (1) Wages must be raised to increase effective demand: (2) Less surplus value must be extracted: (3) Products must be distributed without regard to effective demand: or (4) Products that cannot be sold must not be produced at all. The first and second alternatives result in a reduction of profit; the third is capitalistically impossible (except as a political stopgap); and the fourth means depression.

Surplus Labour

What is most remarkable and ought most to emphasized about Marx's theory of capitalist breakdown as we see it at this point is its great latitude and flexibility. Cataclysmic crises rising to a revolutionary crescendo are only one possible variant of the breakdown process; and indeed, Marx lays little stress on this type of crisis in the *Grundrisse*. For every possible tendency toward breakdown, Marx names a number of delaying tendencies; this list includes the development of monopoly, the conquest of the world market, and, significantly, Marx mentions the payment by capitalists to workers of "surplus wages."[10]   All things considered, Marx's breakdown theory in the *Grundrisse* provides important amplification of the statement in the Preface that "no social order ever disappears before all the productive forces for which there is room in it have been developed."[11] When one considers the requirements that must be met, in Marx's view, before the capitalist order is ripe for overthrow, one comes to wonder whether the failure of previous revolutionary movements in Europe and the US is not imputable simply to prematurity.

The great historic role of capital is the creation of surplus labour, labour which is superfluous from the standpoint of mere use value, mere subsistence. Its historic role is fulfilled as soon as (on the one hand) the level of needs has been developed to the degree where surplus labour in addition to necessary subsistence has itself become a general need which manifests itself in individual needs, and (on the other hand) when the strict discipline of capital has schooled successive generations in industriousness, and this quality has become their general property, and (finally) when the development of the productive powers of labour, which capital, with its unlimited urge to accumulate and to realize, has constantly spurred on, have ripened to the point where the possession and maintenance of societal wealth require no more than a diminished amount of labour-time, where the labouring society relates to the process of its progressive reproduction and constantly greater reproduction in a scientific manner; where, that is, human labour which can be replaced by the labour of things has ceased."[12]

Noteworthy in this long sentence, among many other things, is the statement that the capitalist order is not ripe for revolution until the working class—far from being reduced to the level of ragged, miserable brutes—has expanded its consumption *above* the level of mere physical subsistence and includes the enjoyment of the fruits of surplus labour as a general necessity. Instead of the image of the starving proletarian slowly dying from an 18-hour day in a mine or a sweatshop, Marx here

[10] *Ibid.*, p. 341.
[11] W13:9 and *Selected Works I.*
[12] *Grundrisse*, p. 231 and R:91.

presents the well-fed proletarian, scientifically competent, to whom an eight-hour day would presumably appear as a mere waste of time. In another passage, Marx goes further; he envisages a capitalist productive apparatus more completely automated than that of any presently existing society, and writes that nevertheless, despite the virtual absence from such a social order of a "working class" as commonly defined, this economic organization must break down.

"To the degree that large-scale industry develops, the creation of real wealth comes to depend less on labour-time and on the quantity of labour expended, and more on the power of the instruments which are set in motion during labour-time, and whose powerful effectiveness itself is not related to the labour-time immediately expended in their production, but depends rather on the general state of science and the progress of technology. . . . Large industry reveals that real wealth manifests itself rather in the monstrous disproportion between expended labour-time and its product, as well as in the qualitative disproportion between labour, reduced to a pure abstraction, and the power of the productive process which it supervises. Labour no longer appears as an integral element of the productive process; rather, man acts as supervisor and regulator of the productive process itself . . . He stands at the side of the productive process, instead of being its chief actor. With this transformation, the cornerstone of production and wealth is neither the labour which man directly expends, nor the time he spends at work, but rather the appropriation of his own collective productive power, his understanding of nature and his mastery over nature, exercised by him as a social body—in short, it is the development of the social individual. The theft of other people's labour-time, on which contemporary wealth rests, appears as a miserable basis compared to this new one created by large-scale industry itself. As soon as labour in its direct form has ceased to be the great wellspring of wealth, labour-time ceases and must cease to be its measure, and therefore exchange-value the measure of use-value . . . With that, the system of production based on exchange-value collapses . . . Capital is its own contradiction-in-process, for its urge is to reduce labour-time to a minimum, while at the same time it maintains that labour-time is the only measure and source of wealth. Thus it reduces labour-time in its necessary form in order to augment it in its superfluous form; thus superfluous labour increasingly becomes a precondition—a question of life or death—for necessary labour. So on the one side it animates all the powers of science and nature, of social co-ordination and intercourse, in order to make the creation of wealth (relatively) independent of the labour-time expended on it. On the other side it wants to use labour-time as a measure for the gigantic social powers created in this way, and to restrain them within the limits necessary to maintain already-created values as values. Productive forces and social relations—both of which are different sides of the development of the social individual—appear to capital only as means, and only means to produce on its limited basis. In fact, however, these are the material conditions to blow this basis sky-high."[13]

This passage and similar ones in the *Grundrisse* demonstrate once again, if further proof were needed, that the applicability of the Marxian theory is not limited to 19th-century industrial conditions. It would be a paltry theory indeed which predicted the breakdown of the capitalist order only when that order consisted of child labour, sweatships, famine, chronic malnutrition, pestilence, and all the other

---

[13] *Ibid.*, pp. 592-94 and R:209-211.

scourges of its primitive stages. No genius and little science are required to reveal the contradictions of such a condition. Marx, however, proceeds by imagining the strongest possible case in favour of the capitalist system, by granting the system the full development of all the powers inherent in it—and then exposing the contradictions which must lead to its collapse.

The Unknown Pivot

The gradual emergence of the *Grundrisse* out of obscurity into the consciousness of students and followers of Marx should have a most stimulating influence. This work explodes in many ways the mental set, the static framework of formulae and slogans to which much of Marxism has been reduced after a century of neglect, 90 years of social democracy, 80 years of "dialectical materialism," and 70 years of revisionism. To put it more pithily, the *Grundrisse* blows the mind. A number of conclusions seem inescapable.

First, this work will make it impossible or at least hopelessly frustrating to dichotomize the work of Marx into "young" and "old," into "philosophical" and "economic" elements. Hegel-enthusiasts and partisans of Ricardo will find the work equally stimulating or, conversely, equally frustrating, for the *Grundrisse* is so to speak the pineal gland through which these two great antecedents of Marx engage in reciprocal osmosis.[14] It contains passages which formulate Ricardian ideas with Hegelian language and Hegelian ideas with Ricardian language; the intercourse between them is direct and fruitful. Although we have not here examined this point in detail, a reader of the *Grundrisse* will find a direct line of continuity going back to many of the ideas of the 1844 *Manuscripts,* and from the perspective of the *Grundrisse* it will not be clear whether the early manuscripts were indeed a work of philosophy at all or whether they were not simply a fusion of economic and philosophical thoughtways for which there is no modern precedent. Likewise, from the perspective of the *Grundrisse,* the often apparently "technical" obscurities of *Capital* will reveal their broader meaning. Between the mature Marx and the young Marx the *Grundrisse* is the missing link.

On the other hand, the fact that Marx makes a number of fresh discoveries and advances in the course of the *Grundrisse* must make students and followers of Marx more sensitive to the economic deficiencies of the earlier works. The *Grundrisse* contains the graphic record of Marx's discovery and systematization of the theory of surplus value, about which his theory of capitalist breakdown is constructed. If it was not already clear, a reading of this work makes it clear that the theory of surplus value was not a functional element of the economic model on which the *Manifesto* is based. Marx was aware, in 1848, of the *existence* of a surplus; but certainly he was not aware of the *importance* of this element. There is evidence of Marx's awareness of the Ricardian theory of the surplus in other early economic writings (the *Poverty of Philosophy* and *Wage-Labour and Capital*), but these works equally demonstrate that the surplus-value theory had *not* become a functional part of the economic model on which Marx based his predictions. Marx's early theory of wages and of profits, for example, is clearly a function of a supply-demand model of the economic system; and it will be necessary to re-examine this early theorizing

---

[14] The editors have provided a most thorough index of all overt and covert references to Hegel, as well as Marx's index to the works of Ricardo.

critically in the light of the later surplus-value model. In at least one important problem-area, the question of class polarization, it can be demonstrated that the prophecy of the *Manifesto* is explicitly contradicted by Marx on the basis of his theory of surplus value in a later work.[15] How many other such discrepancies exist, and how many of them are traceable to the differences between the early market-model and the later surplus-value model, is a question which ought to be examined not only for its own sake, but also to clear up the confusion which often results when it is asked what precisely Marx had to say on the question of increasing impoverishment, for example.

It follows that the most important Marxian political manifesto remains to be written. Apart from the brief *Critique of the Gotha Programme* (1875) there exists no programmatic *political* statement which is based squarely on the theory of surplus value, and which incorporates Marx's theory of capitalist breakdown as it appears in the *Grundrisse*. No grounds exist to reject the 1848 *Manifesto* as a whole; but there is every reason to submit all of its theses and views to critical re-examination in the light of Marx's own surplus value theory. Many startling surprises might come to light, for example, if an edition of the *Manifesto* were published containing thorough and detailed annotations drawn from the later writings, point by point and line by line. Clearly the theory of surplus value is crucial to Marx's thought; one can even say that with its ramifications it *is* Marx's theory. Yet how many "Marxist" political groupings and how many "Marxist" critics of Marx make the surplus value theory the starting point of their analysis? The only major contemporary work in which the surplus plays the central role is Baran and Sweezy's *Monopoly Capital.*[16] Despite the deficiencies of that work, it points the way in the proper Marxian direction and forms the indispensable foundation for the type of analysis which must be made if Marx's theory of capitalism is to reassert its political relevance.

Unfortunately from several points of view, *Monopoly Capital* ends with the conclusion (or, perhaps more accurately, begins with the assumption) that domestic revolution within the advanced capitalist countries is not presently foreseeable. This argument can and must be confronted with Marx's thesis in the *Grundrisse* that all of the obstacles to revolution, such as those which Baran and Sweezy cite, namely monopoly, conquest of the world market, advanced technology, and a working class more prosperous than in the past, are only the preconditions which make revolution possible. Similarly, it cannot be said that Marx's vision of the central contradiction of capitalism, as he states it in the *Grundrisse,* has ever been thoroughly explored and applied to an existing capitalist society; here *Monopoly Capital* fall short quite seriously. The results of such an analysis might also contain some surprising insights. In short, much work remains to be done.

That, we may conclude, is after all the most important conclusion to be drawn from the *Grundrisse.* Because this work underlines the deficiencies of the earlier economic writings and throws into sharp relief the fragmentary nature of *Capital,* it can serve as a powerful reminder that Marx was not a vendor of ready-made truths but a maker of tools. He himself did not complete the execution of the design. But the blueprints for his world-moving lever have at last been published. Now that

[15] Cf. Martin Nicolaus: "Hegelian Choreography and the Capitalist Dialectic: Proletariat and Middle Class in Marx," in *Studies on the Left* VII: 1, Jan-Feb., 1967, pp. 22-49.

[16] Paul Baran and Paul Sweezy, *Monopoly Capital,* Monthly Review Press, New York, 1966.

Marx's unpolished masterwork has come to light, the construction of Marxism as a revolutionary social science which exposes even the most industrially advanced society at its roots has finally become a practical possibility.

WHY WE FEAR PEASANTS IN REVOLT

Barrington Moore, Jr.

Not so long ago, it was possible to claim that the United States, for all its shortcomings, was at least trying to solve the main problems of the 20th century without resort to massive cruelty against its own population or that of other countries. This seemed to be the characteristic that most sharply distinguished American democracy from totalitarian regimes and even from those European democracies that held remnants of a colonial empire. If the American capitalist machine showed some tendency to charge around out of control, at least like no other in history it had solved the problems of pressing material want.

Meanwhile, in response to popular demands, the government from time to time took measures, so it appeared, to bring the capitalist machine under control and soften very considerably its impact upon its victims. Intelligent people knew that America had an ugly race problem, but there was obvious, if painfully slow, progress in that area too. Slums, billboards and television furnished Americs's critics with an ugly and depressing spectacle. Yet it seemed that the ugliness, perhaps even *some* of the continuing injustices, might be a price worth paying for a society that attacked its problems without deliberate cruelty. By moving slowly, and it was hoped steadily, the United States had at the very least avoided the fate of Nazi Germany, of Stalinist Russia.

With the first Cuban crisis this comforting view of America's behavior in the world began to seem dubious. It became apparent then that the United States would use its military power to try to crush regimes that made revolutionary demands for a better life, if it deemed these regimes a threat to its own interests. Vietnam and a number of other related events, among them American action in Guatemala, the Dominican Republic and Brazil, revealed the United States as the military bastion of counterrevolution, willing and able to rain fire upon those made impatient by hunger. So far, the main victims of the American way of life have not been Americans (though our casualty lists are beginning to grow). They are foreigners, but they are victims of American policy in exactly the sense that the inhabitants of concentration camps were the victims of Stalinist policy.

How has this come about? The key lies, I believe, in the great wave of peasant revolutions that has swept the world in the past half-century as part of the still larger sweep of post-capitalist industrialization, and in the American decision to resist that wave with armed might.

After the Russian Revolution, and even more after the Chinese Revolution, it became impossible to speak in neo-Marxist terms about the idiocy of rural life or to regard the peasant as a mere object of history, something acted upon by historical forces but contributing nothing to them. Nevertheless, it remains true that the main contribution of the peasants to these great events was a destructive one. Agrarian distress furnished the explosive that brought down the old order in both Russia and

China, and enabled the Communists to usher in a new phase of history. To the work of constructing a new social order the peasants have been allowed to contribute little or nothing. Instead they have been its major victims.

Furthermore, the peasants' role has differed sharply from one country to another in accord with varying historical conditions. In Russia, still overwhelmingly agrarian in 1917, the peasants' part in the overthrow of the old order was immense. At the same time, the Bolsheviks had no following among the peasants and came to power on the backs of a segment of the industrial workers whose revolts in the big cities brought about the final collapse. Chinese Communists took power in a manner much closer to a pure peasant revolution. And in other cases, the peasants have not risen, though they had reason. In India, the peasant has remained mainly an object of history. Japan made the transition to a version of modern industrial capitalism without a peasant revolution, indeed without any violent revolution.

Because of the present tendency to regard Japanese industrialization as a success story, and for even more important reasons, it is necessary to look at this case more closely. In straight economic terms Japan's nonrevolutionary entrance into the age of industrial capitalism was indeed a remarkable success. So for that matter was the corresponding entrance that Germany made, after the abortive revolution of 1848. Politically, however, these victories may have been disasters, leading in time to fascism and World War II. Without claiming that the march toward fascism was inevitable, one can trace a connection between the survival of pre-industrial social formations and political habits, the corresponding weakness of the bourgeois impulse, and the ways in which Germany, Japan and other countries succumbed to fascism. Comparative historical evidence is not firm proof; nevertheless, it is suggestive that the three states where parliamentary democracy become most firmly established, England, France and the United States, went through a period of revolution (or civil war; the distinction is mainly verbal).

On the basis of this record it is possible to draw two conclusions. First, the widespread notion that a revolution is somehow a prerequisite to industrial growth is false. Before one can draw comfort from this point, however, it is necessary to take account of its corollary: for modernization to mean progress in human freedom a revolutionary break with the past seems to be necessary. Again, one cannot prove the necessity; one can only note connections between what has taken place with and without revolutions. Nor does a revolution guarantee success in establishing a freer society; it only creates some of the possibilities. However, with these limitations and qualifications it is correct, I believe, to regard the peasant revolutions of the 20th century as the successors to and even the continuation of revolutionary processes that established Western democracy.

The main propelling force behind modern peasant revolutions is often called parasitic landlordism. Political landlordism might be a better term because it suggests more clearly the central features. Over most of the Asian continent the native landed upper classes did not take up commercial agriculture. Their response to the coming of the modern world was almost the exact opposite of the one familiar to Americans, i.e., increased use of machines, bigger units of cultivation, a sharp reduction in human toil. In China and India, Western imperialism helped to prevent this kind of transformation, but geographical factors and social structures inherited from the past were almost certainly much more important reasons.

Throughout Asia the landlord antedates the coming of the West. Rising population, together with a lack of opportunities for work in the cities, under Asian conditions forces more and more land-hungry peasants to bid for the right to cultivate smaller and smaller plots of land. Where this happens, the landed upper classes are strongly tempted to avoid risky innovations, to sit back and allow the pressure of events to drive up their rents. In order to take advantage of this situation they must employ political levers, including customary sanctions inherited from earlier days, to keep the peasants working and paying. As traditional sanctions gradually lose their effectiveness, the landlords resort more and more to the police and the army until the government becomes little more than a vast rent-collecting agency, as was finally the case under Chiang Kai-shek.

The misery produced by political landlordism is obvious; almost as obvious is the fact that by itself such misery will not produce a revolutionary outbreak. In the past century the Indian peasants have suffered just about as much in a strict material sense as did the peasants of China. But in comparison with the Chinese peasant the Indian peasant has been docile. There is at least moderately good evidence that this difference extends far back in time. Some types of society and historical experience are likely to generate peasant revolts and eventually to favor a peasant revolution; others are quite unlikely to do so.

Among the factors most apt to be relevant are the social structure of the peasant community and the character of the institutional links between the peasants and the upper classes who live off their labor. Partly because the Japanese village was a solidary unit that muffled dissident voices among the peasants at the same time that it was penetrated by many influences from the upper classes, the Japanese were able to make political landlordism into one of the devices for what Marxists call primitive capitalist accumulation. The Japanese Government could make the peasants pay the costs of industrialization and still contain revolutionary tendencies, a feat that helped to produce the Japanese variant of fascism. In India, the caste system was the main mechanism through which the landed upper classes extracted an economic surplus from the countryside. Caste rendered a central government unnecessary from the standpoint of local elites; it was an excrescence and the product of intermittent conquest. In China, the central government did play an essential role in shaping the social order and extracting a surplus, and the different functions of government in China and India help to explain differences in the behavior of their respective peasant masses. To sum up these variations, although political landlordism has been a basic trend in many parts of the world, it has produced major revolutionary upheavals only in Russia and China.

At least that is the case so far. Will the revolutionary wave continue? I do not know enough about the other underdeveloped parts of the world—Latin America, Africa, the Middle East—to speak with confidence. Still, there are persuasive general grounds for believing that the revolutionary wave may have passed its peak. Just as generals often base their strategy on the previous war, so may Chinese Communists now base their hopes and strategies on their earlier victory. The economically backward parts of the world today, including India, are politically and socially fragmented. This may mean that a revolution, even if it succeeded, would have vastly less world significance than did the revolutions in such potentially powerful countries as Russia and China. A revolution in Cuba is mainly important for Cuba; a revolution in Algeria important for Algeria, though of course there is some resonance.

Why then is the American Government quite literally trying to burn these revolutionary movements off the face of the earth? There are three possible answers. The first, accepted by both the Administration and its radical critics, is that these movements constitute, along with Chinese power, a mortal threat to American capitalism. A second possible answer holds that these revolutionary movements do not constitute a really serious threat, and that the moves to exterminate them are monstrous irrationalities of American policy. These aggressive reflexes can be interpreted either as a manifestation inherent in modern American capitalist society (as the radical critics say), or—and this is the third answer—as policies whose real causes are in large measure contingent and accidental.

An absolutely clear-cut choice among these answers is impossible. Though the weight of evidence points toward the conclusion that American policy is by no means the inevitable expression of American society, and that the threat it faces is no mortal one at all, there is small comfort to be had here. The longer these policies continue in force, the more will American society *become* dependent upon its counterrevolutionary role. Since there is no now foreseeable prospect that these policies will change, the radical image of the United States—despite any flaws in its analysis—is likely to become the correct one.

To dispute one version of the radical thesis, it seems highly unlikely that American capitalism depends upon imperialist exploitation. In particular, the American stake in the exploitation of backward areas of the world is probably far from crucial. It is well known that the advanced capitalist countries are one another's best customers. Though figures on these matters are far from dependable, the estimate of the French economist Robert Frossaert that imperialist superprofits form no more than 1 or 2 per cent of the national income of advanced capitalist countries helps us gain a perspective on the question.

May the revolutionary movements on the other hand, be no more than preliminary skirmishes in a straightforward military threat from China? But the United States is desperately trying to establish vital interests close to China rather than to defend interests it already has. Under the conditions of warfare in the missile age, when the United States has bases on Guam and in the Philippines and a fleet of Polaris submarines, the notion that Americans need another base in Vietnam is hard to swallow.

But the fact that it is difficult, if not impossible, to explain American policy through any narrow conception of economic or strategic interests is not a powerful counterargument to the radical thesis. If anything, it strengthens the most tenable of the radical arguments: that modern American society is inherently destructive. Behind such reasonings, too, are certain currents of Marxist thought. Baran and Sweezy, for example, conclude that American monopoly capitalism precludes any humane and constructive use of America's productive power that would go beyond mere sops to keep the underlying population in line with prevailing policies. To a non-economist their present diagnosis does not look very different from that of many liberal economists who have discussed the causes of stagnation in 20th-century capitalism. The key point is that under modern conditions the big firms have difficulty finding ways to reinvest their profits. (That this is not the case at the present moment does not damage the general argument.) Unlike the liberals, however, Marxists hold that no real solution is possible within the present framework of American society. Since serious constructive moves are blocked by the character of the system and the dominant interests it serves, the technological power that it nevertheless creates pours out in destructive ways: war and waste.

It is possible to agree with this radical description and condemnation of American society without being sure that the diagnosis of the causes is correct. A glance at the historical record is enough to raise serious doubts. Up to a point, the Marxist argument makes sense, but at a crucial point it collapses.

The Second World War, it is widely agreed, pulled capitalism out of the depression. Fascism too, one can argue, was in part a consequence of capitalism, though in my judgment, and for the reasons given earlier, a particular form of capitalism that had grown up as a result of a non-revolutionary entrance into the age of modern industry. This feature modifies the Marxist thesis considerably, though one still must agree that the Second World War saved democratic capitalism from the embarrassing task of having to find out if it could solve its own problems peacefully. Since then the United States has been almost continuously in some form of war boom. In *The Postwar American Economy,* Alvin Hansen, certainly no Marxist, asserts that between 1948 and 1963 "defense played twice as powerful an expansionist role as private investment." Clearly the economy was sick, and the war boom has been the main "cure."

The question nevertheless remains whether the illness of the economy, as the Marxist argument maintains, was the main *cause* of the war boom. To believe that it was it is necessary to deny that Stalinist socialism played any significant part in bringing on the cold war. From that it would follow that under Stalin the Soviet Union constituted a freer and more humane society than did the capitalist democracies in the years after the Second World War, and for a long time previously. It becomes necessary to believe that at the end of this conflict Stalinist Russia was so much a satisfied power that it would have made no moves against the West even if this part of the world had completely disarmed. It is necessary to believe that Western, and especially American, business circles forced through a rearmament program against a danger to democracy that was almost entirely imaginary. There are people who can believe such arguments, but doing so puts an enormous strain on the organs of credulity.

It is probably closer to the mark to hold that the conflict between capitalist and socialist states, rather than their domestic social institutions, has been the main factor behind the deformations of socialism and liberal democracy. This conflict may be seen as the modern manifestation of the age-old system of competing sovereign states. Under such competition the only way for a state to gain "security" is to become stronger than its potential rivals. Rivals that must be taken seriously are those that are themselves strong, regardless of their social structure and doctrinal predilections. Conflicts occur among states with similar social structures at least as often as among those with different ones. Hence the system of international anarchy itself often imposes "aggressive" policies upon states whose domestic structure might incline them in peaceable directions.

This explanation cannot be applied universally. Domestic factors played an important part in the aggressive policies of Germany and Japan in their Fascist phase, and in other times and places as well. My sense of the situation in the United States is that business interests did their best to climb aboard the defense juggernaut rather than set the monster in motion. Now, however, it is here and firmly entrenched, a major factor in the American political climate.

To put the point another way, both socialism and democratic capitalism in and by themselves might be a great deal more capable of change in the direction of a moderately decent and free society than anyone has ever suspected. But socialism and capitalism have never existed in and by themselves; hence we are unlikely ever to know what possibilities they contained. Stalinist policies helped to destroy affirmative policies in American society, to change the United States into the affluent version of the garrison state. In turn, the United States now blocks off the prospects for greater freedom which have begun to appear in Russia.

Now the conflict between the United States and the Soviet Union is gradually ceasing to be the main axis of international conflicts. Chiefly as a result of American policies, the international arena is becoming a stage for a conflict between those states that have achieved industrial civilization and and those that seek to achieve it by revolutionary methods. As the latest comer to the industrial world, the Soviet Union balances precariously between the two camps, anxious to avoid the nuclear catastrophe that could destroy civilization. Each step America takes in escalating the war in Vietnam destroys whatever confidence remains that it will not be the first to resort to Armageddon for the preservation of "freedom." Every bomb that falls on helpless peasants destroys the clearest claim upon humanity's allegiance that Western democracy once could make: that it was no terrorist society, that for all its defects it was a way of solving problems peacefully, and for that reason well worth defending. At bottom, this was perhaps always an illusion. Now, at any rate, each day's headlines shatter it. Such talk no longer carries with it the hope of the future, but the stink of death.